Dave

Hitchhiker's Guide to the Speedway Grand Prix:
One Man's Far-flung Summer Behind the Scenes

Jeff Scott   *Yours M Shale*

methanol
press

Cardiff 2019

for Jess, Oscar & Fleur

First published in Great Britain by
Methanol Press
2 Tidy Street Brighton East Sussex BN1 4EL

For a complete catalogue of current and forthcoming publications please write to the address above, or visit our website at www.methanolpress.com

ISBN 978-0-9568618-5-6
A catalogue for this book is available from the British Library

Editor in absentia: Michael Payne
Word Wrangler: Graham Russel
Book & Cover Design: Vicky Holtham

Printed in the UK

"It is difficult to get a man to understand something when his salary depends on his not understanding it"

Upton Sinclair

Contents

Introduction

"It would be great to see Scott take a look at the sport overseas. His experience of camping in the forests of Malilla or taking in the action at the Marian Rose Motoarena in Torun would take the series in a whole new direction."

Paul Burbidge

OFTEN written off prematurely, speedway regularly survived talk of its demise and threats to its existence. These took many forms. Waxing and waning popularity. Health and safety regulations. Audience decline. Unnecessary rule and regulation complexity. And change. It was the endless mainly pointless change that irked. There was naughty late 20th century capitalism – particularly as it applied to competition from different and more exciting entertainment options. More expensive bikes, equipment and tuning reared their shiny glamorous heads. The dissolution of the family as the basic unit of domesticity further kicked in. While, at the same time – inevitably – the stable but retro speedway consumer demographic of white, male and stale remained in force. But, as these people aged over 50 got older, they eventually died and, mostly, were not replaced. The faint glow of rider power got a bit brighter. Promoters self-harmed and failed to invest. Maybe even feminism was a factor. Actually, no, feminism isn't really permitted within speedway circles other than on an individual case basis by proud dads with headstrong daughters. Even the weather took some blame even though speedway is one of the sports that could benefit from the long summer certainty global warming may increasingly provide. There were also many other actual and imagined warning signs, too numerous to list but including cleaner-smelling fuel and silencers that impacted how the bikes rode and raced.

Having survived so much talk of decline, fans, riders, the speedway media and even British promoters (initially, anyways) were ripe to believe and also seize upon the promise of a bright new future when offered it on a plate in the form of a reinvigorated Speedway Grand Prix series. Backed by new people with reputedly applicable Formula 1 experience, global ambitions, substantial pockets, bold plans, strategic plans, and extensive television connections. Thrusting executive outsider people prepared to gussy up, re-brand and restore then turbocharge speedway into mass market popularity in new and existing markets plus, thereby, land a bazillion brand-name sponsorships. That was – for sure – what the strategic plans, public statements and press releases promised. Not just in Europe. But globally. New exciting markets were everywhere. Everyone recognised and seized upon the first concrete signs of this really bright new future when it arrived – for the first time in 2001 – in the form of a specially built temporary track inside the "magnificent" [TM] Millennium Stadium Cardiff. The stadium was the prestige stage that we collectively knew befitted the status speedway really deserved and merited. Build it and they will come. This message was good enough for Kevin Costner in Field of Dreams and it could be true too for speedway. Casting aside hints of uncertainty, let alone anxiety or scepticism, British Speedway collectively celebrated and deep dived its adoration. Backs were slapped. Joys were unalloyed. Success was quickly seen, claimed and proclaimed

The visionaries behind these bold plans and the Cardiff decision were the new rights holders of the Speedway Grand Prix Series (and also the Speedway World Cup they "reinvigorated" at roughly the same time), Benfield Sports International (BSI). They were quickly hailed as saviours. The words, utterances and statements of an unknown bloke by the name of John Postlethwaite – who had, apparently been so HUGELY successful at F1 he abandoned it for the easy contractual pickings of speedway – were treated as holy writ and gospel. These tablets from the mountain with a shale rather than moral, spiritual or religious emphasis were the route map for our thousand speedway suns to truly dazzle. It was widely greeted – especially by those who had or could soon manufacture their own vested commercial interests in lock-step with the savvy new kids on the block – as destiny. Naysayers were completely absent or, if they existed, appeared to have no voice or platform.

Of course, Cardiff didn't just happen overnight. Wales and its history had had to happen first. But, running the development of the Welsh nation close, BSI and their rights ownership of the Speedway Grand Prix series was a close second. Appending the word series on the end of the SGP became obligatory. And gave things a certain majesty. Interestingly, the Tour de France more elegantly describe theirs as an "edition". Of course, before all this could happen, the GP supervisory body – the Fédération Internationale de Motorcyclisme (FIM) – had to be persuaded and, you imagine, conduct extensive due diligence, analysis and stress-testing of the BSI SGP product proposition. And, boy, did they like what they saw. Global markets. Expanded television coverage and rights sales. New, renewed and reinvigorated sponsorships. Likely from big brand names. More cache. More money. More trips to exotic locations and, where possible, upscale hotels and restaurants on expenses. Whatever BSI said or wrote was so truly impressive, the FIM immediately dropped their knickers and granted the keys to the speedway harem of the Grand Prix series rights until 2020.

But what was promised? Or thought to be promised. We are lucky enough that sufficient time has passed to provide some sort of perspective. Time has passed. It is roughly a "Wenger" since BSI became the rights holders for the SGP. Though from a different sports discipline, a Wenger is the ideal unit of measurement, arguably (according to Arsenal fans) too long. Arsene reigned at Highbury and then the Emirates for approximately 22 years. He took a club with a rich tradition and transformed it to make it way, way better. He won trophies and in a new era of broadcast rights and the world wide web he cemented Arsenal's place as a global brand. A brand known for its skill and its creative expressive style of play. Most importantly of all Wenger arguably changed the environment that surrounded him – the British football scene forever. Arguably revolutionised. His approach spawned imitators at domestic and international level in the UK and beyond its many shores. His influence is everywhere. It is irrevocably different to when he started here. Wenger did this through his actions rather than his words. He was obsessed with rest and nutrition before it was fashionable or proved effective in football as well as open to innovation and new tactics. He had a passion for detail and researched relentlessly. Significantly, the latter years of his tenure required him to continue to develop, field and maintain a successful team without significant monies for squad replenishment since corporate strategic goals dictated these finances were primarily almost wholly focused upon infrastructure investment. He subsumed short- and medium-term team building needs – without complaint – in order to play his part in securing the future with a serious investment in a state-of-the-art magnificent stadium. A venue fit for the 21st century that also symbolised and supported the club's financial growth ambitions with a stage suitable for their style of play and status. I write all this as a neutral Sunderland fan. When the history of late 20th and early 21st century British football is written, the impact and influence of Arsene Wenger will shine through. He will be a towering figure who influence will ripple forwards in time for many years beyond his actual life and tenure.

BSI have – according to their boosters – enjoyed similar years of performance plenty and their company accounts reveal similarly – albeit in diminutive speedway scale – floods of cash in revenues and profits. Comparisons are likely to be instructive and are another underlying aspect of my travels. Measuring the historical and structural impact of BSI and their SGP (and their version of the Speedway World Cup) against these standards obviously requires a discount for the fact that this is speedway not football. Our importance let alone our share of mind space (or history) in the national, European and global public consciousness is completely different. It is an apples with oranges comparison. But; but BSI – especially their original chief executive John Postlethwaite and to a lesser extent his even more nondescript successors Paul Bellamy and Torben Olsen – have talked an exceptionally good game in public (and private with the FIM and trade media, apparently). They were grandiloquent and ambitious. Impressively they had ambitious goals and plans. Highly unusually for speedway with its reluctance for record keeping the tax man might espy, backed up with spreadsheets and PowerPoint presentations. They knew what they wanted. Nothing less than a revolution. The tired speedway present was contrasted to a glorious speedway future. It wasn't just a pitch about the status and cultural importance of the Grand Prix – it was about all of speedway. Everyone. Riders and fans. Promoters and sponsors. Restoring speedway to its rightful place in the pantheon of great sports. Casually glancing at the small print, this revolution was to be driven by the bright lights of publicity and broadcast performance. So, this revolution would definitely be (globally) televised.

At the outset, before isolationism, cost-cutting, paranoia, and secretiveness took major irrevocable hold along with the pretention and frightening over-confidence, we weren't even short of specifics. BSI specified a menu of strategic milestones and behaviours. Usually in breathless conversational interviews or on-the-record quotes faithfully transcribed by a willing but supine trade media keener to further ingratiate itself within the bubble of the SGP charmed circle. These specific goals included:

International stagings

Breaking speedway in new countries and on new continents

Rider celebrity

Mass media broadcast coverage

Modern big city centre stadia

National capital stagings

Household name big brand sponsors – both domestic and global

State-of-the-art purpose-built tracks

Best/top riders

Premium entertainments

Comfortable seating

Quality food and drink concessions

Extensive and luxurious toilet provision (hopefully with luxury three ply toilet paper, except wherever BSI break speedway into in the Middle East)

Excellent transport links

Weekend city break locations

Global impact

In a nutshell, the arrival of the Speedway Grand Prix across the globe would see lion lie down with the lamb of Judah. Luckily, Judah was one of the new markets BSI's extensive research had identified as ripe for development and exploitation. Big brand sponsors would flock to beauty contest auctions just to associate their name and products with the raging glamour of these – often young and newly minted rather than those currently available wannabe – shale heroes. Riders would have to fight off the sponsorship cash – hence the eye-wateringly low rates of prize money pay per GP negotiated by BSI with the FIM – and hire security vans to transport it to their (most likely offshore) bank accounts. Security wouldn't only be needed to guard the dosh but to protect the actual riders from the grasping hands (and vaginas) of the adoring hordes. Normal life would no longer ever be normal, it would be celebrity. The terms and conditions noted that these bright lights of fame would apply to pre-existing speedway markets as well as those newly opened by the persuasive frighteningly dedicated and Star Trek like "conquering new frontiers" spirited franchise and advertising rights execs apparently already on board at BSI.

Rightly or wrongly, ever since those early apparently all-conquering heady days, expert analysis of this new era of the Speedway World Championship has had an obsessive focus upon the present, near future or immediate past. The current season. The original BSI ambitions have been ignored, claimed to have been met in full, excused or re-written. History only intrudes when it comes to co-opting the current version and format of the contest by associating it with past glories. Arguably this is a false comparison since a one-off final to determine the whereabouts of the crown differs from one awarded to the rider with the highest points total from a series of meetings. Rather than descend into the black hole tear in the space-time continuum that is the bald-men-fighting-over-a-comb nature of this debate about which is "better", let us just say that they are different and modernity requires institution change in every walk of life. It is what it is and the current system of operation for riders to actually win the thing. They can only race in the format currently used and plan accordingly.

Given speedway is a sport that relishes numbers – race times, averages etc. – and often makes a fetish of their arbitrary but absolute nature to determine team compositions, the absolute number of World Championships won is an understandable comparative measure to use. Many know that Ivan Mauger won the world crown six times and Ove Fundin five. Even members of the general public – aka non-fans who don't go to speedway meetings (or watch it on telly) – will have heard of these people. The triumphs of the present need calibration against the victories of the past. Along with easier less challenging stuff like event locations, this is as far any speedway expert or commentator – whether in print, broadcast or online – allows history to intrude into their analysis of the Speedway Grand Prix. Consequently, we only really get to learn worthy but anodyne history stuff. "He is the first American champion since [add name] in [add date]" or "it is his third crown and he plans to retire when he has won seven". Thinking beyond very simple metrics is definitely verboten. We don't really get deeper reflection since most experts are freelancers who directly or indirectly depend upon the largesse of the rights holders so such wild talk might well scare the BSI executive horses sufficiently to punish miscreants with loss of employment or access. If history has to studiously remain at a just about there in name but only at a basic Janet and John level when it comes to rigour, the language allowed to be used to describe any to do the SGP is even more strictly clamped down. If judged by the SGP website content, social media accounts, official DVDs, broadcast commentary and *Speedway Star* reportage. It is an informal system of self-monitoring and group think rather than being officially codified in written form. There is no need to issue regulations if everyone voluntarily pulls any and all punches (except, of course, when this orthodoxy is challenged).

Gossip is completely frowned upon by the rights holders. Given they hitch their knickers at both actual analysis and incorrect eruptions of unauthorised history, any hint of real salaciousness – and there is much to easily choose from – sees them crush their pearls to dust rather than clutch them in their figurative tiny hands. It goes without saying that the wider media and new (mass market) audiences love "bad boy" memes to drive attention, interest and attraction. Sex, drugs and rock-and-roll sells. If it bleeds, it leads. Even if and as they profess otherwise with breathless confected moral outrage. Curated speedway news on dropped sexual assault cases, stabbings, county court judgements, theft, vandalisation, failed drugs tests, police chases and the like aren't respectable topics but do garner attention. Anyways, even if we ignore this gossip red herring, the net overall result is that analysis of the SGP tends to suffer but always wearing stabilisers or only swimming with armbands. It remains stuck in a world of carefully crafted spurious claims that are only ever narrowly true at best. It is a rather trite world of fey but loud astonishment, feigned wonder and various glorious "best" and "strongest" evers. It is a continuous present of over-statement that only really references the past as a yardstick of events won rather than as something to compare with. The SGP website even abridges its own history with a results section only going back to 2010. Many corporate entities practice serial forgetting, not just the SGP rights holders or the drive by brown-nosers of SGP-embedded media. People and businesses regularly happily curate their memories to their own advantage or as befits their current view of the world.

This all said about the ongoing deliberate lack of analysis and proper use of historical context, I will leave others to write either the proper fully authorised sanitised histories of the SGP. Life is too short to want or need to do so. What might be fun and, hopefully, is the book you hold here is an *ad hoc* one season (2018) dive into the current state of the SGP series. One that seeks to look at its present and past as well as to analyse, find, establish or draw various connections. I was fortunate enough to be kindly gifted some behind-the-scenes access as well as having the time, inclination and masochism to go to all the SGP meetings of the 2018 series. We fans were doubly blessed as we even mostly lucky with the weather and also the absence of unforced cataclysmic organisational error by the rights holders or their chosen franchisees.

When it comes to supplementing the lived experience of the continuous present with the stuff of history, there are many possible sources – with differing degrees of access and availability – of print and online records containing various accounts, interpretations and summaries of past statements, plans and events. Such accounts can be found in past programmes and season guides, the pages of the *Speedway Star*, promoter and rider autobiographies, BARB, speedway forums and websites as well as Companies House. Though, like my erstwhile fellow SGP media colleagues, I won't be using these sources in any depth, I will selectively acknowledge their existence and use them for occasional context. Primarily this *Hitchhiker's Guide to the Speedway Grand Prix* is a snapshot of a season of SGP by a fan. It makes no claims to impartiality or comprehensiveness but, when I am feeling pompous, does seek to question some orthodoxies or suggest other ways we might see or (currently) look at all things SGP as well as its past, present and future structural relationship with British speedway. Mainly based on what I saw, heard, witnessed or found but also rounded out with a dash of the critical thinking others with better access and more influence could have the honesty, integrity or independence to have done so much much earlier. And more often. In a nutshell, this is a book about the clothes the King wears. About how the SGP and its various advocates, heavy breather media boosters, helpers, hyperfanatics, sponsors and staff have helped to set in train and magnify the destruction of the institution of British Speedway. Or, at least, helped turbo-charge its market driven, societal and self-inflicted wounds. It is an attempt to query the mis-direction of fans, promoters but especially the specialist trade media – of all stripes (print, broadcast and online) – who continue to deliberately chase red herrings in their attempts to resurrect and save British Speedway from itself while ignoring the elephant in the room that is its most important and damning structural – but toxic – relationship issue.

CHAPTER 1

Warsaw SGP 1 – 12.05.18

"Where is all the money allegedly paid to the FIM for rights and assets that arguably were not theirs to sell? Because I see no benefits whatever finding themselves back into speedway racing."

John Berry, February 2003

THOSE who wonder if speedway still exists or has gone the way of white dog poo, hotel in room trouser presses or multiple visible love bites are in the majority in the UK, but not in Poland. Though no longer the national number one sport it was, speedway is a robust part of daily conversation, both sporting and otherwise. Poland is what counts as a Mecca for bikes without brakes racing on oval-shaped shale circuits. So much so, the rights holders of the Speedway Grand Prix World Championship series stage 30 percent of their events there nowadays. Doing so means that they are guaranteed near sell-out crowds, fanatical fans and robust media coverage. Two decades back when the Fédération Internationale de Motocyclisme (FIM) granted the sports consultancy company Benfield Sports International (BSI) staging rights. Talk was cheap and optimism ran riot. So much so that capital city deluxe stadia stagings with great seats, food and toilets lapped up by large crowds were held to be the future standard recipe to roll out globally. According to BSI, the FIM and various trade media admirers, this was the formula that would unlock widespread public popularity, transform knowledge of its exciting credentials and propel speedway as a sport back from the dark recesses of the margins – that it had been flung to by societal change and/or self-inflicted wounds – to the bright lights popularity and fame of centre stage. Like a poor man's version of F1, only with bikes not cars. Given F1 is notoriously totally boring to watch – live or on the telly – this was always likely to be an ambition that sells speedway badly short.

On a sunny lunchtime in the hubbub of the tourist hotspot that is the remaining small section of Old Town Warsaw, there are even small visible pockets of Polish speedway fans in replica shirts taking selfies with the PGE Narodowy Stadium as a distant backdrop. Despite its cultural significance, even in Poland, speedway is a provincial rather than metropolitan obsession. Its robustly beating hearts are far removed from the big city bright lights and, instead, are scattered across various smaller – but big name to shale aficionados – regional Polish towns. Warsaw has no speedway team or real shale tradition. The majority of fans for the inaugural event of the 2018 series are visitors from elsewhere within Poland or farther afield. Though wildly popular, with over 50,000 seats to fill, there still will be empty spaces visible tonight in the nose-bleed upper tiers of the PGE Narodowy Stadium. Nonetheless, for the third year running the Speedway Grand Prix (SGP) series starts with an almost full stadium and its highest attendance. In, arguably, its most impressive stadium. Definitely the newest built. One that ticks the various boxes of the original founding grandiloquent aims of newly minted rights holder's BSI: namely, meetings staged in (global!) capital city deluxe stadia stagings to adoring crowds. Sadly, counterbalancing this and completely defying its original manifesto, one key strand of the SGP series rights holder's strategy nowadays is to primarily stage their events at locations in obscure hard-to-get-to places with ambition and budget to pay to stage these meetings rather than in lovely major cities like Warsaw. Where bigger stadia are still used, the racing takes place on notoriously temperamental one-off temporary tracks. Over the years, frequent practice installing them has ensured that the standard of these has improved, though they regularly still provide variable conditions not conducive in terms of size, shale and track quality to consistently produce excellent racing from experienced riders at or around the peak of their talents.

Anyways, one of my key reasons for travelling to each and every meeting of the 2018 series is to see, experience and savour the full glory and potency SGP event vibe first hand. To survey the castle ramparts before entering the palaces within to, hopefully, separate the reality of the lived experiences from the colourful hyperpartisan but apparently plausible media fantasies. What better place to start any Speedway Grand Prix journey than Poland? The number one country nowadays for speedway fanaticism and associated buzz including crowd size, meeting razzmatazz, full-throttle all out competitive racing, the best riders, top rider pay and monies owed. They often get full or nearly full stadiums here on a regular basis. In fact, practice in their lower leagues sometimes gets bigger crowds than the less popular clubs in the top tier of speedway in Britain. But, sadly, these are matters for another book rather than this one since I have a thrilling season of SGP meetings across Europe to savour ahead. I will either be lolling about on the periphery of the pits (or pits lane in one-off venues) on race day savouring the privilege of inner sanctum access to "star" riders (and mechanics) as they prepare to race for Speedway World Championship glory. Or else lurking on the terraces fully imbibing the joys of each meeting.

Close to the city centre and well-served by convenient public transport links, on a hot but breeze-cooled afternoon that also blows wisps of blossom from the trees, PGE Narodowy Stadium basks in bright sunshine ahead of the inaugural event of the 2018 Speedway Grand Prix series. The stadium is and looks 21st century but, true to the incipient political authoritarianism of the country, has avoided the bourgeois decadence of excessive contemporary flourishes in its eye-catching but still mostly utilitarian design. It is more upside-down birthday cake meets the London Millennium Dome with a hint of the Birmingham Bull Ring than something wildly unfunctional and studiously weird by Zaha Hadid, the late Will Alsop or Anish Kapoor. Six hours before the precisely scheduled first race time of 19.04, when it comes to indulging any unslaked nationalist feelings they may usually struggle to hold in check, fans arriving from the metro station heading to the stadium environs are spoilt for their choice of Polska-themed memorabilia street stalls. That said, the Polska merchandise is mostly generic and would suit patriotic football fans or more show-offy theatre goers as much as speedway ones.

The dusty car park area outside the stadium main gate serves as the sponsor village Fan Zone and also the drinks/catering area. It is already thronged with fans eating, drinking, savouring the sunshine atmosphere or getting face-painted. Different sponsor and merchandise stalls are in various stages of set-up completion, but are already fenced off by a labyrinth of currently unrequired crush barriers. Even if we ignore its noise and size, the crowd is similar to its UK equivalent for its age range (from babies to OAPs), but notably different for its sheer volume. The large number of female fans is particularly notable too. Speedway in Poland seems to truly appeal to all its people. Over the far side of the fan village, the banal beat of high-energy music where electronic-meets-lite-rock loudly blares out from the "Monster Area" sound system to apparent complete disinterest. When shorn of its staff and adulating crowds, the logo-emblazoned colour-branded open-sided tent structures of key SGP partner and sponsor Monster Energy looks incredibly forlorn sat in bright sunshine. The relentless insistence of their atonal playlist only adds to its abandoned look and feel.

The stadium itself is in impressive lock down. Such is the cachet of the event, let alone the popularity of the sport, security is extremely stringent. We don't need access to the results of Stanley Milgram's famous prisoner psychology experiment to know that – the world over – security uniforms and hi-vis tabards instil officious over-zeal or power-trippery in those given the authority to wear such garments. The architectural mood music of impressive military-base style perimeter fencing and over-manned gated entry points (with reluctantly operated barrier bars) furthers underlines the impregnable security. Until the stadium entry gates officially open to the public at 4pm, only those with proper accreditation can gain entry. Part of the appeal and cachet of these credentials is that they are subject to regular sometimes painstaking examination. Nothing signals inner sanctum access better than stringent security procedures. At the main pre-meeting entry point (Gate 7), the 50 or so fans gathered with cameras and autograph books get to watch everyone – riders, workers, guests, sponsors, hangers on and notables alike – get stopped to show their colour-coded accreditations. Rather revealingly for a sports marketing company with global television rights sales ambitions, the so-called media village is really just a locked white portacabin plastered with A4 sheets advising on the queueing procedures and the exacting paperwork they require (up to and including passport as well as two recent utility bills) when it finally deigns to open as advertised at 3.30pm.

Staging an event of this size and complexity requires significant organisation. Series rights holder's BSI have considerable previous when it comes to painful levels of bureaucracy for riders and their staff as well as sponsors, guests and media attendees. They particularly love complex instruction manuals, contractual demands and extensive bureaucracy for their franchisees. This is necessary and understandable as there is a need for control in order to guard the integrity and consistency of the presentation of series events and guarantee the effective execution of its many component parts. Of course, speedway promoters do this every week Europe-wide without such a song-and-dance, albeit in a fixed location rather than being a travelling circus. Since this in-town-for-one-night-only-with-top-speedway-talent is the *raison d'être* of the SGP series expansion as well as the means by which they drive BSI revenues by extracting franchisee payments from ambitious sub-contractors and pliant local government tourist offices, there can be no cause for complaint. Said protocols and complex instructions also enable BSI to afterwards deny culpability then apportion blame for the various peculiar often self-inflicted snafus that, invariably, arise. That all said, BSI notoriously take themselves very seriously so rarely turn down the chance for some over-elaborate sweaty-bottomed bureaucracy. Ideally in combination with rigorously enforced hierarchy, pampering for chosen executives, form-filling and, nowadays, rigorous cost control of make-the-pips-squeak parsimony.

The entry badge system for the 2018 Speedway Grand Prix series (not just this meeting in Warsaw) is a case in point. There two different wristband colours – green or pink-and-white striped – along with a dizzying range of seven (also) colour-coded numbered badges each permitting varying degrees of access and entitlement. It is a system apparently based on the mid-1980s approach to company car entitlements with a range of optional extras awarded according to the real or imagined status granted to the temporary keeper/owner to disguise that really we all have the same basic model. Security have handy cut-out-and-keep wall charts they Blu-tack up in the window of their sentry boxes. Said visual guide displays an image of each pass type and below lists the various entitlements of the different colour codes. Like all contracts, instruction manuals and A4 (or bigger!) laminated SGP signage provided by BSI Speedway IMG, irrespective of the country staging the event, everything is – unhelpfully – only ever written in English. It is an old-school colonial approach that hardly burnishes the think-global-act-local credentials of these World Championships or, for that matter, completely fails to recognise the I for International contained in the BSI name or that of their parent company IMG. If the security team can read English, they certainly don't speak it. The authority of their uniform and the barriers they stand behind communicates sufficient authority, while their brusque inspection of credentials and carry bags further confirms it.

I am delighted to have been gifted the lowest level pass: the purple flashed "Guest" version that is provided in Warsaw with its accompanying green temporary wristband. My pass grants limited unlimited access to the pits on practice day ("until 30 minutes before practice starts then 30 minutes after practice finishes") and race day ("until 105 minutes before the opening ceremony"). It is a huge privilege to be gifted this behind-the-scenes access to the SGP. Like bees drawn to the scent of pollen, even in countries where speedway is not really popular, individual Grand Prix speedway meetings attract an excess of rubberneckers, geeks, big cheeses and fans with the right connections all keen to gain free access and bathe in the bright reflected glory of the closest the sport has to the glamour of the F1 pit lane. Though, colour-coded race-day passes and wristbands are BSI's existing SGP caste system to properly distinguish the truly important (mainly sponsors or wannabe sponsors) from the bigger tide of self-important hangers-on, to my mind there is an urgent business case for a premium ultra-VIP badge. Short of a badge fitted with pulsing light (not red in case when worn in the stands it distracts the riders), my design recommendation is a gold glitter polka-dot flash to help the BSI commercial team and execs better identify, target and love-bomb their bulging pockets throughout the hubbub of race day.

Disappointingly for the riders, though at every meeting in the series collectively they are the stars of the show, individually they get a strictly controlled number of complimentary passes from the organisers. Twenty of the guest variety and seven of the highly sought-after access-all-areas unlimited time versions. The limited availability of these badges results in an unofficial barter system amongst the competing riders to avoid or reduce the need to purchase the additional guest passes that BSI will only too happily sell them. Rider demand for an increased number of guest passes varies from meeting to meeting dependent upon its location as they are more valuable to an individual rider in their home country and/or where they have extensive sponsorship contacts and contracts. This is particularly so for those with the most commercial support or those most ambitiously in search of it. Riders from more popular countries/locations are disadvantaged when it comes to getting additional passes for sponsors, friends, hangers-on and those who have helped them without further cost compared to riders from less easy-to-get-to less-populated countries. Effectively this helps Slovenian champion Matej Zagar most as he can parlay his unwanted passes throughout the series into a bonanza of "free" guest passes for his extensive roster of Slovenian sponsors at the Krsko meeting held in his home country. Additionally, the higher up the SGP ranking riders finish or the more years they compete in the various speedway leagues, the more geographically dispersed sponsors they tend to have. "Tai wanted five of Craig's passes – cos he rides here – for his sponsors."

Whatever your colour pits pass, once through three waves of security, guests gain the freedom of stadium access tunnel. This in turn leads to the section BSI grandiloquently designated as the "pit lane". The tunnel is shady and comparatively cool after the heat of the day outside. In reality, pit lane is the far from glamorous below stairs stadium service tunnel-cum-car-park. Or, given this is speedway, van park. Its lengthy car-width passageway is lined either side by marked parking spaces occasionally interrupted by fenced off and heavily guarded accessways that lead upwards to the amphitheatre bowl of the stadium proper. Viewed from the tunnel, curved stadium tiers loom impressively in a riot of brightly coloured seating to dominate the skyline. Though there is no threat or forecast of rain, the retractable roof is closed so the stadium amphitheatre is comparatively shaded. If you are brave enough to walk up and glimpse over the shoulders of the hi-vis security guard of honour, what can be seen of the lush red shale of the temporary track sharply contrasts with the primarily orange and black standard colour palette of the SGP air fence signage. Completely unoccupied except for an impressive random tangle of metallic furniture, the fairy tale artificially too-bright turquoise of the centre green apron further spurs my anticipation for the racing ahead.

If this were British speedway, I'd have no anxiety about pits etiquette and it definitely wouldn't be pretentious enough to style itself as a pit lane. But, since this is the global speedway stage, beforehand I consult speedway author and journalist Brian Burford. He advises, "If you've got a pit pass, get there as early as you can." I have partly defied this advice with some compulsory yomping in the sunshine outside trying but failing to find my way in because of my lack of Polish, the lengthy stadium perimeter and confusing gate signage. Knowing you can get into the SGP pits before tapes up is one thing, but the possibly sublime mystery of what actually happens there beforehand is another. Brian quickly and accurately punctures this particular excitement balloon. "Nothing much! There'll be a whole load of bikes lined up with no wheels on waiting for the tyres." In fact, by the time I arrive, I have just missed this particular lunchtime thrill so, sadly, the excitement of the tyres getting issued and then fitted, eludes me. This year the SGP series again has ambitious new sponsors who – I'm going to guess – won't continue to do so for that many seasons once they realise their costs and expectations are so out of kilter with the reality and actual commercial advantages of their experience. In this case, the FIM Speedway Grand Prix series now has what it terms an "official SGP tyre supplier" – Turkish manufacturer Anlas – to "invest in the sport for the future years to come". BSI relentlessly offer various different SGP sponsorship packages and levels. Effectively all differently shades of vanilla, albeit variously priced. My life is too short to check out the specifics or attempt to find the breathlessly worded press release about the revolutionary significance of this particular deal on the difficult-to-navigate news section of the official SGP website. But, and I guess-summarise here, this changed tyre supplier news was greeted as on par with a major scientific breakthrough in the fight against cancer or similarly life-threatening disease currently imperilling humanity. Doubtless newbies Anlas expect increased global recognition for their tyre brand as a result of this "World" Championship sponsorship and, hopefully, further brand differentiation in online searches from Anusol. Sadly, of course, even attentive viewers won't gain any noticeable visual brand awareness since speedway tyres are too fast-moving and narrow to effectively display manufacturer names. Obviously too, this pyrrhic dream also ignores the brutal reality that the SGP is actually nothing like F1 so there is really no mass global broadcast audience for ANY other brand on display either. Anlas also have the additional obstacle that speedway riders like to stick with the tried and tested tyre supplier(s) they know or else innovate on their own volition rather than having such equipment changes thrust upon them.

Arguably one of the most commercially minded riders in the SGP series, as well as an intuitive understander of how to gain then treat sponsors, is Greg Hancock. Even or especially, if they are not currently signed up as yours. Later in the season once he has stolen a comprehensive march on his rivals, self-congratulatorily drinking deeply from the well of his career-long self-proclaimed "quest for speed", Greg reveals on his podcast that he is a serial helper-cum-love-bomber of Anlas in their quest to seize the speedway tyre future. Effectively Greg has endorsed their ambitions by blind-siding their research and development boffins with expert talk on the science of rubber compounds and track surface physics that, inevitably, requires his extensive (paid) testing. Crash helmets off to Greg for snuffling out yet another sponsorship income stream other riders ignored or failed to recognise. They only saw a tyre they didn't want to use and weren't currently required to use by the current FIM regulations. Unlike Greg, they completely lacked the vision required to efficiently parlay these new tyres into yet more of the green folding stuff via some tactical interest and theatrical showmancing. For sponsor ears or those of the general public – who randomly tune into his lengthy podcasts – Greg's experimentation on behalf of a no-hoper product is dressed up as public spiritedness and yet another example of his personal career-long pursuit of fractional speed gains through technological innovation. Ever the showcaser of and virtue signaller for his sponsor brands, Greg even manfully tried out Anlas tyres during one of his practice session rides the day before. Before, obviously, immediately discarding them. Understandably keen not to massively disadvantage themselves from the get-go, every other SGP rider continues to use tyres from Mitas – the company whom, notionally, this new SGP sponsor eventually hopes to replace in pits everywhere with its "superior" products.

This is kind of the SGP in a nutshell – big initial promises to attract the client and open their wallet. Quite a bit of jazzy – but, ultimately, ineffective – song and dance then follows before the realisation dawns that deliverables (of whatever stripe: market share, acclaim, audience, reputation etc.) are always going to fall short of both promises and expectations. Pitifully poor returns on investment are always hard to justify or spin over the medium to long term, no matter how good the mood music or ambitious and foolhardy the sponsor/patron. It also could be predicted from the get-go since, even though tyres are one of the few things statutorily supplied free to SGP participants as a mandatory FIM obligation. Rights holders BSI would always have a tough ask in getting riders to experiment with an unknown variable in any round of the World Championship series, let alone the opening one. Not to bother to even unpack them, never mind use them, is a commonsense decision from the riders. Given success in the SGP depends on steady points accumulation plus the fact that riders nowadays expend so much effort searching for fractional or incremental advantages in their equipment, preparation, nutrition, fitness and psychology, why then saddle yourself with an unknown and untested product that could be the racing equivalent of a square wheel? If I were these new wannabe tyre suppliers, I would soon be drafting a strongly worded email to BSI demanding both explanation and significant refund. Amazingly, it is said, Anlas fully expect their campaign for rider mindshare to require patience and further years of SGP sponsorship. Unless this is all along really a clever tax write-off ruse, even if every speedway rider in the world suddenly switched to Anlas, the reputational boost and additional revenue streams thereby created would remain more or less invisible to the naked eye. BSI just love to find then milk these kinds of transient, ultimately disposable, ambitious deep-pocketed sponsors. The rights holders bank the sponsorship dosh fully aware that even total immersion in the warm bath of SGP glory by association, this relationship will deliver the square root of close to nothing in terms of increased market share or consumer mindshare for such partners.

Beyond gazing on enraptured at the tyre-fitting, what tips does Brian have to ensure that I have some sense of purpose or belonging in the pits? "Just do what everyone else does – look important! Or stand by Craig Cook's pit bay? Do you know anyone?"

"No."

"Do you know Steve Brandon?"

"Is he the bloke who used to shout at the riders, so they kept to the TV schedule timings?"

"He does look after keeping things on time."

"Isn't he called @talkingbum, or something like that, on Twitter?"

"I'm not on Twitter. Do you know Bert Harkins?"

"Yes."

"Stand by him then. He knows everyone. If anyone asks, say you've come to see how it really works. Most people who are there are hangers-on. It only really gets interesting an hour beforehand and your pass means you won't be allowed to be there then."

"I get thrown out then?"

"When the riders turn up. It's Poland so they'll have a lot of meetings with sponsors to do. Or signings for Monster Energy. Or else they'll be back in their rooms either feeling like superstars or trying to psyche themselves up with positive thinking and thinking that'll make the difference."

"Won't it?"

"Not really. There's no need to race any longer, you can just ride around. Mainly because there's so many meetings in a series. For a time – when they had sudden death and you could get eliminated by finishing third or fourth – they really raced. That definitely made it interesting. Nowadays, it's the same old faces racing each other again and again and again, just in different places."

As Mr Burford predicted, mostly while I'm in the SGP pit lane there are no riders to be seen. Not even all the mechanics are there though, of course, the bikes are. Albeit in various half or three-quarters built stages of readiness for the racing ahead. If standing next to or even, heaven forfend, touching these spotlessly gleaming speedway bikes (without riders) is your thing, then this pits access is a wet dream come true. With around five hours to tapes up, the only rider anywhere to be seen is Britain's Craig Cook. Even he is some distance from his bikes. Craig is slouched in the passenger seat of his van with feet up and mobile in hand. Instantly disqualifying myself from an alternative career as an ophthalmologist, I completely fail to notice what Phil Lanning in a later interview describes as, "those translucent Barbados beach blue eyes". It is Cook's first SGP and to be here this early is a basic rookie error. Not only does it give him endless time for pre-meeting nerves or anxiety but also everyone can see him as they pass by heading towards the rider pit bays. Given both the lack of other riders plus the warm feelings Craig engenders, many well-wishers stop for a word or else shout encouragement as they pass. Hardly conducive conditions for relaxation or, indeed, getting into the zone (wherever that is), if that is your preference. Like pretty well every other Brit, I stop for a chat. Craig is modest and polite. I have previous randomly photographed Craig in his van a few years back at Workington. Kissing a Jack Russell dog, after a meeting. Though it means something to me, it won't have registered with Craig so, as a conversational and comparatively non-speedway ice-breaker that should have positive associations in a strange and unfamiliar place, I remind him. With hindsight it is, perhaps, not the best choice of topic in search of Craig's happy place as the dog died last year, aged 13. It wasn't his dog either but his dad's. "I thought she'd live longer. Dad's bought a mini-dachshund, Molly. What a character! She makes you happy just looking at her!"

Switching topics, I congratulate Craig on his innovative speedway fan-led SGP sponsorship programme. In order to compete effectively in the SGP series, you or your family and sponsors need really deep pockets. Initially more so, just to metaphorically stand still. Back in the mists of time (well, 2003), one of the founding SGP riders – American Billy Hamill – unilaterally withdrew from the series at the last minute citing the sheer cost of competing in it compared to the earnings. "I have been unable to put together a racing budget to compete in the Grand

Prix...I just wouldn't be on a level playing field with the other guys, and it's hard enough when you do start equal." Many fellow riders were expected to follow suit but didn't. Even at the time, FIM Race Director Ole Olsen was indifferent to Hamill's withdrawal knowing, like London buses, that there would be another along in a minute, "There are plenty of young kids out there pressing to get a chance to compete in the World Championship". The stark reality is that competing in the SGP initially costs much more than it repays or will ever directly repay in prize monies and new sponsorships unless you attain the dizzy heights and holy grail of regular climbs on board the Top 8 gravy train. To get to that stage, as a rider you need substantial investment in equipment, systems, talent and skilled backroom staff as the *de facto* business model of SGP rights holder's BSI is predicated on exploiting or piggy-backing upon the financial commitment of others without reciprocal obligations. In order to properly mine the financial riches currently on offer in Poland, riders already require the sponsor support, bikes, engine tuners and mechanics they then also use to compete effectively in the Grands Prix series. Harder still for new(er) entrants, riders regularly riding in the SGP Top 8 (or Poland) have often already sewn up the best engine tuners and mechanics as well as the best or richest sponsors. Before you get the stable sponsorship income streams that breaking into this Top 8 upper echelon can provide, riders have to somehow overcome or square the vicious circle that a good number of GP podium finishes or, better still, some wins requires significant prior investment rather than just talent. Aiming for these notable finishes isn't for the pitiful prize money on offer – these sums mostly remain frozen in time – but for the notional status this confers in the minds of your existing or would-be sponsors and employers. Of course, even the lure of these sponsorship riches could also be a chimera similar to the oft-highlighted massive worldwide television audience promised by BSI (and the FIM) that didn't ever consistently arrive so, sadly, never got to complete the equation supposed to drive legions of admiring global brand sponsors into the welcoming arms of the riders. Indeed, the initial robust interest and growing SGP television audiences there were have slowly withered on the vine. In this context, as he and his dad Will already well know, Craig's decision to compete in the 2018 SGP series is right for his career and psyche. But also remains a very significant six-figure financial gamble without any guarantee of a good outcome. In addition to seeking commercial sponsors – mainly, so far, it seems existing clients or companies based in Cumbria or the North-West of England – Craig has a "GP Support Squad" of over 200+ supporters who have signed up to this scheme at a minimum of £50 per head. There are various tiers of fan membership. Arguably the popular aspect of this fan support – in addition to personal letters, birthday cards, regular communications via email, shout-outs on social media and prize draws – is the thoughtful recognition by Craig of the value of their support by displaying all their individual names on his British and Polish vans as well as his SGP race suits. Craig tells me, "Being sponsored by lots of fans is cool. It's nice to be appreciated. And you've got to be in it to win it."

The fact that Craig rests up in an unmarked grey van without the fans' names on the side is something Plymouth-based speedway fans Andy Riddle and Julie Sweet notice and immediately take up with his van sponsor Richard Cotton of Rentruck. Richard is more worried about passing attention, "Craig needs to get into his own zone for tonight without distraction." There is a rich tradition of riders' vans having livery that reads: Joe Bloggs Speedway Rider. Indeed, for a long time, once you got good enough to race in a few countries, it was a rite of passage to pimp the signage of your van with news of your newfound international status. Who can forget when Linus Sundstrom added "International Speedway Rider" to the side of his van? Or, at least, I think he did. I certainly suggested it to him on Twitter back in the day when he wondered on there how you knew when you'd finally really made it as a speedway rider. Nothing says this – or that you have status anxiety and haven't quite got where you say you have – than making this signage rite of passage.

Richard is an affable man and sponsor of quite some note for British speedway riders as he provides 45 different riders with vans. Most vans have no livery nowadays. Because of the expense to Rentruck but, more importantly, "Riders don't like to advertise that they have 20 grands' worth of equipment inside". Even if riders are lucky enough to have sponsorship, annual van insurance doesn't come cheap, "It's £1,600 a year for speedway riders to insure the vans." You can understand why actuaries might charge speedway riders a premium – their youth (Greg Hancock excepted), long-distance driving, late nights, as well as a deserved reputation for a love of thrills and speed. Arguably, their mechanics are more full-on riskier drivers. Luton Town FC scout, football writer and speedway fan Andy Riddle explains that getting sensibly priced cover is a nightmare generally for sports people. "Sports stars have difficulties getting car insurance. Effectively they're freelancers. Even non-league footballers have a nightmare. It's not so much their actual loss of career earnings but who they might have as a passenger in the car as a result of their work. I know he's not what he was but, say, they had an accident with Rooney in the car as passenger for example? The pay-out would be horrendous so they guard against that." Litigation in such circumstances doesn't just deal with loss of earnings. "They say Chris Holder litigated for a crash at Coventry speedway. Against them and the Tony Briggs air fence. His claim listed not just loss of earnings due to injury but loss of sponsors, future loss of sponsors, reduced level of future sponsorship due to uncertainty about the level of his recovery from the injuries – would he be the rider he was? – and loss of function. The financial value of such claims can really be incredibly high."

Andy's partner Jules is a speedway fan of three years since Andy first took her. Though not of long-standing, she's a passionate fan. Earlier in the reception of the centrally located Novotel Warsaw, they caught a few words with Craig Cook as he chatted amiably with fans, friends and passers-by. The hot-off-the-press news is apparently Craig has slept poorly but aims to recover with a good breakfast and afternoon of rest. Quite why he decided to put his feet up at the stadium on display in the front seat of his van is something of a mystery. Andy and Jules also bumped into Nigel Pearson yesterday in the Old Town. The long-standing telly commentary team take different approaches to their ongoing research for the SGP. "He was having a Guinness. Kelvin had gone to watch the practice, but Nigel doesn't as he finds it boring watching two riders at a time do four laps each." Though they missed getting to chat to Mr Tatum MBE, they had bumped into him in Poland at the SGP in 2017. "Kelvin told us at Torun last year that with Lakeside he went to a BSPA meeting but – because of what was going on there – he walked out and didn't want to be part of it."

Though fans are an essential part of the Speedway Grand Prix stage dressing and furniture, given diminishing attendances generally, the series – like many sports – is increasingly primarily staged as a television spectacle. As a result, much more attention is paid to the look, layout and styling of their pit lane booth by more of the riders than was the case in yesteryear. Of course, since individual tasks directly related to or associated with speedway racing generally – whether skilled, specialist or grunt work – are increasingly sub-contracted out to specialists, this will have been sourced and organised by their family or staff. Whoever has done the actual work, the look and feel of each rider booth is more than just the place they prepare, repair and finesse their bikes or rest between heats. It's the stage upon which they strut their stuff for the benefit of the "worldwide" television audiences served by cameras they know can focus closely upon their various reactions during the course of the evening's racing. Consequently, pit lane has the look and feel of trade sales display booths, albeit at an obscure specialist trade exhibition. It is a blizzard of garish but nondescript logos that shout attendees are here for a heating and ventilation accessories trade event or, possibly, a lubrication and cleaning fluids convention. Only the prominent display of speedway bikes suggests otherwise. Stood ready, these impressive gleaming machines add an incongruent note of drama in an otherwise bland presentational landscape of individually unique yet dully uniform booths.

While some riders' work stations are already meticulously presented, others are a half-built work-in-progress or else notably bare. Most riders' bikes are in situ, others are absent or else clustered swishly together close to the tyre-fitting area. Many riders have what looks to be three identical bikes ready for action. There are bottles, cannisters, tool boxes and containers galore too. Almost every available surface displays a logo or could do so if the price was right. It is a visual storm of brightly coloured signs, logos, stickers, whooshes and snappy messaging. Mostly companies no one has ever heard of, offering unknown or obscure services in mystery locations. Collectively these sponsors are the winds that hold the riders SGP ambitions aloft and, if negotiated sensibly, windfalls that partly land in their bank accounts too.

Ignoring comparative investment levels in equipment and rider bay fixtures and fittings, rider booths are laid out in the seniority order of the final 2017 SGP classification standings. This means the current World Champion occupies the bay closest to the track access point. Furthest away from the shale in comparative Siberia is Craig Cook's spartan booth along with those of the meeting wild card (Krzysztof Kasprzak) and meeting reserves (Maksym Drabik and Bartosz Smektala). The look, feel and equipment in each booth sends its own message, whether explicit, implicit or by comparison. Tai's booth proclaims him as "Tai Woffinden World Champion". These are the words that viewers will see every time the cameras linger on Tai's pit booth. Given that this signage doesn't happen by accident – let alone that Jason Doyle currently holds that title – this is either a confident prediction or else a bad typographical error. Or, possibly, trolling that you just know Nigel and Kelvin – should they deign to notice – would contractually enthusiastically hail as a bit of Mensa-meets-Chess-Grandmaster "psychology". Of all the booths, Freddie Lindgren's is the most notable. Mainly for its use of a blown-up upper-body photo whose focus is his new hairstyle. With only this super-sized image on display to guide us, it appears Freddie's new hairstyle is a restrained Mohican cut that rocks his new Billy Whizz meets straight-to-DVD camp thriller villain look. Glancing at this hard-to-miss image, Rentruck Richard says *sotto voce*, "If that's what it takes for him to become World Champion!" Amazing given the size of the image, later it transpires this Mohican is actually a miniscule pony tail put up in a headband. Whatever it is, and ignoring either are tonsorial style crimes, Freddie's photo is striking for all the wrong reasons. His hair and the notionally menacing nationalist-extremist night watchman pose is more likely to prompt laughter rather than fear amongst his 2018 SGP rivals. Though subject to helmet hair on a regular basis, it is striking how few speedway riders are bald, let alone at the SGP. What riders might lack in height or stature is more than compensated for with fast reflexes, bravery and luxuriant hair. Come to think of it, even receding hairlines are a rarity. Hardly anyone springs to mind off the track either. That said, once seen no one could – obviously – ever forget Stoke speedway promoter Dave Tattum's flamboyant comb-over. Tai Woffinden's staff – well, Nigel Pearson or his muscular mechanics – favour a military buzz cut, but that's about it. Perhaps, it was hair availability that first lured hairdresser made good Matt Ford to Poole Speedway? Whatever their genre of baldness – whether receding hairlines, premature, pattern or old-school complete baldness – the follicly challenged the world over do amazingly often push the (I'm guessing spurious) claim that it is actually a known biological indicator of virility and masculinity. Possibly, hyper-masculinity. If this is so, speedway riders – worldwide – appear to lack this particular masculinity gene.

Though very much in charge of his own hair, arguably, the worst-looking rider booth belongs to current World Champion Jason Doyle. It is a mish-mash of new and pre-loved. Worse still, it appears to have been constructed by design-don't-wannabes keen to graduate as design-don't-knows, on day release from a mandatory work experience project for a qualification they don't want that no-one recognises anyways. Whatever motivated them to do this to Doyle's work space, they have more than fulfilled their brief to deliver maximum confusion and ugliness in the smallest possible space using the largest possible number of obscure brightly coloured sponsor logos. It is either sabotage or just bashing things out without thought or preamble. If anything sends a message of psychological trouble ahead in the defence of his title, Doyle's apparent indifference to the professional visual presentation of his SGP pits booth is very telling. While we don't expect design flair or, indeed, style leadership from riders [1] we do expect basic commercial good sense. The endless quest for additional discretionary monies surely dictates existing or future/wannabe sponsors like to see everything look the part whenever they pass by or see it on the telly?

After entry to the demilitarised zone that is the stadium grounds, overzealous entrance security staff fuel the incipient paranoia of cyclists everywhere by making them dismount to gain access. Deeper inside the bowels of the stadium, however, it is a complete free-for-all. Absolutely no attempt is made to slow down. Bikes zip past, while the plague that is the hipster mode of transport *du jour* – scooters – shoot about the highways and byways of the service tunnel network with the flamboyance of skateboards when fast ridden by riders' oily handed staff. Bartosz Zmarzlik's mechanics have motorised scooters, while it's the foot-powered variety for those of Przemyslaw Pawlicki. Apart from Craig – and, with an endless stream of well-wishers crowding up to his van window his being here more and more looks like a trip to the zoo – all the early arrivals are conspicuously not the riders but rather those connected to their performance, well-being, glad-handing or sponsors. With his son's drugs ban long since forgotten, Patryk Dudek's dad is already in situ as are various mechanics including the recently arrived Jacek "Jako" Trojanowski, Tai Woffinden's tall number 1 mechanic. He's rake-thin and youthful for someone so highly regarded: "Tai trusts him absolutely with his set-ups. If he says go down a tooth, Tai does!" Jako studiously surveys his empire for the night: the Woffinden pit bay. With time to kill and perfection to attain, he grabs a pair of Tai's diddy-sized already ultra-clean kevlars off their hanger and proceeds to meticulously brush them free of imaginary shale dust. Jako obsessively grooms said work clothes with the painstaking fastidiousness usually seen when rats groom each other. He continues zealously until it meets the dust-free cleanliness standard required pre-operation by surgical garments. Having a highly skilled mechanic in your pits corner is all part of the riders' investment arms race generally – but especially for those racing in Poland or the SGP. Success in regular Polish speedway is way more cut-throat than the staler, zest-free, more collegiate endless rounds of the SGP series. Though risks are and will be taken tonight and elsewhere at the remaining nine events of the series, they are at a minimum and on an altogether lesser degree of magnitude to riding in Poland. This is a function of the sheer level of financial reward on offer in Poland but also because – once qualified – SGP riders can't be cut from the series nor dropped during the year. Nor are SGP riders subject to a repertoire of contractual fines for micro-infractions of a wide and minutely specified range

[1] after a lesson in the correct use of *there* and *their* from another Twitter user, Doyle replied, "I race a bike for a living. I don't need A grade punctuation to reply to a tweet."

of performance, attendance and presentational variables. Competition in top level Polish speedway is so intense that marginal gains of all stripes are aggressively pursued. When chased at all costs, inevitably the pursuit of the spoils of career success means corners get dangerously cut, "not in the GPs but, they say, some Polish riders are riding without their body armour in order to reduce weight and go fractionally faster."

Even closer to the track than Jason Doyle's pit bay and almost adjacent to the track entry/exit point is the cordoned-off space that serves during meetings as the televised rider-interview area. Though the logos change, the colour scheme of the interview backdrop in SGP livery (primarily black and orange) is a familiar sight to the diminishing band ("global audience") of World Championship speedway TV viewers. Sadly, despite the volume of hot-take interviews, real insights over the season are stunningly rare but things are occasionally pepped up by instances of inadvertent live swearing. Given nowadays there is a warning system to penalise riders moving at the tapes that can – at the second offence – result in their exclusion, it might be fun to instigate a similar system for interview banalities? This would have to be cumulative and series-long to be truly effective. Come to think of it, perhaps the FIM or BSI could implement a word bingo competition to aid concentration on what the riders are actually saying rather than just – as now – hear and consume it as background white noise? Obviously, certain words or phrases would have to be automatically excluded including "taking each race as it comes", "taking each meeting one at a time" or "left me room to race". And, though highly correlated with the number of Australian riders competing, "stoked" must surely be permanently banned as a descriptor? Extending things slightly further, Greg Hancock wouldn't be allowed to fake smile, fist bump or say "rad". Additionally, all riders in the Monster Energy team would have to open and then down a full can of said sponsor's fluid in one go before each and every interview in order to be allowed to wave any item with Monster branding (especially drinks bottles). This would be easy to organise as, close to the rider-interview space, is a Monster Energy booth stocking the full range of their garishly coloured cans. According to the *Guardian*, each can of Monster contains an artificial boost to your system equivalent to 13 four-gram sugar cubes and two expressos. Monster have the pits lane drinks concession at every SGP this season. All their drinks are provided free and, based on nothing more than casual observation, drunk enthusiastically by security operatives, pit booth staff, mechanics, people with guest passes or those without taste buds. Innovation in the actual product itself (to a non-user like myself) appears to be primarily new can colours, mixes or flavours that fail to ameliorate its trademark noxious taste and after-sip mouth feel. Part of me wishes for a Scottish SGP so that Irn-Bru could take over the gratis soft-drinks concession and, thereby, provide something exponentially more palatable.

Over three hours before tapes rise, the main man behind SGP sponsorship partner Monster Energy's Eastern European head honcho "Monster" Joe Parsons (MJP) arrives. Based in Torun since 2013, Parsons is officially Director of Special Projects, Eastern Europe, Middle East and Asia. In large US-based corporations such as Monster Energy, the Special Projects title is usually the supernumerary position given to those whom you don't trust with the keys to the stationary cupboard but still want to give an important-sounding title to. Such is the paucity of SGP partners or sponsors with any hint of marketing smarts (let alone élan) or thought leadership, in the past few years, Monster Joe has come from nowhere to bestride European speedway like a colossus. The mental image of his bestriding effectively means his testicles teabag Poland. Judged by his actions and often his words too, MJP has little respect for the some of the more frustrating old school practices, traditions and values of speedway. That is his prerogative, of course. And who wouldn't – if encouraged or enabled by their employer to live and say things LARGE? Especially if still desperately clutching by your fingertips onto your lost youth. Or, indeed, ersatz distant echoes of and reminiscences about your California roots? Permission to hog the live camera at every opportunity during work hours would be hard to resist too. In a nutshell, it is imperative Monster Joe keeps the marketing wheels turning in Monster Energy's primary East European market – Poland – in approved traditional Monster (bad/rad) attitudinal fashion. World Championship, World Team Cup and World Pairs speedway sponsorship to whatever depth or chosen stripe consistently remains the convenient and cheap option. With SGP rights holders in cost-cutting mode and desperate for cash to be given almost free rein by them – and one remove the FIM – makes excellent strategic sense. For quite some time, BSI have been totally relaxed about co-opting responsibility for the supply of most SGP meeting entertainments and also its notional off-track glamour to a third party. MJP has effortlessly exploited this opportunity to bend the competition to dovetail with the Polish market needs of his employer without apparent push back, restriction or question from the rights holders. Effectively, the Monster tail wags the BSI dog and, in turn, the BSI tails wags the FIM dog. In this dog analogy, SGP fans who pay to attend are the dirt under the toenail cuticles.

Fresh in from the bright Warsaw sunshine, Joe is tanned and casually dressed in his usual age-inappropriate surfer dude attire, albeit in Monster Energy brand-compliant dark hues of black with splashes of their distinctive fluorescent green. Parsons is of speedway rider height but greater girth. Part middle-age spread, part extensive travel and entertainment, but also newish parenthood. Apart from his swagger, the satchel slung across his back is the only concession towards his authority and status. It is easy to forget as they nowadays seem such a part of the SGP furniture that it is only a few years since this corporation first broke onto the SGP speedway scene. As ever, when it comes to new avenues of sponsorship coin, ever-present SGP series rider Greg Hancock was the prime mover. He was the first to be so often seen conspicuously waving Monster Energy beakers around in his televised SGP interviews, pits pre- and post-race reactions or during his intermittent televised semi-final and final lane selections. From 2012 onwards, Monster has run with the hares and hunted with the hounds by sponsoring certain SGP riders. This created the first speedway "team" of the BSI era in what is – after all – supposed to be a solo championship that pits individual versus individual. They have simultaneously fried bigger fish through their various degrees of SGP series and World Cup event partnerships and sponsorships. This is arguably much more significant as they have got huge bang for their marketing buck with little overall innovation, simply by the shrewd strategic step of easily persuading series organisers BSI to increasingly sub-contract the look, feel and pre/post-meeting off track entertainment options and provision to what is really just the standard Monster template. Apparently lifted verbatim from their corporate brand identity manual. This almost seamless co-opting of World Championship Speedway into their own advertising activities and branding needs, looks more and more like canny negotiation, shrewd exploitation and good execution by Monster. Especially since to subsume the SGP into the Monster Energy brand really only required they roll out their base level – with minor tweaks – tried and tested "extreme" and "dangerous" sports event template that they so successfully operate elsewhere when sponsoring other obscure and niche but so-called adrenalin-based "sports". I hesitate to use the word "danger" but the sports they choose to sponsor do have a strong jeopardy and measured madness quotient. Or, at least, the appearance of said same. Inevitably, where there is real, imagined or feigned risk, there are invariably strong associations of derring-do, thrills and glamour – to either manufacture or exploit. Monster compound these perceptions by also providing a bevy of tightly clothed promo women to complement the spectacle. Almost universally, their marketing collateral and videos – as well as the sports they choose to sponsor and demographics they target – assumes a male gaze.

Though SGP organisers BSI have a long track record of more often persuading pre-existing sponsors from elsewhere in speedway to take the GP sponsorship plunge rather than researching, finding or sourcing original ones for themselves, Monster nowadays comprehensively wear the trousers in this relationship. And have for a long time. The next day, Torben Olsen – son of Ole – "vice president and managing director of BSI speedway" indulged in some reciprocal nether-region smoke-blowing with Parsons in a jointly authored press release with no real new "news" that received little specialist press coverage beyond headlining their own websites. However, what it did contain in the quote from Parsons was explicit acknowledgement of their business strategy with regards to their investments in speedway. "Monster wants the speedway fan base to look at us as one of them and supporting their sport; as really authentically ingrained into speedway racing. We are extremely happy with the relationship that we have built with BSI Speedway over the last six years, and look forward to furthering the development of the sport and exposing more fans to our products." Setting aside the inadvertent horror mental image of Parsons exposing himself to anyone with good eyesight, you have to admire his candour here. It is something increasingly rarely seen in the gamed, tame and stale freelancer-filled speedway media reporting. Namely, that Monster are not one of us ("speedway fans" or people) but, merely, pretending to be so for business reasons. This is hardly a shock revelation but bears repeating given their almost all-consuming visual and organisational dominance. Just as all political careers suddenly end in failure, so too will the Monster-SGP commercial relationship and, when it does (the current contract expires in 2021), World Championship Speedway will struggle to cope or resurrect its battered reputation from the after-burn and wreckage of its demise.

Back outside the stadium, while they wait for the gates to open, an already impressive number of fans – judged in comparison to attendances at British speedway meetings including the Cardiff Grand Prix – enjoy the sunshine. The bright bubbly atmosphere echoes the warm weather. In the tented entertainments area, a musical celebration of Guantanamo torture-suite playlist classics continues to blare from the Monster stand to little attention from the fans. Instead they throng the popular bars and stand chatting or enjoying their food in the sunshine. Others obediently join the sizeable queue for the portable toilets or else await the pending attraction of a visit to the stand of his sponsor Boll by reigning World Champion Jason Doyle. Interacting with a crowd of people for whom English is a third or fourth language probably pitches the conversational insights and joy of a Jason Doyle interview or autograph-signing session at just the right level of nuance. Like so many riders in pursuit of the oft-illusory marginal gains that will establish or underline their dominance over their putative rivals, Jason pays close attention to his nutrition. Judged by his even leaner appearance this season (and last season he was noticeably gaunt), Jason is definitely hitting his target low body-fat percentages and may even have lost bone density. Consequently, he has the visibly disproportionate lantern lower jaw size commonly seen in people with more severe eating issues. This isn't to decry his dedication to gaining further World Championship glory or the current achievement of his nutritional fastidiousness *per se* (especially notable since Jason is disadvantaged by being one of the rarer taller SGP series speedway riders) but to note the visual impact of one of the current prices of seeking success nowadays. Clearly, modern lightweight bikes do often require complementing with modern lightweight riders to optimise their power-weight ratios. Given Jason is reigning World Champion, the idea that you must or can diet your way to SGP glory is a message impressionable younger riders need no second invitation to wholeheartedly follow. The crowd parts and the hubbub rises as Jason strides towards the destiny of his autograph session closely escorted by two Boll pit parade women. All three wear skin tight uniforms that stay rigorously on corporate message with their rictus smiles and tight-fitting appropriately be-logoed clothing. My ignorance, of course, but I have absolutely no idea what product Boll involves. Nor have the interest to find out. I think they make those retro cocktail drinks: Snowballs. One of these Advocaat-soaked cherries would slip down nicely so am half-tempted to wait my turn but the sheer size of the queue puts me off. It is said that lobsters are the only creatures that urinate from their face and, judged by the look on his face at his first sponsor obligatory SGP appearance of the season, Jason copes with his reluctance about public autograph sessions by channelling his inner crustacean.

Rather amazingly and seemingly in all seriousness, this brief fan engagement on behalf of his sponsor Boll would be blamed – in addition to concussion he never mentioned at the time from an early season Polish league meeting crash at Gorzow – by Doyle as a key reason he didn't retain his World Championship crown. "There are a lot of people wanting to talk with you and interact with you before a race meeting," he told a credulous and unquestioning Paul Burbidge. Taking an onion from his pocket and apparently confusing racing speedway with the responsibilities of brain, spinal or cancer surgery, Jason continued, "It's not like any other job when you can just go there and chat to people, still get on with your job and do it 100 per cent." Except for the very rare occasion he had a mandatory circa 30-minute signing session in the fan zone, given that Doyle is, subsequently, notable by his absence from pit lane prior to 17.15 (when the majority of guest pass holders leave) at every meeting throughout the 2018 SGP season, the lived reality is that Jason effectively had almost none of the distracting fan and sponsor interaction he so decries. Warming to his theme, Doyle claims speedway fans and sponsors don't know they are born in comparison to, say, fans of rallying, stock cars, giant wheeled truck racing, F3 and clown-car demolition derbies, "In speedway, you're very lucky to get up close and personal with the riders. It's not like that in other major motorsports." After bemoaning his shyness at length in public, Doyle notes, "That sometimes might make people think I am arrogant and not wanting to talk. That's just how I am and how I have been for the last 10 or 15 years I have raced speedway." I can't pretend to know what people or fans think but I do know that contemporary SGP riders do not really get to interact with speedway fans in the way they used to at either World Championships or elsewhere during the season doing everyday bread-and-butter league meetings. Gone are the days when fans and riders were cut from the same cloth and lived in the same communities. Amazingly, some riders are even tax exiles nowadays. There is no more talking in the car park or motorway service station nor drinking in the bar afterwards like there used to be. Serendipitous interactions with upper echelon riders (racing weekly in multiple countries) are almost completely absent unless you share the same plane flight as a rider. Even then it is unlikely. Or discourteous, in my opinion. Chance meetings over the macrobiotic yoghurts at the hotel breakfast bar are as likely as it gets to the chance to accidentally chatting with SGP riders. Even then riders can, of course, avoid this by getting room service or bringing their own food. At every SGP, officious security ensures that NO genuine paying fan WITHOUT guest pass accreditation gets anywhere near let alone access to pit lane. Those there with guest passes are sponsors, staff, media, friends of sponsors, giftees, hangers-on or else they are the chosen few with good connections. And, of course, lucky prize winners. Or those who have them in an attempt to make up for service shortfalls they experienced at previous SGP meetings. (Anecdotally, these historically really swelled the pits lane crowd.) Like most SGP riders, Jason only arrives in pit lane after the real rush has gone. This is sensible. It is his workplace and he has work to do. Concentration to maintain or develop. No one really wants to go to work in a place crowded with rubberneckers, hangers-on and the needy getting under your feet. Never mind misguided enough to think to offer words of encouragement or to dare to speak to you. The great mass of fans at SGPs – around 85,000, for example, at the well-attended bigger events of Warsaw and Cardiff – get absolutely nowhere near their heroes or admired riders. Even if they did somehow manage to elude security and penetrate the VIP area of pit lane adjacent to Doyle's race booth, he either wouldn't be there or else his fierce manner and resting bitch face concentration would discourage interaction.

Worse still, when it comes to fan interaction in the SGP era, riders don't even bother with warm-down or victory laps nowadays. Primarily due to the dictates of the tight live broadcast television schedules and concomitant costly satellite access, this requires at SGPs the majority of riders to head straight back to the pits without so much as a wave, let alone the traditional lap of acknowledgement. The easy courtesy of regular crowd/fan acknowledgement has gone the way of all flesh in the BSI World Championship era. Even the rider parade is primarily staged with the armchair audience in mind, so lacks the coherence of the traditional side-by-side start line rider introductions. Thankfully BSI have failed to deliver the big stadium SGP series they promised so it is only at Cardiff and Warsaw where for many fans their distance from the track means that the riders and the racing often appears like ant-sized models circuiting on a faraway brightly coloured board game. In essence, Jason's privileged position (and the pressure for success that brings) sounds like not only it has made him lose sight of his speedway roots when it comes to interacting with the fans, but also made him come up with a poor retrospective excuse for his 2018 SGP underperformances. Not to put too fine a point on it, the underlying sense of entitlement of these complaints reflects poorly upon him. As excuses go, they are pretty poor too. Jason had genuine fan sympathy when injury robbed him of the 2016 World Championship that should and would, rightfully, have been his otherwise. Offering up such graceless and ill-mannered comments about the very few curious fans who somehow managed to get close to him during his failed championship defence to a tame dictation journalist definitely doesn't show true World Championship calibre character, judgement or temperament. Tai Woffinden surrounds himself with an admittedly expensive but nonetheless professional SGP back office team so is easily able to tell apart the hangers-on and fair-weather friends – like World Championship crowns, Woffinden probably has more of these than Doyle too – from his actual mates. The next time Jason opens what passes as his heart and speaks his mind to a dictation typist in lengthy but dull two-part four-page interview, these are easy topics to avoid.

Rather than watch the autograph session, the shade of the stadium service-tunnel-cum-pit-lane lures throngs of rubberneckers of all stripes. There is only around an hour of validity left on most passes before these pits guests get banished from the hollowed turf (well, concrete) of the inner sanctum. With action, time and riders at a premium, the vibe is frenetic and, with the sheer volume of people making space and politeness levels suddenly limited, the push and shove greater. The rise of the selfie and the ubiquity of the cell phone urgently requires objects of attention. These opportunities are at a premium. Already dressed for action, the Monster Energy promo parade staff have sensibly recused themselves too for a few moments of respite before they join the melee outside for the Monster rig rider-signing session. They don't talk but stand sternly together close by the off-duty firemen who rest inside or prone on top of their fire engine. These Monster women are still subject to walk-by ogling and paparazzi-snatched photos. There are six Monster promo women. Strange when only five appear on track? Perhaps, the sixth is – in SGP parlance – the meeting reserve or, playing to male adolescent fantasies, the wild card. More likely, having a substitute on hand is how they practically manage any need for toilet breaks during the meeting. It doesn't say much for fan observation skills and also speaks to the innate misogyny of their interchangeability as commodities. Also distaining interaction with the *hoi polloi* guests of others, Monster head honcho in this part of the noxious drinks universe Joe Parsons ignores the crowd around him to swagger purposefully out of the pits area at the head of his own fawning tribe of sponsored pocket-sized increasingly waif-like speedway Diddymen; in this instance, Tai Woffinden and Greg Hancock. They have a sunny date with destiny, otherwise known as a brief but hugely popular – since this is Poland – autograph-signing session. Under the auspices of his employer, Monster, even something as simple as signing autographs is grandiloquently staged in abrasively theatrical fashion. Solely for the benefit and unalloyed delight of the fans, of course. Though such time-limited sessions are a distinctly modern invention and SGP "innovation", even this ultra-brief meet and greet departs from accepted historic norms and is much more spoon-fed than yesteryear. Fans no longer even require autograph books! If they can't afford the official SGP programme – for once, very reasonably priced – with its many autograph boxes to fill, Monster even provide pre-printed rider cards for signature.

When it comes to advertising on the riders' body suits, current exercise, nutrition and dietary fashion has shrunk the available space. Televisual editorial norms also dictate that certain areas of the body feature more often than others when they cover the racing. Consequently, rider's heads, hands, arms, shoulders and backs are the billboard areas as these much more readily find themselves in shot than calves or, to a lesser extent, legs. Every square inch of the bike has been intensively farmed for these purposes since a long time back but nowadays advances in technology mean this is done with more vim, precision and colour. Successful speedway riders tend towards the diminutive, often bordering on the petite. Getting up close to them in the flesh finds them smaller and scrawnier than they even appear on the telly. Sadly, for the taller of the rider species, although there is more space for sponsorship, often there is less demand on the basis of the hard currency of results. Plus, as in our increasingly digitally saturated lives, some people are just more attractive and visually appealing so get more attention and sponsor dollars. The positive emotional appeal of some riders is hard to pinpoint or manufacture beyond the endless sweet nothings they get blown up their bottoms from the specialist media. Or that their publicists claim or ascribe for their employers. Negative emotions come much more naturally to the perception of certain riders. Nicki Pedersen springs to mind, wherever and whenever he rides. Like the wrestlers of yesteryear, Nicki plays up to his pantomime villain status in cartoonish fashion. Of course, some antipathy from fans and riders alike is merited. Yet similar on-track transgressions from other riders regularly escape with less complaint or notoriety. Along with his innate competitiveness and career results, this gives Nicki endless attention and mindshare. It is lucrative too as, apparently, the reflected glory of his "bad boy" reputation and skilled performances are something many long-time loyal sponsors also enjoy and, possibly, relish.

In terms of actual availability, with only hours until the tapes rise, all the Polish riders competing here tonight are notable by their presence and visibility in the pits. None are dressed for action but, since in Warsaw they compete on home national turf, they are fully and patiently available for photos, autographs and brief conversation. Freddie Lindgren is also here but telegraphs unavailability with a stern manner and studious focus upon industriously adjusting the innards of his bikes. It is an increasingly unusual sight to see SGP riders actually at work on their own bikes as the norm is to leave that to others or, at moments of great stress during the meeting, bark instructions about their requirements at their skilled mechanics and assorted technical staff. Ignoring the risk of greasy splatter, Freddie is stylishly dressed in well-cut black-and-white clothing more suitable for a Charlie Chaplin tribute event than mechanical adjustments. Crouched on his haunches and bent over with screwdriver in hand, the thinness of Freddie's shoulders and his prominent collarbones are sharply visible. As is the close attention bordering on adoration of Freddie uber-fan Laura Chalmers. Her Glaswegian mum Alison confides, "She didn't eat at breakfast as Freddie was on the next table". There are many familiar faces from the British speedway scene. Wolves team manager

Peter Adams sits alone morosely scrolling through his mobile in the Tai Woffinden pits bay. Apparently dressed for terrace drinks at sundown in the colonies, Gordon Pairman walks confidently through the crowd barking "no interviews" into his mobile. Gordon was one of those who helped save Glasgow Speedway the time before last and has also been a promoter at Belle Vue and Poole. An auditor by later life training and a tax exile on the Isle of Man, until recently Pairman represented the British Speedway Promoters Association (BSPA) as a member of the Speedway Control Bureau. A thoughtful man of many parts, I understand that Pairman is also an investor in the Tony Briggs air fences authorised (homologated) for use at the Speedway Grands Prix. Rather like the US President is escorted everywhere with the nuclear football guarded by the secret service, perhaps, Gordon is here with the special repair kit these fences require whenever bikes puncture them?

As it is getting closer to witching hour, other riders flit by briefly including Chris Holder – with his increasingly ubiquitous brother Jack – appearing cheerful despite what journalist-in-the-know-but-I-can't-tell-you Paul Burbidge endlessly refers to in the *Speedway Star* as "personal issues". These are widely believed to be fractious and complicated child-access dispute matters regarding his young son Max and were said to have badly impacted his 2017 SGP performances. Seriously enough to find due sympathy with BSI and the FIM during their end-of-season closed-doors wild-card selection deliberations. So much so they temporarily went all Fathers for Justice and judged his suffering of sufficient depth to merit the reprieve of his 2018 wild card selection. Also, being a Monster Energy team rider was undoubtedly also a factor, albeit unconsciously or implicitly as we are regularly told this has ABSOLUTELY no influence on the impartial judgements of the wild-card selection committee of Armando Castagna, Torben Olsen and Phil Morris. These blokes are so inspiringly independent and judicious, it is a wonder that they haven't yet been co-opted to negotiate the terms of Britain's Brexit from the EU. To compound his woes and also bizarrely, given that he is an Australian citizen rather than from the Caribbean, plus now lives/resides in tax friendly Andorra, it is claimed because of Windrush, Chris now also has passport and UK visa issues. To the extent that he nearly couldn't stay in the UK. Or dare leave. Or re-enter. Burbo's behind-his-hand reporting never quite made sense nor found clarity for "confidential" safety reasons. The drums of speedway gossip and rumour give many different, always more lurid reasons for these visa issues including unspecified behaviour matters; hostility of British immigration authorities towards British speedway given the historic laxity by promoters; leverage in a dispute with Poole promoter Matt Ford over team selection ("never trust him when his lips are moving") or just plain bureaucracy. Whatever the ins, outs or reality, Chris appears cheerful enough. Though his speed around the pits area – with posse in tow – as well as his look-but-don't-touch body language clearly indicates that he isn't up for interaction with any adoring guest punters this afternoon.

Rider lane access provides the opportunity to investigate that oft-asked burning speedway question, "Do riders wash their hands at meetings?" If the line of portaloos adjacent the rider pit bays are any indication, the answer is a resounding and definitive "no", as these temporary toilets have no mains connection. Plus, their maintenance is such that, although there are sinks and dispensers, there is no en-suite water or soap provided. Even Stoke Speedway stretches to running water in its toilets, so this is a poor show by BSI at a so-called World Championship. Though, as befits the standard speedway-men-are-men oily handed daredevils narrative, though riders don't expect their path to be garlanded with flowers or deluxe toilet paper, they could reasonably expect some better provision of the basics. Based on my inspection visits to four different booths, there is no loo paper, soap nor water, and there is a heady farmyard bouquet along the lines of pig-farm aroma meets the musk of freshly sprayed silage with added strong notes of sun-baked manure. Laughably, these toilets are unisex. Though I am reliably informed that the fairer sex do toilet, these are only for the urgently desperate of either gender. Perhaps, BSI's idea is to encourage the swiftest of visits during the meeting and, thereby, for the benefit of the live broadcast audience at home, ensure maximum rider visibility throughout the meeting. Long used to basic facilities, sleeping in their vans or changing by them, spartan provision is par for the course for any experienced speedway rider. And, arguably, better than some places too. Obviously, it rather undercuts the oft-cited claims the BSI foundation myth of relentlessly seeking out the best-of-the-best TV deals, sponsors and equipped modern stadia. Doubtless the stadium houses state-of-the-art changing rooms with showers and lockers elsewhere so, hopefully, the SGP riders don't completely lack for creature comforts. However, during the cut and thrust of the meeting, all hands remain resolutely unwashed. Given his eye for the unusual or opportunistic sponsorship opportunity, surely this situation cries out for Greg Hancock to test then launch some innovative speedway-centric anti-bacterial hand wash? He is definitely the man to proclaim improved throttle grip or other nebulous health and hygiene performance benefits ("the handwash of champions"). Perhaps, like they do at key hospital entry points, brightly coloured sponsored dispensers could get prominently fitted in each rider pits bay and, thereby, regularly caught on camera? Rather than just ostentatiously swig some (I'm hoping and guessing) water up a straw from his Monster bottle, perhaps Greg – should he qualify – could thoroughly disinfect his tiny hands prior to each race and choosing his semi-final or final gate position? That would definitely prompt facile speedway media talk and garner attention for his hand-washing mind games, plus it might be a sensible external precaution to counterbalance the danger posed to rider biomes by the forced ingestion of sponsor beverages?

Moments before pit lane closes earlier than the advertised closure time, Nicki Pedersen arrives with a half-peeled banana and smartly dressed woman. Judged by the cut of her stylish red leather jacket and dark skirt, she could well be his manager but is, more likely, his latest girlfriend. What has happened to the world when speedway riders' girlfriends cosplay as their therapists or wealth fund managers? Though completely unafraid to publicly throw himself into the luxury lifestyle of his early mid-life crisis (especially on Instagram) – and who knew there was such a thing as seven-star hotels in Dubai? – Nicki is much more reluctant to press the flesh with his more traditional speedway admirers on an *ad hoc* basis. Such is his cache, star status and raw appeal Nicki is immediately mobbed and surrounded by pits lane admirers he ignores as he slowly picks his way to the sanctuary of his pits bay. Security marshals then throng at the perimeter of his pits bay until moments later they get the signal to shoo them from the stadium service tunnels. By the bikes rather than the bike shed, oblivious to the hordes of onlookers, Nicki and his friend canoodle with gusto.

Back outside in the baking heat of the later afternoon strong May sunshine, all the entrance gates are finally open. Face painters do a roaring patriotic trade in expertly daubing cheeks with the Polish national flag. Though there are three official Speedway Grand Prix stalls dotted around the perimeter of the stadium, none of them sell programmes for the Warsaw SGP. Worse still, they seem insulted at the idea that they might. What they do stock is a range of SGP branded merchandise, general memorabilia and "official" clothes that – on closer examination – don't uniformly appear to have been manufactured with the quality materials the upscale pricing suggests. Though unlikely to be much in demand on such a hot evening, in the interests of market research I try on the 2018 edition – in a selection of sizes – of the SGP hoodies. Local price tonight 140zl. Though matt in appearance the material feels coarse, the cut is boxy and the logo is fractionally above ironed on. It is the type of garment that you know will deteriorate quickly from the first wash and, though hard to believe this is possible, also lose further shape. [2] Though many future grands prix locations this season require mandatory camping or caravanning in order to stay in the vicinity, amazingly there are no SGP branded tents, sleeping bags, mosquito nets or primus stoves on sale.

On a hot evening, making fans compulsorily play hunt-the-SGP-programme makes no commercial sense when the biggest grand prix crowd of the season is on hand with spare cash to spend in the local vicinity. Faced with a thronged stadium with a capacity of over 53,000, Kelvin Tatum can't help but spuriously claim a complete sell out beforehand on social media. Predictably enough, later on there clearly remain empty seats in the nose-bleed sections of the grandstands. In the face of limited independent verification, the SGP has a rich tradition of rounding up or just plain getting attendance figures wrong by the odd thousand, five thousand or ten thousand. Whatever feels right to bolster the gravitas is said or reported – either sincerely or cynically – and then repeated as proven fact by others thereafter. This self-confirming hyperbolic virtue cycle is either based on belief or scant evidence. With such a notably sized crowd inside the PGE Narodowy Stadium, quite what motivates this need to shade this truth for the wider speedway public is difficult to fathom. Built in 2008, the national sports stadium of Poland is an impressive venue at which to watch any sports event. The sight lines are tremendous, the seats comfortable and the aisleways comparatively spacious. What can only be put down to a deliberate design feature of the stadium – its perimeter metal slatted effect perimeter walls – somehow appears to provide a cooling breeze undetectable elsewhere but surprising effective once sat down inside. So much so that experienced Polish attendees carry jumpers, jackets and sweatshirts for later when the temperature "cools" further. This may just be for locals and at the discretion of the skin of the beholder since it remains balmy throughout by British standards for May. The stadium is tiered with concourses at different levels. For the first-time foreign visitor, the catering is a curiosity since, though predictably they sell burgers and the like, it nevertheless punches above the weight of UK stadia (football) fare. Partly in terms of variety but definitely in terms of price. Old Iron Curtain habits die in Poland, like they do in many parts of Eastern Europe, so cash defiantly remains king. Visiting speedway fans do not have to battle cashless transactions, like we did (in ahead-of-its-time German fashion) when the SGP briefly staged meetings (or tried to do so) in late mid-noughties Gelsenkirchen. Disabled-viewing facilities are excellent as it is for anyone who prefers to stand and watch events. Though the security into the stadium is stringent, there appears to be a complete lack of be-uniformed jobsworths keen to assert their authority once fans gain entry inside.

When BSI took over the SGP rights, their Chief Executive John Postlethwaite promised to deliver what the fans apparently demanded: new markets, big brand name sponsors, worldwide television broadcasts, rider celebrity, city centre stadia with good views, catering and toilets. Leaving aside most fans actually demand things he failed to mention (good tracks and lusty racing) or we assumed (competitive formats and financial investments), it was complete news to anyone schooled in regular speedway that we set great store by the calibre, cleanliness and quality of our toilet provision! This was – in fact – amazing to learn. And still is. Until visionary Postlethwaite hove upon the scene, who knew that this was the secret ingredient we had all been so badly missing? I am sure that we have all lost count of the times a night of brilliant speedway has been marred by toilet facilities complaints. If that ever were so – and it wasn't in any of the major or minor speedway nations – then on this particular aspect in this particular stadium the majesty of Postlethwaite's vision for speedway

[2] Given the range of SGP clothing on offer is extensive, it would be hard to judge the quality and feel of all items without proper inspection. My 2018 series tour T shirt softens and wears well after frequent washes.

toilets-we-could-all-truly-be-proud-of has come to fruition unimaginably impressively. He has really over-delivered on these laudable ambitions in Warsaw. Obviously, I am ignoring that it was his successors Bellamy and Olsen who actually delighted speedway fans' bottoms everywhere by delivering these deluxe toileting facilities. For those not afforded the privilege, the PGE Narodowy Stadium gents toilets have large heavy access doors better suited to a FTSE 100 boardroom or ambitious non-denominational church. Once inside they are spacious two room affairs with similar space given to a completely separate area for hand-washing as well as the other more traditional relieving activities. They wouldn't look out of place at a new build shopping centre, I can praise them that highly. Sadly though, they are not the ahead-of-their-time solar-powered eco-toilets run on environmentally sound principles – and using recycled(!) water – found inside the Etihad Stadium at the Melbourne SGPs. Everybody lapped up – fans, promoters, the FIM and media alike – the various strategic ambitions and moon-shots BSI promised as speedway's path to global dominance. Mostly the King remains naked and rockets haven't worked but, praise where praise is due, Warsaw really does provide the toilets promised.

Viewed from anywhere inside the stadium bowl, the colour combination of the advertising, air fences, fluorescent artificial green centregreen apron and red shale of the track completely draws the eye, and adds architectural spectacle to the pre-meeting anticipation. As too does the television satellite aerial tribute-statue-cum-installation the stadium designers magically suspended over it from wires. Quite how this relates to the retractable roof is unclear and, with no rain forecast, it remains open so sunshine glints off its exterior. With such great facilities, the real shame is that the meeting is raced upon a temporary track. In the tried and tested diplomatic vocabulary of speedway euphemisms, it is a "technical track". Aka it has had to be temporarily installed to fit the stadium pitch dimensions so is notably small and all turns rather than straights. This badly impinges upon rider speed and requires the riders to make close to continuous tight broadside turns. Despite improvements over the years from hard-won experience laying these temporary tracks, though it looks good at the outset when pristine, once in actual use the surface condition soon deteriorates to provide riders with random lumps and bumps in unpredictable locations that will scrub off their speed, induce possible falls and prompt compulsory course corrections. Whatever way boosters spin it, and though of course it is the same for every rider, the BSI strategy is to choose to stage World Championship meetings on tracks not suitable for its august "World Championship" status, let alone conducive to enthralling racing. Maximising commercial revenues through big stadium stagings structurally requires that the rights holders knowingly provide or nod through sub-optimal and often sub-standard racing conditions. This short-changes the viewing public, whether there in person or watching on television. Though the MCC could further maximise their attendance revenues by staging test matches at Wembley on a temporary pitch rather than at Lords or the Oval, they don't. The reason is simple: it is a proper sport. I won't say well administered but still better than speedway at the SGPs or, indeed, by the BSPA in Britain. The current (falling) level of cricket popularity would make public outcry at such a decision inevitable, since it would deny its history and provide meagre fare as a spectacle. In comparison, SGP-era World Championship speedway only has the occasional sweet but empty words about its past lustrous history and, since that was before the rights holders' time, it is irrelevant except when invoked as comparative benchmarking of performances or atmosphere. Traditionally speedway promoters, fans and media alike prefer to nostalgically recall their speedway past in touched-up fashion through rose-tinted spectacles. Those these memories often involve or invoke some element of tactical white-washing, BSI prefer to act as if the current SGP set-up is so glorious that World Championship history before their time never happened.

In the bright sunshine as a big crowd amiably filter to their seats, it is a fabulous stadium to wait in for the first signs of impending SGP action of the 2018 season. First out are a swarm of hi-vis jacketed photographers. They amble determinedly for best position like a staid but corpulent stag party with overloaded wheelie cases keen to arrive first at their shared Airbnb to bagsy the best place. Given the lack of mainstream media outlets publishing almost anything on any speedway grand prix event (whether written or pictorial), it is one of life's great mysteries: why there are always so many photographers in attendance? The rules state that there can only be two per bend in field during the meeting with the rest grouped together on staging platforms which ensures they rough get all the same photos! This massive oversupply of photographers – let alone the inverse relationship between photos taken and those published – is, it seems, a feature of all speedway meetings everywhere, but especially at SGPs. If you put the metaphorical gin of a speedway rider on a track anywhere, then the tonic of a corpulent bloke with a fluorescent bib, many big lenses, spare expensive cameras, a stool and a dull conversational line on apertures and shutter speeds floods the glass. Given the screening process those media types specialising in writing words – they invariably fail to get published outside the specialist press – undergo in order to get a press pass from BSI (they have to prove their undying fealty to the SGP ideals via a blood sacrifice or equivalent in order to gain their media accreditation) – it is weird how many photographers manage to so easily convince the same said gatekeepers of their necessity and relevance. Perhaps, I am underestimating the promotional power of photographer websites? While remotely located tribespeople confronted with "explorers" avoid having their photos taken in case it steals or compromises their souls, perhaps it works the opposite way with speedway riders? Unusually, given the SGP prides itself as the home of celebratory unreconstituted sexism, there are also some official female photographers. This laudable storming of one of the last bastions of male dominance, albeit one of the nerdier bastions, by photographic girl power is badly undermined by one woman in micro-cut-off denim shorts. Apparently she is contractually obliged to act out the lyrics of her favourite Right Said Fred song. Until she changes position mid-meeting, said photographer aggressively wiggles her tush, laughs theatrically during mutual shouted interactions with the crowd behind her and – I assume – takes photos. It is tiring work as she also frequently needs to relieve her aching hamstrings with extensive slowly executed deep bends. It is definitely different. Though not good different. It is hard to see how far this (hopefully brief) "Rise of the Good Fun, Slightly Slutty Photographer" is going to improve the photos taken or work as a career move at the SGPs? Arguably, Warsaw is the wrong SGP audience too as the speedway crowd demographic and composition here tonight is the most multi-generational, youthful and roughly gender even of the whole 2018 series. It is definitely not the primarily middle-aged or older male crowd usually found in the stands (or camera in hand on the centregreen) in Britain. This dirty old man aesthetic of her pantomime performance doesn't even stack up favourably against the new school objectification of the more "empowered" Monster start line staff.

With 15 or so minutes to go before tapes up, the riders get driven round on a circuit of the track to wave at fans before they dismount from the SGP parade vehicle of choice: open backed pick-up trucks with gleaming black bodywork. The riders then muster on the centregreen ahead of their individual introductions to the crowd. A giant image of each competitor dominates the stadium screens as they walk up to the podium area in series line-up – aka 2017 SGP finish order plus the add ons: wild cards, qualifiers and local flavour selections. The riders do this with varying degrees of enthusiasm in Noah's Ark fashion (albeit one-by-one) along the narrow pathway garlanded by lines of yet more Monster Energy branded boxes. Some riders appear already badly jaded, despite this being the first meeting of the SGP series season. Though well practised in big gesture faux enthusiasm, despite the brand name of the most-advertised sponsor of any World Championship event, there is remarkably little energy for this formality from the riders. In sharp contrast, the crowd collectively impressively amps itself up into fever levels of anticipation ahead of the action. Or, possibly, this is just an outpouring of our shared joy in the unique but hideously awful design of Neil Kristian-Iversen's SGP race suit with its pointless but truly distinctive one fluorescent cerise (left) arm motif? If Dadaists did breakdown repair uniform design, this would be the design outcome.

Before the meeting goes any further, in a rare but also extremely brief pro-forma acknowledgement of the history of the World Championship, we are all asked to give way less than thirty seconds of silence in memory of the recently deceased Ivan Mauger. Though a shabbily brief acknowledgement given his six-times World Champion status, giant screen lustrous photos of Ivan in his pomp and action shots of speedway racing from a different (60-70s) era are marked in comparative silence by the large boisterous crowd. If he had a sense of humour, Ivan would have appreciated that the possible gravitas of this commemoration was undermined when his surname was – as usual by strangers seeing it for the first time – completely mispronounced as spelt! "Moor-Grrh" serenades his final World Championship appearance. Like the subtle micro signs and signals exchanged by Freemasons but unknown by the ordinary public, knowing to say "Major" when confronted with "Mauger" is what sets the true speedway fan apart from the rest of the world population. As well as any new, arriviste or wannabe speedway fans (should such beings exist) and, of course, this Warsaw stadium announcer. Anyone glancing in the official programme in search of a proper fulsome tribute to Ivan is sorely disappointed. It is not like the Poles don't know, respect and reverence their speedway history. Arguably they do it best. Ivan's record is currently only equalled by Tony Rickardsson. It is worthy of celebration and recognition. Of all riders, Mauger probably did the most to practise and, thereby, inculcate the wide-ranging structured professionalism – for himself, his preparation and equipment as well as back office staff – that nowadays modern riders know they must attain as a minimum standard if they are to stand any chance of career success, let alone World Championship triumph. This lack of speedway touch – based on wilful corporate ignorance and the gleeful contempt for tradition in the pursuit of commercial gain – is the ongoing lived reality of the BSI era of World Championship speedway. Any venue, rider or era prior to their controversial purchase of the World Championship and World Cup rights from the FIM and their arrival on the scene is unworthy of almost any (never mind appropriate) recognition. Like Sky think Premiership football history only really started with their first broadcast so too it is with BSI and Speedway World Championship history. In both instances, the epoch before their arrival is lengthier and more lustrous. Though every era is different, this deliberate forgetting is BSI/IMG corporate policy. As a great speedway rider as well as thinker and innovator, in retirement Ivan obviously engaged critically with the various bungled iterations of the SGP structure and the variable quality of its product or self-inflicted mistakes in its staging. However, this lack of recognition isn't punishment for the temerity to think independently but pig ignorance. Strangely, though later in the year Ivan's long-time agent and ghost writer Peter Oakes will again ride his obsessive *bête noire* and berate the BBC Sports Personality of the Year awards for failing to mention Ivan's achievements or passing; he conspicuously fails to admonish the series rights holders for their shockingly lackadaisical attitude towards appropriate recognition and commemoration of Mauger's achievements. Given BSI never shut up about Greg Hancock – who has only half of Ivan's crowns – perhaps Peter could have a word with his grandson, and Greg's Boy Friday, Josh Gudgeon to see if he can put a word in with Burbo for the SGP website and social media or else complain to head honcho Torben Olsen? After all, it is not as if the Olsen family don't know Ivan either. Especially as Ivan reputedly taught Torben's daddy,

Ole, to ride a speedway bike in 1966 before they lustily subsequently competed for the World Championship crown on a regular basis throughout the 1970s. With Warsaw the first chance since Ivan's passing for the SGP to properly commemorate Ivan's status, achievements and glories, it was bungled at the meeting. And failed to even make the programme or gain mention in the relentlessly anodyne welcome columns of Vito Ippolito (FIM President) and Torben Olsen (Managing Director BSI Speedway). Worse still, Ivan's passing, let alone his World Championship achievements, completely fails to gain mention any of the ten official programmes – mostly edited by Nigel Pearson – of the 2018 SGP series.

Prior to first race tapes up, sweet wafts of methanol exhaust bouquet drift into our collective nostrils only to then disappear for the remainder of the meeting. It is a heady and evocative aroma. Nowadays the fuel is no longer old-school methanol as it is synthetically produced. Perhaps, this explains why it no longer lingers throughout meetings like it once did. To state the biologically obvious, whenever we luckily but rarely get a whiff of methanol on the breeze at a SGP meeting - usually only the first race - it is because actual tiny particulates in the air are ingested (aka smelt) by our noses. This smell brings olfactory joy to many speedway fans. The entrepreneurial Ian Corcoran once got quite close to introducing a line of bespoke methanol scented candles before fire hazard worries saw product development shelved. I reckon they would have sold strongly. Arguably there is also a speedway sized gap in the fragrance market for a methanol scented after shave, *eau de toilette* or body spray. Possibly considerable demand for all three. To underline the retro nature and roots of speedway, maybe even a methanol scented soap on a rope would enjoy sales success? Anyways, evolution means particulates and our noses are so in sync we equally enjoy many pre- and post-industrial era smells: new mown grass, freshly laid tar, aviation fuel, speedway journalism or toilet areas. Tiny particulates. Circulating in the air. They say hearing and smell are the last two senses to desert you before you die and, while methanol no longer salts our nostrils, the merest sweet whiff is enough to evoke the muscle memory nostalgia in almost any long-time speedway fan. Briefly transported to the happy place of my teenage speedway years, the spell is soon broken, when after all the anticipation and build up, the first race of the 2018 SGP World Championship series only makes it as far as bend four. Pawlicki changes line and looks for the trademark but, in this instance, impossible-to-see close-quarters Jason Doyle shove-cum-shoulder-flex. The referee excludes the Australian and, though the series is only a lap old, this lack-of-luck element immediately suggests that the universe has taken against the lacklustre design of his pits bay. Jason's uncharismatic defence of his world title finds itself in jeopardy from the series get-go. Given the blind enthusiasm for the idea rather than the act of Przemyslaw Pawlicki's "victimisation" by the dastardly Doyle, it is also clear that the Warsaw crowd is going to be proudly partisan and loudly patriotic throughout the evening.

It quickly becomes clear for those actually present in the crowd for this SGP in Warsaw that the format of the night is almost solely predicated upon the enjoyment and experience of what remains of the television audience elsewhere. It is true enough that the noise and enthusiasm of the crowd as well as the atmosphere of this impressive stadium makes for a memorable experience if actually attending. It is one of the nicest places I have ever been to watch speedway racing with its great sight lines, feel of proximity to the action, good seats and stadium facilities. Despite all this, nonetheless, it is clear we are still just the atmospheric backdrop for those watching on television. There are a number of factors that confirm we are just here in our capacity as human scenery since they run counter to the usual lived experience of enjoying or relishing a live speedway meeting. First and foremost is the programme. This is the cornerstone upon which all speedway meetings are built. It is often said that if an alien landed on earth from another universe at any speedway meeting staged anywhere in Europe, that they would probably quickly assume that the post-race completion of the programme after each and every race was a ritual act of worship component connected with our participation and faith in the speedway religion. Such is the power of the speedway programme – and setting aside both its paraphernalia or innate collectability for a moment – that within a minute of the end of any race the majority of fans will turn their eyes (and hands) downwards to either its completion or study, probably both. Completing the programme as you go along is something you learn how to do over time. It is an initiation rite of passage in your final induction into the faithful congregation that peoples the speedway church. It is also an essential activity to understand and properly enjoy the spectacle at hand.

Leaving aside the lustre or otherwise of the specific printed content of the 2018 version of the Warsaw SGP programme, as a tool the organisers sell these in the full knowledge that they are structurally and methodologically flawed for their specific purpose since they arrive with completely blank scorecards. It is like a football programme without the team line-ups or an election ballot paper without the actual candidates listed. A few years back in order to supposedly increase the "drama" and random mystery of the draw for race order, BSI in their marketing wisdom decided that this draw would be held on practice day rather than conducted anonymously many days beforehand (as previously) somewhere deep in the bowels of their suburban office. This revised system means that the programme can go to press days, weeks or even months beforehand – a cost saving compared to later more last-minute printing – and also (allegedly) that track preparation can't be gamed. Theoretically this protects race order integrity as it eliminates the remote possibility of track prep persons unknown using their local expertise and race order pre-knowledge to try to fix the track to benefit certain participants. This unlikely circumstance can be completely avoided if said decision about what races each rider will race in and their helmet colour, gate position etc. is not known long in advance. Most importantly, since fans can't arrive at the stadium with their own pre-printed scorecards, it also serves its real purpose to protect sales volumes. The make-do-and-mend cost-conscious culture of speedway fandom inevitably some will bring their own sheets to fill out rather than go to the expense of buying a meeting programme. But here is the rub, those fans that do buy programmes have to dedicate time to besmirching and uglifying their own memorabilia with extensive hand-written entries. Looking to the bigger picture, arguably it is good BSI force us to do some handwriting since, in the age of the smart phone and keyboard, handwriting itself in general under threat and is a comparatively dying art. Beautiful or legible calligraphy even more so. Notorious for their back-page *Speedway Star* SGP adverts sometimes rather wonderfully featuring riders racing turning the wrong way, despite the increased proofreading time available, SGP rights holders BSI continue their rich tradition of lack of attention to details with this same unforced error on the front cover of the Warsaw 2018 programme.

Whether you bring your own scorecard or buy a programme on the day, the end of each race requires some degree of programme completion in order to effectively follow the event scoring and, thereby, grasp the subplots or real/imagined drama as the action unfolds. Yet despite the pride the organisers, BSI and media boosters take in the size of the 50,000 plus crowd, the timings, duration and big-screen replays of the event for those watching live is completely suborned to the needs of television viewers in locations unknown, TV interval advertisers and, worst reason of all, the high cost of the satellite time incurred by the series rights holders. Rigorous event schedules with split-second timings mitigate broadcast and satellite costs as well as ensure advert schedule timings go smoothly. Experiencing the event from inside the stadium, attending fans must choose what they do or watch in zero-sum fashion. They can try to go for programme completion by waiting for the slow-build big-screen graphics of the official result – with, sadly, race times an afterthought (if they appear) – to flash up as if it is a banned but important subliminal message. Or they can check what they thought they saw live away in the far distance with a close half watch of the total mish-mash edit that is the house SGP big- and small-screen presentational style. What we can see on the Warsaw big screen are replays of how the VT guy saw the previous race to try to figure out the precise result for ourselves. After these many years staging experience, the race action replays shown are an imprecisely practised editorial art in the hands of SGP tech people who are, apparently, still without enough speedway knowledge to immediately select then show the key moments or highlights (if any) of each race. Instead, since these pictures are the watched as live or highlights package picture content all SGP broadcasters get served, the race is always relentlessly re-shown from the start as a chronological narrative. Aka two or three different angles of the riders racing to the first corner, some tracking shots, whatever side-by-side racing vague action moments there were – possibly even an overtake if, heaven forfend, one actually happens – plus some last corner action and two or three different angles of whoever takes the chequered flag. Possibly more if there is need to confirm any contested result of the race completion. Anyone with access to the edit suite buttons and some speedway intelligence would, instead, surely show the key moments of the race action rather than all the scene-setting flimflam? Finding compelling race action is a big ongoing product problem for the SGP VT people since race thrills, handlebar-to-handlebar close contests and actual overtakes are increasingly rarely seen. You can only showcase what you get. Sadly, for a long time now, the choice of staging venue and the calibre/quality of the tracks means that most races lack the grit in the oyster of lusty contest and overtakes so, in lieu of thrills to show, the extensive use of tracking shot and visual waffle has become the fixed narrative style of SGP race presentation for viewers everywhere. What gets shown is also not a useful or conducive experience for viewers inside or outside the stadium but, worse still for the long-term future of speedway generally, is hardly likely to find new audiences or convert the sceptical. Clutching at straws, one benefit from attending is that we just get served the big-screen replays without having to endure the interpretative commentary and analysis British and world viewers suffer. That said, if you do watch these stop-start, blink-and-you'll-miss-it style replays on the large stadium screens, you definitely miss seeing the set-up of the next race on the track as SGP riders are rigidly choreographed to immediately emerge from the pits at the moment the others from the previous race depart the shale stage. Though rider activity as they line up at the tapes only provides a modicum of "entertainment" or insight, it is a standard component of the rhythm, rhyme and metre of the symphony of any speedway meeting. Of course, every speedway fan understands the need to run a tight and efficient meeting but, at the SGP, the balance is disproportionately way out of kilter. Rather than enhancing the live fan experience, it detracts. Effectively the flow of the SGP meetings BSI require for broadcast dictates they treat the stadium crowd as pliant along for the ride speedway groupies. We get to enjoy sets of foreplay-free rapid-fire workmanlike sets of four races prematurely ejaculated forth in staccato fashion. The finish is very quick but rarely happy. But always followed by lengthy bouts of post-coital introspection during the formation tractor displays that ensue. All this grooming lasts much longer than the actual. It is a dull spectacle hardly enlivened by what counts as flirtatiousness: namely some begrudgingly soporific rider mumbles and chitchat about what just happened or what happiness and excitements might happen ahead. What a time to be alive, share and live through the brash adolescent romance of our global speedway future.

The buzzy crowd atmosphere is great to experience but does not substitute for the structural problems of having to ignore either the programme, screen replay quality (surely one of the most ineptly handled key additions of attending BSI-era SGP meetings live) or the staccato rider to and fro (ditto). As 21st century citizens, every member of the crowd is already media savvy enough to know that the television audience will understand and see nuances and aspects of the action and drama that we won't, whether it's live or via replays and interviews. This mitigated visual screen experience is the primary consumption model for pretty well all sports nowadays. Tiny happenings that otherwise would get missed live are caught on film. Then endlessly focussed upon and analysed by experts. Almost every sports performer nowadays – mostly deliberately – enacts a heightened theatricality in the full knowledge that micro-expressions, gestures or moments will be caught and magnified by the presence of the cameras. The paying audiences who turn up to watch many lower and mid-tier sports the world over have been holed below the water line by their decision to take the broadcasters blandishments and television contracts. The effects are particularly deleterious if the sport is contracted to be exclusively shown live on a specific satellite broadcaster as these are often the viewing equivalent of Siberia. The needs of attending fans are regularly ignored the world over. But, at least, these decisions usually result in the monies from these contract payments being retained within the sport or by its governing bodies rather than, in the instance of speedway, sold and revenues retained by a private business entity. Speedway has suffered twice in order for BSI (and their various hangers-on) to prosper. SGP-era speedway has hollowed out the fan-viewing experience but also the sport generally has been metaphorically robbed in plain view of both its share of the revenues and of the speedway spend that otherwise might have found its way into British speedway club coffers. The cost of one annual visit to the British Grand Prix in Cardiff could pay for a season ticket at almost any British league club. With speedway fan spend tight, this has almost become a zero-sum financial game. Whenever BSI win this spend, speedway in this country loses. Badly. Compared to other nations, British speedway has suffered especially egregiously. That said, there are increasing signs that the two SGPs a season they stage in Sweden nowadays is badly impacting available spend and, thereby, attendance levels in all tiers of Swedish club speedway. It is not a surprise that things have to come to this pass, as it was hardly ever a mystery that selling speedway television rights is BSI's purpose and business model as they are a sports marketing company. Their SGP policies, contracts, identity manuals and procedures all flow from this business activity focus. Their work is selling rights and associated rights that follow from their exclusive contract until 2021. Their work is NOT selling speedway or its appeal *per se*. Neither in new markets or old. While the FIM's rules and regulations govern the sports aspects of its staging, their substantial royalty/contract payments from BSI ensure that corporate governance and supervision matters generally stay on the back burner. Or primarily concern themselves with actual meeting administration – getting it on within the existing racing and safety rules – rather than strategic philosophy, tactics and execution. In essence, the entity (FIM) that notionally supervises the SGP (and World Cup) rights holders (BSI) are so comprehensively in bed together that the relationship lacks independent oversight. This could be deemed working together smoothly for the good of the sport or, judged on almost any metric apart from revenues or royalty payments, badly falling short of agreed strategic ambitions.

With the broadcasters and their audiences plus franchisees and local governments, their actual customers, BSI both don't understand the real drivers of the speedway fan live experience and don't care about any collateral ("global") damage to speedway as a sport generally either. It is definitively the case that the best way to experience any SGP is to watch it live on screen. This is the consumption medium the organisation and presentation of any SGP meeting is designed to serve, primarily to deliver the attention of the viewers to the massaging and imagery of advertisers and sponsors. Attending fans are very much bottom of a long list. Given we only get limited sight of some additional action and "behind the scenes" in meeting pits pictures via the stadium big screen, I can't help but be impressed that Krzysztof Kasprzak has somehow managed to prominently fit three different sponsors' logos onto the compact surface area of his water bottle. KK flourishes it with the abandon of a newly won World Cup trophy during the post-race interview after his rapturously received (and all fans who don't like Poole) Heat 2 victory. As is the way of these things, I can't recall these sponsor names only their number. At the SGP, and testament to their ongoing colonisation of the competition, only Monster really occupy any SGP fan mindshare amongst their bland roster of obscure advertisers. Particularly so since, as they say in the surfer dude circles it comes from, h8ters are always going to hate.

Ever the showman and always keenly playing to the crowd, Greg Hancock falls of his own volition on the second bend of Heat 3 before then theatrically telegraphing his virtuous decision to race on rather than stop the race. If true acts of charity are best done in secret or without publicity, then Greg is the equivalent speedway opposite. He is regularly seen grandstanding or signalling ostentatious acts of sportsmanship. Invariably small, often without material impact beyond further burnishing his own reputation or, more importantly, finding new routes to further make or turn a dollar. Some say of Greg, "he's too nice to be that nice." The second tranche of heats (5 to 8) rush by unmemorably, except for the ongoing lusty enthusiasm of the crowd for Polish riders. And, from a British perspective, also for SGP debutant Craig Cook securing his first point of the series with a third place in Heat 8. The second interval of the evening drags. As usual the tractors are on track for longer (around eight minutes EACH interval) than the riders. What their work accomplishes beyond the appearance of doing something to the track is negligible. The giant screens show a fast drive-by welter of instantly forgotten updates and tables. Though boisterous, knowledgeable and probably predominantly Catholic by religious background, the predominantly Polish crowd aren't Americans so imploring them to perform some slick dance moves for the "dance cam" is doomed to failure. Those that gamely try to "entertain" us are impeded by the seats or their egos so barely progress beyond throwing a few basic dad dance moves.

Though visually the stadium landscape, centregreen and track look top notch, the polite speedway euphemism of it being a "technical" track starts to more and more rear its ugly head. Effectively this translates into a spectacle with limited passing, tight turns and the ongoing arrival of more unexpectedly positioned lumps and bumps for the riders to negotiate as the track deteriorates. Though highly skilled, the randomness of these emerging holes discombobulates riders enough for them to lose race speed or track position. As if to disprove the handicap of the surface while illustrating his determination to succeed, Heat 9 sees Freddie Lindgren almost double the number of overtakes tonight with two in a single race including an unappreciated – by both crowd and rider – hard last-bend rough-housing of Maciej Janowski. The mood of the crowd isn't improved by an unpopular exclusion of Kasprzak in the next race. His dismount badly punctures a section of the airfence yet, such is the professionalism of the organisers to ensure that meeting delays don't see expensive additional satellite time needlessly incurred, a small cadre of track staff have it repaired within about five minutes. The re-run sees another example of final-doors last-bend bossing, this time from Emil Sayfutdinov on Greg Hancock. It has taken only an hour to stage the first ten heats of this opening grand prix. Heat 11 sees what looks like a tactical engine failure from Nicki Pedersen when already badly trailing off at the back. Craig Cook gets another SGP point in a race he initially led until he invites an easy pass from Bartosz Zmarzlik by occupying a mid-track no-man's land. Heat 12 sees the referee decide it is "all four back" when really Patryk Dudek should have gone for touching the tapes or, possibly, the style crime of riding with green metallic alloy wheels. Predictably, this is not deemed a wonderfully wise or judicious decision by the stadium crowd. Apart from the patriotism, to middle-aged male English eyes schooled in the gender profile of British speedway, the sheer number of women of all ages – but mostly younger (under 35) – in attendance continues to stand out as a very notable feature of the Warsaw SGP.

Heat 13 actually features an exciting pass from Zagar as well as signs that track bumps are getting more of a factor, albeit a random one. Back in the Grand Prix series courtesy of a wild card and after overcoming a possibly career-ending serious back injury, Nicki Pedersen adds fuel to the "psychological questions remaining" fire with a fall from over-riding when ahead in Heat 16. Sixteen races take nearly two hours to complete, after the first ten were completed in the first hour. With the last tranche of four heats (17 to 20) determining who reaches the semi-final stage, suddenly aggressive over-riding becomes the norm amongst the more something-to-prove daredevil, comparatively younger ambitious up-and-coming riders. This is particularly so amongst the Polish riders, especially Zmarzlik. Though harbouring significant career and 2018 SGP series goals himself, Craig Cook has not been even a tiny bit bitten by the win-at-all-costs bug, if judged by how easily the others pass him as they together exit bend two of his last race. That said, it is all in the eye of the beholder. One person's over-riding is another person's thrilling speedway. If so, heat 20 must just about count as a thrill since it features two laps of noticeably wild riding. Starved of overtakes or even mild thrills, the crowd lap up the spectacle and drama that this over-zealous energetic racing provides. Like everywhere else, speedway racing that is red-in-tooth-and-claw is the approved local vernacular and style in Poland. After the tedium of the earlier paint-drying heats, it definitely notably amps up the stadium energy and buzz to the level you would like to think all enthralling speedway meetings would naturally generate. It is a privilege to be suddenly borne aloft by this sharp injection of atmosphere generated by the passion and engagement of these fans. We pretty well all stand for both the semi-finals and finals. The wild over-riding continues to make it feel like these last few races actually mean something slightly more than another day at the office to the riders. Though over-used in press reports, the semi-finals seen live feel like something approaching "great" races. They fully engage many attending fans, for sure. At least, for once, great effort is expended anyways. Or appears to be. Matej Zagar even manages a wheelie-cum-crash after he finishes the second semi-final. After looking a shadow of himself during his first two rides, Tai Woffinden wins the meeting by generating more and more momentum – to match his projected confidence – as the meeting winds and rushes towards its conclusion. Arguably, Lindgren would be the worthier winner for neutrals, while the majority of the crowd bay for some local/Polish rider glory. The final race takes place serenaded by the atmospheric thrill of a powerful wall of crowd stadium noise. Never shy of hyperbole, fawning or inaccuracy, afterwards tame but florid SGP media types claim it drowned out the sound of the engines. Personally, that wasn't my experience. For the majority of the meeting, stadium microphones caught and amplified the engine noise to a level much louder than the crowd reaction.

The noise, buzz and atmosphere are a significant upside to the closing heats of the big stadia SGP experience. Especially so since Warsaw is almost full rather than regularly half-empty like Cardiff. Even better, the wall of noise is made by humans rather than the airhorns that provide the soundtrack of the British SGP meeting in Wales. Though we think of airhorns as a "foreign" sports-spectating accoutrement, come to think of it, I don't recall even hearing one throughout this evening in Warsaw. Despite the upside of three final heats of great atmosphere, plus the stadium really is a pleasure to use (cooling breezes, great sight lines, comfortable seating, good provision of toilets, excellent public transport links etc.), many of the authentic speedway experiences expected by fans are completely absent or deliberately evacuated from the scene. On track, there are few overtakes and even less lusty competitive races. Off it, the smell of methanol is confined to a single waft before the first race and replaced thereafter by the smell of commerce. Getting showered in shale just doesn't happen. And wouldn't even if we were closer to the action since both the modern era speedway bike rider-owner-manager-entrepreneur and also the SGP rights holders prefer their surfaces – whether indoors or out – Brazilian smooth going on bald to minimise racing delays. Lack of shale also ensures that advertiser logos mostly remain pristine and fully visible for the cameras.

After an impressively swift journey back into the city centre from the stadium, the man behind the takeaway sushi bar counter spots my programme and immediately wants to know more. And know it now. "How did Bartosz Smeklata do? And Maksym Drabik do? Tell me first about Smeklata!" News that both scored two points but Smeklata did this from only one ride gains a wan smile. "I am not really a fan of the Grand Prix but of Polish riders. We don't have a team in Warsaw so the GP is it, for here. That is why it does well. Though it is not proper track, people go anyway or come from elsewhere to see."

> **Winner:** Tai Woffinden (15 points)
>
> **Second:** Maciej Janowski (13 points)
>
> **Third:** Fredrik Lindgren (16 points) [3]
>
> **Fourth:** Artem Laguta (13 points)

[3] And here, above in the points totals, is the nonsense of the format created and used by rights holders BSI to administer its Speedway World Championships. This plain stupidity has been hiding in plain sight for so long that we no longer question it but take it for granted. How on earth can the rider who wins any SGP event manage to get less points that the rider who finished third? Or, conversely, how can the rider that scores the most points in an individual competition not win? This format is symptomatic of deeper problems with the organisation, rights ownership and administration of the series as a whole. While it masquerades as a true sporting event and sports competition it is effectively uses a format that makes it more of a circus-style entertainment put on for the financial benefit of rights holders BSI/IMG who are – when it comes down to it – just a television sports marketing company who rent these SGP rights. Ultimately no benefits flow to the wider speedway world, the riders or its fans in terms of enhanced popularity, reputation or benefits. Riders and fans alike are all just the evocative scenery or backdrop to a rentier business that in 2016 alone extracted from its "speedway" activities £3,255,882 that it then – perfectly above board and legally – remitted to its parent company as an intercompany "dividend" payment. While, as it has done throughout every single year of its free rider existence, also directly contributing a big fat zero (£0) to – for example – any European speedway national governing body, young rider development or injured riders helped by the charity SRBF (Speedway Riders Benevolent Fund). While they milked the pre-existing speedway audience with riders obligated to ride by the FIM, BSI have created no new markets and no new audiences. In fact, they quickly lost the initial bump in attendances and television audiences exercising these rights initially gifted them so easily. Sadly, given where we find ourselves now, the long-term damage BSI's business strategy has inflicted upon the sport possibly means that the SGP poo can't and won't get put back into the speedway donkey. To mix metaphors further, they may well have milked our speedway udders dry. In order to take the current temperature, as far as you can as an uninvited independent observer, of the current state of the Speedway World Championships as well as get a hint of what really goes on behind the scenes without solely consuming its significance via all the marketing hyperbole, media images, obfuscations, exaggerations and lies – the following chapters continue are my account of my travels on public transport to every staging location of the 2018 SGP series.

CHAPTER 2

Prague SGP 2 – 25.05.18

"It's the ugly stuff that drains you in speedway, never the racing. That's always a pure rush and fun. But it's the endless journeys, airports, vans and bike washing that eventually kills you."

Jason Crump

IT is a beautiful sunny Saturday morning in the centre of Old Town Prague. Refreshingly devoid of tourists too, which makes it all the nicer. A small crowd of fans, friends, sponsors and support staff gather outside ye olde Hard Rock café to collect pits passes ahead of, for some, breakfast there. Many wear items of CC111 branded clothing and assorted memorabilia including T-shirts with its distinctive "Cookie Monster" design motif. Others wear baseball caps with different allegiances. Worn backwards is apparently a stylish but carefree option. Craig's friend Simon Thurlow helps out with pass admin to make sure the 38 pits passes requested ("if we order ahead, we can have as many as we want") get correctly allocated. Simon looks fresh, despite staying out until 07.30 this morning. "Our taxi back was CZ2,800! They ask to see your identify documents and, once they've got your passport, you've no choice but to pay to get it back. What a rip-off! But, to be fair, it's cheaper than a taxi back to Carlisle from a night out." Other friends over from Cumbria also took a hit to their pockets with fines of CZ800 each for travelling on the metro without a ticket (price CZ32) last night. "There was a group of them just waiting there – for tourists, like us." Despite these transport wrinkles, and with an Airbnb costing £30 each for two (but shared by six), Simon approves of Prague prices, "when we went to Cardiff last year with fuel it was over £500!" Belle Vue fans with a good-sized flag on hand for display at the Marketa stadium later, Ian Winston and his partner are in Prague for a SGP for the third time, "it's cheaper than going to Cardiff and we can have four days here." Ahead of Craig's rumoured pending arrival, talk turns to what happened at practice yesterday. Simon reports, "Craig didn't have a good practice – he only got two laps". "How many should he have had?" "Six. His kill switch – it turned out – was interfering the first two times so he only got in the last two laps. It's a new engine too! The first race will be the test."

Friday night in Prague old town before the Grand Prix are, apparently, the witching hours for speedway star spotting. The quality and range of possible sightings varies. From Nigel Pearson and Kelvin Tatum MBE out drinking – Philip Rising suggests on the British Speedway Forum they are to be easily found talking loudly in the Irish pub on the Main Square that "does good breakfasts" – to the current World Champion: "Jason Doyle popped into the restaurant we were in last night."

"Jason Doyle and restaurant aren't words you expect to hear together nowadays?"

"He wasn't eating! He was only getting change for his taxi. The riders are all on sports nutrition things now."

Talk soon turns to who might win tonight. Simon won't make forecasts but Ian suggests nearly a third of the competing riders might triumph, "I think it'll be one of the Poles – they go well here – or Tai or, maybe, Zmarzlik. I think Craig will do better here, maybe four or five points?" Widely respected and knowledgeable BT Sports compere and speedway broadcaster Natalie Quirk's parents, Stockport-based Belle Vue fans Elaine and Mike are also here in Prague to watch the meeting. But also to access the pits with guest passes courtesy of Craig Cook. Understandably Elaine is proud of her daughter, "She's been going since she was eight. She was a member of the Joe Screen fan club."

[Mike] "When you think that she goes three and half hours without any script."

[Ian] "So you're the Quirkmeisters!"

[Jeff] "Speedway needs high-calibre broadcasters who are knowledgeable but also likeable."

[Mike] "She's fortunate that's what's wanted now."

[Jeff] "Speedway needs that generally so good to have someone so at home with the medium, the sport and with people. She comes across well. She's got a calm style too."

[Elaine] "She's no diva!"

Prague is the longest-serving Speedway Grand Prix location. The meeting is held at a traditional speedway club rather than in a stadium better suited to other sports purposes rented for the night. The track itself is under the new management of Pavel Ondrasik (taking over from his dad Petr) who has long-serving King's Lynn rider Tomas Topinka on board as employee as stadium manager. Just as talk turns to (incorrect) rumours that, sadly, this may be last Grand Prix held in Prague, Craig Cook arrives looking fresh. Despite sharing a double-bed with his dad Will the previous night. Last-minute travel bookings meant it was that or sleep in the van. Though Prague is a good value, popular destination – too popular you could argue, if you spend any length of time in the old town – on a (UK) bank holiday weekend flights and accommodation are still pricey since availability is at a premium. Still, we are all here and, as friends, rider, mechanics, helpers or fans, collectively look forward excitedly, even Craig seems chilled as he – with a relaxed breakfast ahead before he heads off to the track – meets, greets and mingles with friends and well-wishers in easy-going, friendly fashion.

Taking the local temperature with *ad hoc* but completely unscientific research, my airport taxi driver had heard of speedway but had never been. From his reaction he wasn't going anytime in the near future either even though he had the weekend off. The concierge at my high-rise out-of-town hotel – where speedway tours specialist Travel Plus Tours (TPT) locate themselves this year – tells me that she'd never even heard of speedway until lots of the TPT guests started asked her about the whereabouts of the stadium location, despite there already being a coach organised to take them there and back. The track is located on the far outskirts of the city close to what looks like a forest to a visitor's eyes but may well count as a small wood round here. It is easily accessible by public transport. In this case, old-school two-carriage trams used by locals to travel the many outlying Prague hills rather than the swish central city two-line network of metro trams premised upon tourist use to monuments and sites of interest festooned with multi-language admonitions to "beware of pickpockets". During my brief ride on this brightly coloured contemporary tram transport system, the primary language spoken is English or German rather than Czech. Across the aisle, a woman is lost in a book with the back-cover strapline, "what if charisma could be taught?"

After you leave the far-flung metro stop and walk around some of the perimeter of a dense forest/wood that invites getting accidentally lost, the Marketa stadium suddenly looms ahead. It is part of a tree-rich residential area of low-slung quite desirable multi-storey blocks of flats. The stadium abuts parkland and the wonderfully peaceful tree-lined sloping graveyard of the Basilica of Saint Marketa. Originally this was all part of the grounds of the Brevnov Monastery founded in 993. To the casual observer, it appears the Marketa Stadium is an organic part of this verdant community rather than having been inserted as a resented later intruder. On the road that leads towards the stadium, there is already an uproarious mid-afternoon tailgate party of middle-aged male drinkers in full swing held at the back of one of the few vans currently parked up in the fenced-off visitor car park. Slightly unnecessarily large-lettered English language signage ("Entry Guest Passes") with directional arrows guide arrivals past military-smart uniformed police at a checkpoint where they completely ignore pedestrians but zealously stop and direct the few vehicles. Walkers run the gamut of crash barriers that separate the pavement from an almost traffic-free road. Two waves of recent mums amble past in deep conversation pushing babies in buggies in the opposite direction to the speedway. Ageing family cars already occupy all the residential on-street parking along with an illegally parked dusty silver Opel with an advert that fills its back window about the date, time and location of the Grand Prix tonight. Though it won't interfere that much with driving safely, it is an inefficient tool to stoke significant demand as would-be punters only get see it if they drive behind it or see it when parked. It is an approach to marketing that shouts proud and enthusiastic local speedway club rather than BSI contract terms. Despite a good number of uniformed police and security people, the more human scale of this part of residential Prague has a less officious, more relaxed feel than Warsaw.

Whoever commissioned the large-size stadium information maps clearly loves them enough to place a big bulk order. Every few yards there is yet another handily displayed on a wall or fence. Quite who could get lost or badly confused is a mystery since the rough layout and dimensions of the Marketa are easily gleaned just by standing outside. The stadium is compact and old school so lacks covered grandstands. The tallest visible stadium building is the main grandstand with a rooftop "VIP" terrace overlooking the start line. The track is set in a bowl and viewed either from brightly coloured permanent metal seats or else from temporary stands erected to supplement seating capacity for this big occasion. Out on the centregreen, all the usual Speedway Grand Prix furniture, advertiser signs, meeting paraphernalia and equipment are either already installed or else laid out ready for later use. In the bright afternoon sunshine with close proximity to a proper permanent track, the ostensible surface glamour of the SGP feels dialled back and much more workaday.

Inside the Marketa pits, it is a surprise to see Ronnie Russell. Quite what his role here is unknown to me but he certainly projects a strong air of officialdom as he wears his SGP lanyard, wristbands and a scrupulously ironed shirt with pride. So much so you'd wrongly half-suspect Ronnie has a military background or did National Service. His look radiates authority and is a long way from his casual dress for his regular track curation work for Swindon Robins speedway club at Blunsdon stadium. Historically, until the change to fixed race nights this season, the limited interchange time between the finish of the dogs and the next night staging of the speedway often saw Ronnie kip on the floor of the cramped changing room in order to start work (flattening and removing the shale?) at 4am. Afterwards it turns out that Ronnie is here to try to persuade those with power and authority – aka the FIM – that the revolutionary air fence he designed, produced and tested is far better and safer than the Tony Briggs model currently homologated for use at the SGP. Though beauty is in the eye of the beholder, Ronnie's design has merit since it overcomes the occasional possibility that riders and bikes can still disappear at speed beneath the skirt of the existing widely used air fences into unknown but dangerous solid objects that may lurk beneath. Anyone who goes to speedway regularly knows that contemporary air safety fences massively improve rider safety and boost their confidence about falls into them but are, nonetheless, currently still not flawless. Every aspect of the SGP was long ago sub-divided and contracted so it could be monetised. Air fences are no different. The combination of sufficient safety, homologation and friends in high places probably remains potent. Even (or especially) at speedway, possession remains nine-tenths of the law. Doubtless air fence approved supplier status is no different. Any notional, real or imagined, advances in rider safety will have to wait until finance or accidents dictate otherwise.

With four hours to go before the official start time, all the action is adjacent to the pits area outside a single-storey ochre-painted building. There mechanics patiently queue with bikes (usually three) and helmets awaiting their official Technical Control inspection inside. Once formalities are successfully completed, as if on a promise elsewhere, once back outside they race to fit newly issued tyres with great speed and dexterity close to the inspection building exit doors. A spares van with tall piles of unwrapped unused Anlas tyres aplenty sit there forlornly as rival manufacturer tyres get fitted by skilled mechanics in speeded up Benny Hill film fashion. Hopefully, no Anlas senior executives are on hand to witness the complete and utter rejection of their extensively Greg Hancock tested products, despite them being the "official" SGP series tyre.

Lacking riders or the urgency of a meeting, the pits area basks serene in the sunshine except for the occasional clink of tools. The club has proper rider pit bays – open-fronted cubicles with a flat corrugated iron roof – again (like Warsaw) laid out in 2017 final table finish order. All riders have easy access to the track from these pits. On a sunny day, allocating bays by current world ranking disadvantages the top six riders – Doyle, Dudek, Woffinden, Janowski, Zmarzlik and Sayfutdinov – as their notionally prime position location takes the full glare of the sun whilst other bays remain shaded. Each rider booth has a television monitor that relays the SGP feed. These are switched on and currently show a pristine but empty track. Behind the six primary rider pit bays – of the home team whenever they stage league racing here – runs an elevated concrete path up to a pre-race rider muster point with floor markings in red, blue, white and yellow helmet colour order. When broadcast live later, though officially the muster point where riders sit ready waiting to race, informally it is yet another SGP stage for FIM Race Director Phil Morris to strut and fuss about in full view of the cameras. Previous incumbents in the same role – Ole Olsen and then Tony Olsson – preferred to do their jobs quietly and efficiently so shunned all real or manufactured opportunities to camera bomb or accidentally appear in shot.

By the track exit, the broadcast interview booth is primped for later action but currently lacks riders, interviewer or film equipment. From the splatter of sponsors of logos shown, it seems Turkish company Anlas are again the event sponsor. Kind of pretentiously, the Speedway Grand Prix even has an "official watch sponsor" I haven't heard of nor can remember. Though, obviously, if we are looking for spurious synergy, it is the case that each and every speedway race gets timed. For the nerdier fan, this needs to get recorded in the programme. To my mind, even if they still wear them, almost any speedway fan in any country is not likely to buy a fashion watch nor consider upgrading from their existing cheap imitation Tag Hauer. Though there may be the odd fan who takes great pride in their use of a stopwatch function at speedway meetings, they are unlikely to want to upgrade their disposable specials to the pricier official SGP watch. When it comes to the riders, they will have no interest in time. Except where it comes to airline schedules, if they have it off, serve it or, of course, when they race in Poland where squad selection is often determined by the brute force results of weekly teammate-versus-teammate four lap race times.

Helped by the conspicuousness of its sponsorship activities and pits stall of free drinks in different bright can colours, Monster Energy again is the most prevalent brand trademark seen at the SGP. Whether this is reality or a function of the eye-catching nature of their florescent green fork logo is hard to gauge. Fair play to them, at the Marketa they rather innovatively even have a retro-look water bowser cannily and stylishly kitted out in their corporate livery on hand for curatorial duties. As a positive branding exercise, this will only fail to be memorable if they over-water the track or if rains torrentially. With experienced track curation staff on site and bright sunshine, this anxiety seems moot. The stadium speaker sound check gets conducted at an ear-splitting volume. Later when there are fans actually in the stadium, they play them at an ear-strainingly muted volume, as if conducting some sort of weird free mass-hearing test. The sound check person is either a patriot or optimist – possibly both – as they have the Czech national anthem on a repeat loop. The lowlier tech guys from the SGP broadcasts sub-contractor have the professionalism smarts to check out the semi-final and final gate position draw graphics for any colour separation issues. They do this with admirable fastidiousness for each and every individual rider image for all four helmet colours. Since some riders (I won't name) or the meeting wild card and reserves almost certainly won't make the last eight, checking their images in each helmet colour is a thoroughness and degree of professionalism that borders on anal retentive. However, these are checks well worth completing since some helmet colours do indeed refract or blur when confronted with certain rider images. For reasons unknown, the yellow helmet plays particular havoc with the stern Freddie Lindgren SGP stock photo.

Next to the bike inspection building is the Marketa clubhouse. It boasts a small raised viewing terrace that looks towards (rather than overlooks) bends three and four for those members keen to test their distance vision. Through an open set of double-doors, there are four infant school style wooden benches laid out perpendicular to each other in front of two sparsely filled trophy cabinets (three trophies in each) along with some sparsely-filled bookshelves that face the entrance. Because this one night only the clubhouse also serves as the "Jury/Briefing Room", every access point has Blu-tacked A4 laminated temporary notices with large no smoking symbols stylishly done in the corporate identity manual compliant SGP series official livery of orange and black. There are signs that warn apocalyptically – given much greater urgency by the use of bold capital letters, "NO ENTRY WITH STEEL SHOE". If the clubhouse is off limits to all but club members, SGP officialdom or competitors, then the building next door surrounded by crash barriers with photocopied A4 signs painstakingly attached that designate it as the "VIP area" keeps out the unwelcome but doesn't add much to its appeal or cache. Indeed, viewed from afar, this low-slung "VIP" building looks like a community centre. Albeit one that serves alcohol and has a small grassed area out front with good access to (possibly "VIP") seats that overlook bend 4 of the track. Some men lean on the crash barriers for a chat and smoke in the sunshine as they half-heartedly watch for the comings and goings of the speedway great and the good who – so far – are conspicuously failing to materialise at this early late afternoon hour.

If there is a broadcaster arms race, then in presence and investment terms this was won hands down a while back at all SGPs by Polish television with their specially constructed raised spacious outdoor studio. In addition to room for commentators, it also boasts seats for guest experts too. It makes the Sky Sports speedway commentary high-rise window cleaning cage effect scaffold pole studio of yesteryear – during their Billy Big Bollocks of live broadcast speedway in Britain before the sharply declining audiences really kicked in – look as retro as Stonehenge. Sensibly, given the rain delays speedway sometimes suffers here or elsewhere, it has a well-constructed sloping roof. That said, given the metal of its construction, fixtures and fittings, let alone the array of cameras and mikes, this studio wouldn't be your first choice of location as the best place to avoid lightning strikes. Luckily, this evening Prague's skyline enjoys only distant lurking dark clouds.

In the final hour before the more widely issued lower status "guest pass" access dematerialises like Cinderella's slippers at the ball ("105 minutes before the opening ceremony"), large numbers of speedway fans, hangers on, sponsors, media types and rubberneckers suddenly and rather excitedly rush to fill the pits area. Many of these same people were also in Warsaw, which either possibly calls into question how they get allocated. Then again, maybe just like speedway riders are really just a travelling troupe of freelance performers for hire across Europe, so they get followed round by an equivalent posse of pits people? On hand is the Polish dad-in-impressively-bright-red-trousers with his family in tow again manically keen to get selfies with every competing Polish rider while animatedly discussing prospects. Or, possibly, since I don't speak Polish, the weather, track or likely chances of the embers of proletarian rebellion flailing into a dictatorship of the people from their humble roots at a speedway meeting. There is the back-packed photographer with the many choices of whopper lens who – having framed and conceptualised the never-to-be-seen-again perfect atmospheric photo – rudely pushes aside any people with the temerity to notionally interfere with its capture for posterity. He also just loves to dive amongst the fans' feet onto the floor for yet another of his signature notionally "quirky" but pathologically predictable and creepy fast-shutter series of upskirt shots. I have yet to see any of these evocative from the vantage-point-of-a-child photos published anywhere. Talking of children, the SGP pits really are the place to go if you want to see insouciant mechanics and middle-aged men with impressive beer bellies ride shiny scooters at speed for only a few yards in a very confined area. Also here again are the two women in Union Flag dresses whose function, it seems, is to enthusiastically touch, closely hug and pose for selfies with Phil Morris as soon as he hits the metaphorical red carpet of his mind that is really the SGP pits and track environs. Having last seen Phil in the flesh in a Polish nightclub, 21-year-old SGP and Eastbourne fan, model and veterinary student Sinead Bacon is surprised by the age profile of these women. Sinead is here with her mum, Jackie, and a friend from Wolverhampton. Their guest passes come courtesy of one of Freddie Lindgren's mechanics. Sight of Joe Parsons – discombobulating in this instance, since he's incongruously stood next to child in a pushchair rather than gurning for the camera – prompts Jackie to despair of the pre-meeting entertainment. "I can't believe that they still do the Monster rig everywhere? It was old hat when they started it years ago!" In World Championship speedway circles, the recent SGP tradition of the rig still counts as entertaining and respecting the fans via cutting-edge truly innovative marketing.

Though some of the officer class start to grace us with their presence, most riders remain conspicuous by their absence – except for permanently fan-friendly Greg Hancock who is immediately collared by a cheery group of Rzeszow fans. After initial faux reluctance, they persuade him to pose with them for a group photo behind the giant club flag they expertly unfurl. Stupidly, they then elect me to take this for posterity so only get a series of distorted and blurry smartphone photos. They greet this discovery with disdain, incredulity and glares, apparently unaware their flag is too long to fit them all into one shot without a wide-angle lens function. Height differences also play a big part too as in the centre of their group Greg strains on tiptoes to be barely visible above the flag. Notable for his English paleness and body-art starter kit of extensive upper arm tattoos, Hancock's panjandrum Josh Gudgeon guards against health and safety infractions, as he waits patiently to escort Greg to other carefully scheduled pre-meeting appointments elsewhere to smilingly press the flesh. Ivan Mauger's ex-manager and speedway journalist Peter Oakes regularly proudly opines about his grandson Josh's clients (and even the reach – whatever that is – of his tweets) as if it is breaking news in his lengthy weekly *Speedway Star* columns. Some of its few remaining readers, like to regularly play Spot the Josh Client Coverage. Apparently something of a prodigy according to his granddad's write ups, it is rumoured misplaced loyalty saw Josh get a Monster Energy tattoo – whereabouts unknown – to celebrate the "motorsports consultancy" work he landed with the company in 2012 aged 18 while also studying full time for his degree in journalism from the acclaimed University of Hollister. Readers also regularly learn of Mr Gudgeon's star rider friendships but also his changing work responsibilities. Latterly, Josh's job title in respect of Greg Hancock has, sadly, shrunk. Apparently though he self-identifies with the much more grandiose sobriquet of "manager", the reality was soon subsequently corrected in a later column to the lesser and more prosaic "road manager". Though in Prague Josh is only a humble roadie-cum-Boy-Friday for Greg, 24-year-old Josh's meteoric rise elsewhere continues to be well promoted and documented by his proud grandfather. According to Oakes already "a well-known figure and face around the tracks", Josh landed the exciting new position of Director of Communications with the freshly-minted private limited company (owned by Rob Painter and Vicky Blackwell) nowadays with the rights to run the Great Britain speedway team organisation. It is a position that will add further authority to Gudgeon's social media persona as an advocate of real or imagined wishes and needs for both riders and fans (usually against dunderheaded hydra of vested promotional interests). It would be a stunning achievement for the sport in this country if Josh could manage to boost the currently pitiful level of press coverage British speedway enjoys with the national media to a mere fraction of the adulatory comments written about him by his granddad.

Though Bruce Penhall played midwife with his initial introduction of his fellow southern Californians Hancock and Parsons, without Greg's sponsorship search zeal there arguably would be no Monster Energy sponsorship at the SGP. Ever cannily professional, Greg has been finding and seizing lucrative commercial sponsorship opportunities in speedway since before Josh was born. Though the liquid may taste "toxic" to some, the Monster Energy sponsorships – for their level, extent and duration – have been incredibly sweet. I am going to guess based on no real insight at all, arguably, in total billings getting on for one of the most lucrative of Greg's career. It has been an opportunity that Monster – under Joe Parsons – have seized and also then leveraged to the full. In the temporary bike and equipment overflow area for the riders behind the pits, I spot – from an earlier less slick, uglier era some Monster-branded Greg Hancock towels. One is folded over a crash barrier and another laid out, possibly drying, on the grass. In addition to this towel based visual exhibition of the Monster brand evolution, his continued use of these towels confirms Greg's parsimony. But also, his connection to, part in and understanding of what is – in the final analysis – the practical, make-do-and-mend approach that is the hallmark of speedway culture generally. Ultimately, just as all political careers inevitably end in failure, so too do all speedway sponsorships. They end. Often suddenly. The lucrative easy days of yore quickly return to the nothing of comparative destitution. How it happens varies – whether through non-renewal, loss of confidence or, worse, family illness or career ending/limiting injury. If (like Greg) you ride, come from, work or stay in the speedway world long enough, like death and taxes, feast turns back to famine. For me, that Greg Hancock still owns, has and uses these superseded Monster towels is much worthier of respect than his studied bonhomie as well as much more authentically symbolic of what his life in speedway really is or stands for than his oft-lauded World Championship wins.

Earlier in the old city, Craig Cook's team spoke with incredulity about how the Prague SGP was "completely paper[work] free for environmental reasons". The only visible paper in the pits are a couple of autograph books (they still exist!) and numerous programmes. Compared to Warsaw, programmes are readily and easily available as well, at a bargain price CZ120 too! Further underlining the green credentials of this Prague SGP meeting, there is an extensive range of recycling bins. Each with a specific but mystery purpose including a selection of multi-coloured ones lined up in helmet colour order supplemented with some additional rogue non-speedway colours from elsewhere in the rainbow. There are also numerous metal bins and drums with funnels with various instructional shouty notices in English regarding their specific terms of use. Though suddenly very crowded, Emil Sayfutdinov weaves purposefully through the pits crowd with speed, skill and dexterity similar to that shown when on his bike. In the interview area, Nicki Pedersen stands ready in ideal camera position (sensibly designated by the pink cross on the floor) awaiting his interview with the SGP's pits "colour" interview woman Kiri Bloore. She is a new addition to the broadcast team and already, from her Twitter feed, travels the world to various forms of motor car rallying from more exotic countries (but equally out-of-the-way locations) than visited by the SGP. There is no visible chemistry or bonhomie between them. Kiri studiously ignores Nicki to concentratedly scroll through her phone until, given the signal, both then suddenly animatedly converse for their various pre-recorded interviews like very matey old friends. After each interview concludes, another different logo microphone cover gets selected from a nearby box. Once the correct replacement microphone cover is fitted, their interview repeats with both similar and variant questions. In total Nicki pre-records three packages of banal Prague SGP anticipation. While all this goes on, Tai Woffinden's press wallah Nigel Pearson pigeonholes the next waiting interviewee Niels Kristian Iversen for some hail-fellow-well-met platitudes and pleasantries. Nigel's backpacked (with understated Monster logo!) commentary partner-in-crime Kelvin Tatum walks round from pit bay to pit bay checking the pre-meeting preparations of the various mechanics until buttonholed by Gordon Pairman. Kelvin mostly nods as Gordon animatedly holds forth while festooned in a full complement of SGP lanyards and wristbands. They clash with his colonial vibe cream collared summer shirt attire. Understandably Gordon long ago stopped paying to get in the SGP so, sadly – his later season career highlights interview with Peter Oakes reveals – reveals that he labours under the false impression SGP admission is priced at bargain basement levels compared to the eye-watering admission costs of (allegedly) rival international sports events.

Though the pits are mobbed, there is a noticeable lack of curiosity in or glad-handing around the Craig Cook pit bay. The pits layout dictates that his bay location is, in relative terms, the equivalent of speedway Siberia so is already a backwater in footfall terms. There are so few people it is almost like Cook has been quarantined, sent to Coventry or else an unofficial exclusion zone operates. Craig is on hand but focuses on his bikes with two CC111 branded (probably) mechanics for company along with a waiting bloke who sneezes continuously for nearly five minutes. Down a steep path behind this section of pit bays is an impressive fence, some woods, a large and fully occupied rider van parking area and, in comparative shade, a bank of temporary toilets. In my role as secret shopper of the SGP rider temporary toilet provision experience, though there is no running water here either, at least these have paper. They are also a hugely improved sensory experience compared to the noxious gas variety of rider toileting facilities supplied in Warsaw.

The Marketa stadium turnstiles open well before tapes up. Traditional mass market, albeit with a euro feel in its selection, music blares distantly from the stadium speaker system. The pre-meeting atmosphere benefits from the sunshine as well as the welcoming community feel of the staging club. There is easy access to the stands, friendly staff, the soothing balm of bargain-priced Czech beer, the smell of comparatively edible food and the sounds of a live brass band joyfully winning its musical competition with the pre-recorded variety. By my grandstand steps, highly unusually for speedway (at this time of the evening), strong alcohol has completely pole-axed four blokes. They lie, nationalities unknown (though I'm guessing not Czech), comatose and totally oblivious to all around them. Next to them is a scrawny topless old-age pensioner struggling to master the buttons of his retro-look mobile phone. He too is oblivious to quizzical stares or judging eyes. Afterwards, long-time obsessive friends of all things SGP, writers Rising and Burbidge (of the *Speedway Star*) both kindly acknowledge in passing that the racing on offer at the Marketa is often poor so, instead, make a virtue of its history and location in their encomiums. Apparently, Prague is a wondrous bargain-break city location for speedway fans keen to halo their bank holiday weekend with a below-par bout of processional SGP racing.

My seat in the open to the elements grandstand – booked via speedway tour specialists Travel Plus Tours – is in prime position and overlooks the first bend. Our group of older fans provides an immediate boost to the average age in our section. Like us, our metal seats are old-school. They are durable, rigid and noticeably narrow as well as built for an era of body shapes and bottoms without access to 24/7 on-the-hoof convenience eating. After only five minutes in these uncomfortable seats, the night ahead takes on an unexpected additional element of endurance and could well leave us with lumbago as a lasting memory of this Prague SGP. We are luckier than the second bend dyslexic Poole fans who have, weirdly, hung out three generously sized different flags that read Opole. From a distance it looks like they have similarly rigid seats in prime viewing positions with the added bonus of hot bright late afternoon sunshine. Though on the night, to untutored eyes the Marketa Stadium doesn't look full, afterwards BSI Speedway Managing Director Torben Olsen will laughably hail Prague as a "sold out" crowd.

If any Speedway Grand Prix is really only about the riders, then this message doesn't appear to have been communicated to FIM Race Director Phil Morris. It is quickly clear that he is in unofficial competition with "Monster Joe" Parsons for the most attention from the live cameras through each and every SGP. Parsons has various ploys. His best is the spontaneous orgasmic outbursts of celebration any low-attention-span but over-excitable "true" [American!] speedway fan would overwhelmingly feel if there to witness it live. Mostly Parsons exploits the privilege of his access-all-areas series sponsor partner status or else the fig leaf of the various Monster rider sponsorships as reason for his relentless SGP camera-bombing. Presented with endless star-farking camera opportunities, Parsons's standard repertoire includes high fives, moments of tense, studious concentration followed by excessive glee and last-minute hand covered (to thwart imaginary espionage) wise words of whispered encouragement wisdom to soon-to-race riders. He looms into shot so often you half-suspect his frequent vanilla virtuoso "accidental" photo-bombs are part of a complex performance-related bonus scheme. Suggestions that the tiny SGP is the convenient stage upon which his giant ego runs rampant is increasingly hard to pass off as just a conscientiously done day job. Like his apparently much more successful role model boxing promoter Don King, Parsons likes to arrive at every event with the World Champion on his arm and leave with the World Champion on his arm too, though not necessarily the same person. Ever since Parsons massively expanded his set-list of vaguely justified camera-bombing appearances, this presents a problem for all similarly attention hungry rivals except Phil Morris. His position as FIM Race Director gives even wider access to absolutely anywhere in the stadium but especially the track as well as the fig leaf of pressing or structural work reasons/excuses to pop-up on camera absolutely anywhere. Ostensible vital work easily parlays into numerous opportunities to parade his importance to riders, fans, sponsors, friends, himself, other officials and – such as they are – worldwide television audiences. If the best referees are actually the ones that you don't notice doing the job, then the FIM Race Director position has gone the way of all flesh since Phil took over from the previous race director incumbent Tony Olsson. Unobtrusive efficiency has given way to OTT virtue signalling performance. Invariably on camera. If only there had been some clue regarding his hunger for celebrity and televisual fame prior to his appointment? Minimal investigation quickly takes anyone to the Morris Wikipedia page. It reads as if written by his alter ego or a VERY close family member and lists his many achievements as well as his numerous post-speedway racing career television appearances on *The Weakest Link* and *The Colour of Money* plus his speciality pub quiz and intelligence-led popular programmes *Brainbox Challenge*, *Are You Smarter than a 10 Year Old?* and *Eggheads*. Space is also found for his karaoke win in Prestatyn that subsequently saw him appear on Channel 5 with Sinetta. As a keen singer and dancer, Morris has also strutted and crooned his stuff in his key role in the Welsh Boyzone tribute band Boyozone. Popular demand has seen them so acclaimed they headlined the Barry Island festival and even re-formed with a different all-star line-up for a one-off by popular demand gigs in Porthcawl.

Obviously, though apparently it long ago got forgotten by BSI, actually having a raceable and/or useable track is the most important pre-condition to successfully staging a competitive speedway meeting. Anywhere. Over many seasons the SGP rights holders deliberately downgraded the minimum tariff that defines "success" away from conditions that deliver thrilling races (and, thereby guarantee some form of entertainment) towards providing a ridable surface that ensures the meeting is staged to some form of mundane completion – even on wet shale – to fulfil all contractual obligations as well as remain within the allotted satellite time booked. If SGP meetings lack real excitement, thrilling racing or close contests – as, sadly, most do since these variables are more the exception than the rule – then the embedded co-opted house-trained relentlessly excited media on hand will massively compensate with Orwellian hyperbolic claims otherwise. The situation is compounded by BSI's strategic decision to stage some meetings in the series on temporary (man-made) tracks. Additionally, the changed nature of contemporary era speedway bike and rider needs dictates that their "best" track surfaces are nowadays comparatively shale free. Within this context, since he took on the position of FIM Race Director in 2015, Morris has met the implicit operational brief of his job description to effectively stage manage trouble- and thrill-free SGP meetings to timely completion. The dirty but barely disguised secret remains that the majority of these meetings lack real thrills or jeopardy as a contest while staged on gate-and-go tracks with shale levels barely above those normally found on the (insert your own favourite tarmac road here) M25. While riders, media and fans mostly all collectively look the other way on this badly missing fundamental X-factor of good race track provision (while, simultaneously, bemoaning why no-one takes speedway seriously), Phil appears to increasingly and immodestly believe in his own exceptional brilliance as he struts his many hours on and off camera upon the SGP stage. Doing this stage management job effectively clearly requires that Phil project confidence in his own abilities but, in an SGP world where failure is never acknowledged (or rarely even publicly alluded to unless it is immediately then brushed under the carpet), so enjoyably drinking your own bathwater is not a good look.

That said, his antics are hugely enjoyable to watch in lieu of exciting on-track action or, better still, to pass the many rigorously scheduled pre-meeting and intra-meeting longueurs. It is also an unacknowledged fact that around 40 per cent (sometimes more) of the track action in any and every SPG meeting features tractors circuiting repeatedly but accomplishing little, under the close directional supervision of Morris. Since speedway fans notoriously love tabulation and record-keeping, whether or not they are in the stadium or watching elsewhere, there is an untapped but genuine marketing opportunity to institute a series-long buzzword-bingo-style game of "Where-is-SGP-Wally?" With spotter scorecards on hand, concentration levels and interest levels too would collectively go through the roof as we actively scan for further random sightings of the virtuoso peacockery of Phil or Joe in SGP action. While his access builds to match his confidence, Josh Gudgeon could perhaps work towards becoming the occasional wild card with more alfresco photo-bombs throughout the series. Obviously, there would have to be some sort of handicap system to reflect their respective comparative rarity with, say, six Morris sightings being the equivalent of a single Parsons, plus some sort of additional marking system for virtuosity of incongruous, truly flamboyant or rarely seen camera-bombs. For example, a trademark Parsons shout-at-the-moon celebration of a Red Bull race and/or event win; a crash scene with Phil staging an actual medical intervention; Joe seen on camera with Greg Hancock crying or, maybe, with either Peter Adams or Patryk Dudek's dad laughing. Complex but distinctive routines should also get proper acknowledgement. There may even be no need of a prize as anything that increases the enjoyment of watching any SGP is innately in and of itself its own huge reward. If there must be a grotesque mangle of glistening metal to pass off as a commemorative award, Monster already have their World Cup trophy designers on speed dial.

Hand-in-hand with the modern workplace tradition of job title inflation in lieu of a pay increase that reflects these extra responsibilities, has been the inexorable rise of the name tag and its similarly intrusive but slightly less prevalent cousin: the work uniform. Throw a name badge or uniform at it often serves instead of a coherent strategy. Since club level speedway tends to be tight for funds or parsimonious in orientation (except the initial months of the Bob Brimson era Eastbourne Eagles), it usually errs on the side of the branded team shirts halfway-house side of the equation. At this SGP, they have gone so far as to issue the track stone pickers with one colour of team clothes (grey) while their supervisors wear an altogether more managerial colour (black). With 45 minutes to go until the tapes rise, four pickers march purposefully out onto the track in rough formation except for the bloke pushing the wheelbarrow. Without preamble or foreplay, they immediately set about industriously picking the large stones from the track surface with their bare hands. Even to untutored eyes in the grandstand, the sheer volume of visible stones (of varying sizes) marks this out as a thankless but ambitious Sisyphean task. Initially they go at their hand curation in hammer and tongs fashion on the fourth bend of Marketa track. Their gusto quickly goes flaccid almost as soon as they leave vicinity of the pits gate and begin to head clockwise round towards the finish line. Rather helpfully, the stadium giant screens begin flash up a "warning flying track debris" message in English and Czech. Never one to let the chance of some additional crowd attention go to waste, wearing his FIM authority heavily Phil Morris strides out to give ostentatious superfluous directions. It's a theatrical performance that serves no apparent real function but skilfully manages to mix his trademark large flamboyant gesture version of mime with some strong elements of pantomime. Phil performs watching the stone pickers. He checks the contents of their barrow, while he showcases the side-to-side head movements of an especially nervous but attentive chicken. He strides about the track manfully checking for perils unknown. It is a disciplined performance. In front of the main grandstand, with a flurry of kicks and scrapes Phil attempts to smooth a puddle into a larger damp patch. It is part SGP performance art and part last-minute fine-detail micro-curations. Naively, I assume this must be what track director know-how dictates must take place in order to enable the racing on this surface delivers a thrilling spectacle. With the track suddenly to his apparent satisfaction, but still incredibly stony, Phil returns to both real and imagined supervisory duties in and around the pits. By this point, this speedway version of The Flintstones sees hand curator numbers swollen to ten. Though their numbers and collective speed increases, their quality control has departed, if judged by the contents of the wheelbarrow – as it passes my section of the grandstand – looks all track dirt rather than large stones. Somehow Phil misses this heaven-sent further opportunity to simultaneously mime his managerial authority and displeasure at the range, variety and quality of the rocks collected. But them's the breaks when the red transmission light of the cameras starts to blink elsewhere in the Marketa Stadium.

Out on the centregreen, a female singer with a guitar accompanied by a drummer blasts out some incomprehensible rockier numbers in Czech. Despite the complete lack of crowd reaction, polite cultural difference assumptions initially suggest that this must be the style and calibre of musical entertainment locals love to hear. In the all too brief intervals between songs, clearly operating under the delusion that we have paid and actively sought to see them, the singer shouts greetings ("come on, Prague!") or insists on reaction ("let's hear you!"). When the band switch to English language "classics" – "Simply the Best" is brilliantly murdered ("Is there an album on sale afterwards?") – the veneer of projected cultural difference quickly melts away to reveal they are really just pretty awful. "It's like a really bad pub band." In the years prior to the advent of the Monster rig with its stage-managed rider-signing sessions accompanied by start women and loud youthful pre-recorded music, the SGP rights holders used to provide musical pre-meeting entertainments inside the stadium rather than outside it. Cardiff crowds enjoyed the delights of known or, at least, notorious artists. Albeit often well past their prime. Tony Christie the summer after his "(Is this the way to) Amarillo" re-issue enjoyed chart success. Welsh superstar singer Bonnie Tyler decades after her fame ebbed away. Latterly cheaper wannabes, nonentities, tv show runners-up or never-have-beens have replaced the once-greats. In this context, the treat of having around 45 minutes of musical murder provided gratis along with the price of entry evokes faint nostalgia for the more optimistic SGP era of yesteryear. The gung-ho glory years before rights holders BSI gave up and either left it to the local staging promoter to organise the sounds or else went down their all-costs-must-be-ruthlessly-cut from all departments including musicians booked route.

By the time they reach the back straight, the track sifter team numbers an impressive twelve. Better still, these dirty-handed workers are smartly attired. The local love for uniforms continues with the arrival of a large troupe of schoolgirl majorettes. More workwomanlike in their moves than choreographed to Busby Berkeley standards, they provide another welcome distraction from the sheer discomfort of the metal grandstand seats during the lengthy wait for the meeting to start. It also gives another chance for Mr Backpack Cameraman to dramatically fling himself to the floor as though evading snipers for some more of his unique camera angle shots that the less charitable could deem crotch shots of the schoolgirl dancers doing their routines. Some further unintentional entertainment – throughout the meeting – is provided by the slightly hammy bilingual announcer. On a night of few overtakes or close racing, to my mind, he is worth the admission money alone, even though he follows a consistent half-incomprehensible format. First, we get lengthy bursts of Czech followed by noticeably much briefer descriptions in English. Their levity is partly the content – often ridiculous exaggerations and claims made all the sillier by his stilted English – but also how his natural bored *sotto voce* delivery in translation fights his professional desire to sound thrilled. As the majorettes depart their centregreen stage, a long-winded statement in Czech is followed by news in English that we have just witnessed some "wonderful artistic impressions". Lengthy filler descriptions in Czech continue interspersed with random gems apropos of nothing evident going on inside the stadium such as, "Tai Woffinden and Jason Doyle are big fans of SuperX or FreestyleX", "there is many ways to go" and my favourite, though I was distracted when I possibly slightly misheard this, "a track excitement to get moist". After introducing Tomas Topinka to the crowd in Czech (and before we later see him in action driving the bowser), we're then told he nowadays helps curate the track with, "such great racing lines what the track is known for since Greg Hancock in 1997".

Before the riders come out for their introductions, the local promoters make an unforced category error with some introductory parade laps from what appears to be the local chapter of portly middle-aged Hells Angels. Pregnant but proud astride their gleaming monster bikes, this sight might inspire Deliveroo to do things differently from now on in Prague with extra Angels style. Like many speedway fans, I really couldn't give much of a toss about seeing other motorbikes – of any sort – at a meeting. Historically (in the UK at least) though the riders, media and fans/aficionados of other bike disciplines sometimes make polite noises of interest or nod towards an invisible shared common bond, there really is no automatic synergy or crossover appeal with speedway. If anything, the catatonically slow Marketa Hells Angels drive-by parade leaves time to wonder: have things in the Czech Republic really modernised since independence if this is classed as a good night's entertainment here? When did Hells Angels start to eat so much? Or start to allow women to ride the bikes rather than their owners? Did Harley Davidson really file for Chapter 11? And, one for Josh Gudgeon given his career-minded Monster Energy tattoo, is it true that Harley Davidson are still the company where more of their employees voluntarily have company logo tattoos than any other? (It is, appaz!) Whatever the answers to these pub quiz questions, sight of these weekend Hells Angels luxuriating in the final echoes of their sub-cultural significance is, at least, likely to delight the bloke three rows down. He is here proudly wearing the collector's item of a gun metal green T-shirt that rather neurotically reads, "Hells Angels – Tel Aviv Israel". Later in the evening, during news of post-meeting winner presentation celebrations and the promise of "exciting fireworks", the announcer promises the return of these bikers and reveals them to be wannabe weekend plastic Angels from "Auto Klub Marketa" rather than the full Monty devilishly wild real thing.

Instead of the usual awful grandiloquent SGP standard introduction format of brief minor pyrotechnics, deafening sound track and light show led lengthy catwalk style of individual rider presentations beloved by BSI whenever meetings are held in big stadia, we get an old-fashioned rider parade. This happens in draw order so requires that the riders wheel out their bikes in race appearance order before they then line up next to their machine and each other close to the start line. Each rider gets a fleeting individual introduction before they reward us with a wave or two. Greg Hancock, of course, milks the opportunity and plays to the crowd adulation he expects rather than gets. Greg takes so long waving and smiling to his public that you half suspect it may be a Farewell Tour since he's still doing so when the next two riders following him have long since settled back down. Ignoring the remaining rider introductions, exuberant waves over Greg then leaves his place in the line-up to do some *ad hoc* gardening of the track by gate 4. Though this will be his first gate position of the night, it is not until Heat 4 so, ignoring that the track is rock hard and littered with stones, the impact of his handiwork will be minimal by the time the tread of his tyres nestles down upon the gate 4 shale. Being generous, it may be useful to Greg as a pre-meeting psychological comfort but looks for all the world as the kind of unnecessary attention-seeking "professionalism" and virtue-signalling behaviour that his boosters in the media would portray as yet further confirmation that Hancock is a true "showman". No sooner is Greg back in line than Nicki Pedersen breaks ranks to garden the few yards in front of gate 3 (his starting gate position in Heat 3). Maybe this attention to tiny detail is what made them both World Champions? Or, possibly, what ex-World Champions in their 40s anxiously do to try to even things up in a world that pits them against younger thrusting rivals? Predictably enough, the backpacked cameraman lays on the track to take more of his trademark uniquely-angled mole's-eye-view photos. Or, possibly, this time does so to exaggerate the stature of his often diminutive SGP subjects? Rider introductions over, the Czech national anthem is sung by a choir. We don't get to hear them until halfway through when they switch the stadium speakers back on. Round me some suspect they got turned off as a safety precaution against the headline band. Though not quite so dramatic on a stadium big screen or the little screens at home, this old-school rider parade does the job for fans inside the stadium and feels the normal order of things.

Before the racing gets underway, BSI's love of SGP staff clothing meets its match in the form of the Marketa zeal for colour-coordinated staff uniforms. Peak Speedway Grand Prix uniform arrives in the unlikely guise of dress-alike centregreen marshals. They march out of the pits in precise formation that, along with their age and gait, suggests that they definitely saw military service. It is an impression enhanced by the sharp cut of their dark uniforms. An image of diddy Len Silver leading out at military medium his more raggle-taggle platoon of Rye House track staff springs unbidden into my mind. The announcer's enthusiasm at their arrival, "please welcome your speedway marshals!" is greeted in studious silence by the crowd. What before the racing starts seemed the perfect grandstand position – overlooking the start line, the first corner action and in shade away from the still blinding sunshine – unbelievably suffers from a badly restricted view. From this vantage point we are unable to see the rider in gate 4. Whether up at the tapes or taking the chequered flag there. To compound matters, unfortunately there are a couple of serial nationalist standers. One is predictably enough Polish and the other a less easy-to-forecast Russian. They are both frequently seized by the patriotic need to adulate and, thereby, block any sight of any race finish involving riders from either of their countries. With four Poles and two Russians racing in every SGP of the 2018 series, this requires a lot of exultant or encouraging standing. There is soon something of a Poland v Russia patriotic arms race between them that requires they stand throughout any and all laps led by their fellow countrymen. By the time of the final four qualifying races, any race where a Russian or Pole isn't stone cold last requires passionate expression of their undying love.

Worst of these two offenders is the Russian fan who stands ramrod tall to then better make love to his national flag. He has a definite choreographed routine. His base repertoire requires that he leap to his feet proudly holding his flag with two hands in front of his body. As his rider enters the apex of bends three and four, he draws the sensual material of the Russian flag in a tender caress down his tummy towards his crotch area for a brief pause before a final meaningful lingering patriotic caress of the flag on his jeans prior to a Three Amigos style penetrative thrust of his hips. Split-second synchronicity sees his orgasmic finish coincide with a final triumphant arms-length flourish of the flag as it raises like a modesty screen to cover some further rapid hip thrusts. Any race with a victorious or nearly victorious Russian rider adds further frenzy to his already crazed Happy Finish celebrations. There is little doubt he is definitely his own most amazing lover. In contrast, the Polish man lacks panache or schooling in the ways of patriotic lurve. Plus, he is fatter as well as basically a traditional jumper up and downer. When particularly exultant, he occasionally supplements his jack-in-the-box routine with a jiggle finish or a slower more measured Anthea Redfern twirl. Unlike the Russian man, he isn't here alone so has partners-in-crime to perform for who endorse and critique his performance. As my mum would say, "he doesn't make a very good window". Given the current speedway fashion for obsessive body consciousness, perhaps, BSI could launch an SGP-branded rhythmic gymnastics exercise programme with optional flags?

Sadly, for my particular section of the home straight grandstand, these zealously patriotic celebrators ensure that seeing the finish of almost any race is impossible unless you wait for its probable but not for definite replay on the stadium big screen. Even if it is shown, by that point – as is traditional whenever attending any SGP live – there is a zero-sum game choice for fans. Either watch the replays of the last race finish or else choose to watch the new set of riders come out and mosey up to the tapes. You watch said replay in the hope that this particular camera operative understood enough about speedway beforehand to direct their camera to capture the key or contentious incidents of the previous race. And, having hopefully done so, that the replay operative then has the editorial wherewithal to decide to show these key moments. Whatever goes on, every heat is also played back as a copious montage of fractionally varying tracking shots of the first few yards from the start – shown from different angles – in tandem with some first corner action, some side-by-side back straight action with optional slo-mo sprays of shale, overtakes (if any), a brief flash of the last bend action (if any) and then the race finish. Then, of course, there is a slo-mo of the lead rider crossing the finish line, even if said result is completely certain or ruthlessly mundane.

Strangely, as at Warsaw, before the first race you can smell wafts of methanol but not thereafter. Out on the track, the highly improbable event of a Niels Kristian Iversen last eight qualification takes a major blow with an immediate warning from the referee for moving at the tapes. This new initiative dictates that there is no further warning for future infringements by any rider on a warning but only summary dismissal from that programmed race. Two strikes and you are out! Predictably, throughout the SGP season ahead, no referee has the courage to dismiss any rider for any such (often obvious) repeat infractions. Given the majority of races here will likely be won from the gate (FTG) by the rider who starts/ reacts quickest away from the tapes, having to remain stock still while other riders possibly twitch in anticipation is – theoretically – a disadvantage. That said, this ruling has arguably had the opposite effect of encouraging every SGP rider to try their luck at predicting the rise of the tapes in at least one race – especially later in the meeting – safe in the knowledge that the downside of a vague-slap-on-the wrist warning is the only outcome to weigh against the much greater upside of professionally "cheating" your way to a race win. As some worried and others predicted, all four of the first set of heats are won from the gate by Tai, Emil, Nicki and Maciej. Prior to the first three races, taking a leaf from the always rigorous Pearson-Tatum satellite broadcast commentary playbook, the stadium announcer hails the "fantastic line-up here". A series of processional races is sub-optimal entertainment. Rather amazingly, afterwards Paul Burbidge will claim in his *Speedway Star* "trackside" report on the meeting that television audience criticism and complaints (on "social media" aka Twitter) were misplaced as although the meeting was turgid(!) the atmosphere experienced live by the fans was breathtaking! This rare but rather wonderful sighting of the-product-was-shit-but-you-should-have-been-there-live defence is unusually refreshing and, let's be honest, kinda dim but also strangely inspired.

Perhaps, a better defence would be that viewers at home get treated throughout to the extra helping of bonus sightings of FIM Race Director rushing self-importantly about the pits, trackside or out on the track cajoling, explaining to, smiling with (helmets prevent us seeing their smiles and grimaces of response) or encouraging riders. Though home viewers miss nothing of Phil's various involvements, attending fans are deprived of the full range and majesty of his repertoire. For example, both the pits and the elevated stage of the pre-race ramp can't really be seen from most sections of the grandstands. Suited and booted riders on or off their bikes are all the raw material Mr Morris requires to strut his notionally managerial stuff. There are too many personal favourites to choose. It's always a delight to watch whenever Phil relives the athletics promise of his youth (hat tip: Wikipedia) to foot race almost any and every fallen SGP rider, especially younger ones – Greg rarely falls off, nevermind that he definitely never runs nowadays – from the track or centregreen on their run back to the pits. Notably "fit for his age and fitter than many younger than him", Morris generously gives them a head start before inevitably he manages to overtake. Sight of Phil ("fairly tall at six foot") in magnificent full flight signals to us all that his duties are so important and numerous and well-executed that he has to run to do them all. Overtaken riders (or loudly mentored trackstaff) are just collateral damage for the greater good of any SGP show. Inspiration for men in their 40s everywhere, Phil bests the riders on regular basis despite all their personal training, psychology coaching, exercise and nutritional regimes. Mainly because they wear a steel shoe on one foot and Phil doesn't or that they don't know they are always racing whether they are off their bike or on it. Apparently unaware that all this running actually suggests the opposite of managerial effectiveness and control, like a thinking man's Welsh Forrest Gump, Phil runs everywhere. Of course, as Peter Oakes revealed in his *Speedway Star* column, Phil was a gifted schoolboy sportsman and used to run for Welsh Schools. In contrast, the Marketa crowd have to wait until just before the start of Heat 4 for their first big-screen sighting of Monster Joe Parsons. The need at most SGP meetings for the cameras to relentlessly rove the pits in search of drama to compensate for the lack of it on the track inevitably gives the stay-at-home armchair audience the benefit of many more sightings of Joe and Phil in attention-seeking action (or Peter Adams evading it) throughout any season.

There are, of course, vague nuances to note from the first set of four races but these are slim pickings as the thrilling close racing alleged to be the lingua franca of the SGP series is only notable by its complete absence. Rather enjoyably, the loud confident forecast from the bloke behind, "I fancy that this is Milik's GP to lose" takes an immediate bad blow when he runs a first heat last. The Travel Plus Tours customers I'm sat with take quiet understated pride and some small measure of satisfaction in Craig Cook's Heat 2 second place. Some then claim they see it as a psychological corner turned. Sadly, though he also starts some other races impressively too, these are Craig's only points of the night. The first race interval features a lengthy water and grade of the track. On the big screen, we get treated to a couple of pretty inaudible rider interviews and, best of all, an advert showing – by association with the derring-do of the participants in the wide range of other obscure motor "sports" events it sponsors – just how thrillingly wonderful Monster Energy is. It is typical Monster fare: high-speed, fast-action, fireworks, thrills, evocative optimistic camerawork, achievements, close finishes, stunning location backdrops, enthused crowds and, of course, logos galore. More revealingly, since it is a generic composite of all the motorised and equipment led – aka non-proper – sports they sponsor, speedway really doesn't feature in the first sponsor motion advert – by a key partner-cum-sponsor – shown at supposedly one of its major world speedway events! Despite how Monster Joe bangs on about thr importance of speedway to the company/brand, all it gets in terms of its prominence in this all-action advert is a glimpse of close finish and a banal relentlessly cheery but hammy thumbs up to camera from Chris Holder. Monster probably contractually demand so many thumbs up per meeting from their sponsored riders. The provenance and location of this pro-forma joyousness from Chris is unknown. Recent years would see Chris get a thumbs down from the paying public after a couple of seasons of him riding like a shadow of his former self. With around 18 months' worth of below-par SGP performances, it is ironic he is the smiling face of speedway they choose for the 2018 edition of the Monster-sponsored sports advert montage. Anyways, the clear message from how little speedway features in their latest showreel style advert is that – for Monster – speedway is more-or-less a complete afterthought and an irrelevance to its brand development everywhere but Poland. Which we already knew, anyways. If speedway sponsorship (even at SGP prices) hadn't been so cheap and Polish SGPs so frequent (three this series) in such an important geographic market for Monster, the business case for involvement would soon evaporate. Though the drinking sports buddy friendships Joe enjoys with Aussie riders from the Monster sponsor team are fun – and though, it seems, their speedway careers then taper down in contrast to off-track bonhomie and larks – these aren't relevant to a sustainable long-term business model either.

For the next few heats, the main entertainment on offer remains finely calibrated around zero beyond seeing how individual riders decide to fight the track. Extensive further interval curation appears have had no impact upon the surface or the processional nature of the racing. Races continue much as before – pretty much still all won from the gate. On many speedway tracks around the world – much as fans vehemently deny it as a cartoonish mischaracterisation by outsiders – the first rider away from the tapes often/frequently wins the race. This is particularly so at Marketa tonight, but also often the case too at other stone or shale-lite locations in the SGP series. As an exception that then re-proves the iron rule, Heat 7 takes three goes to complete and does – in comparison to the previous six races – have a brief but gentle hint of overtaking drama. First time out reigning World Champion Jason Doyle gets warned for moving at the tapes. Throughout the season Doyle will be a perpetual chancer in this respect. In the re-run, Doyle is third going into the first corner and appears to deliberately lay down his bike. This is the speedway equivalent of a professional foul. Doyle is playing the percentages and, by so doing, hopes to persuade the referee that "first bend bunching" caused his dismount. Doyle does this, if he did, knowing that on the Marketa track third after the first corner is going to be third at the chequered finish flag too. Doyle's swallow-dive-cum-fall happens right in front of us. In real time, the right decision looks to be to exclude him. This would likely happen to the wild card or meeting reserve but, instead, the referee gives the current world champ the benefit of his doubt. At the third time of asking, we finally have a race with overtakes. Sadly, there is no need to lie down with the smelling salts to recover from the excitement since these are of the unexciting vanilla kind. Technically they are overtakes but without any drama, thrills or ingenuity. Worse still for Cumbrian speedway fans, they involve Craig Cook as he is effortlessly passed on the first lap by Tai (bend 2) and Doyle (bend 3). In what is already look like his SGP series signature move, yet again Craig was first from the tapes and into corner. Whether it is equipment, confidence, tactics, mid-track position, psychology or a varying mix of all these factors – Craig often fails to capitalise on the advantage at the start his natural ability and fast-twitch reaction reflexes provide him. It is as if – when only yards away from the tapes – he and his bike then encounter some invisible barrier that then somehow fractionally slows his forward progress. Though easy to notice (or mis-identify as a non-rider) from the stands, Craig's track positioning appears off. He leads but rides in the no-man's land of mid-track where riders can pass either side of him before he even exits from the second bend. To the untutored eye, Cook also looks tense and stiff on the bike. Not exactly nervous but, possibly, internally questioning so not wholly comfortable or graceful. Once relegated to the rear of the SGP race, Craig immediately rides with the grace and power we so often see but seems to lack until he finds himself at the rear. By the second lap, Craig's bike also sounds bad so even this aspect of his racing élan disappears later doors. Heat 8 sees Niels Kristen Iversen's night get worse. After waiting six further heats since his first race, the pressure of the warning for moving at the tapes sees him badly rear, almost wheelie, at the start line. This race too does – in strictly legal terms – also feature what a pedant could count (if viewed through rose-tinted binoculars) as an overtake on the first bend, albeit again of the thrill-free variety. If asked to recall it afterwards, it is unlike that Janowski will hardly have noticed, let alone remember, it.

The second interval sees the promotional video from Turkish tyre manufacturer and Czech SGP event sponsor Anlas take centre stage on the stadium big screens. Apparently run in order to make the Monster video suddenly look brilliant, Anlas treat us to evocative sun-kissed close-up shots of tyre knobbles before the camera slowly pans back to reveal that somehow a motocross bike is the only surviving vehicle in some kind of post-apocalyptic Mad Max lite dusty mountainous desert hellscape. This doesn't seem good news for the future survival chances of the human race, let alone the market success of the Anlas brand inside or outside speedway. Formally the new tyre supplier to the SGP, though the riders make positive noises and, maybe, even get photographed next to a box-fresh pile of them they definitely won't want to compete using them. Well, except Craig Cook who decides to give them a go. For his rivals, this probably further confirms his current unsuitability for the World Championships as well as his vulnerability to their collective strategy of making sure to swarm him out of contention from SGP glory this season. And, thereby, straight back out of the SGP series next year unless he again succeeds in the qualifiers. Being picked on as the new kid is a rite of passage in school life and also in this series. New SGP entrants don't have the knowledge, experience, bikes, sponsorship revenues/support, track or general series smarts and savvy that longer-term participants gain though the inertia and lack of churn that longevity in the top 8 automatic qualification places give them. In the zero-sum game of final rankings, any new or up-and-coming rider who can be eliminated by killing their ambitions, enthusiasm or confidence with tough experiences in the initial meetings of the series, thereby, better maximises the percentage chances of the remainder of the riders in the field to automatically play again next season. Craig's decision to use or, at least, try Anlas tyres in an actual SGP race illustrates the very qualities of curiosity and openness to continuous experimentation that riders require to succeed. Should Craig win races on these tyres, it will suddenly look like the brilliantly shrewd seizure of a future possible sponsorship opportunity (or, at least, putting himself in the frame for one) that the other riders – except Greg Hancock – in the series have stupidly forgone by not using them. Sadly, all the signs are that the tyres aren't going to deliver any competitive edge. Given speedway riders generally and SGP riders in particular rarely shy away from trying to love-bomb naïve prospective sponsors into moments of money madness, the lack of attention Anlas get should give their senior execs pause for thought. There is a rich tradition of excessive one-season sponsorships across the sport that rarely deliver the reputational benefits promised or implied and so, often, don't lead to renewal. In the case of Anlas, rumour has it that they will also be the SGP series "official tyre sponsor" next season too so they are clearly either gluttons for punishment or else have both low expectations and deep pockets.

Also, on the big screen is the chemistry-free pre-record interview Nicki Pedersen did pre-meeting with Kiri Bloore. the specific content of which the stadium sound system muffles to keep suitably mysterious. With Pedersen paying so much more attention to his nutrition, training, girlfriends and appearance nowadays, the interview is much more notable for the hint of Hitler moustache Nicki sports along with the mandatory five o'clock shadow buff that European silver foxes usually wear to suggest they are experienced men of the world. Quite whose boat this overall get up rocks will, doubtless, become clear on his Instagram feed later. With little of note or excitement so far to discuss, the much better amplified live rider interviews focus upon track feedback. Ever the professional, Greg Hancock is diplomatic, "It's okay – normal Prague for this time of year – you just gotta make the starts!" This isn't exactly a ringing endorsement nor does it bode well for the likely quality of the races ahead. Tai Woffinden is blunter, "It was good early on but I don't know if all the fresh dirt has gone and it's just rocks?"

Just when prospects don't look good, Heat 10 is actually exciting to watch and, be still my beating heart, possibly even counts as a proper speedway race. We get to see the highly talented but unpredictable Matej Zagar reel in the fast-starting Jason Doyle over the four laps with track craft, bluff and guile. In any race that lasts less than a minute between experienced gifted fellow professionals, on a track offering no help or zest, it is hard to pass, let alone comprehensively out-fox them when they are ahead and fully intent on blocking you. It is a delight to watch. Equally, it is frustrating for all long-time Zagar watchers to again witness his speed and talent on a bike – particularly notable for one so tall (in speedway terms) – knowing that in the next race he will probably ride with lacklustre disinterest. Amongst his generation of speedway riders, Zagar has made the "mercurial" tag his own with his inconsistently fickle performances. Matej has the ability to be one of the dominant top-level riders of his era but, equally, often it appears can't be sufficiently bothered to apply himself. Often wonderful on the track, Zagar is sometimes less so off it. There are so many off-track rivals for difficult behaviour it would be unfair to currently award this to Matej but continuing to part own this awkward mantle is still quite an achievement. Obviously, to succeed in any sport, great self-confidence is often a prerequisite to go along with talent and opportunity. For a while, some wondered if Zagar's off-handness – that some experienced as arrogance – was a function of cultural difference or, perhaps, language difficulties where something along the line kept getting lost in translation. Apparently, it is really that Matej has little or no edit function. Whatever crosses his mind, no matter how touching, banal or undiplomatic, gets said. Many who know him better, relish his honesty and find it refreshing. Particularly so in a sport where behind-the-scenes straightforwardness isn't the order of the day.

Normal absolutely no thrills first-from-the-gate service resumes in heat 11 with a Nicki Pedersen starting wobble that relegates him to fourth within two bike lengths and also sees the crowd get coated in a thin film of shale dust. Heat 12 is similarly decided and dusty. British SGP hopeful Craig Cook again starts quickly and is in the mix right until he approaches the second bend and then drops from contention. More disturbingly for the series ahead, his bike looks too slow for the Marketa track compared to those ridden by his rivals. After another protracted interval the SGP rights holders schedule to race the agricultural vehicles for around ten minutes and also show adverts to its various international television audiences, we get more from the gate speedway in the next set of races (heats 13 to 16). Despite the meagre fare, the announcer continues to find delight. His declaration after heat 14, "so another phenomenal race!" prompts the speedway rarity of grandstand laughter. There are nuances. Tai battles his way through the field from last to finish second in heat 15, plus there is an actual overtake in heat 16, albeit of the dull dutiful workmanlike kind when Doyle passes Nicki battling his mind and bike on the third bend of the first lap. Yet another long interval then passes slowly. The big screen obsessively flashes up its dual language "beware flying debris" warnings unaware that pneumoconiosis from the dust is a likelier health threat for the crowd. In between rock warnings, we get given a big-screen masterclass about 21st-century-speedway-experience-in-a-digital-age. Namely the thrilling news that we can find out about the SGP on some new-fangled things the youngsters use apparently called "Twitter", "Facebook" and the "World Wide Web". Various word formations flash on screen. Insultingly low level if you are familiar with internet access on your phone or home computer; totally baffling, if not. Actually, to be fair, given the speedway crowd age demographic in most countries BSI choose to stage the SGP doesn't make understanding and use of social media necessarily a given. Big-screen advice includes that we can, "use social media to see different ways to communicate in the world of speedway!" Who knew? For once, too, such ground-breaking news justifies their use of an exclamation mark.

With points still required by many riders to ensure they make the Prague SGP top eight and qualify for the semi-finals – and as is traditional at every meeting throughout the series – over the final four races the competitiveness of the racing hots up. Or heads towards hotter. This is the point in the meeting that less experienced, younger or Polish/Russian riders in need of points and qualification suddenly tend to wildly over-ride. Often to the point of danger – for other riders not just themselves. This intensity is supposedly how each and every race in the "World Championships" will always get ridden but, of course, in reality aren't. With fast action reflexes the key ingredient for success at the Marketa track, the edge is even taken off the benefit of wild aggression as a tactic to try to save the day. The evidence of the previous 16 races still doesn't stop the less thoughtful or more ambitious riders from chancing their throttle hand with the SGP equivalent of some hit-and-hope one-club-golf. Though in his first race of the night Doyle had fallen theatrically when he thought it would influence the referee, in heat 17 he decides to remain on his machine when taken very wide rather than risk the exclusion that would end his semi-final qualification hopes. Instead – and peculiarly given his age (30s) and riding seniority – Doyle rides wildly out of control (or in signature dangerous style according to critics) across Laguta on lap two to secure the third place point that both needed to obtain to qualify. Like the previous race, heat 18 is also won from the gate. In this instance by Nicki Pedersen through sheer willpower on a slow and slowing bike. Craig Cook is taken wide on the first bend by Milik to relegate him to the rear. It seems the riders are taking it in turn to bully Craig or else that the SGP rider hive mind intuitively knows this tactic works effectively. Tai wins heat 19 from the gate though is, at least, highly pressured by Zagar until the Slovenian rears massively and out of contention on the final lap. The last heat (20) is the best race of the night since it pitches two young wild over-riders keen on putative glory – Dudek and Zmarzlik – in direct head-to-head competition. Dudek needs the win to qualify, while Zmarzlik appears desperate for the pride of not letting him do so, as no amount of points from this race can ensure Bartosz makes the semis. The first semi-final proceeds dully from the gate until a trailing Nicki decides to celebrate making a SGP knock-out stage (something of a rarity, nowadays) by throwing himself off his bike in theatrical fashion after contact from imaginary invisible forces. Any hope of getting a rival excluded or managing a better position in the re-run is dashed when the referee fails to fall for the opportunism of his professional dive. For the last two laps of the re-run Freddie and Tai stage an actual proper race and compete against each other as though they mean it. The second semi-final is from the gate too albeit with the bonus thin-pickings that the front three riders remain in close proximity throughout.

Butterflies pass on a warm breeze just prior to a final Lindgren wins on the line from Dudek. With standers galore, it is a finish our section of the grandstand only sees on the big screen after. Just before that, we do all get to clearly see Tai get squeezed up on the first lap by Freddie on the back straight. With the gap between his bike and the fence narrowing, Tai is deliberately not left what nowadays is called "racing room". This is a mythical corridor talked of in hushed tones as something akin to a cross between a sacred space and the ultimate measure of respect. Though without agreed dimensions, like implicit parental favouritism between siblings, riders tend to both notice its absence and know it when they see it. Riders, commentators, pundits and fans – often those with an explicit or implicit dislike of Nicki or Pedersen's historically combative approach to gaining race advantage – valorise this as mandatory and the correct etiquette for good/clean speedway racing. It is not a requirement of the rules but, in a career where everyone is freelance and wishes to ride another day, does guarantee everyone rubs along nicely enough to manage to do just that. It definitely isn't the winner-takes-all philosophy World Championship speedway boosters claim animates the riders and their SGP racing. After you, Claude. You win today, I'll win tomorrow may suit rider earnings but, perhaps, could be seen as mis-selling or slightly misleading the paying public.

Anyways, judged by his gesticulations after his sudden bail out, Tai considers that the referee should halt the race to punish Freddie for the crime of without holding his birthright to a track safe space by deliberately squeezing him up on the back straight and leaving no room to pass. Though Tai's Monster Energy fellow-sponsored riders probably would have left room, Freddie is not his team mate nor a works rider. He is one of Tai's putative rivals for the World Championship crown. You would expect such career glory to be taken seriously. I always understood track positioning, knowledge of physics and geometry, use of the throttle, control of line and speed to be standard elements of competitive speedway racing, even at the SGP. On the telly, Tai's multi-tasking publicist and long-standing television SGP commentator Nigel Pearson apparently – after over three decades watching the sport – splutters outrage and refuses to believe he just witnessed this vague hint of hard riding. Let alone how this scandal thereby lost Tai the opportunity of another final win. To impartial observers, it just looks like competitive speedway racing. Rather fabulously, Nigel's genuine rather than his usual confected heat-of-the-moment outrage led him to forget his number 1 press agenting client's surname and briefly re-christen him "Woffington". This basic but Freudian error – not automatically knowing your client's name – may symbolically explain away the ongoing mystery of Tai's comparative lack of UK media coverage, despite being two-time British World Champion and putative "superstar" rider in his own birth country. Given the protracted nature of the SGP series and its race format, excluding re-runs or race-offs, Woffinden and Lindgren are scheduled to potentially exchange on-track pleasantries a possible further 24 times before the 2018 SGP concludes. They say it is defeat that clarifies and brings character into focus. When things don't go his way, Tai still appears too brittle and quick to anger or petulance to merit the greatness his media boosters and ghost writers relentlessly ascribe. Though I have no actual insights to back up this impression, it is off the track in the focus upon and love of his wife and daughter – plus how he regularly prioritises them over the demands of these salad days of his meteoric career – as well as in how he sincerely relishes their life together that Tai really impresses and stands out.

The post-race interview with the victorious Freddie is inaudible ("shambles – the PA here is an absolute shambles"). On the podium, Lindgren looks hot, happy and rocks his distinctive newly transplanted hair look as he receives congratulation and ugly – one more of those special "edgy" designs commissioned by Monster – trophies from "the Deputy Major of Prague and the Deputy Minister of the Interior". It is a sign of how far the perceived status of the SGP nowadays has fallen in the eyes of local political bigwigs and dignitaries that only the deputies overlooked for promotion get sent along to the Marketa to award the trophies. That said, two DIFFERENT Prague Mayors have columns in the programme. Quite why there are two is unexplained. Perhaps, the rise in tourist numbers coming to Prague places so many ceremonial demands upon the holder that a job share is needed to avoid wearing them out. Nonetheless, it is peculiar. Even the army only requires one regimental goat per battalion. Though the announcer warns us of "fantastic fireworks", these initially get going as the damp squib you would be embarrassed to stage for safety reasons for curious hyperactive toddlers in your back garden. Eventually they ignite into what could well be a dry run for the loud (rather than colourful) plea for independence by frustrated wannabe big-wigs from the local municipality with close connections to the Marketa speedway club. Sadly, we leave before the fireworks finish on the Travel Plus Tours coach back to our hotel on the remote outer ring of Prague city centre. Tour guide and trip organiser David Goodchild takes to the microphone(!) to soothe us on our way back. He diplomatically claims to the assembled throng of 50 speedway devotees (and two other TPT staff), "it was an enthralling meeting if not an exciting one."

Winner: Fredrik Lindgren (16 points)

Second: Patryk Dudek (14 points)

Third: Emil Sayfutdinov (15 points)

Fourth: Tai Woffinden (16 points)

CHAPTER 3

Horsens SGP 3 – 30.06.18

"Over 200 countries* worldwide cover the SGP series in various formats from live coverage to news bulletins"

John Postlethwaite, FIM Media Guide 2005

PETER Adams draws on his cigarette with the deep satisfied relish of someone who learnt to smoke in a closed severely rule-bound institution. Though it is scorching, he projects the dark air of a man with some mysterious deeply scaring knowledge who has seen too much so also knows too much. Something best avoided full stop, let alone spoken about in polite company. Everything about Peter shouts reserved. From his lack of eye contact and bonhomie to his studied quietude. Peter keeps himself to himself. It is also his shield of choice for dealing with the always inquisitive and talkative speedway general public. Projecting this do-not-enter-here warning definitely works with me and simultaneously also burnishes his mystique as an accomplished guide of Speedway World Champions as well as guards his discretion. I'm told, if you know "Pete" well enough to be trusted to be part of his inner charmed circle, he's warm and witty. He is one of the people I would like to know better in speedway. He smokes adjacent to the half-full car park of the "best hotel in Horsens". This is not a phrase you get to hear bandied about that often in the world of travel and hospitality or experience. In reality, it is one of the lesser status but still swish properties of a regional hotel chain with upscale pretensions located in a comparatively obscure part of Denmark for the casual tourist. Adams is here for the Speedway Grand Prix rather than the renowned annual crime festival they hold at the former prison hereabouts. Under the terms of the boilerplate BSI contract for staging promoters, the best two hotels in the area (if they exist) get block-booked and pre-paid. As a consequence, most overnighting riders plus the great and the good of the SGP world – rights holders staff and their co-opted tame media posse plus sponsors or the well-connected – often briefly get to stay together on the series circuit. It is a kind of speedway scout camp with an in-room iron and kettle but no badges. Adams attends as the mentor-cum-manager for two-times World Champion rider Tai Woffinden. Mr Adams is an astute judge of speedway flesh and its runes, who allies the strategic use of this knowledge to his good understanding of motivation and human nature as well as the equipment, rules and regulations. Tai is the third rider Peter has helped guide, mentor or inspire to World Championship glory (after Olsen and Penhall). His reputation is an astute speedway thinker, arguably the best and brightest in British speedway. Though that it is a category with few credible rival candidates, it doesn't undermine his status. Though deludedly some still think they are rivals – and, cannily, Adams doesn't correct them – doesn't often get borne out by results or lessen his achievements. All other things being equal, in any speedway experience or knowledge head-to-head situation Adams provides the intelligent and hard-won shale savvy that delivers the marginal percentage gains that tend to give greater chance of glory. He is a shrewd hire by Tai. Actually, a re-hire as, for a while, Tai went his own way but, when – predictably – that didn't work out, came back for more. Doubtless, Peter has an ego but in this, as some many things, he keeps it hidden.

* Very good going when – by 2019 - there are still only 195 countries in the world….

Only yards away, Tai is stood in reception patiently waiting to enquire about postage stamps for his postcards. Success and good management mean Tai charges top dollar so has to some extent stepped off the always-chasing-the-money speedway meetings treadmill most riders subject themselves to during the season. To do so, Tai dropped racing British speedway a while back. Since he "only" rides in Poland, Sweden and the SGP, Tai has used a brief gap in his schedule to go away on holiday with his wife Faye and one-year-old daughter Rylee. Small, confident, extensively tattooed and relaxed – Woffinden is dressed for comfort in trademark Australian style – shorts, sleeveless dark T-shirt, cap, flip-flops, sunnies, mobile and zip purse-cum-wallet. Though born in Scunthorpe and a relentlessly emphasizer he races as a patriotic "British" champion, prior to the first SGP of the series in Warsaw, Tai's social media vocabulary choices show his roots to remain totally Australian when he posted the shock news on his Twitter and Instagram accounts that, after four years happily travelling the globe, "my left thong blew a plugger". This isn't a sudden horror any Brit would easily understand or talk about. Luckily there was a photo of his newly broken industrial strength flip-flop. It is a rare, welcome flash of the man-behind-the-facemask his high confidence levels, sometimes stilted humour and public statements usually mask. Like Australia, Denmark is a slip-slap-slop nation of keen sun worshippers. In the ultra-relaxed parkland grounds of his hotel this afternoon, Tai's attire would actually count as over-dressed, given the sheer number of sunbathers including smatterings of chestnut-heading-to-teak coloured really ancient male old-age pensioners. These either sit with their lifelong partners or else strut – legs almost akimbo – around topless by ponds. Some stand, as half-naked senior sentries, watching the world go by close to the many hedged or tree-lined secluded spots suggestive of the promise of a quick bout of carefree naturist ping-pong, fondling or swingball. Even with all this on offer, Tai instead retreats to the umbrellaed shade of the outside patio for a quick chat with Peter Adams prior to heading off to the stadium.

Either all packed and ready to head off there too or just arriving is rival rider Emil Sayfutdinov with a heavy red metal-effect wheelie-case. Sadly, like so many guests in this hotel before him, Emil finds that the catacomb of passageways, random stairways and dead-end corridors that is the layout of this converted country house and stables confusing. Just getting away from or back to reception can be difficult. Diminutive and toned, Emil grumpily flits to and fro from the relatively formal table-clothed dining area or back and forth up the stairs to the passageway that leads to yet more stairs to the comfortable ocean-liner effect bar. Emil leaves but almost immediately returns again before doubting his decision to retrace his steps in the wrong direction once more. Hopefully, he will eventually find his way to his room and the stadium. At the best of times with a pending night of work ahead, off-duty speedway riders aren't overly chatty. Since I don't speak Russian either, my cheery "I got lost earlier too" greeting is a step too far for his conversational English or else a badly unhelpful intrusion into his pre-meeting psychological preparations. I get a full-beam "who-the-fark-do-you-think you-arc?" go-away stare. Based on their comparative mindfulness and Zen levels three hours before the tapes rise, Emil is unlikely to trouble Tai too much tonight.

Fifteen minutes away on the much more suburban far side of Horsens, for the fourth year the local CASA Arena football stadium has been transformed to host the third round of the 2018 Speedway Grand Prix series. Unusually, in the increasingly sub-contracted universe of this series, this is an event promoted and actually put on by the rights holders BSI, albeit with sufficient inducement from the local municipality to do so. Though they (BSI) were the ones who grandly claimed that the views, seats, better bogs and edible catering offered by big modern sports stadia in city centre locations was the way forward for global consciousness/acclaim for speedway, as well as what speedway fans were told they secretly truly hankered for and really, really wanted. BSI rarely bother with the responsibility, pain expense and faff of doing the event staging themselves and continue to find sufficient mug promoters or local government bursaries prepared to pay them for the honour of doing so on their behalf. Whatever the promises or, words, the realities of this strategy, Horsens is a peculiar choice. And faraway from the madding crowd. Even by Danish standards. Founded in 1994 from the combined ashes of two other local soccer clubs with much longer histories, AC Horsens play football in the Danish Superliga. The front exterior design of the stadium is grandiloquently modernist. In additional to excellent sight lines and facilities rather than the traditional full set of four floodlights it boasts two over-sized signature floodlights shaped like a mid-nineties Bang & Olufsen record stylus arm developed for exclusive sale to wealthy Germans without much self-awareness. Symbolically echoing rights holders BSI's SGP reign, if you look beneath the glitzy surface appearance of the exterior the otherwise identikit stadium quickly falls short of its promise and ends blandly as nothing to write home about. Beyond the signature floodlights, it is a traditional multi-windowed soccer stadium with low-cost new-build budget-hotel-meets-teens-detention-centre aesthetic. BSI Speedway Managing Director Torben Olsen's column in the programme thanks "the city of Horsens" for their "support" which strongly suggests they have again crossed IMG's always grasping palm with silver from public funds but failed to get a prophecy beyond pending future empty coffers.

Admiring the stadium aesthetic and getting inside are two different things. It is quite a task as poor Sellotaped signage and laughably unclear directions sees many ticket holders make a series of abortive access attempts at the "wrong" main entrances. At least we enjoy multiple desultory security checks from the bored staff before being sent elsewhere or back beyond from where you originally came from to repeat the process. Fans mill about like agitated ants unable to access their nest. Or else wander down rough-hewn dusty paths towards the impressive Meccano effect under-scaffolding of the array of temporary grandstands erected specially for the SGP tonight. Later, these overflow seats will remain quarter-empty and blighted by blinding sunshine. Once you finally gain access, the full glory of the architecturally design-free concrete built-in-a-hurry construction look awaits as do the back straight grandstand seats with a good view of the pitch/track. Only having two floodlights, three stands and one open end gives the stadium a decidedly lop-sided feel. The two main grandstands run parallel to either side of the pitch and shout previously neglected lower tier professional football club after a half-thought through post-season redevelopment makeover. Amazingly, internecine football politics sees Horsens selected as a 2020 European Championships venue as it is a Danish slap in the face chosen in deliberate preference to better stadia in Sweden. For this evening the pitch is ringed by a narrow and compact – more squashed circular than oval – temporary speedway track made of reddy-brown shale. Football clubs and speedway tracks rarely make good bedfellows if the original pitch shape retains dominance. Ringed by an advert festooned safety airfence, the tightly-fitted track is more bijou than expansive so passing, if the surface even permits this, will be at a premium.

Though you'd expect – since the series rights holders are both organising and promoting here – that everything to do with the Horsens SGP – right down to the last carefully observed detail – is going to showcase the gold-standard of all that is fabulous about their World Championship, the reality falls badly short. Quick to contractually demand nothing but the very best (and then more still) from the other promoters who sub-contract from them to stage these events elsewhere, BSI are content to just go vaguely through the motions in Horsens. They deliver their base level off-the-shelf, tried and tested for-one-night-only speedway presentational mousetrap to the punters. They get it over with, take the money and run rather than bother pursuing positive word-of-mouth by delivering excellence or extra touches that delight. By all accounts, there are a lot less punters expected this year than for previous SGP meetings held at Horsens. Over recent years, in search of the elusive tourist krone, Horsens reinvented itself as a cultural destination and self-styled "home of crime" by hosting an annual crime literature festival in its former prison. In oblique tribute, BSI have made ticket prices for the Horsens SGP an actual crime. The price of my nearly £90 ticket is nothing to do with exchange rates or the Scandinavian cost of living but where the economic reality of fallacious premium product claims meets falling actual SGP attendance levels. Obviously, the embedded specialist media coverage – whether print, broadcast or online – remain studiously in denial (either contractually or voluntarily) so talk otherwise even when the evidence of their own eyes shows otherwise. Even carefully framed television pictures can't help but shows empty to sparsely filled grandstands when the camera pans to follow the racing. Criminally high-ticket prices – well, high for any or all proper speedway locations holding league racing but not for any other SGPs held elsewhere – continue to maximise revenues even as/if attendances fall. Plus, if even the smaller capacity "big" stadia aren't going to sell out, sensible yield management practice automatically means higher prices prevail too. Where once BSI claimed to want to try to spread the speedway word so priced keenly; nowadays they want to claw out every penny or cent given what they know – despite the new jewel in the crown of Warsaw – to be the truth, lived reality and trend of declining SPG numbers of paying attendees.

When faced with declining demand, sensible businesses assume inelasticity of demand so premium price to maximise revenues without care as to the medium- to long-term consequences for the market size. BSI's World Championship rights contract with the FIM runs until 2021. This effectively means BSI/IMG aren't necessarily in it for the long haul so have no commercial imperative to show any duty of care for the future of the World Championships or the frippery of fan goodwill. Whatever their contract length, BSI are safe in the knowledge that numbers through the turnstile is not their sole revenue stream and not always the dominant one either. BSI turnover come from various revenue streams including the sale of television rights, licensing, sponsorship and advertising plus ambitious sub-contractor promoters or subsidies from local municipality and government bodies. Additionally, local, seriously committed or completist punters will still attend SGPs anyways in vaguely sufficient numbers and are so keen they clearly prepared to pay almost any price up to and often including being gouged to do so. In fact, entry prices for Horsens are deemed so high that, even in a country where tax systems and wage levels ensure that what to British eyes looks like a norm of countrywide perpetually high pricing, fan discussions in various Danish speedway Facebook groups express enough outrage to propose a general boycott in favour of watching it on the telly. Not unreasonably, even the most committed Danish speedway fans are forced to conclude that for the price of family admission, you could get a budget holiday week away in Majorca or similar sunny destination. With so many Danes of all ages sporting healthy tans, the chance of further sunshine is going to be hard to gainsay in favour of what, in previous years, has been a carnival night of relentless processional speedway racing.

According to the local programme sellers, in previous years the grassy area in front of the main grandstand used to be buzzing prior to the meeting. "It is quiet. They usually have food and drink stalls outside with crowds but, though the weather is perfect, this year they didn't bother. I don't know why? It is a shame." I think we can safely guess it is a mixture of cost-cutting and inattention to detail. There is, of course, the obligatory Monster Energy "Fanzone". The Horsens iteration looks forlorn and isolated. Something further emphasized by the amount of unneeded security fencing and crash barriers that surrounds the riders' autograph table. Even with three riders carefully chosen for their local appeal (Tai, current World Champion Jason Doyle and Dane Michael Jepsen Jensen) plus the pro-forma glamour of the start women, it is ludicrously over-engineered for the very small number of people who can be bothered to queue. Indeed, the riders (three), riders' staff, hangers-on, start line operatives (five), security and the officious SGP shirted staff with their barely suppressed sense of entitlement, walkie talkies and access-all-areas lanyards, together add up to almost outnumber the queue of fans wanting photos and autographs in the blazing sunshine. With fan numbers so low, these autograph hunters at least for once get a less chaotic, more personal, face-to-face and altogether less corporate SGP rider experience. There was, of course, a time when fans and riders mixed easily, regularly and randomly. In the pits, in the bar, out in the car park, at nearby or en route petrol stations, service stations and takeaways as well as out on the road. Even rider access at everyday run-of-the-mill UK league meetings is more restricted than it historically was but, at the SGP, something has been badly lost when it comes to close fan connection. Access is verboten in all but the most strictly controlled circumstances. At many SGP venues nowadays, it is even impossible to overlook and watch the pits in *ad hoc* fashion during the meeting. This used to be an almost God-given right. Apart from the three riders (out of eighteen competing) pre-chosen for the 20-minute race day Monster fanzone autograph-signing sessions or serendipitous fleeting encounters as the riders hustle by on an imaginary red carpet escorted by their minions through the security-guarded designated pits/rider access point, ordinary fan and rider interaction only really gets to happen mediated via the medium of screens. Whether computer, phone, television or big stadium screens. Or for fans who have paid to enter and watch SGPs, the possibility of the odd brief pro-forma wave, thumbs up, theatrically broad smile (if it is Greg Hancock) or nod to those seated closer to trackside before or after individual races. In the bigger stadiums even these gestures are lost to even the most keenly sighted. Rigorously tightly timed race broadcast schedules brought on by costly satellite live uplinks dictates that even a full post-race win celebratory lap is an increasingly rare sighting, while celebratory wheelies are even less so still. Whereas once you could ask a rider afterwards in the bar or car park their thoughts or views, nowadays they are cosseted away and their (often pathologically banal) but specially composed words relayed as *bon mots* and faux insights on tablets brought down from the mountain by their personal freelance army of third-rate press officers and social media managers. Given their season-long relentless European travel schedules – mostly Poland, Sweden, Denmark and Britain – racing the speedway, the best opportunity for a chance encounter with riders is at the boarding gate or deplaning. Even then riders are still comparatively elusive since, as very regular travellers, they have frequent flier status and privileges with airlines so can again avoid the *hoi polloi* with access to airline lounges or priority boarding and seating.

Predictably, with around two or so hours before racing starts, the pits are becalmed and the riders absent elsewhere unless booked and scheduled to sign autographs or meet sponsors. Most of the mechanics are elsewhere too as their preparation work is mostly already done as far as it can be done until they begin to warm up the bikes ahead of the meeting. There is the odd clink of mechanical activity in some pits booths – aka those used by obsessive compulsive, experimenting, panicking or the only racing here tonight for this event riders. Namely, the meeting reserves, wild card, Artem Laguta and Craig Cook's pits booths. Craig's mobile is glued to his ear while his dad Will and a mechanic fret over the equipment. Most pit bays have bikes parked up on show that gleam in the sunshine. For Nicki Pedersen, the bikes are his stage props and the pits his backdrop. Nicki casually sits side-saddle on one to film an interview in English. Nicki's manner is calm, his tone measured and words mostly self-deprecating. Nicki is arguably the second-best speedway Grand Prix word farmer. He gives good, varied sound bite. In different languages too. He is vastly experienced at the media game. In the English language, no speedway rider has the fluency, enthusiasm and interview ease of Greg Hancock in front of the microphone or camera. Nor his studious trademark, allegedly confected, pathological niceness. Greg has the gift of the gab. The skill to make what sound like new but continuous off-the-cuff and insightful comments that, when listened to dispassionately in the cold light of day, are roundabout platitudes that really say absolutely nothing. Though, at the time, they manage to sound original, sincere and profound. It is quite the media skill. Chris Holder has a camera-friendly fluency that quickly runs dry once he's run through his usual repertoire ("stoked") of speedway-meets-surfer-dude Australian colloquialisms. Tai is getting lots of interview practice and, when his words echo his on-track significance and gravitas, will gradually become the rider who gives best (English language) interview. That will definitely be the case once he loses his standard strong opinion pre-prepared statement bombast or, worst of all, his trademark studious shoulder shrugs of indifference. Tai is even, allegedly, learning some Polish. And, more surprisingly, Swedish too. Even if he gets to "track strong", "I fast bike" or "more money", this would – by traditional English rider standards of language fluency in foreign tongues – make him one of our greatest-ever speedway linguists. His ambition to learn is be applauded culturally but is also commercial common sense given that Poland is where all the real money and interest in him is.

Like the inevitability of death and taxes, the embedded speedway media need no second invitation to wax lyrical about the skill involved in laying a temporary speedway track inside a stadium built for other sports purposes (usually football). Descriptions quickly get so grandiloquent about its "creation" that you would be forgiven for seeing it as on par with the construction difficulty of building the pyramids or begin to see it as the eighth wonder of the world. After so much practice over the years building one-off temporary tracks they dismantle immediately afterwards, there is no doubt that standards have risen from execrable and inept to mostly professional. Whatever standard they build, these temporary tracks are not conducive to thrilling racing or much passing on account of their size, typology, inconsistency and lack of shale. There is, of course, also much to be said for purpose-built facilities in speedway which, historically in the UK, mostly share stadia with dog tracks, stock cars, rugby league and football clubs. Of course, stories of SGP temporary track snafus could fill their own book. When the accredited sock puppet media are in charge of the reporting, if there is any acknowledgement or mention is made, it is only in passing and then quickly forgotten in the lava flow of hyperbole and general suck-uppery that masquerades as comment or honest opinion. Though the choice is wide, my all-time favourite temporary SGP track cock-up is the infamous abandonment of the Gelsenkirchen *indoor* meeting (with roof!) because of wet shale. I think we can all agree that the basic issues that bedevils such one-off tracks is that they lack space and are prone to break up during the course of a meeting. Worse still, these track lumps and bumps interfere with rider progress and, thereby, race results as they randomly occur in both vital and unpredictable spots. Admittedly, track conditions shouldn't really bother highly skilled professional riders but, though hardly sinkholes, meeting wear and tear sees ruts and holes suddenly appear that cost race position and points without rhyme, reason or warning.

Historically, the best bodge solution has been to compact the shale to mimic the smooth surface of a newly laid road. Historically, shale (dirt) on the tracks is the accelerant required to deliver optimal speedway racing conditions. Nowadays, the lack of shale suits both the riders and their highly-powered modern speedway bikes since these are so super-tuned for all-out speed that a modicum of shale depth will either kill their speed or make them dangerously temperamental to ride. These are predictable moot points. By all accounts, the

Polish riders in Horsens have been complaining loudly during practice that the track is the "size of a saucer" and that will be hard to overtake on or ride quickly. Given the position of the stands, size of the football pitch, the need for safety (air fences for the riders, fences for the fans) and the overall space available inside the stadium, CASA Horsens was never going to have the dimensions of a bigger-sized Polish track.

A man whose name I don't quite catch – it could be Hans – has happy memories of living and mechanicing in Britain from sharing a house in Coventry with fellow Danes, riders Alf Busk and Jan Staechmann when he was starting out in the sport. Stood intently peering over the airfence, he admires the handiwork and track surface, "It should be good! It has been laid for fifteen days, last year it was only six days. The wind was different direction yesterday. It was opposite – 180-degree change. It is has been well watered – we have only had ten millimetres in the month of June so far – but with the sun and wind, there may be some dust." The shale BSI use here will get ripped up overnight and, by 6am, will be able to go by lorry to Cardiff for the indoor meeting there in three weeks. The nature of temporary tracks and their construction dictates that practically all race winners in Horsens will start from gate 1. The track shape and slope along with gravity ensures that moisture invariably leaches towards the inside. This further maximises the positional advantage gate 1 already gives in the race to be first into the first corner. An advantage that the lack of space to overtake then compounds further. Whichever way you look at it, the generous inducement of local council financial support that underpins BSI's choice of this venue structurally severely limits the ability of the riders to deliver thrilling racing here – defined generally and loosely by most fans as fast, close and competitive WITH overtaking – before a wheel has even been turned in duty, competition or anger.

Things have changed since speedway life in 1980s Coventry. In world terms, national speedway fortunes wax and wane. Danish speedway dominance took over from British and has itself now given way to Polish. "Speedway is so hard in Poland. Poland is very very hard, the hardest it has ever been."

"Is it the money?"

"Of course! Everyone looks to get advantages. Alf Busk – he still does the engines – says when you are on top there no one can do enough for you. Nothing is a problem. But as soon as you are no good, in the end, you are completely on your own."

"Who do you admire now?"

"Tai is the cleverest rider, I think, he waits his time and then passes on the third lap. The others are race race race and all speed."

"After his bad injury, why does Nicki still ride?"

"Because he is mad! People say now Nicki is too old but they are wrong! He is still close to number one in the averages in Poland. You cannot do that unless you are very good."

"There is no money in the SGP. Prize money is small and costs are higher than earnings, why do they do it?"

"They can say I rode in the World Championships! You can say I am 'sixth or ninth in the world' and that will help with getting good sponsors."

"Have you heard some Polish riders race without body armour to reduce their weight and improve power-weight ratios?"

"Yes. It is stupid. There are air fences now, of course, but there are still bad injuries. There is hard riding and there is dangerous riding – Freddie has crossed the line, I think. People complained about Nicki – they are both nice off the track – but Freddie is something else now." But what of the future? Nicki's career is nearly done and, without him strutting his stuff, things don't look so bright for Danish speedway, its media coverage or, indeed, its place on the SGP schedule. "Nicki is very good at getting on the television and in the media. He doesn't do well at small tracks but speedway in Denmark needs him to win. When it goes down, like it has, there is no attention. Only for Nicki. He knows how to deal with media. To keep their interest. To say new things. The rest of them struggle, they try but still struggle to get any media interest." From the translation of his Danish programme notes on Pedersen into English, Erik Gundersen doesn't sound like a fan or bosom buddy of his fellow Danish three-times World Champion. "I've noticed after his bad knocks that he's not making the hard moves on track, he's not taking the sort of lines that we see others doing nowadays." After admitting that "speedway needs characters", Gundo (as Phil Lanning matily calls him elsewhere in the programme) opines, "he wants to do this so bad. He's got a personal trainer that he hires for so much money to keep him fit at his age."

Back in the pits, Workington-based Steve and Alison Mills believe Tai Woffinden hasn't – to date – been overly welcoming towards fellow Brit and his newly minted erstwhile SGP competitor Craig Cook. While obviously success in the World Championships is a zero-sum game and dog has to eat dog to ensure position and success in the rankings, apparently, Tai's SGP track and set-up advice has been non-existent. Worse still, apparently, was his approach towards his race partner at the recent but ineptly named "Speedway of Nations". Alison definitely wasn't impressed, "It was awful the way Tai spoke to Craig on TV. Craig was nice and positive and Tai just blanked him. He just wanted to ride with Lambert." Steve sees things similarly, "He didn't even look for Craig in the first race, he just went off. Every race after that – when Craig was replaced – he looked for Lambert. I can remember when Tai rode a couple of times at reserve for Workington. Maybe [Craig] riding in the Premier League is too much of a comfort zone. It's a huge step up but, then, it's not so long ago that Doyle and Cook were riding for Somerset and Edinburgh yet they're here now." Craig has found points hard to come by in the SGP series to date. Alison notes, "Steve did the analysis and Tai only got an average of four points a meeting in his first GP series but, like so many, he's forgotten all about that now."

Like the pits at every SGP to date, Horsens wouldn't be complete without the massively backpacked photographer. This afternoon he has a box-fresh Monster Energy cap but isn't bothered about scuffing it up as repeatedly brushes aside bystanders in order to (bravely) dive onto the ground. It is as if, in his mind, he is reporting while under fire in a war zone so needs to seize every opportunity to snatch his trademark unique ant's eye and up skirt/shorts shots of riders, tyre changes and handlebar grip replacements. It also wouldn't be a SGP without officious clipboard-holding types dressed in dark corporate clothing bustling hither and thither for no apparent purpose beyond parading their sense of purpose along with access-all-areas lanyard, badges and wristbands. Apparently cloned in a dank backroom in BSI Towers, these people relentlessly escort and fawn over actual or would-be sponsors and occasional ultra-minor dignitaries. Otherwise, they cheerfully bark out orders or provide banal notionally informative platitudes to nonplussed or disinterested visitors. A blonde mahogany tanned woman – who looks like a Dane but speaks in an incongruously strong Scots accent – breathlessly explains "the pit lane" as if elucidating a mystery on par with finding the recipe for the secret elixir of eternal life. "It's quite technical. Often, after each race, they'll come back and make adjustments to their bikes." Hold the front page! As she guides her small but eager newbie audience over towards the television area with red, blue, white and yellow stripes currently projecting onto its screen backdrop, the Noddy-level explanations continue, "it is used for many different things including interviews." [1]

When it comes to confidently bombastic low-information experts, few can hold a candle to Monster Joe Parsons when he speaks his brains and holds forth. To be fair to the bloke, though suspiciously over-tanned for his age, he is skilled with people, occasionally gives good sound bite and, most significantly, can bend almost any aspect of the SGP race day schedule, presentation and appearance to suit the visual or commercial needs of his employers Monster Energy. Whether every series event "partner" should get to so extensively and relentlessly showcase their brand – to the extent the SGP nowadays is in the eyes of fans and those consuming the event on screens almost synonymous with Monster Energy – is another matter. In this Kingdom of the Blind, one-eyed Joe is definitely king. So far this series, he's dressed like a heavy metal roadie, brought a pushchair (with child) to the pits, shaken hands like an African-American raised in the Bronx, tweeted tosh and, especially when the cameras are on him but also not, reacted to minor on track triumphs for "his" sponsored riders with a glee that would make Diego Maradona's goggle-eyed allegedly performance-enhanced late era of goal-scoring celebrations look understated. Living this drinks brand 24/7 appears to require large-sized ugly tattoos, dark clothes, braided colourful wristbands of various age and provenance closely allied to theatrical signals of excess enjoyment. It is as though living life in Monster Energy World is always experienced as the equivalent of perpetually exploding stickily everywhere like a just-opened thoroughly shaken bottle of a nondescript but brightly coloured fizzy fluid skilfully engineered via a secret process that adds complex chemical compounds and way too many three-digit E numbers to even attempt to list.

This sunny afternoon Chris Holder's pit is currently Joe Parsons' temporary stage. In fact, and kudos to him for his industry and marketing savvy, Joe Parsons leverages each and every Speedway Grand Prix meeting to the full as the backdrop for love-bombing distributor and key customer as well as giving them their own individual behind the scenes up close and personal SGP tours. Plus Parsons also very regularly invites along the top talent and performers whom Monster Energy also sponsor in other extreme sports disciplines to feel the speedway buzz but also to feel part of the larger Monster lifestyle brand family. This afternoon Joe struts his stuff before a rapt audience of four similarly aged but vaguely curious blokes of indeterminate significance. Likely, Monster Energy valued customers. They all confidently clutch different coloured cans of the non-alcoholic beverage equivalent of novichok. With audience in tow, Joe speaks them his oft-repeated standard intro guide to speedway. They

[1] Any involvement in SGP event management sounds nightmare work if judged by the job advert placed in 2015 by the rights holders for the role of "Event Manager – BSI Speedway IMG". At a basic level said work requires "planning and executing event and hospitality activities". The specific tasks involved range from the banal to the predictable via way of the pompous and ridiculous. High up the list of key responsibilities is the production of "event collateral" (accreditation passes, wristbands, lanyards, photographer bibs and trophies), "event signage" (scoreboard magnets, venue signage, grid girl boards and rider race jackets) and also "ordering event related equipment" (radios, big screens, PA systems, hospitality wallets). Things get slightly sweatier bottomed when it comes to "managing relationship & approval process with official SGP merchandise partner" before going full on power trippy over "onsite event management". This part of the brief is so wide it includes staff catering, briefing & managing security, managing the draw plus accreditation for every wo/man and their dog. The minefield of "arranging all flights, hotels, transfer and logistics management" for the BSI Team and "arranging additional hotels for riders & Officials for BSI run events" sounds easy as it slips off the tongue but is – given the locations, egos and personality quirks involved – doubtless a total joy. There are also the branded seat cushions and overhead compartment compliant wheelie cases for BSI Speedway IMG senior executives or favoured up-and-coming but ambitious middle managers to consider. That's before sorting such stuff as the "National Anthem Singers" or "opening or closing parade vehicles or fireworks". Predictably a very long way down the priority list of key event management responsibilities is "co-ordinating all Health and Safety Management between BSI Speedway, promoters and venues". There is also the small matter of the "vetting of suppliers" before even getting to overseeing the "hospitality programme in Cardiff with a Hospitality Executive reporting to me on this". Ominously, and usually a leading indicator of a dysfunctional or toxic work environment are the dreaded "mandatory" requirements: "ability to work long hours and also work in a stressful environment" plus "must be a Team Player". While "previous promoting of events", "understanding of health and safety" and "exposure to hospitality" are only "desirable".

stand agog forgetting that when they were first told of their exclusive back stage access to a premium motorsports event, it is unlikely that speedway in a temporarily converted football stadium in an obscure provincial Danish town sprang to mind. "They race here, then Poland on Sunday before going back to wherever they are based, Monday in Britain and Tuesday in Sweden, maybe Wednesday in Denmark. They're always on the road during the season. Do you wanna see the track?" Like a bearded roadie sheepdog, Joe takes his meek lambs out onto the centregreen Monster podium where he continues to gesticulate Phil Morris fashion for another 15 minutes or so. His listeners clutch their brightly coloured cans of Monster close and sip often. Doubtless a sensible precaution to avoid sudden onsets of drowsiness during Joe's lengthy peroration about all matters shale. Who knew that there was so much to learn about speedway? Away from the sporting talent and client glad-handing Parsons' job requires (and he excels at), there is much more to Monster Joe than meets the eye. After an early hardscrabble working life that took in a variety of temporary and short-term jobs including a paper round, Avis ex-rentals work, Big Law tyres (was Firestone) and temp agency Kelly Services, Joe Parsons got taken on staff at Toshiba. Since then hard work, studying for technical qualifications, good timing, curiosity and smarts saw Parsons fight his way up from the unpromising backwater of the chaotic Toshiba bulk Returns Material Authorisation department to various positions of power where website programming knowledge and technology savvy intersects. From marketing for Toshiba to building the Monster website for their parent company the Hansen Beverage Company in the early 2000s. On full-time staff since 2002, Parsons' web marketing and general promotion talent and abilities allied to his perceptive handling of the actual (surfer and skateboarding) sports talent Monster sponsored was spotted, encouraged and endorsed by its drink/brand inventor Mark Hall. Nowadays, Monster Special Projects Director, deeply schooled and ahead of his time in the intersection of web marketing and lifestyle sports brand promotion management, MJP is hard-working and street wise enough to cannily VERY easily bend the SGP to the current needs of his soft-drinks employer.

In a lengthy interview with Greg Hancock on the Reel 45 podcast Parsons gives some background to his subsequent involvement in speedway rider sponsorship and the SGP. "I just came from the internet farking BS. I had to get content from riders and athletes for the web [and eventually] I got involved in motorsports management.. making sure these guys they got their hat, their bottle, their sticker". Monster Energy have a well-honed, tried and tested marketing model for the less mainstream, obscure, backwater, superseded and overlooked sports they adopt and bend to their commercial needs. "It's not rocket science, once you know how to bake the cake you don't need a recipe anymore...our brand capitalises on the content and we can leverage back into our advertising...you are a conduit to those cultures [whether surf; skateboarding; motorsports], you walk the walk and talk the talk with riders of that space. When you look at Eastern Europe, what is a cool motorsport that resonates with our brand? Speedway. And you have the recipe. You dial in the ingredients based on the landscapes...You get involved with individuals rather than the sport itself. Anyway, Speedway was a category that was a cool motorsports in Cosa Mesa [California] too. I had a relationship with Bruce Penhall at this time and our CEO sent me over to Poland and Eastern Europe and I looked into speedway." Warming to his own triumphant life story, Parsons continues, "I made sure to get involved at the GP level however we can. I had managed to get a contact at IMG/BSI and we ended up being able to negotiate a comfortable commercial deal that I think has worked out great for us. That's worked out. I'd like to say the fans are happy in what we have done for the sport. Some fans are not happy with, maybe, how much success we've had with it!" However, the future Monster Energy relationship with the BSI/IMG SGP isn't necessarily set in stone for ever more. "I think there are limits and thresholds to what you can and can't do. And tweaks and balances you can make provided the environment is susceptible to that. There are a lot of rules that you might want to change as a rider and a lot of rules you might want to change as a fan...Some of the things I'd like to see in the GP aspect of it is more on-board cameras; fan interaction. Things, you know, that work. Locations, good tracks, healthy riders. These types of things is only going to make the sport good. Whether it's a rider we endorse or our enemy, a competitor does. We try to figure out a way to keep the riders healthy but not take away from the racing. We always want to keep it fast and dangerous and on the edge, because that's what it is all about. I want to smell that engine. I want to see that rubber burn. I want to see the crashes. I want to see the highs and lows, the controversial aspect! But, first and foremost, I want to see a bunch of healthy riders." Sad to admit, and though he would want nothing to do with such a task, if British Speedway is to definitely be saved for future generations as a robust sporting cultural entity, some believe Parsons needs to be helping to organise this future as – like him or loathe him – at the SGPs he has a proven track record of easily and successfully managing to get the tail to successfully wag the dog. Often against its better or own commercial interests. If we ignore those infamous extremely ill-advised Frankfurt airport tweets, giving him a go – should Parsons do so sincerely (it is hardly a product promo op given the ageing British speedway demographic) – could hardly make things worse given our current lack of game-changing ideas or impressive talent.

Abutting the outside area adapted to be the temporary pits that houses all the rider and television interview bays is a large white canvas tented structure lined with plastic window side panels that looks better suited to corporate hospitality catering at a minor tennis tournament or, perhaps, staff dining and rest area for the new Downton Abbey film than speedway. Its purpose is also hard to intuit to curious casual outside observers as, unusually, given the organisers like nothing better than slapping up officious SGP branded instruction notices on all available surfaces, it lacks Blu-tacked temporary signage. The fact that FIM Track Director Phil Morris stands in its doorway offers no further clue beyond the likelihood that all sorts of "importances" (people, conversations, decisions, egos, key officials or sponsors etc.) lurk within or hereabouts.

The discovery, administration and rigorous enforcement of bald-men-fighting-over-a-comb importances – whether of people, designated areas or systems – is something of a specialist area for the SGP rights holders BSI. Though you can usually count the things that Nigel Pearson is impartially and unambiguously "right" about on the trademark index finger he uses to interact with critical fans on Twitter, completely avoiding Friday practice is one of them. Generally best left to riders, mechanics, Kelvin Tatum MBE, selected key officials and inattentive but pathologically friend-free speedway reporter types, apparently yesterday at Horsens the unveiling and soft trial of a revolutionary new timing device using "transponders" fitted to the bikes was the exception to prove the rule. Quite when or, indeed, how a new-fangled high-tech stopwatch is going to save speedway, amp up the entertainment factor or bring the crowds surging presently back remains shrouded in secrecy. A good rule of thumb for new ideas that promise much but then accomplish nothing or turn into a shit show is the level of enthusiasm and frequency of Paul Burbidge's advocacy. After the meeting, in the "report" pages of the BSI in-house company magazine otherwise known as the British trade publication the *Speedway Star*, SGPs very own but less likeable Forrest Gump, Paul went all in. Just like he had for the various previous hapless so-called innovations. Often superficially instantly appealing upon closer these "revolutionary ideas" have varying degrees of eptness, realism and cost. They include examination squads, fixed race nights, listening to fans, attracting back the "top stars", track covers, local government funding of new stadia, pink helmets colours, doing whatever Matt Ford says, Scottish independence and, best of all, combating the vague whiff of homophobia at BBC Sports Personality of the Year show (but not its much stronger smelling variety in speedway circles). I often wonder if I am the only one paying close attention his ramblings? Whatever their real quality as analysis, widely spreading them about – with the manner of a keen gardener with access to free fresh horse manure and a plot of wilting prized plants – in a specialist motorcycling trade publication with a sharply declining circulation and no longer stocked in Smiths effectively keeps them secret. It is the sports "journalism" equivalent of a witness protection programme. Anyways, barely able to hold back from spraying his premature word orgasm everywhere, Paul hails transponders as a "huge leap forward" in the measurement of lap times. Both likely to presage the second coming of Christ and to provide "new data that could unlock a world of options for the sport's top riders". In life as in speedway, most sensible people initially shy away from new-fangled options they didn't know about or want. Quite how this would happen, sadly, isn't specified over a series of breathless but prolix articles that include extensive positive but vague or bland quotes from Phil Morris including, "It's a joint FIM-BSI venture. The SGP Commission, which is BSI and the FIM, will discuss going forward with the project." Though some SGP riders barely register gratitude if a sponsor transfers five-figure sums into their bank account or provides a free fuelled-up new transit van for their exclusive use throughout the duration of the season, Paul asks us to believe that, "riders buzzed around the scoreboard in the pits like bees around a hive, fascinated to see the times they were recording". And who, putting hand or cloven hoof on heart, wouldn't be "fascinated" by the "chance to see which bike or lines on the track perform best, without having to rely on pure instinct"? Setting aside that – apart from location – track conditions at any Friday SGP practice bear zero relationship to the track riders then experience in the actual competition on the Saturday, this innovation is highly likely to fall foul of BSI's legendary parsimony. A strange look for a go-getting outfit that once was seen as the new motorsports Golden Child of the world's biggest sports marketing company IMG. According to SGP social media and website news guru Burbidge when cosplaying as a reporter in the pages of the *Star*: the future is all systems go if, and it is a big IF, BSI manage to "recruit a partner to meet the costs of using the software and obtaining a transponder for all 54 bikes." Even if we assume that transponders do in some shape or form get effectively rolled out in Friday practice, how exactly is something most fans don't see, can't see and couldn't care less about going to increase attendances, boost TV audience viewing figures or drive social media engagement, let alone satisfy existing sponsors or find new ones? Quite how BSI turn the question "what can we think of to be seen to be doing something truly innovative in the speedway grand prix?" into the correct answer "transponders" is precisely why their revenues continue to decline. It is the kind of thinking that suddenly makes the idea of holding a competition to design a SGP emoji – and, thereby, get young people flooding to watch speedway and/or talking about the series IRL or on social media – look credible.

Over weeks of issues, Paul marvels at length about the wonders of "transponders" without pausing to consider the surveillance implications for that most notoriously shy of form-filling and tax-paying creatures, the speedway rider. In the glory days of yore, cash in hand spoke many languages to riders and promoters alike. Indeed, one of the most authentically speedway things BSI do – like British speedway promoters since time immemorial – is to no longer report SGP attendances. Though their website if filled with statistical guff and notional analysis (the all-time average points per race by rider inside leg measurement table is my favourite), attendance figures definitely don't. Returning to rider confidentiality and secrecy matters, in a world where (high tax regime) Swedish and Australian riders are prepared to go into tax exile in Andorra, the chance for The Man to track and record them at work is likely to be as popular as an emergency ten-year audit of all their records and receipts.

In the excitable but knowledgeably reverent tones of acne-plagued "top stream" hormonal teenagers discussing their practical knowledge of the clitoris over an after-school Dungeons & Dragons session, Paul is too excited by the heady rush of transponder developments to reflect further. More relevantly, of course, even if the usual triangle of BSI ineptitude – cost, futility and implementation – doesn't quickly kill this idea or see it delivered stillborn, then news of early results showing "there was actually only a third of a second between the top 13 or 14 guys" should surely do so? Ironically, after all this guff about taking speedway race times into the future depths of 21st century technological wizardry, BSI then completely forget to ensure they give ANY heat times out over the public loudspeaker system during the Horsens Danish SGP. Given that announcing the race results only requires knowing first, second, third and a heat time forgetting 25 percent of the information equation it requires to be meaningful is, at best, poor attention to detail. As the saying goes, first they came for our watches then they came for our Fitbits. It might only be transponders they are fitting today/tomorrow but, once the Pandora's Box of vaguely justifiable micro-technology deep-state (or BSI) tracking is opened, then the slippery slope of custodial sentences, the chilling of free speech and democracy plus further enhancements to stir and spur SGP audience engagement soon beckon. Before they know it, all in the name of entertainment, riders may find BSI Speedway demand surgically embedded micro-chips to go along with their many tattoos? Although body art can't measure heart rate or neurological activity it is a leading indicator of a willingness to experiment. On this basis, Tai Woffinden is the ideal candidate to become the first fully robo-rider of this speedway generation.

Back in the dim mists of time, SGP organisers BSI flamboyantly but speciously claimed that their big stadium strategy responded to grassroots fan demands to zhuzh up the sport though, historically, we tend to prefer our stadiums dilapidated and our tracks top class. Though you can't have everything, we would like these circumstances to also come along with some exciting, close racing with lots of passing from the best, fully engaged, brave and skilful riders available that season. Should culinary excitement be my speedway thing, the pitiful catering here – own label hot dogs, ready packaged hot drinks (just add boiling water) and obscure crisp brands – would struggle to float even a model boat. Though I'm not really expecting that Denmark's most famous culinary hero Rene Redzepi has a satellite branch of Noma at AC Horsens, given talking up the food quality is a key part of the BSI SGP speedway entertainment offering, the calibre of the catering on offer at the "Salgsbod" is, putting it politely, on the austere side of spartan. To drown our culinary sorrows, there are many varieties of beer and lager on sale, albeit, like the food too, local prices to British, Polish or Czech eyes are criminally expensive. That said, beer googles are mandatory if any fan wants to truly appreciate the racing at any SGPs and, with overtaking once again at a severe premium, Horsens is no exception to this iron rule.

When it comes to stadium directions, every expense has as usual been spared in all areas by BSI. My "section 5" is identified by a poorly copied unlaminated colour A6 sheet stuck on a wall above a collection of brightly coloured wheelie bins close to a few pallets laden with various sized unopened cellophane-wrapped boxes (contents unknown). Glancing in the other direction from the lee of the grandstand, there is impressive array of abandoned full-size movable football goals. It is a schoolboy's kickabout dream as they come with metal posts and netting too. About ten are dumped close together in overgrown grass, apparently organised as a surrealist maze or an end-of-year art display that captures the essential futility of soccer when set against the inexorable passage of time. In the intervals between each set of four SGP races, tractor-shy smokers rush out among these posts and nets to have a fag and a pee. Like homing pigeons draw back to their home loft, male fans – smokers and non-smokers alike – rush over during the intervals to piss in synchronised almost perfect harmony all over them. So much outdoors sprinkling goes on, I half suspect it is either *ad hoc* but cost-neutral BSI urine-themed SGP entertainment or an initiation for speedway Druids (Danish section) to gain blessings against rider injury by ceremonially waking dormant goalmouth spirits. At the top of each steep-flighted staircase on the back straight grandstand rests a decorative steward. They dish out flags rather than advise on your location in a sea of yellow plastic terrace seats or adjudicate the pissing contest. At every Grand Prix, so far without fail, fans seated in areas deemed key camera shots get given a cheap mini-national flag of the staging country of that event. Probably produced cheaply *en masse* in Asia. As it is highly unusual for BSI to incur additional unnecessary costs, clearly this isn't for the benefit of attending fans but purely to fool the broadcast viewers about the degree of the spontaneous diehard nationalism and fervent enthusiasm of SGP crowds. If a picture paints a thousand words, then little beats slow panning shots of a spontaneous sea of waved flags pre-supplied for this purpose. Poland is the only staging country where there really is no need to pre-plan this as rampant ("Polska!") fans need no second invitation to bring their own flag or happily get their face painted on upon arrival. Tonight, irrespective of our nationality, we all get given a Danish flag. Though, they say give a wo/man a flag and s/he will wave it; mine won't get waved but, cultural sensitivity and diplomacy plus environmentalism, dictates I won't casually discard it either.

The front two rows of the whole length of the grandstand in my central section remain noticeably empty. For once, Polish speedway fans are conspicuous by their absence. If judged by the lack of bought or homemade Polish flags (team, rider or national versions), general bonhomie and shouting, red and white coloured wigs and clothing or groups animatedly taking track-facing selfies. The fabled multi-generational, inter-generational nature of the speedway is dialled down a notch but still on display – granddads, daughters, sons, wives, mothers-in-law along with grandsons and granddaughters – are all here and already seated. Mostly quietly. Sharing sandwiches or snacks with some low-key murmured chatting. Patiently waiting, slightly bovine, definitely more dutiful and crushed than enthused. If measured by the primary language spoken, mostly Danes and, most likely, regular speedway fans here to experience first-hand – despite the prices – the only SGP staged in Denmark this season. Unusually for big stadia sports events of any stripe nowadays, there are also many smokers. Militant lifelong smokers, in fact. Openly so and proud too since, apparently, it is still allowed in these stands. There may be informal courtesies about minding your smoke but, if there are, these go studiously unobserved. Most smokers are blokes, mainly OAPs or the shop-soiled late middle-aged. Perhaps, one of the real appeals of GP speedway in Horsens is the chance to smoke and watch the racing just like it was still the 1970s? Albeit sitting down rather than standing. It is amazing how quickly you forget the unpleasant intrusiveness of cigarette smoke, especially when these wafts come from users who just don't give a toss. I don't recall the BSI new era SGP modern stadia strategy template promising endless belches of cigarette smoke as part of their revised entertainment proposition?

Though guff from Torben Olsen pre-thanks us fans for our "fantastic atmosphere", there are many empty seats. Interestingly, though Olsen also congratulates us on our "passion for this event" which has "allowed it to be a continued success", Horsens is dropped without ceremony from the 2019 SGP series schedule when, I'm guessing, Horsens city council no longer help financially support it. With spare seats aplenty, there is space to move into comparatively smoke-free but completely empty first two rows of seats closest to the track. It is such a good idea that the biggest chain smoker immediately follows and manspreads two seats. Side saddle. Possibly to let the gentle summer breeze waft over his unfeasibly large testicles, while he billows intricate warning smoke signals to curious distant eyes. Weirdly, sat in this manner, his back is half-turned from the race action (such as it is). All the better to concentrate upon his copious drinking and obsessive borderline manic chain smoking. He smokes with greater intensity than Peter Adams. Right down until the burnt filter taste immediately prompts yet another light up. Even experimental beagles aren't forced to smoke this much. It doesn't seem to provide much satisfaction as he exudes intense sadness with his eyes glassy, mid-distance and defeated. The noise, proximity and speed of the riders racing close by draws most gazes but not his. His scuffed leather blue-laced boots are only done up half-way and speak to a long-forgotten element of dashing vanity. Many middle-aged men at the speedway hereabouts appear to have been issued with the same slightly too small flattened oval-shaped spectacles of the type that were briefly fashionable well over a decade ago in Australia. They continue to get worn with pride at unfashionable pastimes of yesteryear like speedway and, possibly, the dogs and stock cars. The look of these spectacles shouts the opposite of chic. More impulse buy in an out-of-the-way petrol station on an overly sunny day. It would be no surprise to see Nigel Pearson or Kelvin Tatum wear them in the commentary booth. Around this grandstand, they are mostly perched jauntily on heads as style items, almost après-ski fashion, rather than used purposefully as tools to help see or read. The more radical exponents of this sub-cultural tribe wear two sets of glasses simultaneously – one invariably shaded – on their heads. From a breeding point of view, I suspect this will attract mates who value dexterity and vanity. Amazingly, another newly arrived smoker is soon drawn to these two rows of empty seats too. It smells and feels like I am suddenly watching speedway on the set of *The Towering Inferno*. Perched at the opposite end of the row, this bloke dresses more well to do, though he is studiously ruffled and rumpled. He smokes languidly but draws deeply and rocks this look with the confident manner of sophisticated middle-aged men of leisure everywhere if still convinced they are a sure-fire babe magnet.

Before you know it, the stadium announcer interrupts the pyrotechnics and smoke show to ramp up the excitement, "ladies and gentlemen, please welcome your marshals and medics!" Nothing quite thrills like the arrival of the help. Or, for that matter, riders making the quarter-lap journey from the pits gate to the Monster Walkway of Fame. Aka a section of the centregreen that leads to a winners' podium edged and divided up by small black Monster branded boxes. To ensure yet more thrills, the individual rider loudspeaker introductions are badly out of sync with the giant screen pictures. It is as if there is a slight time delay in sympathy with the essential time warp unchanging nature of speedway. The audio-visual time lapse sees Przemyslaw Pawlicki take to the shale just as Chris Holders looms cheerily from the screen. Or Matej Zagar ignore the fans while Craig Cook smiles-cum-grimaces in giant size. These two are arguably the closest there is to a matching pair. Both have Belle Vue connections and neither smile easily. At the other end of the spectrum, the toothy wattage of Greg Hancock's smile – if properly harnessed – could power a sick children's ward for week. Never a man to pass up a long lingering look in the reflection of the shallow bath water of fan adulation he imagines greets him everywhere he rides, Greg is the only rider who takes it upon himself to ride a complete introductory lap. The bovine crowd reacts to Hancock with sustained silence, as if collectively just stun-gunned in the abattoir kill suite ante-room. With helmet off and Monster Energy cap on, The Good Ship Greg sails on round the track oblivious to milk the vague eddy and ripple of catatonic indifference his passage prompts. If the crowd are low wattage, Greg is extremely high energy for a man of his age so gives full reign to his extensive repertoire of perma-smiles and hip-hop inspired hand gestures. In one slow lap, these run the whole gamut of waves, salutes, thumbs up and, look mum no hands, open arms greeting. It is as if, in his mind, Greg has just completed a brilliant solo operatic performance of *Hamlet* (is there such an opera?) and sustained applause forces his return for a second curtain call, albeit for some strange reason taken astride a gleaming speedway bike. The few rogue fans who do acknowledge him do so in the polite way some motorway drivers and passengers reply wave back to schoolchildren stood on a passing bridge or waving from the window of a minibus trip going in the opposite direction. Ignoring the ego required or self-fulfilling self-aggrandizing aspect of thinking you are the most popular man in speedway, it is also a form of gamesmanship to go along with the notional fan-friendly sportsmanship. The art of coarse speedway. Oblique one-upmanship. That must partly be the implicit judgement of the announcer who deliberately calls out Greg to the crowd as "the grand old man of speedway". It is a moniker that runs counter to the wild, living life on the edge, daredevil high-octane image the sport and Greg's main sponsor Monster like to project about all things Grand Prix speedway. Pre-meeting laps of honour are also frowned upon by the walkie-talkied BSI supervisor who strides managerially from the centregreen onto the middle of the track to block any further copy-cat riders – most likely Nicki – who wish to milk the moment with some additional yards in search of adulation. She is also in charge of the erection of the tubular scaffolding effect proscenium arch that BSI pretentiously but briefly raise over the podium before and after the meeting. When originally sold in by its designer it probably sounded like it made for greater majesty and sense of occasion as well as guaranteed to add lustre to the official event press photos released afterwards to a mostly unexpectant and indifferent world. Seen in its full silver scaffolding-pole glory, at best it looks mis-placed and pretentious. These are precisely the add-no-value pointless touches of notional tinsel that BSI bring to the existing speedway proposition to allow them to continue to believe that they are somehow entertainment innovators and widely respected iconoclasts.

Crowd reaction inside AC Horsens to almost anything seen on track enjoys a default setting of badly muted unless it hails from Denmark. Despite his many talents, Greg is not Danish. Nicki Pedersen is and so are the crowd gauged by the excessive roar that greets him, the brief quarter-lap parade of meeting reserves Mikkel B Jensen and Mikkel Michelson as well as that of wild card Michael Jepsen Jensen (so good, as they say, they named him twice). Despite the long-standing swirl of Michael Jackson child-grooming allegations, Phil Lanning's interview article (imaginatively headlined: "Michael Jepsen Jensen is The Thriller") with MJJ in the Curtis Sport official programme makes ponderously heavy work of a random tenuous "Bad" and shared "Thriller" connections with Jepsen. Lanning writes, "Just like his namesake [?!?] Michael Jackson, he's got all the moves. Whatever MJ could do, MJ is the shale shamone." Ignoring wtaf is a "shamone" when it's at home? Or, indeed, what on earth is it doing in an IMG company speedway programme edited – always proudly – by Nigel Pearson? The answer probably is that no one at BSI cares enough or bothers to closely vet the copy prior to publication. Whatever the tenuous journalistic reason for crowbarring in some Jackson songs and albums references, "Michael Jackson" Jensen subsequently bemuses any Danish youngsters inside the stadium keen to spend time in his company with a less than thrilling four points from his five rides in this Horsens SGP. Anyways, vague moot psychological advantage aside, all Greg's spontaneous lap of honour accomplishes is to further throw out the flow and co-ordination of an already stuttering pre-meeting old-school race order line-up of riders and their number-one bikes in front of the home straight grandstand. Understated choreography chaos rules. The stadium announcer sounds a hired-hand stranger to speedway flesh so flounders rather than recovers. If he were a twitcher, his broadcasts would identify sparrows as eagles. Post-introductions over, riders immediately rush back to the pits while ground staff race past them in the other direction to speed dismantle the arch scaffolding. For the duration of the meeting, the silver scaffolding of said arch languishes abandoned and forlorn in pieces on the centregreen. What better metaphor for the collapse of the pompously stated dreams and moon-shot strategic ambitions rights holders BSI once held for their management of this re-engineered SGP competition in their early era press statements?

According to the programme cover and, later, the announcer, tonight's sponsor are WD-40. Though their name suggests they a vile tasting lifestyle-oriented energy drink aiming to rival then dethrone Red Bull or Monster; in fact, they are what is known in trade circles as a "penetrating oil". How pleasantly retro to have a speedway meeting sponsored by a company product that may really get used by the riders in the course of their work. Newcastle Speedway once had – and, maybe, still do – a long-time sponsor (Lawrence Heppell) who ran a piano-tuning business. These are the kinds of very committed financial fan/business backers speedway clubs treasure as the return on their financial investment in their favoured club (or rider) will only ever really be imaginary or infinitesimal. It is a rare bird amongst any flock of speedway fans who after they glance at the programme scorecard and spots the advert suddenly think, "Cripes, is it me or did the piano sound out of tune when Tammy played his scales this morning?" Indeed, the sight of high-tuned gleaning chrome speedway bikes ridden by colourfully attired athletic riders flashing past the grandstand seats might not quite be sufficient entertainment to stop distracting thoughts of tight or damaged nuts and bolts back home intruding into the idle reveries of the fans here in Horsens this evening. Such is the subliminal power of product placement and advertising. Though hardly subtle, it definitely plants a seed with me about rusted bolts that grows throughout the meeting and remains increasingly hard to shake off for the remainder of the summer. Prompted in no small part by the chance to drift off during the all too predictable processional racing served up on this latest Danish iteration of a specially made SGP temporary track. Even in a world where fans are inured to the fact that most SGP races are won from gate, the bias in favour of gate 1 – aka the rider wearing the red helmet colour – nonetheless still stands out as incredible in Horsens. Although SGP gate positions are randomly drawn, only a fool would bet against red winning. Afterwards we learn that apparently this is not the fault of BSI deciding to use a temporary track or any construction errors but of physics due (dew?) to gravity ensuring moisture inevitably leeches to the inside according to the SGP's ex-FIM Assistant Race Director (and *Speedway Star* Managing Editor) Phil Rising's painfully tortuous explanation-cum-justification post on the British Speedway Forum. Whatever the nuance or explanation, the plain fact is that another SGP again sees the majority of its races won from the gate while featuring little or no exciting, meaningful competitive overtaking. So far, so typical for the SGP this season and many previous. Hardly notable, just something not spoken about in polite company. Or else reported in a manner that implies its diametric opposite by the embedded heavy-breathers who provide the "official" speedway "journalism" on TV, digital and social media or in print. Both during and afterwards, the mere threat of a pedestrian pass is all that is required to react with ecstasy and acclaim. Worse still, overtakes don't even really need to happen, as the pro-forma recipe for almost all media descriptions of SGP meetings and/or races deals primarily in a perpetually excited vocabulary of top/star riders, thrilling overtakes and daredevil races to the chequered flag. If BSI or their tame media helpers ever went in for honest public statements about the SGP: short relentlessly processional races, few thrills, rare overtakes and a stale too lengthy format are difficult attributes to make sound catchy.

I am sat in seat that costs enough to either buy half a season ticket at any British speedway club or else could be spent to gain admission to around five different speedway meetings of my choice staged anywhere else in Britain. That said, as a long time and genuine speedway fan, there is still a thrill to watching here, albeit SOLELY due to my proximity to the action. The Horsens back straight grandstand reminds me of a posher version of the now demolished

Newport Speedway in the salad days of Tim Stone's fan-turned-promoter reign there. Indeed, the AC Horsens grandstand seats are appreciably closer to the track and also better overlook it. Perhaps, BSI's plan for the Speedway World Championships was all along to create a more deluxe Newport Speedway? If so, and though they kept very quiet about these most laudable of their stretch goal ambitions, they have delivered in full. And, talking of Newport, given the execrable fare on offer at the Horsens Salgsbod, how I'd welcome one of those past their sell-by-date Tesco sandwiches Tim allegedly used to dumpster dive from work in order to later serve them up to slake the hunger of less-discriminating Wasps fans drawn to the Newport speedway club snack bar. Thoughts of food aside, it is my sheer proximity to the speed, vibrancy and colours of the passing bikes and riders that prompts my enjoyment. It is definitely not the calibre or competitiveness of the racing. On a warm, almost balmy night with an uninterrupted view sat slightly above the action, I can almost (but don't) reach out and touch the riders. The power of the bikes, the skill of the riders, the velocity added to the concatenation of noise and colour makes for an irresistible combination. All that is missing are overtakes, competitive racing and a nostalgic whiff on the heady bouquet of methanol. As a die-hard speedway fan watching some racing abroad, all is right with the world. I appreciate the meeting for what it is: a colourful vaguely exotic pretend contest – like wrestling on bikes without brakes – between men and machines. Perhaps, being wreathed in cigarette smoke also stirs a deep primal teenage comfort memory? I enjoy this speedway high for what it is – fleeting, bounded and here, now. Its total meaninglessness is its charm.

Sadly, as a contest, it lacks dynamism beyond the speed of the participants since it is totally processional. Almost every race sees the riders strung out like the proverbial line of speedway washing. Arguably, it is proudly and relentlessly processional. There is little or no drama. This is no spectacle to attract, let alone retain, the neutral observer or those fabled mythical first-time visitors they so often speak about in hushed reverent tones on the telly as if they actually still exist in real life. Nowadays new fans at speedway are seen as often as unicorns gambolling playfully about at Horsens central bus station. If these die-hard-fans-of-tomorrow-in-waiting-deeply-aroused-by-the-majesty-and-amazing-spectacle-of-speedway-grand-prix-racing do exist, where do they come from? Or if they do how, in the wild of the normal world, do they randomly get to even hear or learn about it? The idea that newbies are going to lash out the best part of £100 (if you include purchase of the programme) just to sample the speedway action they rarely mention or no longer really report on in the mainstream media is an utter nonsense. And, even if such easily persuaded wannabe fans do exist, disillusion quickly sets when they experience the thin gruel that BSI ensure gets served up to actual attendees in sharp contrast to the grandiose grandiloquent boasts and claims made about the superlative quality on offer. It is like discovering that despite Basingstoke's claims to be Paris it is just a posher version of Hemel Hempstead. To be at this particular Horsens SGP meeting for your first time ever trip to speedway indicates you are either lonely, unlucky, stupid, lost, invited by family and friends or come as the +1 of a sponsor or guest with tickets to spare. Or else you definitely have more money than sense and no friends. If that is so, this immediately makes you ideal future sponsorship material. Glancing around behind me, in demographic terms, you will be male, close to God's waiting room and no longer in possession of all your faculties, hair or teeth and, most likely, good eyesight and erections are both a distant memory. However, you will have brought your own sandwiches and carry a jumper in case it turns cold later. This all said, I am thankful to be alive to see, hear and experience this SGP in all its flawed glory. It may be mostly dull, but it is the speedway dull I choose to seek out and savour. This is my tribe. Though different nationalities, we have in common our shared shale passion. Like all true speedway fans, I watch the action in rapt attention, delight at minor manoeuvres or moments of real or imagined virtuosity, moan between heats or afterwards and, invariably, claim it was better in the past. And it was, for sure, at Smallmead in Reading in the mid-70s. Sat here in the present moment, there is much unintentional pleasure to be gained just watching this over-confident, sometimes inept often too self-regarding SGP world go fast flooding by in all its technicolour close proximity glory.

It is fortunate that I am so Zen, given the follow-my-leader racing, lack of actual drama and the awful price-entertainment ratio. Things start well for a partisan crowd when Nicki wins the first heat from the inside gate on a slithery track. Danish flags wave in joy and abundance. Nicki looks fast and confident. Maybe it is – finally, again, yet again – going to be his night tonight? Before heat 2, we get to see an impromptu fat mechanics race across the (proscenium arch-less) centregreen. Panting breathlessness abounds. Like breakdowns and mechanical gremlins, these foot races by the portly used to be all the rage until outsourcing to much more svelte professional third-party tuners and mechanics killed off this particular speedway side-show fun. Modern SGP mechanic have colour co-ordinated race suits tailored to fit their effete and/or muscle-bound gym bunny bodies. These exotically tattooed himbos are ubiquitous. Always on, always lurking close by or hyper-concentratedly staring over the air fence pimped, primed and coiled ready to spring into spanner twirling action. Any and all false starts require a flock of mechanics and helpers to surround man and machine to re-fuel, tinker, cajole or tweak. The quantity of staff surrounding any rider on the track is a function of their status, pocket depth and implied expertise of the hired help. Hopefully, like so many people within speedway, they work on a voluntary basis. Otherwise, along with criminally high costs detailed on tuning invoices, their presence further boosts the base level overheads required to effectively compete in the SGP series. The world over, obligatory regulatory requirements, health and safety, industry procedures, design features, mandatory supervision, staff costs and cultural requirements are used as (financial) barriers to entry to prevent the arrival of new, cheaper, talented, younger, iconoclastic or stiffer competition. Speedway is no different and a roster of mechanics beside you in the pit bay (or on the track) are all part of making that ladder so much harder to even reach – let alone climb – for SGP newbies and wannabes.

When it gets underway, heat 2 looks fast but on this iteration of the Horsens temporary track it remains incredibly hard to overtake. Rider struggles with this one-off specially made shale stage continue into the third race. Though there are flashes of elegance, the racing remains a pernickety, battle between man, gleaming bike and grunky random surface elements. The "grand old man" Greg Hancock sufficiently masters conditions to briefly treat us to a double pass before the fourth race settles back into its processional but jittery tempo. The track clearly needs some interval tender loving care but, despite the available manpower or extensive range of agricultural and construction equipment on hand, the die of its quality and performance was (again!) cast before a wheel even turned. All that remains is for the roster of track staff to go through the motions of pretending to be able to influence conditions. It is a role and stage that FIM Race Director Phil Morris never hesitates to relish or theatrically perform upon for the cameras, his bosses and those of the attending public who bother to watch. No sooner is the pits gate open to re-admit the riders than Phil slips his leash to get out stamping about on bends 1 and 2 like an angry bull keen to trample any available matadors. He waves, signals, directs and generally dashes about. To minimal end or effect. Morris embraces and channels his inner Marcel Marceau, albeit the grandly unsubtle version more suitable for the big-screen age. He is joined by a gaggle of purposeful men equipped with natty headphones and mouth-mikes, muddied climbing boots, protective gloves and dark matching boiler suits. This local curatorial tribe is led into unproductive labour by their gringo Chief Morris. Sadly, based on their collective lack of impact, like native peoples everywhere, harsh dispossession and possible near extinction awaits. But, we live for the moment without thought of history, tomorrow or future travails so, at an event with minimal spectacle, we get our speedway entertainment kicks wherever we can. And, for sure, Phil is where we can. Even without a ribbon on a stick or frequent twists and tumbles, the manic dance of his energetic shale inspired rhythmic-gymnastics-meets-speedway-charades invariably draws the eye. Well, my eyes and that of the broadcast editor sat in front of an array of screens. With one of his trademark circle waves transitioning into a salute, Phil tries to signal "one word, first letter" to a passing tractor in such a manner that it briefly slows – possibly to figure out if this is a film, book or play – until Phil impatiently fires off another of his virtuoso one-armed man juggling a hoop impatient gestures of rebuke. Given how the track staff then – in fast and extremely efficient short order – so over-water the track they swiftly create a sticky, truly glutinous impassable gloop, I am guessing that the mystery instructional word for this interval was either flood or smegma.

Such as it is, the racing resumes. The riders battle the greasy surface and never look totally comfortable. The next series of four races stand out only for not standing out except for the tricky conditions. Seven of the first eight races get won from gate 1 by the rider drawn to wear the red helmet colour. To then try to resolve or better balance things, we get treated to another emergency extensive track grade. An impressive amount of agricultural equipment – tractors, graders, blading or smoothing implements – yet again trundles back out onto the track. Phil Morris works more of his mime magic as well as stands stock still, like a Rodin statue (albeit one with a head and arms), on the centregreen infield closely "studying" the crime scene getting made much worse at his specific direction. There is much industry for questionable end product. Keen to seize the moment and pass time, a group of merry Polish fans rush down to the front row to film the apparently inexorable tractor action at some length for posterity. Unable to slake his need for crowd attention, Morris barely makes it back through the pits gate into the hallowed sanctuary of the pits to plot further track curation boobs when heat 9 comes under orders. After these latest ministrations, the track is so slippy that Tai's bike slaloms and snakes woozily from the tapes until he falls-cum-dismounts on his own accord onto the damp shale of first bend. Amazingly, rather than exclude Tai as he should (to my mind), referee Craig Ackroyd calls all four riders back for the re-run. It is the kind of benefit-of-the-doubt reprieve that riders outside the favoured few or upper echelons rarely get. If that had been Pawlicki, Cook or a meeting reserve, their comparative lack of exalted status makes it much easier to decide to instantly exclude them. Craig Ackroyd has notable previous when it comes to peculiar SGP decisions. The most notably influential of these contentious decisions dictated the course of 2012 World Championship when he decided not to exclude Chris Holder in the last GP of the series as he lustily battled Nicki Pedersen for position and the whereabouts of the crown. The decision not to exclude Holder, as Craig should have done, is widely seen as robbing Nicki of his third World Champion title while also helping gift Holder his one and only glorious win to date. In a further ironic twist, neither rider has since scaled these heights. Given his dominance this season, so far, Tai needs no special favours in his quest for his third World Championship triumph. Though the solitary point Tai gains from the re-run is moot over the long run of this season, it is nonetheless a lovely present from the referee. More peculiarly, given perceptions that Monster Energy riders explicitly, implicitly or subliminally follow team orders, "grand old man" Hancock and "youthful" Woffinden actually appear to race each other semi-seriously. Coming back this season from injury, Greg certainly needs to start racking up the cumulative points after an indifferent opening to a series he only competes in this year due to the award of a wild card. Nicki finishes comprehensively last and spends much of the final lap yet again ostentatiously bereft at the real (or imagined) underperformance of his engine. Over recent seasons, it seems Nicki has never run a last that was ever his fault but is always that of his bike, the track, the ref, the rules, other riders or the iniquities of a malign universe. It is amazing how often his highly-tuned bikes go from wonderful in the pits beforehand to execrable when out on the track. Given how often these psychological engine issues crop up, perhaps, Nicki suffers from the speedway equivalent of golf's putting yips? It is definitely a problem – seemingly without solution – and possibly even beyond the bolt loosening or penetrating remit of meeting sponsor WD-40.

Heat 10 actually prompts loud cheers – sadly, caused by chip-on-the-shoulder Danish nationalist feelings towards Sweden rather than the race action – when Swede Freddie Lindgren tries to predict the tapes' rise but instead breaks them. His exclusion costs three possible points from his highly fancied campaign to podium finish his 2018 season but, more worryingly for Lindgren, reveals a strong undercurrent of anxiety that his rivals – but especially Tai Woffinden – won't hesitate to recognise and aim to exploit. Freddie has previous in starting a SGP series as runaway the most in-form rider before vulnerability, back luck and injury derails his campaign. Unusually for a rider back from serious injury, Freddie is nowadays much more aggressive rather than – as is the norm – notably less so. Setting aside that this level of serious on-track aggression will get repaid by his fellow riders over the SGP season, and much as I'd like to see him finally get to become World Champion, the flattering-to-deceive warning signal is suddenly flashing bright red.

Though relishing my proximity to the speed and colour of the action, there is so little actual speedway entertainment, I'm tempted to stay afterwards to see the evocatively-named "Trouser Snake" – or whatever the local band BSI booked on the cheap – are called play their exclusive centregreen concert. This would, at least, get further bang for my krone and fractionally notional entertainment value – albeit of the unintended kind – from my investment in a premium-priced Horsens SGP ticket. Three meetings into the 2018 SGP series, even the flamboyant interval track curation directed via the medium of inspired Morris dancing begins to fail to cut it as a compensatory distraction. Sadly, for anyone wishing to watch the adverts rather than another lengthy track grade, poor local weather knowledge and attention to detail by BSI sees the bend 1 big screen obscured by the bright evening sunshine. When they pitch the low-spending wonders of the speedway audience demographic to actual or wannabe advertisers, it is unlikely that any mention is made by the salespeople that they will ensure your prized film narrative (or still images) get showcased on the big stadia big screen but only seen by the fan number equivalent of an empty darkened room.

When racing resumes on the extensively re-dowsed ultra-slithery track, Nicki Pedersen's huge popularity with the Danish crowd gets reconfirmed once more. Though a pantomime villain for UK SGP fans at Cardiff, and despite living for so many years in Stevenage (which surely, almost, makes him as British as Tai Woffinden), adulation levels for Nicki are off the scale. Plus, since this evening we occasionally get to see a facsimile of glory-era Pedersen rather than the Man-Who-Stares-at-Engines imposter of recent years, Nicki treats us to the rather pleasing spectacle of some virtuoso rough-housing of every other rider in his race. It is an immutable law of speedway that if you give an in-form Nicki the chance to ride you hard, then he will! Unlike the Monster Energy SGP speedway team in general – Tai, Chris and especially hissy-fitter-in-chief Greg Hancock – who are serial Nicki non-handshakers, Artem Laguta has been brought up to expect an element of rough-and-tumble out on any speedway track, so sportingly congratulates his hard-riding opponent afterwards. That said, and to be fair to the Monster lads, Nicki race wins are increasingly rare in the SGP, so their opportunities to self-righteously studiously ignore him are no longer what they were. Even their erstwhile Monster leader, Mr Joe Parsons himself, especially now that Darcy doesn't ride, no longer bothers to endlessly slag off Pedersen on Twitter with the obsessive frequency that he once did. Their collective sense of aggrieved entitlement about Nicki ignoring their imaginary After-You-Have-As-Much-Room-As-You-Like-Claude "underwritten rules" hasn't dissipated but, sadly, though his zest remains, Nicki's mechanical or psychological SGP struggles means he is no longer so often close enough to deliberately defy this speedway heraldic code of honour. In his pomp, though far greater box office in every (serious) speedway country than any of the riders Monster Joe chooses to have represent the fluids of his "edgy" brand, it widely mooted that Parsons' antipathy towards Pedersen is partly based on righteous animus over Darcy's failed Latvian SGP alcohol test as well as the fact that Nicki's pre-existing major sponsorship packages with blue-chip Danish companies meant he was never available for hire by Monster. Of course, while Parsons dresses his sour grapes up as a critique of Nicki's imputed lack of respect for rider safety and on-track fairness, it still looks more like Nicki is too much own man to be so easily biddable. Plus, of course, the fact that Nicki is heavily sponsored by Polish energy drinks manufacturer NGine must also play a part in Monster Joe's regular public antipathy towards and criticism of the Danish rider. Sadly this combination of circumstances means that Nicki is, thereby, unavailable to be brought in to play his small part in the high-fiving moody/smiley live human adventure meat Monster requires for foreground shots in their filmed 'extreme' sports advert montages. In the ultimate speedway Sliding Doors moment, nor is Pedersen available or invited to those famous hair letting-down sessions the Monster Energy Aussie rider posse sometimes enjoyed chez Parsons.

Heat 14 is won easily by Tai Woffinden after he slips by current World Champion Jason Doyle on the first lap. By the low standards of this dull meeting, any run-of-the-mill pass counts as an apocalyptically thrilling overtake, especially if done with a vague element of panache. Patryk Dudek endures a forgettable meeting, possibly partly brought on by indecision over which of his three bikes to ride. To help choose which machine to race on, Dudek rides one bike out onto the track before calling for another to be rushed out by his mechanical team so he and his dad can inspect them both alongside each other in front of the back straight grandstand. Last time his choice brought him third place, this time he runs a last and, as a bonus, also gets to enjoy some harsh riding from Freddie Lindgren. You wouldn't want Patryk choosing your lottery tickets. It is a race won from the gate by Hancock. As an equal opportunities harasser, Lindgren also tries to bully Sayfutdinov but gets short shrift when Emil cannily slow rides the inside white line to make passing impossible. If Craig Cook wasn't having bad luck, the perception he would have no luck at all continues after he makes a brilliant start to heat 16 only to get – in my opinion – unfairly called back by referee Craig Ackroyd. In this mini-battle of the Craigs, Ackroyd then doubles down on his error and harshly – but as the rules require – warns Cook for moving at the start. Any future such infractions will see the Cumbrian disqualified from the heat. To prove that not everyone off gate 1 in the red helmet colour wins tonight, Cook finishes second in the re-run after some virtuoso racing from the visibly in-form Zmarzlik. For reasons best known to himself, Bartosz decides to initially hang back – apparently so he can deliberately bump Janowski's shoulder at speed as he passes – before then reeling in Cook on the final lap.

The next interval sees Phil Morris out with alacrity to ostentatiously stamp down random patches of imaginary loose shale on bend 1, but also unveil another addition to his unique SGP repertoire of track grade instruction hand gesture for passing tractor drivers. Though naysayers may doubt speedway tractor drivers tasked to circle a speedway track for eight or so minutes need so many different complex instructions, Morris truly begs to differ. He really hoes his own row when it comes to relentlessly issuing complex irrelevant gestures that –

even if for a moment we don't try to recall the infinitesimal number of superlatively prepared SGP tracks delivering wonderful racing under his or previous race director supervision – add almost nothing to the tasks undertaken. If properly used sign language is a godsend for the deaf, beyond the obvious interpretation of a Welshman pleasuring a well-hung elephant, Phil's motions are altogether harder to understand, let alone put into practice. On the subject of working with animals, verbal slurry suddenly gets blasted out over the stadium loudspeakers when – though, he lives in Sweden nowadays and the meeting is being staged in an obscure Danish football stadium temporarily (badly) adapted for speedway – Greg Hancock tells us, "I feel at home here so I'm getting my groove on!" In the same way it is mandatory for Englishmen living overseas to get more ridiculously quintessentially English, at least Greg's mail order purchase of his "Speak like a Teenage Californian" dictionary gets more good use. Whether this affected vocabulary is contractually required by Monster – so that middle-aged men can sound down with the kidz (hyperactive ones at that, if they drink the product) – or is used out of a barely hidden anxiety about the deep sense of loss felt for his vanished youth, it simultaneously manages to sound false and affected as well as corny too. Worse still, in the next breath Hancock also wants to simultaneously play up his "Old Man River" speedway longevity as his unique selling point by crowbarring in as many great Danish rider references as possible into thirty seconds of conversation to enrapture the locals in his favour. Speedway in Denmark might not be what it once was in terms of stars or attention, but Greg is here to happily evidence and explicitly remind everyone what it once really was like. Elegantly but apparently effortlessly finding new reassuring clichés, Greg verbally soothes the long-time patriotic fans in the crowd with a quick burst of piquant nostalgia involving the rapid fire incantation of Danish star rider names from yesteryear that echo in the memory like the distant familiar chimes of a fondly recalled childhood ice cream van. To nearby listening dogs, his faux reminiscences sound like, "blah blah blah I was so lucky blah blah blah Hans Nielsen blah blah blah Erik Gundersen blah blah taught me so much blah blah blah and I came out a man." This is so effortlessly trite, when Greg's speedway career finally ends, writing schmaltzy lyrics is a possible future forte to immediately seize.

Continuing to stage his valiant one-man campaign to temper the "rider in the red helmet on gate 1 at Horsens" win statistics but also provide the hint of overtaking that the meeting so badly misses, Craig Cook again leads the field into the first corner of heat 18 before spending a lap and a half then ceding position until he finally finds himself back in last place. To accomplish this, Craig rides his SGP trademark stiff mid-track no-man's land race line. It is as if he's voluntarily agreed to help the police with ongoing enquiries by agreeing to appear as bait in a staged reconstruction that aims to lure (suspected) thieving riders into repeating the crime of stealing his hard won but easily lost race points. Discarding the nice guy persona he had just spent good waffle burnishing in the pits, even Greg Hancock piles on the agony by deliberately giving Cook a thrusty back wheel in order to pass the visibly disconsolate Englishman. By the end of this evening in Horsens, red-helmeted riders win 17 of the 23 races staged with Craig Cook providing a third of those gate 1 non-wins. Even when finishing a competitive second in heat 16, a distracted Cook fails to perform his obligatory "that-was-a-close-race-mate-aren't-we-quite-something" handshake with Zmarzlik and, instead, immediately returns to the pits without reaction for further tinkering or bike repairs. After bagsying his last latest last place, Cook glides to a halt by the pit gate to wait for it to open so he can as quickly as possible disappear from the Horsens shale stage. What figure a depressed temporarily out-of-sorts rider might cut isn't something that automatically springs to mind but, if one is needed, Craig is definitely providing the archetype. Even during the races, Cook's usual fluid expressiveness and confident elegance when racing at high speed on a speedway bike appears to have been replaced with a hunched, tentative stiffness that shouts ongoing battle with his equipment. Post-meeting Craig would note that despite significant expensive investments in top gear for his 2018 SGP campaign (helped in small part by an innovative fan fund-raising initiative), highly regarded top-class engine tuners all remain unavailable. Flemming Graversen, Jan Andersson and Ryszard Kowalski are all just too busy working for rival SGP riders to tune his engines. Despite such set-backs, Cook continues to cast around the pits for advice and opinion afterwards, "I spoke to the other guys and my sprocket has two teeth less than anybody else's." It is a trying mechanical situation that a few splashes of meeting sponsor WD-40's "penetrating" oil can't solve alone.

The final race of the qualifying heats is well worth watching (but still can't in any way justify the stonking ticket prices) for the track management skills and speedway smarts shown by Tai Woffinden. First he bests Laguta and then intelligently shadows the red-helmeted Freddie Lindgren until this inevitably provokes yet another predictable hard riding manoeuvre from the Swede that Woffinden wanted to elicit then evade in order to ease past and escape. I would hate to find that going to all the SGPs somehow outs me as a born-again closet Woffinden fan and bandwagon jumper. It is, after all, already a very crowded shouty bandwagon. That said, watching Tai during his first few apprenticeship league racing seasons in British Speedway was genuinely exciting to see and something I sought out. Like I also tried to watch – for example – Chris Holder or Darcy Ward wherever and whenever possible. There is something truly thrilling about seeing obviously talented but still fearless young riders during their initial Bambi baby-step apprentice league racing seasons. To marvel at how fast they race without fear or favour. Sport arguably thrills most when it showcases emerging youth. Greg Hancock's longevity within the SGP is, arguably, symbolic of everything that is wrong with the BSI SGP series and its format. It is a bug rather than the deluxe feature claimed by BSI and the house-trained media. Sure, it is a good story to milk and, after all, motorsports is slightly different so has seen older winners before (for example, though not all comparable, Fangio won his fifth Formula 1 title aged 46). But, essentially, Hancock is a bed-blocker. His continued participation in the series is a fault of the format and system rather than their triumph. Top 8 automatic qualifications as well as a quarter of the field additionally given over to wild cards places – matily chosen by BSI and the FIM to secret unpublished criteria – add up to a dull recipe of inertia and decline. Regular blasts of the zest, jeopardy, excitement and thrills younger, lighter more ambitious riders could and would inject into the World Championships are structurally excluded. BSI only ever want their SGP pot to simmer not boil. Anyways, in a mediocre field in a prolix series, not only does Woffinden (along with Zmarzlik) stand out but also catches attention and focus whenever he rides in full flow rather than just professionally go through the motions. We all know that Tai has the best equipment as well as a tendency nowadays to pass rather than overtake or race. Despite all this, he still draws the eye. Well, my eye. As if to disprove my enthusiasm with a nod towards the cronyism and "one-rule-for-one-and-one-rule-for-another" favouritism that infests the SGP on and off the track, Tai gets a flier in the first semi-final that, if he were a meeting reserve, Pawlicki or Cook, would more likely get stopped and called back. Here, though, referee Ackroyd once more lets it go.

In the first running of the second semi-final, Nicki Pedersen gives Bartosz Zmarzlik a masterclass in how to gain advantage by manufacturing a speedway professional foul. Looked at in real time, Zmarzlik appears to clip Pedersen as they compete for the all-important second place that secures a place in the final. The big screen replays show that Bartosz did clatter Nicki's leg and, thereby, knocked him off so should be excluded but – and the but is important – Pedersen had also deliberately slightly slowed to make himself available to get clattered. Ignoring the rules don't cover fractional in-race delays, Pedersen did so safe in the knowledge that the referee would weigh him being ahead and Zmarzlik behind against the hard-charging velocity of the Polish rider. In a split second, Nicki skilfully assessed comparative speeds and on-track race positions with the accuracy of a human speedway Satnav; while simultaneously calculating the collision trajectory percentages to decide it was well worth taking the risk of having a theatrical "crash". Nicki also knew that he really had nothing to lose as over the course of the entire race, even on this extremely hard to pass on Horsens track, the faster Zmarzlik would likely overtake him. With only a small outside possibility this coming together and fall would be adjudicated by the referee as Pedersen's responsibility, it is a tough but everyday lesson in SGP knock-out stages gamesmanship that Zmarzlik needs to learn from quickly.

While we wait for his mechanics to dust the shale from Nicki's bike (and, hopefully, for once, manage to avoid suddenly introducing surprise last-minute mechanical gremlins into its engine), to pass the time we are treated to a brief big screen but platitudinously dull live pits interview with Chris Holder. A fraction of a second after its conclusion – apparently unbeknownst to him – the camera continues to lovingly lingering in time-delay fashion on his head and shoulders, Holder contradicts his bonhomie to aggressively, almost angrily, rip off and discard his sponsor contract interview compliant race bib and Monster Energy cap. Holder is definitely a long way from a happy camper. Though Pedersen gave himself the chance to play again while also sabotaging the ambitions of a rival rider, in the semi-final re-run avoiding third place in a three-rider race proves beyond Nicki. On what looks to be a fading and underpowered bike. Nicki gives getting to the final a good go with guile and the hard-won track craft of a long and successful career started many moons back as a training track junior. Despite drawing upon an impressive repertoire of jinks, sudden decelerations, changes of racing line as well as curious angles of entry and exit at each bend, Nicki is nevertheless still out-thought by Artem Laguta in their mini-competition for second. With atmosphere levels in the crowd, mostly at the deflated level of a badly punctured Space Hopper – except when Nicki rides – Pedersen's failure to make the final further dulls the collective tepid enthusiasms of a notably torpid crowd.

The final features an extended bout of tapes area gardening from all competing riders. This is more of a triumph of hope over reality, given the bone-hard surface and bias towards the inside gate 1. First time out the race is stopped and sees Woffinden nearly take off Laguta. The processional re-run is dominated by Tai after a super quick start. No sooner is the race done than a good portion of the crowd head for the exits rather than wait for the proscenium arch to be re-erected, nevermind the presentation of the ugly "trophies" Monster apparently provide in order to try to make these triumphs in ten different locations over this SGP series look vaguely memorable. Fewer fans still then linger to see or savour the act BSI booked – Big Fat Snake – play at The Forum after the podium presentations. With BSI band selections made on cost and availability grounds rather than musical ability, quality or demand, staying to listen feels to me more like a threat than entertainment but, strangely, afterwards, I regret not experiencing the joy and full banality of their set.

The only road to leave this part of Horsens runs parallel to the stadium. Before heading off for destinations unknown, many blokes take their final chance to smoke and piss artlessly outside (wild-pissing, as they call it in the Netherlands) in the overgrown grass amongst the stored-cum-discarded goal posts and nets. It is a peculiar micro-rebellion to choose in lieu of using the more convenient, fit-for-purpose and relatively spacious stadium toilets. Once the hallowed ground of the AC Horsens outside storage has been ceremonially dowsed, it is then quite a trek to retrace our route to escape the stadium grounds. It requires going past the underside of the temporary stands and negotiating the crowded narrow uneven-surfaced walkway alongside the security-fenced holding area that serves as the riders' van car park. It is a speedway truism the world over that, the moment any rider finishes their last race, they pack away their bikes and equipment with the speed of thieves snatching jewels with loud alarms ringing and the police already called. If they have help – whether family or staff on hand – often the job is already half done before they even pass the chequered flag. It is a rigorous approach to time-keeping regularly seen in reluctant learners at school but also brought on by the relentless season-long demands of long-distance travel – mainly by van and plane – and the huge number of hours it inevitably eats up. Given that in-demand riders such as these SGP ones hop from country-to-country on an almost daily basis, the next work location is rarely just around the corner. Given speedway tracks are more often flung to the periphery of their towns and regions – as a function of noise, space required and popularity – this all adds to the distances involved. Security in Horsens is tight. What a few hours ago kept fans and ne'er-do-wells alike out, now keeps the riders and mechanics locked in while the stadium empties. All the riders and mechanics stood around by their already loaded vans didn't make the knock-out stages of the meeting. They lost. FIM rules require that all riders and bikes must remain on hand in a neutral zone (parc ferme) for half an hour afterwards in case their equipment needs to be officially inspected for real or imaginary rogue elements or being subject to paid formal protest from rival rider camps. Having to aimlessly hang around rather get on to the next gig adds insult to injury and further underlines their poor performance or comparative lesser status here this evening. Even after the top three celebrate on the podium, pose for photos, give interviews to the tame embedded speedway media and maybe even have a shower, if they are lucky, these waiting discarded riders will only just have left. By then, the traffic jam-cum-queue on the almost gridlocked road will hopefully also have long subsided.

It is three kilometres back through town to the rider hotel. Walking easily out paces the jams of escaping vehicles. After the roar of the speedway, crossing the parkland grounds of the hotel at dusk feels particularly serene. The ducks are in complete command of the empty park grass and ponds. Similarly, stood exactly where he was seven hours earlier, Peter Adams draws deeply on his cigarette and savours his commanding view of a now stilled hotel car park. As I didn't see him on the walk back, quite how he beat the traffic gridlock is a mystery. Then speedway is founded upon secrets and hierarchy. Its in-crowds and out-crowds. Its real insider knowledge in sharp contradistinction to its for public consumption statements. I don't for a moment believe that Peter left early without watching Tai race to victory in the final. It is as if he somehow got beamed back from the stadium via the Starship Enterprise. If so, he's playing the Bones role – though he's better suited to Spock – as the doctor is the more likely smoker. Peter nods hello. Nigel Pearson is also back too and, though the evening is warm, announces that he is off to his room to collect his jumper. At reception Kelvin settles up the personal extras on a hotel bill otherwise paid for by persons unknown from event/competition he reports on as an independent journalist.

"What room is that?"

"518."

"You're staff, aren't you?"

"Yes."

"Then there is nothing to pay there."

"I had lunch earlier."

"Ah, 384 Danish Krone for lunch and the gift shop."

"Gift shop?"

Scanning Kelvin's large eyes and his naturally shocked resting bitch face gives the receptionist no clues as to his real state of mind. Especially since he's just finished three hours intensive live commentary work screech-reacting and running the full gamut of human emotion from D minus to D. "Gift shop."

"I got nothing at the gift shop."

Staring harder to mellow this misallocation, Tatum continues to wears the shocked look of a man without belief in the afterlife unable to shake off recent new knowledge about the futility of human existence brought on by seeing graphic images of the true full horror of Hell that now – apparently – permanently occupies his every waking thought and peripheral vision. "You bought nothing from there? [checks] It was a coffee."

"I had a coffee after but it wasn't in the gift shop."

"We put down coffees as 'gift shop'"

"You confused me with the gift shop when I'd bought nothing from there."

Rather than go all Hotel California on KT ("you can check out any time you want but you can never leave"), the receptionist opts for the politic path of least resistance. "Do you need a receipt?"

"I don't need a receipt."

Winner: Tai Woffinden (19 points)

Second: Artem Laguta (12 points)

Third: Greg Hancock (16 points)

Fourth: Jason Doyle (12 points)

CHAPTER 4

Hallstavik SGP 4 – 07.07.18

"Trying to become an FIM Speedway Grand Prix World Champion is like trying to bake a cake without a recipe."

Speedway Star

THE first ever Speedway Grand Prix held in Hallstavik is a feather in the cap for Rospiggarna speedway club but also cause for excitement for a small town also famous for its paper mill and, of course, a local resident who came second in Swedish Idol in 2010. By all accounts, the SGP riders enjoy the multiple racing lines they find in Hallstavik but, then, they regularly talk up even the most mediocre SGP tracks before they race on them. Even if a poor-sized crowd shows up, they will likely near double the usual population of Hallstavik. Away from the edges of its major cities, to the untutored eyes of visitors, Sweden quickly turns more assertively into an elemental, green and spacious countryside of fields, forests, mountains, lakes, rocky landscapes, villages and remotely located homesteads. The town and country contrast is notable.

The Duke of Edinburgh Award scheme meets the Scouts ethos that apparently determines the SGP rights holders choice of speedway event location gets into gear with this compulsory trip to obscure parts of regional Sweden for the first time this 2018 season with tonight's meeting in a wood on the edge of a picturesque small town at Rospiggarna speedway club. Given most of Sweden is in or close to a wood, this isn't the exotic or distinguishing feature it sounds to less attuned ears of urban tourists. Travelling to these SGP meetings by public transport requires detailed pre-planning. My trip today is by train then bus having already taken the plane the day before. Given that Sweden is the third (or second depending on who you speak to) most significant speedway market in Europe – well, the world – you would kind of half expect that its major cities of Stockholm or Gothenburg would fit the BSI big stadia bill. Interestingly, the disputatious fiasco that ended its three-year stint in the Ullevi Stadium in 2004 has yet to see the bikes return back there. BSI did stage the Scandinavian SGP at the Friends Arena in Stockholm for five years (2013-2017) but then – as so often with their own big stadia strategy and choices – failed to spark sufficient interest to turn the profits required. Though inconvenient for fans, at least the Swedish SGP spectacle won't be spoilt by the vagaries of a one-off track – like it was in both Gothenburg and Stockholm – since league speedway is regularly raced on the track at Rospiggarna. Looking at this relocation to existing clubs in the countryside decision more dispassionately, it strongly suggests that the gilt has mostly come off the popularity of the Speedway Grand Prix lily when it comes to big stadia stagings on one-off tracks. Only Cardiff and Warsaw remain vibrantly on the roster. A litany of failed big city stadia stagings that invariably end in fiasco, failure, dispute or no speaks. (Whether attempted in this part of the world or the warmer climes of distant continents.) Promoters have handed back the keys in both Sydney and Melbourne rather than continue with the staging losses their BSI contracts entail. Stockholm went the way of all flesh and Gothenburg finished ignominiously too. Both locations suffered from the same difficult but easily predictable equation - given the fare served up and how big stadia are inevitably unsuitable venues for staging thrilling speedway meetings - namely falling crowds and exorbitant stadium hire costs. Switching to lesser cities is no guarantee of success in Scandinavia or the Nordics either. After three early 21st century stagings (2002-2004) at the Olympic stadium in Hamar – hardly the place that most springs to mind whenever you think of Norway – the series has yet to return to that country full stop. If the SGP is a big stadia disease prone to infect the speedway body politic, its standard symptoms of bilious nausea accompanied by industrial quantities of heartache, boredom and financial disaster never get cured by BSI doctor's extensive documentation, advice or ministrations nor made more palatable by palliative lashings of tame media BS. Luckily however, over recent years, if self-medicated with total abstinence, the initial virulence rarely bothers the central body but is flung to the far extremities of the limbs with only occasional fever dreams of riches and acclaim to remind us of past naivety and our collective failure to take adequate precautions.

Thoroughly schooled to nowadays mostly expect speedway grands prix in far flung but not exotic locations, from Stockholm I set off on Swedish railways to Vasteras – apparently not a *Game of Thrones* twin town – to wait an hour for the connecting bus I booked to Hallsta vägskäl. Despite prior weeks of above average temperatures and endless sunshine, upon arrival in Vasteras it rains heavily enough to reduce even the most robustly prepared track to slime. Luckily it is some distance away. Sheltering under the trees of the still lush park nearby the central rail/bus station, many 50s and 60s vintage cars drive by. Judged by their motors, it seems the locals like nothing better than to weekend drive in big horsepower vehicles built in an era when the US car industry still had confidence enough in the joy of the open road to exhibit this excitement in the flair of its designs. The passing retro vehicles are beloved, gleaming but practical rather than showier muscle cars. The rare racier ones are much more *Grease* era than *Starsky & Hutch*. With the benefit of the nostalgic distance of time, even the well-kept bigger berth family-oriented cars look like stylish knights of the road. Either open-topped cars were in their infancy back then or the vagaries of Swedish weather discourages their wider ownership. From the transport terminus, the bus quickly finds the edge of town, exhausts the string of low-slung industrial estates to find endless mostly cultivated fields whose low crops bask bright green in the blistering sunshine. The driver speaks no English and, strangely, though I am on the correct 569 bus, Hallstavik completely fails to appear amongst the litany of obscure Swedish place names on its electronic route planner. My choice of potential English speakers amongst the two other late lunchtime passengers is a nervous old lady who avoids eye contact and a bearded heavy-metal fan looking bloke with pounding music seeping from headphones who, apart from his middle-age, wouldn't be out of place setting up on the Monster Energy SGP fanzone stand.

He is helpful and speaks fluent English so consults with the driver to identify and agree my request stop. "You are lucky I was here to ask otherwise as he did not understand you or know you wanted that special Hallsta stop." My good Samaritan knows and once relished going to speedway but is shocked verging on amazed to discover that he hadn't even heard that a major international individual speedway meeting is going to be staged in his neck of the woods this evening. He suspects that rampant World Cup fever – recently severely heightened to a crescendo by unexpected progress and this afternoon's Sweden versus England quarter-final match at four – has displaced news of all other sports on the streets and in the media. Though patriotic and proudly Swedish, his natural antipathy to ball sports has been further stoked by this nationwide outbreak of wall-to-wall football fervour. If he wasn't working later, he'd definitely join me at the speedway. "Speedway is unknown, little known, here. Mostly, no one knows! But I admire the riders, they are sports people who do it for the love. Anyone can be good at ball sports and choose the one that makes them the most money but speedway is different. Do you know of Tony Rickardsson? He was World Champion many times but he would only get paid a million crowns a year. It is a sport for Poland, Sweden and England and Denmark too. They have to travel so much but it is a real community. Do you know of Tomasz Gollob? He rode in Poland, Sweden and England to make a living. You have to work hard and travel much."

My speedway further education is cut short when the bus slows to a halt by a request stop in the middle of nowhere with green but featureless fields on either side. And also a wood whose regular rows of trees and general geometric shape indicates it was newly planted two decades back. The driver unnecessarily points to the only adjacent narrow road and a sign on the village limits that says Hallsta. It is a place that immediately prompts closer inspection of my travel ticket pdf where it is rather grandly described as Hallsta vägskäl. Though, I anticipated Hallstavik to be small, rural and remote, where I stand looks ridiculously so. On a dark winter's night, it would make a good setting for the opening scene of a horror movie. Even in bright sunshine, there is a sense of desolation. Apart from the narrow road to the village, the surrounding fields are also cut through by a curved section of dual carriageway that needs substantial crash barriers to manage high speed of passing vehicles that zoom past on this nowhere section of road. It is gloriously sunny and, apart from the occasional air displacement whoosh of a passing car, notably quiet. Nothing stirs except my feeling of dread. There is no sign at all of a paper mill on the horizon. It looks like a no-horse village. Actually, to be fair, it is so rural, they probably do have horses. Though fancying myself as something of a travel expert with Mr Google at hand, it is clear I have most likely badly boobed in my travel arrangements and totally vagskalled myself! If moments ago, when I stepped off the bus I had 99 metaphorical red balloons then 98 suddenly just punctured prior to release.

A short walk takes me to the nearest property – more John 'Boy' Walton homestead in the Swedish countryside vernacular than family house – to ask for directions but find no one home. Like a thirsty man in a desert, sight of two women carrying stuff from their car into a larger sized but gated house makes me sprint up the narrow road ahead in case they suddenly disappear again. With all their doors open and packages in hand, the two women are guarded and suspicious. The suspicious sight of a stranger is tempered by the sound of spoken English. Their three fair-haired daughters stop playing to briefly look on curiously. My statement, "I have come from England for the speedway" only gets further blank looks. "Where am I?" prompts a thaw in their reserve and frostiness. "You are in Hallsta, where should you be?" Saying "Hallstavik for the speedway" aloud brings immediate broad smiles and barely suppressed laughter, "Hallstavik!?!?" They proceed to roll the suddenly remarkably different sounding – now they are spoken correctly accented and out loud – pronunciations of Hallstavik and Hallsta with delight round their mouths. I may have accidentally stumbled upon a new Buddhist mantra for them. Though, I suspect, its incantation would amuse too much to allow them to the appropriate levels of mental emptiness required to begin to find Nirvana. After quick consultation of a map of Sweden, they flourish a mobile phone screen, "Look, you are here in Hallsta and [scrolls bigly] there is Hallstavik! Quite some way away! Many, many kilometres away." Though no longer unexpected, the news is quite a blow to my Sherpa credentials but also my chance of getting to the speedway GP I came for having left England to do so on Thursday morning. It is a doubly embarrassing unforced error too since I could have booked the whole trip with Travel Plus Tours. Worse still, the TPT coach actually leaves to the meeting from my Stockholm hotel this afternoon. They very kindly even offered me a lift there to go with their kind post-meeting lift back. If only my mis-placed intrepid traveller confidence along with a desire to fully use the prized gift of pit lane guest access hadn't lured me away, I could have had four extra hours sightseeing as well as avoid the financial and psychic cost of marooning myself miles away in Hallsta too. Plus it also now means I'll miss watching Sweden play England in the football live at the stadium too.

"You are 145 or so kilometres away from Hallstavik! How did you get here?"

"By train from Stockholm then bus from Vasteras. When is the next bus back?"

"[consults phone] Three hours."

"Three hours!"

"If it sees you, it will stop. Sometimes they don't stop as they don't see you. It is a special stop."

"I'll hitch back."

"No one will stop to pick you up. That is certain. It is dangerous. There have been robberies."

"By hitchhikers?"

"By people pretending to need help by broken cars."

"Not hitchers, though?"

"They will not stop for you, even if you have no broken car. What time does your event start in Hallstavik?"

"Seven."

"You will be able to get there today from Vasteras but maybe not in this four and one half hours."

Feeling a potent mix of chastened and angry at my silly error, I say thanks and head back to what – now I'm going to hitch and feel the All-American lure of the open road – I'll call the freeway. There is a short pull-in-cum-halt to stand by that is really just the turn into the one narrow road to Hallsta village. As they warned about the discretionary bus stop, its placement is such that you would have to know it is there or else be an extremely observant but brave driver to manage to both see me and then safely stop in the distance available. I pray for a helpful driver with wonderful eyesight, exceptional reactions and advanced motoring skills. It seems that I have managed to invent my own equivalent of a common budget airline airport location fiddle – convinced that I am going to land in London only to find myself two hours away at London Birmingham. In British Speedway terms, I have attempted to go from Oxford to Eastbourne speedway in Arlington and, instead, somehow ended up close to a small similarly named hamlet in North Norfolk. If this were really the case, given the state of the privatised local bus and train services operating in England nowadays, I would have absolutely no hope of making an immediate spontaneous trip to my correct destination from such an improbable and poor starting point on local public transport on a mid-Saturday afternoon. There just wouldn't be the service, let alone any possibility of the various services connecting in an integrated fashion. And, even if there were, the walk-up price would be astronomic.

I call my good speedway friend in Manchester and, from their swift internet searches, learn that trains and buses could get me there in time for the start if – and it is a big IF – I can get back to Vasteras quickly. Sadly, there aren't many cars going in either direction and, on my side of the road, the few that do are going at quite a lick. Yet amazingly, hallelujah, within just minutes a car going in the other direction slows, crosses the freeway and manoeuvres into the turning lane for Hallsta to pull to a halt to pick me up! Astonishingly, I have only waited five minutes. The kindness of strangers! How wonderful. My good Samaritans totally restore my faith in human nature AND also the kindness of strangers. My heroes and generous guardian angels are Dennis and Emma. They are on their way to the apparently famous vintage American car rally event held annually in Vasteras but specifically turned round to get me having glimpsed me as they originally shot past. I'd seen those retro cars already out in force in Vasteras earlier but didn't know why. Dennis has gone along for 22 successive years. It sounds a fun relaxing afternoon. Emma is on a high too having very recently been the birth partner for her best friend ("she has no mum but my mum is like her mum"). She marvels at the extremities and sheer wonder of the birth. Emma delights in telling me about baby Joseph as she drives. She just can't stop going to see and marvel at him further. They haven't heard of speedway and aren't tempted by my offer that they drive me to Hallstavik this afternoon in order to get their first taste of some shale action. They also confirm my incredible good fortune.

"We saw you but couldn't stop but he said 'turn round'."

"But why did you stop? I was told people wouldn't."

"You were in the middle of nowhere. Who would be here who didn't need help?"

"I feel like crying with happiness and stupidity."

"We feel like laughing at your stupidity!"

They too roll the pronunciations of Hallsta and Hallstavik around their mouths and, again it has to be said, with great difference and clarity. On his phone, Dennis looks up a range of possible travel options from Vasteras to Hallstavik. The best option goes in 30 minutes and is a four-change journey by train, train, bus and bus that – if all connections are made – sees me arrive at Hallstavik bus station with 20 minutes to spare before the SGP starts. "We will drop you as close to the bus and railway station as we can. Usually we would be there in 20 minutes but not only are there all the cars – though it is still early so we may be lucky that there are not so many – but they turn off all the city traffic lights in Vasteras. So that can cause delays too." Upon arrival in Hallstavik, Google maps suggests that my walk is then 15 minutes to Rospiggarna speedway club. Dennis and Emma remain sceptical, "If you don't get lost!"

There is, in fact, a good choice of public transport travel modes and routes to Hallstavik. The station staff recommend the two bus cross-country version with a change in Uppsala (the closest railway station to my destination). They are apologetic that I can't buy the cheaper two-hour ticket but, since the journey takes four or so hours in total, they have to sell me the 24-hour unlimited bus travel ticket. Though everything feels like a crime in price terms in Sweden, this is surprisingly good value at around £15. Even more amazingly – for someone used to the impact of privatisation on rural bus services – is the existence of a regular walk-up service. Plus since it is run as a service by a single controlling entity rather than separate competing profit centres, bus and/or train routes integrate with each other at station interchanges. In this case, the university town of Uppsala rather than either just end; require further long waits and expenditure, taxis or the private vehicles of friends and family. To be honest, it is a big disappointment to be in Sweden while England play them in the (football) World Cup quarter final and not get to actually savour the patriotic fervour watching the game on their home turf with random Swedes. I had planned to leave the Hallstavik pits to do so at the stadium on the big screen they had set up for this purpose. That said, I already pre-resented the additional admission charge – on top of my standing entry ticket – to do so. Before departure there is even time to watch convoys of beloved gleaming vintage American cars and small-sized trucks slowly promenade the streets. These vehicles also look good when viewed from above on the upper deck of my first bus. Their stately speeds along with a few bottlenecks give time to properly savour the sight of these eye-catching vehicles from a different more confident era and culture. Silly to claim on bus routes used and road driven many times every day by local residents, but my bus trips feel like a once in a lifetime journey. Not only is it absorbing since I am a stranger to this part of the country but, because of the football, though almost everywhere is bathed in bright sunshine the roads are surreally empty. It is as if some post-Rapture apocalyptic future has arrived here now. Think *The Leftovers* without all the depressiveness or the threatening religious cult in white clothing. Viewed from the upper deck, it looks like all the humans (and, weirdly, most of their vehicles too) who once swarmed the houses, businesses, farms, fields, villages, towns and countryside have been permanently relocated to an alternative unknown dimension. But left everything they used and owned – especially their national flags – behind when the Rapture apostle Paul described suddenly struck. Our progress is stately and serene, albeit flag patriotism rampant. A stickler for the specifics of its published schedule, the bus even takes time to linger at various deserted stops even though we don't pick anyone up. Sweden has collectively stopped to spend time with its flags and to watch the football indoors on its screens.

Even the station interchange at Uppsala is almost deserted of waiting passengers and none of those waiting wear Sweden replica shirts. An impressive number of almost empty buses still run, driven by moody drivers with radios blaring the match commentary. They are understandably irked at how their rosters randomly impinged upon this particular once-in-a-lifetime possibly momentous afternoon. The staff in the railway station restaurant and bar – with the upscale French furniture and decor vibe but no screens – easily outnumber their two customers, so stand chatting. They direct me deeper into the town centre to slake my football lust but don't hold out hope that there will be room at any bars there showing the game. The shopping streets are deserted and, strangely for tourist eyes on a Saturday afternoon, the shops are shut. Defiantly so. Pragmatism, patriotism and community sentiment clearly culturally trumps the capitalist profit motive here. This wouldn't happen similarly in Britain, any longer. If they exist, our high street shops are open and trading in their battle to the death with online shopping as well as out-of-town malls and shopping centres. Like the villages that surround it, Uppsala feels deliberately shut to collectively enjoy the football. Sight of an extremely crowded side street O'Neill's bar on foreign soil makes me suddenly come all over speedway media in-crowd but I fail the induction test when I don't drink a Guinness. It's fun to briefly embrace some cultural travel philistinism and go in. Usually I don't understand why you would go abroad to a foreign country and then choose to drink in an ersatz version of an Oirish bar when many more authentic and local experiences are also available. The urgent need for access to a big screen quickly compromises any sincerely held informal principle. England are already one-up and, though the two screens have a 20-second time delay between them, that was sufficiently long ago to have missed the replays of the first goal too. Instead I am treated to the sight of Sweden doing a good impression of playing like a superior version of Sunderland, albeit in yellow and blue with more collective commitment and imagination. Indeed, there are more ex-Sunderland players on the pitch – across both teams – than any other English league team. On screen, England showcase their new found alleged "game management" skills with professionalism and swagger. In reality, most long-time fans of the national team suspect it is probably the shallow confidence of a flat-track bully and soon to be revealed as a false veneer when facing better opposition. But, for now, it quiets the sea of yellow with blue trim in this pub. Concentration levels and emotions are high, but the atmosphere remains actually and metaphorically warm. Though young and old, men, women and children wear their national team shirts with swagger and pride, people still find time to look away from the action to give a quick polite welcome to late newly arrived strangers. Aside from extended families, either lots of people already know each other in this small town or else the joy of Swedish football overcomes them with matey bonhomie. The barman talks in an impenetrable polyglot garbled accent that turns out – when he asks me to guess – is a distant mangled echo of Scouse via 20-odd years in Uppsala. I only have time for ten minutes either side of half time. Nothing much happens beyond the well-researched and tutored grinding professionalism that is currently hailed and lauded as Gareth Southgate's signature style. Just like watching the SGP meetings in a foreign language (Polish) at home, the England match-viewing experience here is much improved without the jingoism or prolix platitudes when listened to in Swedish.

Apart from the driver, the next bus has only one other passenger and we pick no-one up as we ride the sun-kissed ghostly cross-country roads in serene isolation. In a spooky premonition of processional SGP races later (and everywhere), we don't overtake the slow but faster-starting lorry we find ahead of us as there is no room to pass. Instead we interpret the purpose of our journey to be to settle for the points we have and escort it home. Indeed, my bus driver makes little or no attempt to overtake – even when the speed limiter and fleeting opportunity allows – but sits there content on just finishing. He switches off the radio when Sweden go two-nil down, while the other passenger has a very bad sneezy cold at odds with the weather. The rural idyllic countryside has a picture postcard quality and beauty. It is all cute isolated homesteads, wooded valleys, glistening lakes, rocky outcrops, worn winding desire paths, well-tended roadside villages and lush green fields. Hardly any other vehicles pass in either direction. Fitting the cliché of years ago when Abba ruled the roost, most that are out look like they are Volvos. I don't see a single person outside after we leave the outskirts of Uppsala. No one. Nothing. Nada. On the side of a barn, the word SWEXIT has been painted in giant letters. It is hard to imagine that this appeared without the permission of the farmer or land-owner. Like the UK countryside and Sunderland, the awareness and fear of migrants is at its highest where none or hardly any actually live. I am going to wildly guess – and also use the evidence of my own eyes in Stockholm – that new arrivals of any stripe in Sweden are going to tend to congregate in more densely populated metropolitan areas rather than flock to live in glorious isolation in more rural ones. Brexit is an ugly word in keeping with the ideas that underpin it. Despite the widespread 'good' Swedes narrative, Sweden has a much darker second world war history than it admits to itself. So, perhaps, this Swedish nascent desire for greater autonomy from the (so-called) European super-state driven by its exceptionalism should not surprise. Recent years have seen Sweden become less welcoming and hospitable to cultural otherness. Combining country names prefixes with exit makes ungainly words that don't infer intellectual or linguistic elegance either. If or when such retro-nationalism stirs more widely in mainland Europe into formal opposition and inchoate but emotional opposition to the EU, there will be reams of these ugly neologisms. Itexit. Spexit. Luexit. Esexit. Bexit. Nexit. Should they go down this route, and so soon after joining, Slovenia and Slovakia (or Poland and Portugal, for that matter) might have to flip a coin or lose voters in the Pexit and Slexit confusion. If these campaigns are going to underscore their strong emotional appeal, more evocative choices of independence safe word may be needed to rally these various sincerely held demands for autonomy.

Hallstavik bus terminal is a grandiose way to describe its reality. It is a purpose-built stopping point of concrete, bus stops and basic shelters close to a crossroads that looks over-sized for its purpose and traffic volumes. This grandiloquence is probably dictated by the staffing requirements of the nearby paper mill as its workforce are unlikely to solely drawn from town residents. The generous extra width of the road – and accompanying pathway – from the bus terminal to the nearby paper mill is definitely suitable for fully laden large lorries, whether with timber beforehand or paper after. The mill chimneys dominate the horizon and catch the eye as they belch out impressive clouds of Saturday evening white smoke. The SGP is around a 15-minute walk away according to the other bus passenger. Typical of the all-expenses-spared parsimonious approach BSI take with its sub-contracted outlier events, the first fan experience 'touch-point' and only real concession to razzmatazz is a single laminated A4 sign with a SGP-branded background compliant with the colour palette and layout requirements of its corporate identity manual. Though this manual is kept permanently handy in the desk drawer of a slightly sweaty-bottomed middle-manager tasked with brand supervision back at BSI Towers in suburban London, out in the Swedish wilds on SGP manoeuvres its power remains undimmed. Hopefully there is sufficient mobile signal to enable all the power-trippy compliance checks required. Stuck to a lamppost and beneath an advice arrow point onwards, the only A4 laminated notice I find anywhere around the bus station states "Parking and Camping". Though brevity and honesty aren't words you associate with BSI, the SGP or its media boosters, this isn't an overly helpful sign for anyone not driving to the event but using public transport. Given its size, it isn't overly helpful for passing drivers either unless viewed as a sight exam or reactions test. There is no-one around to ask for directions. Except for two teenagers with a basketball walking ahead of me, everyone must either be indoors or already at the speedway. They suggest I follow them down one of the few roads off the main drag. The first impression given by the family homes, lines of parked cars, heat and deserted tree-lined road is of isolation and how it feels like an end destination, albeit a homely one. Everyone going to the SGP must already be there. Sensible really, given there is only about 20 minutes to go until the religiously rigorous regular scheduled start time of the first race at 19.04. Though the track is nowhere in sight, through the trees there is the comforting sound of amplified music. These distant wafts are occasionally broken up by announcements whose specific wording is lost into the ether at this distance. After so much (self-inflicted) hassle to get here, the standard pre-meeting sounds and music of a speedway night ahead reassures and soothes but also fires my anticipation.

The comfortable family houses, school, playground, sheds, garages and other dwellings that line this narrow countrified tree-lined residential road make it an unlikely suitable route to a regional Swedish speedway club stadium. Let alone what the ever-modest FIM race director Phil Morris grandiloquently styles on Twitter as the "biggest global speedway event the FIM Speedway Grand Prix". As the street climbs a gradient it quickly loses its roadside housing which dies back in favour of more trees. The darker shade of a thick tree canopy blocks out some of the bright evening sunshine too. But for the width and quality of the road surface or tightly parked cars and vans lining both sides, it feels more like a walk into the wilderness and woods rather than the way to a major international speedway meeting. The road narrows further to transition into a tree-lined pathway. Reassuringly, I can see other late-comer stragglers ahead. At the crest of the final section of sloping path, the stadium suddenly appears ahead displayed in its full glory. At first sight, possibly because it is seen from a tree-surrounded clearing, the impression is more of a holiday camp in the midst of minor celebration than the oft-proclaimed "world" championship. It is the first ever SGP to be staged in Hallstavik and a sign over the main entrance to the stadium proclaims this location as the "HZ BYGG ARENA" with the added swagger of a suitably large typeface. Predictably, as with many size claims, the club is at best compact rather than bygg. The word "HALLSTAVIK" appears underneath the location warning so we are left in no doubt about exactly where we all are right now. This is handy as, even for regular Rospiggarna league meetings, according to the Greg Hancock "Reel 45" podcast, "most people come from other places" and only 11 percent of attendees actually come from Hallstavik.

The local speedway club adapts to the "global" demands of the SGP big day by indulging in a frenzy of temporary fencing and crash barriers. These divide the site into specific fan-, staff- and rider-designated areas as well as guard the privileged while guiding fans round the stadium on the specially constructed one-night-only walkways. Though we lack armed uniformed guards or gun turrets, the psychological impact of all this paternal fencing gives a warm fuzzy safely secure feeling. That said, whoever decided to loosely gift wrap the stadium environs in temporary fencing has taken their understanding of the precautionary principle to ridiculous lengths. They definitely brought a smile to the faces of wherever they hired these fences and barriers from. Despite all the demarcation and security fencing, the combination of low-slung buildings, natural surfaces – grass, gravel, sand and outcrops of local stone – and warm evening sunshine gives things a friendly family-holiday feel. Even the comparative blizzard of what the photocopied laminated A4 signs claim is simultaneously the "RACE OFFICE" and "MEDIA ACCRED" centre is really an open-sided canvas roof on silver poles more suited to a garden with a small table, two chairs, and a bunch of boxes underneath. This "office" is supervised by friendly staff in colourful lanyards with their bikes – one mountain, one sit-up-and-beg – parked ready for a quick getaway either side of their temporary work station.

Once through the extremely light-touch security check at the entrance to access the spacious grassy, gravelly and steep rock outcrops of the Arena grounds, the skyline is dominated by the scaffolding of the temporary stand, various national flags of the competing riders and a yellow crane. Concession tents are scattered about but, this close to tapes up, only have small gaggles of committed drinkers or hungry punters. Behind close-mesh fence, dawdlers eat and drink at wooden tables very adjacent to some tightly packed portaloos. According to the official programme, there are 25 toilets on site. Tickets for the permanent and temporary seated areas of the stadium sold out almost the instant they went on sale. For a short while, it seemed that that would be that until additional "open standing" tickets for steep rocky slopes with good views then also became available. First mover advantage, bring your own comforts and local knowledge sees these free-standing areas transformed by fans into seated picnic areas. Perhaps, given how comfortable well-prepared everyone appears, this is the way local fans traditionally consume their Rospiggarna speedway action on a sunny night? The relaxed atmosphere definitely makes me want to come back for a league meeting and find out. Whatever vantage point fans' tickets authorise, we all get to overlook the track as it is laid out in the natural bowl below us. Deeply probing questions from Nigel Pearson in the official programme printed by Curtis Sport that he edits prompts reigning World Champion Jason Doyle to admit the Hallstavik track has a "nice shape". Its brown shale definitely looks a deep hue and contrasts to what remains of the parched grass on the centregreen where the only bright green colour is the artificial fluorescence of the Monster logo in its giant floor version. There is a smaller subset than usual of the regular SGP centregreen furniture of rostrum, proscenium arch and advert boxes. There is, of course, still the full set of various flags FIM rules obligatorily require on hand[1] in order to officially run a speedway meeting. To avoid cluttering up armchair views of the sponsors' centregreen adverts, though essential these flags have temporarily been shunted off onto a smaller grassy area that also serves as a small practice track (possibly for juniors or learners) when the SGP isn't in town.

In the absence of anyone else wishing to advertise, the unsold predominantly bright black-and-orange air fence panels bristle with SGP adverts in corporate identity compliant background and lettering. As ever, big brand sponsors or their logos are conspicuous by their total absence. Set overall against the background of the crowd, surrounding trees and bright blue sky, the colour of the air fences somehow catch the eye more than usual in this

[1] The flags required by the FIM include the country flag of each competitor, the referee and the FIM along with the flags used by the marshals – under the instruction of the referee – during the meeting including the chequered flag, yellow last lap flag plus the red and black flags.

compact stadium. It is the second proper regular speedway track used this season, so far. After the maintenance staff emerge from the pits gate ("please welcome the FIM Speedway Grand Prix marshals") a medley of pre-recorded rider interviews blast out over the stadium speakers. Either as a form of lite Guantanamo-inspired mental torture or to overcome early onset somnambulance amongst the noticeably high number of older people who appear to form the dominant age group of this particular SGP meeting audience. A man for whom coherent strings of words come hard to find in interview, Jason Doyle goes to his equivalent of a safe space with any crowd and waxes lyrical about the local track. "So many racing lines …it's a very good race track, it's special, it's a fast one!" To be fair to him, the number of SGP meetings when statements such as these could even be half-true is so small that even the most studiously optimistic professional rider can rarely honestly utter them, except in bad faith. The English language broadcast media have no qualms about hailing every track – no matter how ill fit for purpose – as wonderful. One of the joys of my SGP travel has been not having to listen to this relentless product promotional cheerleading as it masquerades as journalism or sincere honest opinion. Rather ambitiously, Tai tries to mix psychology with faux modesty under the mistaken impression that his fellow SGP riders actually listen to this piffle on his current state of mind, "I've the same aim as I had at the start of the season … just keep on progressing, progressing, progressing." Perhaps P isn't the best letter to select from the ready-drafted statements of ambition thesaurus but, at least, it does have potential if re-purposed as meditation chant. Next up on the mike but apparently forgetting that he is a tax exile in Andorra – to live there requires accommodation and a €50,000 bond in order to then only pay 2% tax on your earnings – and how much the football World Cup quarter-final defeat badly harshed the patriotic buzz, Freddie Lindgren addresses the crowd (in English) Swede-to-Swede, "It's my home crowd, Swedish crowd, hopefully they'll cheer me on a lot."

I have been very kindly gifted VIP tickets to go along with the free-standing ticket I bought. This is lucky as all late arrivals (like myself) to the packed standing areas would find little or no space as well as poor sight lines. It's another first-hand real life lesson that possession really is nine-tenths of the law. The VIP section is almost completely empty. It is hard to know if this is the unpopularity of this Speedway Grand Prix, the obscure event location or hard won previous experience. The VIP seats overlook the third and fourth bend as well as the elevated trackside temporary studio favoured by (nationality unknown but I'm guessing Polish) live broadcasters with big budget, ambition and the audience size to support the grandstanding expense of between-race expert colour comment made while sat closely around a table that overlooks the track. They are certainly positioned right on top the last bend track action as well as bathed in the glare of possibly much too bright sunshine to make for easy working conditions. When someone talks of VIP seats you imagine excellent views from the kind of plush padded wide seats you get nowadays in upscale cinemas. The HZ Bygg Arena takes a much more egalitarian approach to the notionally Very Important by providing a stepped gently raked grandstand of wooden planks albeit zhuzhed up by affixing formal "seat" numbers. Amazingly, in an almost empty grandstand, two of my prime back row four seats are already occupied by interlopers. Out of respect for my elders, I clutch the small plastic Swedish flag I have been issued with by the steward who checked my tickets to sit in passive aggressive silence next to them making no acknowledgement or mention of their infraction. Afterwards, I wonder if an administrative error by BSI – highly unusual, I know – has seen all the VIP tickets given the same seat numbers? Interrupting this ticketing conundrum, the riders take to the track for a proper – in comparatively understated fashion by SGP standards – old school introduction. Indeed, they actually ride their bikes round to the start line and park up for their introductions rather than indulge in the modern television friendly way of theatrically mounting a centregreen stage. Sight of the riders on the track is, apparently, the "unofficial" permission signal for fans currently viewing elsewhere within the stadium to suddenly swarm the deserted tiers of both VIP stands. Suddenly, it goes from spaciously empty to thronged in moments. My new closest companions are some weekend Hells Angels studiously kitted out in meticulously observed full regalia. All they lack is the threat of menace and greater self-control around food. The Swedish national anthem plays. Nowadays, these are apparently incredibly stirring and soothing sounds to Greg Hancock in his adopted country he tells Phil Lanning in the official programme. "It's really strange because the hairs on the back of my neck stand up when I hear the Swedish anthem."

Despite looking only pleasantly moist while enjoying the ongoing drying effects of the warm sunshine, for the first set of four heats the track defies pre-meeting praise to ride as if heavy, cloying and wet as an otter's pocket. Joe Parsons must have been too distracted by his traditional search for the best pits camera angles to issue Monster Energy team-riding orders as heat 1 sees third-placed Greg Hancock – who lives locally – cut up Chris Holder to overtake rather than escort him round the track. Ahead of them, Tai wins easily from the gate – in the fastest time of the night – while behind him the other riders jostle gamely without impact. Heat 2 looks much faster (but isn't) mainly due to the different high speed close to the fence wide outside race line ridden by Bartosz Zmarzlik. Piotr Pawlicki zooms from the tapes in heat 3 but locks up so often he gradually relegates himself down the field and somehow manages to snatch plum last in the race to the finish line. Heat 4 sees Craig Cook battle his bike, track and confidence at the back of the race to come last.

No sooner has chequered flag stopped waving than two of the Monster Energy start women sprint to the pits with an altogether less comely gait than seen during their parades prior to each race. Another ungainly runner – when racing to supervise emergency track repairs or sprinting past steel shoe shod SGP riders – FIM Track Director Phil Morris passes them going at military medium pace in the other direction. It only takes the blink of an eye before Phil resumes his traditional management role of sternly shouting instructions at the bend three and four track rakers. Phil's notoriously tough-love management style looks too harsh for the curatorial tasks at hand and is the type of retro staff motivation so often absent from the contemporary workplace. Pretending afterwards it was all a pose to get the job done and we are all still mates almost probably makes this treatment feel much worse. Judged by the tracks served up this season to date in the SGP (and also in the 2017 series), there is probably a good case that either of the Monster Energy women could job swap with Phil and, thereby, ensure end up with much better track preparation results on race day. Staff motivation would definitely improve. Sadly, much as he likes to pose for the cameras or performatively work, Phil would be an altogether less popular or effective as a start person substitute.

Next to me are Per-Arne Bernhardsson and his wife. They are here as guests of the highly regarded engine tuner Jan Andersson. With the differences between success and failure getting ever tighter, collectively riders lavish considerable sums on getting their bike engines tuned into a state of (alleged) perfection. The time taken between tune ups has shrunk so ridiculously that engines are only seen slightly more often at the track than the tuners. The ongoing engine-tuning arms race between riders continues to push up the cost of each service as well as lead to demands for exclusivity. As prices and praise have grown so has the status, gravitas and pretentiousness of some tuners. It is an immutable law of speedway life that often riders expend more mental effort and anxiety on the complex travel arrangements for their engines than they do on their own race strategies. The timely to and fro of their finely tuned engines is one of the major considerations for success on the track in Poland and, as a result, the SGP free rides on these rider engine-tuning investments. Like the mystery that surrounds the secret ingredients behind the success of Coca-Cola, tuners especially – but also riders – jealously guard their engine-tuning methodologies, recipes and formulas as well as the current status of their engines in the tuning cycle. One day in the future, only logistics, time and expense will prevent engine tuning between races. While the fashion for frequent engine tunes and its mystique continues, wealthier or more ambitious riders in search of glory often only consider using newly serviced and tuned engines in all the truly lucrative meetings they race.

Ex-Reading Racer Jan Andersson's engine tuning career had humble beginnings. "Jan started tuning for Per [Jonsson]. Now he works from eight to eight seven days a week with his engines. He is still doing them for Nicki, Hancock, Doyle, Emil and Dudek." Rider obsessiveness – when the chance to earn big bucks is involved (aka in Poland) – applies to many areas of their work and preparations. Weight is one of those key issues, whether of the bike or the rider. It is said some riders in Poland discard the safety of lightweight body armour and, instead, favour the scantier, less reliable protection offered by the modern airfence in event of a crash. The extreme focus upon exercise and nutrition is increasingly an epidemic for all riders at any level of speedway, whether they are beginners or riding in the SGPs. Ignoring they no longer interact socially with fans, a free post-meeting pint would immediately get refused on the basis of its empty calories alone. In horse racing, the importance of the weight-loading aspect of power-weight ratios has long seen diet and calorie control the order of the day for jockeys. This is increasingly the case for speedway riders too. "What about Kolodziej wrapped in plastic sat in his car with the heater on before meetings?" ponders Per-Arne.

Critical observers of Tai Woffinden highlight that his success is built upon a small but sensible repertoire of "professional" race strategies rather than the riskier, more intuitive old-school speedway technique of all-out chasing down the back wheel of the rider ahead in order to try to find the speed to pass. With significant financial incentives for in-demand riders to remain injury free – beyond the common-sense self-preservation need to do so – playing the percentages is good for both safety and earnings throughout the season. Beyond his talent, skill and technique on the bike, Tai's main drivers of success are – to channel my inner live speedway commentator alter ego and state the obvious – riding faster bikes than his rivals; gating and going; passing under strict racing conditions approved by Monster Joe Parsons (aka when given the width or "racing room"); lingering behind in apparent defeat in order to spring a surprise fast pass on the race to the line as well as – most important of all – his signature first bend cutback. Though eminently predictable, Tai does this with aplomb time and time again. Heat 5 is a case in point. Third on the first bend, out wide Tai bides his time – he almost idles for a fraction of a second as he waits for a gap to appear – then cuts back through the field on bend two into first. Woffinden goes on to win by half the length of the straight to almost no reaction – audible or otherwise – from the crowd. "Hallstavik make some noise!" implores the meeting presenter over the stadium speaker system. Though they are both in denial, time waits for no man and the future calls in heat 6 when Nicki Pedersen and Greg Hancock race intensely for the chip-shop money of third place rather than the triumph and glory of first to the chequered flag that they still both see as their rightful natural position.

For the first two laps of heat 7, Craig Cook gets the competitive bit sufficiently between his teeth to threaten Holder for third-place before he falls back like a Duracell bunny whose battery suddenly badly faded. Zagar also fades on the run in to the chequered flag to nearly lose the win to wild card Andreas Jonsson. Though he no longer competes regularly in the SGP series, Jonsson was the last Swede to taste any success in the SGP (he finished second in 2011). He still rides regularly so has the guile, track craft and shale smarts to succeed at the

SGP level. What was noticeable on parade and now during his races is how much "bigger" Jonsson appears than his mostly younger and rigorously calorie-controlled rivals. It is as if Andreas – without really changing from his fighting weight of five or so years back – has been somehow super-sized in the interim compared to his younger studiously sylph-like rivals. This could partly be a psychological and visual effect of Jonsson's dour bike livery and kevlar colours but there is definitely something more lumbering and less fluid about him. The shapes Jonsson cuts still please the eye and drive the bike with elegance but, compared to the next generation of riders competing here, there is still something noticeably heavier and yesteryear on display. Time catches up with all speedway riders in its own ways. It could be argued that despite his comparative youth Chris Holder's trademark exaggerated throttle twists and thrusty broadsides are, unless he gates, more for show than effect nowadays. Over the last two seasons his oft-mentioned but never properly specified UK visa and child-access problems have relegated Holder into the category of a more-often-than-not-off-the-pace-rather-than-on-it rider. Though publicly exponentially more likeable in his laid-back surfer dude pomp than contemporary fellow Australian riders such as Troy Batchelor or Darcy Ward, Holder's SGP career is unlikely to enjoy a renaissance any time soon. Heat 8 sees the briefest hint of wind tunnel physics inspired entertainment when Maciej Janowski slipstreams the fast wide-line riding Zmarzlik before he catapults past him for the race win.

By SGP standards, though this latest series of four races has been comparatively "thrilling" as it featured a vague hint of racing drama, the real winner continues to be the track rather than the riders, fans or viewers. Heavier cloying conditions badly interfere with the smooth functioning of contemporary highly-strung high-powered highly-tuned temperamental speedway bikes. The riders have fought a tough track and, so far, the track has won. If this were boxing, the referee would stop the fight. Within seconds of the latest interval starting, the man in charge of this victorious track – FIM Race Director Phil Morris goes out to perform in front of his indifferent public backed by a 70s and 80s rock-cum-lite-metal soundtrack blaring out over the stadium speakers. As usual, Morris delivers elaborate overwrought choreography of instructions, mime gestures, strong imprecations and complex unintelligible signals to uninterested track staff. This interval, Morris appears to be angrily drowning a litter of unwanted kittens. It is all part of a series-long display that sees Morris manage to simultaneously take complete responsibility for another sub-optimal racing surface while ostentatiously evading and denying it. All season, the ongoing futility of all his actions and attempts at always-much-too-late marginal-if-any improvement to the prevailing sub-standard track conditions is there for all to see. Though they regularly stage top level Swedish league speedway meetings here, SGP track preparation requirements appear to have contractually killed its normal zest in favour of rendering it heavy but tame. After a brief flurry of gestures, even Morris can hardly rouse himself into his standard frenzy of ineffectual intervention. Instead, he picks up random big lumps of bend four shale to closely inspect as if it's an archaeological find only to immediately throw it back to the floor as worthless in the disgusted manner of a sommelier who repeatedly serves swigs of corked wine. As he walks at much faster than his usual military medium back to the pits, Morris thoroughly wipes his soiled hands with the concentrated conscientiousness of a vet moodily scrubbing up ahead of a routine operation on a vicious dog.

Heat 9 sees Tai idle in traffic on the first bend before he executes yet another of his trademark sharp cutbacks to – this time – gain second place as the riders exit bend 2. Woffinden does this move so often it is a wonder that his relentless financial hunger hasn't seen him try to register some sort of SGP copyright? If the definition of a fool is someone who does the same thing again and again but expects different results, then Tai's rivals collectively have its distant cousin equivalent since they are endlessly caught out and repeatedly bamboozled by this entirely predictable manoeuvre. Possibly, it proves that in the speedway kingdom of the unintuitive or blind, the one-tactic rider is World Champion? After the race, it is announced that the referee has issued a warning to Woffinden for moving at the tapes. The strengthening breeze and tannoy requests ("Hallstavik make some noise") begin to stand out more than the racing. Though most races are still to happen, the meeting has settled down into a bland mush of processional wins that are hard to recall or distinguish apart beyond widespread ongoing struggles with the cloying shale of the track. Dudek excels in this respect as he flamboyantly fights with the track surface as well as a particularly recalcitrant bike. Though recovered from his latest serious injury gained last season, Nicki often appears to be on the back foot in the battle of wills with his own psychological demons rather than being defeated by his rival riders. On these nights, his decision to return to race speedway – let alone the SGP – looks questionable and is sad to see. Heat 12 is a case in point. Nicki appears to ride the wrong racing line. Worse still, he fails to do so either quickly or effectively. Other riders sail past. Or, in the case of the bulkier looking Andreas Jonsson, easily boss him aside by dint of his choice of a superior racing trajectory rather than the audacity of chunkier kevlars. In forlorn races such as these, it is nowadays obligatory for fourth-placed Nicki to performatively signal that he rides defective equipment with various exaggerated throttle twists and pantomime unloving downward stares at his engine. It is invariably a gestural prelude to a retirement or else a slow ostensibly under-powered last lap to eventually crawl past the chequered flag half a lap or so behind the third-placed rider. Looking on impassively, *sotto voce* Per-Arne notes, "Jan says all the riders are fine with their engines but Nicki always says they are shit. If it's not the engine, then it's the track, the other riders, the bike, the ref or the rules, never Nicki!"

Apparently mesmerised by the use of two-minute countdown clock on the centregreen, and though we can all see and read it for ourselves, like a child who has just learnt to count bigger numbers, before each and every race the stadium announcer tries to instil a sense of urgency and drama by chanting, "one minute left of the two-minute time allowance". Though illustrating that what gets measured gets too often spoken about, it is a warning no spectator or rider really needs heed as – series to date – there have been no exclusions for exceeding the time allowance! We do, of course, have an "Official Watch & Timing Partner of the FIM Speedway World Championships" but – inevitably – they get no mention though to do so ("brought to you by Aztorin") would have vague "organic" justification. Though by its nature, exceeding the two-minute time allowance is one of the more forgettable rule infractions, though it is very hard to recall any such exclusions in the SGP we and Aztorin – whose products apparently have "attitude inside" – live in hope of such excitement. It would definitely be more thrilling than their handsome "Milk Tray" man wannabe catches a delayed helicopter from a remote formula 4 race track SGP big-screen commercial. Heat 13 sees Woffinden so busy bossing Dudek about (relegating him to fourth) that he inadvertently allows his current main title rival Freddie Lindgren to escape for the win. The last Swedish SGP world champion was Tony Rickardsson in 2005. Talked up in leaden fashion by the trade press and bored interviewers for the last decade or so, there are still apparently high hopes that Freddie might be the next one. The programme doesn't go into all the specifics but since Freddie broke his vertebrae in three places in Manchester in September 2017, "Lindgren has gone to great lengths to find his happy place." Though Sayfutdinov races to victory in heat 14, behind him Hancock conducts a masterclass in diligently riding a slow blocking lines to kill the speed of his pursuers to secure his second place. The Slowway World Championships has less of a ring to it than the Speed version. Heat 15 serves another battle between the 2018 series wild cards so sees us (again) witness the further gradual sad decline of both Chris Holder and Nicki Pedersen from their previous exalted levels of grace, power and greatness on their bikes. In their micro-battle for a distant second, Holder is all theatrical throttle hand and slow locks on the bend exits to further delay and try to hold Nicki back in third place. To add insult to injury, the referee issues Pedersen with a post-race warning for moving at the start. Heat 16 has the dubious excitement of head-to-head clash between the two remaining scoreless riders of the night, Messrs Cook and Pawlicki. Belying his duck, Craig looks really competitive for a couple of laps before he is jostled aside by Laguta and is, thereby, badly thrown off his metaphorical stride. Nonetheless, in the battle of the zero-point riders, Cook still holds off the close attentions of Pawlicki for the healing balm of a solitary third place point.

The interval is notable for the sight of FIM Jury President Tony Steele out on the track at the start line as another wannabe archaeologist inspecting the cloying shale for long-buried treasures unknown. After some fruitless sifting of the claggy surface matter, Steele picks his way through the slalom of temporary fences that protectively wall off VIPs and officials from the rough attentions of the hoi polloi. Away from the SGP cossetting of VIPs – mainly officials, media, key sponsors and assorted hangers-on – Tony and FIM Jury Secretary Mick Posselwhite spent £842 on two tickets to fly on the same British Airways flight as (the better seated) Jason Doyle after their original SAS flight home was cancelled. "We have a really good travel agent who got us the last two seats. They like us as we pay straightaway and don't cancel our plans. They are a corporate travel agent and do clients like Fred Perry." The closest most people get to either Jason Doyle or Fred Perry (deceased) is seeing other people in shopping malls wearing their branded clothing. Actually, catching sight of Jason Doyle "69" clothing in the wild away from speedway is something of a rare event akin to winning the lottery. Strangely, even at speedway GPs where he is reigning World Champion, Doyle's 69 brand identity number is much less popular among the child face-painters than many of the "signature" number brands of many lesser riders. Quite how the riders choose their universal but specific SGP numbers is often something of a mystery. Or else so pathologically mind-numbingly dull that many fans would rather get intimate body art from the work-experience tattooist than have to learn their creation myth stories yet again in the pages of the *Speedway Star* or Nigel Pearson Media staff programme notes. The very fact that riders have or chose these number designations (for example, who springs to your mind as number 54?) is both part of the end-of-days madness of rider power but also massively delusional since such affectations have zero mind share amongst the speedway fraternity, let alone wider real world. Perhaps the corollary of the confidence required to be a speedway rider requires equivalent delusional belief that these random numbers will somehow magically sear themselves indelibly on the impressionable minds of prospective sponsors, the public and media in way that then magically generates additional sponsorship monies? Amazingly, BSI even have complex hard-to-explain rules about how these SGP numbers can be recycled and subsequently inherited after riders cease to be part of the series. In rough terms, after a rider absence from the SGP series of two years, the existing number can then get used by other less imaginative riders. Given the number choices currently theoretically range between 1 to 999 quite why there would be a clamour to use 55, 108, 69 or 89 defeats all observers except numerologists and astrologers.

News that the 50/50 draw has been won by "green series ticket number 549" – the first such quaint announcement of the 2018 SGP series – obliquely underlines that we are watching racing at a proper speedway club track rather than one of the ersatz temporary varieties! Better still, "the winner can collect in the clubhouse – the yellow building on bend three". Further confirming their actual real speedway club credentials, when the tapes break with only one minute remaining on the stop clock before heat 17, the start marshals swiftly replace them with the spare set already on hand with practised expertise, skill and speedy efficiency. Craig Cook then gates and leads for nearly three laps until Tai eases under him for a win in the slowest time of the night. An out-of-sorts Pedersen retires disconsolately without finishing having only scored three points in total all night. With the first corner bathed in bright late evening sunshine – possibly blinding the riders as they exit the second bend – Per-Arne peers at second-placed Andreas Jonsson through spectacles missing their right-arm stem as if judging a Mr World competition and pronounces him, "too heavy for this". Though seemingly little different to when he was in his pomp, compared to most of his nutritionally pimped but starved gym-bodied contemporaries, Jonsson looks more and more over-sized for a speedway rider as the meeting progresses. Emil's control of heat 19 is so easy, he can indulge us with a rare hint of thrills by riding a fast exciting wide line for the last lap of the race. Per-Arne worries for the future, "Everyone talks about these [SGP] riders as if they are the best but young, gifted and fast riders don't get a look in as they can't afford to fix the engines or hire the tuners. Engines need fixing after three goes! The fans are working people not lawyers, they think all is good seeing what they see but there is no feeder route to the Speedway Grand Prix." Jason Doyle bullies Dudek on the opening lap of heat 20. The diminutive Pole fights back into contention only to receive yet harsher treatment from the current reigning World Champion Aussie. By the final laps, last-placed Dudek is content to pull a series of straight-length wheelies. Doyle often employs an effective roughhouse racing style. It is widely critiqued as deliberately much too aggressive when practised by Nicki Pedersen – especially by Monster Joe Parsons and Darcy Ward – but endured without cavil by fellow SGP riders. It was often hailed by the speedway media commentariat as commendably competitive and robust whenever (often) ridden by Doyle during his world-champ-in-waiting media-darling phase these last two seasons. With Doyle badly off the pace this season, suddenly it looks more calculatingly brutal and violent. Nonetheless, Doyle continues gets no negative public feedback on or off the track. At the death, Janowski snatches first with a hard ride that also brooks no dissent.

Arguably the race of the night comes in the re-run second semi-final. First time out, Emil Sayfutdinov gets in a tangle with his compatriot Artem Laguta on the home straight when they race hard for third. Sayfutdinov is granted an unexpected reprieve when the ref excludes Laguta. It is hard luck on Janowski and Zmarzlik who have to race again having just been on the cusp of qualification for the final. Next time out Bartosz Zmarzlik executes a brilliant last corner overtake when he nudges Sayfutdinov aside at high speed. Stirred by some exciting racing, while we wait for the final Per-Arne worries about the combined impact of SGP ambitions and rider power on domestic Swedish speedway. "Do you know Tommy Rander? He likes to fight the high people. In the past, he fixed the team and monies but riders wages went up and up – and they spent it on things like tuning – and now, in a big city like Gothenburg, we have no team to watch." The notional fairy tale for the local media of a Swedish winner of the first Hallstavik FIM Speedway Grand Prix of Sweden fails to materialise when the fast-riding Janowski beats Lindgren. Though Woffinden runs a last in the final, he extends his overall cumulative championship lead by a further point from his nearest rival (Lindgren). With six events in the series left to go – there would have been seven if BSI's Australian contractual terms hadn't made the meeting due to be staged there so commercially unsuccessful – it already looks like Woffinden's title to lose.

There are no end-of-meeting fireworks to mark this Polish triumph. Whether this is for further BSI cost-cutting reasons or neighbourhood noise regulations – unlikely in a forest in a very small town proud of its new-found international speedway credentials – is unclear. The smattering of fans here from Poland celebrate in very good voice without them. Most other fans make a quick initially easy exit from the stadium knowing that, like Colditz, there is only one way in or one way out of these Hallstavik woods. Sadly, that narrow road is already clogged by an assortment of nose-to-tail barely mobile vehicles. The car park is similarly grid-locked and slow-moving. In the Travel Plus Tours midi-bus back to Stockholm, while becalmed we are graced with the speedway celebrity presence of Bengt Jansson. In the Sarf London accents that suddenly spring to audible life on the bus, Bengt is hailed as an "ex-'ackney 'awk" when – to me – he is always only an ex-Reading Racer. Tonight he has Bert Harkins in tow. Both are affable and cheery. Bengt seems the more tired and emotional of the two. But, equally, maybe this is just speedway pensioner modesty when it suddenly encounters adulation. Bengt and Bert wave, exchange a few affable words with those seated in the forward rows of our mini-bus and are gone to destinations or SGP after-parties unknown. We most definitely aren't going anywhere until fraternal handshakes see our driver suddenly discover the whereabouts of a secret second tree-lined escape route.

At this time of the year in Sweden, it stays lighter later. The dusk half-light refracts and takes on the colour palette of its surroundings. Further north, the rocks give a yellowy hue. Hereabouts, as our mini-bus wends its way back to Stockholm, the woodland and lush green fields in this part of the Swedish countryside graces the world outside our moving windows with an hour or so with a beautiful dark-hued, green bluey tinged dusk light. This deep glorious green-tinged light casts a hypnotic spell in a dark monochrome subset of technicolour. It envelopes all who gaze upon it from the passing windows of Travel Plus Tours mini-bus in its trippy wonder. Marie Kondo asks of our possessions: "Does it bring joy?' Well, while the Hallstavik SGP didn't deliver joy, the fading light of journey back does that and much more. Tour guide Claire Dunn briefly takes to the microphone with a loud rhetorical question, "Do we think Nicki should retire gracefully?" that has a half-life that lingers in the half-light. If we take the lessons of his poetry and lifestyle, Dylan Thomas already trod this path with a resounding NO! Nicki should defiantly continue to rage, rage against the dying light. The transition from youth to senior, light to dark has many wonders if only we remain alert enough and alive enough to see them. Though his speedway racing retirement is definitely nowadays in sight nowadays for Nicki, his decision to return after further serious injury – when other saner voices counselled otherwise – further reveals his indomitable spirit but also guarantees more colourful speedway times ahead for us all before his career is finally done. What a time to be alive to see and savour these end-of-era meetings and races. Though tonight disappointed, the unique warm green glow of this seasonal Swedish dusk already haloes these memories ahead of their later transformation into nostalgia. Perhaps, when all is said and done, long after this version of the World Championships inevitably collapses under the weight of the flaws of its contractual rights ownership, current format and execution, dull processional SGP nights like these will only be remembered as if bathed in their own soft-focus magical but imaginary green twilight.

> **Winner:** Maciej Janowski (18 points)
>
> **Second:** Fredrik Lindgren (15 points)
>
> **Third:** Bartosz Zmarzlik (13 points)
>
> **Fourth:** Tai Woffinden (16 points)

CHAPTER 5

Cardiff SGP 5 – 21.07.18

"You should aim at helping your own guys. You don't cut your neighbour's lawn before you do your own."

Peter Ljung

ONE of the current biggest sponsors of UK speedway in terms of pounds per season spent are Clean Filtration Solutions. They currently sponsor Dan Bewley, Craig Cook, Swindon speedway and the British under-21 speedway team amongst others. The people behind CFS ("Peter Johns is a customer") are husband and wife team Derek and Val Baker. They also sponsor riders in other motorcycle disciplines including moto-cross. Outside the Principality Stadium Cardiff, they are accompanied by the tall, tanned Fred who they travel with to MX and also sponsor. He has had more broken bones than it is easy to quickly name unless you are studying as a medic. It is par for the course, apparently. They arrive at the riders' and guest entrance outside the Welsh city centre venue where the British Speedway Grand Prix is again staged this evening. There they are met by a key member of Craig Cook's off-track team, Ian Corcoran. They chat amiably, get their access-all-areas accreditation (wristband, badge and SGP lanyard) before he guides them through the intense scrutiny of the heightened security checks required in response to the state of modern UK and international politics to access the stadium.

Derek and Val were Poole Pirates sponsors until what they felt and sounds like some shoddy treatment and reaction by Matt Ford that abruptly ended their association. Almost straightaway after they took the opportunity to sponsor ("we leapt at the chance") what has comparatively proved to be the much more professional and welcoming Swindon Robins speedway club. This was a particular disappointment for Val who is, actually, in real life a Pirates fan of 40 years' standing. Derek is equally knowledgeable, well-researched and enthusiastic about all things speedway though he has currently only served 14 years as a fan. Remission for good behaviour in the form of their sponsorships has given them many unrivalled insights into the sport, its politics and current exalted status. When they were associated with the Pirates, they got to sponsor Craig Cook on a one-off basis at the Gary Havelock testimonial meeting at the beginning of the 2014 season. After a slow start to their first centregreen face-to-face meeting, their collective shared interest in moto-cross broke the conversational dam and they have not looked back since. Sponsors since 2014, they follow Craig's progress and results closely. Having a rider they back, trust and think so highly of competing in the SGP indicates their good judgement of speedway flesh when it comes to rider sponsorship. Derek and Val set huge store by the traditional values parents look for in prospective marriage partners for their children – sincerity, character, manners, courtesy and honesty. They value these traits as much as or more than actual or latent talent. Val tells me that she great store by manners and approach when it comes to deciding who to sponsor. Polite approachability are as essential as is the desire to progress and get better. At one point, they tried to sponsor Tai Woffinden. Sadly, their initial email fell on deaf ears until eight days later when a woman – they took to be his mum Sue rather than his wife

Faye – from "Tai Woffinden's office" rang to say, "You know it starts at £5,000?" Derek's reply, "Why are you telling us that?" likely prompted the follow-up DVD in the mail notable for the Post-it slip on it warning against copyright infringement as doing so may spur possible legal action. Val wrote back stating that there was no danger of copyright infringement since it had gone straight in the bin without being watched. Given the close-knit nature of the sport, companies offering rider or team sponsorship are going to get noticed by others in the community. "Other riders have approached us – Scott Nicholls, for example – but we are looking to sponsor the up and coming, the younger ones not the older ones."

By some accounts, Tai Woffinden is not a team player. This is completely understandable when you have his currently marketable talents but, equally, there have been talented individual riders before who have managed to either be or pretend to be genuinely supportive of other lesser riders. Worse still for Tai there are strong rumours that last season – when he was on no speaks with Alun Rossiter nor riding for team GB (ostensibly over a dispute of Rosco's choice of dining for the team) – he approached Australia team manager Mark Lemon to explore riding for the country he grew up in and also has the greater lifestyle affinity with, if compared – for example – to that enjoyed in and around his birthplace of Scunthorpe. Lemon reputedly rebuffed the idea with the memorable quote, "You'd be hated in two countries then!" It is certainly true that Tai inspires strong feelings for or against. People are rarely indifferent. Fans can make the argument both ways. Refusing to ride for your country for whatever (real or publicly stated) is rarely a good look. Whether it is better than putting up for sale some of the Team GB (or whatever they were called back then) paraphernalia and gear you wore racing for your birth country on eBay is also open to debate. While on furlough, after kebabgate (which never really stuck as a pithy descriptor of the Rosco-Woffy nutritional spat or its real reason), Tai showcased his commercial acumen and ambition as well as his unique future vision of speedway in the UK – if you listen to his advocates and freelance media boosters – by offering to buy the rights to Team GB from the BSPA. Whether this was just the tonic the sport in Britain requires or a hopeless ego-driven misjudgement didn't formally get to be tested in the marketplace since Tai never submitted a proposal so saving the BSPA the trouble of turning down the offer. Having only watched since the mid-1970s, and despite speedway being best experienced/watched as a team sport, I would question if there is sufficient fan interest or patriotism to make this commercial venture a long-term success compared to, say, the SGP. Even at BSI, team speedway in the form of the World Cup or the now revamped Pairs ungainly re-christened as the "Speedway of Nations" are the runaway poor relations.

Anyways, since then the BSPA have had a change of heart about the privatisation of the British national team and this season subsequently decided to license the rights to Revolution Speedway run by Rob Painter and Vicky Blackwell of VRX Motorsport. The new Great Britain Speedway Team organisation have an extensive staff roster featuring an innovative and unexpected new job title within the speedway world – Data Analyst. This position has fallen to well-regarded and knowledgeable sports journalist David Rowe. The role is widely understood as someone to explain the FIM rules to team manager Rosco, tell him when to make rider changes or play the tactical joker as well as fill in his programme. According to naysayers, Rosco has previously struggled to fully master these aspects of his position. Painter, Blackwell, Rowe and Rossiter aren't yet quite in sync, if judged by the decision to publicly sack Craig Cook from the Pairs – aka the Speedway of Nations – in favour of Robert Lambert by text message. Having done so, Rosco was only to then discover that the minimal but very confusing rules there are actually didn't allow such a move, even if sent by text. Little data analysis is required to see this as arguably one of the most demotivational decisions ever by any national team manager in any UK sport. Though subsequently rescinded, it could be argued that in reality from that point onwards Rosco had initiated the slow process to sack himself. Trying to recover from a self-inflicted own goal, team co-owner Rob Painter drove to Cumbria to apologise face-to-face (after Rosco had pleaded bleatingly – some said cried – on the phone for forgiveness) to restore Craig Cook to the team and also "explain" the decision. The style and management tone for the newly independent commercially run national British speedway team had been seen to fall badly short of its proclaimed ambitions at the first (self-inflicted) hurdle. Subsequent actions rather than sweet words – aka only giving Craig the first race and then using Robert Lambert in his place throughout the rest of the two-day event – was also viewed by some as very revealing of the organisational ethos. Though finishing runners up allowed this further mis-step to be swept under the carpet in the faux euphoria, or else claimed to be a justifiable pragmatic decision, the smell of stinking fish still lingers. It is all a far cry from the initial trade press (*Speedway Star*) news coverage when the newly appointed Commercial Director's well-connected granddad wrote a double-page exclusive about the privatisation of the national team by a comparatively unknown company that he chose to hail as something akin to the resurrection of Christ, albeit from the ashes of the dreams previously frustrated either on the track or inside the BSPA boardroom in Rugby. Unable to ever quite leave behind his tax inspection roots, Derek Baker's scepticism has led him to look into Rob Painter's directorships publicly listed at Companies House. Unlike many speedway promotions whose choice of company name (or frequency of company name change) defies most rubbernecking by wannabe researchers, apparently Rob is much more transparent about his companies and company directorships. Though he hopes otherwise for the good of the sport in this country and its riders, Derek has reservations, "I am not sure that they will have a long-term future." He is also mystified but quizzical about public rather than Companies House claims about how much that the organisation has spent: "It can't be £350,000 already?"

Inside the bowels of the stadium that serves on race day as pits lane for the British SGP, there are very few mechanics and no riders. Some riders' bays are still just forlorn shells without any signage other than that of the place holders that designate the space as belonging to individual but absent riders. It seems strange to attend the mandatory practice (that is, in fact, discretionary) the afternoon before but then not to at least begin to set up your pits booth at that point? Such is the speedway mindset in some quarters. That said, it is not yet 10.45 so many riders remain back at their hotels or other accommodations calorie counting, going through their sports psychology exercises, resting or, if old school, having wild unprotected sex with groupies. Aside from the mostly volunteer ground staff, stadium security and sponsor staff, the only regular SGP professionals here are the Monster Energy start women. They are already in full regalia for the day and evening ahead being objectified. Long-time member of the Cardiff track curatorial team, Graham Cooke, rushes by with a colleague on a mercy mission. "Sorry can't stop, we have to go and get some lime!"

"For vodka or soda water?"

"No for the track! No one thought to bring any! It's used to mark out the gates and the start line."

And to think people have the bare-faced temerity to dare to unfairly criticise organisers and rights holders BSI for basic event-staging errors without knowing that there is always budget available for last-minute vital contingencies. Even in 2018, it is permissible for staff to use their initiative to buy essential items from the nearest B&Q superstore (if stocked) to ensure SGP events go ahead superlatively. If only naysayers deigned to acknowledge this empowerment and continuous programme of improvement through additional investment, these few vocal critics would surely hang their collective heads in shame. Shortly afterwards, I bump into the wife of the King's Lynn start marshal as she waits by one of the central city car parks for her husband to return. Having worked at a couple of Cardiff SGPs previously, he isn't at all shocked to discover that the curatorial team had had to go out on an emergency run for lime but was adamant that they had chosen the wrong solution. "They need spray cans not lime to make the start. You keep it behind the Monster Energy logo in a box on the centregreen so, like the flags, it doesn't spoil the pictures by lying around in shot." Like all voluntary unpaid positions at the SGP, competition to do the job for nothing as well as experience the event first hand from a unique vantage point is intense. Recent years has seen the British SGP start marshals drawn from King's Lynn, Mildenhall and Leicester speedway clubs. "One year you shadow and then you do the next. I did last year and have been advising the Mildenhall start marshal this. When you're out there you think 45,000 fans are looking at you but they're looking at the riders. They only look at you if you make a mistake!" He is in awe of the bespoke start equipment used at SGPs, "The starting gate is a beast. Ole Olsen made it! Well, a friend of his. It has wireless activation and everything." Sadly said starting gate is most remembered by fans for its catastrophic failure at the inaugural Warsaw SGP a couple of years back. This saw a number of adverse and farcical starts before the estimated 50,000 crowd got to see most races started by green light starts. Not exactly a science or scrupulously fair but, then, quality and integrity are not always leading performance indicators within speedway circles. Ian Corcoran recalls that night vividly, "You remember Warsaw? Ole Olsen has an instruction manual for everything – it's very specific, detailed and exacting – including the start gate. They were supposed to have two but didn't. But what they hadn't predicted was that it worked okay when the stadium was empty but, the power demand when it was full, meant they didn't have enough power trackside for it to work properly." As often before, BSI apologised profusely but offered zero compensation as well as made various empty promises. In this instance, to always have two start gates on hand at every future SGP to ensure it never happens again. Obviously, they subsequently forgot about said promise almost straightaway after the initial furore subsided. Though my position and distance away means I sometimes might be mistaken, despite lessons allegedly fully learnt, most 2018 Speedway Grand Prix events bravely re-tempted fate by having only a single set of start gates to use.

Back out in the heat of the main drag outside the stadium, the official and unofficial merchandise stalls compete for impulse purchases from passers-by. Stand-out item on social media is the official British SGP cap movingly made with the wrong date for the meeting. The cap claims it is to be held next week and, weirder still, these commemorative caps want to innovate with a Friday staging (27.07.18) rather than the more traditional Saturday. This is the relentless all-encompassing focus on excellence and attention to organisational and merchandising detail by rights holders BSI at their showpiece event that so many cherish. Sadly, I don't manage to get my hands on th is once-in-a-lifetime collector's item. I don't buy any SGP-branded merch or anything from Tai Woffinden's popular stall next door with its range of 108 logoed products. There is a much more tempting range of vintage, retro and contemporary speedway goodies for sale at the nearby Collector's Fayre held annually at Cardiff Rugby Club in a room overlooking the adjacent Arms Park. It is less crowded with both punters and stalls (four) than yesteryear so is cooler and easier to browse. Amazingly petty-mindedly, given their inattention to detail elsewhere, someone connected to the SGP itself deliberately stood for most of the morning and stopped would-be Fayre attendees (entrance fee £1) to try to redirect them to the Fan Zone a considerable walk elsewhere in the city by listing its many "free" notional attractions. Typically, Nick Barber – until recently

Mayor of Felixstowe – remains sanguine, "I've been here 13 or 14 years now. The SGP don't like this Fayre, they never have! If I was them I'd pay the rugby club a thousand pounds not to rent out this hall to me but they don't cos they're too tight. It costs me to hire and to pay for it. I have four stalls and the entrance money. It is not what it was. For example, no one – including you – does books any more. Tony McDonald does DVDs. People think they're getting racing from the 50s, 60s and 70s but they're disappointed when they find that they're only getting interviews. He doesn't come any more since he told me that he wouldn't pay to come but would advertise his attendance on his website for free. That was an offer I could turn down! Maybe this will be the last year I do it? I don't know. Speedway isn't on the up. If they want anything, it's the GPs what everyone wants nowadays. Though even that isn't certain." The Fan Zone also isn't the must-see pre-meeting magic bullet BSI, Monster Energy and their social media boosters claim. Long time (Redcar) speedway fans, Keith and Mandy Mason are disappointed: "It was too hot and not that full as most of the events are on too early."

The Millennium – nowadays Principality – Stadium in Cardiff city centre is the key strand in the origin myth of the brilliance of John Postlethwaite's leadership and vision for the Speedway Grand Prix. At least it is according to *Speedway Star* Managing Editor Philip Rising. He used to work at the SGP as FIM assistant race director and his company Pinegen – who publish the *Star* – for some years had the lucrative gig to produce various of the SGP programmes. The SGP was and continues to be their biggest advertiser – BSI take a full-page advert weekly. So, whatever way you spin it, he is hardly an impartial observer. Nonetheless, Rising hails the BSI initiative to stage events in big city stadia (some with retractable roofs) on one-off temporary tracks – apparently forgetting that this was first down in the ballroom of the Blackpool Tower in 1957 – as a "miracle", "extraordinary" and something that "made the impossible possible". I don't know about you but I would hail a visitor from the future or a cure for dementia as a miracle but see the logistical challenge of building a small track inside a stadium you have hired as something of a slightly lesser order of magnitude. Then this claim is emblematic of the acres of uncritical coverage and endless hyperbole his supposedly editorially independent trade magazine has consistently lavished upon rights holders BSI and all their events. No statement has been too silly or banal to repeat as gospel, no major snafu (and there have been many) has been too big to diminish, ignore or dismiss. Even contractual disputes or falling attendances – something we only ever hear about afterwards, if at all – are never the fault of BSI. Worse still this thrill at and coverage of all things SGP, no matter how dull, is nowadays coupled with an endless advocacy of latest bright shiny new idea to (re)solve BSI's real or imagined commercial needs dressed up as reflective analysis on the true needs of British Speedway. Nowadays these are usually written by Paul Burbidge but read like they were dictated by any of BSI's over-confident chief executives: John Postlethwaite, Paul Bellamy or Torben Olsen. Whether it is "top riders", fixed race nights, compulsory razzamatazz or squad systems, invariably said ideas are uneconomic, impossible to implement or just plain catastrophic for the progress and interests of the British speedway clubs. It is to be remembered, of course, that Philip Rising hired SGP mouthpiece Paul Burbidge who is – along with the similarly hard-working Nigel Pearson – arguably one of the most editorially compromised sports journalists in speedway from an independence of opinion perspective. Though, of course, we must note the caveat that their "happy talk" views are always strenuously only ever their own sincerely held honest opinions. Quite how the hyperpartisan Burbo can be simultaneously employed by the SGP to write news for their website and banally operate ("manage") their social media Twitter account while also reporting at length on the said same events for the *Speedway Star* is above my pay grade and confounds greater minds. If nothing else, the double-dip of one hand so conspicuously washing another is usually a very big no-no in credible media circles or, at least, if it goes on is hard to then justify as being independent analysis. Fears that this may lead to lack of investigative zeal, difficult questions unasked or sycophancy have – on the whole – proven founded.

In print Burbidge repeatedly rides BSI hobbyhorses and is often either hugely critical or else barely disguises his thin-lipped disapproval in his various "analyses" of goings-on in, around or within British Speedway in a manner that deserts his mind or keyboard whenever similar critical analysis is required for the SGP. Worse still, he doesn't just avoid sensitive SGP matters but actively reframes their presentation to the presumed benefit of his employers (and/or the series riders). His writing seems to only ever try to cast things in their best light for BSI. This is, of course, a laudable skill if acknowledged as BSI marketing content or grandiloquent PR but less so when it masquerades as "journalism". It would even be less bad if British speedway was so often unjustifiably praised too rather than primarily judged harshly. It can't be right that the Chief News Writer of the only English language UK magazine published about contemporary British (and world) speedway is – over a decade into the job – still writing up accounts of his first-ever visit to some UK tracks. Doubtless too, there are even currently operating British tracks who have yet to be graced by his presence. [1] If nothing else, it betrays a spectacularly zealous incuriosity supported and endorsed as so willingly accepted by the owners and management of *Speedway Star* magazine. In contrast, not only has Burbidge been to every SGP track staging events that he reports from but – unlike the time he gave a blow-by-blow shock-horror lengthy account of poor track conditions at Belle Vue (versus Poole) without being there (but reporting as if he was) – would rarely dream of reporting said meetings remotely without the benefit of his own physical attendance.

Now that British Speedway is so obviously in an increasingly parlous state – and probably requires thoughtful but dramatic change – with regard to attendances and general public mindshare, it follows that sales of the *Speedway Star* are also falling badly. Consequently, Rising has now suddenly found the Sword of Truth he had previously mislaid in order to (self-interestedly) bleat on about the need for collective action to save the sport (and his circulation!) apparently oblivious to his own possible culpability with regards to his long-term editorial advocacy of, commercial or personal involvement with and extensive valorisation and coverage of all things BSI and SGP. Maybe this is what the SGP editorially once merited as the newest, shiniest or best new speedway game in town but bigger pinches of editorial salt would not have gone amiss over these last nearly two decades. Anyways, while the history of the *Speedway Star* and Pinegen's various close or interconnected relationships to the SGP can't be unwritten, the status of the Cardiff GP on the speedway social calendar is what it is but also clearly didn't happen by accident. Or, more importantly, solely because of its allegedly superior quality to speedway meetings elsewhere in Britain. Its significance and appeal rests on a nexus of commercially influenced factors and circumstances that can't be gainsaid by merely highlighting these ongoing pungent whiffs of compromise and complicity or the hours/acres of accompanying uncritical comment. It also must be noted, that going to Cardiff has never been about the calibre or quality of the racing. It is often knowingly staged on a sub-standard or poor track. The logistical difficulty of building a track for one night only could prompt sympathy but doesn't as it is really a self-inflicted revenue-maximising key strategic decision taken long ago by the SGP rights holders BSI in the heady days at the start of John Postlethwaite's reign. And continued ever since. To be fair, said track construction has been

[1] Paul Burbidge finally made it along to Stoke speedway club in spring 2019 to complete his decade-long background first-hand research into what he notionally primarily reports upon. Heaven forfend the idea that he would miss out on going to any SGP location for over a decade for pressure of work reasons.

mastered nowadays by Ole Olsen and his curatorial acolytes. While things have improved from poor to acceptable, the racing is still mostly mediocre.

Strong security means that the queues to enter the Principality Stadium are again slow and lengthy this year. The queue delay is something of a surprise once you get inside the darkened arena as visually crowd levels look badly down. This is especially disappointing as the tickets for 2018 have been on sale for 364 days! Doubtless the lack of fans is partly an illusion created by the size of the stadium but, even just prior to tapes up, there are still huge swathes of empty sections and bays as well as numerous unoccupied seats. The upper tier along the length of the home straight is almost people free. Then again, perhaps better informed fans than myself had been pre-warned about the entertainment provided by a massively over-amplified pub band playing what sounds like refreshingly bad Stones covers for around 45 minutes. Over the years, a mix of revenue maximisation founded upon relentless sub-contracting, cost-cutting and parsimony has seen the appeal, quality and calibre of the musical acts booked by BSI that appear here go into sharper and sharper decline. Where Cardiff speedway fans were once serenaded beforehand – and often at the interval too – by the likes of comparatively skilled, mostly famous musical artistes such as Tony Christie, Belinda Carlisle, Bonnie Tyler, Tony Handley, and Jamelia. Nowadays, after the recent era high point of the annual performances of The Magoos, who also famously got to play two sets at Chris Morton's wedding anniversary celebrations, things have gone badly downhill. Imagine claiming to friends that you are a musical promoter only for them to then discover your job is to book third or fourth-rate musical wallpaper acts for an uninterested crowd of speedway fans. Arguably worse than the band is the screechy woman compere. Apparently, her job is to rouse hard-of-hearing fans from their pre-meeting torpor – understandable given the heat of the day and follow-up warm darkness of the under-lit stadium bowl – into a delirium of barely supressed rampant joyfulness. Making a potent combination with the band, she manages to keep things on the catatonic side of chill. It is enough to prompt fans to put in their ear plugs early or else move from the designated quiet areas to the air-horn sections in the hope that their klaxon screech might somehow mitigate the noise pollution currently being emitted from the stadium sound system.

How many people are there here? This is a hardy perennial of a question British speedway fans repeat like a soothing mantra at almost every track they attend. Reading Racers historian Arnie Gibbons is an impressive estimated counter of crowds. Possibly something to do with his work background and the rigour of his accountancy training. The sheer scale of Cardiff would test his skills, even if he were here with me which, sadly, he isn't. When it comes to the Cardiff SGP, the shared oft-repeated *ur myth* is to conflate attendance claims with reality on the basis of no evidence beyond the grandiose claims made either by the rights holders or their willing media helpers. They make fewer wild claims about Cardiff crowds nowadays, partly because they are obviously (to the naked eye) less than they once were rather than because modesty or honesty has finally triumphed. The years of bullshit has, however, seen this foundation myth widely accepted without independent verification or corroboration. Namely the Cardiff crowd is always 40,000, or more (!), even when plainly it isn't. There was, of course, the widely unacknowledged embarrassment of the rights holders BSI "accidentally" giving an "official" attendance for a Polish SGPs held in Torun (16,000) and Bydgoszcz (20,000) that were a total of 2,500 fans higher than the official stadium capacities (15,500 and 18,000 respectively) they listed on their own SGP website!

Though always happy to make wild, specious, dim-witted and/or unverifiable claims and statements in the trade press or on their website that suits their current real or imagined commercial purposes via the willing keypad of their tame stenographer-in-chief Paul

Burbidge. BSI actually aren't short of willing industry figures and media helpers unafraid to compromise their notional integrity and authority by bothering to check the content of their authoritatively uttered or written piffle about the SGP. This applies to so many claims about the SGP it would take a lifetime to fact-check them. This tendency definitely happens in spades when it comes to Cardiff attendances. In speedway circles it is a truism that Cardiff attendances are 40,000. Or, with a pinch of salt, 45,000. Sometimes even 50,000. For example, Tai Woffinden has the cachet and status to make florid statements that get reported and, given their variety and volume, appears to like to do so. Racing at Cardiff – so he tells the meagre number of press people contractually obligated or forced to cover it – is something "special" and, he says, the volume of the noise of the fanatical and adulating Cardiff crowd is particularly notable. So much so it makes his hairs stand up. Ignoring the trite Janet and John level of such piffle dressed up as first-person athlete reaction, this is especially impressive when you consider the noise-deadening characteristics of any crash helmet. Tai is regularly adulated and adored by fans and the specialist trade media so can, sometimes, also happily bandy about the completely unverified and improbable 50,000 figure. Actual paying attendance has never got remotely close to this number. Nevertheless, even the official Cardiff 2018 programme edited by Nigel Pearson and produced by Curtis Sport claims attendance will be "about 50,000". It also contains news that the stadium has "82 sets of toilets". This seems much more *bona fide* and, of course, fulfils BSI's original SGP dream to give the fans the toilet facilities they were apparently crying out for at speedway meetings to go along with the seating comfort and the premium catering offerings we apparently also so badly resented not having.

It would be easy enough to properly verify attendances since the barcode readers at the entrance turnstiles of the Principality Stadium accurately record exactly who enters. The stadium owners release these official figures to whomever they should at whatever body uses the facilities, whether it is the Welsh Football or Rugby Association or a concert organiser. Most sports events then publish these figures. On the British Speedway Forum, Philip Rising claims a doubtful transparency by insisting BSI advise the media of the official attendance at/ during Speedway Grand Prix press conferences. Whether they do or don't, BSI mostly strictly control the actual media attendees [2] and, thereby, influence messaging so – except for the Jewel in the Crown of Cardiff – it fails to ever appear in print or online. The remaining very small cadre of actually "independent" media folks – I'm thinking Ben Findon of the *Telegraph* – don't mention it either. If they are fans of speedway and they mostly are – if attending and also working for a national media outlet that even then still doesn't cover the sport regularly – failing to do so accurately ensures they won't find their way onto the rumoured infamous BSI blacklist. Setting aside lack of space or conspiracy theories, maybe it is just that no one wants to know exact information? This is lucky as we don't get it unless the professionalism (or pride) of stadium owners releasing said figures somehow accidentally finds its way into the public domain. That was certainly the case in recent years in Australia, when attendance figures for the Melbourne SGPs held at the Etihad Stadium could be learnt and seen in the full glory of their decline. So much so that this event suddenly – well, eventually, as it was common knowledge in Poland months before official confirmation that it wouldn't go ahead – disappeared from the 2018 series calendar. The Aussie staging promoters recognised a hopeless un-remediable situation when they saw one, so did the speedway promotional equivalent of walking away from the mortgage payments they had already made; so just handed back the keys to the metaphorical Speedway Grand Prix house in order to evade the exorbitant costs of their future staging obligations.

[2] Rather delightfully, it is said that sometimes media SGP press pass applications even get run past Paul Burbidge prior to authorisation.

Weirder still, not only do the football and rugby report their (higher) attendances at the Principality Stadium in Cardiff on their websites (and in the media), but they are never the suspiciously rounded numbers attributed to the SGP. These are almost invariably exact thousands (40,000!) or, on a bad more modest day, hundreds (41,800). Taking Cardiff 2014 – as a random example – attendances were reported in the *Speedway Star* as 41,800 "official attendance" (Philip Rising), "more than 40,000" (Andrew Skeels) and "pulled in around 50,000 fans" (unattributed). Back in the mists of time of 2010 when fictitious SGP attendances were still on some reporting agendas, Peter Oakes in the *Speedway Star* relished the "near 45,000 Millennium Stadium throng", Paul Burbidge hailed the "record breaking 44,150 crowd" on the SGP website, while the *Sunday Times* (where they have fact checkers and legal people to consult, if required) had an altogether different story: "the 32,000 attendance was disappointing if hardly unexpected". Though legendary numbers of free tickets are given away at Cardiff by BSI, that still doesn't fully explain away the difference between 32,000 and 44,150. If records were being set or Cardiff did manage to get 50,000 through the turnstiles, you just know that rights holders BSI would relentlessly trumpet this loudly far and wide. Further bad news for anyone with a swish scientific calculator is that the probability of such rounded numbers appearing in a time series as exhibited by official Cardiff SGP attendances will quickly break your device. Even if you had access to the computational firepower of the super-computers at CERN, such a time series would be hard to calculate quickly, let alone express succinctly using standard mathematical notation. In layman's terms, the chances of such a series of Cardiff SGP attendance figures actually occurring in real life has a smaller probability than simultaneously winning both the national lottery and Ernie, aliens visiting Eastbourne speedway and Nigel Pearson growing dreadlocks all on the same night.

Eventually the band desist. The stadium is fuller but is still noticeably emptier than the glory days of yore. Boosters will always boost or else have an unconvincing vaguely plausible justifying story about the lack of people. These vary from the banal to the creative. It was sunny and garden barbeques were too much of a lure. It was wet [the stadium has a roof] or started too late to take young children. The netball was on elsewhere. The last trains leave too early. The hotels are too expensive. The wrong British wild card has been selected. There are too many motorway roadworks or not enough riders born under Pisces. One story that has never been whispered, let alone explored, is to suggest that there might be actual declining popularity. Though only umbilically related, UK television viewing figures certainly show that the trend and numbers are inexorably downwards. These are provided by BARB: the official industry measure and standard by which all advertisers and television companies agree to measure their comparative popularity and audience sizes. Obviously enough, along with the evidence of their own denying eyes, many speedway (GP) fans don't accept these figures either. Instead they prefer to query and pick apart the industry accepted and statistically significant methodology BARB use to collate and determine these figures. Or else they cite always unavailable, unverified but different – invariably better – viewing figures put about by someone with access to confidential commercial information at Sky Sports or BT Sports to those in the know (who, in turn, post them anonymously on the British Speedway Forum). The mere sight of these burgeoning lusty proportions invariably prompts instant strong but long-lasting erections in all advertisers – whether existing or wannabe – who gaze upon them. Weirder still, there is an ex-practising auditor on the Speedway Control Bureau who even advances the exasperated claim – via text message – that British speedway viewing figures (or viewers) are such a special shy beast that they need special statistical treatment to better understand then represent the pitiful brute numbers. He believes (sincerely, I gather) that some sort of additional weighting is required to artificially show these actual BARB numbers in their true rightful glory. However, it is chosen to be spun, fewer fans nowadays attend

Cardiff. Does anyone think for a moment that if, for example, the turnstile records showed that 48,574 came through that this (wonderful but never going to happen) achievement would be kept quiet? We would never hear the end of it. It would be the SGP attendance equivalent of the endless annual happy talk nostalgia about Chris Harris winning here. So oft repeated, it is a memory pebble worn smooth by waves of its own re-telling. In speedway circles, like with so many sports memories, faux nostalgia regularly adds lustre and exaggeration to subsequent descriptions of supposedly canonical or legendary happenings that ignore their comparatively nothingburger reality at the time.

Something it seems that is impolite to mention as a possible explanation are the ticket prices charged. Though I paid an eye-watering sum to see the meeting in Horsens, I can try to vaguely justify this expenditure to myself with the foreignness and notional exoticism of the location (but not the forgettable football stadium venue). Though exciting too in its own way, with its array of well-known identikit city-centre shops and a castle, Cardiff feels much more ordinary and everyday to (UK) visitors. Yet there are tickets here that cost £105! Wtaf! For that you are ringside and, if on the back straight, each lower tier seat has been issued by the organisers with a Union flag to create the requisite enthusiastic patriotic television pictures broadcasters require to halo their live-action visuals. It almost goes without saying that ongoing cost-cutting by BSI means that – unlike on some previous occasions – every attending fan is no longer provided with their own individual flag. This parsimoniousness provides yet another one-off cost-saving. To be honest, if I didn't go to watch the Speedway Grand Prix live, I don't think I would hold a cheap plastic flag from one year to the next. It has to be said that – really – if BSI behaved consistently with regard to their flag provision at each of the 2018 SGP venues then they would provide Welsh flags to the selected few to wave for the cameras (or whenever the inclination and fancy takes them). Some may say in extenuation that there are no Welsh participants but that would ignore the centre-stage role the erstwhile "action man race-director" (TM Paul Burbidge) Phil Morris invariably animatedly hams up for free at each and every speedway GP meeting.

Interestingly, there is a good-sized (doubtless legal current health-and-safety compliant after making and recording full risk assessments) gap between the track, track safety air fence and the premium-priced prime location back straight seats. Nevertheless, the only additional protection the fans have from serious injury or death as a result of any flying speedway bikes are these cheaply produced plastic flags to deter a possible "tragic accident" perfect-storm-in-waiting at Cardiff. Setting aside, Jason Garrity is riding at reserve this year so the chance of some form of the speedway equivalent of either skittles or Rollerball is necessarily massively increased, even the normal order of things at this venue is a matter for theoretical concern. The combination of the proximity of the best seats to the restricted space dimensions of the track; its notoriously inconsistent surface (ruts and bumps invariably appear); the sheer power and temperamental nature of the modern speedway bike and how many contemporary riders are full-gas full-throttle merchants without complete control of their high-octane machines is potent. Like for all speedway meetings, fluke tragedy remains a possible outcome. Given this is a temporary track deliberately installed as a commercial decision by organisers BSI for one-night only, surely the precautionary principle requires them to bear the cost, difficulty and expense of putting in proper or better protective fencing? Before there is a tragedy rather than after. There are many existing higher fence or bigger gap examples across European speedway to follow too. From hard won stock car experience, for example, at King's Lynn where big metal catch fencing prevents spectator injury from flying equipment or rogue detached bits that could land in the crowd and cause injury. If fencing is a cost too far for BSI, then surely they need to substantially increase the safe distance between the fans and the track? Of course, this would mean some loss of income for BSI from the premium-priced back straight lower tier seats. And, when it comes to copying British speedway clubs, in the past BSI have had no hesitation doing so when it comes to speaking to current sponsors. Though they do forage for some of their own, BSI have historically liked to borrow or persuade existing ready-grown speedway sponsors to desert the shallows of their initial British speedway league club roots for the bright lights of the SGP's erstwhile "global audience" deep end.

As if to prove the point of how far speedway bikes can fly, later Craig Cook's airborne bike flies an impressive distance over the air fence before it crashes (harmlessly in this instance) to writhe like an upended dying beetle in front of the slightly panicked photographers perched on bend 2 with apertures and ginormous lenses at the ready on their stand-cum-galley gantry. The more dedicated souls among their swollen number snap a bazillion shots of said flying bike few will ever see in the ongoing elusive quest of this Tog tribe of their reputation-making money shot. For the fans sat close by, doubtless this just appeared as further colour and entertainment. Though most of the photographers flinch in unison, for their work they were already stood up (or crouched) so had a much greater chance of evasive action than anyone wishing to start their evasive action from a seated position. If such a thing should happen, there would be split-second time between bike take off and its high-speed crash landing amongst the punters. That said, SCB Referee Chris Durno completely rejects the very idea that there is any real danger for attending fans at Cardiff, "the idea a bike flying off into the crowd is totally nonsense to me. Of all the GP circuits, I perceive Cardiff as the one that puts in the most consideration for flying bikes and shale." If this very statistically unlikely event ever happened, luckily Nigel Pearson and Kelvin Tatum would be broadcasting live during the incident on whatever obscure straight-to-DVD satellite channel have currently taken on the oft-discarded British television SGP rights, so could mark any serious injuries or deaths with the appropriate hyperbole, due seriousness and gravitas required. Kelvin could utter something along the lines of "these life-changing injuries/deaths were out of the top drawer". While Nigel – temporarily donning any number of his many speedway work hats to comment with authority – could feel the great sadness in, for example, his BSPA Press spokesperson capacity but also point to the soaring popularity of speedway and its crowds as extenuation for the odd regrettable death here or there. If available, tearful estranged children or grandchildren could opine, "it's the way [insert name] would have wanted to go! He always really loved speedway!" all the better for the subsequent human angle aspect of the news stories. And, for once, this would guarantee speedway appears in the national news headlines. Should the bike veer off to strike the photographers, hopefully, they have the smarts to keep shooting to get to that vital lens-filling epitaph-shot a fraction of a second before the fatal impact. Though not the most mobile of the shale species even when not stood on a gantry, if only a wounding transpires then, at least, the thin comfort exalted status in speedway photography circles – rather than national fame or generous commendation on the latest invite-only Tog WhatsApp group – awaits.

If the pub band can't "get no satisfaction" killing a few Stones numbers, then at least the crowd do gain a measure of contentment when they finally stop playing. Admittedly that pause in the aural torture is then the signal for the screechy woman with access to the stadium loudspeaker system to resume and further ramp up her joyous whoops and relentless demands for additional fervour from us. In my section, most fans sit in quiet almost bovine contemplation or else focus on not spilling their beer trays as they negotiate the steeply raked steps to the nose-bleed seating in the very back row of the stadium. Crowd noise levels are muted. There appear to be fewer Polish fans in general so boisterousness levels are massively dialled down. The increasingly desperate attempt to inject atmosphere might be a contractual obligation of the rabble-rouser job description but is an exercise in futility that mainly falls on deaf ears. According to breathless proudly uncritical trade press reports, Cardiff – apparently – sets the gold standard for the quality, drama and zest of its carnival-like party vibe. Eat your heart out, Rio! Like the 1960s, you have to have been there to truly experience the majesty of its full glory. To be frank, the entertainment style served up at Cardiff tends towards the portentous and grandiloquent. Think mid to late era Rush, albeit without the double-necked guitars. It is the sporting musical accompaniment equivalent of a migraine. It tends to the derivative: all fanfare, dry ice, open-topped stretch limos and wildly flickering coloured lights serenaded by loud soundtrack modelled upon the dramatic choruses found on American 1970s quirky chart hits. Cardiff rider introductions usually take their cue, attitude and visual repertoire from WWE wrestling, albeit the poor man's budget version choreographed by an intern while also having to handle calls on the complaints hotline. How this came to be the required BSI stadium event signature house style is something of a mystery. Most likely it is a format dreamed up by Soho-based brand consultants who have never been to speedway but are briefed by other middle-class executives who despise themselves for their association with anorak-wearing speedway fans to make such a lucrative living.

Weirdly, either BSI have gone completely against type, history and tradition and attempted to "innovate". Or else, and much likelier, even the meagre expense of the usual brightly spotlit but subtly condescending rider introductions is nowadays proving too dear for their shallow pockets in a stadium of this size. That said, when the lights dim, like a crowd of saliva-free but nonetheless expectant Pavlov's Dogs, we are trained to look pitswards at the herald of musical fanfare that, usually, greets the arrival of the riders as they are borne aloft on some kind of exceptionally highly polished aspirational vehicle. Catching us all unawares a voice cries out, "It's Jason Garrity!" Given that the general public couldn't name let alone pick out even notionally famous riders in a reduced-sized identity parade of three suspects, it is rather ambitious to expect even a knowledgeable speedway crowd to be able to instantly recognise then applaud Jason. Especially if hidden amongst 30,000 or so fans. Before we know what is really going on, the voice then trumpets excitedly, "It's Dan Bewley!" Quite where Jason was, Dan is or what they are doing defies human understanding. It is only really Belle Vue fans who would easily be able to put a name to Dan's face. As most in the crowd nowadays are one-off speedway meeting attendees drawn to the bright notionally glamorous flame of Cardiff by its reputation as much as its reality, this is way too stern a test. And hardly "entertainment". Practically all won't ever have seen him ride in the flesh or, given the poor BT Sports viewing figures, on the telly. Let alone pictured or interviewed. Even those that have – luckily, given his talent – seen him ride often won't have seen him without a helmet on. To add to this degree of difficulty, it is hard to break our training – by all the SGP rider presentations of yesteryear – of scanning the pits exit and track expecting Dan and all the other riders to appear there. Randomly chosen stairwell summits on the home straight apparently are the stages deemed to best introduce the 2018 Cardiff rider roster from to us. And where, apparently, Dan is already stood waving. If we had the compound eyes of a fly, we might have a caught a fleeting glance of Dan. To make things doubly or trebly harder, the lighting operatives appear to have shaky hands and heavy metal stadium concert light show ambitions as well as a keen desire to induce epileptic fits so excitedly strobe their glare of spotlights madly about the pre-darkened stadium seats. Just guessing which stairwell the lights are supposed to be illuminating is a game in itself and instant reaction eye test. It is a kind of scarf-free speedway version of "Where's Wally?" meets "Whack-a-Mole" via a "Spot-the-Ball" competition format. Even with the helpfully reduced crowd size that BSI's relentless but dull marketing messaging has engineered, we collectively struggle in needle-in-haystack territory. And, after all, who would honestly notice – let alone recognise – Artem Laguta or Bartosz Zmarzlik (unless he spoke) if we stood next to them in the queue at our local supermarket ?

In some ways, this wild spotlight format is a huge step forwards as the introduction ceremony is mercifully brief compared to the usual bombastic but funereal-paced affair. Plus there is a certain perverse joy to not seeing the riders but only hearing their names. I am managing to – completely accidentally – glimpse one rider in three. The riders are introduced to the crowd in pit bay order aka according to their final 2017 standings. Few knew it was possible but this format is arguably an even more superfluous way to introduce the riders than normal. Predictably, pantomime villain Nicki is booed, while more surprisingly Tai is loudly cheered with a jingoism that convoluted explanations from his press team about his formative Australian Perth childhood often appear determined to kill off. The only rider who manages to milk the spotlight, lengthen his time there and generate a second wave of adulatory applause is, of course, Greg Hancock. At the other extreme, though he is the only SGP rider to currently race in British Speedway, reigning World Champion Jason Doyle is greeted in comparatively lukewarm fashion. Though it is only the fifth event in the series, after a slow start to its defence, Doyle's chances of retaining his crown remain statistically possible but, in reality, are already effectively over. Being the last to be introduced to the crowd at every event in the series is only going to psychologically further underline this rapid decline to Doyle.

Thankfully something that hasn't changed at Cardiff is that Kevin Coombes is still, despite initial aural appearances to the contrary, event compere. Kevin is knowledgeable, professional, enthusiastic and a mild-mannered rabble rouser. When he first got the Cardiff gig, some grumbled at how much frothier and dumbed-down his presentational style became at the Millennium Stadium compared to his regular, long-time presenter work at Arlington Stadium for Eastbourne Speedway. In contrast to what is around him at Cardiff or served up on the telly during any live broadcast by the commentary team, Kevin comes across as rigorous, informed and affable while fully engaged but without totally compromising his impartiality. More John Craven's Newsround than shouty poorly drawn import cartoon that is increasingly the television commentary house style. Though Kevin no longer presents at Eastbourne, he has been re-hired for the 2019 Championship incarnation of the club. Before they were even fashionable, Kevin had a portfolio career that involved some work with the police – in a capacity I never quite got to the bottom of (it was either the glamour of forensics or the tedium of stationary supplies) – speedway presenting as well as spinning the mobile disco discs along with friend and Eagles timekeeper Barry Geer on his free weekends and throughout the off-season. Bookings taken for weddings, celebrations, works events and birthdays. I seem to recall Coombes took up some kind of weekend but competitive hobby car racing and also became a proud slightly later-life dad. In a nutshell, Kevin is an approachable and friendly bloke but still kinda somehow manages to be shy bordering on private rather than aloof. Just hearing his dulcet tones on the stadium mike adds authority and increases my enjoyment. This is lucky as racing at Cardiff – like at one-off temporary tracks almost everywhere – can tend towards the mundane and processional. The bijou confines of the track along with space-restricted racing lines inevitably means overtaking is at a rare premium. What also adds to my enjoyment is the atmosphere in my part of the stadium. The cheap seats. £19! In SGP terms, it is a complete bargain! Especially based on the number of races, unique surrounds and calibre of the riders but, sadly, not the racing thrills. Beyond their proximity to the track, quite why more expensive seat tickets appeal is a conundrum to me. And many others too – given how crowded my particular upper-tier cheap-seat section is yet again this year. It has to be said that your £19 gets you ant-sized riders staging races on a far distant but brightly coloured track. Once inside the stadium, apart from the odd clampdown year, the stadium staff on duty generally turn a blind eye to fans moving about elsewhere to their choice of free upper-tier seats. There are always a huge number of these to choose from. This year it appears even more so. It is also possible to move to prime viewing areas that – if seated lower – command bigger (often huge) prices. You can get champagne views – albeit elevated ones – for only cider spend. Equally, if proximity to others isn't your thing, fans can move to empty sections where they can really spread out and sit completely alone, like birdwatchers without a hide, in splendid sweet isolation.

Given the distance many fans are from the track action, what also adds to the spectacle and lustre of the experience at Cardiff (alone) – and praise where praise is due rather than exaggerated as a right for commercial reasons – is the extra behind-the-scenes footage that is shown on the giant stadium screens you can actually see! It is a shame that BSI don't invest similarly at other locations to improve the overall fan experience. As is usual elsewhere at SGP meeting big screens, we are subjected to pre-recorded frighteningly dull rider interviews; generic graphics; explanations of speedway for that shyest and most mythical of beats – the newcomer; rapid build cumulative score charts; race results; advertiser videos, messages or listings; safety notices; pointlessly whizzy hard-to-interpret almost context-free race action montages; along with endless slow motion replays that obsessively study all starts, race leaders and all finishes (whether close or uncontested) in preference to properly focussing upon the key moments of any race. However, what we additionally get in Cardiff – and, since it works well, is a real bonus – is intermittent live footage from the pit bays, pits lane and the walkway that provides track access. I suspect that these are the pictures broadcast live on the "world feed" that are usually withheld from fans inside SGP stadiums. As a result at Cardiff: we catch glimpsed sight of riders, mechanics, hangers on, press officers, BSI staff, BSI approved chancers, key sponsors, competitors' family and also a smattering of FIM authorised officials as they loll about the pits, ingress and egress the track perimeter or its general environs. Whenever there are frissons of dispute, anger, premature celebration, time pressure or irk behind the scenes or pit lane rather than the track is its real *mis en scène*. Obviously, the bright glow of possible televisual celebrity often attracts, draws out or prompts larger-than-life reactions as well as luring out performers, attention-seekers, the puffed up and narcissistic to the bright glare of possible TV stardom. Moody poses, photobombing, manly heterosexuality, ultra-branded clothing and snappy but ugly haircuts abound.

Are these camera lens ineluctably drawn to "accidental" SGP screen stars or they to them? For sure, it is a philosophical question beyond the understanding of mere mortals. These SGP screen hoggers appear so often you half-expect news that their performances tonight in the Cardiff pits are in fact also some kind of an unofficial audition for parts in the pilot episode of a new speedway sitcom. When eventually crowdfunded, it'll be shown heavily edited on an obscure early hours weekend-only pay-per-view satellite channel. The basic premise of the sitcom appears to be ambitious, confident but information-lite slightly delusional not-quite-loveable speedway characters (some but not all with a modicum of knowledge and expertise) get to decide the future direction of the sport using a combination of charades, unfashionable dress styles, their volume of social media likes, breathless mentions in the news pages and/or "Off the Beaten Track" column in the *Speedway Star* along with a mimed shale version of blindfold pin-the-tail-on-the-donkey. This in turn decides the choice of random buzz words they must crowbar into the script as well as use to create their innovative but bespoke manifestos to either "save" or boost the popularity of speedway with the general public. Apparently, they say that this sitcom idea is currently being secretly final trialled outside the already over-subscribed SGP live broadcasts – albeit on a much smaller scale soft-launch basis – with the newly privatised Team GB franchise. If successful, many of these star speedway characters will get a longer West End run or something much more consequential and celeb than camera-hogging or photobombing a few means nothing Test matches or SGP rounds.

Sat watching the big-screen action in the light breeze small gaps in the stadium architecture thankfully provides for those close to the pigeons in the back row of the third bend cheap seats, the full glory of the red shale track and artificially bright green centregreen furniture is laid out far below us in all its colourful majesty. Admittedly, from this height and distance, the track staff look sized more like specks than people, while the riders astride their bikes seem more like animated gaming console figures than flesh and blood. This whole upper tier section of the stadium is packed out with animated and boisterous value-seeking fans pleased just to be here. In my row (and later that in front), we are joined by a group of six lads in their 20s all dressed up as 1970s athletics head-banded and moustachioed David Bedford look-a-likes. It is a get up made infamous by the 118 118 adverts. Rather than wear the telephone directory 118 numbers, these blokes have instead cleverly substituted Craig Cook's 111 SGP race tabard number onto their clothing. It turns out they are all mates of Craig Cook visiting Cardiff from Cumbria. Clearly here to have a good time, they also to give Cook their wholehearted support as well as revel in the experience of his (latest) SGP appearance in the Principality Stadium. This time as a fully paid-up member of the series rather than a one-off participant. I saw them earlier in the pits laughing and joking with Craig, Craig's dad Will as well as the 111 pits team of helpers and mechanics but didn't realise their personal connections. Perhaps they sit elsewhere in the stadium or no longer bother to come since his appearance in the SGP series is so workaday normal and frequent, but whereabouts are Tai's local, joyous and supportive mates sat inside the stadium tonight? As a conscientious and newish dad, perhaps they have melted from the scene, still live in Australia or, maybe, such strong social circles were what the Woffinden family also sacrificed when they transplanted themselves back to Scunthorpe in their dedicated, single-minded laudable quest to try to (so fabulously) fulfil Tai's career dreams and ambitions? Wherever they are or aren't, it is my Cardiff good fortune to have these boisterous loud and proud Cook 111 fans decide to also sit around whereabouts I am located. Then again, when Tai battles the tricky track surface to win a workmanlike and processional heat 1, a bald bloke by the aisle a few rows down leaps to his feet in joy, performs a jig and is in such a state of ecstasy that veins bungle menacingly for his health on his shaven head. So, perhaps, Woffinden fans are actually really like God and are everywhere, albeit not his actual mates.

On the subject of transient or "plastic" mates, there are so few young British speedway riders with the latent talent and poten ambition tial to also be competitive on the international stage that, whenever, these do appear on our shores they are relentlessly lauded and prematurely hyped. It does seem that there are currently quite a few riders aged twenty or under who have the nascent talent and speedway ability that might see them manage to make this leap upwards. This being speedway, like horses expected to win the Grand National, at this age they may currently look like favourites for later World Championship success but circumstances, time and luck can all intervene. They are also young, lithe, fearless and light as well as yet to be psychologically tested by injury. Best of the current bunch by far is Robert Lambert. Age 20 and an Aries, Lambert is talented, single-minded and very much his own man. If judged by the strength of his opinions but also his teenage decision to take a German licence at 14 to progress his career when the UK authorities wouldn't let him ride senior speedway until aged 16. Lambert is exciting to watch and hoes his own row. He also performed very well when thrown in the notional deep end – if you are good enough, you are old enough – at the recent two-day World Pairs tournament that is currently ridiculously and also rather pretentiously known as the FIM Speedway of Nations. Earlier this afternoon, Robert was passionately snogging his Berlin-based girlfriend Jessica Gast in his pits bay. Sadly, I caught no sight of Robert's ultra-involved and legendarily ever present Tiger Mother, Helen. Many feel "dads & lads" aren't always the best combination for guaranteeing shale success when the pressure mounts and tempers fray so, hopefully, the rarer "mums & sons" combo is a more empowering and less combustible long-term set-up speedway career-wise.

With the number 16 wildcard race tabard on Lambert's back, family, fan and media expectations run high. It is never easy being the New Great Hope for the Future of British Speedway. From the big-screen pits feed, it appears this evening that Robert has also attracted some extra motivators on hand in and around his pits bay for his Cardiff SGP debut. One of these motivators is Team GB and Swindon Robins Team Manager Alun "Rosco" Rossiter. Apparently operating under the misapprehension his role and experience is akin to that of England football team manager Gareth Southgate, Rosco has cannily assumed the role of advisor and mentor, albeit of the someone who has seen it but not done it variety at the World Championship level. It's a self-elected position which also gives Rosco the chance to bathe in the likely reflected glory of Robert's possibly triumphant Cardiff SGP participation. As well as possibly burnish his nascent reputation as the go-to-speedway-guy for big night obvious motivational advice ("go faster"; "give it large"; "go on son"), direction ("gate well") and tactics ("win or finish second"). Alongside Alun this evening is his partner-in-crime: Team GB's newly minted personal training guru, who is still so comparatively new-fangled within the sport that his name still escapes many fans including me. Nevertheless, he is, apparently – on the basis of a runner's up medal at the Speedway of Nations and a number of off-site training days – at the forefront of revolutionising the nutrition and exercise plans of talented young British speedway riders everywhere. In social media pictures, this great leap forwards appears to involve young riders sitting in classrooms discussing diet plans or happily standing around red-faced in gyms close to various new-fangled bits of equipment whose true function is hard to easily glean. Or else, judged by social media footage, he gets random riders to warm up for international Team GB meetings by catching various randomly chosen balls from different U.S. sports while fellow rider colleagues throw shapes or stretch holding long elastic bands. All this happens with the riders already dressed for action in their box-fresh matching team kevlars. Of all the newbie motivators on show, it is impressive how some bloke that got Neils Kristian Iversen skipping and doing "down dog" poses as part of his personal training regime when riding in King's Lynn area a few years back has so quickly transformed his status, authority and reputation into that of National Team Exercise Jedi Master. Without his usual Team GB team manager status and monogrammed team shirt, Rosco lacks formal verifiable functionality at an SGP meeting, so has been reduced to sporting a new – gauged by Twitter photos before tapes up – age inappropriate hairstyle. He also has on a camera-friendly quirky collared "personality" shirt of the kind that took over from statement socks worn at Christmas. These "quirky" – some would say garish – shirts were most often seen in the wild during the mid-90s in regional wine bars, primarily worn as talking point in lieu of conversational abilities or verifiable personality. Aka loud and proud in their colour palette but with enough of a hint of oddness in the design to suggest the wearer vaguely has a hinterland as well as, in their own mind, something of a subtle Ladies Man and all round bit of a larf. More likely, these shirts are an attempt at sartorial competition with the (unstated) aim to either echo or outshine the more expensive obscure designer but slightly less garish shirts Scott Nicholls relentlessly advertises on Twitter and Instagram but also sports on telly back in the BT Sports studio whenever he is on live SGP colour comment duty. If FIM referees were to adjudicate, Rosco would be excluded from the meeting for taste and style crime reasons. Some suggest Scott requires a final warning too, but his innate natural charm means no one plucks up the courage to do so.

No matter who is beside you in the pits, obviously enough, it is what you do on the track that counts. Sadly for Robert, he starts with an engine failure at the tapes after his chain comes off. Like many in the crowd, Craig's mates are incredulous, "How the fark did that happen?" Though by their very nature, mechanical problems occur randomly (or lie solely in the imagination of the rider), this is bad news on such a big night especially when you would expect no preparational stone left unturned. Still, Robert's misfortune, is meeting reserve Dan Bewley's good fortune. Dan is another – even younger – racing talent attracting overly big predictions for the future because of his performances for Belle Vue, especially at home but also away. Bewley has skill, speed and verve on his bike as well as a currently fabulous power-to-weight-ratio based on his slight teenage frame and jockey stature. Even when completely wet, Dan won't weigh a ton. Sadly, though regularly described as racing like he's on a runaway horse, Dan's Cardiff debut dream also quickly descends into something of a nightmare too when he finishes last after getting passed easily by a sluggish Janowski on lap three. Doubtless, if he were bothering to watch, the Great Britain Speedway Team psychologist would mentally cut and paste some happy talk about racing on the big stage for his next lengthy audit, milestone and envisioning meeting with Dan.

Of course, there is a rich tradition of trying to remotely influence equipment and people through mind control and extrasensory perception. Always enthusiastically embraced by the military on both sides during the cold war, it also found its way into sports "science" and chess to psychologically help or hinder top performers by the 1970s. Russian psychic Nina Kulagina could reputedly stop the heart of a frog just by staring at it. Perhaps, the privatised Great Britain Speedway Team already secretly have such employees on staff to send thoughtwaves to Tai Woffinden, Robert Lambert and Dan Bewley. Equally, maybe, distances within the Principality Stadium and also the need for confidentiality about our psychic secret weapons means Rosco is the chosen intermediary for these thoughtwaves so has to remain close at hand with these riders at all times? There is a slight delay to heat 3 for tape repairs. It could be for wear and tear reasons or, possibly, a no consequences – as no Brit riders are in this race – rehearsal of a clandestine aspect the audacious GB Speedway Team strategic development plans to mind control all types of speedway equipment getting properly field tested. When this race finally gets underway, in the rush to the first corner Pedersen has Doyle appear to touch-cum-clip him just as Hancock also cuts across too. The net outcome is that the reigning World Champion is unceremoniously dumped onto the shale. Whether this is by accident, design, play-acting or intrusive extrasensory perception is for German FIM Referee Christian Froschauer to decide. Peculiarly he elects to sit on the fence by warning Doyle (for moving at the tapes) but having all four riders back. The stadium noise hasn't really got going since the warm-up musical act stunned us into collective silence and even the environmentally friendly airhorns they allow here hardly get any use in their specially designated sections. It is so becalmed that while we await the return of riders from their tinkering, apparently unaware that BSI cost-cutting means that most of us don't have them, Kevin Coombes is reduced to asking us to wave our flags. Their first bend bundle first time out prompts Nicki and Jason into a follow up two lap duel for second position. As ever, the compact Cardiff track size dictates passing is at a premium while early doors slippery track conditions compounds things further. When it comes to lusty passing and overtaking you would always want to see in any speedway race, pickings are so thin that this brief battle for second position means this heat counts as the most exciting – aka least processional – race of the evening to date.

Almost wherever he has raced this season – Britain, Poland or the GPs – Craig Cook has been reluctant to bother the scorer too much in his opening ride. Geed up for Cardiff, this evening is very different. Craig wears his gating gloves from the off. Despite the start area already starting to rut up, he makes the perfect start to fire away from the tapes and his rivals with grace and speed. So much so that ref Froschauer immediately stops the race. Next to me, the joyful whelps of the "Cookie Monster" supporting athletics team 111 quickly turns to loud disbelief phrased in the common language of men. When giant-screen replays show zero movement and a perfect start from Craig, incredulity swiftly turns to anger. Words to the effect of, "What the goodness is he thinking?" are uttered angrily at an unfeeling world. To make this poor decision much worse, the referee also warns Cook. Said warning system is notionally designed to discourage rolling starts and is new to all FIM events this season. A second warning sees the guilty (or otherwise) rider disqualified from the next heat if he again moves. Of course, since this is Grand Prix speedway, this has yet to happen. Advocates claim this shows that the system works effectively. It certainly ensures that any warned rider stays stock still at the tapes – too still, often – from then on. It is almost an immutable Law of Speedway that the rider in the lead when a race is incorrectly stopped often struggles in the re-run. Whether it is this jinx, hyper-stillness prompted by his warning, the accelerated heart rate of justifiable anger or a return to normal service, Craig finishes last to collect his traditional big fat SGP first race zero. Given how hard it is to pass here, if Craig hadn't been incorrectly hauled back, the diametric opposite of a race win almost would most likely have been the outcome. On such poor random decisions does the fine difference between glory or cumulative failure to reach the end of season automatic qualifying top eight slots depend. Craig's mates definitely can't see past the injustice of the ref's original wrong decision. There is nothing for it but to get in more beers. It is a long walk and even longer interval queue. One of the group has bought his humorous outfit a little on the too tight and skimpy side. Going up and down the steep stand stairs, thereby, becomes his catwalk. Totally accidentally, of course. The expense and importance of those beer trays require slow, careful progress so we can all (if we so choose) admire the taut, tanned masculinity – just the right side of vain gym obsessiveness – he affects nonchalant obliviousness about. With the such regular lengthy intervals, maybe, the SGP organisers should another year formally add "hot" waiter/waitress-at-seat-service to all those magnificent Cardiff entertainments they so keenly celebrate beforehand? This trial run gets enough casual glances to suggest there is a sizeable market of fans not wholly absorbed by the big-screen adverts. With a minimum of five lengthy (circa eight minute) intervals for track grades, there is time aplenty to fill with distractions.

When it comes to ogling the big screen, the speed edit and vibrant colours of exciting action shots of the 2018 iteration SGP Monster Energy commercial would be harder to resist if speedway weren't almost wholly absent from its fast-paced montage of other nearly motorsports no one really knows or cares about either. To help calm the few heart rates vaguely elevated by sight of all this frenetic Monster-inspired danger and glamour, the big screen plays logo shots of tonight's event sponsors and partners on an endless loop. Apparently, just as the rider pits bay allocations follow the final 2017 standings, these adverts appear in a priority order dictated by spend level. Each ad gets the same duration to forever burn its product offering, status and standing upon the impressionable minds of this captive speedway crowd. But who, exactly, are these major UK/global brands and high street names keen to gain further mindshare with shale fans? Naturally there is Anlas ("Motorcycle Tyres

Only"). And, of course, Adrian Flux – if their logo is anything to go by – the horse-grooming specialists brilliantly discovered by the bods in the BSI advertising team after extensive research looking through British speedway club programmes in search of pre-existing sponsors. It is a research model that famously saw Poole sponsor Meridian Lifts offered "special" Cardiff sponsorship and executive box package opportunities under the mistaken apprehension they were a big business like Otis Lifts rather than a small regional enterprise. Though easily lured by the opportunity to showcase their brand at the big tent signature event of the "global" speedway season, tonight's sponsors will almost certainly gain zero verifiable new business from their guilt by association with the lustre and glamour of the Cardiff SGP this evening. After all, who can afford to own a horse nowadays as well as also buy SGP tickets and cover the cost of the associated travel?

The most pitiful of all the almost unknown (outside speedway circles and inside too, despite these efforts) ineffectual sponsors involved in financially backing the 2018 British FIM Speedway Grand Prix is surely – if only from a Welsh taxpayer point of view – is the Welsh Government. What the goodness are they thinking? They clearly have more money than sense and clearly no real oversight beyond lip service from their taxpayers or patriotic citizens. Ignoring how few Welsh people attend Cardiff, even less of them would notice the stylised "Part funded by the Welsh Government" dragon boldly shown on the big screen. Though I usually hold that the BSI sponsorship team couldn't fight their way out of a wet paper bag, the ongoing contractual financial support from Welsh government to help ensure BSI's continued use of the Principality Stadium is quite something to behold and admire. Whoever is in charge of "negotiations" in Cardiff on behalf of the government should not be allowed out unsupervised in public. I can't be bothered to go through the rigmarole of sending them a Freedom of Information request about the terms and duration of their financial support but will, instead, draw upon the lessons of SGP history. It would be clear to a blind man on a galloping horse that these public servants do not introspect about previous decisions, poor use of marketing budgets or bad agreements but view their responsibility to be to slavishly continue them. The last time I looked, speedway fan and diligent SGP researcher Charles McKay wrote in *the Voice* (issue 44 in 2011) that the Welsh government had a five-year agreement to pay BSI a maximum of £850,000 from 2012 to 2016. This largesse by the First Minister and Minister for Business, Enterprise, Technology and Science was granted under section 61(j) of the Government of Wales Act which allows elected officials to do anything they consider appropriate to support sports and recreational activities relating to Wales. Even if the Welsh Government have managed to negotiate this figure downwards in the meantime, the ongoing sponsorship of BSI to continue to use the stadium that is the strategic and Hollywood bling cornerstone of BSI's hugely profitable empire beggars belief. The latest available accounts (to end of 2016) at Companies House for BSI show its turnover at c.£8.6m, operating profits at £422,651 and inter-company dividends paid at £3,255,882! Welsh tax payers could be forgiven for wondering about the necessity of their contribution to this BSI or IMG parent company happiness. Another equally bonkers explanation for this largesse is that this payment could be to gain a contractual obligation that restricts BSI moving the "British" SGP to a stadium elsewhere or preclude any decision to expand and stage a second UK SGP. The idea that the "BSI Speedway (An IMG Company)" – as the big-screen adverts bill them – executive team would voluntarily make the decision to kill off their sacred Cardiff cash cow that provides the biggest percentage of their UK annual revenues is – despite their extensive track record of failure to fulfil their publicly stated strategic ambitions – too inept even for them.

Even if we assume that there is some positive word of mouth and reflected glory for Welsh Tourism from the Visit Wales adverts in the programme and on the air fences as well as the continued use of the Principality (previously Millennium) Stadium in terms of visitor numbers and their associated spending, BSI Speedway have for a long time actively worked against these Welsh Government aims and ambitions. Indeed, the rights holders moved the long-time Cardiff SGP start time back from 7pm to 5pm – earlier than all the other events which all still start at 7pm local time – a decade ago and have kept it earlier doors ever since [3]. This decision was made by their then "Managing Director of BSI (Speedway)" Paul Bellamy and explained as part of an ongoing fan care programme and listening project initiative usually most notable for its complete absence. Man of the Speedway People Bellamy apparently wanted to ensure fans and their children/families could leave the city early evening (or catch the last trains out to London and other destinations), get to bed at a reasonable hour, only enjoy protected sex and also avoid the expense of staying in Cardiff hotels the night beforehand and/or the evening after the event. It was a decision that the supportive *Speedway Star* sympathetically hailed at the time in an "exclusive" interview with this great man of world speedway as, "a move specifically designed to combat the price of hotel accommodation in the Welsh city". This was after Bellamy speciously claimed – without the evidence of independently verified attendance figures or hotel price comparisons – that, "the British GP has been a victim of its own success". When the people you help fund to stage their event decry the ability of your city to accommodate its punters without gouging them – when they themselves can only half-fill your National stadium – surely questions really do need to be asked by Welsh taxpayers and voters? We all know that most SGP speedway fans only arrive in Wales/Cardiff on the day and also leave on the same day. That has always been the case. These fans spend the majority of their time inside or around the stadium. Worse still, the advent of the "free" Fan Zone and its extended duration means that time spent in the city centre as well as the level of food and drink expenditures made there by SGP fans – ignoring any austerity tightening of wallets or home-made sandwiches – has also been severely reduced. The organisers structurally deliver for Cardiff (and Wales) a perfect storm of "love-you-but-leave-you". So, though there are, indeed, additional visitors to Wales that might go elsewhere if BSI decided to relocate to another UK city – highly unlikely for a variety of reasons not least stadium availability or stadium owner reluctance – currently those that come don't provide either the Wales-is-amazing word-of-mouth paid for or the incremental discretional expenditures within the principality that surely the Welsh government expects as an unstated *quid pro quo*? Of course, part of the Cardiff SGP culture is to hit the city centre bars (well, that iconic Welsh pub the Walkabout) after the meeting with the added lure of seeing riders, ex-riders, mechanics, media personalities as well as past and present national team managers on hand with drinks in hand. With Poland the next day for serious riders as well as the current widespread fashion for exercise, nutrition, performance app data, special diets as well as weighing then probing the contents of your stools even this isn't what it once was. Ignoring too that there are regularly almost twice as many fans at rugby and football events held at the stadium to go on the lash and, thereby, boost the financial health of the Welsh national economy after.

[3] If staging SGP at a sensible time to help fans and their children/families travel at a sensible hour and save unnecessary costs was a sincere or genuine BSI Speedway opinion or strategy, surely this should apply to much more remote SGP locations such as Hallstavik, Horsens, Teterow, Krsko, Malilla and even Gorzow too? Given Cardiff is a capital city with excellent transport links as well as extensive hotel, restaurant, bar and cultural options, it is perverse to choose it as the hill to die on in a fake quest to get the kiddies to bed on time while also reducing fan expenditures and mitigating travel hassles? Especially when Visit Wales are only in their second year of their latest (five-year) contract – that runs to 2021 – with BSI to stage the British SGP in Cardiff? That said, the spurious justification for a wonkily early start time typifies the make-it-up-as-you-go-along nature of executive decision-making at this IMG company (that they call "innovation") but also – yet again – highlights yet again how the tame speedway media fulfils their role as promotional note-takers-in-chief rather than deign to rouse themselves to anything more investigative or analytical.

Better still from a sponsor care point of view, BSI Speedway's "Official Merchandise" trumpeted on their website online and sold from a number of bright orange concession tents at each and every Speedway Grand Prix meeting indicates the real FIM and BSI attitude and commitment towards this long time sponsor. BSI, the FIM, IMG and Visit Wales can bang on beforehand and afterwards all they like about what this financial commitment to the Cardiff SGP delivers but stuff they actually sell as merchandise either fails to mention this event or else goes one much better and lists it as "Cardiff, Great Britain" on the commemorative 2018 SGP series tour T-shirts. As the capital city of Wales, surely the least that could be expected of an event the rights holder also rather damningly officially call the "British Speedway Grand Prix" is a correct listing on the official SGP merchandise tour clobber as befits their status as a proud nation and valued event sponsor? In a nutshell, Visit Wales have a sponsorship partner who encourages speedway fans NOT to stay in the country and then compounds that by no platforming them on their series collectables. It comes across at best – given strong independence sensitivities in the region – as dismissive and insensitive or possibly even virtuoso trolling. Given BSI famously give ruthless attention to any and every detail of their contracts, brand, corporate identity and event instruction manuals, the decision to designate Cardiff as Great Britain rather than Wales can only be calculatedly deliberate. With a repeat customer roster of (often obscure) event partner companies nowadays, BSI have moved on from their pump and dump, here today gone tomorrow approach of yesteryear to something approaching stability and professionalism. Sensible given declining television contract values, falling attendances and the end of their rights contract for the SGP in 2021. Given this context, no matter which way they look at it, Visit Wales surely must recognise BSI nevertheless still view them as a locational convenience with significant revenue benefits to still be exploited rather than a founding integral partner of their whole World Championship expansion project. When it comes to public acknowledgement of Wales, the best this sponsorship gets attention-wise is (when not preening for the cameras) FIM Race Director Phil Morris who is rarely ever far away from underlining his pride in his national identity to the embedded speedway media. Of course, by extension, this also foregrounds his status as one of the all-time great Welsh speedway riders. Ah, oh, apart from Port Talbot born Freddie Williams who had the ability to actually ride and compete in the World Championships as well as win it twice.

Slippery conditions when the racing resumes sees another sub-standard Cardiff indoor track yet again confirm as laughable Burbo's claim that this event is a "cauldron of intensity". Instead we see Woffinden just about control his move over into Lambert during the first five or so yards before this manoeuvre halts the race. The big-screen replay confirms my initial distant surmise. However, referee Froschauer sees things differently so wrongly excludes the young Brit. Lambert's Cardiff dream has already been lived as a nightmare with two rides and two exclusions garlanding his big stage debut. Rosco's motivational presence and thoughtwaves definitely aren't working their magic for the young Brit. In the re-run, the Speedway Gods intervene by having Tai appear to stall at the start. By the time he remembers to turn on his fuel, Tai is last in a three-rider race by half a lap or so. Turning on the fuel and attaching the cut off are the basic requirements of any pre-race rider checklist. Afterwards, on the stadium screen, we see Tai bollock his tall lead mechanic Jacek Trojanowski who shrewdly takes one for the team by submitting to the anger and mis-directed blame. He even mouths a superfluous but tactical "sorry". It is sad to see that even in the carefree daredevil speedway universe, like the world of work everywhere else, you sometimes have to word-fellate or brown-nose your boss. Heat 6 sees Craig Cook again gate with alacrity to lead. Behind him Freddie Lindgren and Chris Holder have a battle royale for second. So much so that their distraction effectively gifts Craig an unpressured first ever SGP race win! In the fifth event of the series. The stadium crowd booms its approval and Cook celebrates enthusiastically while his mates spill their lagers over their athletics gear as he takes the chequered flag and they jump, hug and dance with the kind of ecstasy they probably don't usually show on a big night out in Barrow and Workington. Their celebrations and collective joy continues throughout his subsequent warm-down victory lap. What a time and place to record his first SGP race win. Fans in the posher lower tiers wave the Union flags provided with patriotic gusto.

Jason Doyle's World Championship defence started poorly and hasn't really improved. After a single point and warning his first time out, Heat 7 sees him rear when close to a bucking Pawlicki who then takes off the nearby Janowski. Predictably the ref excludes the wrong party, in this case Janowski. On the buttons Christian Froschauer is marvellously consistent, albeit wrongly so. He has now had three decisions to make and has made three wrong calls. The FIM like to occasionally flourish their power in the area of referee selection to remind their elite FIM referee pool who rules the roost. Such decisions keep actual and wannabe refs pathologically enthusiastic. It takes much service, experience, elite examinations and politicking to become an SGP referee. There is a strong element of a closed shop as well as peer selection – almost to masonic standards – by FIM committee and other retired ex-top FIM refs. Age-related retirements are also rigorously enforced by the FIM (at 55) so referee career expectancy at an international level is often short as a result of the time taken to climb the greasy pole to big event preferment. Plus the widely felt desire to officiate at the highest levels means that competition is intense. Even if a referee makes it to the top grade, while they might get to run elite level FIM events, these selections might never include any actual SGPs. With only 10 (or so) SGP opportunities in any one season, some favoured refs do still get repeat bookings. Given his performance so far, it is going to be a while until referee Herr Froschauer gets another invite to repeatedly bungle in front of the SGP series cameras.

Greg Hancock wins heat 8 in the fastest time of the night. As usual, he milks both the real and imagined adulation of the crowd. It has taken 75 minutes to run the first eight heats. Slow by the vigilant television broadcast satellite cost clock-watching standards of the SGP. After a wait of over two hours, to go along with the lengthy formation tractor displays fans finally get the treat that is the joy of an Anlas tyres commercial. No matter how many times shown, it still instantly draws the eye with its leaden mix of visual clichés heaped upon the lustre and implied faux exoticism that panoramic views of any gravel pit inevitably inspires. Especially notable are the glamorously metallic green tinged tyres that suggest either the colour resolution of this commercial is slightly off kilter or that the product is made from inferior rubber. If it was shown without graphics ("Motorcycle Tyres Only") and a different end product shot, it could just as easily do service selling something else entirely. The rugged countryside backdrop could double underline the implied adventurous lifestyle users of an aspiring new strongly smelling men's shampoo have or else showcase the freedom a range of barely detectable incontinence underwear grants wearers, if only you can rely on them to always keep you dry.

With the sponsorship partners adverts back on repeat on the big screen, there is time to glance in the official programme. Buried on pages 74 and 75 is a wonderful article on what is laughably rather grandiosely called "the SGP Academy". After close on two decades of failing to invest anything beyond sweet words back into British speedway (or anywhere else for that matter), this year (and last) BSI have finally kindly deigned to let the Poultec rider training initiative (originally started at King's Lynn under Buster Chapman) have a room for free inside the stadium BSI have already paid to hire. The total cost (if any) to BSI is, possibly, some stationary and light refreshments for this unoccupied room. These constitute almost the sum total of their meagre investments in British Speedway since they first got involved systematically exploiting the sport in this country two decades ago. Without being told to do so, Phil Lanning understands his journalistic role is to spew out some written pats on the back towards BSI (in their own Curtis Sport produced, edited by Nigel Pearson official programme) for the brilliance of their vision in so generously helping the unnamed but aspiring young British riders that "are being nurtured right now". Before giving good written head – and in arguably the most thrilling section of the whole programme or, indeed, any programme of the 2018 series – Phil projects us collectively forward into a particularly more-or-less-the-same-as-now near future. It is 2028. Fans arrive in "pure electric cars, taking selfies on virtual reality phones while robots police the roads". Setting aside what this rather limited vision of the future tells us about Phil's unconscious, apparently there is an outside possibility that there will still be British riders in contention for the World Championship in a decade's time. Given the current state of British speedway and likely switch to semi-professional riders, even by imaginative futurology or science-fiction standards, this does sound ludicrously far-fetched. Some attendees of the SGP Academy are devote believers. For example, Kyle "hot Brit prospect" Bickley went last year (aged 15) so is massively keen to hail the benefits of the tuition offered and unspecified insights gained. "It was pretty cool to be honest. I learnt so much in one day. Most of that was behind a desk like being at school again which was unusual."

Ex-rider Olly Allen "36" is an enthusiastic teacher ("we could be training up future World Champions") only too happy to pass on his expertise, experience and knowledge via the SGP Academy to the next generation of riders. He is especially keen to help them overcome the real or imagined "stigma" of "using a skipping rope in the pits". In basic terms, the key assumption underlying his vision of the aims of the academy appears to be the need for greater professionalism. The toolbox of any aspiring but savvy young speedway rider apparently requires "managing your social media" and "looking after sponsors" properly but seems to be primarily founded on the idea that like all "top athletes" these young adults can somehow exercise and diet their way to becoming World Champions. Given contemporary riders everywhere starve themselves (like jockeys) nowadays in order to be fractionally lighter on their bikes and, thereby, improve their power-to-weight ratios, food has become something of an all-encompassing obsession. Even Olly has it on his mind when explaining the curriculum, "it's like putting pieces of a pie together". Given it is still in its infancy, though the accompanying mood music is loud ("revolutionised"), any transformational outcomes the SGP Academy has so far delivered are currently hard to specifically identify as the pay off – if it comes – is way down the line. In a sports world where incremental gains are increasingly the aim, luckily Olly can already report some incredible dietary success, "a lot of parents said after our Academy in Cardiff last year that their kids had changed like eating brown bread and not eating white, stuff like that."

In perfect synchronicity, while nutrition, psychology and diet looms larger and larger in the lives of the increasingly lean professional troupe of current SGP riders, the entertainment menu served up to the fans on the track for over a decade or so has been increasingly thin pickings too. All very factory-produced own-brand white bread so looks right and is regularly consumed but is invariably bland and unsatisfying. Of course, the embedded (mostly freelance) media and organisers' staff celebrate each SGP event as if they are excitingly innovative, never-to-be-forgotten three-starred Michelin meals. As if to confirm this dull state of affairs, Tai gives us an *amuse bouche* of a win in heat 9 with a from-the-gate victory won with dull ease by virtue of riding a wide line on what appears to be a faster bike than his rivals. The saintly Greg gets warned for moving at the tapes in the initial attempt to run heat 10 before winning the re-run. Of more interest is the ongoing debacle of the Lambert debut. His first mercy of the night – a re-run after a shockingly unconfident leaden start that has one of Craig's mates perceptively but gleefully remark, "Lambert's having a terrible night. He's lost all rhythm" – sees Lambert hold third at the second attempt right until the penultimate corner. There he gets another speedway lesson in competition at this level from Freddie Lindgren who (predictably) aggressively cuts him off in order to pass and relegate him to last place. A three race princely minimum of zero points did not feature as part of the pre-meeting Lambert media script. Back in the pits, with unglory infecting all who gaze upon Robert, the big-screen cameras suddenly fail to catch sight of any pitside Rosco advice photobombs. When Craig wins heat 11, his Cumbrian friends add delirium to the frenzied roar of the stadium crowd to greet his second successive win of the night. Seeing the series form book to date thrown out of the window is the cue for the 111 athletics team crew to party with the abandon of a long-planned bank holiday night out in Manchester rather than Carlisle. They dance, shout and loudly swear to greet the sudden lottery win they all knew was inevitable. Almost unnoticed in the mounting euphoria, at the other end of the spectrum, an out-of-sorts Nicki concedes early and coasts the fourth lap home for third place. Though Craig has often found himself at the back of SGP races this season, in contrast he continues to wholeheartedly race each heat to the chequered flag. Professionalism dictates he mostly save his irk, disappointment and despair for other more private off-stage locations. Maciej Janowski wins heat 12 in imperious fashion. This next set of five starts but four races has taken 22 minutes to complete.

The Monster commercial again heralds in the latest interval. One of Craig's mates sensibly beat the rush to the bar by missing heat 12. Yet again, his beer tray laden return is a languid affair that lingers just the wrong side of posy. The steep stairs are his catwalk in clothes that allows for the accidental display of taut thighs and biceps. It is a physique he admires enough for us all but still wants to share. On the subject of posy Phil Morris is out on his own much more highly visible FIM mandated catwalk, this time by the pits entrance area of bend 1. As ever, the Cardiff track is rutting and cutting up. All over. But especially unpredictably on bends 2 and 3 as evidenced by sudden occasional bike wrestles for the riders. Phil telegraphs his curatorial concern and heavy touch management through his usual elaborate series of stamps, gestures and brief shale caresses. As these interventions with or instructions to staff fail to have noticeable impact and the condition of the temporary track progressively (as they do) worsens, this display is once again all fur coat and no knickers. Over the stadium loudspeaker system and on the big screens, it is announced that Cardiff 2019 tickets go on sale tomorrow. Fans are clearly getting so hard to attract to Wales in the sufficient numbers of previous stagings that BSI need to leverage, then harness whatever spontaneous enthusiasm the faint euphoria of the day-after afterglow that this experience of the meeting briefly generates in some of its punters. Next year Cardiff is going to (weirdly) be in September. So, really, BSI are dragging back revenues into this year for an event next year that is still over 450 days away from being staged. In comparison, though it is less than two months until it is scheduled, tickets for the 2018 Slovenian SGP are still yet to go on sale on the SGP website. So, in this instance, the sub-optimal customer journey and overall experience BSI love to in obscure locations has yet to even get underway. It is easy to figure out that BSI get all Cardiff revenues whereas their staging-cum-royalty-cum-management fee from the Slovenian promoters for their staging of that event is fixed and (probably) already paid so there is little financial incentive or customer service imperative to further maximise sales revenues. In both instances (Krsko 2018 and Cardiff 2019), what fans want comes a long way last. Stranger still, BSI Speedway put it about that the date change to the autumn is part of that old canard: a strategic initiative to attract newcomers to the Cardiff SGP. Namely, the under-25 demographic aka students. Sadly, BSI have once again failed to do their research properly as the influx of returning and fresher students to Uni doesn't start until a week after the event takes place. Doh! Worse still from a BSI point of view, if they were serious about the need for this Cardiff change to the autumn, they failed to check, book or secure this date moving forwards as normal timings for Six Nations fixtures resume in 2020 (as there will be no Rugby World Cup). This forced switch back to the summer months in 2020 means that there will be two Cardiff SGPs in around 21 months so overall revenues are likely to fall.

The already bubbling 111 crew go wild when Craig Cook wins heat 13. It is his third successive win. Craig is so high up the SGP leader board a metaphorical nose bleed threatens and his qualification for one of the SGP semi-finals for the first time is almost guaranteed. The lads punch the air, shout and group hug. Horns blare in cacophony elsewhere in the stadium. Though passing space in the seat rows is almost as restricted as on the track, Craig's crew mingle and interchange seats and rows with abandon. Luckily they are all dressed in athletics gear for the Brazilian (via way of Cumbria) carnival style flamboyant energy they expend in their celebrations. They seize and live in the joyful moment. The time for contemplative appreciation is later with heat 14 already up at the tapes. It is a vanilla SGP heat – processional, dutiful and forgettable. Apart, of course, for the track increasingly entering into the equation by cutting up and catching riders unawares with its random bumps and divots. The next two races are also unmemorable too from a thrills point of view. That said, Robert Lambert does gain his first point of the night when Martin Vaculik has an engine failure in heat 15. Back in the pits, to avoid the taint of failure by association but keep the door open in case of race win, edge-of-screen camera bombers Rosco and trainer bloke migrate their ongoing mission to offer unsolicited advice and congratulation from the vicinity of the Lambert pit bay more towards the Cook one. They always had every faith in Craig though they made no public statements to that effect beforehand. Memory loss apparently brought on by the proximity of live broadcast cameramen afflicts Rosco sufficiently that he temporarily forgets only weeks ago firing Cook from the national team for the Speedway of Nations by text message. Prior to then re-instating him when it turned out this wasn't permitted in the rules that surely no national team manager could be expected to read or know. Heat 16 sees Nicki's engine "problems" briefly abate long enough for him to spend two laps battering Holder and Zagar – aka using his "experience" and "track craft". These ministrations and exertions engineer him a second place finish.

Say what you like about Tai Woffinden but, sometimes, he is really committed, almost bravely so. After a comfortable heat 17 win in the fastest time of the night, with no apparent thought to any of the consequences, back in his pits bay we all see him riskily open a can of Monster and actually drink from it. Properly. It is an actual gulp-cum-drink rather than a tentative sip. We all see it on the big screen and, I suspect, collectively silently gasp to our ourselves at his understated everyday heroism. According to the latest research by the British Nutrition Foundation published by the *Guardian*, each Monster Energy 500ml contains the rough equivalent of 13 or so 4g sugar cubes and a double espresso, irrespective of the can colours. Tai must either be an experienced drinker of such fluids or only actually ingest a tiny amount to avoid the inevitable over-stimulation side effects of surfer dude hipness, jitteriness and palpitations in his later races. It also takes sponsor care and management to new amazingly self-sacrificing levels. Visual speedway rider platitudes in the area of product placement are endemic and have a long history. The proximity and surfeit of cameras nowadays has taken peacockery and virtuoso display to new levels, to the extent that there is almost zero scope for innovation. When you think that Tai flounced away from riding for his country (Britain) and declared future unavailability – since rescinded when the team got privatised and the pay percentages got sorted – because of a dispute (allegedly) with team manager Rosco over nutrition and diet that fell short of Woffinden's need to at all times treat his body as a highly graffitied temple. Whatever the nutrition merits or otherwise of kebabs, though Rosco supposed made his managerial culinary choice for motivational team-building reasons – and, after all, as a long-distance lorry driver he is going to know how to avoid dodgy food and restaurants – Tai took in water over these particular doner kebabs. Perhaps, it was symptom of deeper problems in their relationship? But, equally, when it comes to nutritional militancy, let us not forget that Stoke speedway promoter Dave Tattum remains the one of the earliest and most hugely persuasive speedway role models for the benefits of vegetarianism in a life well lived. Tattum was British speedway's second most important vegetarian after Tony Steele though, such is the fashion for controlled diets, many riders are possibly even closet vegans or, at least, regularly v-curious. Whatever the ins and outs, by actually drinking some of this Monster fluid Tai is suddenly sets the bar way higher with a new standard of what insouciance about your own personal safety in the face of frightening danger looks like at work. For the benefit of the cameras, fellow team rider Greg Hancock has spent many years pretend suckling on drinking straws protruding from plastic vessels festooned with the Monster colours and logo. Or waving it about in an exaggerated fey way that often borders on St. Vitus dance proportions rather than merely just the melodramatic. Rather like badly acted alcoholic drinks in feature films, it is often hard to believe that the drink in question Greg holds aloft has not been substituted with more palatable but fluorescent hued coloured water. Of course, for film stars this is often a matter of sobriety rather than taste. Anyways, with his bold deep draft drink, Tai has moved the sponsor care Overton window from mere bottle waving towards verifiable ingestion aforethought.

There is, arguably, a case for extending the limitations on advertising energy drinks at active and sporty young people to include banning impressionable and increasingly anorexic younger speedway riders from its use. The contemporary obsession with bike power-weight ratios has seen exercise, diet and nutrition come massively to the fore. Given daily caffeine and sugar suggested age health limits for children's consumption of energy drinks like Monster and Red Bull are really a function of comparative body size and weight as much as cognitive, skeletal and muscle development, the current trend towards the miniaturisation of speedway riders bodies surely means that they deserve similar protections? We demand SGP riders wear kevlars, crash helmets and neck protection yet allow Monster to provide a free bar for these often increasingly skeletal young people in the pits. Admittedly, and luckily, these riders aren't going to get pregnant or breast-feed and also often already have travel-induced sleep problems but their little bodies could still suffer from the hyperactivity, jitters, head and stomach aches. Strangely, the exciting Monster montage of thrilling events didn't cover any such alleged side effects let alone any weight gain and bloating. Or talking to God on The Great White Telephone, something almost as technicolour – albeit along with diced carrots and tomatoes too – as their can colours and advert film image montage.

Heat 18 sees Nicki experience a *bona fide* engine failure rather than one of those imaginary gremlins that so often beset his equipment but would fail to convince even the most favourably inclined court. We know it is genuine as Nicki's bike actually judders on its second lap and, thereby, sees him slip from nearly first to fourth. Usually Nicki is already last before he suddenly "discovers" the lost power or internal engine equipment failure with his special mechanically hypersensitive X-ray eyes. All the remaining riders also judder too but that choppiness is due to the mogul runs and bumps of the Cardiff one-off temporary track. For once, the third place rider – Fredrik Lindgren – is the unhappiest soul post-race.

He needed a win to get sufficient points to progress to the semi-final stage. Failure to do so effectively means that – after only five meetings of a ten meeting SGP series – his ambition to be 2018 World Champion just ended. Barring injuries to other rival riders, of course. Freddie's has been a quick decline from the early heady days of optimism around the time of the initial SGP meetings in Warsaw and Prague. These saw Lindgren ride and get talked about as the rider most likely to challenge or even – heaven forefend – end Tai's oft pre-heralded by his agent Nigel Pearson while cos-playing as a journalist during his live speedway commentary work three-peat World Championship ambitions and ascension thereafter to further greater glory. Obviously, the media won't breathe a word about the extinction of Freddie's hopes or those of every other rider vis-à-vis Tai's already significant cumulative total points tally. One of the many unwritten rules of speedway churnalism is to never admit the identity of the pending World Champion isn't a mystery or that the series is a lame duck until every extreme outside mathematical has been relentlessly talked up to exhaustion. At that point, attention must mandatorily switch to exploring the ineffable mystery and magic of the competition for eighth place. I don't know about you but I always celebrate and can instantly recall who finished eighth at Wimbledon, in the Open, Premier League, Cricket World Cup and the Grand National? Back down in Lindgren's pit bay the mood is grim and the disappointment (or anger) barely suppressed, if the live images flashed up on the stadium giant screens of Freddie's 1000 yard stare tell any story.

Heat 19 sees Greg Hancock (48) make the perfect start. So much so, that the referee instantly stops the race to call it back. However, this is not the real significance of the moment. When historians look back in depth over annuls of world speedway, the minutes after the initial false start of heat 19 will go down in posterity as the time Greg's hired hand and Gamma proxy Josh Gudgeon left the shadows of his formal job responsibilities to finally bestride the shale film stage with grace and authority. It also further confirms the full-service world top speedway riders enjoy nowadays while they are otherwise occupied at the track and/or busy racing. Savvier wealthier SGP riders such as Greg Hancock sub-contract their complaints and public displays of anger to other hired hands positioned at trackside. Joe Parsons automatically does this for all his Monster Energy sponsored team riders: complaints primarily for Greg, celebrations for Patryk and Tai, commiserations for Chris. It is the way Parsons lives his job description. Parachuted into the upper echelons of world speedway on a fast track while still at Hollister University while still without real marketing/PR experience, purpose or function – during actual 2018 SGP meetings Josh has taken it upon himself to add his theatrical emoting to the Greg complaints party cause too. Afterwards this helps validate his self-elected role as the fans' and riders' representative true voice on speedway earth that he channels via the medium of pithy tweets. Casting aside the more humdrum formal day job aspects of his care-in-the-community role as Greg Hancock's "tour manager" and hyper-dedicated amanuensis for the benefit of the SGP live cameras, heat 19 sees previously risen without trace Josh burst forth fully formed from his chrysalis to – thereafter – ceaselessly but authoritatively emote for Greg. We get the happy photobomber version in the rare instance high-five celebrations are needed but are mainly served up the angry/frustrated/sad version, whenever real or imagined injustices strike. Confirming the old adage, why bark yourself when you have a dog to do it for you, on the stadium big screen we collectively see Gudgeon grow into the borrowed halo of authority he would otherwise mainly lack without the endorsement of Hancock's employ to excuse his yaps and gestures into the watching lenses on Greg's behalf. Like a less-likeable pits lane Bambi taking those first faltering steps, the camera is inevitably drawn to those imploring out-stretched arms as they direct righteous indignation towards referee Froschauer. Come Judgement Day, the heinous crime of falsely adjudging Greg "Twitcher" Hancock for moving at the tapes will gain the greater punishment of eternal damnation rather than the speedway equivalent of opprobrium for putting on the red stop lights before the riders had even made it to the first corner.

Josh is resplendently eye-catching in his newly dyed camera-friendly bright bottle-blonde hair. He theatrically pantomimes his strength of feeling and instant intuitive blood-conscious awareness of the speedway reality of the situation. Impressive innate skills to immediately flourish when looking over an airfence towards the start line from an oblique wrong angle from around 40 or 50 yards away. Without questioning his eyesight and unconscious bias or, indeed, need to even watch the big-screen replays to check his appearance or the veracity of his opinion that a truly scandalous crime had been committed against the adorable and saintly Greg, Gudgeon quickly summons a depth of outrage usually found for heart-rending television pictures from a poorly run dogs home just after maltreated but unwanted cute puppies have been discovered shivering in unsanitary condition in their small cages. It is outrage so volcanic, Josh briefly manages to out-outrage the Maradona style eye-bulging apoplexy Monster Joe regularly delivers on cue to the cameras over any decision that goes against his sponsored SGP riders. In Parsons' world, every real or imagined slight against his heroic team of sponsored riders is an unforgivable actual and/or thought crime. Though as a Monster Energy team rider Greg already has guaranteed lava flows of indignation on hand to spew forth from Monster Joe upon hint of the merest of any track *faux pas*, it is a sign of how keen Hancock is to grab the further glory of a Top 8 SGP finish that he co-opts Josh as his on-hand permanent joker to double the outrage, whenever required. Rising like a Colossus to the occasion of an active camera lens, Josh gives the watching thousands his version of priority boarding levels of emoting. It is even more visually stunning on the big screen than his earlier unreciprocated attempt at speedway bad-boy youth culture which took the form of a spontaneous but failed fist-bump of consolation with Maciej Janowski seconds after his exclusion from heat 7. It was a rookie error to assume SGP riders who don't employ Gudgeon give a toss for his opinion or find comfort in his consolation. It also wasn't indicative of his fabled speedway smarts to pick such a poor moment – just as "Magic" strides angrily away from the track towards pit lane – to try to remind all us viewers of his hard-won extensive rider connections. Nevertheless, finally, after the best lengthy apprenticeship riding the nepotism magic carpet can muster, heat 19 sees Josh come-of-age with his righteous-indignation-for-fans-and-riders-everywhere televised moment. He is Liz Hurley in that dress to Greg's Hugh Grant – albeit ranged against the dark forces of referees and unscrupulous promoters that – forever – change how we view the speedway world thereafter.

It is a such a masterly and dramatic show of confected rightful indignation that even referee Herr Froschauer can't ignore or fail to act upon it. And doesn't. First off, the referee dutifully orders a re-run with all four riders back before then refusing to warn Hancock. Weirder and more uniquely still, we are told by announcer Kevin Coombes that the "referee has apologised". It is an apology that won't stop the FIM quietly ensuring that he never – barring illness or unexplained favouritism – gets chosen to adjudicate another SGP as punishment for his virtuoso series of bungles here tonight. I can't recall ever hearing or having heard of a mid or post-meeting public apology by a speedway referee? Though nice to have, they are nonetheless still useless. Worse still, said apology fatally undermines the air of authority and judgement that haloes the power of all referees. Just like we don't want our heroes to be found to be fallible (or learn how those delicious tasting pork pies really get made), we want to be able to selectively hate our officials without any glimpse of their common humanity or vulnerability. Typically, of course, it further illustrates the one rule for the chosen (or Monster sponsored) SGP riders and another rule for the less exalted other riders. Craig Cook made a similarly swift start to heat 4 and the replays also clearly showed that the referee had incorrectly stopped this race too. Yet ref Froschauer failed to apologise and, instead, doubled down by warning Cook. In that re-run Cook finished last. Though counterfactuals are often a quick way to early madness, if things had been otherwise Craig could possibly now have four rides, four wins and twelve points. What a huge SGP confidence boost, possibly lasting onwards throughout the remainder of the 2018 series too, that would have been. Instead, though creditable, Craig is on nine points with three wins from four races and Greg gets a re-run. Further fuelling uneasy feelings of injustice, inevitably Hancock doesn't win but does display some on-track ongoing irk by riding successive hard third bends on laps one and two. All four riders struggle for bike control on a lumpy track. Glowering by the pit gate, Josh appears fractionally less theatrically aggrieved.

The last qualifying race of the night sees Craig Cook vie for second in the first corner only to have his bike accelerate and spear skywards over the fence towards the flinching buttock-clenched photographers snapping away on their bend 2 elevated stand. After abrupt take-off, the bike flies through the air to land in the neutral area between track and crowd before writhing to a stop. Wherever high-powered speedway bikes get raced, the possibility of wild escapees firing towards to centregreen staff or the crowd is ever present. In the heat of moment and thick of the racing action, riders are going to open up the throttle to gain race position without fully gauging the narrowly confined context. Some tracks have better safety precautions than others. By its very nature, any temporary track is going to install all its furniture, safety measures or facilities on a one-off basis. On a tight technical track like Cardiff really opening up the throttle by accident or design is going to cause problems. Historically this indoor track notoriously cuts up and deteriorates. The next day Tai Woffinden would describe the track in national print press reports as "gnarly" rather than dangerous. Given dangerous rarely exists in the speedway rider parlance or, apparently, their dictionaries – except on rare occasions or unless, of course, it is the inaugural meeting at the new Belle Vue – perhaps gnarly is an antonym for dangerous. Or, possibly a euphemism. There is no doubt that the combination of lumps and bumps plus superfast bikes without brakes is a potent eye-catching cocktail when the racing area is constricted and restricted. By their nature, freak accidents are unexpected but shouldn't be unexpected or unprepared for. Though organisers BSI do regularly block off some lower tier seating inside the Principality Stadium for flying shale reasons and also have a modern fully homologated air fence for flying bikes and riders, sadly they don't also install catch fencing to further protect the fans. While they maximise their revenues by premium pricing said lower tier close to the track/racing seats, fans have no additional protection against outlier flying bike accidents other than the flimsy plastic Union flags so kindly provided by BSI Speedway. Anyone entering any speedway stadium usually finds that their ticket warns them that they have entered the stadium at their own risk. MY Cardiff ticket fails to state this, though legal small print in the programme does advise speedway is dangerous and attended at my own risk without any responsibility by the staging parties. Quite how anyone who doesn't buy a £10 programme – and many understandably don't – learns of their jeopardy at the Cardiff SGP is unclear. Since they have not been advised of their (lack of) rights, have BSI Speedway still legally eluded all possible obligations in the event of accidents involving fans? Eating your tea or walking in the street entails risk of injury or death too, though no one draws your attention to said unlikely dangers. Doubtless the organisers are compliant with the letter of health and safety regulations that apply when staging speedway meetings inside this stadium, they have chosen to not further minimise the remote statistical chance of spectator injury (or, worse death) with additional safety features – such as catch fencing – above and beyond their full legal compliance. Obviously, this both saves costs and maximises revenues at their showpiece event with only freak outlier downside risk borne by the fans.

On the track, in a fraction of second after seeing the crash and wild bike ahead of him, Robert Lambert lays his bike down with lightning reaction. This almost intuitive speed of reaction marks Robert out as possessing the high calibre gifts of vision and twitch muscles usually required in successful speedway riders. Craig is down on the track for so long that Tai comes out to check on his status. The 111 crew are aghast and temporarily silenced. Always keen to find new audiences or expand existing ones for his SGP charades show, Phil Morris leaves the track to go over to the photographers' gallery to mime a completely new set of expressive gestures that appear to request that photos of the incident and flight of the bike are to be incorporated into the Welsh Olympic dive team practice programme. And should be emailed to him afterwards for fuller consideration before they are then completely forgotten about. Craig eventually rises to his feet to applause from the stadium and also his Cumbrian mates. Though excluded from the re-run as the cause of the accident, Cook needs to quickly physically and psychologically brush himself down in order to prepare for his first ever SGP semi-final. Craig must race this most important heat of his SGP career (to date) without his now inoperable damaged winningest SGP bike.

In the re-run, second placed Jason Doyle is surprised by a Lambert pass on the first bend of the last lap. The 2018 series so far has been an ongoing struggle with anything and everything for the current Aussie World Champion after two seasons as the supremely dominant SGP rider. In this instance, Jason locks-up-cum-tumbles from his bike in an awkward fall that is made much worse when his bike follows and lands heavily upon him. Doyle is down for a considerable time. Amazingly, the nightmare night for FIM referee Christian Froschauer continues to bungle when he again wrongly excludes Lambert. It is a debut Cardiff SPG night to forget for Lambert compounded by mechanical gremlins and daffy decision-making by the ref. Ever keen for attention and chance to further virtue signal his professionalism, rather masterfully – given another rider lies injured – Greg Hancock comes out to the start line to ostentatiously garden gates two and four. He chooses this activity rather than offer words or emotional support to the stricken Doyle. It goes without saying that it is completely pointless preparation work that serves no purpose as, before the semi-finals get raced, not only will the track be graded but Greg doesn't know which semi-final he'll race in or from what gate. It is pure look-at-me theatrics. You could say showmanship if there was any entertainment value in watching such shale gardening but, I'm going to suggest, there isn't. After considerable medical attention, Jason Doyle is loaded into an ambulance which then proceeds to do a lap of honour. This is plain weird and slightly comic. Only those with X-ray eyes can see Jason wave (if he is?) or nod (if he does?) to acknowledge the cheers of the crowd. If Doyle is lying there in agony, the ambulance interior and pain likely muffles the applause. Given that the strict timings and expense of satellite access requires a ferocity of SGP race frequency – sets of four races raced in quick succession before lengthy commercial breaks mostly unrequired by any racing need at the actual live event – usually dictates that the riders generally don't often do traditional laps of honour/celebration, this ambulance run around the track is even more peculiar. Looking to the bright side, at least it indicates Jason isn't life-threateningly injured. This ambulance lap of honour aside, the lack of SGP race victory celebration laps is yet another area where attending fans are regularly short-changed for the needs of sponsors, advertisers and those not doing so.

This lengthy delay gives further opportunity to peruse the official programme and wonder why its editor Nigel Pearson chose not to find space to commemorate six times World Champion Ivan Mauger? Given, it is the first British Speedway Grand Prix since his death on April 18 2018, it is astonishing that there isn't some sort of tribute or feature included. Ivan and Tony Rickardsson jointly hold the record for the most World Championship wins. Space is found for three pages of Nigel's "informative" interview with Phil Morris but none is available for an actual World Championship legend. Such an omission is a surprise given Nigel's expertise, knowledge and love of the sport. It is also further confirmation of the contempt current rights holders BSI Speedway (An IMG Company) have for almost any history of the World Championships prior to their involvement. If only giving Ivan 15 seconds at the Warsaw SGP (and mis-pronouncing his surname) was scant recognition of his World Championship contributions, this is much worse. Especially given Ivan's contribution to the status, development and professionalism of speedway in Britain too (arguably Mauger set in place the high standards template contemporary riders mimic or extend). Or, indeed, given Nigel is his press agent, how often interviews with Tai reference equalling or exceeding Ivan's achievements when he has yet to reach half that number. Though we all know that historically televised speedway has always been shown on commercial stations (and featured on the first night ITV ever broadcast), when the BBC don't mention Ivan or Ronnie Moore (who passed away in August 2018 so couldn't be honoured in the Cardiff programme) on their Sports Personality of the Year programme in December Peter Oakes brands them "REAL losers". Oakes criticises the programme maker's "ignorance" and opines, "the fact that two of speedway's greatest legends, deserved their place on the In Memory slot" but didn't get a mention is "scandalous". Given Peter's oft-cited work in the 1970s as Ivan's agent, let alone his authorship of *Ivan Mauger's Speedway Extravaganza* (the first speedway book I owned), this omission from the official FIM Speedway Grand Prix programme for Cardiff surely deserved similar if not greater criticism in his *Speedway Star* column at the time or, indeed, in his six page Winners & Losers end of year compendium article? But, then, unfairly bashing BBC speedway coverage plays better to the gallery and is the safer prejudice confirming option with influential speedway power brokers.

Without announcement and possibly against the rules(?), three hours into the meeting it turns out that heat 20 has been awarded. Inside the stadium, we learn this when the riders get on with the semi-finals. Across the aisle from me, two blokes from Bournemouth cheer Tai on throughout. "The racing is always exciting here. Our tickets were £19 each. You go to Poole and you could spend 30 quid and the racing is dull." Zmarzlik wins semi-final 1 with ease and power. Afterwards, I am asked whether I noticed that his bikes had specially adapted shorter frames for the tighter more technical turns required at Cardiff. I hadn't. Though my eyes are mechanically untutored, my ears do recognise that Bartosz speaks in a fabulously high register of almost Alan Ball-esque proportions that might sometimes attract dogs or other beings with high-frequency hearing. To the disappointment of the 111 crew in athletics gear next to me, Craig suffers an engine failure in semi-final 2. The heights he scaled this evening both confirm his abilities at this level and halo an afternoon and evening of joyful celebration for his mates. Before the final, one them – Mark from Workington – introduces himself. He "used to race motorbikes" and even tried speedway training session, "I had a go with Craig Branney". He remains wary of the sudden dramatic dangers the lure of speed and adventure on such high-powered bikes poses, "Two of me mates are paralysed". With his cunning plan of foreshortened bike frames to match the proportions of the track and his diminutive body, Zmarzlik deservedly wins the final. Woffinden is second and, with five meetings in the 2018 SGP series to go, is already 20 points ahead of his nearest rival rider. Even by SGP standards, this is much too early in the series to be World Champion elect and retain floating interest in the SGP as a serious competition. Historically, the whereabouts of the SGP World Championship crown doesn't go down to the wire and often is all over bar the shouting two or three events before the series concludes. Clearly something is wrong with the series structure as a competition – but completely fine as a proven television and commercial rights revenue maximising format – when only once in the last decade has the series really gone down to the last to determine the overall winner. Tai could take at least one SGP off and still win massively easily this season.

Winner: Bartosz Zmarzlik (19 points)

Second: Tai Woffinden (16 points)

Third: Maciej Janowski (12 points)

Fourth: Greg Hancock (12 points)

Landshut SGP Qualifier final – 28.07.18

"The one thing I wanted to read about was what
Scott thought of the Grand Prix itself"

Paul Burbidge

FOR a small Bavarian town less than hour away from Munich airport by bus, Landshut has a lot going on this weekend if the circular advert post outside its utilitarian but austere railway station (rather than the conspicuously empty streets and sleepy town vibe) is any indication. Last night Ringlstetter & Band (me neither) played the Landshut Sparkassen Arena while tomorrow (Sunday) night Anastacia plays the Ringelstecherwiese as part of her Radl Tour. The big event tonight is, of course, Die Nacht Der Entscheidung Speedway Grand Prix Challenge at the One Solar Arena.

Every rider competing in Landshut tonight can possibly join the 2019 SGP series as the top three riders (who do not finish in the top 8 of the 2018) qualify for it. To get to this final qualifying round, competitors have already had to ride well in obscurely located qualifying meetings elsewhere. These would all score well at Scrabble. They were held in Zarnovica, Slangerup, Lonigo and Abensberg. On the whole, the SGP series is a closed shop that admits very few new entrants not chosen or co-opted by rights holders BSI Speedway (An IMG Company) in consultation with the FIM and informally consulted elite sponsorship partners. Whereas all new riders in SGP qualifiers are nominated by their respective federations, albeit limited by their permitted qualifying allocation of the 64 places. The involvement of the FIM is the fig leaf that allows BSI to pretend that there is both an element of open qualification to these "world" championships as well as a smidgeon of independent decision making behind their choice of wild cards. Any and all influence that key series partner Monster Energy might apply is, of course, strenuously denied as merit, circumstance and complete coincidence saw their sponsored riders Hancock and Holder get two of the three 2018 wild cards.

The possibility of random unanointed riders getting into the series based on current form and ability or their stellar performance at one-off meetings doesn't fit well with the psyche or control freakery of BSI's series management. Even for this meeting, in consultation with the carefully weighed opinions of the tame independent decision makers at the FIM, BSI have given out wild cards for this meeting to those it (currently) favours. The riders getting a second go despite failing to qualify to ride in Landshut from qualifiers elsewhere are Robert Lambert, Vaclav Milik and Piotr Pawlicki. [1] If ever there was a clear buy signal about how BSI would like this evening to go, then these selections are a good guide to who they might like to join the 2019 series. Not satisfied with already making over 80 percent of the rider choices for the SGP series, rights holders BSI really can't help themselves meddling, even in the 'free and fair election' portion of the World Championship. Though it is deemed impolite to mention it in rarefied SGP circles, Tai Woffinden has never qualified to ride in the series. He

---

[1] These riders were all picked as they were on the younger side – with good stats and results in the senior leagues around Europe – and also as they had proven themselves in the sister FIME SEC series. Additionally, these riders also have the back up and finances needed to compete at GP level. Thought and calculus evidence goes into the selection of these riders in case of the need for demonstrative defence against any formal counter protests.

has been specifically chosen by BSI whenever he has not made the ongoing sinecure that is the automatic re-qualification for any rider that finishes in the top 8 rankings.

Given almost every rider here is capable of finishing in the top three on their day and also ultra-keen to do so, the appeal of this meeting for fans is that almost every heat has significance so will be raced lustily by all the riders. Sadly, that is no longer the case in the ten-round SGP series itself, where numerous processional run-of-the-mill races compliment the endless diet of "another day another dollar" run-of-the-mill ho-hum meetings. Full-on racing from the get-go – rather than media claims that is the case – invariably whets the appetite of any true speedway fan. It is why, like so many other fans, I am here. We fully expect to see many of the best Speedway Grand Prix races of the year/season here in Landshut tonight. The weather Gods must feel otherwise since – after many weeks of 30 degree plus temperatures – three hours or so hours before tapes up torrential rain and thunder of biblical proportions hits the area. Even the most-experienced track curators struggle with the after-effects of monsoon-like rain.

The helpful and efficient staff at the Tourist Information office have never heard of speedway but do roughly know what a motorbike is. Thankfully they also know the whereabouts of One Solar Arena but advise that is out in the country quite a way from downtown Landshut and located in its satellite sister village Ellermuhle. Formally and officially known as Landshut-Ellermuhle, it is in Landshut the same way Gatwick or Stansted airports are in London, albeit East Croydon distance away. Though not well served by public transport, there are buses. These are infrequent and the equidistant bus stops closest to the speedway are both still a good walk from the stadium itself the Tourist Office staff kindly pre-warn me. Later, sat on one of only two buses that will actually get people there this afternoon or evening, there are almost as many posters advertising (three) the meeting as people actually going there (four, if you include me). We are initially accompanied by two mums with shopping, pushchairs and young children who get off in the outlying residential communities before we can persuade them about the child-soothing joys of speedway. To the first-time visitor looking out the bus windows, a succession of residential areas soon give way to freshly laid looking bright black tarmac country roads that service new-build strip mall style out-of-town shopping centres, various distribution centres or give access to endless fields of impressively tall close-to-harvest lush corn. It is a hugely popular local crop grown for bio-fuel rather than human consumption.

Ellermuhle village looks like the kind of place you decide to bring your young family (or ageing parents) if you are worried about the big city ways of Landshut. Its streets are narrow, tree lined and lush. The houses comfortable and prosperous with well-tended gardens. Given the residential nature of the area, the immediate vicinity of the nearest bus stop to the event doesn't exactly shout speedway. When the three other German-speaking fans (probably because they removed then pilfered all the posters he had on display on his bus) get off, the driver insists I stay on so he can drop me off closer to the One Solar stadium at a crossroads further along the route of the number 9 bus. Though he would like to do so, work shifts mean that the driver is unable to attend this SGP-lite event tonight. He is very knowledgeable about previous recent and historic speedway World Champions as well as Martin Smolinski ("he has a Polish father"). The driver waves away the poster theft, "They left over 50 at the station, we couldn't get rid of them as really no one was interested to do anything with them but me!" From the crossroads, the stadium is visible in the far distance. The land is flat and fields closer to the track are grassy or else have already been harvested down to stubble. Marshals direct a steady flow of early arrivals to designated grassy parking areas that bestride the road that curves away towards the stadium. If this were a fairy tale it would go uphill and eventually lead to a castle. Sadly there is no fairy tale as it is flat country hereabouts. It is no surprise to notice the runway tarmac and airfield field markings peak through the overgrown grass of this small current working airport. There are already a good number of fans making their way on foot. Though the sun has broken through again after the torrential rain, sensibly many carry coats along with their bags laden with food and drink for later. It all adds to the comfortable family feel. As does the incredibly high incidence of thermos flasks. Even more notably, the essential local speedway accoutrement hereabouts is definitely to bring your own foam seat – more like a swimming float than a child rear car seat – to make the predominantly grassy banked viewing available inside the stadium more homely and comfortable.

Upon closer inspection, the stadium lives up to its One Solar designation in spades as all the available roof space is taken up with solar panels. This is innovative and commendably eco-friendly as well as, given the lush fields and traditional local climate, optimistic given most are non-heatwave summers. Everything about the stadium from its infrastructure, layout to stewarding shouts club or speedway community pride. Signage and guidance are nearly as plentiful as the volunteer staffing. From arrival to departure everything about the fan "touch points" at Landshut indicates forethought. It is a proper fully functioning speedway club with family and community values centre stage along with understandable pride about its hour or so strutting its stuff upon the international stage. Once through the turnstiles, the young women clad in tight bright green lycra greeting fans strike the only jarring and incongruous note to the dominance of these more traditional and homely surroundings. These women magnanimously offer the chance to sign up for something that I still don't understand what the product is or does, even after they explain twice. I do gather that if I take the plunge and sign up, then I am also automatically entered into tonight's draw for the consolation prize of a big box of popcorn. Posing for selfies with them (while also having intense product discussions) draws quite a crowd as does the other popular entrance area attraction – the speedway bike on display on the impressive Martin Smolinski stand left there for fans to climb aboard for their action photos and selfies.

Martin is the self-proclaimed and actual best currently racing German speedway rider. He bestrides the German speedway scene like a colossus. At least in terms of attention and sponsorship, if not in world status and rankings. He is the local hero round here too. That said, Martin only rides tonight as he – rather than Kai Huckenbeck who gets the nod for the German SGP in Teterow instead – has been given ("awarded") the German wildcard for this meeting. There is terrace talk that the new shale that dresses the Landshut track is specially laid to informally help with his qualification chances. Martin has good previous SGP experience as a both a full-time and regular wild card member of the series. And has also won a Grand Prix in New Zealand. Albeit that the – legal at the time – technical innovation to his bike that allegedly allowed him to do so was swiftly outlawed afterwards by the FIM authorities in revised regulations following grumbles and informal complaints by fellow SGP competitors. Nowadays Martin mostly gives his racing attention to the FIM Longtrack World Championships and only really gets to ride the SGPs by dint of these wildcard invitations. Though, like everyone racing here tonight, he could theoretically qualify to do so (again) as of right with a top three finish. The prize money given to any SGP winner is so pitiful (but FIM approved) that it reputedly cost Martin more to win that one SGP event than he got back in winnings. The basic economics of SGP racing requires that you leverage your "world" status and cache for sponsorship dollars. Martin does this with zeal and aplomb in Germany as well as with local businesses. It helps that the German language market is both large and monied but also that he lacks similar status competition from other speedway/longtrack riders. Kindly providing your bike in full regalia for photos is one of many savvy fan-facing initiatives from "Smolly". Though these touches are commercially astute, Martin also comes across as genuinely very fan-oriented and friendly. He works hard to be open and available as well as build interest in the wider community. In the 1970s, Germany did have a World Champion – Egon Muller – but also had other riders during that era who plied their trade overseas but did not make the same exalted grade. Even as a mere Reading Racers fan, German riders such as Hans Wasserman and Seppi Angemuller immediately spring to my mind. With a small speedway talent pool – compared to the size of the country or spill-over German language populations in Austria and Switzerland – to compete against from the juniors upwards, actually achieving world class standards is that much harder for talented and aspiring German speedway riders.

Also in the close vicinity to the turnstiles are a wide variety of stalls including a traditional track shop with an impressive range of merchandise that includes clothing, posters, programme boards, rider models, badges, mugs and other assorted retro or old-school memorabilia. The event programme is the traditional A5 size and produced by the club rather than sub-contracted to favoured SGP supplier Curtis Sports. As a consequence, it is informative and features original bespoke (rather than cut and pasted or auto-pilot) content. It is also reasonably priced by SGP standards for events held outside Eastern Europe and even comes with a free pen. With the best bumper crowd of the Landshut 2018 speedway season expected tonight, food and drink stalls scattered throughout the stadium grounds do brisk trade. Even without the aromatic wafts from the barbecue, it would be a crime to come to Bavaria and not try the local sausages (or beer). They are delicious. Though the local soft drink of note Cola Mix sounds a really unpromising combination of Coca Cola and orange juice, it is surprisingly thirst-quenching and extremely moreish but also hugely popular with the local wasps too. They just can't get enough of it so swarm the *ad hoc* wooden bench seating area. There they have met their match. In a virtuoso and mesmerising display of nerve and precision steady hands, a bloke opposite me called Rheinhold endlessly and effortlessly catches flying or landed wasps by their (long) wings as a prelude to crushing them under his thumb on the table. Once caught by their wings between his thumb and forefinger, the wasps frantically lash the air in search of a surface to sting before they meet their sudden death foretold on the table. Alongside him, his friends simultaneously conduct an informal wasp rescue effort for those stuck inside empty (refundable deposit) glass bottles that litter our section or else vainly try to shoo away keen landing wasps blithely unaware of the killing machine in their midst.

Rheinhold is here tonight with his friend Eric and another shy bloke whose name I don't catch. They met through their shared love of speedway and motorbikes as well as motorsports generally. All have been mechanics at some point and ridden to various degrees of enjoyment or professionalism. Eric used to mechanic F1 bikes and the other man Longtrack in the 1980s. They have spent and enjoyed years on the road – whether in the pits, on the track or in the stands – being involved in multiple capacities with various bike classifications and types. Though no longer doing the rough-and-tumble time-pressured pits work, they look back fondly. They travelled "only 60 kilometres" to get here this afternoon and now savour the moment sat at these benches on a lovely warm night drinking beers, eating local produce ("welcome to Bavaria") and chatting to friends old and new. They keenly anticipate the speedway ahead and are tremendously welcoming as well as keen to proudly describe the club, local area and Bavaria generally. In their role as unofficial reception committee and Tourist Information, they want to know the purpose of my visit and sympathise at the replacement bus service travel complexities of weekend journeys on DBahn. They also very kindly offer me a lift back into Landshut after the meeting. Eric tells me exactly where to meet ("by the big gate over there everyone leaves through") and I have absolutely no doubt his word is his bond. When it comes to the come-as-you-are friendship, fraternity and community ways of the club speedway world, even/especially as a visiting foreigner, I am immediately at home and accepted just for being a fellow like-minded soul. "We have got to know each other and made friends. It is a community we have been coming here for years. Look around you, people are workers enjoying themselves." Landshut stage seven or eight meetings a season including league racing, pairs and junior events plus individual competitions of which this is the most prestigious. "It is one of our two big events, everyone is here. There is new shale they are using for the first time tonight."

With less an hour to the meeting, FIM Race Director Phil Morris gets very animated – even by his own grandiloquent standards – about the newly laid shale with the Landshut track staff he gathers round him for this purpose on bends one and two. Though it looks pristine and perfect to my untutored eyes, Phil angrily demands sweeping changes. In fact, he wants all the newly laid shale scraped off and removed to the edge of the centregreen where it soon creates a burm, if not a ridge or, in parts, mini-hillocks. Under his instruction, visually the track goes from picture perfect to gravel pit in short order. It definitely looks like panic stations have struck the big cheese FIM non-locals. Phil summons out his boss and Director of Track Racing at the FIM – Armando Castagna – onto the track for an extensive repertoire of gestures and directional waves as if trying to explain how to pack an especially large parachute interspersed with wistful stares at the progress made so far by passing grading tractors. Armando and Phil used to race together for my club and, out of earshot in some circles, are seen as the Reading Racers Mafia. When all is said and done, Morris's job is to make sure that Armando looks good by ensuring that the FIM fulfils its contractual staging obligations to all interested parties – promoters, rights holders, sponsors and riders – by making sure that the SGP racing goes ahead. While also adhering to existing rules and regulations as well as health and safety requirements. On the whole though, whatever anyone else thinks is irrelevant so long as Castagna supports and approves of the work and approach of his protégé. Despite the sub-standard nature of the processional SGP racing nowadays and the wilful obscurity of its track locations (let alone the falling crowds and declining TV audiences), the Welshman is tipped for great things at the FIM. Armando's star also remains bright. Indeed, the FIM are already leveraging Morris's expertise elsewhere at their Ice-racing events despite his ice and deep-freezer credentials extending little beyond occasionally re-filling the ice-cube tray of his fridge at home.

With his boss on hand to grandstand for and impress, Morris goes into curation management overdrive. He demonstrates how to use a rake. He stands on top of a serious-sized grading blade to jump up and down. Ex-rider and another FIM honcho of some description, the knowledgeable and friendly Jan Staechmann comes out to join the ongoing in-depth conversation while work creating the dry ski slope of the centregreen ridge carries on around them unabated. Phil runs hither and thither. He signals and semaphores with wanton frenzy. As do selected members of the Landshut curatorial team, most likely notionally senior staff or managers. Instructions fly in all directions and two languages. The earthy common language of men is flung about with the same abandon as the shale removal. Phil is comfort hugged by what appears to be FIM Track Racing Committee member (and ex-SGP referee) Tony Steele, though it is hard to tell at a distance. The number of FIM officials and job titles appear to have encountered a rip in the space-time continuum so now multiply to fill all available corners of the known universe! Despite being one of the most obscure global sports governing bodies in current existence, any bigwig autograph hunters allowed backstage are in serious luck here tonight in Landshut. Phil's ministrations look frenetic and supremely last minute as well as in complete defiance of the actual preparations of the local track staff. If you are going to have a serious World Championship decider meeting with the big boy riders, then it comes with the territory that the FIM big cheeses are going to congregate then throw their (probably homologated) weight around too. Say what you like though, it is not often that fans get to see the centregreen get graded too! I can't recall ever having seen it dressed like this before. So much shale has been removed that they have to smooth these mounds too in case they create a mogul run for riders who hug the inside line. Indeed, the inside line gets repainted but skirts the shale berms so now has the wonky geometry of a young child trying to draw a perfect circle. German fans sat close by kindly complain bilingually (for my benefit) that they reckon that the excess shale would definitely have favoured local favourite Smolinski if it had remained in place. We know that the remedial track work is finally complete, when Phil Morris starts manically running about removing the tarpaulins that cover the air safety fence adverts. In his enthusiasm to get this further instalment of his One-Man Track Show on the road, he nearly knocks over bemused but loitering local track staff in the process. Though earlier I did see a couple of blokes with a bulky camera and long boom mike in matching black team shirts with "FIM Broadcast Crew" written on the reverse, tonight's meeting isn't being shown live by any of the regular obscure pay-per-view straight-to-DVD satellite channels SGP rights holders BSI use to broadcast the actual events but streamed live by the imaginatively named FIM-Live TV on You Tube. FIM Broadcast Crew apprenticeships may one day lead to working in a very minor capacity on future Monster Energy commercials, the current equivalent of speedway Hollywood. Meantime, they too rush hither and thither with the authority and power of their status here clearly and magnificently displayed to all in large letters on their backs.

Slightly late, the riders come out on some flatbed trucks to greet the fans. The stadium looks comfortably half full. Afterwards Eric will say, "The crowd was around 5,000 when we expected 10,000! This is disappointing for German speedway". On bend three, where the majority of the Martin Smolinski fan club gather, they go bananas when the lead truck containing their local hero approaches their position serenaded by "Oxygen" blasting out over the stadium loudspeaker system. The first in a series of pleasingly retro playlist of old-school speedway stadium songs ("anthems" in SPG media speak) on tonight. Martin is totally in his element. He smiles and waves with gusto. Air horns parp throughout the stadium. Flags get waved. Though brief, his celebrations stop just short of ecstatic. In notable contrast to Martin, the rest of the riders collectively glower, look remarkably glum or bored senseless on the three trucks that follow behind. Only Krzysztof Kasprzak could possibly be mistaken for concentrating intently rather than being pissed off. The riders dismount by the start line for their introductions. It is refreshing to see a traditional rider parade at an SGP meeting, albeit one missing the riders' bikes. Probably because English is at least his second language, the announcer makes the introductions in a monotone usually used after a prized vintage car got wrote off in a hit-and-run accident en route to the meeting but professionalism dictates they still continue, despite the upset. Apparently while also struggling to sight-read out strange riders' names in number order they have not seen before from a jumbled information sheet printed faintly in a much too small typeface. In the line-up, Matej Zagar and Jack Holder really stand out. Holder because he looks so small even when compared to the diminutive standards of his not exactly tall contemporaries. In marked contrast, not only is Zagar the tallest rider here but he also draws they eye because of his total disengagement from his surrounding, never mind the monotone introductions. Earlier in the pits, Matej had (unusually) seemed all jokes and smiles when dressed in his smart but summery casual civvies while sporting a rather sharp – obviously hot off the scissors – new haircut. At the far end of the line-up, while every other rider stands ready to wave and grimace in a forced rictus smile, Zagar stands in a what appears to be the drug-induced trance pose his kidnapper required he adopt. Shortly after, Zagar kneels down onto his haunches to pick up then run the shale through his fingers as if he is a toddler discovering the magical feel of sand for the first time. Zagar is well known for being his own man. More especially for his blunt honesty since he apparently lacks any time delay or edit function between any thought bubbling up and immediate articulation of that thought into language. It appears studied indifference is also one of Matej's distinctive speedway behaviours.

In complete contrast, the crowd, track staff and the start girls appear absolutely delighted to be here if judged by the zeal with which they work or watch. Undermining the stereotype of German punctuality, the meeting gets underway late. Though he has completely altered how the local club planned and set up their track, Phil Morris continues to fret right up until the last moment. He urgently flaps his arms like the wings of an under-confident seagull struggling for lift off at staff and riders alike to aggressively signal them to their respective action stations. It is amazing how every Grand Prix staging is somehow hijacked into becoming another variation of the Phil Morris show, albeit one where drama and magic are instead exchanged for endless returns to centre stage for further attention-seeking struts of his ineffective stuff before studiously indifferent crowds. If the sign of a good referee is not noticing them, then this isn't a message that resonates with Morris around any FIM track. The main result of his Landshut intervention is a late start accompanied by distinctive piles of shale on the centregreen. Not only is there a reddy shale burm adjacent to the inside line but also a succession of randomly placed accompanying mini-hillocks too. Even the most studiously steady handed track curator is going to struggle to paint the all-important inside white line with finesse and accuracy. Phil Morris still isn't happy with what he sees, so demands further correction. Sensibly the Landshut line drawing team continue to adapt to prevailing conditions so create a shape more akin to tracing the outline of a newly fallen autumn leaf in infant school art class than the perfect oval. Infractions over this particularly wonky inside line will be hard for referee Christian Turnbull to properly adjudicate. Obviously, without penalty cannier riders can and will exploit this peculiar typology for the extra drive these additional shale mounds provide, if opportunity, bike temperament or bravery allows.

The meeting starts with an electric gate from Neils Kristian Iversen that ensures victory though he is pressed onwards by an on-the-gas Lindback. After all the pre-meeting talk hyping up the likelihood of a Robert Lambert triumph, he finishes comprehensively last. Unlike Cardiff, he actually completes his first race. Craig Cook has a similar bad habit of failing to score first time out at many meetings this season too not just grands prix. Heat 2 sees the Cumbrian fire from the tapes into the bend only to get pushed wide into third and remain there until he retires on the penultimate corner of the last lap. It is a race won easily from the gate by Martin Smolinski. So much so that he can indulge his adoring public with some early doors showboating. Smolinski's third bend fan club lap up his exaggerated throttle twists and speedy slight front wheel raises. Though it doesn't seem possible, the manspreading amateur photographer bloke next to me – with an impressive and extensive range of big lenses – thrusts his legs wider in perfect time with each joyful throttle twitch of Smolinski's celebrations as if taking part in a particularly vigorous but invisible exercise class.

It is no fairy tale to claim that Hans Andersen could definitely have been a speedway World Champion. Every season – if they ride in them all – there is a youthful talented rider whose form, pace and verve sees them suddenly dominate everyone else in all the major speedway leagues (Poland, Sweden, Britain and Denmark). Not winning or being thereabouts is the exception not the rule. With the confidence of inspired performance and youth can come outspokenness too. Sadly for Hans, during his brief supremely confident time in the speedway sun he (in passing) questioned the structure and organisation of the Grand Prix (especially its qualification process) and, thereby, the management effectiveness of its hyper-sensitive rights holders BSI. Given the GP fields are primarily made up of the installed base of re-qualified top eighters or those the organisers BSI decide choose to invite (after "consultation"), if you make your face not fit by revealing you have a mind of your own then the call to compete often conspicuously fails to come. It failed to arrive for Hans anyway. Well, until it was too late – after his golden era of superlative form had evaporated as, inevitably, it does for all suddenly "hot" new riders. Whether it is equipment, confidence, fortune, pragmatism, hype or injury, something changes and the scorching declines to lukewarm. A blind man on a galloping horse could see Hans merited inclusion via one of the permanent wild card picks that year but, no matter how convoluted or thoughtful the reasons given, it looked like punishment that this just didn't happen. The message from the rights holders was clear and easily seen from outer space. As the Chinese saying goes, shoot one and a thousand obey. Since then arguably the only rider to go his own way has been Emil Sayfutdinov. For him the boot was on the other foot as he kept turning down BSI's entreaties (for three seasons) rather than not receiving them. Though the reasons Emil gave were understandable, along with some injuries his decision has, thereby, probably robbed him too of the high probability of becoming World Champion many times. That said, this comparison slightly fails as Hans was winning everywhere rather than being talked up as the next great thing likely to win everywhere.

Back in the present, Hans gets a massive unpunished roller at the start of heat 3 but is so badly off the pace against the next generation of shale whippersnappers that he is only third by the time he reaches bend two. Though really only a journeyman rider nowadays, nonetheless, Hans appears to have a made a good living at the sport and his Twitter account posts suggest a happy and contented life (albeit with lots of commuting and occasional injury). By general repute there are two Krzysztof Kasprzaks. Sadly the defective can't-really-be-bothered one has wrongly been sent along to compete in Landshut so, inevitably, finishes an impressively long way behind Hans. Heat 4 sees Zagar deliberately line up incredibly close to Janusz Kolodziej at the start line. If this was supposed to intimidate or off put the Pole, it fails completely when Janusz gates sharply to win easily. Defying the trend for greater colour and wild or intricate patterns, Kolodziej's kevlars are primarily dark army green, as if he has decided to race this season in an advert and decal-free undercoat version. It definitely isn't the usual speedway rider look. I kinda like his night-fisherman-expecting-wet-weather vibe. If Janusz qualifies for the 2019 SGP, there is definitely lots of space still available for sponsor adverts on both his kevlars or matching dark military green bike cover.

No sooner has the fourth race finished than what sound like randomly chosen radio adverts suddenly blast out over the stadium tannoy system. Once these urgent sounding but incomprehensible (to non-German speakers) messages end, pleasingly retro 1970s rock music resumes as the backing track to our between-races down time. The first interval is around 10 minutes, which is more than enough time for Phil Morris to managerially parade about the track, issue orders and supervise activity to little apparent effect. The bowser gets most of his attention and, despite this, still provides the most excitement. After initially parking up on the second bend, once given Phil's permission to water, the driver appears to want to set his own bowser track record. I don't think I have ever seen a bowser (or any other speedway curation vehicle) at any track driven so fast for so many laps. Perhaps, the driver is a frustrated boy racer saddled with the wrong vehicle or, maybe, there is a record distance travelled before the bowser tank runs dry to beat? As the bowser roars round the track, it defies UK convention in this matter with powerful sprays of water jetting from the front of the vehicle rather than the rear. Maybe front-watering vehicles have to be driven quicker in order to water better? Or, possibly, like punts get steered from the front or rear dependent upon whether you went to Oxford or Cambridge University? Perhaps there is some other obscure but meaningless historic freemasonry-sequel type differentiation? Whatever the origin story, on principle, Phil Morris continues to gesture hard to interpret step-by-step but complex instructions on what appears to be "how to install your own CCTV cameras without a stepladder" towards the bowser vehicle. Morris does this with energetic barely suppressed fury, despite knowing that – from the drivers' seat – these gestures will pass fleetingly by the speeding windscreen in a blur. Overall, it is hard to imagine that all Phil's sound and fury accomplishes much other than to badly disconcert the mood of the local track staff and, thereby, put them collectively off their usual rhythm. That certainly appears to be the case as the riders go back out before the start gate white lines have been painted or the tapes reattached. After a quick bout of shaky line painting, getting the tapes back into their standard position nearly sees the start girls get decapitated. Should there have been a start operative tapes fatality, you can imagine it being said at the funeral or the wake something trite along the lines of: "What a way to go! She died being objectified while doing something she really loved". Though in their tight-cut green lycra clothing they look the decorative lane-identifying object heteronormative chauvinism dictates, these women clearly primarily identify as speedway fans first and foremost. Not only do they fill out programmes but, unusually, another films many of the starts. Either for posterity or for quick-posting You Tube in despair at the calibre of the meagre available pictures from FIM TV. To my mind, other than actually riding the bike, there are few places more exhilarating than the centregreen to watch competitive professional speedway riders race in the flesh.

Almost as quickly as he rushes to get out onto the track, Krzysztof wants to come back. He stops racing after a single lap and pulls onto the centregreen to wait briefly opposite the pits gate for Milik to win the race he started so fast. Bad KK is definitely here tonight. It is not a good look. On the subject of distinctive looks, one of the green lycra crop-top women lane operatives has also innovated in start-line body art terms with an impressive side tummy tattoo. Watched from side on in the main grandstand, it regularly draws the eye (well, mine) as the riders line up and fiddle about digging what little shale remains after Phil Morris demanded its removal from the track and placement onto the centregreen. Despite his curatorial finickitiness, Heat 6 is notable only for the struggle the riders have with the track surface. Robert Lambert continues to find the step up in class an issue, despite giving it full bore from the tapes. Ahead of him, Zagar pulls alongside Pawlicki at speed but fails to intimidate before he then hits the track bump that ends his challenge for race supremacy but also his further participation in the event. Zagar's exclusion quickly becomes withdrawal too once the physical and psychological after-effects of this heavy fall kick in. In the re-run Lambert gates into clear air but is swiftly brushed aside by Piotr Pawlicki before they have even exited the first bend. Pawlicki looks fast with his bike and kevlars pristine perfect as he coasts to a comfortable win right until sudden cunning pressure on the last lap corner sees Lambert nearly snatch victory on the line. Craig Cook wins heat 8 after a big blast on the third bend easily sees off the challenge of the frenetic but diminutive Jack Holder.

On the subject of blasts, at the interval radio adverts resume to excitably serenade us with breathless news of exciting products unknown (or prize-draw popcorn consolation prizes). Despite further track ministrations supervised under the watchful hand gestures of Phil Morris, racing on it continues to prompt bad struggles for some riders. David Bellagio cuts through the heat 9 field on the first bend with ease only to then get relegated to last, but shows great skill to somehow manage to stay on his wildly bucking bike. Heat 10 sees the experienced and fast-looking Antonio Lindback definitively prove that there is no additional traction or grip if you decide to ride aggressively out wide. Cook lines up so close to KK before heat 11 that the Polish rider takes to repeatedly nodding (in vain) at the start marshal to do something about this proximity. Despite this wordless pre-race semaphore, KK gates with alacrity only to have the dull-kevlared Kolodziej immediately sail past to win easily. Instead of battling back, Krzysztof elects for another early retirement on the third bend of the first lap. At this rate, KK will complete all his rides on only slightly more than one tank of methanol. Neils Kristian Iversen looks superfast in the next race and wins so comprehensively that he even starts pulling celebratory wheelies on the back straight of his last lap. Despite the late-ish start, the first twelve races are raced in 75 minutes.

The interval aural experience again features pre-recorded adverts urgently voiced in the important anxious manner of emergency traffic news followed by more well-chosen speedway track music classics from the 1970s and 1980s with a rock and soft metal emphasis. A small group of men in matching collared black shirts with "CREW" and "FIM TV" written on the back storm through the main grandstand to destinations unknown with their camera and fluffy mikes held aloft as if auditioning for the SAS (Outside Broadcast Division). With no sign of breaking news in the referee's box, there must be drama to record for posterity elsewhere. Possibly at the nearby Smolinski promotional stand or, perhaps, it is the record-breaking length of an impressive ladies toilets queue notable for its comparative proximity to Landshut.

After looking so good in the earlier races, Heat 13 sees Kolodziej gate as if half-asleep or forgetful that he is supposed to compete. Luckily, Janusz is in such superlative form tonight that pace and track craft soon see him recover the lead from Milik. Heat 14 features an outrageous rolling start from Craig Cook that still only finds him placed third into the first corner. Possibly because he expects referee Turnbull to call him back. Though Craig doesn't look at all fluent on a slow bike, he fights back through traffic to take second. Heat 15 is worth the proverbial admission money on its own. Lucky as it is the only exciting race of the whole night on a surface made to the exacting requirements of FIM Race Director Phil Morris. Turning back the years, Hans Andersen thrillingly passes Jack Holder on the third bend to lead. Behind the Australian, Robert Lambert's pace increases. So much so that in the approach to the third bend on lap three, Holder deliberately elbows Lambert in an effort to discombobulate and, thereby, impede his increasingly speedy progress. Far from deterring the young British rider, it spurs a double overtake of both Andersen and Holder as they all exit bend four and rush down the home straight. At high speed, Lambert dips his handlebars to power through the oft-fabled non-existent fractional gap minimally available by the safety fence. He easily glides past the visibly surprised Dane. It is virtuoso, thrilling skill that augers well for Lambert's speedway future. With Zagar (withdrawn) and Kasprzak (not fussed) both absent from heat 16, the German reserve riders finally get a chance to show their mettle. They race hard for the third place chip money, while far ahead of them Iversen wins his match race with Bellagio (on a sick sounding bike) to – given the races ahead for his rivals – almost guarantee his place in the 2019 Speedway Grand Prix series with the cushion of a race to spare.

In the Speedway Grand Prix proper, the last four programmed races are usually fractionally more competitive than the soporific heats that precede them because riders still in contention for qualification for the semi-final (and possibly, thereby, the final too) ride harder as further participation often rests upon good results in these races. If that doesn't happen, then there is always the next event in the series to shine at instead as points accumulation trumps event wins in the quest for the putative glory of an end of season top eight finish. The nature of the SGP is that it is a series rather than a one-off event. In Landshut, the metrics are totally different. With only four races left and no further racing after (unless a run-off is required), the speedway truism of "go hard or go home" is – for once – true. Many riders still remain in contention for the all-important qualifying top three places. Fire in the belly and handfuls of throttle remain the order of the night. Wins or, possibly, second places are vital for almost everyone except, perhaps, Neils Kristian Iversen and Janusz Kolodziej.

Possible contenders often feature together in the same race and so need to gain these crucial wins racing against each other. Equally the mathematical chance of qualification can just evaporate while you are sat in the pits waiting to race your last ride. At this late stage, it is almost a zero sum game where victory for one rider is effective elimination for another. There are many possible permutations remaining including a possible four rider run-off for third. The announcer doesn't even try to describe the competitive landscape before these concluding decisive races but sensibly prefers the vanilla neutrality of just stating the line-ups. Craig Cook gates with alacrity to win the treat of a five lap heat 17 to take his points tally to 10 and, thereby, give himself an outside chance of making the run-off if luck and results go his way. The same is true for Antonio Lindback after he wins heat 18 imperiously. The Swede has got faster and faster and more dialled in as the meeting progresses. In order to book his almost certain place in the SGP series next season, Max Fricke really just needs to continue doing more of the same. Ahead of his final race, the omens look good as Fricke has the comparatively weak rivalry of Bellego, Lambert and the meeting reserve to best. Sadly, speedway is a capricious and contrary beast when an engine failure almost immediately robs Fricke of the place that his form until then made rightfully his. As it is, Lambert follows up his thriller last time out with another electric win. It is too little too late. But again bodes well for his future. Crowd sympathies lie with Fricke who may never again get such a golden opportunity to gain automatic full-time entry to the SGP series. His engine failure is possibly good news for Lindback and Cook.

That said, though heat 20 has a strong line up, if they finish in their ideal permutation of Pawlicki, Kolodziej and Iversen – all three qualify. This being speedway, even at a sudden-death FIM-supervised event like this, the possibility of a gentlemen's agreement in the pits might miraculously somehow fortuitously transpire. It would make sense. But doesn't. First time out, Kolodziej's massive roller at the start sees the race stopped by FIM referee Christina Turnbull. Luckily for the Pole, referee Turnbull surprisingly doesn't exclude him and, thereby, end his SGP automatic qualification dreams. In the re-run Pawlicki immediately throws away his chance of another possibly abject SGP season (if his 2018 form were to continue) by making a truly terrible start. The rogue, only guaranteed non-qualifier in the race, Martin Smolinski certainly didn't get the memo as he rides hard, dangerously and aggressively under Iversen. It is as if Martin is both fired up and offended by his own subpar performance this evening on home shale in front of his expectant and passionate fans. Doubtless, they will forgive him. Of almost anything, if judged by the joy that greets the race win from this rejuvenated three Weetabix for breakfast version of Smolly. Iversen enjoys the good fortune of qualifying while in the pits as the other results go his way. Smolinski remains sanguine too, at least on the sponsorship front, given his fluent strong performances elsewhere in a different high speed motorcycle discipline. Namely, the much more popular than speedway in Germany Longtrack World Championship. If he avoids injury and remains competitive, Smolinski is likely to become 2018 world long track champion or, worst case scenario, just miss out.

Excitingly, the peculiar finishing race order of Heat 20 means that the sudden-death qualifying meeting gets the added bonus of an elimination winner-takes-all match race between Craig Cook and Antonio Lindback for the final automatic qualification place in the 2019 SGP series after both tie on 10 points in third place. For British speedway fans of a certain age, it has echoes of the Mano-a-Mano competition of the Golden Helmet, albeit over only one race and served up as palette-cleansing post-meal sweet treat rather than as an *amuse bouche* pre-meeting appetiser. In fact, much more is at stake. In terms of possible future adulation and glory but, more importantly, enhanced sponsorship appeal and revenues. Based on my heart, I want Cook to win. My head says Lindback as he's got faster and looked more in form as the meeting developed. After some faff but minimal supervision by his standards of the track grade by Phil Morris, the riders get to wheel back and forth as they dig for glory by the start line. With only two riders rather than four in this race, they each enjoy incongruously large gates to animatedly last-minute garden into whatever they deem ideal condition. Continuing her generosity towards riders making moving starts, referee Turnbull lets Craig Cook's obvious roller go unchallenged even though it provides him with serious first bend advantage. Ominously, Lindback looks graceful, noticeably fast and in gloriously synch with his bike. Man and machine in complete fast motion harmony. Just thinking such stuff, often prompts a capricious universe to deliver an immediate engine failure to the object of your attentions (Lindback) but, in this instance, doesn't. In comparison to his Swedish rival, Cook cuts a workmanlike and ultra-wary figure astride his machine. With Lindback in close pursuit, it is only a question of whether Cook can respond after he is inevitably overtaken. When the Swede with the Brazilian roots effortlessly fires past the Cumbrian Brit on the third bend of the second lap, sadly Cook has no comeback answer. Though he gamely tries to stay in contact, his race is run. On the final corner, Cook elects for the mechanical fig leaf of a sudden Pedersen-esque "engine failure" to visually try to explain his match race defeat to the crowd and, possibly, himself.

Lindback celebrates his win and qualification but not excessively. He has been to the SGP rodeo before so knows the reality of a likely tough season ahead, never mind all that glitters in the BSI universe definitely isn't gold. Sometimes Lindback's star has shone brightly, other times not and, sometimes, verged on the pitiful. Perhaps now with a calmer lifestyle off and at the track, hopefully Antonio is just about to enjoy great late SGP career longevity and his own Hancock-style decade of on track competitiveness and financial triumph? Craig is wrenchingly close to automatic SGP qualification for the 2019 series. The margins really are so fine between SGP participation or exclusion from the circus. Common sense should dictate that – having narrowly lost out in a Europe wide qualification process over two rounds against all the available competition – that rights holders BSI Speedway (An IMG Company) automatically choose him as the first reserve for the SGP next season. Sadly, their selections are made much more on a grace and favouritism basis. If your face fits, you are in. If your sponsor has clout, often you are somehow in too. If you just miss out on the only proper route to qualification by a figurative hair's breadth, you are definitely out.

With only one road out of Dodge City, clutching their programmes, bags, thermos flasks and obligatory (here) individual firm foam seat-cum-cushions-cum-swimming-floats fans rush for pole position in the car park dash. They are off out through the exit gates almost as soon as the chequered flag has been re-sheathed in its holder alongside the rainbow of other different coloured flags required to effectively run any international speedway meeting. Apart from the pre-recorded interval adverts, throughout this event felt like an old-school proper speedway meeting – albeit one so modern that the stadium runs on solar power – rather than a bog-standard SGP one pretending to be something more glitzy and significant than it actually is. After we collectively avoid stumbles to premature death in the car park gloom, Eric reveals he wasn't overly thrilled by what he saw. Partly it is the disappointing crowd size. But mostly at the loss of a copper-bottomed bona fide excuse to go to more speedway Grand Prix meetings throughout Europe in 2019 following Martin Smolinski. It was the guaranteed qualification his home track advantage should have provided but, sadly, didn't. In English for my benefit, Eric says, "Smolly was scheissen!"

Qualifiers

First: Janusz Kolodziej (12 points)

Second: Niels Kristian Iversen (11 points)

Third: Antonio Lindback (10 points)

Non-qualifier: (after run off)

Fourth: Craig Cook (10 points)

CHAPTER 6

Malilla SGP 6 – 11.08.18

"I have had two broken backs since then!"

Nicki Pedersen

THE talk of breakfast was the sighting two nights previously of Monster Energy sponsored SGP riders Tai Woffinden and Chris Holder staying in our hotel. Given the surf dude argot both flourish in press interviews, technically we should probably say "the Boyz are in Da Howse" or something similar. They unexpectedly arrived at the Best Western in the sleepy Swedish waterside town of Vastervik two nights early because of the threat of industrial action by the Swedish pilots of Ryanair for an event held 90 or so minutes' drive away in the woodlands of Malilla. The fly-commute has revolutionised and maximised the earning potential jobbing life of speedway riders. Freelance workers who ply their trade Europe-wide, they soon find planes, airports, associated security checks and boarding procedures its bane. Though clearly riders get frequent flier status (where and if available), on the whole they enjoy budget airlines flying to obscure locations from less glamorous airports. They most definitely know their way around the perpetually crowded Luton (voted the UK's worst airport for the third year running) and Stansted airports. While they do the air miles, their mechanics usually travel with the bikes by road. That said, riders are not averse to trying to take speedway engines and other essential bulky equipment on as carry-on for the overhead locker.

There is a track on the edge of town here – once you have driven past the impressive churches, parks and crazy golf – that doesn't stage SGPs. The local club Vastervik race on Tuesdays in the Swedish League. As regular competitors in that league and as the only decent hotel in town, Tai and Chris must have stayed at this Best Western many times before. As they were both brought up Australian, they will cope better with warm summers and the stifling heat that lingers in the air-conditioning-free rooms here. This disrupts the sleep patterns of the predominantly seniors crowd that makes up the backbone of this particular Travel Plus Tours (TPT) group also staying in the hotel. If the heatwave temperatures aren't keeping up residents, then the sound of the torrential overnight rains on the signature central glass show roof should do the trick. The breakfast buffet is plentiful but, nowadays, mostly verboten when it comes to speedway nutritional experts. Even the studiously continental range of breakfast ingredients including delights such as salads, raw fish, extensive natural yoghurts and gluten free multigrain bread doesn't have sufficient dietary appeal to tempt Tai or Chris into a further public appearance. They also weren't in the compact sweatbox of a hotel gym earlier either so didn't get to see the topless Frenchman lovingly exercise in front of its mirrors. If they went out for a run, cycle or constitutional walk around the pretty Vastervik shoreline, they would need to negotiate the maze of crash barriers that segment the town ahead of its annual highly regarded triathlon.

According to all the digital forecasts – anyone connected with speedway is invariably going to get a repetitive strain injury as they check quite a few of these frequently for updates – now the endless heat of this heatwave summer has finally cracked, it is really going to get broken this evening with some torrential downpours in the vicinity of the FIM Scandinavian Speedway Grand Prix. Malilla is, like Sweden generally apparently (according to locals and seasoned visitors), notorious for its summertime rainfall patterns. Water and speedway don't tend to play well together. To compound matters from a spectating point of view, the staging stadium grandstands lack roof cover. TPT tour guide Alan Crooks describes the joys of speedway at Malilla succinctly, "Fast track in a forest with no cover accessed by a single track road". The fact that it is a proper club regularly staging competitive top-league Swedish speedway bodes well for the quality of the track provided as well as their ability to cope with all weathers. It is a shame that dampness tends to scrub off the velocity of any fast track due to its impact upon prevailing conditions and rider enthusiasm. This is the fourteenth consecutive season that an SGP has been held in Malilla.

We muster in reception and manage not to get mixed up with the wedding party also meeting up there. Befitting the age demographic of the sport, if available, the hair colour of our group tends towards grey. What we lack in youth, we make up for a wide variety of speedway-themed T-shirts. These often commemorate previous TPT tours or SGP trips, often both. They are often barely disguised humble brags about our visits to more exotic faraway speedway locations. One of the smallest men in our party sports a collared checked shirt that defies the fashion regime. He is the only ex-speedway rider in our party. It is an exalted status he wears very humbly, though his pedigree is known to the regular trip cognoscenti. "That's ex-Newport rider Brian Woodward. He rode with Phil Crump and used to get away maximums at Exeter. He guested for the Falcons and rode with Ivan Mauger. He broke his back and, when he takes his top off – we were in Australia, in case you ask – has visible plates. Last year he broke three vertebrae in his neck mountain-biking but has recovered." We leave for the stadium in good time to enable most of the tour to enjoy the 31 guest pit passes available to our party. These are kindly left for TPT by Julie from BSI for collection from the race office. As there are 36 of us, mostly couples, there is a draw on the bus. Well, actually, Alan announces the draw he made in secret earlier back in his room at the hotel. Predictably there are many winners. They often greet the good news with a barely suppressed whoop or cheer. I am one of the unlucky five. Some winners already have pit passes so, like good fishermen, throw their catch back into the re-draw. Tension mounts. Finally I am drawn as third reserve but then also decline mine as I too (luckily) already have a pass. In the end, by my calculations, one person out of the whole group misses out on a pass so, with that kind of luck, isn't the person to ask for betting tips. Alan gives sensible advice on the likely pits etiquette ahead, "Don't forget that these guys are working. If they tell you to piss off or won't talk to you – it is not personal, they have work to do."

As we get closer to the stadium, the overcast skies progressively darken until they are angry and jet black overhead. The stadium is in a forest and has a single access road. Predictably, the heavens open as we arrive. The rain is on the right side of torrential but is still worryingly heavy when you hope to run a speedway meeting. On a coach filled with organised speedway people of a certain age, there has been much planning aforethought so there is an extensive range of wet weather gear handy or worn ready for our de-coaching. Some tour members dress as if about to go deep sea fishing; very few are totally unprepared. Though they may remain dry, things don't look auspicious. Even the passes aren't where they are supposed to be picked up from. Given the comparatively remote location and its size (only 1800 people live in the town), many fans camp at Malilla. BSI and the *Speedway Star* recommend this option to get the full Malilla SGP experience. The pitched tents in the vicinity of the G&B Arena look especially forlorn in the heavy rain. You can imagine even those enjoying the smugger luxury of mobile homes or camper vans are currently sinking into boggier ground.

If you are a fan of angry skies and dramatic fast-moving cloud systems, Malilla definitely is the place to be this evening. On the ground, anywhere you look it is sodden. The usual speedway uniform of warm weather wear has more or less vanished. Every style and colour of practical wet clothing is on display. It is raining so heavily that the supervisory staff in full fluorescent waterproofs combine notional authority with a level of dryness that can't help but get covetous looks, especially now it feels much cooler too. Luckily, it is a stadium where they expect inclement weather. So much so they have a strict umbrella ban. This news – as so much other information – failed to make the SGP website travel advice so many fans still think their compact brollies might evade bag searches. Given the impressive pile of brollies, they are clearly one of the hot search items for the security people. As this is Sweden, rather than said treasured compact brolly being lost forever the genuine expectation is that people will re-collect them upon departure. Though harshly enforced, there is an admirable egalitarianism to this protection of the public commons for the pleasure of all. Everyone can watch the speedway meeting from the open grandstands without a few selfish but well-prepared people blocking their view with an umbrella in order to stay dry.

Though Sweden is a country where the standard of living and the exchange rate means few things ever feel inexpensive to visitors, the club does a roaring trade in see-through multicoloured anoraks-cum-cagoules at a bargain price of 20 krona. Gaiety isn't the word that you would traditionally associate with groups of people sitting disconsolately in the rain waiting for it to stop. The range of bright colours makes the sodden crowd seem much less cowed. The track itself is completely covered with impressive expanses of tarpaulin weighed down with a similarly notable number of big heavy-looking agricultural tyres. These covers were borrowed earlier this morning from Vetlanda speedway club and put in place before the rain arrived. There are many puddles and pools on this glistening plastic barrier. In fact, there is so much lateral water that, if this were golf, temporary rules would allow a free drop away from the water hazard without the usual two shot penalty. Sadly, this is speedway so, despite the preparations, things don't look at all auspicious. Worse still, practically every weather forecasting site and app predicts bands of heavy showers to continue for at least the next hour or two. These app rain timings are ludicrously specific but vary. Resorting to an old-fashioned look upwards at the sky shows fast moving dark clouds rapidly skittering by. On the horizon, in the direction the wind comes from, these distant clouds look lighter and whiter.

There are no public announcements inside the stadium and, since the UK television coverage is yet to start, updates texted from home are currently unavailable. As they offer dry shelter and a roof, the pits are exceptionally crowded. Partly with riders, mechanics and various staff but also with all the guest visitors with passes who, for once, can't be thrown out at exactly 105 minutes before tapes up as when this might actually be remains conspicuously unknown. Even the most observant detective and optimistic student of human nature would struggle to read the runes of the riders' body language. Earlier the mechanics ventured out to a tent close to the pits to collect the race tyres for use tonight. In every pit bay, bikes gleam ready to race, if conditions permit. Very few riders wear their kevlars and, those that do (Emil, Maciej and Matej), must be doing so out of principle to show support to their sponsors. The majority of the SGP talent stubbornly remains unchanged. Many seem to believe that their hoodies are waterproof. Tai wears his hoodie hood up over his Monster cap. Some anoraks are new season current sponsor compliant, others are practical but loved historic garments. Greg Hancock and his amanuensis Josh Gudgeon sport matching but incongruous see-through baby-doll style anoraks. These garments are either sponsorship logo opportunities-in-waiting or else are discards from a highly specialist soft-porn film session.

With torrential rain following brief respite following torrential rain, the pits get much cosier, well beyond maximum capacity limits. As this is speedway, people stand and gossip or stare morosely into an imaginary dry weather distance. We are collectively becalmed. Riders mooch on their chairs. Mechanics chat or try to look busy without really anything to do that they hadn't already done. The Monster Energy start women stand and wait together. Within but apart from the pits throng. For one of the first times this summer, they have broken out their corporate anoraks. These are designed more with fashion and advertising than warmth or comfort in mind. Rules dictate that since this is an FIM event, once the competing riders signed on for it then this meeting takes priority over all other speedway engagements they have elsewhere this weekend. This code speak means that this SGP and its pitiful prize money takes priority over any more lucrative speedway work going on in Poland tomorrow (Sunday) until it is finished, deemed completed or cancelled. The pits hive mind consensus is that if Malilla doesn't run tonight, they will stage it tomorrow late morning at 11 or 12. There is less agreement on how many races need to be run this evening "in order to declare a result" aka not have to any refund tickets for not running the full complement of the (23) programmed races. This rather lawyerly phrased officialese gets uttered in the pits and speedway promotional circles whenever fans have paid to enter the stadium and a lower number of heats than programmed are going to be ridden (rather than raced). My understanding without evidence is that SGPs require 16 heats to be raced to avoid any admission monies refund requirements (though it was only 12 heats in Warsaw). All fans are here on a buyer-beware basis when it comes to any extra travel costs any delay, abandonment or postponement creates.

Even though the rain abates to drizzle, if I were a betting man, I would say that the meeting is still going to be off. Text news from England is contradictory. A friend of a good friend of a competing rider says the riders have had a meeting and it is postponed until tomorrow. While on the telly, apparently they are saying the start is delayed by 30 minutes. Over the stadium speakers, there are bilingual announcements, "We are sorry for the delay, the new starting time is 8 o'clock." Seventy minutes before the revised start time, the ground staff start to remove the track covers under clearing skies in lighter drizzle after a rider meeting where the riders initially fought against riding before they rather morosely collectively agreed to give it a go. As the covers come off, a good-sized gaggle of riders stand on high in the pits viewing area keenly watching the track staff. They are grumbling almost as much as their tummies. Noticeably, though the riders study the track intently, they remain dressed in their civilian clothing. Though it can't take long to change, this is a clear indication of their current reluctant mindset. Some riders venture down to bend 4 for a closer first-hand inspection of the moisture content of sections of shale recently exposed by the covers removal. To my untutored eyes, the track looks in remarkably good condition. Some water did escape from the covers. The most sodden sections of track are bend 4, the mid-section of bends 1 and 2 plus the exit of bend 2 to the middle of back straight. Whether this piebald damp is good or bad for racing according to the riders, I don't know. Judged by their glum faces, I suspect bad. Though the impressive giant suction vehicle they have on hand in Malilla goes out onto the track it merely parks up then returns again shortly afterwards unused.

While FIM Race Director Phil Morris often appears completely surplus to requirements at most SGPs when it comes to influencing track conditions, this is definitely the evening to shine and really earn his corn. As usual, he showcases an extensive repertoire of instructional arm gestures interspersed with on-track conflabs supplemented by angrily barked instructions for the (often) bemused track staff. Tonight though, to my mind, Phil rises to the occasion to fulfil the track prep aspect his job specification. There is an impressive amount of motorised curatorial equipment parked up ready to use alongside the human variety already out and about in zealous action. When I worked on the ground staff at Wimbledon tennis sweeping up and pulling the covers, we spent a huge amount of our time on cloudy days waiting for it to rain or waiting for it to stop raining. Speedway people are similarly obsessed and blessed. We watch the sky, the track activity or refresh the weather forecasts on our phones. The track staff here are plentiful and busy. They show great purpose and expertise. They are so organised that it appears that they even have a head curator for Phil Morris to gesture complex but detailed instructions at like an angry rogue robot on a car assembly line. In turn, this head curator has his own assistant on hand to receive the translated version of whatever the current marching orders are for the track preparation and staff support roles. Track activity is certainly intense and done with skill. There is no doubt about the commitment of the club to get the track to a standard to get the event on should the weather hold, especially now after the riders grouchily agreed at their earlier meeting to give things a go if the weather permits. With little else to watch, the choreography required to fold the wet track covers is quite a spectacle even for those without origami leanings. Once all these covers have been folded then loaded by a fork lift onto a flatbed lorry, we get treated to a precision display of shale replenishment by an expertly driven dumper lorry. It is a virtuoso exhibition of controlled tipping. One load of dry shale takes a few laps to deliberately distribute with almost delicate care and accuracy rather than the more traditional get dumped in a hurry in one run. Just after the shale is down, word sweeps the pits that Malilla staff did this on their own initiative without permission from Mr Morris. It is a universal law that metaphorically bald men will fight over any comb available. This applies to matters of shale curation as much as any walk of life. My late beloved mum used to despair of the intense politics involved in routine cleaning work.

Australian photographer Chris Horne isn't surprised at the expertise, skill and thoughtful track preparations on display. "Most Swedish tracks are used to the wet, much wetter than this! The shale they just put on is specially prepared. They use fine dust rock from this area that is then ground smooth. It rides well in the wet because it combines with the damp shale to go like cat litter – into little balls – that they then grade smooth. The riders will be able to race on the track here tonight!" That must be the plan as the riders have finally gone off to get changed into their kevlars. Zagar, Sayfutdinov and Janowski are already in their work gear so mooch about the pits. If nothing else, more riders getting race ready shows willing. Beneath the assorted colours of their wet weather gear, the crowd sit patiently and wait for further news or tractor action. Instead, just as the track looks fit and ready to race at the revised 8 o'clock start time, there is a further heavy shower. Not quite torrential but heading in that direction. It certainly undermines the last 70 minutes or so of skilled hard work laying a new surface on the track. Whether working, watching or on duty here tonight, once again the covered pits area crowds out to exceed its maximum capacity. People again moodily stare off at the rain, huddle cosily or chat amiably to pass the time. In a vain attempt to ramp up the excitement, over the stadium speakers they play pre-recorded rider interviews. Greg tells the sodden but patient fans his usual spiel. Greg gives good earnestness, bonhomie and positivity so could make tossing a coin sound melodramatic. Surprisingly for a team rider who managed to get thrown out of an Australian SGP for suspiciously slowing down to let his Monster Energy team mate Chris Holder pass, Hancock claims, "when you come to GP, you don't have any team mates."

After all the hard work on the track, though it has again stopped raining, the intervention of the latest batch of inclement weather seems to dictate that the meeting won't go ahead. That would find good agreement amongst some of the SGP riders who are well known (understandably) not to like damp conditions. Many speedway riders have a proven record of struggle in the wet. Phil Morris calls a public rider meeting in the crowded pits. He has a large but sceptical audience. Given the height of the riders and the elevated soles of Phil's black boots, there is an element of teacher instructing and talking down to an eager reception class. These are the self-styled "bad" boys so, in front of their rebellious friends (mechanics, support staff and assorted hangers-on) there is inevitably some answering back. Occasionally in the blunt, common language of men. But there is also pragmatism and professional recognition that complex travel itineraries means that it is better that the show goes on rather than inviting the logistical complexities of doing otherwise. Despite Greg's claim that it is every man for himself at any Grand Prix – ironic given he is a member of TWO SGP sponsored teams: Monster Energy and his own speedway team (named Team Haj after his long-time lead mechanic Rafal Haj) – the riders suddenly temporarily coalesce into a collective "Union" body when it comes to negotiating about track conditions and whether or not the meeting goes ahead.

It is an informal voluntary alliance brought on by circumstance and self-interest. A speedway trade union has often been dismissed and dissed by the powers that be as they prefer to divide and rule without impertinent questions. More experienced and public-minded riders have periodically valorised trade unionism as essential but still struggled to gain formal power due to spotty membership, support and acceptance among the riders. The last meaningful iteration of the Speedway Riders Association was run and headed up by the well-respected Australian rider Shane Parker. Though a genuine and persuasive man, he found widespread traction hard to gain. Sadly, in any era, collective negotiation over pay, health and safety as well as terms and conditions won't find a receptive audience with bosses (promoters). They much prefer to divide and rule, negotiate individually as well as act capriciously and upon whims to protect what they deem as the best interest of their individual club business. Structurally the way British speedway teams are constructed, assessed and managed ensures short-termism rules. This approach fails to build for any future much beyond the next meeting or two. Everywhere you look in British speedway, there is frequent chopping and changing of the line-ups, which inevitably leads to significant random rider churn and erodes trust with the workers. Promoters also have additional fig leaves of higher collective authority of group decision-making to hide behind. Either their trade association (BSPA) or its separate rule making body (SCB) which itself is in turn responsible to the ACU and FIM. Another force pulling against riders acting in concert are their own individual commercial interests. Given they are all self-employed freelance workers with transient frequently unenforceable contracts, when push comes to shove it is a zero-sum game of behaving according to your own needs and your assessment of your current best interests. Such decision-making tends to be in the now and short-term in emphasis rather than strategic. The bread on one rider table often comes at the expense of there being less or no bread on another table. It is standard practice for riders in the same team to be on completely different rates of pay. However, tonight in the Malilla pits, the rider hive mind is currently briefly temporarily united. Though they are quite some way from best buddies and serially reluctant to wet race, Greg Hancock and Nicki Pedersen – as the elder statesmen spokesmen – work in tandem together to negotiate on behalf of all the SGP riders here tonight. Even when stood close by, the crowd around the FIM Race Director is such that these pits discussions are mostly inaudible except when Phil shouts agreed actions, "We need another 15 minutes to prepare the track."

In basic terms, this promise effectively means that the track staff industriously scrape away the shale they recently so carefully newly laid. While this goes on, Nicki gives a live pits interview in English to Polish television on the present state of thinking about tonight's SGP. The heavily made up and besuited regular (male) interviewer eagerly translates the news that the track is going to be re-prepared and then this handiwork re-assessed on a further track walk by the riders. As good as his word, after ten minutes Phil Morris shouts, "three minutes, riders" as a signal that they muster ahead of their group track inspection. Once out on the shale, the riders meander and linger. Mostly unlovingly, if their body language, arm waves and disconsolate foot gardening seen from the safe distance and dry of the pits and the terraces is any indication. To say they make a slow leisurely circuit of the track giving it a disgruntled thorough inspection is an understatement. It is almost as if they wish to run down an imaginary clock provided the Official SGP "Time Partner" Aztorin (who?) and, thereby, delay things long enough to give the rain chance to return. Afterwards, Paul Burbidge reports in the *Speedway Star*, "a number of riders forcefully voiced their concerns over conditions prior to the action". Joined on their walk by Phil Morris and assorted members of the Malilla curatorial team, consultation is the order of the day. Nothing is too much for the curatia (my new collective noun for a dusting of speedway curatorial staff) to try to get it sufficiently "right" to allow the riding – if not the racing – to go ahead. When not carefully listening and consulting, Phil Morris also can't help himself so indulges in some gratuitous but trademark barks and shouts of unintelligibly complex track care orders. The skies decide to clear just as the track finally gets more-or-less scraped down to the base layer of its foundations. So much so that sparks fly up almost continuously from the grader as it laps round and round the circuit. To patient watchers and waiters, it suddenly looks a foregone conclusion that the meeting is going to proceed, especially since the skill and expertise of the grader tractor drivers shines through in their dexterity.

When I was a student, Fred's (or Fredericks as it rather poshly noted on the sign but no one said who went there) was the on-trend and trendy place to go for your haircut. Owner Fred would diligently consult at length about your requirements and listen patiently to your replies. He would then proceed give you the haircut he was always going to do anyways – a flat top with number two on the sides – irrespective of whatever you had specifically requested. Here tonight Phil Morris definitely channels the spirit and memory of Fred. The riders can have any track preparation they want so long as it is this one. After their 15 or so minute track walk, upon their return the riders call an impromptu team meeting at the pits gate. Every flavour is available to them from the FIM endorsed and accredited event management team, provided it is vanilla and ultimately, it turns out, doing exactly just what they are told. Namely, riding. "Giving it a go" as it is widely known in optimistic it's-a-job-not-a-sport parlance that is the lingua franca and vocabulary assumption of all in-the-know insiders. There are some riders who don't bother with this track inspection including Woffinden, Dudek, meeting reserve Oliver Berntzon and Zagar. Afterwards Matej tells Burbo, "I knew the track was alright. I didn't understand people whinging and complaining about the track. We've raced in worse conditions." A key backroom member of Craig Cook's team, Ian Corcoran watched the rider deliberations closely from afar, "You could virtually lip-read Nicki not wanting to ride. I didn't think it would be on. It wouldn't be elsewhere!"

To the same muted reaction from the fans that greeted news of the delay, the meeting eventually gets underway at 20.45 – a full hour and 45 minutes late. Well, 101 minutes late if we use the organisers traditional but exact start time of 19.04. The stadium is only half-full but the range of waterproof clothing worn adds brightness and colour to the stands in the gloaming. Rather than the dour boggy cloying shale affair that the struggles with the weather would lead spectators to expect from a track after such a delay in Britain, Maciej Janowski looks incredibly fast when he wins the first race comfortably in a time of 59.9 seconds (the joint second fastest time of the night). Well behind him, Craig Cook bosses Swedish wildcard and Jason Lyons look-a-like Peter Ljung in the race for third. Now that the meeting is finally underway, missing media culprits must be ruthlessly hunted out by staff from rights holders BSI. That is definitely the impression given by a stern-faced woman in the full uniform of SGP branded attire. She looks the kind of woman who smiles as soon as she wakes up in order to get it out of the way. Channelling her sweaty-bottomed inner grouch, she barks authoritatively into her walkie-talkie, "It would be good to look at the media accreditation list and see who didn't turn up!" Hopefully media accreditation list supervisor Paul Burbidge, if asked, has an explanation for no-shows. To be fair to any wannabe "accredited" media attendees, Malilla is a comparatively remote location that is a struggle to get to from inside Sweden, let alone from more distant countries. Even if you lived in Sweden, the look of the weather and the forecast of thunderstorms would give an extreme optimist due cause for concern about the viability of the meeting going ahead or, at least, the calibre of the entertainment served up if it did run. No Swedish media outlet, let alone any serious media organisation worldwide, is going to reserve space or airtime while desperately hanging on for the latest news on the weather, meeting delays or latest track repair happenings. In news or feature terms, SGP speedway reporting doesn't even make the status of a nice-to-have-on-a-really-slow-news-day-when-there-is-space-to-urgently-fill and it is well over a decade away from the vaguely must-have it sometimes was during the era when Tony Rickardsson was in his pomp. Indeed, currently, Tony was last Swedish World Champion way back in 2005.

More relevantly, organisers BSI appear to run their press accreditation programme to keep independent minded but suddenly interested media people at bay with a ludicrously bureaucratic and intrusive "official accreditation" system that requires your inside leg measurement, the sacrifice of your second born, your grandmother's maiden name, audited circulation figures and an extensive bibliography of your previous speedway reporting. Copy approval is not sought but the palaver to gain a press pass makes it tacit. Most likely, BSI worry in case a proper journalist gets access to the SGP crown jewels and then, heaven forefend, report the banal turgid reality of what they actually get to see. Rather than what they are implicitly told they must see in order to continue to gain access. Apparently, no reporting is preferable to independent-minded reporting. BSI much prefer to operate with a restricted carefully selected roster of tame or gamed "journalists". An almost in-house newsletter style media who can be relied on to dutifully report races and comments in enthusiastic but anodyne fashion in obscure trade/specialist media outlets in a manner that never (or rarely, as news occasionally sneaks out by accident) frightens the BSI executive team horses. After years of practice, the BSI photographer and media accreditation team keep speedway and the Grand Prix series secret with the jobsworth zeal of prison guards everywhere, if judged by the serial non-appearance of staff and stringers from proper, respected or serious media organisations. In a world where the *New York Times* once sent reporters to Berkshire to cover the first-ever modern press printing of the *Reading Evening Post*, Speedway World Championships barely even make the results section of national outlets. Personally, I feel that any media person who registered to attend Malilla but then didn't show up should be publicly birched. Possibly by Joe Parsons with different coloured Monster Energy branded sticks matching whatever the new-look can design is this week approved by head office. These sticks could be passed to him by the Monster start crew women and ticker-tape fired into the air in celebration as the punishment strokes are administered in the fanzone area while – as is traditional – derivative EDM blasts out to mask the screams. After said public punishment, journalist miscreants then get given a lifetime ban and are forced to copy-read all of Burbo's copy in search of factual accuracies as a form of best-practice brainwashing. Thinking about it, maybe no serious media organisation ever comes along because they are already blacklisted by BSI? Whatever this BSI media guard woman hopes to accomplish with the threat of her media curiosity – other than virtue signalling her attention to irrelevant detail and power to her underlings and bosses – with her investigations into media non-attendees is hard to understand? It is indicative of the ubiquitous fitted-as-standard delusional holding-the-telescope-the-wrong-way-round superior attitude groupthink and arrogant mindset that generally besets the BSI Speedway management culture. Less fur coat and no knickers but more SGP-branded see-through baby doll pac-a-mac (as modelled by Josh and Greg earlier) and Y-fronted incontinence pants.

Out on the track, the first four races are all won by the yellow helmet rider from the outside gate 4 position. Though it is still amazing that the meeting has gone ahead, the races are often from-the-gate processional affairs. Visual entertainment is at a premium. Watching the taller blonde-haired Monster Energy woman briefly dance along with the music on the centregreen each time she returns from her start line duties is, arguably, the highlight. At the interval, possibly due to the damp atmosphere or to mark her sorrow at seeing the bike Piotr Pawlicki chose of the two he brought out pack up at the pits gate before the start of heat 4, she gives her hair a lengthy and enthusiastic mermaid-esque comb. Imagine as a rider, you wait all that time, then when the meeting finally gets underway, your bike fails and start women slowly brush their hair in celebration. What a world we live in. Luckily nowadays, every SGP rider has a stable of alternative bikes to use provided your mechanics can get you on one before the two-minute time allowance expires. With entertainment in short supply, some fans look back nostalgically on the second lap of heat 4 as the only hint of competitive speedway action. And then only for third place when Pawlicki races hard with Greg Hancock, after he survives a predictable first lap violent cut-across manoeuvre from Nicki.

To make up for lost time, there were incredibly sharp changeovers – even faster than usual – between the first four individual heats. It is perfunctory with a capital P. In sharp contrast, the interval break is, as usual, leisurely. This tardiness is purely to suit the television companies – as they can run the commercials of their various obscure advertisers – but is not ideal for attending fans. It also allows further extensive track curation notable for its intensity but also for the impressive showers of sparks that fly from the grader as it scrapes along on the track base. These free pyrotechnics are arguably better than some post-SGP meeting firework displays. The spark showers are so violent it is almost as if they are welding the shale to the track base. Further confirmation that SGPs have an exponential effect upon job titles and jobsworthness, I spot someone wearing an "Assistant Clerk of the Course" jacket watching these tractor activities closely. Stood alongside me watching the sparks rather than shale fly is Nataly from Russia, who is on a speedway tour with her husband Igor. He runs a speedway memorabilia museum in Moldova. They have come along with their good friend Ove. Though he is five times World Champion, Ove Fundin is a modest, unassuming and friendly man who belies his age and feels no need to draw attention to his celebrity or canonical status within speedway circles. Rather he prefers to sit, savour the action and chat with his friends rather than play the Big I Am. "The first four races it was yellow, usually it is red that wins here." Ove is hale, fit and alert, "it is my first GP of the season. I'll be going to Torun too. It is my favourite!" The winning yellow helmet spell is broken by Craig Cook when his tapes-touching jump start earns him an exclusion. Ove Fundin yelps in delight at Jason Doyle's cunning high-speed attempt to snatch third on the line in heat 6. Amazingly, given the earlier sessions of heavy rain and talk of postponement, heat 7 sees some sections of the crowd enjoy copious billows of dust! Just as notably, the next race appears to suggest that we have the confident, imperious and aggressive prime era (rather than mechanical gremlins of recent vintage) Nicki Pedersen out racing for glory in Malilla. With track craft aplenty allied to canny situational awareness, first Nicki pinches up Vaculik by the back straight fence on lap two before repeating the medicine on the fast-racing Zagar in more-or-less the same spot on the next lap. These pincer manoeuvres see Nicki easily win the heat. Watching a keen-to-win Nicki with a fast bike and his dander up is a joy to savour but increasingly rarely seen. Injuries (bad), age (in denial), attitude (variable) and equipment (unreliable, appaz) have all intervened over the last few years to conspire against Nicki to varying degrees. Though Nicki can dish it out on the track, he can also take it. Almost alone amongst the SGP riders, Nicki does so without complaint. This is handy as he is a serial disher-outer. At the SGP or elsewhere, Nicki is an equal opportunities beaster. He does so without fear or favour and, often, reason. As a result, in each and every heat Nicki races – whether SGPs or anywhere else – competing riders invariably raise their game in order to try to best him. With Pedersen alongside them at tapes, this combative Dane usually gets full-bore, full-gas competition. There are no gimmes or mulligans offered or, indeed, expected. No favours are given though some are returned with interest. It could be argued that Nicki Pedersen is the only rider of the current crop – and one of the few of his generation – who has had to properly race almost every single one of his heats throughout his career in the SGP series in the winner-takes-all manner and full-bodied style of the old one decisive meeting World Championships format.

It is certainly true that in the current structure of the SGP – the sheer number of events (ten, minimum) in each series and the frequency of races – has eliminated the need to really go for the on-the-night one-off triumph when calculated points accumulation is the sensible and winningest strategic approach. In speedway animal terms, it favours weasels, squirrels and snakes over sharks, lions and tigers. Additionally, the advent of multi-rider sponsorship by – most visibly – Monster Energy in the SGP has created the perception of an alliance of commercial interest that, if not formally operating as a team in an individual competition, leaves open the occasional possibility of unconsciously acting in concert. Various incidents over the years suggest these suspicions could be well-founded albeit not formally proven. Between races Ove questions my background to get a handle on my speedway provenance.

"Where do you live?"

"Brighton. Have you been?"

"Of course! You have no speedway team, who do you support?"

"Eastbourne are my local team. Reading are the team I supported."

"Did you go in the Reg Fearman time?"

"I first went in 1975 when Smallmead opened."

Ove is very knowledgeable about British speedway and places in Britain generally but passes modestly and quickly over his own extensive and very notable UK pedigree, "I started in 1952, then was there from 1954 to 1966 and again in '67." When it comes to watching any speedway meeting, Ove explains to Nataly that to get the most enjoyment out of it, "You have to have someone to keep your fingers crossed for. I really enjoy Maciej Janowski." The racing comes at us so thick and fast our occasional conversations are snatched. The third set of four races gets underway with heat 9 only 40 minutes after the delayed meeting started. In that time there have been eight races and two track grades. The pace continues on the track as well as off it when Tai Woffinden serves up a blistering first lap to complement an aggressive version of his traditional first corner cut back. It is amazing that his fellow professionals continue to remain either oblivious of this race tactic or unable to counter it. Unfazed by conditions even before he took to his bike, this successive heat win already takes Tai to seven points this evening and further boosts his cumulative championship leading total. Ferocious speed and aggressive passing manoeuvres continue in vogue in heat 10 when Emil fires from fourth to second and monsters Doyle in the process.

The dull next race is only notable for how Greg Hancock bullies aside wild card Peter Ljung for the third-place chip-shop money. Almost universally according to media accounts, Greg is that rare beast – a gentlemanly speedway rider always keen (except when allegedly cheating in Australia) to help and share his knowledge with other riders as well as always provide sufficient racing room to his fellow racers. Fans know that Greg is notoriously a good gater with fast reactions who prefers to win straight from the start rather than battle his way through traffic. From my observation of the series to date this season, in addition to his fast reaction from the gate, points-scoring Greg cannily accumulates all the race points he can from the notionally "weaker" SGP riders, whenever and wherever he faces them. Against these particular "lesser-light" riders, Greg races them very hard and often passes aggressively. The only love given by the American is tough. As the cumulative points total is the key top eight qualification metric, overall it makes strategic sense for any rider to treat each heat as a zero-sum game. Points I get, you don't get. It takes shrewdness to realise – as Greg clearly does – that these are more easily gained against overawed, less experienced, wild card, reserve or generally less -GP-capable opposition. In these heats, the oft-referenced avuncular lots-of-racing-room Greg gives way to his harsher racing, sometimes tactically bullying, alter-ego. Automatic SGP qualification – ideally without need of a wild card – ensures ongoing and/or better sponsorship contract values, achieves sponsor financial incentive targets and, hopefully, attracts more sponsors. Points realised against the "weaker" riders count just the same as those much harder to win points gained against SGP series regulars, star riders or in-form up-and-comers.

The most exciting and wildest SGP rider of the moment and, arguably of the 2018 series, is Bartosz Zmarzlik. Winning heat 12 he looks simultaneously imperious and an out-of-control accident waiting to happen. Bartosz has a memorable racing style notable for how often he takes his right foot off his footrest to point it forwards. It was unique but, nowadays, some other riders also do this this too. Bartosz appears to do this whenever at full speed – executing dramatic full-throttle passes and overtakes, when exhilarated or showboating in the lead. It defies speedway convention and looks wrong but is how he races his bikes. Though generally mild and positive in his opinions (should he express any), Ove definitely isn't a fan of Zmarzlik's leading leg. "I hate to see that. It is not nice. You are not in control. You are a passenger!"

One of the few riders not to walk or fret about the track, Matej Zagar looks quick and confident imperiously winning heat 13. In contrast, Nicki Pedersen closely examined track conditions beforehand and also voiced forthright and forceful concern on behalf of all the riders. Firing from the gate for heat 15, it looks like Nicki too has had three Shredded Wheat for breakfast. He rides with vim, vigour and zest. Almost because he can and, of course, because his give-no-quarter image almost requires it, as an afterthought Pedersen nearly takes Ljung's leg away. It is almost like watching in-his-pomp earlier era Nicki. It also wakes up Peter Ljung who chases him hard to get his first points of the night after three last places. Nataly and Igor watch as "fans of Russian riders and Zmarzlik". Zmarzlik is on fire. Heat 14 was his fourth straight race win. Of their Russian compatriots Emil and Artem, only Laguta gets to see the chequered flag (once). Possibly as a good luck charm but more likely a combination of over-anxiety and mechanical under-confidence, Piotr Pawlicki brings out two bikes for every race he competes in then impulsively selects one out on the track according to unknown criteria. His performance in this Grand Prix and the SGP series to date suggests his cumulative points total would be better if he were more often short of a bike rather than spoilt for choice. The bike Piotr finally chooses then fails at the pits gate. No one else has suffered such bad luck but it is his second pre-race engine failure of the night. The extra machine on hand fails to calm his nerves but his Tourette's level twitchiness at the start line lures Janowski to wreck the tapes and, thereby, get excluded. It is a circuitous way to ensure that you stand a better chance of a point to go along with your earlier warning. Without even a practice lap to acclimatise, meeting second reserve Joel Kling still bests Pawlicki to take third in the re-run. Rather optimistically given BSI's approach to media coverage, Ove asks, "I saw you were taking notes for every race, what newspaper are you writing for?".

"I'm not. I'm taking notes for my book, so I don't forget."

"I'm like that."

"You have an excuse."

"You mean – I'm old!"

Actually, engaged, alive and living in the moment are some of the words that – along with five times World Champion – spring to mind to describe Ove. He is definitely 85 years young.

After the interval, Pawlicki is out quick with his two immaculate looking bikes to choose between in an on-track beauty contest. After sitting astride his first-choice steed, with the two-minute clock ticking down towards zero Piotr suddenly decides to switch to the second machine. This bike actually manages to go the distance and his third place point boosts his meeting tally to three. By his recent SGP standards, this represents a stand-out performance. Piotr and Craig Cook appear locked in a death spiral of serial underscoring in their unofficial contest for the not-so-coveted 2018 SGP series wooden spoon. If defending World Champion Doyle didn't have bad luck in his title defence, he would have no luck at all. This continues with a tapes exclusion in his next race. Doyle hasn't relished conditions and his four points total reflects this scepticism. The re-run of Heat 18 is notable for the sight of Nicki out gardening at the start line beforehand without his bike while his mechanics stand beside him to direct his trademark portable cooling hairdryer-cum-engine-cooler-fan towards his face. It is already after 10 and the evening has cooled so either Nicki gets tremendously hot and sweaty in all meteorological conditions or else some weird heat-and-hair-related sports psychology obsessiveness dictates its use. The security blanket of Nicki's regular between races ostentatious use of this hardly compact black coloured fan has – over recent seasons – not shown much impact in his actual results. But is one of the few pieces of his race night equipment that – unlike his bikes, apparently – works very reliably. We all know Nicki likes nothing more than blasts of intra-meeting blast cool air between race re-runs but to see two of his mechanics give it large trackside in total synchronicity is a sign of how serious Nicki is to remain "in the zone". Whether it works is open to question since Nicki then finishes third in a three-man race won by meeting reserve Oliver Berntzon to comparatively lusty but nevertheless still notably muted cheers from Swedish fans in the crowd. Berntzon won after a compelling no-holds-barred, no-quarter-given battle for second with Andorra-based fellow Swede Fredrik Lindgren. Pedersen and Lindgren are by some distance the two most aggressive riding riders in the SGP. Arguably Freddie out-Nicki's Nicki nowadays. When added to three seconds and a race win this hard won third-place point is enough to guarantee further ostentatious use of his fan as Nicki qualifies for the semi-final. Once almost taken for granted, Pedersen making the knock-out stages of any SGP meeting nowadays is getting something of a rarity. Even more worth treasuring is the manner of Nicki's getting there. As has been the case for a few years now, Nicki isn't as fast at the SGPs he once was. Though he still stars in Poland and Sweden for his league teams so definitely still has the velocity to combative shrewdness, basic physics dictates it is much harder to boss other SGP riders around if they are comfortably ahead of you on the track. Tonight the faster slow-version

Nicki has been in the thick of the rough and tumble throughout and, more importantly, then remained there without real or sudden onset fictional bike gremlins for every single race. Pedersen has flourished his skills, virtues, aggression and experience to maximise his race positions in each heat. Faster riders should often have been able to pass. But trepidation allied to the canny forceful geometry of Nicki's race line selections quick-quick-slows the pace waltz fashion to his advantage. Or, else, he compresses the available space to only leave fleeting options for passing manoeuvres for those riders confident or brave enough to decide to risk an outside pass. A determined and almost on-form Nicki is what the Speedway Grand Prix craves, needs and has badly missed for some considerable time.

After an out-of-sorts evening getting bested by actual or imagined conditions, Greg Hancock finally looks competitive in his last programmed race. For two and half laps he leads fellow Monster Energy sponsored rider Tai Woffinden in their personal mini-race for second. With Janowski leading comfortably, Woffinden definitely needs a second place to ensure he makes it through to the semi-finals. To do so Tai executes an impressive outside overtake – something of a collector's item tonight and, sadly, even at most SGPs this season – past Hancock who immediately slows. If this were Nicki you would expect immediate imaginary bike problems brought on by a combination of sulk and insult at finding himself last. Greg's problems mystify Ove, "I don't know why Greg slowed? The engine was still running and the chains were still on?" Experienced long-time Speedway Grand Prix riders such as Hancock, Holder and Doyle all struggle and underscore tonight. If the issue isn't mechanical or meteorological, it must be psychological.

The initial attempt to run the first semi-final sees Lindgren take Zmarzlik's left leg (rather than his flamboyant frequent flying right leg) on the second bend. Watched from my position on the fourth bend, it seems to me that Bartosz's fall was gamesmanship as he slightly waited for Freddie and made sure to make himself available for this collision. Once touched Zmarzlik collapses like a dying swan. Watching the same incident in real time from the same vantage point, Ove Fundin is clear that Lindgren is the guilty party for taking Bartosz's leg away. Replays on the big screen aren't conclusive enough for either of us to change our opinion. Referee Craig Ackroyd astonishes Ove by deciding to exclude Zmarzlik. As is traditional, the stadium crowd get no advisory information at all on this decision, while the English language telly audience enjoy the treat of excitable "analysis" from Tai's publicist Nigel Pearson and ex-rider Kelvin Tatum. Afterwards, it turns out the referee adjudges Bartosz was not fully in control of his bike. If this need for full control criteria were regularly applied, Zmarzlik would get exclusions aplenty at each Grand Prix. Talk of ongoing lack of control from Zmarzlik is something that, in normal circumstances, would get a sympathetic hearing from Ove but in this instance doesn't. By the time the end of the SGP season arrives, these semi-final (and possible final) points lost because this contentious decision may cost Zmarzlik the chance to become World Champion. Or, at least, stymie his challenge to do so.

Though there is minimal competition for the accolade despite histrionic embedded speedway media claims otherwise, the re-run of the first semi-final arguably serves up the most memorable race of the Speedway Grand Prix 2018 season to date. It even beats the only previous dramatic race of the series in Prague where Tai threw his toys out of the pram at the ref not stopping the heat after Freddie cramped him up by the fence. Apparently to Tai's mind, even though it is the World Championship, there can't be tough but normal racing manoeuvres when he is out there on track intending to stroll to further glory. To further double-underline his presumption and underlying attitude of entitlement, tonight's Malilla semi-final re-run is a further case in point. This evening Nicki is something like the old Nicki but, like Brer Rabbit, as the meeting has gone on, in the face of his own slowing and slower bikes the experienced Dane has had to really fight for his points with cunning, guile and his trademark over-boisterous (some naysayers would say unfair or dangerously aggressive) tactics rather than rely on the advantage of sheer speed. It is not a Tomasz Gollob style racing masterclass spirograph of stylish intelligent racing lines allied to shrewdly exploiting fleeting and imaginary gaps to turn them into real ones. Instead it is Nicki's own elemental version of said same: where the hyperawareness and track craft gained through thousands of laps intersects with an attitude of dare-to-pass-me-though-I-know-you-can-and-possibly-risk-a-bad-fall. It is not the more straightforward normal vanilla speedway Grand Prix fare of highly tuned fast bikes ridden by full-throttle merchants playing catch up from the gate processionally while vainly chasing behind quicker reactions rivals.

Tai and Nicki start by vying so wholeheartedly for first corner supremacy that it blocks Freddie. Lindgren has the vision and smarts to react with a deliberate *ad hoc* but surprisingly ungainly passing manoeuvre. It simultaneously takes him out of trouble, allows him to somehow change lane and, thereby, catch the preoccupied Pedersen and Woffinden completely unawares with an overtake-pass-cum-intersecting charge to the front into the race lead. After a season watching Tai race the SGPs live (and previously on the telly), he appears to gain most of his points via the use of noticeably faster bikes allied to his signature first bend cut back to the inside. His other more oblique but also relentlessly successful strategy is to spend a couple of laps apparently straining to get the speed to pass but failing to do so only to then – on the last lap or bend – suddenly zoom past on the much faster bike he was always riding but pretended he wasn't. These cut back and feint arrows in his quiver appear to endlessly surprise other SGP riders. It is a puzzle why his rivals mostly don't or can't anticipate these stratagems? They say it is hard to kid a kidder and, though he doesn't possess bikes as fast as Tai's, Nicki has been to the rodeo before so knows enough to predict what is likely to happen on their closely fought race to the finish line for the vital qualifying second place. Sure enough, with horsepower apparently to spare, Tai sufficiently winds up his speed on the last lap back straight to begin his manoeuvre to overtake Nicki the long way around the outside. Rather than wave his rival through with a doff of his helmet visor, instead the noticeably slower Nicki rides an angled racing line across the last corner to the chequered flag. It is a trajectory that inevitably occludes Woffinden's run between Nicki's bike and the safety fence. Pedersen's instantaneous but intuitive fine calculation of velocity and angles exploits the laws of physics and trigonometry to block Woffinden by using his own tactics and momentum against him. It is a masterclass in precision situational awareness. Speedway Tai Chi, if you will, against Tai. This is red-in-tooth-and-claw competitive must-win World Championship racing and is definitely not collegiate, let alone close to the "respect" and bonhomie of team mates or team riding. Judged by his histrionic reactions, it is a manoeuvre that frustrates Tai's sense of proprietary as well as his ambition to qualify for the final. When things don't go his way, Tai tends to cut up quicker than a one-off SGP temporary track. They say real champions reveal their true character in adversity. If so, despite his beatification in the tame speedway media by his publicist and other embedded enablers, for Woffinden rough going discombobulates him exponentially more than the steady state of smooth conditions and predictable racing.

Setting aside the wider context, Nicki's race-winning World Championship manoeuvre definitely massively offends Tai's sense of entitlement to safe-space speedway racing. The unwritten rule to "leave space" is preached as a necessary courtesy and "professionalism" by, amongst others, Greg Hancock (except if up against lesser SGP riders) and Monster Energy's Joe Parsons (usually on social media) but does not appear in any rule book. In the same way an alcoholic is someone you don't like who drinks the same amount as you, then a truly dangerous rider is someone who rides like <insert aggressive rider name> (for example, Jason Doyle in 2016 and 2017 SGPs) but is called Nicki. Speedway is a competitive adrenalin-based sport. In the heat of the moment, feelings can run high. Inflamed passions provoke strong reactions. Heat of the moment outbursts and passion are par for the course. What can be overlooked and forgiven when it happens once is graceless petulance. Especially since many sporting champions require bloody singlemindedness and steel so don't – when push comes to shove – usually always play nice by the Queensbury rules. When temper, petulance and lashing out come fitted as standard when things go against you, it throws into question your World Champion credentials. Sadly, when it comes to overcoming temporary bumps in his often plain-sailing SGP road, the Tai Woffinden Speedway Legend jury still remains very much out undecided, if judged by how badly he takes the manner of this third place. In the warm down lap, Tai aggressively gestures, rides close, knocks helmets and repeatedly keeps flicking his back wheel in petulant anger towards Nicki. Putting it mildly, he does not react in a statesmanlike manner to his disappointment. No angel on the track by a long chalk, Nicki defends himself and his personal space throughout this unexpectedly strongly contested warm-down lap.

If this heat of the moment warm-down lap contretemps were where it stopped, then such is competitive speedway racing and so be it. But. And it is a big BUT. When the riders reach the pits gate, Woffinden's mechanical staff wait there ready and keen to get involved to defend their rider's (putative) honour. In the SGP pits, Woffinden stands out for the look, professionalism and composition of his pits team rather than just their number. Other riders are similarly staffed in terms of numbers. Like many, Tai's pits crew dress smartly in their (predictably primarily black) team outfits. Colourful, branded co-ordinated uniforms or team shirts are the spray-on professionalism of the contemporary speedway scene. To the envy of his rivals, Tai's crew includes current top mechanic Jacek Trojanowski. While any six-footers look tall in the SGP pits, Jacek is really tall, notably slim verging on flamingo-leg thin. He comes across as detailed, professional and hard working. Tai apparently trusts him absolutely and an important part of his SGP racing success is built upon this key relationship. While you should never judge a book by its cover, everyone does. The two other members of Tai's crew look like bouncers. They are peas from the same pod when it comes to looks and attitude. They project an air of quiet, strong menace. I take that to be their intention rather than a reticence brought on by shyness or language difficulties. Before racing gets underway, they often joke amongst themselves or with other mechanics and do, sometimes, even smile as broadly as their biceps are big. Mostly they glower and keep themselves to themselves. As a mechanical team, they appear to work hard and well together with fluency, expertise and swift confident capability. They are both key members of an efficient highly professional back room team. It took me a long time to realise that there are two similar looking gentlemen. They look so alike they could be mistaken for brothers. But aren't. Though hard to tell apart to casual observation and too young to have seen Kojak, one of them sucks a lolly. They are no strangers to the gym. The size and development of their chests and biceps get noticed, not least by themselves. They take pride in their work and appearance. They are strapping lads with closely shaven heads of the kind you see in the shadows of nightclub doorways, at body-building contests or in those who feast on gym supplements. It is hardly subliminal but the message I get from the contrast in Tai's size to theirs is that – should the going get tough – they are there to help and protect him from threat, attack or violence. Some could rather unfairly say they look a bit thuggish. They clearly train hard in the gym. Often. To show that nominative determinism is alive and well in speedway, one of them is called Darwinski. There is definitely something primal and Darwinian about the way they strut about and hold themselves. Should they ever commute on the London Underground, they would definitely belong to the commuter army of man-spreaders with legs akimbo to air off their unfeasibly large testicles.

At the pits gate – whether it is adrenalin, protectiveness, rage or need for retribution – Konrad (or, maybe, his brother from a different mother Robert Ruszala or, since there is never a BSI SGP name badge when you need one, possibly Leszek Wisniewski) and Jacek wish to greet Nicki's return with a few well-chosen words of advice and comment. As Tai has already been eliminated from this SGP, Woffinden's mechanics must also be keen to immediately get on with bike repairs and maintenance duties for the next Grand Prix at the pits gate – rather than in Tai's pits bay – as he has very diligently brought along one of his big shiny spanners. It is a non-adjustable spanner of the double-headed variety made for loosening big circumference hexagonal nuts. Despite having zero experience doing mechanical work on speedway bikes, I can't say I can recall ever seeing a nut of this size on any riders' equipment. It looks badly unfit for purpose. Strange when so much that happens in any speedway pits bay nowadays is so meticulously planned and organised to ensure everything has its place but remains instantly on hand. Maybe it is the spanner required for the nut in Frankenstein's neck or to open the chest cavity compartment where they store Monster Joe Parsons' matchbox-sized sense of humour? Whatever its actual use, Tai's mechanic staffer gaily waves said spanner about like a prized trophy in Nicki's vicinity with some gusto. Though I am close by, I can't hear what is said. Since he seems a man of few words, I am guessing it is either "Me Monster sponsored rider's monster", "Golly, I say old chap, that was a bit rum", "Look my nice shiny spanner for you!" or, "Can I help prepare your bike for the final?". He has definitely spat out his trademark actual lolly along with his metaphorical dummy.

After frequently wondering what the actual verifiable purpose of the frequently ornamental FIM Race Director Phil Morris is, it turns out that – unofficially – his job responsibilities also run to that of part-time boxing referee. With lightning speed, Morris inserts himself between the tool-wielding mechanic and Nicki to push Tai's black-suited staff member away before his words and brandished spanner can translate into action. Given how often Phil bangs on about his Welshness, there is also an element of loose ruck about his intervention that distantly recalls some primal sporting aspect of these oft-proclaimed cultural roots too. That said, in sporting terms, after the initial push back on Tai's mechanic, Phil creates the tactical blocking human shield more frequently seen in the elaborate choreographed plays of basketball or gridiron. Pedersen's manager Helge Frimodt – albeit spanner-free – briefly joins in this toys-out-of-the-pram fray. Morris restores order quickly and effectively. He dampens the possibility of a bar brawl with his prompt physical intervention. As Phil's apparently self-penned Wikipedia page modestly notes, "his physical strength also attracted attention from a Wrestling promotion who wanted him to train with the legendary World of Sport Wrestling great Kendo Nagasaki". Having separated Nicki from the threat of assault, Morris pushes the Dane away and back up the pit lane back towards the pits. He wears the officious but slightly put-upon expression of a supply teacher forced to abandon their exam marking in order to adjudicate a school-gate flare-up between harassed parents over parking spots.

Just as hostilities start to subside and at the moment the possibility of confrontation had been averted, Tai's lead mechanic Jacek decides to give a quick jostle too – possibly just so that he can say that he did so afterwards – on the periphery of this post-race *ad hoc* SGP discussion group as if he felt keen to get physically involved too. With the boxing build of a lightweight stick insect, albeit with impressive long reach, it is hard to know whether to see his attempted intervention as delusional or laughable. In fact, it is far from funny. Collectively Tai's team have lost their shit over a predictable low-level racing incident. It is in a different post code to statesmanlike and is even further from befitting the behaviour of an ex-World Champion or a repeat world-champion-in-waiting. It definitely highlights a precious sense of entitlement, precarious mental attitude and lack of street smarts that media reports claim it was part of Tai's Grand Prix manager Peter Adams' remit to guide and counsel against. Then again, the most extreme act of pits violence I have ever seen was at Wolverhampton speedway club involving their club security guard and, as luck would have it, Nicki. As ever, no one saw anything. Here that cannot be said. Some of the confrontation is caught on camera. And spoken about in the BT Sports commentary box. Kelvin theatrically hitches up his metaphorical skirt, while any of Nigel's thoughts are – as usual – hopelessly compromised in their authenticity, status or power by his ongoing role as Tai's publicist. On and off the track, everyone already knew this was highly likely to be the most exciting event and talking point of the entire Speedway Grand Prix series this 2018 season. Afterwards, it is pretty well the only incident from the whole 2018 series that merits future place on SGP promotional showreels. Subsequently, it is shown in heavy rotation on You Tube too.

Film of the incident quickly gained traction and comment. BT Sports twitter was quick to cash in on any potential virality with an edit of the on-track discussions that bore little or no relation to the reality of those interactions. The initial hot off the VT BT Sports version somehow managed to portray Nicki putting his arm out to gesticulate and protect himself from Tai (and his repeated aggressive wheel flicks) as a surprise escalating violent blow upon his "victim" rather than an angry gesture in response to post-race aggression that it really was. In the same way Tai's staff initiated and led confrontation at the pits gate, it was originally Tai who escalated and led this style of fraught response during the on-track warm-down lap discussions. Yet, somehow, BT Sports managed to de-contextualise this as its opposite. With so little on-track SGP action to vaguely tempt let alone thrill their stay-away armchair audience, in the absence of the need for veracity or authenticity, they clearly decided to ignore the actual sequence of events in order to big up the cartoon of Nicki as their go-to pantomime villain. BT Sports certainly need something significant to boost their speedway audience viewing figures. According to BARB, the statistically valid industry standard assessment model used by all television stations and programmes, UK SGP viewing figures have hugely declined since BT Sports took over from Sky Sports to show these World Championship meetings live. This massive drop is understandable to some extent since there is a significant difference in the total subscriber numbers between BT Sports and Sky Sports. Also, some sports attract big interest and others don't. That said, BT's annual report to shareholders did reveal that after they massively invested in the sure-fire winner of showing live (British) Premier League football, they only managed to add 7,000 new subscribers. This is a pitiful audience increase in brute numbers terms, let alone given the size of their financial investment in the purchase of these football broadcast rights and the outside broadcast equipment and staff then required to exercise them effectively. If football can't move the dial, then no number of replays of minor speedway fracas is going to make any difference. To solve the problem, from mid-summer 2018 BT Sports STOPPED submitting their viewing figures to BARB. Even a blind man on a galloping horse knows that IF the figures were notably good, they would continue to report them.

Worse still from a timing point of view, BT Sports have got involved at a time when the UK speedway audience has been in serious and long term ongoing decline for well over a decade on any satellite broadcaster channel. Indeed, it was Sky Sports who initiated and then presided over a precipitous and accelerating almost decade long decline. Live broadcast speedway of any stripe, whether British league racing or, of course, the SGPs is in likely terminal decline, despite the odd dead cat bounce. It is said – by me, actually – that most SGP meetings are primarily shown on televisions on a compulsory basis in institutional settings: such as service station toilets, hospitals, remand and respite institutions, Police waiting rooms. Places where the pictures are shown as pacifying wallpaper and, even if they wanted to, viewers can't choose or change the channel so there is no choice but subjection to the inanities of the associated chatter. Even if they are lucky enough to watch with the sound off, they still get served up the glitzy effects and packaging of VT guys obsessed with the glamour of first corner spinning back wheels and the associated flying shale shots. It's an endless show reel of oft replayed starts and dull finishes leavened with fast motion evocatively framed processional back straight racing. Given CNN have the global airport franchise locked down and most prisoners go to bed too early to catch more than the start of the live broadcasts, televised SGP speedway apparently mostly plays unwatched in the background to the equivalent of coma victims (and their distressed visitors). Another important category of regular SGP viewers – those suffering with locked-in body syndrome – go through seven types of hell trying to spell "please turn off the sound" or "Rosco looks sillier than Scott in that shirt" one painful letter of the alphabet at a time through laboriously convoluted eye movements. The only possibility of escape from this torture requires that they be lucky enough to have someone close who loves them enough to have the patience to gain the brilliance of understanding required to note these blinking silent desperate cries for help.

Quite how many of these forced viewer survivors, if they finally ever recover, then decide to drink Monster or fit some new Anlas tyres to their scramble bike remains uninvestigated. Even worse, I was excitedly told earlier in Malilla – as if this is an impressive figure – that they were saying in the "SGP media centre" – otherwise known as the musty smelling damp tent with Wi-Fi and some stale snacks no one risks eating located close by to the pits – "it will go ahead: there are 637,000 worldwide subscribers waiting to watch this SGP!" If that is the current worldwide audience officially claimed by BSI (in the media centre) for the Speedway Grand Prix, given their track record of struggle with accuracy in statistical matters surrounding attendance levels, then this could well actually already be something an exaggeration. For the purposes of discussion, let us accept that this may – for once – be an accurate assessment rather than a random inflated figure selected from thin air to impress the unwary, naive or prospective partner/sponsor. Even if we allow for time-zone differences and events being shown either as live or as highlights, with a possible 196 countries in the world available to purchase rights to show the SGPs, this is a pitiful number. No wonder, beyond Joe Parsons vicarious lifestyle investment of only a small portion of his total Monster marketing budget into his speedway plaything, genuinely serious global brands are going to swerve the sponsorship opportunities if all that is on offer is an audience reach of this risible minitude. In global audience terms, this number is so infinitesimal that, more often than not, it will fail to register other than as a rounding error. Proper global brands would avoid involvement even if this 637,000 were solely the UK audience size. The keyword to note here is "subscribers" – rather than the more common expression of viewers – since this implies what is being counted is those who have (pre-)paid for a package of various products and (satellite) channels rather than those that actively watch them. This mis-counting happens elsewhere in other sports too, of course. For example, football clubs with half-empty grounds regularly count all the season ticket holders in their official attendance numbers, even if said fans don't attend. But, at least, they are still declaring them and seeing them printed/recorded. Obviously, enough, things have been bad for so long at BSI-run SGP events that they don't even publicly provide any "official figures" for attendances or television audiences. And why would they when it makes such grim reading? They must be shocking when BSI no longer bother with the independently unverified numbers they once so loved. Even the FIM stopped mentioning them around a decade or so ago in their annual report on speedway. It is also worth recalling that erstwhile SGP publicist manqué Philip Rising once amazingly claimed on the British Speedway Forum that the SGP had two million viewers in India alone!

Though to most untutored eyes, Nicki is the victim in the scenario that just played out before us, Ove Fundin isn't so easily convinced of his blamelessness. "Nicki has always been a dirty rider. If it hadn't been stopped then there would have been a fight. It was something interesting to see." Back in the tent that serves as the nerve centre of race-night operations at the SGP in Malilla otherwise known as the "media centre", Paul Burbidge clutches the mobile phone via which he frenetically stabs to issue his trademark trite, hackneyed and dull hyperbolic phrases as heat-by-heat commentary via the official SGP twitter account. It is so banal and far from Shakespeare that for a long time many thought some basic form of chatbot deliberately programmed with an excitable but extremely limited laddish-cum-Boys-Own vocabulary must churn out this guff about "powered past", "brought the roof down", "crowd go wild" and "burst past <insert name> to win" on auto-pilot. Even Burbo can recognise this altercation might be news and vaguely stir interest so reports as a memo to self in giant letters for his other day job at the *Speedway Star* afterwards, "the incident will unquestionably build excitement for the next time these giants of the sport meet". Given how often these riders race against each other in the various leagues (Poland, Sweden and Denmark if not any longer in Britain) or SGPs, excitement levels are likely to be muted at best with the wind behind us on a sunny day. Whatever degree hearts race or don't, it is highly unlikely to add anyone extra fans through the turnstiles at Gorzow (scene of the next instalment of the SGP) or draw new viewers to seek out the screens showing the future SGP meetings or races in hospitals, prisons, airports and care homes. Given the comparative lateness of the hour and though the ambient temperature is cool, concentration levels, heart rates and anticipation levels see sudden boosts in the Malilla crowd and selected rider pit bays. Indeed, it is rumoured afterwards that Nicki is cowed by no man so immediately sought to resolve matters with Tai's mechanic but was prevented from doing so by wiser counsel.

The second semi-final features some wild riding from Patryk Dudek on his Swedish home track. He appears to lock shoulders with Maciej Janowski on the back straight of the first lap but is soon shaken off. The intensity of their mini-battle eliminates both from contention and qualification for the final in a race once again won imperiously by Matej Zagar. The entire meeting has taken just over two hours to run as the riders come round to line up at the start tapes for the final at 22.50 local time. Based on his form and speed up until this point, Matej Zagar would ordinarily start as favourite to win but for the presence of Nicki Pedersen with his dander up and long-time indifference to on track controversy. The veteran Dane definitely rides a hard first lap that involves dramatic rough-housing cuts across the racing lines of both Zagar and Lindgren. As intended, this impedes their progress – especially Zagar's – and slows them. As always, Nicki is an equal opportunities even-handed serial aggressor. The lead and distance his first lap antics create remains under continuous threat but, using force of will and track craft rather than brute speed, Nicki holds on to gain his well-deserved triumph. He celebrates with an ecstatic victory lap. Rather than then head back to the pits in search of praise or spanners, Nicki leaps from his machine to climb into the first bend stands to wildly – if hugs can be wild, then these are them – his girlfriend, friends and family who just watched and cheered his latest triumph. Beforehand Nicki was seventeen-to-one with the bookies to win. It is his first Grand Prix victory since 2015; particularly notable given the succession of spinal injuries that placed his long-term mobility and health, let alone his speedway career, in serious doubt. Interviewed inside the stadium over the stadium speakers ("It is a long time since you won a GP"), Nicki is buzzing and proud, "It is. I have had two broken backs since then!" Looking tired, sweaty and dishevelled but ecstatic, Pedersen thanks and briefly namechecks all those who continued to believe in him for their help in getting him back on top of the podium yet again. His fulsome praise is so severe it even extends to inanimate objects he had earlier strongly doubted, "It's a proper track, so a good track." His ongoing real and imaginary mechanical travails are briefly forgiven and forgotten in the afterglow of triumph. Displaying the attitude of champions in sports everywhere, Nicki clearly has and continues to believe the rostrum is his rightful place in the SGP even if the actual results in the World Championship over recent years indicate or imply otherwise.

Winner: Nicki Pedersen (15 points)

Second: Matej Zagar (16 points)

Third: Fredrik Lindgren (13 points)

Fourth: Martin Vaculik (10 points)

CHAPTER 7

Gorzow SGP 7 – 25.08.18

"I suppose lesbian sex is a bit like the SGP, in that it goes on for ever and there are a lot of men watching it at home, alone, on the internet."

Catherine Bohart

THE friendly women receptionist behind the check-in desk at the Sheraton hotel in Poznan asks with what sounds like genuine curiosity, "Who is going to win the GP?"

"I dunno? Tai?"

"I think Tai."

The much-travelled David Goodchild of Travel Plus Tours is also waiting there, "I think Zmarzlik," he says before turning towards me to advise, "always say a local rider!" Poland is a speedway nation so it is not wholly a surprise that people talk about it in – what to British ears – are unexpected places. Namely ordinary everyday life. After two decades of BSI allegedly spreading the Speedway World Championships gospel, in the UK speedway is a well-kept secret. [1]

Other than inside a speedway stadium, I have never seen anyone read a *Speedway Star* in – as it were – the wild. Yet on the direct midday Poznan to Gorzow train, there is a bloke in glasses sat by the window on the opposite aisle from me reading the latest issue closely. And I mean closely. He is totally absorbed. He studies with the intensity of someone who knows they are about to come across a life-changing revelation. People read the *Speedway Star* like that. Weekly. Part specialist publication, part trade journal, part in-house newsletter, part promotional catalogue and, of course, part bible. Until recent years, it was never afraid to leave the difficult questions unasked or real news unmentioned. Even now in the current era of comparative Glasnost, the SGP mostly remains in a bubble of relentless celebration and kept sacrosanct from hand-wringing analysis. Hence its reputation as a kind of cheerleading speedway *Pravda*, mostly printing what the "official line" or orthodoxy dictates rather than the reality of any given situation. Many promoters and those who operate within speedway's inner sanctum (plus some knowledgeable punters) refer to it as "the comic". This has always struck me as an unfair sobriquet but, possibly, reflect how it combines narrative plausibility with cartoonish fiction and touches of hyperbole. Of course, for any student of the politics of the sport there is a detective almost forensic appeal in the hours of weekly fun to be had reading it to discover what has been said, isn't said or has been obliquely implied or nodded

---

[1] Something that is similarly secret is where the euros and zlotys but not my pound cash went from my wallet? It is a theft that defies the imagination as well as requires the illusionist and escapologist skills of a Derren Brown or David Blaine. The manager of the Sheraton Poznan remains adamant his investigations reveal they are completely exonerated of said crime though my wallet never appeared – freely – in my possession outside. During my Sheraton stay it either lived stored throughout in my locked Sheraton Poznan room safe or else padlocked inside a wheelie case I had with me at all times after I left the hotel to walk to the railway station to get my train. But still got emptied. My personal recommendation would be to not stay at the Sheraton Hotel Poznan. Or, if you do, store any money or valuables via reception in the hotel safe. Sensible travel safety practice is also not to discuss the timings and specifics of your travel plans in public areas unless you are happy to be overheard doing so.

towards in passing in its pages. There are a great many photographs too, albeit within an implicitly agreed slightly self-conscious limited repertoire of standard poses. Invariably the money shots are mostly of crashes, spectacular overtakes, evocative handlebar-to-handlebar landscapes (featuring from two to four riders) as well as individual portraits (of riders and/or teams) in the pits, environs of the stadium or in live action out on the shale. Seriously declining circulation has seen the *Star* rouse from its editorial slumber over recent seasons with regards to asking harder questions about or making Dutch Uncle observations with regards to the real or imagined travails of British speedway. Commercial self-interest now sees impassioned editorials appear and even lengthy analysis of endemic easily identifiable (but less easily solvable) possibly structural problems besetting British speedway league racing. Particularly falling crowd numbers and their less frequent corollary, closing clubs. These issues and strategic problems have been unavoidably obvious for some time but often escaped the attention of the *Star* until around the time its circulation declined to perilous levels and, thereby, became an obvious scapegoat and explanation for its ills to its (part) owner and Managing Editor Philip Rising.

Strangely, said extensive analysis of speedway's ills completely fails to mention the era-defining deleterious impact of the SGP. This is something of an omission, given how the magazine owners Pinegen Limited once printed SGP programmes while the actual magazine was also giving acres of uncritical coverage. This breathless suck-uppery has continued even after the lucrative programme business went elsewhere. Pinegen shareholder Mr Rising has historically had his own close involvement with SGP rights holders BSI too. Whether in official capacity as FIM assistant race director or his subsequent unofficial capacity as an *ad hoc* but relentless independent interpreter-cum-happy-flappy-spokesman for all things BSI and SGP on the British Speedway Forum. Given all this experience and insider knowledge, you would expect more joining of the dots by Rising or his editorial colleagues about how the SGP has emasculated British speedway, hastened its decline and ensured its penury. But, when it comes to almost any aspect of the SGP – one of its remaining regular full-page advertisers – the *Speedway Star* still remains faithful and tactically comatose when it comes to questioning almost any structural aspect of the series. Preferring instead to publish detailed but anodyne rabble-rousing copy – whether reports, interviews or "opinion" – mostly written by its Chief News Writer Paul Burbidge who in a spooky coincidence is also employed by BSI to write similar news, reports, interviews, comment and assorted guff for either their website or spectacularly hyperbolic social media account.

If the *Speedway Star* magazine editorial really is the canary in the mine (as it likes to masquerade as nowadays), then all we had was a long dead dusty skeleton by the time it roused itself enough to seriously call out to Houston with regard to some intractable or serious problems. Every print edition is nowadays full colour and – laudably, to be honest – extrudes thousands upon thousands of words weekly on a minority declining niche sport. If you include its digital edition with enough words and pictures to fill at least another magazine plus you then add in all the other speedway forums, social media accounts and websites, British speedway still generates a phenomenal number of words – often low quality (this book included) - on a daily basis. It is a sometimes toxic lava flow completely disproportionate to its declining active fan base aka those that bother to pay at the turnstiles to actually attend meetings. Until the *Star* decided to withdraw from the circulation services of WH Smith as a cost-cutting measure - citing a saving of £12,000 per annum – that was really the only place it could be regularly seen in the wild. Except of course, for apparently randomly selected mid to discount level supermarkets located in the vicinity of speedway tracks or general area of where they used to trade before going defunct. For example – and hello – Tadley Sainsbury's

12 or so miles from the now derelict Reading Football Club overflow car park that once was better known as Smallmead Stadium. Whenever the weekly issue of my annual subscription arrives late (aka not on Thursday), I could still immediately get my fix in WH Smith branches in Brighton or London Victoria. To be honest, I often liked to have a good glance through in Smiths on my Thursday morning walk home for the sheer thrill of it not just in case it didn't make it through that day in the post. No other of my magazine subscriptions enjoys this urgent intensity or thirsty interest. The immediate need to be notionally informed about the fine detail of results, news, political spin, forthcoming meetings and injuries is a very hard speedway habit to kick. But, sadly, other people it seems increasingly have the full busy lives and willpower to do so. Of course, the *Star* remains a vital and hallowed institution, albeit an increasingly hollowed-out one that more often belies its status as one of the biggest jewels in the speedway crown. But sadly, like hanging, national service and smiling village bobbies, its halcyon days are over and times have changed. Harsh realities intrude. Not only has speedway has been flung to the far reaches of the periphery of the public imagination but its primary demographic is either declining or ageing badly. Hand in hand with this often literal die off has also predictably gone the circulation of the *Speedway Star* magazine. The past is a foreign country. If the only old ways and views are firmly held onto out of romance or nostalgia, these can prove terminal. In the context, the only new game in town throughout the twenty-first century has been the Speedway Grand Prix. Anyone who is anyone has hitched a ride or jumped enthusiastically upon this bright shiny bandwagon. But, like life, things are rarely straightforward and all that glitters isn't always gold. How the SGP cuckoo ate our speedway young while it feathered its own nest; the reality of business model and practices or even how willing quislings – blindly or willingly – helped it hollow out British speedway is the subject for another book, another time. Though, obviously you may have noticed, I am a bit of a moth to this particular SGP flame so can't stop myself from sideways glancing upon some aspects of these ongoing thought crimes throughout this book too.

Anyways, the only place I have ever seen a fuss made of the *Speedway Star* was at Poole (a Wednesday night track) where its arrival and the cache of buying and reading it a day earlier than subscribers receive it in the post – it is formally published on a Saturday – sufficiently spurred interest and sales for its publishers Pinegen to make sure bulk copies arrived at Wimborne Road every week. As the most successful team of the past decade or two, it didn't hurt that Poole Pirates attracted large to good-sized crowds keen to read extensive coverage of their star riders, successes and impending triumphs. Poole even had a magazine seller wandering the terraces and bars during the meeting hand selling the magazine. Though on sale at all clubs elsewhere, no other speedway track appeared to enjoy this sales volume or the buzz of this hot-off-the-press cachet. So, to actually see someone – a younger person too (white, male and, less predictably, in Poland) – studying it closely on a regional train in Eastern Europe is nothing short of amazing, even given that our final destination will tonight stage a round of the Speedway Grand Prix. To read it so intently in a second or third language is so stunning, it immediately makes me remember Kevin – who I used to stand by at Eastbourne well over two decades ago – who used to bang on admiringly about the exotic ecstatic passion the Poles held for all things speedway ("they are so mad for it, even the birds love it!").

As far as I can see, this crowded noon train to Gorzow – the last that arrives in time for the Grand Prix – has no birds mad for it (or otherwise) obviously going to the speedway. However, there is a gaggle of boisterous Piotr Pawlicki fans in bright red replica shirts with his number 59 and name emblazoned on their backs. The forgettable and weirdly incongruous numbers selected by SGP riders as their identifying brand numerals – apparently often chosen for their person significance – seems delusional. From a memorability and market size point of view. Maybe this is the number of the house where he and his brother grew up? Stranger still, given their ineffectiveness but not BSI's legendary officiousness, there is even a BSI rule about said rider numbers which says they can be retired by BSI and then given to other riders after two years of non-use in the SGP. The bigger question is does 222, 692, 108, 54 or 111 really help anybody stand out? The answer is a resounding no. I don't expect it will be that long before one of the next generation of riders chooses 666 as a condition of his Monster Energy sponsorship.

Ours is a slow but direct country stopping train. Calling everywhere, it feels like. Many stations are just platforms with a sign without shelter. Some have impressive civic station buildings but most don't appear to have the footfall to warrant investment in further infrastructure. About half-way, with no announcements, pretty well everyone gets off to join a train on the platform opposite. Even the Pawlicki fans. The only one of this group who speaks broken English tells me that the train opposite is now the one to Gorzow when I pop over to consult him. If I hadn't done so, the *Star* reader and I would have sat patiently in the sunshine like slowly ripening lemons while the last train to Gorzow that arrives in time for the SGP left without us. Clearly this amazing Polish fan reading in a second or third language isn't actually a Pole but must be a stranger here too. In fact, he is James Hawkes from Stevenage. He's a Tai Woffinden, SGP and Rye House speedway fan so in mourning at the sudden recent closure of his club. Though Woffinden no longer deigns to race in British speedway and also has ridden a roster of different clubs in different leagues, James is definitely keen to claim Tai as a Rye House rider for his couple of seasons' racing there a decade or so ago in 2007 and 2008. Given his ongoing absence from league racing in Britain, by Tai's standards his time in Hoddesdon almost merits a long-service gold watch. Many clubs and fans like to suggest Tai's pedigree as a rider and/or World Champion is based upon the apprenticeship time spent at their particular club. Given riders race for so many different British clubs during their careers, there is a rich tradition of clubs retrospectively claiming successful or famous riders as obviously supremely talented from the outset and truly a product of "X" club despite its (usually spotty) rider development pedigree. Some of the most amusingly ridiculous of these "we developed this rider by giving him his first steps in speedway" claims is usually made by Derek Barclay on behalf of the Conference League "plc" incarnation of Wimbledon Speedway (2002-2005). Apparently almost any rider who once fell off in a second half race there or, possibly, even rode an actual league meeting at Plough Lane as a visitor to their troubled gate-and-go track owes all their later career success to this wonderful, hugely formative experience. History tells us that – in this instance – this is likely an impossibility for Tai since he started racing Conference League in 2006, while Wimbledon went defunct in 2005. According to the man who bungled the stadium contract renewal negotiation live, their demise was due to the pending demolition and development of Plough Lane (this finally happened over a decade later) rather than the stadium owners for reasons best known to themselves refusing to accept one of the highest weekly rent payments (£2,000) paid in British speedway at that mid-noughties time. It would still be a high weekly rent even now, to be honest. Perhaps, it is actually NOT racing at the Conference League incarnation of Wimbledon that eventually made Woffinden World Champion? Even two years spent enjoying strong home advantage racing at Rye on its compact slightly peculiar contoured track is a hard pedigree to directly correlate with or translate into success on the SGP stage, except through a very powerful rose-tinted telescope on a sunny day.

With ambitious new owners, Rye House speedway club moved up into the highest British league last year but, sadly, went under this year in mid-season with fixed race nights and a standoff with the authorities over changing these blamed in the media and on social media for their demise. James is saddened but not surprised. "Running on a Monday doesn't work. The crowds disappeared. We are a Saturday night club. Under Len Silver – he was a bit old school – it ran like clockwork. It was either on a Saturday or not, if the GP was on." Fixed race nights is one of the many quarter-witted ideas Paul "Bungalow" Burbidge was allowed to bang on about relentlessly in the pages of the *Speedway Star* for many years as an initiative to miraculously "save" the sport. According to the convoluted mostly fact-free logic of Burbo's recommendation, fixed race nights would be both a panacea and route to the sunny uplands of booming attendances by attracting back the SGP "star" (or "top") riders. It was definitely a strategy that also suited BSI Speedway - his other employer – as it further entrenches their deleterious (for British speedway clubs) Saturday night monopoly as well as bonus haloes the notion that there is something uniquely attractive and special about any riders who grace and race in the SGP. This solution was always more myth and delusion than sensible but didn't stop the upper echelon British speedway clubs eventually half-arsedly trying it out while also granting some clubs exemptions. So, every Elite League (or whatever their diminishing number league was called that season) club raced on the fixed race nights of Monday and Wednesday bar Swindon who sometimes did but also continued to hold some meetings on their traditional Thursday race night. Predictably, although this solution succeeded every time it was suggested in Burbo world, it fails in real life. The obvious reality is that more money is what would attract back these (self-employed) riders to race in the UK (and, ideally, Britain not being an island). Money in British speedway is in ever shorter supply due to a complex vicious circle that – on the one hand - sees costs on the rise, less attractive race nights available and (actual or perceived) rider quality diminish. While, on the other, attendances along with the sponsorship and TV monies needed to pay for any radical structural change are simultaneously all in steep decline. As ever, what didn't appear at length in the pages of the *Speedway Star* about the demise of Rye House is as significant as what did. Namely, authoritative rumours that the club could have survived if only the governing trade body of the sport hadn't allegedly rather intransigently put the integrity and authority of its decision making above the ongoing commercial existence of one of its members. It is not a good look so, hence, it fails to make the pages of the *Star*. With debts owed within speedway circles and, subsequent news of its parent company in receivership, the ins and outs of their demise is, of course, both hard to exactly trace and moot since they have irrevocably been consigned to history.

Tai's major commercial and sponsorship market is where he makes sure to race and, thereby, earn most: Poland. James tells me that Tai is so keen to culturally attune himself that he has already learnt some basic Polish words and phrases. Though learning the lingo, it isn't known if Tai has taken his own personal ultimate step of commitment via his favoured medium of expression: body art. Speedway themed tattoos in Polish would be quite a statement of his commitment. Quite what phrases to then choose is much harder. Generic Tai-centric phrases such as "heat leader", "tapes infringement", "sponsorship packages available" or "enough room to pass" in Polish could really add something unique and very speedway to his existing body art. Not visibly similarly tattoo minded, James is also keen to visit Poland more often and generally study all things Polish. Its (military) history sites, culture, league racing and language particularly appeal. "I might learn Polish over the winter. I don't think it is the easiest language?" To my mind, the omens for exciting speedway fandom and also his future linguistic success look good, "If Tai can learn it, you can learn it."

Twenty-six-year-old James is in the early stages of SGP ground-hopping with the permission and encouragement of his wife. It also a break from his regular work for F1 Auto Centres ("we have 103 branches") as a Pricing Manager where he puts his service management degree - which included a dissertation on "service branding in football" with the MK Dons as his dissertation case study – with an accounting minor. The starter-level SGP addiction gateway drug of choice (Cardiff) then led James onto to harder stuff of Torun in 2015. The next year his burgeoning addiction saw him re-visit both locations and also add Prague into the mix. By 2017, James was hooked, and re-visited all three previous highs as well as also going to see the SGP in Stockholm. This year it is Cardiff plus all three Polish SGPs (Warsaw, Gorzow and Torun). At this rate, should the BSI iteration of the series manage to survive until then, James will run out of new SGPs to attend by 2024. Defying its long history of ending in a damp squib before all the meetings of any series are completed, James optimistically hopes that this season the SGP series remains live as a competition until the very last meeting, "It would be nice if Tai could win [become World Champion] in the first race at Torun". James is an enthusiastic SGP advocate and traveller. "I haven't been to a bad GP yet! Prague is a fantastic city and the track is unbelievably good. The stadium holds eight or nine thousand so the atmosphere isn't as good as Warsaw. Stockholm had six or seven thousand in a 20,000 capacity stadium. Cardiff seemed to cut up. You could see little bits coming up straightaway and then really from heat five or six. The SGP TV coverage is brilliant but the British League racing is awful with only two fixed camera angles." Again without warning or public announcement, our second direct train journey suddenly ends at another remote rural station. We again follow the gaggle of blokes in red Piotr Pawlicki 59 shirts to decamp in hot sunshine onto ageing replacement coaches to Gorzow so crowded that many people stand awkwardly in the aisle for the remaining journey. Like James, Nicki Pedersen famously lived in Stevenage for some years with his wife/partner Anna Metta – before they separated – and their two children. Partly for its travel convenience but also because of the guaranteed anonymity of Hertfordshire compared to the hassle his fame brought in Denmark. My question, "Did you ever see Nicki in Stevenage?" reveals the area as something of a speedway rider mecca. "Believe it or not my grandfather – who has lived there all his life – knew of him so I got to meet Nicki and got my picture taken with him when I was 13 or 14. I believe Krzysztof Kasprzak lives there too! Well, Hitchin, which is nearby." Aside from the SGP, like so many fans, James is completely definite that the centre of the speedway universe is in Poland and is likely to remain there for any aspiring riders for quite some time. "You have to ride in Poland. They go so fast. If you don't catch up, you go home!"

After a series only staged in the warm summer sunshine – except the last GP in Malilla – the Gorzow forecast across all the weather websites is late afternoon thunderstorms and torrential rain. For once, multiple online weather forecasts of differing complexity and accuracy are unanimous that rain will be prolonged and torrential even if the thunder and lightning somehow evades the Edwarda Jancarza stadium. Speedway and rain don't mix. If the meeting is staged rather than postponed or abandoned, damp tracks usually produce processional and less confident racing from the riders. It is hard to believe that the SGP races could become more processional but heavy rain could make this impossible bad dream come true. Under the auspices of series rights holders BSI Speedway, the oft-used "top riders" and "World Championship" descriptors imply the pursuit of excellence and exhilarating lusty competition. Sadly, in the current SGP series, this translates to mean "professional". It is a competition graced with skilled riders who can be relied upon to get the meeting on, irrespective of the track racing conditions. Competitors who understand that their primary purpose is to attend, put on a show and perform a minimum of sixteen races (to ensure there are no ticket refunds) no matter what the prevailing conditions are at any event. Given the expense and distance fans travel to watch any SGP series meeting – whether they are from the staging country or further afield – any possibility of postponement is bad news.

When it comes to broadcaster, rider, rights holder and staging staff, any re-staging comes with considerable logistical and financial pain. Even though FIM gives any (next day) re-staging of the meeting priority over all others – to ensure that SGP riders don't bunk off for elsewhere (read: Poland) – the broadcasters, organisers, riders and staging clubs operate on the tacit (verging on the explicit) understanding that the meeting will go ahead no matter what. Unless actual rain interferes with vision and, thereby, safety. Even the concept of "dangerous" is flexible, fungible and mutable when it comes to SGP meetings. Brute costs, packed demanding schedules and lucrative Polish (Sunday racing) pay days ensure that when it comes to SGPs it is always a case that "the show must go on" no matter how dull or workaday that decision to proceed ensures it becomes to participate in or watch. When bringing this circus together for one Saturday night in one-off often remote locations, taking the money, sticking to rigorous schedules and staging what can afterwards be deemed and reported as a World Championship speedway meeting trumps all other considerations – completely regardless of the calibre of "entertainment" it then, thereby, offers. So, in SGP speedway as in life, it pays to travel with optimism aplenty as well as savour and enjoy life to the full in the moment, whatever you are given.

Over the wide Warta river that bisects the river port of Gorzow, there is an almost festival atmosphere nearly five hours before the scheduled start time that's not subdued by the encroaching threat of distant dark skies. Half a mile or so away from the stadium, memorabilia, food and drink stalls line the road and walkway that run parallel to both the river and the residential housing. Inevitably, there is a notable amount of red-and-white Polska themed clothing to go along with the sunshine. Polish speedway fans wear their nationalism and speedway rider adoration proudly. Stalls already do good custom. Smoke wafts from open grills over families, fans and friends enjoying themselves at the temporary tables and benches or relaxing on the grass slopes down to the river Warta. This is another Polish town that knows and lustily celebrates its speedway pedigree. On the edgelands of the market stalls before the walk through the housing estate towards the stadium begins, there is an impressively long line of bright blue coloured temporary toilet booths plus a smattering of hand washing stations (with water!) at either end of this magnificent parade of unisex public conveniences.

In this part of town too, roads and roundabouts are already blocked to traffic to free up greater pedestrian access. Sensible precautions as the stadium is due to be close to its 17,000 capacity barring no-shows or last-minute impulse buyers kept away by forecast bad weather. Local speedway club Stal Gorzow regularly get large crowds here for their Sunday Ekstraliga meetings. Stal Gorzow was founded when Poland was still behind the Iron Curtain. An essential component of robust civic pride required then and still requires now a successful local speedway club, preferably staged in a suitably impressive stadium. This was doubly so in an era when achievements on the track and sports fields were key global signals of superior status in the ideological battle between the rival social and political systems of communism and capitalism. When I first started going to speedway in the mid 1970s, Poland had the rider talent but not the equipment. How times have changed. Arguably, British riders now have the equipment but not the talent. The Edwarda Jancarza stadium is named after one of their most notable riders and, like proud sports clubs the world over, there is a statue of him in town. In contrast to the mien of the statue, in his programme photo BSI Speedway Managing Director Torben Olsen wears the look of an executive irked to still have to publicly dress in company-branded clothing rather than the more stylish outfits that more befit his income and executive status. Even as he celebrates the eighth year of co-operation between the city, club and the SGP at this apparently "iconic venue", strong rumours suggest that Gorzow have already been dropped from the calendar in favour of a different Polish club (Wroclaw) prepared to pay much more for the privilege of doing so. The introduction to visitors from Stal Gorzow Wielkopolski S.A. Chairman Ireneusz Maciej Zmora in the official programme appears to confirm this not-so-idle speculation. "We hope that you leave Gorzow with tremendous memories of this great speedway event and that you will be coming here in future."

The stadium is surrounded by low-rise social housing built in a pleasingly robust but retro architectural style before accountants with computer programs reduced the size of each flat to minimum proportions to save costs. There is a small parade of shops, a couple of bars as well as some licensed souvenir stalls on the stadium perimeter plus an entrepreneurial man unofficially selling memorabilia from his drive. There are also a posse of drug users trying to sell (two different) bargain bags of cheap sweets to feed their habits. The junkies chase hard currency and footfall so lay these out on the ground at various different key passing points in and around the stadium grounds. Many fans wait by the central turnstiles that won't open for at least an hour yet. Any wire fences that allow glimpses of distant pits activity or the riders' van parking area are already fully occupied by keen rubberneckers. From outside the stadium looks reasonably modern and architecturally echoes the Pompidou Centre vernacular as it is all exposed (silver) terrace undersides and stairways. These in turn buttress the exposed support struts that create its pin-cushion-crossed-with-mobile-telephone-masts roof. Once inside, the bowl of the oval track is surrounded by two tiers of blue-and-yellow all-seater terraces. The upper tiers seat greater numbers of fans at a steeper angle than the lower. Executive boxes (or possibly suites) with sealed windows line the length of the home straight. Stal Gorzow is the only speedway club I have ever visited (so far) with 15 yards of raised flowerbeds. With an eye-catching range of flowers in colourful bloom, these line the access route to the pits gate. They also have an extremely independent-minded pits cat. Going in the other direction, Faye Woffinden walks in conversation alongside Tai's manager-cum-mentor Peter Adams who pushes baby Rylee's black buggy. Peter discourages the incongruous photo of a speedway lifetime with a brief but meaningful flash of his trademark thousand-yard stare.

The pits are yet to get too crowded with the flood of fans, sponsors, hangers-on and visitors who have the most severely time limited pits pass accreditation. Like the Cinderellas they apparently are, access ends in a metaphorical puff of smoke exactly 105 minutes before the tapes rise for the first time at precisely 19.04. These pass holders travel separately but tend to arrive together around 4pm for an hour or so in the pits. Collectively delighted to be invited into the inner sanctum, autographs and selfies are pursued with almost religious zeal. The more technical minded bathe in their proximity to the rider pit bays. These are filled with gleaming bikes, crash helmets, toolboxes, television screen and active or idle mechanics. All the gear but not the real talent. There are also various other usually carefully organised box-fresh accoutrements and paraphernalia that further crowd out the limited bay space. It is a work area during the actual meeting so careful almost meticulous organisation is the norm. Though set up for one-night only, everything has its place and knows its place. Lesser pit pass holders skitter about manically to walk or stand anywhere they choose unless deterred by stares or manners. Some linger by but don't go onto the track that is militantly guarded by firm-minded security people. With riders and mechanics drawn from many different (mostly European) countries, everyone has some degree of language difficulty to overcome to communicate fluently. The ongoing fan-unfriendly design stupidity of the standard SGP programme template and colour palette continues. All keenly sought and rapidly scribbled autographs on the individual rider pages provided are immediately hard to decipher from the murk of the primarily black background but also the signature-resistant gloss paper stock. This structural illegibility problem dents very few ardours. That said, most riders make themselves pretty scarce or appear only briefly during this particularly crowded witching hour. They obviously have good reason as they have to mentally, physically or nutritionally prepare for their races ahead. Equally some riders have other commitments elsewhere – glad-handing current and wannabe sponsors or, for the select big name or locally based few, their pre-scheduled commitment to a 30-minute fan meet-and-greet session inside the Monster Energy Fan Zone. The Polish and Russian riders along with Craig Cook and the always patiently available Greg Hancock are the regular exceptions to this tacit try-to-make-yourself-scarce-around-the-pits until about 17.00 unofficial SGP rider rule.

Since mechanics, flunkies, hangers-on and staff vastly outnumber the scarce talent, whenever a rider arrives they are (politely) mobbed. Often, because of their diminutive height and stature, they are quickly lost in the hubbub. Getting from the pits gate to their individual bay is slow progress even if they have minders in tow. Adulation and demand for selfies borders on insatiable. Much more than autographs. Ignoring writing isn't expected to be a rider strongpoint, graphologists would definitely struggle to gain sensible meaning or insight about their character or future from these cursory dashed-off scribbles. Anthropologists would offer much better interpretations. Particularly if they followed Greg Hancock and tried to fathom the complexity of his evocative handshakes. These are delivered with a flourish to strangers, friends and staff alike. Greg defies his colour, ethnicity, current half of the year Swedish residency and Californian background to hand slap and greet as well as fist bump like he's just arrived from the projects or grew up in the Bronx. Maybe, he's a closet freelance hip-hop disc jockey or, perhaps, there is some sort of mandatory handshake and grooming training programme held at Monster HQ to help their sponsored riders cut the right (Monster Joe approved) style while they get down with da kidz? Despite occasional body parts bumping awkwardness brought on by his compact size, Greg isn't averse to lusty man hugs or ferocious cuddles on – unlike Phil Morris - a gender neutral basis. Based on his frequent availability and regular pits meet-and-greet performances, Greg is a credit to speedway riders everywhere. He is definitely the most willing of the current crop of SGP riders to go the extra yard and patiently glad hand the speedway public at length. Greg gives good smile, glad hand and warm greeting. He is also the most interview friendly of all the SGP riders. Available with fluent dramatic sounding insights and bon mots. These rarely sound ready-drafted, scripted or pre-prepared but spontaneous though clearly Greg's experience and intelligence means that there is still a strong element of disguised studious professionalism. Re-listened to in the cold light of day (rather than the heat of the action), Greg actually says little beyond truisms, what he already said elsewhere or relentless product promotion. Mostly this chit-chat is about himself, his thoughts and feelings as well as his various sponsors. All this is interspersed with reference to some of the notionally more glamorous aspects of speedway life and competition so more as speedway likes to think about and evocatively present itself rather than how it really actually is. This is particularly so whenever the talk focuses upon the product served up by and at the SGP. Greg is relentlessly on message and very frequently available. He is the consummate professional in the pits and effortlessly manufactures brief soothing messages for the fans he bumps into that anticipate or further stoke and stroke their feelings as well as match their preconceptions. Greg is definitely the stand-out star at every formal or informal fan/sponsor/hangers-on meet-and-greet session that the SGP Truman Show requires in and around any World Championship event.

After many years organising SGPs in many countries and venues, the show rights holders BSI Speedway have an efficient mousetrap of lengthy detailed contracts and copious written instruction manual specifics on how to manage, stage and supervise the many different aspects of the circus that combine together to make any individual Grand Prix event. Like staging any speedway meeting – albeit on a grander scale since multiple sponsor, media and broadcast interests need to be accommodated and satisfied – this requires slavish adherence and meticulous attention to myriad details in various quarters simultaneously. BSI staff are the Officer Class while the franchisee provides the big cheque along with the grunts and slaves said event execution requires. For ease these are sometimes paid but mostly volunteer local people assume and project a relationship of helpful subservience. Despite having often more knowledge, smarts, expertise and savvy when it comes to actually staging speedway meetings at the location than these temporary bosses issuing the instructions and notionally supervising or checking their work. This is definitely the case at the Stal Gorzow speedway club. Well used to staging very professionally run high-profile meetings while fulfilling time-constrained and pressured routines, procedures and demands aplenty (particularly so as Polish league meetings are frequently televised), the regular stadium and pits staff exude quiet confidence. For example: the man so diligently and carefully washing then drying the shale-dusted section of the pits area where the bikes line up before each race on their respective four (red, blue, white and yellow) helmet colours pre-race markings didn't need to ask permission or consult an instruction manual to learn how, when or why to do so. Doubtless, at some point, his work is checked but doesn't actually require supervisors – let alone ones with lanyards exuding managerial status in their SGP-branded clothing – to do so as it is just one of those things he does whenever they stage a speedway meeting here.

With little to do until the temporary crowd subsides in the pits but before the bikes fire into life, many fans pass time idling amiably. Two of many Craig Cook crowdfunder fan sponsors, Tom Buckle and Adriana Merrit, arrived early in Gorzow to savour the atmosphere as well as make full use of their pit passes. They also enthusiastically seek the missing 2018 vintage SGP rider autographs they need to complete their burgeoning top rider collection. The surprise early arrival of a banana-eating (when will this nutritional madness ever end?) Nicki Pedersen and his high-heel-wearing girlfriend prompts a scrum of well-wishers that Tom negotiates with aplomb to secure yet another missing signature. Nicki soon cuts short the session with an expansive Phil Morris-esque wave of his hand. Tom and Adriana already have the autograph of the SGPs very own reverse Barry White. "We spoke with Bartosz! He's got an even higher voice in real life than on TV! Sometimes people put on a different voice in public." With a small bottle of water tightly squeezed into his black jeans back pocket and his trusty dictation phone in hand, Paul Burbidge power-poses the pits awaiting his race day interview stenography duties rather than bothering to search out the interesting SGP stories he so rarely finds. He is accompanied by someone who appears to be his assistant or, possibly, an intern or work experience person keen to see how content-free interviews are sourced and recorded. Like myself, Burbs is known to sometimes mangle or accidentally incorrectly transcribe [2] (rider) interviews in the process of his subsequent dictation typing. Sadly this means Paul can encounter reluctance to share a few words with his phone. By all accounts, Tai completely refuses to speak with him. There is rarely a Burbs by-line on any published Woffy print interview or, indeed, beyond what everyone heard at the post-SGP press conference few original post-meeting Woffy quotes in Paul's SGP meeting reports either. You would think being on no-speaks with the current World Champion (and best British rider of his generation in the SGP) might be something of a handicap to doing both or either of Burbo's overlapping "news" jobs for both the *Speedway Star* and the SGP website. Paul ploughs on regardless, churning out guff and fluff like seeds off a field of sun-ripened dandelions on a windy day. Not without cunning, Paul nervously lurks by the reserve and wild card rider pits bays as they are often easy or needy prey. He records an interview with Craig Cook that

---

[2] I sympathise. My own contemporaneous handwritten notes can struggle to be read or understood afterwards, plus the nature of the beast is that errors and misunderstandings do inevitably occur much as you try to guard against them. I apologise in advance for any/all such misapprehensions and mistakes.

discusses the meeting ahead and his intentions for the rival SEC series next year that when it appears in print is something much more pointed about Craig apparently not wanting a wild card for the 2019 SGP series. Such statements would be madness and strongly against Craig's own interests but – if reported – conveniently help build the exculpatory backstory for BSI's almost inevitable commercial decision not to deign to offer Cook that option. Whether Paul wears his *Speedway Star* news writer or his BSI SGP website and social media news hat when writing up this article is, sadly for the sport, a distinction he regularly blurs in his journalism. This is no surprise since Burbo's work often reads as if written – whether consciously or unconsciously – as if to satisfy or advantage the perceived commercial interests of the SGP rights holders BSI. While Burbo works his journalistic magic, nearby Phil Morris rushes hither and thither. Morris briefly enters, surveys then quickly exits various designated – according to the pinned-up photocopied laminated A4 notices outside - "FIM" activity areas. Or else he barks out orders here and there about the pits. He also briefly stops to chat with and glad hand the two middle-aged women in union flag dresses who often appear at this hour in the SGP pits to take selfies with him. Tall pale red-haired opinionated-opinion-maker-in-waiting and Ben Stokes look-a-like (albeit the post-Bristol fight police mug-shot version) Josh Gudgeon watches Rylee Woffinden warily as her mum Faye chats with another bloke. Officially Josh is here to service Greg's every travel need and informally to emote on his behalf whenever he manages to photo-bomb the live television cameras during the meeting. Or, possibly, build upon or make further sponsorship contacts to explore later in his latest new role as the freshly minted commercial director of the recently privatised national speedway team. While he psyches himself up to deliver further joy for Greg, Josh grins and gurns uneasily alongside baby Rylee as if she were some kind of a grey-and-yellow clothed explosive device.

In the far corner furthest from the track, with Craig Cook's bikes already successfully checked by the onsite FIM Technical Control and the meeting tyres issued and fitted, his friendly but taciturn dad Will stands to survey the length of the crowded pits area. I enquire about the SGP series so far. "We're going to these places for the first time and only get four minutes [at practice] to find the set up. It's not a question of track craft but set up. At Malilla, we had the bike just right and then it rained and was slick. We used the second bike in the last race and that was the one we should have used." Will waves his arm expansively, "All the guys here ride all these tracks all the time, some of them didn't even bother to practice yesterday. They are regulars. In the UK, we know all the tracks and what our set ups should be. Here we don't but they do. The differences at this level are fractional. Every year Craig gets better. There is the odd poor meeting but every year he has improved. I think he has had 28 track records? Anything on two wheels, he's good with! Anything. He has the track craft and skill. We started at 21, imagine if we'd started at 16? Everywhere we go, we're finding out what others already know. On the temporary tracks we go well because it is the same for everyone. Other times we gate and then find we have the wrong set up."

In order to try to defray the cost of competing in the SGP series, Craig Cook's backroom team sensibly got financial backing from various commercial or local businesses but also – rather innovatively - from a large number of individual fans. It is unusual for so many to crowdfund a rider but also a sign how his SGP participation generally caught the imagination of British speedway fans. Craig's fan engagement via Twitter and Instagram is notably good. Exploring every route to gain word of mouth, fan interest and buzz as well as putting on a show is the modern digitally enabled way forward for riders and clubs alike. "The Facenna brothers [in Glasgow] know what it is all about – getting the crowd engaged. For Craig's debut, they had a Cookie Monster and all sorts. It got a big crowd and a big crowd talking." Just like his dad, Craig is a proud Cumbrian and advocate for the charms and beauty of the area. "Two or three hundred people went to Cardiff from the villages around us." A group of Craig's close friends dressed as the guys from the 111 adverts. "They're a great bunch of lads. They swear a bit but are great. Only last night, we were looking at the photos from when he was at Buxton and he used to change his hair colour every week for the fans." The issue of the wild card isn't something Will feels comfortable to discuss with the decision-makers or those in potential authority who might influence the decision. "I'm good with the bikes and everything but not talking. I'd say we only just missed out by a fraction in Landshut [SGP 2019 qualifier], it was Craig's first time there. If you look at both years, Craig has been the best British rider. It would be good to qualify top eight for next year but we're running out of GPs. We're learning all the time so it would be good to be back. We know so much and have spent the time and the money finding out. Britain needs more than one rider in the GPs. At the last GP of last season, Nicki Pedersen was there talking to everyone all the night to help get his wild card. He doesn't usually do that."

The pits get cleared of most lower level pass holders with prompt efficiency but without the officiousness sometimes shown elsewhere. Thrown back like unwanted fish, close by the stadium turnstiles are already open. Though it's a good sized stadium, like life itself, there is only one main entrance area but many exits. My souvenir programme yet again confirms how the rights holders BSI only like to price gouge notionally "richer" speedway populations. Consequently, the official programme is again a bargain in Poland. They are in plentiful supply too from a single-storied building with a line of eight greyhound stadium style on-course betting window booths adjacent to the entrance turnstiles. The sky is jet black and it spits onto rain so the joy of reading Torben Olsen's trademark stilted cut-and-paste welcome message to fans will have to wait until later. The local consensus – and back at home in the UK too – is the meeting will definitely go ahead provided that it rains torrentially as forecast rather than continuously. Luckily the rain behaves as forecast with the lengthy kind of apocalyptic downpour befitting the deep black clouds. It is so heavy that drains flood, big puddles quickly appear across the stadium grounds and Noah readies his ark. Torrents of water quickly drive outside beer drinkers back inside their bars, while speedway souvenir vendor Pawel Ruszkiewicz closes his convenient-to-the-entrance stall nearly 90 minutes before the race action starts. Like his staff and stock, he gets completely soaked in the process of reloading his white transit. Pawel used to have the official merchandise concession exclusive at SGP meetings but, though he no longer has, just can't stay away. Many fans decide to run the gauntlet of thorough security and barcode automated turnstiles for the shelter of the stadium concourses. This doesn't seem strategic as they have to negotiate exposed wet and windy open spaces as well as a giant puddle by the stadium steps deep enough to hide monsters or float a boat (should it evade the bag check). The rain is so ferocious it bounces up from the ground. Too many fans seek shelter under the meagre spaces between the metal entrance stanchions, while a tide of groundwater ruins and then sweeps away the junkies' street sweet display towards the flooded drains. They rescue them for an optimistic brief dry before spreading them back out under the turnstile roof next to the huddle of damp fans. The weather in combination with the look of the sweets or their vendors gains no sales, I see.

The rain stops as suddenly as it started and the sky clears. A measure of early evening warmth returns too so the collective mood lightens. Bustle resumes as substantial crowds quickly appear from wherever they sheltered. There is frenetic purpose and laughter. Air horns sound. Drinkers spill from bars to drink outside again. Supermarkets in the nearby parade of shops gain long queues. Visitors leave the nearby church to congregate outside. After the security check, the turnstiles cope easily with the crowd volume before navigating a large puddle causes a bottleneck by the stadium access stairs. Two women in tight predominantly blue start line clothing stand on its edge to advertise a product whose name I don't catch. They pose for endless photos. Rather distastefully various blokes use their professional distraction to reveal their personal crises of masculinity to cop a feel of the front and back bottoms of these perma-smiling women. They laugh with their mates at the wit of their power to humiliate. Though they occasionally reprove these "advances" with stares or exclamations, these women are sitting ducks for such unwanted attention stood by the puddle. Maybe, this drive-by-sexism goes with the territory in this kind of anonymous crowd environment if you do such promotional work. But shouldn't. Glamour girls weren't until recently – when Monster Energy arrived on the SGP scene – such a standard part of the speedway community eco-system or, if rarely so, were kept remote from the public areas for staged centregreen promo shots. It goes without saying that these blokes are hardly prime specimens. They have looks from the bulldog-licking-urine-from-a-nettle end of the scale with bodies to match that aren't strangers to the fridge or bar. It is behaviour that doesn't fit my understanding of speedway values. At ordinary speedway club meetings, the community would soon step in to police the situation. SGP attendees are invariably not local so – sometimes – behave much more lairily if believing they're lost in the anonymity of the crowd. How women get commoditised, treated and coerced by the male gaze is, of course, a wider societal issue. Especially now in our #MeToo era. This recidivist behaviour is tacitly encouraged and endorsed by the SGP rights holders, not least by the objectification of women their key sponsor/partner Monster Energy regularly provide, promulgate and foreground in their start staff. Arguably, setting aside the possible future "innovation" of transponder use at practice, this travelling troupe of promotional women are arguably the most tangible new "benefit" consistently delivered by the BSI era of speedway grands prix over the past 23 years.

What makes this drive-by Neanderthal sexism all the stranger is that speedway in Poland – and here yet again tonight – attracts men and women in roughly equal proportions. There are many families (new, extended and multi-generational) as well as the young and the old, albeit with noticeably many more older people than Warsaw. The dress style is primarily informal. There is an impressive variety of replica shirts or branded clothing and message T-shirts, though there are pockets of surprisingly dressy people too. Though a long way from the majority dress code, there are more suit and evening/cocktail dress wearing fans than I have ever seen at any speedway meeting anywhere else previously. Ditto high heels and – rocking their inner (late) Bob Dugard on his tractor – dressier shoes. It is either an evening out to celebrate with more formal wear or else the perfect start to a longer night out ahead. Carnivalesque is putting it too strongly but upbeat and anticipatory – as if we are all going a party later – sums up the pre-meeting mood and atmosphere of the restless crowd that throngs the stadium concourses and stairwells in Gorzow. Given the rain and likely falling temperatures later, there are also many anoraks and fleeces too. Even the concourse food and drinks choices are varied, if not extensive. Popcorn, hotdogs, difficult-to-describe meat dishes and, since by traditional British summer standards it is still warm and almost balmy, delicious bargain ice creams at only six zlotys for a double scoop. I love a speedway meeting with ice cream even if, sadly, culturally there is no option of a 99 flake. The design of this stadium encourages everyone to muster or walk the central concourse. It feels Mediterranean. And writhes like an especially active ants' nest. The architectural construction style of exposed stanchions and stairways gives the building a work-in-progress Meccano feel, albeit one that everyone wants to promenade around in order to soak up the views and enjoy the really buzzy atmosphere.

As late this spring, I was surprised but delighted to find I could still purchase a third row seat on bend 1. It is a fabulous place to watch FIM race director Phil Morris continue his campaign to win the inaugural "Incomprehensible Distance Track Directions Award" with another virtuoso series of his innovative instructional waves, claps and gestures towards studiously bored track staff. They muster disconsolately as far away from Phil as they can get. Diagonally opposite him on bend three. This is either avoidance or else better to appreciate Phil's re-enactment of how he earlier quickly punctured the water bed back at his hotel with a series of nifty but dramatic stabs of the carving knife. Despite my proximity to another *ad hoc* show of masterly power from Phil, my choice of seat betrays lack of local knowledge. Inside the Edwarda Jancarza stadium, the first eight or so rows of lower tier seats enjoy a much lower slung elevation compared to the steeply rising angles of their upper tier counterparts. With the obligatory SGP airfence already in position, my view towards both the start line and the intimate nuances of the first bend action are, sadly, either occluded or badly obscured. This is a disappointing situation even before the meeting start brings a gaggle of joyous drunken first and second row revellers, dancers and assorted passionate Zmarzlik fans (who stand to plaintively scream their imaginative "Bartosz!" rallying cry) to work their viewing pleasure magic. The roof position also ensures that initial rows of seats are still close to swimming after the earlier torrential rain. Most fans use the A4 sheets provided by the organisers - in the red pantone of the Polish national colours provided in lieu of the traditional SGP cheap plastic flag – to dry or cover them. The shale sludge that coats the track after the earlier downpour looks less easily sorted. Curatorial staff attack sloppy conditions with a zeal and expertise that soon sees the track show significant improvement. Text messages from England – rather than stadium announcements – reveal that the start is (initially) delayed by 15 minutes. Tractors circle towing various different curatorial devices to blade and grade the surface. Many blokes with rakes work energetically. Predictably, though the local track team project strong skills and experience, Phil Morris thinks he is supervising a prison chain gang so goes through his mandatory pantomime of shuttle runs, shouts, inexplicable gestures, angry waves, kicks of random shale piles and authoritative instructions shouted into hand-covered managerial ears. At one point, he even mimes what looks like how to inflate a paddling pool while serving a tray of award-winning exotic cocktails.

Judged by the depth of gloop, the expected rain meant that the track had sensibly been pre-dressed with minimal shale. To be fair, no shale is the *de facto* setting for any and every Speedway Grand Prix. Under the supervision of FIM Race Director Phil Morris, BSI get what they want each time. Namely a smooth surface that minimises disruption to their television spectacle from crashes. Success for BSI, the FIM and Morris is delivering a crash-free meeting that sticks exactly to the television satellite schedule timings – the SGP is, after all, staged purely for the screen spectacle rather than the live fan experience – where the sponsor/ partner logos of the air fence adverts remain unshowered with shale and visible throughout. Speedway fans at the track want to see competitive racing with lots of overtaking so are quite happy to put up with the odd 10-minute delay here or there brought on by race incidents and crashes, Instead, what they get are staccato sets of four heats and the longueurs of seven sets of lengthy track grades supervised by the wildly flailing arms of the attention-seeking Morris. In his role as race director, Phil is always going to be very happy with 23 processional races that adhere to the timings. Playing to the cameras or bossing about the local curation staff who already know full well how to prepare their own race track just adds to his joy in the job. Anyways, what minimal shale there was prior to the downpour is soon scraped off and away to reveal the harder surface of its base. The curatorial work at hand appears to be to re-lay the track with a dusting of fresh dry shale in the manner of frosting sugar on a sponge cake rather than the icing on a Christmas cake. Once the hardcore base has just enough of a thin film of shale, it will provide just about sufficient grip and acceleration from the bikes on this wet grey cement look track. The drop of new shale is quickly distributed then smoothed attentively. Though things quickly come back together, 15 minutes after the scheduled tapes up, the riders are finally allowed come out like a troupe of kevlared Bambis about to take their tentative first-ever steps. After their belly-aching and frequent track walks in Malilla, the SGP inspection rules have been altered to only permit the riders out on supervisory manoeuvres AFTER the track work is complete rather than before or during as previously. This is sensible as, after all, given there will be a welter of slightly differing opinions and required actions. In speedway as in business life, a camel is invariably a racehorse designed by committee. Resigned to their task, the riders either gaze wistfully at distant but diminishing curatorial activity or treat us to their usual gardening repertoire of digging, kicking and anxious hands on hips that usually goes along with philosophical contemplation of life and all things shale-related. Despite the skill and efficiency of these track ministrations, some riders remain extremely wary. Especially the experienced ones. Greg Hancock gives such time and attention to his inspection of the track that you half suspect he's going to apply to become a member of the track staff when his career (finally) ends or else he has been seconded by the local police to investigate a trackside murder crime scene as thoroughly but clandestinely as possible. Nicki Pedersen takes a track walk with a screwdriver in hand. It is a rare sight to see Nicki without his hand-held industrial fan. This screwdriver is either to establish the shale depth or in case he has a chance encounter with Tai's spanner-wielding mechanic.

Further confirmation of how central and significant the clever broadcast camera work is to a SGP presentational aesthetic and anaesthetic that regularly delivers processional racing as "exciting" footage, one of the stadium big screens broadcasts live rider track walk footage. It makes brilliant use of camera angles and close-ups to genuinely make these various rider inspections verge on the breathtakingly thrilling. Whereas watched from our seats it looks dull and unremarkable. This ability to frame then so quickly package something so action-free, banal and dully lame as a stroll on damp shale by blokes in bright coloured kevlars into something daring, evocative and grandiloquent via an exciting created-on-the-hoof live visual narrative that thrills like Noah strolling with pairs of animals through the parted Red Sea is truly special talent. This packaging professionalism and the ability to do all this fluffing up in the moment with an instant edit is the spray-on not-so-secret weapon that enables rights holders BSI – who, after all, are a really a TV rights company staging "sports" events - to continue to sell the notional spectacle of their packaged TV rights (and commercial breaks) to broadcasters and advertisers alike, despite and whatever the track conditions, available competing riders or race action delivers. If you have this spray-on whizzy moving action pictures capability on hand in your black box, ultimately there is no need to go to the expensive trouble of sourcing and fitting out the very best tracks and/or locations to stage these SGP events. Instead, as they do, BSI can themselves put on a couple of revenue-maximising big stadium meetings raced on temporary tracks and otherwise mostly control costs by licensing the promotional right to stage the other meetings in the series to third parties – and supportive local councils – willing to overpay for the honour. As usual, leaving every thoughtful comment stone unturned, man of many speedway hats Nigel Pearson inside this SGP patronage system tells world feed viewers, "It really is a pleasure to be here tonight. As it is at any Grand Prix."

It is an immutable law of the SGP that, if it starts late, then the rush and need not to exceed the satellite time booked dictates that the races of the meeting then get staged with even more excessive hurry than they already do usually. It is as if BSI, riders, media and the organisers have to flee the scene of a crime and collectively take us all along with them, irrespective of how this interferes with the tempo and enjoyment of the spectacle for those of us who have actually paid to attend. Gorzow is no exception to this common "get-it-over-

and-get-it-over-now" mindset. Riders are prematurely ejaculated onto and off the track. As one set of riders depart one heat they cross four others at the pits gate and accessway going out for the next. As ever, SGP races are staged in groups of four. Delays for crashes or false starts aside, the only real respite from the hurried tempo is for lengthy commercial breaks which ,of course, remain sacrosanct but completely dead air for fans inside the stadium. The first race reveals that, despite the torrential rain, the track still looks and seems rideable. This is impressive given the volume of water unleashed from the heavens. The initial set of races fly by unmemorably, except for the vibrant atmosphere and enthused buzz of the crowd. It is particularly loud and celebratory whenever any one of the five Polish riders racing this evening take to the shale. Especially so if a race features Bartosz Zmarzlik as he is currently the club star rider. Martin Vaculik is also a local favourite as he also rides for Stal Gorzow. Heat 4 sees Fredrik Lindgren lose control of his bike and steel shoe on the fourth bend as well as take-off Bartosz Zmarzlik from behind. It is virtuoso speedway violence. Rightly excluded, Freddie feels the full opprobrium of the crowd. After the initial optimism of the first two meetings of the 2018 SGP season, Lindgren's series ambitions have suffered serious attrition. Filmed back in his pits bay with a blown up image of Lindgren with his hair up in a ponytail man-bob as background contrast, on the stadium big screen Freddie looks suitably pissed off and gloomy. Zmarzlik wins the re-run easily which is slightly harsh on Nicki who led the race comfortably first time out.

The interval sees first-among-equals SGP partner sponsor Monster Energy given first dibs to showcase another of their logo-splattered fast edit promotional trailers on the big screen. As ever, it features lots of obscure motorsports, fireworks and smiling competitors. It is possibly the same one they have previously shown at all the other SGPs too but we can't tell for sure as they seem designed to go by in an exciting but eminently forgettable blur. That said, yet again (and, obviously, knowing the enthusiasms of their target audiences better than I do), this Monster commercial again has much more cleavage dwell time than it does actual speedway shots or action. The crowd don't need any third party external help to buy more drinks or really enjoy themselves. They queue on the concourse, make their own distractions or join the seemingly endless Mexican wave. Even the big cheese killjoys large slab of home straight executive boxes fails to impede its rapid progress. The stadium speakers blare rock, trashy electro-pop, naff package holiday hits you'd half-forgotten or Western classics. Queen are just as likely to proclaim their champion status as we are to have a post-sunset chorus of the Birdie song. There is even a dance cam that fans of all ages embrace wholeheartedly irrespective of their fluency, capability, alcohol consumption or size. Never afraid to let some predictable hyperbole badly interfere with the facts, on the telly Nigel Pearson does everyone a disservice when he claims the passion and atmosphere is like The Kop. For sure both are passionate, notable and unique in their own way but hardly comparable in terms of scale, numbers, gender mix, team songs or dancing. But, especially the scarves and singing as both are completely absent here. To the extent both are, of course, crowds at a sports event – it is yet another mastery and evocative comparison from The Voice of Speedway.

Before heat five gets underway, proving again to nostalgic communists in the crowd that capitalism gives us too many choices and makes citizens consume too much, Tai takes to the track with three mechanics and two bright shiny bikes. More isn't necessary better. Tai finishes third after initial struggles to evade strong pressure from Craig Cook on laps two and three. The Jason Doyle of last year appears to be slowly awaking from his hibernation slumber to ride with a greater measure of consistency. So much so he fires from the gate with fast front wheel proudly aloft to lead for nearly a lap until Artem Laguta sails past. Nicki also gates quickly in his next race but Zagar passes him with ease before they have even reached the third bend. Though on a visibly slow bike, Nicki grinds onwards and manfully holds onto his second place rather than theatrically succumb to another bout of his increasingly common phantom engine problems. Though frequently endorsed as "the last true gentleman of the shale", Greg Hancock is only selectively and strategically a sportsman so continues wild card Simon Wozniak's speedway education at the SGP level with a lap of harrying and bullying as well as some free introductions to thrusts of his back wheel. Though Wozniak won his first race to the warm adulation of the crowd, this time out the young Pole soon gets the message and cedes position to the American SGP elder statesman.

Even with a restricted to non-existent view of the first bend action blocked by the airfence or first row standers, the seating discipline around me is awful. And, when I stand to see, the complaints from behind are strong. The front rows only sit down during the interval breaks – dance cam and obligatory Mexican wave permitting. People watching is fun but also instructive as a snapshot of the possible future for speedway in Poland. Sat next to me are three women – mother, daughter and granddaughter. They are without male company and all watch intensely until it gets way past bedtime for the tired youngster. Directly in front of me is a young family and there are also many others to my immediate left and right. So many families are dotted about the stadium that there is no need to designate any one section as the Family Area. Many couples are here too with a trip to the speedway apparently as much a part of the dating scene here as is a quiet meal out together. Though British speedway has romance and also attracts three or four generations of some families out to watch together, as a visitor Polish speedway looks and feels like part of an ongoing living culture rather than an increasingly eclipsed one. That said, obviously I am curmudgeonly enough not to be a fan of free standers in the seats at almost any sports event, family or otherwise. The steep rake of the upper tiers give unrivalled views to all as well as a sense of vertigo that restricts joyous leaping about until, like the silent signal salmon get to exultantly spawn upstream, the races come around the final bend. Apart from the chance to sit down, the lengthy intervals pass psychologically quicker without having to watch tractors endlessly circle doing their track grades. For whatever reason, professionalism, prevailing conditions or the earlier rain sight of said tractors is minimal. So too is sight of Phil Morris relentlessly semaphoring his importance and exulted status to the crowd.

A dusty Heat 9 initially suggests that even Chris Holder has roused himself sufficiently from his ongoing seasons of visa and child access induced torment to actually want to race. Sadly, this rarity is only a temporary illusion as Holder quickly tires and succumbs to his third successive last place. Most in the crowd only have eyes for Zmarzlik. Defying the form book, he is a surprise third behind Janowski and Woffinden. Amongst billowing clouds of shale that could double as a desert storm, the next race sees Craig Cook pressure Nicki throughout in their mini-battle for the consolation of third. It is a literal and psychological battle for supremacy that ends for both without sense of triumph or real satisfaction, while wild card Wozniak again rides impressively for his second win to make it six points from three rides. Greg gates and goes in heat 11 only to see both Vaculik and Sayfutdinov pass easily but dustily before he has even made the third bend. Hancock then rides the white line to both remain out of harm's way and keep the often wild-riding Lindgren safely behind him.

During the third interval, before he heads off to get more drinks, the bloke half of the couple sat directly in front whose young son stands tall on the back of his seat to see and cheer better checks on the time left and "how many races to go?" If this were a search for aliens living secretly among us, then that question immediately marks him out as not from Planet Speedway. Without re-starts, officially there are 11 heats left. As we are just over half way through the meeting plenty of drinking time remains. It turns out he is a lawyer, while his wife Monika is related to Bartosz Zmarzlik. "He is family." Everyone here takes considerable voluble pride in Zmarzlik. In this packed crowd of Bartosz worshippers, actually being related does stand out in one upmanship terms but also must really add piquancy to seeing him in the SGP tonight. Monika is "cousin to Bartosz's mum. We usually go to the pits but today we didn't as it is too important and we didn't want to distract him." Out of sheer helpfulness, I pass on five times World Champion Ove Fundin's assessment that Bartosz's flailing leg might handicap his World Championship ambitions. Obviously, said observation reveals Ove as old school. When translated to Monika it fails to strike a chord, "I haven't seen that? It must be how he likes to ride."

On resumption Matej Zagar wins heat 13. Behind him Tai bests Freddie for second. Back in Prague, Lindgren definitely irked Woffinden but times have changed since then so Tai's default setting of over-confidence has reasserted itself. So much so that he easily evades Lindgren's predictable over-aggression shown here. The comfort with which Woffinden eludes Lindgren's signature on-track violence illustrates in miniature the gulf that currently exists between them. Like a speedway equivalent of a wash-and-go shampoo, Greg again gates and goes to win heat 14. Zmarzlik wins the next imperiously from reigning World Champion Doyle to noisy adulation from the Gorzow faithful. After the riders immediately disappear back into the pits, I nudge the husband of Bartosz's mum's cousin to ask if he clocked sight of the rogue leg or the repeated lifts of Bartosz's foot from his footrest. "Sorry, I was too busy watching him winning!"

The most dramatic flashpoint of this often processional meeting ignites from innocuous circumstances after Maciej Janowski makes an elementary but common speedway racing "error" on the third bend so locks up and, as a result, briefly slows. This hesitation allows Nicki to ride him towards the fence until Janowski manages to relocate his mojo to bump his way back past. It is a standard vanilla speedway tussle for position and supremacy. For reasons unknown, Janowski takes sufficient umbrage to make the time out to twist around to give Nicki the finger during the race. Something Nigel Pearson describes to any poor-sighted viewers watching as "an interesting gesture, a very interesting gesture". Though the crowd apparently love this devilish flash of anger, to neutrals it looks embarrassingly childish that Janowski needs to create a scene about such a nothing pass/incident, let alone double-down on it by blaming Nicki for what is really his own momentary unforced error. Nicki doesn't appreciate the discourtesy if judged by how afterwards he briefly tries to grab hold of the saddle and rear mudguard area of Magic's bike as they both head down the slope back towards their respective pit bays. This grab without smash is quickly repelled by a strong push-cum-wrestling-grapple from an easily angered but territorial mystery member of Magic's pits team. If Nicki and Tai's encounter in Malilla was box office then, in comparison, this is just plain silly. Quite why Tai's bouncer-look mechanic is also there – yet again – lurking on the edge of the thick of the action when his rider isn't involved or even racing in the heat raises questions both about his temperament and judgement as well as his ongoing lack of supervision by Tai's SGP team manager Peter Adams. Maciej's unnecessary petulance sparks the confrontation, yet he escapes scot-free at the time though – when the mystery violent assailant is subsequently revealed as his dad - he is then fined 2,000 euros because – under SGP/FIM rules - he is held responsible for the actions of his pit crew. This seems harsh and inconsistent when Tai's mechanics got a fine of absolutely nothing for much worse behaviour from his pits crew in Malilla. To add insult to Nicki's non-injury, he is later fined 300 euros for "verbal, ungentlemanly behaviour" towards Phil Morris before the meeting. Ironic when you consider Morris' own visual and verbal hair-trigger impatience directed towards random curatorial staff during the many track-grading breaks. It defies understanding why such crew fines aren't consistently levied. This inconsistency effectively legitimises and possibly encourages further physical confrontation by non-riding parties. Points deductions from the riders for any/all undisciplined actions, aggressive intentions and threatening language from their pit crew or staff would soon put a stop such happenings. Of course, these barneys this season are almost all that has sufficiently roused fans from their SGP racing induced torpor sufficiently long enough to make these incidents vaguely memorable. It is a sad state of affairs when fits of anger and annoyance – mostly off the track – are the only incidents (rather than thrilling overtakes and handlebar-to-handlebar races we were promised and gets reported) that stick in the mind about the speedway "product" on show. Though filial pride and passion are often seen as virtues, it once again suggests that dads-and-lads working relationships in speedway pits are rarely the ideal combination for guaranteed success. While people might suggest that Peter Adams shouldn't publicly turn blind eyes towards staff hot-headedness, his ongoing successful mentoring of Tai to World Championship glories is based upon a close relationship of mutual respect and hard-won experience rather than any blood ties.

Almost as soon the first bars of YMCA sound out over the stadium sound system, the crowd forget this minor contretemps in favour of a quick boogie. Such is the collective *joie de vivre* that the dance cam is really only a convenient further reason to strut your stuff. Amazingly, the bowsers come out to water the remarkably dusty track. Apparently unaware it is after the lights-out curfew in most closed institutions, Kelvin Tatum explains the track characteristics to any remaining clueless watchers, "It shows how well this track drains". On an educational roll, Tatum quickly follows up with some weather insights, "It's not a particularly warm night, most people are wearing a jacket or a jumper." The circling bowsers rather than cool air restricts Phil Morris to a brief cameo appearance. The height and position of the air fence Morris peers plaintively over watching the bowsers dowse the track makes him look like Punch in search of his missing Judy. Out in the first race after said dousing, unusually Greg relishes the damp under tread conditions to win heat 17 in style with some aggression. Behind him Doyle bosses Pedersen for a lap in their mini-battle for the consolation of third. Once passed, Nicki immediately conducts his traditional mid-race thorough mechanical review and, by the last lap, manages to discover the "engine problems" that must surely solely account for yet another slow sub-par performance. Leg all over the show but not akimbo, an incredibly fast-looking Bartosz wins heat 18 by the proverbial country mile to the wild joy of the Stal Gorzow home crowd. Bathing in the glow of this latest victory, his lawyer relative goes out of his way to reassure me about doubts I haven't raised, "He is not a crazy guy! He is a common person. He is polite. He has good parents. The sport is wild but he is quiet and has good values." A dramatic low impact spill stops heat 19 when Emil loses control and clatters Maciej Janowski. Despite this forced departure from his bike, both Magic and his dad react without anger or hand gestures. Instead, Janowski calmly dusts himself down while his dad pushes the bike back rather than choose to play his version of bumper-cars with Sayfutdinov. The re-run sees some intense Pole-on-Pole action when Dudek roughs up wild card Wozniak. The crowd is so conflicted, they mostly don't cheer. Craig Cook wins heat 20 without too much celebration though second-placed Piotr Pawlicki makes up for it with an enthusiastic and well-received lap of honour. The tight broadcast schedules of the SGP have almost made the once standard speedway practice of on-track fan-rider interaction and mutual congratulation of fabled "The Lap of Honour" – let alone wheelies – distant relics of the past. Worse still, nowadays fan-on-rider encounters are minimised, eliminated or stage managed rather than being the accidental *ad hoc* but almost guaranteed affairs of yesteryear when no bar, car park or service station within the vicinity of any track was safe from such chance encounters.

Something has been seriously lost somewhere along the line. The theatre the SGP serves up to speedway fans is pre-programmed, timed and choreographed. Consequently, so are these pre-arranged fan-rider engagement tableaux primarily almost solely staged for benefit of the cameras. Apparently only adventitiously done as a professional courtesy on what looks and feels like an obligatory basis – whether we want it or not – for those sat watching at home rather than for those in actual attendance. For sure the few wheelies and waves on laps of honour after (significant or otherwise) race wins were themselves always only ever performances too but were felt as a "spontaneous" part of the shared speedway community vernacular. While WWF style laser lighting, fireworks or on-stage theatrical introductions add to the bombast and notional (television) "spectacle", they are ersatz generic bolt-ons bulk imported from other more showier-minded but other less sporting motorised endeavours. They come across as superfluous and without real tradition, request or meaning rather than being organic extensions of the overall speedway meeting experience. Call me old-fashioned but patiently queueing for nearly an hour in the FanZone for some random rider to scrawl his name on some Monster Energy marketing collateral specifically brought along for that purpose – or, indeed, loud bombastic cookie cutter motorsports meeting style presentations – really don't give out the same buzz. It might or might not – it doesn't for many – add anything to equation beyond an element of unnecessary theatre imported wholesale from mid-1970s to early-1980s era American sports events. But, like the SGP series itself, this throwaway surface presentational glitz comes at the high price of the loss of the easy rider–fan intimacy that used to exist but has now gone missing in amongst all the stage-managed razzamatazz and notional greater professionalism. Without the vital ingredient of close but accidental shared interactions and experiences, "top" speedway riders have increasingly become a – frequent flier – class apart. Riders generally but especially SGP ones are increasingly badly detached from communities they came from and used to rub along with perfectly amiably. Speedway is all the poorer for it, never mind that it signals and symbolises real problems ahead for its future. The speedway patient won't recover in the intensive care unit, let alone return to rude health, if some of its vital organs die off or go permanently missing.

The party atmosphere the Polish crowd spontaneously supply from the joy of just being alive and at the speedway ramps up further with a Polish one-two in the first semi-final in the form of another fast easy win for Zmarzlik and second place for Dudek. In the other semi-final, after another slow start, Woffinden evades traffic then roughs up Hancock to secure the second place he needs to qualify for the final behind race winner Laguta. After a short delay for the alleged drama of picking gate positions, in the most common cliché example of speedway music directly correlating to speedway life, the sound system blasts out "The Final Countdown". This turns out to be wild optimism. First time out Dudek makes a perfect start but referee Krister Gardell mistakenly stops the race for imaginary movement at the tapes. The big screen replays confirm his error and the patriotic but knowledgeable crowd take this mistake badly. All SGP re-runs see extensive further faff and delay as mechanics crowd round their riders and bikes to top up miniscule fuel tanks with methanol but also make various micro-adjustments. We are lucky that the rider nutritionists, psychologists and performance coaches currently aren't allowed out onto the track to offer motivational or dietary words of advice, otherwise we wouldn't be properly able to see Phil Morris plus the delays would be truly endless. If there has been an actual fall or coming together then OCD levels of cleaning and virtuoso on-the-spot repairs get underway. Sometimes a new bike is required and often there are enough people out on track to build one from scratch.

While all this goes on, "The Final Countdown" plays on an endless loop either to serenade or drive us mad. Robbed at the first time of asking, blue helmeted Patryk Dudek again blasts away from the start but makes sure to immediately cut across local favourite Bartosz Zmarzlik. Dudek's attempt to temper the speed and impede the progress of his rival for glory and crowd affection goes awry. With his front wheel aloft and tactically veered left, Dudek is unable to keep control when Zmarzlik resists his sudden but deliberate imposition. Patryk flies into the air fence with such power and speed that he punctures it. To my mind, Dudek tried and failed to clamp down on Zmarzlik then lost control (if he even had it) so is the cause of the stoppage and should be excluded. Conscious of the rules, the context and the passionate crowd, referee Gardell instead opts for the more politic two wrongs make a right route with an "all four back" decision. Bartosz's cousin-in-law is relieved, "I'm a lawyer and I used to be a judge so I like to be straight. Bartosz used his elbow so was lucky there." Though Dudek signals the air fence puncture to track staff within 20 seconds of his crash, it takes over ten minutes of frenetic activity to actually repair it. Phil Morris stand and watches the repairs with the intensity of a Welsh bird of prey. This puncture repair delay definitely scrubs off the fervour of the crowd. Rumours sweep the crowd that Dudek has broken his shoulder – and even make it into English to me – but will continue to ride. At the third attempt to run the final, depending on your degree of fanaticism or admiration for him, Dudek either legitimately anticipates the tapes or else illegally moves. Arguably his easiest and most accurate decision of a seemingly endless heat, the referee decides to warn Dudek about his future behaviour. At the fourth time of asking, Patryk is so studiously still at the tapes, you could mistake him for a statue. After three fast gates and under the pressure of a warning, Dudek's fast reactions completely desert him. Artem Laguta wins with speed and some style. Enjoyment of the spectacle and also speedway itself conquers local patriotism, if judged by how the crowd rejoice with vim, colour and excessive noise in the Russian's triumph.

That Zmarzlik has again got to the final showing superlative form throughout the meeting but then not risen to the occasion is lost in the hubbub. This choking is a worrying handicap to his World Championship ambitions and credentials. If fans notice that Zmarzlik's confidence deserts him for these all-important decisive pressure heats, then it is certain that his rivals do too. Three bad starts from the best gate in the final is less than ideal for Bartosz. Back on the Travel Plus Tours bus, we get stuck in the car park for an hour due to a bad accident only yards away at the road junction outside the stadium that requires multiple blue-lighted vehicles. Tour organiser David Goodchild takes to the microphone, "Twenty minutes to run the final when he should have let it go the first time!" During the journey back to Poznan, our coach catches up with Freddie Lindgren's van in the lane next to us at the tolls. Hand injury restricted Freddie to two points from five rides but not from getting away from the stadium quickly, "It's the fastest he's gone all night!" There is clearly speed left in the old dog yet, albeit in this instance in the wrong vehicle. Hopefully, it is a good omen for the remainder of the 2018 series that Lindgren still wants to race and, thereby, provide an element of grit in the oyster of on-track competition for Woffinden and Zmarzlik for the World Championship crown.

Winner: Artem Laguta (18 points)

Second: Bartosz Zmarzlik (18 points)

Third: Tai Woffinden (12 points)

Fourth: Patryk Dudek (12 points)

CHAPTER 8

Krsko SGP 8 – 08.09.18

"President of the Republic of Slovenia, Borut Pahar,
is the patron of the meeting."

LIKE speedway, the world of work isn't what it was. The job for life has gone the way of the club for life. If they exist at all. Apprenticeships have gone the way of all flesh in preference for being thrown in at the deep end to "learn" on the job. Job titles sound much more important but fail to mask a lack of status or security. Precarity is the order of the day. The rise of the freelancer and zero-hours contracts normalises the temporary and transient nature of much contemporary work. Employers have few obligations to employees, let alone wider social responsibilities. In the UK, nowadays, riders come and go with a rapidity that makes it hard to even keep up with who is who or who is where, let alone when. Even clubs with a long-term view don't build their teams much beyond a monthly basis. Teams get constructed according to real or imaginary short-term business needs due to availability and rider averages rather than obligation or loyalty. This is particularly weird when there aren't enough riders (Europe-wide) to go around. This means that many riders race for more than one club in Britain, albeit with the fig leaf that they are in different leagues. Overall, the British speedway workplace for those that compete on the track is more and more *ad hoc* and transient rather than based on ability or past performance. Obviously, further uncertainty can also be dictated by injuries. Whenever riders get sacked on a whim, they have little or no recourse as they may well rely on that promoter for future work. How these decisions are arrived at and how they are handled is often also poor. They can learn of their termination via third parties or get sacked by text message. Even when riding for their country. Great Britain Speedway Team manager Alun Rossiter sacked Craig Cook by text before the 2018 FIM Speedway of Nations pairs competition then had to do a quick reverse ferret when he then discovered it was against the competition rules to do so. Grovelling for forgiveness afterwards, as Rosco did, is the exception rather than the norm. Riders can learn of their demise on social media. Worse still, like then Peterborough promoter Ged Rathbone did to two riders (Tom Perry and Emil Grondal) at the East of England Showground in late August 2016, they can learn about it at the same time as the fans over the stadium speaker system during the meeting interval! Even better from an employee motivation point of view, Ged still expected Tom Perry to continue to ride in Heat 12 (where he came second) after this news had also reached the pits. With team slots a long way from permanent, collective engagement and team spirit are regularly just empty words uttered on principle that faintly echo a more loyal bygone era. Some riders do pull together and help out. This is partly down to their own character and approach to life but also a function of the collegiality prompted by long hours and the significant travel distances that throws riders together *en route* and in pits across Europe a regular basis. Relentless travel and churn is the collective shared lot of any jobbing, itinerant speedway rider. Though riders may be good enough to be able to afford to formally sub-contract out (on a paid or unpaid basis) various key duties – such as engine-tuning, driving, mechanicing, travel bookings, media outreach, sponsorship research and management – they are really freelance one-man bands with short careers prone to workplace accidents.

Though the world of civilian work is similarly subject to zero hours contracts and casualisation without the safety net of trade unions or effective state support, the possibility of industrial injury or disease at work tends to be minimal. Or, at least, denied and hidden until it is way too late to legally attribute blame or claim compensation. Riders face the additional possibility that they could be badly injured in the course of their work or, even, permanently disabled. To some extent they can insure against this in both their approach to competition on the track but also the insurance policies they take out for loss of earnings off it. In general, the track furniture and equipment used has been significantly improved in its safety aspects, whether provided by their employers – air safety fences, for example – or by the riders themselves (better helmets, back protectors etc.). Ultimately, valuable though these additional protections can be, they are flimsy reassurances out on the track if luck or circumstance go against you. By speedway standards, SGP riders enjoy incredible security of tenure. Though injury can stop them competing, they can't get sacked throughout the whole duration of the (annual) series in question. They can be suspended if, for example, they infringe the blood alcohol regulations like Darcy Ward did. Better still, if riders finish in the top eight, they automatically (re)qualify for the next season. This security of tenure is almost unheard of in speedway circles. Additionally, riders can also be considered for a discretionary wild card nomination if they make a compelling case, their face fits or their sponsor allegedly has an undue influence. Though he didn't breathe a word at the time the wild cards got selected, afterwards even Paul Burbidge joined the dots and figured out that politics and commercial matters off the track could be a factor in such choices. Monster Energy contract negotiations – over their further continuing "partnership" with the SGP – finally prompted this realisation when their out-of-sorts and out-of-form team rider Chris Holder somehow gained selection as a wild card for the 2018 series in preference to other better qualified or more deserving candidates.

Though severe or permanent injury isn't on the menu, the world of work OFF the track at speedway is similarly capricious and temporary for those involved. There are freelancers galore. Those that are paid are the lucky ones. The hours are long and often anti-social to match the obligations or onerous travel distances. Indeed, much work that needs to get done to keep any speedway club just about together as an almost going concern gets done by volunteers without pay (and often proper thanks) out of love of the sport, for the club/rider, family connections or happenstance. Some of this unpaid labour is a privilege to do and provides memorable experiences but is, nonetheless, expected to be done *gratis*. These free at the point of delivery duties are factored into the club profit and loss accounts on that basis.

In the bright early morning sunshine that warmly bathes the holidaymakers, business travellers and airport staff through the impressive glass windows of British Airways Heathrow Terminal 5, the cream of the regular roster of BSI SGP freelancers muster by their departure gate ahead of their flight to Zagreb, Croatia for the Slovenian GP in Krsko tomorrow evening. Upon arrival at Franjo Tudman Airport they will either rush to the track to pre-record some rider interviews or else watch practice. Some may even just go straight to their hotel (bar) in Ljubljana. After staging so many SGP events over these past two decades, rights holders BSI have developed – nay, perfected – various levels of finely tuned organisational and administrative bureaucracy they roll out and deploy at locations around Europe and occasionally (until these end inevitably in failure) in Australia and New Zealand. Talk of finding new markets and exotic countries has been just that: empty talk. Despite having had many American World Champions, North America remains resolutely unvisited and even staging events in comparatively local motorcycle-mad countries like Spain and Portugal has proven completely beyond SGP rights holders BSI's imagination and abilities. It is almost as if they talked a good new market penetration and development game to land their decades-long contract without ever really intending to put their hands in their deep profitable pockets to turn these pretty words into action. The current team of SGP freelancers assembled at this Heathrow departure gate are experienced and skilled at what is required to deliver an extremely slick comparatively deluxe representation of the SGP product for the various screens: telly, social and online media. It is a colourful visual and aural output that (apparently) mostly sates and satisfies the public, broadcasters, rights holders and sponsors. Even if the official BARB television audience UK viewing figures say otherwise. Whether live, pre-recorded or packaged, these televised SGP meetings enjoy a tried and tested house style where hyperbolic commentary verbals get matched with a similarly OTT visual vocabulary of fast-action moving pictures, slo-mos and musical backing tracks. Almost whatever the circumstance, the BSI broadcast template is firmly applied to whatever "events, dear boy" transpires. No matter what is served up on the track – whether exciting, dull, thrilling or workaday – the words and pictures that find their way to our screens follow a rigid commodified template in terms of the narrative pacing and framing of the actual SGP racing and said presentation of the stadium environs.

These talented people mustered by this Terminal 5 departure gate provide the combined specialist skills and abilities to fulfil the various tasks and functions required to get this particular live sports broadcast show on the road and then into the lounges, cells, bars and wards of their viewers. Though their specific skills are often generic to outside broadcast sports work, their SGP experience boosts and embeds their value but, as freelancers, there remains an impermanence to their employment. They are all to a greater or lesser extent biddable since they can be dispensed with summarily according to whatever notionally enforceable notice period (if any) applies to the terms and conditions of their contracts. They are disposable commodities. In almost any line of work nowadays, the reasons for dismissal can be structural or whimsical. Rights holders BSI Speedway make so much profit from staging the events for which they hold the rights – SGP and Speedway of Nations this year; the SGP and World Cup previous years – that cost-cutting rather than sudden loss of cash flow is the likeliest reason behind any such decision. More pertinently, if you don't get with the agreed programme and be seen to be on board and doing so – or, possibly, if your face suddenly doesn't fit – replacement quickly looms. Though all these people are mostly hired by the series rather than the event, unless they have specific skills unavailable elsewhere or are seen by the wider speedway community as an essential component of the show, these freelancers invariably have interchangeable waiting-in-the-wings substitutes. The basic reality is that freelancers everywhere have to curry favour and toe the line – whether they intuit this or, less often, get told explicitly – or else they often don't get invited back to the rodeo for much longer afterwards.

Though the long-serving commentary team of Kelvin Tatum and Nigel Pearson are the public face of the SGP in the English language on UK television but also on the generic world feed used by broadcasters elsewhere. They survived the transition of the SGP UK broadcast contract from Sky Sports to BT Sports (by way of Eurosport) – allegedly by taking a fifty percent pay cut to their freelance contract fees – the reality is that editorially they are – to all intents and purposes – effectively staff rather than working and reporting at the SGPs as independent journalists. Whether or not this compromises their editorial judgement or speaking truth-to-power is a question of taste and opinion. That said, it is hard to recall any ongoing critical analysis, holding to account or pointed comment upon the various snafus that have beset SGP events over the years. If they comment at all, Nigel and Kelvin prefer to describe specific incidents or the current status of rider ups and downs rather than seek to understand or articulate the structural basis and causes. Their analysis is stuck in the permanent present with incredibly strong notes of product placement or sycophancy. If they had a motto is would be: Never *Sotto Voce*. They take things race by race and event by event. History only ever intrudes to keep cumulative score – whether points or titles – rather than provide lessons. Philosophy or strategic analysis don't exist. No matter what does or doesn't happen on the track, their default setting is over-excited. They are never knowingly under-exaggerated. It is world where everything is GREAT and let me excitedly tell you about it – yet again – in more copious detail. Few do enthusiastic heavy breathing about what we just said we saw better than these guys. They say it as they see it and are unafraid to relentlessly say the same things (and 'jokes') again and over again, albeit sometimes in slightly different words. Though they say accomplished sports broadcasters know when to pause or keep silent to let the action speak for itself, neither Nigel or Kelvin bother with such petty indulgences. When it comes to anything beyond surface matters, they stick religiously to what the Polish call, "not my circus, not my monkey".

The pits colour interviewer position is much more precarious, if judged by the frequency with which the people doing that job change. This is a function of the fact that getting rider interviews and reaction – either live or pre-recorded – as well as filming colour packages to slot into the live coverage or online (via the SGP website or social media) requires widely available and transferable general broadcast skills of fluency and expertise under time pressure rather than the specific speedway expertise or knowledge race commentary needs. So along with availability and gender (plus it seems looks), in the absence of SGP fan acclaim or speedway celebrity, freelancers with live events or sports broadcasting experience, expertise and impressive *curriculum vitae* and showreels can challenge any current incumbent in the pits colour/reaction role. Despite the don't-worry-there-will-be-another-one-along-in-a-minute nature of this colour interview position, the experience and media professionalism of current incumbent Kiri Bloore has been noticeable in this sometimes fraught time-pressured, time-poor position throughout the 2018 SGP season. Observing first hand from afar (or on screen), though Kiri hasn't yet fully settled in or got to know the riders as closely or intensely as some others chose to previously, the editorial quality of her on-the-hoof live broadcast work and the product she provides is an improvement on previous freelancers working this position. In her trademark too short shorts Kiri works hard, appears to deliver without multiple retakes and – as much as rider articulacy and circumstance allows – occasionally errs towards the vaguely informative than the relentless bland. Even her unique to camera presentational style of apparently undergoing a dental hygiene exam while simultaneous conducting an elocution test for English as a second language is memorable. That all said, watching SGPs live in person spares attending fans – unless they want to subject themselves to it afterwards – of the need to compulsorily bathe in the loud relentlessly cloying shouty heavy breather word soup that is the primary *lingua franca* of English language live broadcasts. Except, of course, when David Rowe is on the mike. The fact that this perpetually on the edge of an orgasm commentary house style has endured beyond the transition from Sky to BT (via Eurosport) rather undermines the oft-uttered excuse that this happens at the specific instruction and request of the producer for editorial reasons rather than as the presentation preference of Nigel Pearson and Kelvin Tatum. Authoritarians the world over know that you don't have to interfere editorially, if the hired help already know and when to voluntarily toe the party line. Or be so willingly akratic.

Stood behind some of the key members the BSI Speedway executive team in a slow-moving business class queue for a BA flight after an event in Germany some years back, I rather revealingly got to hear first-hand the contempt in which they apparently held the anorak wearing fans we could see nearby. It was as if these rights-holding executives felt soiled by their mandatory weekend interactions with speedway fans as it forcibly reminded them of the manner in which and the sport from which they made their big salaries. Those execs are (mostly) long gone but, it seems, the ethos of condescension their overheard comments implied remains alive within the organisation and its staff. Well over a decade later, it seems this attitude is still alive and well in the first words I overhear at another (different) airport while (again) waiting for a BA flight. Though these aren't executives and, as they are freelancers, travel economy not business, as they muster by the departure ready and wait for our boarding by group announcements these words are hard to forget, "Ready for another weekend of bollocks?" Maybe it is only the early hour that prompts this shared cynicism and this talk of "bollocks" actually carefully masks their excitement for something they really relish and enjoy? Perhaps this is the affectionate argot of mid-to-late thirty TV and media somethings use to affectionately describe the speedway freelance weekend work of their dreams? But I think not, since there is only murmured assent and no push back, let alone dispute.

Like we can question our own families but take against outsiders who do likewise, it is alright for speedway fans to question the sport, its practices or even, heaven forfend, the brilliance of the Speedway Grand Prix. It is possibly our birthright and – nowadays – practically obligatory. Though we know the pursuit of World Championship crown has been devalued nowadays and that the SGP is often bollocks, what doesn't feel quite so alright is those who are paid to attend as part of their job taking the piss and laughing at us behind our backs; while all the while professionally pretending in public that the situation is otherwise. Work is work and theirs is presenting and representing the full majesty and glory (or otherwise) of these SGP events back to us via the medium of the broadcast media. It is definitely poor form and, possibly, bad faith. Though I can also sympathise that if you have no affinity for speedway to start with then being forced to endlessly watch processional SGP races featuring the same competitors in far flung obscure unsexy regional locations on a regular almost fortnightly basis would really start to grate. So many dull weekends would also make you doubt the futility of your existence or, at least, your chosen line of work. Setting aside the challenge of regular interactions with BSI executives or their middle managers, working behind the scenes quickly disabuses the sentient of the far-fetched notion that the SGP somehow represents the crème-de-la-crème, pinnacle and *sine qua non* of modern competitive professional speedway. Indeed, having to entertain such an idea or claim in your work will either drive you mad or will quickly appear ludicrously laughable. After all, no man is a hero to his manservant. Disillusion kicks in even before the sheer random obscurity and basicness of most of the locations chosen nowadays by BSI to stage the SGP events further compounds matters. These far-flung places definitely lack the nightlife or chi-chi big-city glamour and facilities media creative types often require to further burnish and validate their manicured self-image. Even if parties and wild sex with attractive strangers can be found, it is the riders who'll get their brains banged out not the freelance help. If you then add in the cumulative impact of travel logistics, long days, admin, early starts and limited hours of sleep thrills are in such short supply that any remaining hint of a possible buzz is quickly extinguished.

That said, and looked at dispassionately, has anyone employed to help put on the SGP events organised by rights holders BSI ever been acclaimed for their candour in public? They don't mention this on air but, judged by my experiences of the series to date, it is hard to gainsay the veracity and accuracy of this bollocks opinion. The current SGP series format as devised and staged by BSI – under the notionally watchful but really let's nod it through auspices of FIM supervision – is a huge disservice to the image of speedway and an impediment to its future medium- to long-term success. Phil Morris might thank the Lord via his Twitter account that it is "the biggest global speedway event the FIM Speedway Grand Prix" but the reality is that embarrassingly turgid races regularly get served up on mediocre tracks. There is no joy and little overtaking or thrill to the spectacle. The simple high-octane pleasure of four riders going hell for leather on bikes with no brakes against each other for World Championship glory and status has been badly neutered. When fans, specialist tame media and the commentators bang on about how great and thrilling the action is, the evidence presented to watching neutral eyes tells a totally different story. Nondescript races blur together and follow each other repetitively. There are no new break-out widely acclaimed shale heroes; even though Tai Woffinden's PR man Nigel Pearson uses every platform he has available to relentless imply and insist otherwise. Primarily, SGPs blur into each other as an indistinguishable mush with Monster logos and numerous hashtag speedwaygp.com signs. It might be bigger, but it is a long way from best or global. Whole continents remain completely unvisited let alone conquered. Motorbike-mad countries – even easy-access European ones – mysteriously but studiously remain untouched. BSI's strategic vision lacks imagination, investment and ambition. Easy markets are viewed warily and then just ignored since to try the SGP out there initially requires an element of speculation without guaranteed accumulation that they refuse to make unless, of course, they can find regional or local government funding. You would hope that this lack of ambition is because BSI are fully and painfully aware of the unsatisfying reality of the product they offer and how crowds invariably fall off sharply after the first blush of interest. Real *bona fide* on-track drama – rather than fictional claims about its existence – is only notable by its frequent absence. This is spreadsheet speedway served up with organisational efficiency but without pizzazz by a sports marketing subsidiary with the collusion of gifted motorcycle professionals out to earn a crust rather than entertain.

If you never mind the "bollocks", the check-in queue talk is otherwise mundane. Gossip (about persons unknown), offhand terse chat about previous trips, people and locations, the odd war story (travel or work) plus social possibilities and excitements ahead in the brief time they have free beyond their packed work schedule. If they offered Power Pilates classes at Heathrow, Kiri Bloore would be there in a shot. She's the only one secretive or in demand enough at this time of the morning to stand elsewhere to take/make a mobile call. Apart from precious breakable expensive equipment that can't be trusted to the baggage hold, everyone travels light. Nigel Pearson arrives close to boarding time looking fresh and cleanly shaven. Shortly after, his commentary partner-in-crime Kelvin Tatum ambles up with a not excessively packed rucksack slung over his shoulder. With Nigel and Kelvin there too, the talk of the enlarged group shifts from amiable to more perfunctorily polite and anodyne. Group dynamics shift subtly. The tattoo per head average drops dramatically. The age seniority and casual dress of Nige and Kelv makes them look like almost still down-with-the-kids geography teachers keeping things contemporary ahead of their mature students field trip flight. Apart from the isolation and unpredictability of employment flows, they say one of the most difficult things that you give up when working as a freelancer – rather than full-time work attendance in the office, factory, shop or public service institution – is the opportunity to focus any of your free-floating antipathy and anger towards randoms. Usually colleagues or customers. People who are distant from your close family or friends. This is the role critical (or sentient) speedway fans – often derogatively called "keyboard warriors" rather than fans or customers – often occupy for those inside the charmed circle of paid freelance speedway media professionals. Those fans who dare to question rather than swallow wholesale received speedway media opinion frequently get short shrift. Rather than see this feedback as free – possibly valuable – market intelligence, fan opinion is frowned upon, summarily dismissed or completely ignored in the speedway universe by promoters, speedway media freelancers, riders, sponsors and rights holders alike unless it echoes the company line or confirms their latest doomed-to-failure idea/initiative. The SGP is no exception to this dismissive hypersensitivity and, arguably, is even more precious since its obligations and interactions are less onerous and frequent than endured by proper speedway clubs. Since their product platform is primarily visual, rights holders BSI fret obsessively about immediate surface appearances. Stage management and media management are indivisible at the SGP. Much more than anywhere else apart from possibly the Polish Ekstraliga. Turn up, pay up, shut up and be grateful for what you get then fark off is often felt to be the *de facto* expectation of speedway promoters for fans everywhere, but especially so at the SGP under BSI.

Surprisingly this BSI Speedway SGP team of all the talents lacks one of its star performers, namely the legendary Paul "Burbo" Burbidge. Rather like members of the Royal Family don't all fly together on the same plane in case of accidents, perhaps BSI Speedway protect the future of the sport as well as the deification of the SGP by insisting that Burbo travels separately from his colleagues? This would be a faff but, if it ensures the survival of Grand Prix speedway's very own Prince Andrew, then it is a small price to pay. Rather like "Airmiles" Andy, Paul loves his Avios and, of course, the British Airways Executive Club tier points. His years of SGP work trips to far-flung European regional locations (with the odd glamour trip Down Under thrown in) earnt Paul his hard-won British Airways Executive Club Bronze card holder frequent flier status. This exalted status helps anyone jump airport check in and boarding queues, boost their baggage allowances and also, most importantly, provides the cachet of that oh-so-important access to the lowest tier of the British Airways business departure lounges in the UK and elsewhere. Once inside the hallowed portals of the lounge (think SGP media centre with better food and drinks, less damp but more boring people), Burbo can work, relax, drink, snack or even eat a delicious full meal – menus vary by time of day – in the always joyful Master-of-the-Universe company of other time-pressed, stressed but self-important executive frequent fliers. They say it is in these various BA Executive Club lounges that Burbo gets his best ideas to develop and/or save British speedway. Even if they are unworkable, inept, wrong-headed, laughable or catastrophically expensive – it is always there (or else the ideas magic apparently happens in conversation with Matt Ford and Torben Olsen or Paul Bellamy and John Postlethwaite before him) that the visionary Muse strikes him most often. Though Burbo just HAS to attend all the SGPs, he has been a notoriously reluctant traveller beyond the confines of Dorset. After years resisting seeing the British league clubs he is employed to report about first-hand, recent times have seen Burbo venture more widely around the UK and then complain in print – though it is a fraction of the kilometres that riders travel by road – about the mileage he's driven in his subsequent reports. His long-time serial lack of curiosity about the notional objects of his main ostensibly full-time news gathering/writing job (British speedway clubs but especially National league ones) – except when he is misrepresenting them, exaggerating their significance or achievements, directly/obliquely slagging them off or critiquing British speedway in comparison to wild claims about the brilliance of the SGP (or Polish and Swedish speedway) under the guise of candid reporting – has yet to threaten his job security at the nowadays financially struggling *Speedway Star*. The only conclusion can be that the man who appointed him – Managing Editor and Pinegen co-owner Philip Rising – encourages, endorses and condones this "SGP-good British-speedway-bad" approach to news gathering and reporting. Though Burbs makes no secret of his employment with the *Speedway Star* and the SGP in the header of his always compelling Twitter account, it often fails to get regular formal mention elsewhere. This may well be shame, modesty, conflict of interest or just been accidentally overlooked for years, who knows? Looked at generously, Burbs gets to see speedway run in a wide variety of continental European locations so is exposed to other practices worth considering, importing or crosspollinating with the British version. In practice, if there are any, these "new" ideas don't register enough to get relentless mention. It is as if Burbs is on some secret speedway panda-breeding programme where two rare but brash beasts – the SGP and Poole on behalf of all other British speedway clubs – are coaxed to mate to ensure the cash keeps flowing and yet the rest of the speedway species dies out. In this extinction event scenario, Burbs is part fluffer and part matchmaker. It is, of course, a match made some distance away from heaven. Difficult too when both are apparently completely set – internet forum fans often suggest – in the ways of Onan. While romance sometimes almost blooms for them but produces no heirs, their commercial needs react like Rohypnol on the rest of British speedway to further impede its progress or ruin its future.

The bright lights of foreign travel to exotic or obscure European locations and the chance to enjoy the luxuries of gaining frequent flier status would appeal to most genuine speedway fans and, possibly, prove wildly irresistible in comparison to visiting every British speedway club regularly. If this were the military, Mr Burbo would long ago have been cashiered and drummed out for dereliction of duty. But this is speedway, so a mountainous shabby carpet is always on hand to sweep any of these real or imagined short-changing-the-sport nasties under for complete absolution without subsequent acknowledgement or further say so. Like Major Major in *Catch 22* – who is only ever out of the office when it says he is in and only ever in his office when it says he is out – beyond sightings required (until the last year or three) by his dictation typing duties for Matt Ford at his local club the Poole Pirates, Burbo is an elusive speedway media beast to find regularly at most British speedway league clubs on anything like a regular basis. That said, Burbs does travel the UK to go to first-ever meetings (a rare breed nowadays) and last-ever closure meetings (increasingly common) plus deigns to occasionally appear at other assorted "big night" events. Mostly, though, Burbo appears to prefer doing his work remotely in his own company – either transcribing pits interviews or else conducting phone, email and press-conference interviews to record then mis-transcribe before translating into his uniquely heroic and grandiloquent *Boy's Own* meets *Dan Dare* and *Beano* style copy – to any unnecessary speedway travel or socialising. And, fair play to him, drinking a skinful in yet another overseas Genuine Irish tourist bar with erstwhile SGP colleagues would be tough yardage. This dedication to dictation typing mixed with a pronounced social awkwardness makes Mr Burbidge an ideal employee and freelancer – aka always available and able to efficiently meet deadlines. Even better, Paul's investigative powers are of the reduced instruction set variety and, like low information voters the world over, this incuriosity makes for a potent mix of minimal analysis allied to mis-placed but bold wrong-headed assertions.

Like a poor man's shale Zelig, Paul is the ideal mouthpiece for his corporate masters (primarily the free riders at BSI) as – like me – he endlessly writes up and repeats whatever he has just been told with hints of magnificent authority. He rides the blue groove of the approved party line doggedly. It is a safe rule of thumb to do or think the opposite of whatever Paul has been told to advocate or recommend. His various attempts to "save" and/or resuscitate British speedway with brave new plans for the future would invariably further endanger the critically ill almost comatose patient if put into action. Sadly, some of these fast-witted suggestions appear to gain some traction with either BSPA bigwigs or the less thoughtful but frighteningly ambitious promoters. To misdiagnose once is an unlucky fluke, to do so many times is a sign of true genius. Any list of the various nonsense ideas and magic solutions Burbo has floated down tangent cul-de-sac must include: squad systems, fixed race nights, track covers, worshipping the audience pulling power of top/star riders, transponders and – completely ignoring the troubled finances of the country and local authorities, let alone austerity – new UK stadiums built and owned by the state or local government. Fortunately for speedway gaiety, Burbo can also go badly but amusingly off-piste. Without "woke" Paul there would never have been (and though laudable) mentions of homophobia, sexism and Scottish independence within the pages of the *Speedway Star*. Many readers nearly spat out their false teeth in shock. Indeed, some have yet to recover from the shock of sexual politics appearing in the safe-space pages of the *Star* and, obviously, stubbornly still refuse to get dragged by Burbs into the late 20th century. Typically, Burbo fails to be consistent in his woke-ness or join easily spotted dots. After suggesting Tyson Fury should be disqualified from the BBC Sports Personality of the Year shortlist (so SGP World Champion Tai Woffinden could take his place and not win either), after Burbo hitched his new-found metaphorical woke kilt about the boxer's scandalous homophobia and sexism. Yet ire, question or comment about the obvious sexism and misogyny of the Monster start women or the unfortunate incident of Monster Joe's possibly Islamophobic airport terminal tweets came there none. It goes without saying that these "bold" ideas often appear from nowhere without warning or anything beyond a modicum of research. They just suddenly materialise when beamed down from the Starship BSI or Starship Ford.

With Paul unavailable to entertain with his favoured pits persona – startled shy rabbit about to run off impression – Kelvin is left as the only member of the SGP group at the departure gate who appears genuinely excited to be there getting paid to go to the speedway. His anticipation and fascination remain undimmed albeit, obviously, being Kelvin the emphasis is long-retired ex-rider obsessive, technical and geeky not just vanilla anticipation at the pending race action ahead. Kelvin definitely projects the air of a senior venture scout researching one of his many duplicate practical skills badges. Tatum really is just itching to get down to the track to see the bikes in the pits and study them closely. The gossip he seeks will be as much set up, sprockets, specifications, lubricants, technical innovations and track conditions as the political or personal. Watching the other group members, they seem have the workaday "another day, another dollar" slightly crushed put-upon air of regular fliers. The dress code for these mid- to late-thirties blokes is the vanilla normcore surfer dude meets skaterboi garb often favoured by urban techy creative media types. Albeit the more high-street backpacker from Milletts look, rather than the more hipster version they mistakenly imagine these get ups project. The clothing is dark, worn but understated, the footwear is distressed and the facial hair stubble or scraggy. Doubtless they are on brand and provincial trend too, if only I knew how to recognise them. The blokes are work fit. They project confidence in their abilities. They know how to deliver their specialisms but also how to party so are cusping on the verge of slightly too long in the tooth to still pursue this laddish lifestyle. Propped up at a hotel bar or life-and-souling with the SGP in-crowd at an invite-only after-party, they'll seem more shop-soiled than handsome, more shop-bought than authentically individual. They are younger, less branded or successful, slightly buffer weekend warrior clones living their own tangential wannabe indy media versions of Monster Joe's ageing but ersatz roadie lifestyle. Maybe, like so many aspects of the SGP, this look is contractual if you are male and regularly spend time on the road working at Speedway Grand Prix meetings in notionally creative jobs like marketing, product placement, travel management or the broadcast media? John Cooper Clarke warned us a long time ago that in some environments people turn to poison as quick as lager turns to piss.

Obviously, mustered by check-in there are no name badges or employer and job title tattoos. Guessing their specific job function ahead this SGP weekend isn't easy. Given the group is only a loose coalition of people flung together by circumstance, it is often said that birds of a feather usually stick together. Kelvin stands and chats with Nigel, while "bollocks" man spends most time with Kiri. This could be bonhomie, sexism, fascination with Power Pilates, animal magnetism or because they work together. By a process of deduction that won't get me inducted into Police Detective College any time soon, from his mouthiness and loud careworn memories of previous trips, I am guessing he is either the features photographer or else the packages and live interviews cameraman rather than the sound guy. Though, that said, having to wear 'cans' – as I believe the young people call the ear defender looking modern headphones – all day probably means that you probably shout and rarely don't shut up if you don't have them on. So hard to know exactly? The surfer boi look is so universally fitted as standard around the SGP staff roster that, sadly, beyond the twang of Scots in his accent there is nothing memorable about this bloke that would enable me to recognise "bollocks" man again on the street or the pits, even without a camera or boom mike obscuring his face. If this had been a murder scene, he would get away it based on the combination of this surfer dude serial non-descriptness but also my lack of observation skills. I once saw a man badly assaulted mid-morning by four blokes with baseball bats by the pumps of the Wood Lane Esso station close to a satellite BBC building not a million miles away from QPR's stadium. I don't think their dispute was because someone had just pushed in. Afterwards, I could give the Police lengthy detailed descriptions of both cars, the baseball bat makes and the gory specifics of the assault itself but was completely stumped by own vague recollections of the specific identifying features of the perpetrators. It was all useless generalities (black hoodie; blue jeans; white standard Converse high tops; not tall, medium build; short hair; 20s) rather than any more helpful distinguishing features. Nowadays, SGP races react upon the general speedway population similarly. Fans can detail the kevlars, bike decals, sponsor names and even immediately identify the riders from their body shape or the way they hold themselves on a bike but the races themselves defy recollection – let alone accurate description – so remain a samey non-descript blur and unmemorable mush.

With different responsibilities and as the SGP English language world feed live broadcast talent, Nigel and Kelvin face less SGP demands on their hours and time outside the actual meetings than the other SGP freelancers. They long ago perfected their on-air schtick together. In essence, they react to the racing like dogs. One barks at nothing and the other joins in the chorus. They alternate and feed off each other. The clamour quickly gets to a frenzy and stays there. The atmosphere is relentlessly celebratory and self-congratulatory. As they wait in the Group Four and Five queue, Kelvin is keen to establish Nigel's plans for the final GP of the season in a month's time as he plans to fly to Torun on the Thursday to have a long weekend partying with the friends with whom he – apparently – "broke" the hotel bar in Malilla. With various sports broadcast gigs beyond speedway, Nigel has pre-existing darts commentary commitments in Dublin. This sounds genuine rather than just a convenient excuse. Nigel is the "Hardest Working Man in Speedway". Even if we set aside his football and darts commentary work, Mr Pearson is the closest we have to a one-man speedway media empire. Obviously, the nature of freelance work means that you seek to maximise your income as well as parlay your connections and expertise at all opportunities. Speedway is, of course, a sport renowned for many things kept under hats, swept under carpets or known to only those in the know. Unlike, for example, MPs there is no central speedway Register of Interests. If there were such a required listing, you could guess that the entry for the numerous pockets of Nigel's mono-coloured speedway fever dream coat would include:

BT Sports SGP live commentator

BSI SGP World Feed live commentator

BSI SGP Highlights package commentary

"Voices" SGP series DVD commentary

SGP rider interview evening co-compere (Cardiff)

BT Sports Premiership live commentator

BSPA Press Officer

Tai Woffinden PR

Nigel Pearson Media (manages sports freelance journalist team who supply meeting reports, rider interviews; programme content)

Programme Editor (for SGP; BSPA shared events; various British clubs including Belle Vue and Swindon)

Content Supplier to the deracinated *Speedway Star* [1]

Chairman Cradley Speedway

Speaking events – Kelvin & Nigel tours plus *ad hoc* rider evenings (organised by third party)

This may not be 100 per cent accurate but is a good guessed snapshot of Commander Pearson's current extensive range of intersecting and intermingling speedway responsibilities. It is the power and depth of speedway patronage writ large. It is hard to imagine any current non-rider has more speedway hats/helmets to wear or different revenue streams that flow from these job positions and tasks. People wearing too many hats is a common serious problem in speedway that people regularly excuse or turn a blind eye towards. Few people wear as many actual and metaphorical hats. Whatever the ins and outs, Mr Pearson appears to enjoy lucrative off-track earnings – he must be one of the top earners – and also be something of a monopolist without his value of status coming into question. With so many levers of power to hold or manipulate, there is a greater degree of career and financial security than even cannier, well-sponsored SGP riders merit. Unlike those who compete on the track rather than make their living off it, there is no physical risk of injury and, with fingers in so many pies, little reputational danger either. The activities and functions many of these speedway-associated jobs require are self-explanatory though the specifics are a confidential matter of contract, agreement or description with the employer in question. Viewed from afar outside at a basic level, what some jobs actually require is much more obvious than others. For various of these jobs, Pearson is more something of a secretive behind-the-scenes Mr Big Figure – part *Wizard of Oz* and part Ernst Stavro Blofled in *Dr. No* (albeit without the cat) – than up front on centre stage. Whereas, live commentary work clearly involves going to the

[1]This is an expanded 2019 position with partner-in-crime Phil Lanning apparently under a new contract to provide "exclusive" interviews and bland content after – it is rumoured – their bid to do this work for around half the price previously paid in total to long term freelance club reporters previously used by the magazine. These now surplus-to-requirements freelance speedway reporter people supplied individual meeting race reports and weekly club updates before their sudden regrettable sacking – for cost-control reasons – sometimes by email. Though a lower page extent, the new-look "rejuvenated" *Speedway Star* magazine is nowadays big interview led and packed with bigger/better photos (from gifted young snapper Taylor Lanning and various other photographers). There have been many deleterious consequences, among them the 75-year speedway tradition of listing race times (with the heat results) and track records has been disappeared from the historical record of note. On the plus side, speedway continues to have a glossy must-read speedway magazine for fans! And BSI somewhere to place a weekly full page advert in about the SGP.

track/meeting and being heard/seen relating what you see using your knowledge, fluency and skill. Chairing Cradley Speedway requires a mix of strategy, admin, good governance, pressing the flesh and counting the doubloons. Plus there are many unseen and taken-for-granted elements of successfully running any speedway club from staging meetings to finding riders not just the popular image of opening the doors, banking the money and carefully compiling the accounts for Companies House. Without a permanent home, as custodians of the Cradley (brand) name and reputation, important additional responsibilities for the Heathens management team has been building the financial war chest that allows their endless quest researching, costing and pitching new location plans as well as building relationships with the council and their planning authorities. Weirdly, Nigel's Woffinden position is listed on Tai's website but not really acknowledged or spoken about despite him regularly screaming his praise for his employer on the telly. Even more peculiarly, while the BSPA position isn't even listed on their website, it is widely understood in speedway circles that this is part of his media and social media responsibilities. Sadly, both Tai and British speedway remain mostly forgotten or a mystery to the mainstream media of any stripe in the UK, despite Nigel's expertise and outreach activities or the more prosaic task of helping to supervise official press and photographer BSPA pass accreditations.

Of course, there is a long history and tradition of revenue maximisation and entrepreneurship in speedway. In days of yore when demand, interest and crowds were substantial, successful speedway businessmen tended more often than not to be promoters and some star riders rather than the journalistic help. Anyways, the onus upon Nigel (and his *ad hoc* teams) to produce original content is huge and it is unfair to expect that there is enough time in the day to supply it all without either repetition, facile statements of the obvious or some degree of cut and paste along the way. Still, given most who hire Nigel and/or his team want knowledge; reliability (making deadlines); contacts; key suppliers (often Curtis Sports for programmes); content (interesting – aka to a sufficient standard, notionally interesting, fills available space); discretion and keen price, this works well for all parties. Obviously, in order not to scare any of the horses, content errs towards the positive, lobbying, anodyne or uncritical. Even if he wanted to – which he most strenuously doesn't – these circles of patronage are so tightly intersecting that almost anything blunt or critical is going to offend somebody or their vested interests. The net result of such a speedway content empire is that promoters, riders and sponsors everywhere and anywhere can give interviews to Nigel or his team safe in the knowledge that it is more like a playdate than an interrogation. Any stone can remain unturned, either voluntarily/accidentally or by prior agreement. And, let's face it, historically they all pretty well do. This is speedway journalism as promotional heavy breathing. It is a world where everything in the garden is either thrilling, rosy or viewed at its rosiest. Sadly, for the wider interests of British speedway in general, as a narrative style relentlessly employed across print, broadcast and social media it has singularly failed to excite, let alone retain the existing speedway fan base. At the most basic of levels, even if the interviews and comments accidentally vaguely "entertain", it is a cookie-cutter production-line approach that regularly fails to deliver actual insights, let alone scratch beneath the surface beyond the tired platitudes it pretends is doing so. Worst of all, the lava flow of speedway content has completely failed to attract or find new audiences. This is the Mushroom Principle of management specially adapted for speedway fans: feed them allegedly "thrilling" shit but keep them in the dark to see what comes up. Sadly, nothing grows. Attention, interest, numbers and revenues all shrink.

Obviously, there are many factors behind these particularly worrisome declining broadcast audience and paying track attendee figures. Many more serious and intractable than just the endless guff of banal content supplied in bulk. But clearly the narrative style and mores of Pearson's monopolist-in-waiting approach to speedway news, comment and features reporting has been a significant factor in this ongoing slow-motion decline of British club speedway. The "isn't this wonderful?" school of speedway reporting has definitely been the *de facto* house style during a lengthy period when every metric – whether sponsorship monies, audience figures and fan numbers through the turnstiles – has seriously collapsed. It is true that others lustily singalong too, but Nigel happily leads the chorus and congratulation. Sadly, despite the happy-clappy backing track and mood music, throughout his time as a monopolist various British clubs have failed or gone out of existence, the pipeline for new speedway rider talent has more-or-less disappeared (or dried to a trickle) while top riders almost universally boycott riding in Britain. Their absence is a function of a lack of money – like everywhere, fewer fans means thinner pickings – but equally also a function of their own warped spending priorities. Sponsors were and are mostly regional or keen fans with businesses and spare dosh rather than known, high street or global brands. Sponsorship monies of any stripe are thinner on the ground as well as increasingly valued and prized. In the face of declining audiences, most monopolist suppliers would consolidate and eliminate further competition (tick) but also change or reconsider their product offerings. Sadly, only the pull-up-the-drawbridge and eliminate the competition half of this equation is continuously actioned. In general terms, the speedway editorial and comment supplied remains either descriptive or suck up and, given its gaslighting nature, is really a kick down rather than boost for the sport and fans/viewers alike. When the house style relentlessly claims everything is wonderful in the garden and the majority of riders and races are great or amazing even if – or especially if – the evidence of your eyes says otherwise. Going further overboard or into further and further copious (or technical) detail isn't going to convince, win back waverers or find new disciples. Obviously, preaching to the converted or satisfying employers and acolytes is rarely a recipe for increased market share, additional consumer spend or greater mindshare in the contemporary attention economy. If there are debates, these are of a who-just-did-what-when variety rather than of a how-to-grow or why-change-is-needed type. Demographics are against speedway too as its core audience is metaphorically but also literally dying off.

This is not to claim that the facts reported are wrong or events as portrayed didn't happen. But rather that the Overton Window has drastically narrowed and so have the carefully chosen objects, themes and topics Nigel Pearson Media *et al* report. It is a kind of perverse reverse of the John West advert claims, where the best fish are ignored but the cans still get made and sold with what should get rejected. Keeping a media show of this size on the road without it being widely seen that the King has no clothes is quite an achievement. Obsessively blowing all that smoke up so many esteemed backsides is remorseless and extremely tiring but, I assume, financially worthwhile. It is a content model where the revenue streams are discrete but interconnected with a variety payment routes including direct, commissions and gratis. No matter how skilled, ambitious or creative, any new speedway media market entrant is going to struggle for traction or income against such an interlocking coalition of patronage so, consequently, will get quickly vanquished. The barrier to entry of the installed base of Nigel Pearson Media clients is so prohibitive that it defies effective competition. This monopolist position can't be good for either the SGP or British speedway. Even if Nigel suddenly chose to defy his programming and own vested interests, after so much happy talk and ingratiating noise his room for manoeuvre let alone candid or critical comment is almost zero. With fingers in so many pies and hands in so many gloves and pockets, this speedway media house of cards depends for its stability upon the surety that confidences won't be punctured or broken with home truths. In this universe, only random speedway fans without power, authority or status can try to recite blunt truths but, rarely, get anything approaching a proper hearing. When push comes to shove, Nigel Pearson claims the privileges of a "journalist" while exercising the power of a politician. It is hard to conclude anything other than British speedway has a less rosy present and future as a result. Looked at in the round, when it comes to 21st century speedway biggest off-track earners Nigel Pearson deserves to be ranked up there with the likes of John Postlethwaite and Matt Ford. Whether this has been value for money or good for the sport is a question beyond my pay grade. What is clear that the past decade or so British speedway has gone from managed decline to cliff jumps with possible catastrophic failure or irrevocable possibly terminal change pending. Whether more independent much less heavy breathing speedway journalism could have saved the day on its own is an unknown counterfactual. The status quo has and remains unchallenged. Spin, exaggeration and hyperbole done well is something to behold and even admire as it floats many boats. Done badly it sinks them. Nigel has yet to – publicly – see a Curtis Sport programme he didn't like, a race that didn't amaze or delight in some way and any star rider who wasn't a top bloke. Arguably, he is well-suited to working with BSI on the SGP and the BSPA on British speedway as they are both organisations who don't welcome transparency, spade-calling or glasnost. They much prefer relentless positivity even if the observed reality, sums or evidence says otherwise. There is, of course, absolutely nothing illegal whatsoever in this diligent entrepreneurship, degree of control or nexus of relationships, even though they may appear – to the untutored eye – as if they are completely failing to deliver on any reasonable metric beyond *omerta*. Or sometimes give rise to perceptions that such a structure might deliver alleged possible conflicts of interest not in the best interests of the sport of speedway and its representation. In our media age, journalistic codes of ethics are increasingly anachronisms generally but – some still naively say – remain essential to our pre-existing notions of reporting health and its independence. In some respects, Burbs and Nige are two sides of the same heavy breather speedway patronage media coin. Albeit the more experienced practitioner is cannier, monetises the role better and has fractionally less tendency to grandiloquently heroic description than his Dorset-based beta proxy.

The net upshot of the BA "Group 5" seating allocations on this flight to Zagreb is that I can now accurately and honestly say with a straight face "I have slept with Nigel Pearson". Well, almost. Another similarly glamorous claim could be "I slept with Kelvin Tatum". Or, if we go full *Hangover 3*, there is the double-bubble claim to boggle the mind and get as a face tattoo, "I have slept with Nigel Pearson & Kelvin Tatum"! Perhaps there are SGP groupies already with this in mind? It is fortunate I don't fly anywhere from Cardiff or Bristol airports as otherwise I could add regular SGP traveller Phil Morris to this speedway slept with list. During over two decades long-distance train travel with the London and South East branch of the Sunderland AFC Supporters Club to most of our home and away games, I developed an enthusiasm for a fun sideline in "people asleep on the train" photography. Similarly, this flight showcases many deep but discombobulated sleepers contorting themselves into the available seat space while trying to snatch forty winks. Peculiarly, close-by strangers are quite defensive of this perceived invaded privacy of sleepers they don't know, despite the legality of photography in such public areas. The random seating logic of bargain airfares dictates it is nowadays more-or-less impossible to sit with people you work with without extra cost, inconvenience at time of booking and much additional faff. This is, of course, often a blessing and welcome respite. Though Nigel and Kelvin appear to genuinely enjoy each other's company on their Boys-on-Tour long weekends away with additional speedway commentary, curry and Irish pubs thrown in, they too sit apart. Nigel, Kelvin and myself are transplanted by the BA algorithms to the rear of this A320, while their remaining BSI freelance colleagues with greater frequent flier status get to sit further forwards. In the row behind me, Nigel would be the ideal candidate for some public transport sleeper photography as he is one of those typical but fun head back and mouth completely open photogenic subjects whose muscle relaxation prompts occasional severe neck bobble and multiple surprise wake-ups. In the genre of sleeper photography, this common pose is known as The Tortoise. Nigel's close-cropped hairstyle adds lustre to this pose. Kelvin sleeps way more decorously. No surprise as it is definitely an essential skill to master during a long-track and speedway career of snatched sleep in vans, hotels, airports and flights.

Even if you had no knowledge of anything to do with speedway, should they be awake, willing and polite (not a guaranteed combination) you could have a high-level expert conversation with almost any modern rider about flying. Airline by airline and airport by airport, especially obscure and regional ones. They know from often bitter experience practically all the plane configurations, airport layouts (and where to doze or sleep), check-in desk positions, hold and cabin baggage allowances, drop-off points, catering availability, parking locations and booking rules. It could well be their Mastermind subject. Hard-won frequent flier knowledge, tips and tricks is an unexpected expertise thrown in for free for many riders during most careers making their living riding speedway. As we queue to de-plane, from their conversation, I gather that all the SGP commentary team's flights aren't usually quite so scheduled or commodious. Kelvin sings the praises of the chance of some in-flight rest and also some further sultry sunshine in central Europe. From Franco Tudman Airport on the outskirts of Zagreb in Croatia, the SGP entourage gather back together for immediate travel to nearby Slovenia, either to the track in Krsko or their hotel in Ljubljana. If they do go to the track, only torrential rain awaits rather than any practice. So much rain falls, parts of the track flood. Though they lack the range of equipment the SGP organisers in Malilla had on hand to ensure the meeting went ahead, the Krsko track also enjoys the luxury of good drainage with the added advantage of a robust (aka stony) surface. They also have local weather knowledge and forecasts so, despite the flooding, laugh off online anxieties of visiting fans.

The last time I worked in Zagreb was during the war. Madness when you look back. There was war tax (20%) along with equal numbers of prostitutes and drinkers in my hotel bar. Strange to say with the sound of fighting only ten kilometres away, you still felt safe because of thick fogs so dense they were dangerous. As was driving because of the other reckless drivers or confident gun toting police at the mostly "unofficial" checkpoints. Non-eastern European hard currencies were king. Cash was generally. Though Eastern Europe is blessed with beautiful countryside and marvellous train networks, we drove round Hungary and the republics of the former Yugoslavia back then. The borders of, let alone the differences between Slovenia, Croatia, Bosnia and Herzegovina, Macedonia, Montenegro and Serbia were harder to figure out as a foreigner but invariably known to the nearest inch by locals. Generally the people, countryside, buildings, views, food and the wine – though not the bone fish local delicacy from Lake Balaton – stood out. People were welcoming, made do and lived for the day. Visiting Zagreb was a highlight and it is good to return decades later under different circumstances. Bathed in warm sunshine everything looks better. As a non-resident, I have always had a sneaking regard bordering on love for communist era public housing. Viewed from the windows of the (old style) passenger touring coach that serves as the airport shuttle, the city suburbs look lush and prosperous – though the social housing vibe and characteristics architecturally still remains strong. Zagreb city centre appears transformed. The clean stone of its buildings look magnificent and its tourist landmarks are crowded. The flower and fruit market smells lovely. The various ticket operations at the main railway station still work to old-school Eastern European practices and hours so close early and studiously observe their 50-minute lunch and two separate tea breaks. Refreshingly for a traveller keen to go down memory lane, little English is spoken. There are completely separate sections of the building for ticket sales and travel information. Timetables to far flung exotic destinations are on display. Signage and guidance can elude inattentive visitors. There are no ticket machines I saw. Even for the anxious, it is hard to miss the direct lunchtime intercity train from platform 1 at Zagreb station to Ljubljana that travels there via various obscure stopping points including Krsko. On a very warm day, despite forecast thunderstorms, the sunshine bodes well for the SGP tonight. The journey passes through weather-beaten countryside, rail halts-cum-stations and takes around 90 minutes because of a lengthy stop at the border for thorough passport and security checks.

Though it shares billing on Google Maps with Krsko central bus depot, Krsko railway station and its environs are deserted when the last train before the SGP start time arrives to deposit around ten travellers. Once the train pulls off, it is so dead you wouldn't know it was early Saturday afternoon, let alone that the town is staging an international sports event. There are no taxis and, though I only really have a choice of two directions, other arrivals either don't want to help or can't understand me. According to an article by Charles McKay in *The Voice*, Krsko is so obscure it even fails to make the *Rough Guide to Slovenia*, despite the attraction of its nuclear power station or the Slovenian National Speedway Museum housed in the town library. Charles suggests Krsko is a two-horse town where one has died and other is at its funeral. In the baking heat, I want to choose my road direction alongside the Sava river well. Luckily, Ipswich fans Ian and Nikki Gyte from Great Yarmouth have visited before. They introduce themselves and are walking to the stadium too. It is a straightforward 20 or so minutes' walk across a couple of bridges to then follow the lower level bankside walkway that runs parallel to the wide Sava river and a busy road. Our route is mostly lush and tree lined, while the opposite bank is lined with industrial buildings and factories in various states of working order and repair. Known locally for its nuclear power station and cement, some of these industrial building are gloriously dusty (but don't work weekends). Shaking off its deserted one-horse town first impression, viewed from its river valley, Krsko sprawls across the hillsides of this natural bowl. Distant lush green hills beckon with white benign clouds overhead rather than the black and stormy variety forecast. The distinctive coloured (single) grandstand of the Stadion Matije Gubca (the local equivalent of Robin Hood) can be seen ahead well before arrival. The bankside path eventually turns into a side road that runs parallel to various entrances, while the stadium perimeter itself is lined with concession stalls and parked vehicles. Though still many hours before tapes up, there is a low intensity buzz even though workers currently outnumber fans at the event. The usual orange-and-black liveried SGP merchandise stall is supplemented by local food and drinks outlets including the only honey stall of the 2018 series. Samples of this local delicacy taste wonderful but, sadly, I don't make a purchase in case officious airport hand baggage checks will define it as a liquid. There is a summer fete vibe emphasized by the bright warm sunshine, human scale and retro look of most stall. Given the location of Krsko and the travel logistics required to get here, let alone the steep cost of the ticket by local standards, impulse buyers and walk-up custom will be in very short supply. In fact, tickets were hard to buy full stop via the SGP website. Indeed, tickets for Cardiff next year (September 2019) were on sale well before Krsko tickets became available. Setting aside the basic ineptitude, SGP rights holders BSI clearly don't care about such customer-service matters or important details that impact ordinary fans. Once BSI have banked their event fees from sub-licensing the right to stage this meeting to the local club/promoter, gained financial support from the local council and, of course, already received monies for the sale of series television broadcast rights, they just don't care two hoots about the SGP fans or our experience of the various customer-service touch points.

Around the time the Speedway Grand Prix rights got sold by the FIM to Benfield Sports International (as, I think, BSI Speedway were known then) until 2021, it could be argued that the latest iteration of British speedway club scene had already reached its high-water mark in terms of product quality. In Ipswich of all places too. That is certainly often the opinion of many keen Witches fans of a certain vintage. Their team back then had Tomasz Gollob and Tony Rickardsson, plus Chris Louis, Savalas Clouting, Scott Nicholls and that Czech rider almost named after a make of Swedish car Toni Svab. I can almost name these riders without hesitation without even being a Witches fan or consulting Mrs Google. Maybe I don't have the line up quite right or even the year. I am guessing 1998, something like that. Whenever they won the treble. For those who believe speedway is really a team sport – and I certainly think it is – rather than an individual one: which is the style favoured by lesser speedway markets where they don't have really enough riders – America or Australia – or, indeed, the inclination to regularly stage such team racing. "Proper" speedway nations like Sweden, Poland, Denmark, Britain, Germany and other European nations all regularly put on team league racing. Though we didn't know it at the time, collectively rather than just at Ipswich, it could be argued that we never really had it so good since in British speedway in the 21st century. Much more given to real or imagined nostalgia than living in the present, speedway fans and promoters like nothing better than to look backwards to whatever is their particular choice of a golden era. Obviously enough, this is usually determined by their age or when and where they first watched their speedway. Or, more accurately, where they were taken to watch speedway first. For me, then, it is Reading in 1975 and the few years afterwards. In popularity and attendance terms, speedway has robustly flourished many times – post world war two and in the 1970s, for example, before dying back again. This has been the both natural and commercial cycle. Like forest fires destroy the dead wood in order to rejuvenate the flora, fauna and animal life of the woodland, the speedway forest has had its peaks and troughs. It survives the vagaries of fashion, politics and economics. Here, now, definitely isn't the place to rehearse the many theories of why that was or how we might try to engineer a return to these halcyon salad days. That would require another prolix book with too many pages. Though, obviously, to help us avoid unforced errors we do have the handy rule of thumb that whatever Paul Burbidge advocates as possible solutions – squads, fixed night racing – is going to be stupidly destructive and the complete opposite of the correct course(s) of action. Anyways, that Ipswich team symbolised a rare time of optimism. Many teams were strong and crowds similarly robust or, at least, comparatively good, Sky Sports television was about to dip its feet in live SGP broadcasts. As a result of this success, Sky Sports then went on to show British league club speedway broadcasts live too. Arguably, things had already peaked or were about to be destroyed by the sale of these broadcast rights since live meetings delivered the notional cachet of wider acclaim and fame, while also gifting the buntz of significant additional monies to the top-tier clubs. Sadly, the clubs mostly squandered this bounty on rewarding themselves or short-term expenditure items. In tandem with these broadcasts, rider pay rates rose so this meant better standard (aka foreign) riders rode here and stayed longer. For a period, such riders wanted to continue to regularly race in the UK rather than just part-serve their initial apprenticeship here before departing for mainland Europe. Sadly too, there was an inevitable structural tension between "star" riders competing in the SGP and in British speedway. As the SGP series rapidly expanded to meet BSI's commercial ambitions and revenue goals rather than for organic or strategic reasons, choices had to be made by individual competitors and, over time, British speedway lost comparative appeal to the "top" riders so gradually saw its poor relation status increasingly confirmed. Clearly there many other factors too that changed over time and cumulatively set in train the present decline of the appeal of British speedway racing to riders, TV broadcasters, sponsors and fans – from which, finally, there may actually be no long-term recovery – but, arguably, the most significant of these factors is the BSI era of the SGPs and under them the series expansion. This massively expanded roster of events effectively hollowed out British speedway by taking the better riders away on the best weekend (Friday and Saturday) race nights from May to October. More significantly still, it also successfully sold back an ersatz but believable fake big stage/big occasion version of what was claimed to be "top speedway" to the ready-made audience of speedway fans BSI inherited here. Cardiff was a big event endorsed and enabled both via and by the experts and gaslighting editorialising of the specialist shale telly and print media. Both initially and over time, Cardiff drained the overall speedway pound spend away from the clubs towards the one-off signature occasion and event of the British GP. Of course, this didn't happen overnight and required the collusion (both deliberate and sincere) of many willing helpers, not least public fan opinion. But – along with the series expansion and UK broadcast monies mainly spent by promoters on riders' wages – the coinciding eras of televised live speedway and the SGP has been disastrous for the health of speedway in Britain. In competitive sport terms but, more importantly, lost revenues.

Whatever the money taken by BSI running speedway events in Britain – whether the annual SGP or the less frequent stagings of World Cup rounds – it definitely hasn't gone back into the development or running of the sport. Neither at the club level nor into helping junior riders progress in any form whatsoever. Obviously enough, the SGP rights holders have no legal obligation to do so. An informative comparison could possibly be made with Arsene Wenger as he started at Arsenal fractionally after BSI secured the SGP rights and has now finally left the club having been widely judged by its fans and shareholders to have long overstayed his welcome. Prior to being forced to exit stage right, Wenger is credited with "revolutionising" many aspects of professional football in the UK. His impact and influence have been deep and lasting in many areas including tactics, research, player recruitment, care and diet. Indeed, his impact upon nutrition is so ubiquitous and far-reaching within UK sport generally that it has even reached the faraway obscure shores of speedway rider lifestyles. Wenger delivered numerous trophies, developed and signed star players and then also still managed to run and field a team starved of the necessary financial investment while those monies went into building (and servicing the debt of) the best football stadium in Britain. Wenger spurred many imitators at club and even in the national team level in England as well as created an impact and legacy that will outlive his tenure. In the same period, BSI have invested nothing into rider development anywhere in Europe and, beyond annually staging a bigger version of the Brighton Bonanza indoor meeting British riders can aspire to race in one day, had zero positive structural or lasting impact. BSI have contributed nothing to the greater good of speedway in Britain. Unless, of course, if you count that they enabled one of their sponsors to provide a more prestige version of start line girls at their showcase Cardiff meeting and SGP events elsewhere. Worse still, simultaneously, BSI and the SGP have arguably been the most major contributor to the ongoing but slow strangulation, decline and possible demise of British speedway. They have had very willing help from the speedway media – individually and collectively – and fans as well as from the associations and trade bodies (BSPA, SCB, ACU and FIM) tasked with safeguarding and administrating the sport here in Britain. But, fundamentally, if this were a murder investigation, detectives would follow the money in order to see who might have an interest or benefit from the murder. On that basis, the perpetrator is clearly Colonel BSI in the Millennium Stadium with his stuffed-to-overflowing wallet.

Millions have been – and continue to be – sucked out of the British speedway financial ecosystem in plain sight aided and abetted by willing and uninquisitive helpers throughout British speedway but especially in the tame often compromised speedway media. BSI have made their lucre by exploiting the staging rights the FIM, arguably, didn't own to grant in the first place. Whomever received then leveraged these rights inherited a ready-made train set of fans, television audiences, committed-to-appear riders and a roster of pre-existing Europewide venues. If this were politics, this award/gift of rights would also require reward in recognition, significant investments or payments in kind. The FIM have certainly – according to BSI annual accounts filed at Companies House – regularly got fulsome benefit in the form of annual seven-figure "royalties" paid. The executive team of BSI never had the vision or smarts to get away so comprehensively with their audacious putsch without the paid or unpaid help of many willing others with speedway and the FIM but particularly the vision, guidance, hard work, abilities and contacts of Ole Olsen. SGP rights holders BSI have subsequently been very much helped along by a small coterie of freelance speedway media boosters as well as an *ad hoc* ever-changing roster of promoters, sponsors and hangers-on easily satisfied with a few free tickets, back stage access passes along with the notional "celebrity" and reflected glory of the bright spotlight of temporary (for one night only) fame. Almost as bad as the money getting lifted by a private company with no interest or obligation to speedway in Britain, without supervision BSI compounded their offence by expanding the series (from its initial five weekends to as many as twelve) to occupy the prime race nights of Friday (for practice) and Saturday (for the event) every year, often from late April to early October. This took and has taken riders, speedway spend and fans elsewhere. Media boosters – people often employed directly or indirectly by the rights holders or associated service companies (whether broadcasters or sponsors) – have and continue to laud the spectacle while ignoring inconvenient strategic, logistical and financial conflicts. They report what they see and tell it as they see it to underline the masquerade of their editorial independence. Yet, decades into their SGP gigs, they somehow still studiously leave alone posing possible difficult questions or joining the dots about any possible direct connection between the rise of the privatised SGP and the current ongoing decline of British speedway (which they often also try to deny with relentless positivity and empty happy talk). Those with fingers in many pies and hands in many pockets, don't even acknowledge – beyond re-arranging the metaphorical deckchairs or adding Poundshop tinsel to the tree – that there might be serious structural governance and supervision issues to address. Every investigative stone remains unturned, while the SGP monies flood the BSI bank and balance sheet.

Once past security and inside the Stadion Matije Gubca, sun bakes the pits area. Some mechanics work but with bike checks still to take place or tyres yet to be issued, there is a lull in activity. Those who are there rest in the pit bay shade beside bikes missing their back wheels. The majority of the riders have yet to show up. Up the slight incline that leads towards bend one, the coral-coloured track looks in pristine condition. Either bathed in sunshine or dappled by sections of shade thrown by the imposing solitary grandstand, the track looks remarkably dry given the flood that prevented practice yesterday. Upon much closer inspection, its surface layer looks more made from stones and gravel than shale. In fact, the track isn't coral coloured. This is an optical illusion when seen from a distance. Up close grey-white surface gravel stands out against the darker base layer of the track. Out on the sun-bathed centregreen, after posing for photographers, Tai Woffinden does the most British thing I have seen him ever do when he suddenly strips off to go topless and play a very brief impromptu game of pick-up football out there. Though enthusiastic, Tai shouldn't give up the day job. Rather refreshingly in an era of lithe speedway riders aiming for low fat percentages and chiselled gym bodies brought on by copious exercise, catching balls thrown by a part-time PT instructor and their primarily food free nutrition plans, Woffinden clearly puts his main efforts into family life or hours in the tattoo parlour rather than the gym or sauna. Given Woffinden innovates and marches to his own tune in other areas of his SGP preparations, it is no surprise he proudly bucks the latest trend in elite rider speedway physiques. With the inevitable weight gain of new fatherhood behind him, Tai's toplessness and residual slight will-to-paunch also sends another subtle but ultra-confident message to his erstwhile rivals: I don't have to diet and change my life to beat you. While they follow nutrition plans to the letter, obsessively count the calories as well as strain away inside the self-inflicted hell of carefully tailored personal exercise regimes developed by self-promoting regional PT instructors, Tai's body fat percentages reveals that he prefers to spend guilt-free time with his fridge and family. Or supervising work on his house and the many acres of the grounds of his Midlands estate. It must really depress Tai's SGP rivals that while they try to diet their way to his glory, Woffinden prefers to actively seek the everyday normality of an enjoyable family life. Clearly Tai's body is also his main canvas of self-expression via the medium of tattoos rather than exercise. As Tai slowly walks topless off the centregreen, we get a brief tantalising but sweaty glimpse of the full dark ink majesty and wide repertoire of the upper body art that his kevlar work uniform struggles to hide when fully togged up for speedway.

The paraphernalia needed to professionally stage and broadcast a Speedway Grand Prix already appears fully in place except for last-minute checks and snagging. The air fences are inflated. The centregreen furniture and equipment is set out ready and waiting. Even the only innovation of the season is also already on display – Monster Energy's sponsor seating. Though hailed as another thrilling SGP innovation almost on par with the development of the Apollo space programme by Peter Oakes in his weekly multi-page *Speedway Star* column, it looks much more Blue Peter than NASA. Though there is no visible sticky-back plastic, this "innovation" looks more like a discarded failed attempt to make a fairground ride by welding three sets of two surplus rally drivers bucket seats together. Each narrow seat comes complete with full safety harnesses and awaits the snug fit bottoms of its lucky Monster Energy valued-client occupants. Said sponsor seats are positioned in the middle of the last corner quadrant of the centregreen. Though a good notionally safe distance from the track, you have to question whether it is a potential sponsor death trap. It is highly unlikely that any of its users would be able to flee to avoid any high velocity bucking-bronco-esque riderless bike if it ever manages to escape its pilot. YouTube has an enjoyable sub-genre of speedway bikes careering randomly around the centregreen until gravity, fuel, fence or foolhardy fan impedes its wild progression. Even if the people chosen by Monster Joe to be sitting ducks manage to evade said ghost riders, this viewing platform isn't really fit for purpose as its rally car seats welded together design severely impedes all backward glances towards any back straight action. Though watching from the centregreen is a huge thrill and unique way to experience seeing speedway, you have to admire how Monster Energy have taken their self-proclaimed reputation for edginess and given it a memorable twist by their brave decision to invite the remote possibly of legal action from those injured, maimed or – heaven forefend – the family members of those killed in the course of honouring peculiar tasting non-alcoholic beverages by savouring some SGP race action. Arguably, there is more jeopardy for the clients Monster entertain as airfences made of flesh than the air-filled variety riders clad in helmets, back protectors, kevlars and gloves usually crash into. Oblivious to the killer seats lurking in full view in front of them, stadium staff with various coloured hi-vis tops resuming chatting amongst themselves now the brief centregreen topless low-skill football entertainment has finished. With the gates yet open, there are no fans to supervise as they try to bagsy the best positions on the gently inclined grassy banks that surround the track that provide the primary viewing positions for those without grandstand tickets. Arguably the best seats for also seeing the pits action – or, at least, the to and fro – are those in the temporary stand erected in front of some low-slung buildings on the grass banking in the vicinity of the exit of the first bend. These overlook the track in one direction as well as the pits and its track access in the other. If judged by ticket price expense, the permanent grandstand that overlooks the start line and runs almost the length of the home straight from the exit of the fourth corner to the entry to the first bend is the place to watch from. This grandstand structure is a riot of colour – blue and green seats contrast with walkways in bright safety yellow, while banners and numerous Slovenian national flags that line the grandstand base colour compete with the ubiquitous distinctive orange-and-black of the SGP branding.

Back outside the stadium, there still aren't many fans here yet. Those that are look lost for anything to do to pass the time before the turnstiles bother to open. Everyone has a way to busy themselves. They chat with friends, collect tickets, buy programmes, stand by the closed SGP merchandise stall or watch Monster rig staff make their preparations, peer through gaps in the fence at an empty track or, better still, a tented sub-section of the pits where blokes with duties unknown sit resting in the shade. The bright side to BSI apparently deliberately holding down attendances is that the outside stadium café bar unusually still has a choice of free tables and available chairs. Now the locals in the pits have reassured me that there definitely won't be any rain, I can safely sit in the shaded bar area with friendly Ipswich fans Ian and Nikki to watch the SGP world walk by. I have just missed the dressed ready-for-action Monster Energy women relax before their sexually objectifying race day duties fully kick in. Of all the regular parachuted-in SGP staff, and in sharp contrast to many overly serious BSI events people, they appear to genuinely relish and enjoy their duties. And, sometimes, even have fun doing it, albeit not so much during the repetitive, ultra-mundane and mind-numbing parts. Of course, manic perma-smiles come with their job descriptions. The Monster women strike me as focussed and highly professional both in public and also in their behind-the-scenes work spaces. Whenever you encounter them in public, the pits or stadium perimeter *en route* to or back from the Monster rig events they remain ultra-professional. I doubt they are well paid. Plus, I would expect strong competition for the positions so career stability, let alone longevity, is unlikely. To be fair too, the blokes that staff the Monster pits drinks stall at each event are also extremely amiable and very much always on – whether posing for photos or being relentlessly positive, happy and super-helpful doing their jobs. Perhaps, Monster actually formally contract this level of customer delight and engagement that they appear to have their staff genuinely deliver? At least, the Monster women don't have to actually drink the stuff. I forget to ask Ian and Nikki what they did drink and eat.

Ian and Nikki sit are long-time speedway fans and also of the SGP so have seen many changes during their years watching the sport and travelling to European events. In a sense they typify the new breed of SGP fan co-opted by the series as it has been staged by BSI. They already had deep pre-existing club loyalty and went along regularly so were already effectively a ready-made target audience ripe for the plucking. Understandably, many existing fans succumb to the glamour of following riders they admire (and others they don't) as they race elsewhere on the European continent for individual World Championship glory. It is also a weekend away in climes comparatively exotic, watching something they love. Ian and Nikki enjoy the whole experience. "They do hold them in out of the way places. I think it is because the riders don't like temporary tracks. We were last at Krsko ten years ago. We sat by a speaker and our whole bodies vibrated. We met Paul what's-his-name [Bellamy] on the way back and he told us to email him after and he sent us some pits passes for another GP. We haven't been to Cardiff in protest the last two years at the price of the tickets. £75! We boycott it and watched it at home on the telly instead. We used to go to everything on a bike that moved but we don't any more. It is cheaper to go to Prague. It is the price variations I don't get to be honest? Why is Prague cheaper than a home GP? It wasn't in the EU when we first used to go. It is now and it's still much cheaper? Admittedly we booked ahead but we came here for £500 all in including flights – Nigel and Kelvin were on ours – and hotel. We came on the train you did as it's the only one that gets here beforehand. We can just sit and enjoy ourselves here. We still love the GPs but they do rely on the fact that we're passionate. We're STILL waiting for them to go to new places they promised! There's been some cancellations too but, to be fair, they've been fine. In Sweden – Gothenburg – they abandoned it half way through when they could declare a result and not give any money back. It wasn't really racing. It was a lovely sunny day beforehand. We had half an hour sleep in the room and, when we woke, it was pouring with rain. The problem is that most people don't have any interest in speedway. I listen to talkSPORT and Radio 5 and we can have a Speedway World Champion and it's not even mentioned! In Ipswich there's good coverage in the *Evening Star* but that's local. I reckon it's half-and-half not being in the news – half BSI not being interested and half there being no interest. All of us are at the point where our clubs have folded or could fold. At Ipswich, we're lucky. Five or six years ago, we dropped down so are still going. But there's Coventry who are finished. Newport, er, Weymouth, Eastbourne – well, they dropped down even further to the National League to keep going – and Peterborough dropped down too. Lakeside went down two leagues to the National League but have now come back up to the Championship. Birmingham went close to going under. Those are just the ones we know about or can think of. Many clubs are just about surviving. You know that the FIM or the GP aren't putting any money back into the sport. I don't even think the prize money is that much for the riders. It certainly wasn't a massive amount a while back. They used to be able to win a Fiat van or some engines. It was more about deals than cash for them. What they wanted was sponsorship and equipment. To be fair, there isn't the money about like there is in Premiership football but, what there is, they don't see!" Nikki nods agreement with her husband and also reminds us that the musical entertainment on offer isn't what it once was when the GPs first started, especially at Cardiff after stringent cost-cutting took hold. "They used to have relatively big-name performers playing before or during the interval. People like Tony Hadley from Spandau Ballet. Tony Christie when he had a hit again with Amarillo. Bonnie Tyler, Belinda Carlisle, Chas & Dave. Then some weren't quite so good or famous like that X-Factor girl, er, Jamilla or the dance acts. The best one of all wasn't at Cardiff, it was Right Said Fred at Gelsenkirchen. I don't think they have any known singers or performers at Cardiff now. Do you? I don't know for sure as we haven't been."

Though they had a band playing covers loudly at Cardiff this year, rights holders BSI mostly appear to have officially sub-contracted primary responsibility for fan entertainment to one of their main sponsors, Monster Energy. The publicity posters used to explicitly acknowledge this as "the Speedway World Championships, presented by Monster Energy". Nowadays they just assume everyone knows they are a key "partner" or it is just obviously so since Monster provide the start girls, centregreen brand and podium furniture. It is canny of Monster (and good negotiation by Monster Joe) to get this brand dominance WITHOUT paying to be the main series sponsor. More importantly, Monster nowadays are effectively the major component of almost all the "entertainment" on offer beforehand to fans at SGPs. On the whole this is 45 minutes or so of loud music before the meeting serenading two different sessions – one with a sub-set of SGP riders signing autographs onto pre-printed cards or programmes and another earlier one where the Monster women give away various company-branded items including cans, race bibs, T-shirts or calendars. Depending upon the size of the crowd, these are either handed over or thrown into the crowd by the riders present and the Monster women. At Cardiff, they run a so-called "fan zone" for more hours quite some distance away from the stadium itself. This is mainly a few different autograph signing sessions with an extra Q&A, a few old bikes, music, plus free (different coloured) cans of Monster and the odd brief talk thrown in. A few years back the meeting start time at Cardiff switched to an earlier time (currently 5pm) and it now starts the earliest of the SGPs as the remainder all start at 7.04pm European time. The move to earlier was presented by the rights holders as a fan friendly response to steep hotel prices, lack of rooms and, weirdly, the time of the last train to London. Even if we ignore that it is a heroic and erroneous assumption that most speedway fans who use public transport come from London, it is a fact of speedway life there are very few functioning clubs in the whole of the South East full stop let alone the Greater London area. BSI systematically encouraging Cardiff SGP fans to evacuate and completely leave the city, area or region after the meeting is a massive slap in the face for Welsh tourism. Especially given the Welsh Government provide BSI with financial support to help ensure that the British SGP is staged at the Principality Stadium. Indeed, Visit Wales advertise on the giant screens and in the programme, so deliberately discouraging overnight stays is hardly supportive activity by BSI. That said, by unhappy coincidence expanding the fan zone hours until later afternoon and starting the meeting early also really kills speedway fan/tourist spend in the city centre as well as eliminates the need for BSI – as Cardiff is one of the few events they actually deign to stage themselves – to invest in vaguely notable but declining musical acts. Getting inside the stadium early to see the "name" musical acts booked used to be a big part of the advertised SGP proposition and one of the notional "thrills" of attendance. Not putting on such acts is clearly a cost saving. BSI relentlessly advertise Cardiff events in the trade press (aka the *Speedway Star*) for all of 12 months beforehand, primarily through "early bird" discount price promotions that require a degree in maths plus an element of comparing apples with oranges and bananas while counting the number of letters in your star sign in order to arrive at the few pennies specifics of the fractional reduction offered. Almost the only way the tickets for next year could go on sale any earlier than they already do would be for fans to buy them as they exit through the turnstiles. Ian notes, "whether it's what speedway fans want or not, the entertainment at most GPs is majorettes and a few laps from the local motorcycle club plus, maybe, a few fireworks at the end."

Ian and Nikki can take or leave the involvement of Monster Energy at the SGPs. "The Monster girls were here having a drink just after you left. Dressed ready for the meeting. I don't reckon they get paid much. I can't bear any of those energy drinks. Just the taste and sweetness puts me off. That Monster Joe also puts me off too every time he comes on the telly. Which is very often. He seems to like the cameras. They do sponsor their riders quite well, I imagine. There's Greg, Dudek and Holder and Tai, of course. They have had a few World Champions so it is worth it for them. Tai will win again this year unless something unusual happens. Funny that because years ago we were flying back from a GP – to Bristol, I think it much have been, because Nigel Pearson was speaking to The Colonel, they called him – and saying Tai would never be World Champion because he wasn't dedicated and had the wrong attitude. You wouldn't guess that from how he talks about him nowadays!" Given the contractual stranglehold on weekends that the FIM zealously enforce for SGP rights holders BSI, rival competitions and promoters really struggle to get going. Even the four events of the rival Speedway European Championship (SEC) series struggles to grab rider, fan or sponsor mindshare. Though the racing has often been good and arguably very competitive – at least according to their English language commentators David Rowe and Sam Ermolenko – the UK television viewing figures are even smaller than the SGP. Which given the low and swiftly lowering bar is, frankly, hard to imagine as possible. Apparently, you need a microscope to see them. Like many fans, Ian and Nikki initially took an active interest in the SEC. "We watched it, but they seemed more like normal meetings than GPs? It wasn't high profile and lacked proper marketing and merchandising. Emil favoured it for a while but then dropped out." When asked to name some innovations brought to speedway by the executives and boffins behind the rise of the BSI era SGP, nothing really springs to mind. "Air fences? Maybe not. They were starting to come in anyway. There were already start line girls too. Though, to be fair, they have moved on from what they were. It is sometimes on in more exciting places to go to, maybe that's what they brought? Some of them are out of the way but we love the GPs. Thinking about it, if we are looking for specifics there doesn't appear to be any innovations really! Not that we can think of, anyway."

Though Phil Lanning claims in the programme that the 2018 SGP series "has had everything; tears, tantrums and titanic battles. The racing has simply been ferocious, arguably the most competitive SGP series ever". When it comes to recalling most exciting and memorable races from this season, Ian and Nikki initially struggle to recall or remember their own top three really notable races. "Races of the Season is hard. It hasn't finished yet, obviously. In the last GP, Zmarzlik looked like he would walk it and then in the final he didn't get out. I remember that but then I had £80 on it so it was notable for personal reasons rather than any particular race. In my top three would be the bike bouncing over the fence at Cardiff. There was the Nicki and Tai dust up though Nicki did nothing wrong at all. There are very few memorable races unless there is an incident. Looking back, more spring to mind. There's Bomber taking Greg on the last corner to win at Cardiff in 2007. There's Jason Crump falling off his bike on the victory lap, I think that was in Norway. Or the time that Tony Rickardsson did a lap of honour in Norway and everyone thought that was it and he was going to retire and, then, he didn't. Actually there was Prague where Tony Rickardsson got his hand caught in the bike front wheel and Tomasz spotted it straight away. Immediately. And took a spanner and had the wheel off in no time. He was such a good rider. Probably the best, really. Not just GPs, anywhere! There was the Prague meeting that went on until midnight. It was incredible it was on at all, they were still blading it at 10pm." When it comes to memorable meetings one will always stand out above all others for the Gyte family. The first ever meeting "when it opened" at the new Belle Vue National Speedway Stadium track in Manchester. Queueing beforehand with their son and heavily pregnant daughter-in-law, her waters broke in the queue and she was rushed inside the stadium. "She gave birth to Isla in the medical room before it had even been used by the riders!"

With the witching hour of tapes up slowly approaching, cannier fans congregate by the street access gate close to the riders' van parking area adjacent to the pits, that they apparently demolished a multi-storey car park to create. Just as George Best once advised me that you should always lurk in the vicinity of the ladies toilet area in nightclubs to meet the best women, armed with souvenir programmes rather than autograph books or memorabilia to sign, strategically minded fans police the only two ways for riders to enter their business end of the stadium. It is old-fashioned and sweetly optimist to assume that riders will arrive by van. Transporting the bikes, paraphernalia and freshly tuned or specially selected engines long distances mostly falls to the SGP mechanics rather than the performers. Though their vans give some much-needed privacy (and often a makeshift bed) riders prefer to psyche themselves up or rest elsewhere. Some of the great and the good do dribble by. In the company of a similarly blonde woman – who I take to be his 29-year-old girlfriend, guide and positive "inspiration" (it says on his Instagram) Carolina Jonasdotter – a distracted Freddie Lindgren with his hair up high and proud in a small and slightly ridiculous ponytail curled on top of his head (almost exactly like it shows on his pits bay panel photograph) evades all the autograph hunters as easily as he slides past rivals spinning back wheels. Even those signature hunters whose pits passes grant access to the outer sanctum public areas of the pits. After a season that started so brightly it prompted talk of possible World Championship title glory, loss of form, psychological self-pressure and, latterly, injury as well as possible bad luck hairstyling has badly harshed that anticipatory buzz. Never exactly a mega-watts smiler, Freddie wears the mantle of his own disappointment like a badge of dishonour but also as a shield as it really discourages conversation from well-wishers. All five Monster Energy women make a grand entrance from the street, though their progress is slowed by frequent photo requests. They embrace the adulation and all (polite) requests with practised patient smiley professionalism. Along with the more august arrivals are also the anonymous, hard-working and, this being speedway, probably the not so good or, at least, some chancers. Paul Burbidge is also here too but passes by unrecognised with a quick burst of his trademark nervy hunched scuttle. Burbo carries himself with the purposeful fast walking demeanour of man who just knows he is eventually going to be caught, outed then punished for serious crimes as yet unknown. Based on past performance, these are most likely to be against understatement and thoughtful analysis. Nicki Pedersen wanders in with his current girlfriend. If you are only as old as the woman you hold, then Nicki actively seeks eternal youth. His girlfriend has on distinctive trainers. The one foot I notice has LOVE picked out in capital letters made from imitation diamond effect stones. I don't get to see what is written on the other but expect something smoochy rather than the matching HATE that would appear if we were on remand and if these trainers were knuckles and the diamante stones tattoos.

Over on the far side of the pits, Emil Sayfutdinov has been found by the always heavily made up and smartly dressed – unusually not yet attired in his slightly too tightly tailored dark suit – Polish television commentator and is being marched-cum-led to the punishment block otherwise known as the outside interview area. Possibly because he told Phil Lanning in the programme, "Slovenia is a track I like a lot" or, equally, perhaps it was his implausible claim, "this is a fascinating series"? As usual at any SGP, the interview area is set up within the pits close by the track exit/entry to ease gaining instant rider reaction or live off-the-cuff swear words after (or between) races. Closely followed by a roving cameraman, Emil and the interviewer chat amiably (either in Polish or Russian) until Phil Morris intercepts their purposeful path to say, "Emil, Emil, only good things on these!" Emil looks nonplussed. "Only good things Emil," Morris repeats. Emil doesn't usually come across as a barrel of laughs so almost any jovial but thinly veiled instructions in his third or fourth language – even if vaguely funny – will immediately get somewhat lost in translation. Emil shrugs as he walks on by and, as the handheld camera is raised and accompanying large-headed microphone flourishes, is adjusted into position on his cross on the floor by his interviewer. As the pre-record starts, Monster Energy staff stumble by struggling under the sheer weight of one of the two substantial Monster liveried metal post-cum-columns. At each meeting, they place these columns carefully to fully maximise their tangential appearance direct camera shots during the meeting. In this instance, they are placed either side of the pre-race muster area where later riders will sit astride their bikes as they patiently await the instruction from serial camera-bomber Mr Morris to go out on track. Once each column is roughly in position, their placement is painstakingly adjusted to ensure almost constant visibility albeit without quite interfering with riders nervously micro-adjusting their bikes, kevlars or googles as they stave off the boredom of the irregular wait times required to synch up with the broadcast schedules and various interval advert durations. It is only ever extremes. Either the riders are sent straight out or they have to hang about inordinately. To be fair to the SGP, particularly in comparison to the experience at some British speedway clubs (who are staging 15 rather than 23 heats), they often do run very efficient meetings. There is something to be said for this efficiency. Speedway is a simple sport and fans don't come to witness long gaps between races intermittently filled by endless circuits of the track by tractors. That said, SGPs serve up a minimum of 45 minutes of tractors at every meeting too. These efficiencies are television satellite access and broadcaster (advert) schedule driven and led, so come at the expense of the enjoyment of fans attending. Inside the stadium, paying customers get served staccato bursts of sets of four races. Everything is a rush, albeit interspersed with lengthy track work delays – more tractors! – between sets. Riders no longer do victory laps but head swiftly off the track as if in an emergency evacuation almost while the chequered flag still flutters. The SGP spectacle is rigorously co-ordinated almost solely for the benefit of screen viewers located elsewhere. Either absent at home or else forced to watch as a pacifier until lights out in institutional settings and places where you don't choose the channels you watch. The riders pits muster area is the secret sauce of the SGP broadcasting equation since it enables any temporary overruns in the broadcast schedule timings to be massaged and managed on the fly and, thereby, accommodate the inevitable but random delays caused during any meeting by infringements, re-runs and crashes. While one heat races, the riders for the next get lined up ready for immediate action in the speedway stationary equivalent of a holding pattern. These movements are supervised by the ubiquitous Phil Morris. Though, titled FIM Track Director, this is really glorified parking attendant work, albeit done with the fully blown officiousness of a traffic warden with a lucrative incentive scheme. It continues to surprise that Morris doesn't demand a special uniform or salutes. During longer delays, panning shots of riders ready and waiting sends out the reassuring message of impending further action to viewers, while it also helps build a smidgeon of anticipation or maintains the illusion of tension.

Predictably, Greg Hancock arrives in a bubble of well-wishers dispensing the elaborate handshakes that befits the Projects childhood he never had. He is a serial and flamboyant greeter. Of anyone in his path. He is the speedway equivalent of fast-flowing volcanic lava, albeit no one gets burnt to a cinder. Staff, fellow riders, sponsors, media and especially fans in search of autographs and selfies plus random passers-by all risk embrace or the full beam wattage of his perma-smile. Greg is charm, warmth and enthusiasm personified. Patient too. Unlike so many of his scowling SGP contemporaries with toothy delight always at the ready, Greg "The Grin" Hancock gives very good bonhomie. Some other SGP riders do briefly embrace the apparently unslakeable fan adulation but do so dutifully without his warmth or genuine enthusiasm. Some other riders don't even bother to try to fake it or thinly disguise their contempt. Or, indeed, possible shyness. Given how limited, manufactured and pre-programmed these fan interactions are with erstwhile "top" riders nowadays at the SGPs, this is a poor show. In terms of engagement and availability, Greg is World Champion almost every time he sets foot in the pits or in its vicinity. If there were to be a lifetime award for the modern era, Greg would scoop the prize. Lurking close by watchfully is his beta minus proxy and minder Josh Gudgeon. His regularly changing but grandiose job title is often specifically namechecked (and, sometimes, announced) in the "Off the Beaten Track" column of the *Speedway Star* written by his grandfather. Mentions, namechecks and drive by job title announcements happen so often that many suspect that there is some sort of bonus scheme or bingo competition in operation. Guaranteed regular column inches in the

Star for Josh's clients is definitely a competitive advantage rivals can neither best nor boast. Greg learnt and knew how to secure extensive media coverage as well as how to skilfully press the speedway flesh of fans, promoters and sponsors long before Josh was even born. Greg must still feel the need for the extra help, status, prestige and validation that employing such a freelance staffer notionally implies if not confers. Street product demonstrators judge themselves by how their showmanship builds what they call (among themselves) "an edge". Aka the distance from the eye of the storm they occupy to the periphery of the interest they create. The longer the distance from the eye to the edge, the higher the number of punters and, so, the better the chance of a sale. Though Greg has no specific product to sell beyond his friendliness, his currency of acclaim is monetised at one degree of separation in the reflected glory it provides for existing sponsors. Or how it attracts future sponsorship prospects who also fancy bathing in the warm glow of this esteem. Though spacious, even the layout of these SGP pits at Krsko struggle to accommodate the overflow interest as fans and well-wishers hover and worship around Hancock's pit bay. Ever the professional, Greg relentlessly poses and smiles like a synchronised swimmer gasping for air between sub-routines. He signs with swift but practised flamboyance whatever is proffered for signature by fans. Usually his photograph as it appears in the official Nigel Pearson edited Curtis Sport produced programme. Of course, black pen signatures on shiny paper stock against a black background won't ever create either an attractive or lasting memento. Such caveats sink without trace on this tidal wave of Hancock signature requests.

Stood looking onto the hubbub is German based Australian photographer Chris Horne. Though he is an authorised and accredited SGP photographer I ask, "do you want me to take your photo with Greg?" He declines. "He'll often try to drag me into them but I take them not be in them. I could get one. I've known Greg and his family many years and taken many photos of him and the kids. Greg is a charming man. He would give you the shirt off his back, if you needed it!" Talk of Greg's impending beatification is briefly interrupted by yet another announcement in a Welsh accent that booms out over the stadium loudspeakers. "Riders meeting in 15 minutes!" It is the third such announcement. They blast out at five-minute intervals. These are the speedway version of the hammy urgent instructions most often heard on soon-to-be-sunk German submarines ("Achtung! Achtung! Dive! Dive!") in crackly black-and-white war films of yesteryear. Phil Morris – for it is he – wastes no opportunity to remind the riders of his power and their obligations, even though – in this instance – their attendance is mandatory. Giving the current showboaty FIM Race Director greater access to a microphone at SGPs could either be a huge error or a masterstroke. Given how they use referees with microphones to such good informative effect during American football matches, personally, I would love for BSI or the FIM to get Phil throat-miked up. Rather than just interpret his body language or the wild frenzy of his endlessly eye-catching semaphores, we could instead enjoy the additional entertainment of actually hearing him barking out ineffectual track curation instructions or, indeed, passing on refereeing decisions to incredulous riders during the SGPs. Given the frequency of his elaborate on track mimes and general camera-hogging – arguably even more so than Monster Joe Parsons – I think that we can safely say that Phil could soon be easily persuaded of the need to delight us with his *bon mots* over the stadium speakers too.

In the warmth of the late afternoon Slovenian sunshine, these "Attention Punters" announcements definitely give the pits an old-fashioned holiday camp feel. It is as if the Krsko pits have somehow been twinned with Butlins, Pontins and *Hi-De-Hi*. Quite where Phil's nerve centre of operations is located is a mystery. He is clearly there with stopwatch and ego in hand. For now, we will have to make do with these tantalising but slightly desperate urgent softly lilting Welsh instructions. Well, until such a time as the joint decision is taken by SGP rights holders BSI and FIM – after careful due deliberation in those upscale hotel behind-closed-doors bug-swept-room meetings they also use to determine those wrong but sponsor/partner friendly SGP wild card selections – to invite Phil centre stage with his own microphone at every SGP meeting. And we all know that he would relish adding the further gravitas equipment such as a throat mike provides to his carefully unchosen casual race night get up. Even better, surely there must be extra revenues to be had once the BSI marketing team source some new mug sponsor just gasping out there to seize the opportunity to keep their products a secret by becoming the "Official FIM Speedway Grand Prix Amplification Partner"? Or some such similarly meaningless but grandiose description? "Riders meeting in ten minutes!" I ask Chris if he goes? "No, it's riders only. And their heavies. We have our own meeting." In it an immutable law of bureaucracy, that meetings beget further meetings. Especially at BSI style speedway. "Is it about apertures?"

"No we're told where to go, where not to stand in front of the fans or TV cameras so we don't block or interfere with their view. Mostly it is about 'situational awareness' – though they don't call it that – as we are working where there is possible danger. It is common sense but easy to forget when you get wrapped up in the meeting. Have you ever been involved in a high-performance sport? They [riders] are off the scale. At the line, their heart rate is at least 160-170."

"Fight or flight?"

"It's way beyond that. Their adrenalin is rushing, really rushing. They race with that. They have that level off the track too so you really have to look out for them. It takes me – all of us photographers – two or three hours to come down after a meeting. We feed off the energy and adrenalin. Just think what it is like for the riders to come down after a meeting when they have actually raced and competed?"

Though there are bag security people and even ticket checkers before you gain stadium access, they err towards the indifferent and lacklustre. Perhaps, this is an understandable reaction to the lowly status and comparative obscurity of speedway as a sport in Slovenia? Or, equally, just recognition that a speedway meeting on the outskirts of Krsko won't have any real surge of wannabe freeloaders with fake tickets or vest bombers with tickets but bad intentions. Well-informed walk-up punters are also likely to be thin on the ground as the erstwhile star attraction of Slovenian speedway – Matej Zagar – is out injured so won't ride tonight. Apparently ignoring the significant "support" (aka payments) from those Torben Olsen scrupulously name and acronym checks at length in the programme – "AMD, AMZS and the city of Torun" – that ensure Krsko's selection as a series venue by BSI Speedway IMG, some cynics claim that the World Championships only comes here because Matej is in the series. It is certainly brilliant news for his sponsorship income ("without sponsors, things wouldn't be possible" as Paul Burbidge's hard-hitting interview questions force Matej to shockingly reveal), particularly as he has effectively no real national rival on the international stage. Even though Matej is *hors de combat*, to be honest I did – for once – expect to see him throw aside his offhandness and serial reluctance to engage with the public for some tactical Hancock-esque sponsor fawning. Especially since, like a shark requires perpetual onwards motion, Matej states in the programme, "I just look forward, I want to keep moving". In the swap system that the riders unofficially operate amongst themselves, one such fiat currency is unwanted SGP guest pits passes. Throughout the season at meetings elsewhere, Matej zealously trades his in order to amass a bonanza of pits access for existing or potential sponsors in Krsko. The brutal reality is that this rarest of birds – Slovenian sponsors – don't travel much to SGPs elsewhere. Conversely, most GP rider sponsors also don't bother to make the journey to out-of-the-way and unglamorous Krsko. Though, I fail to catch sight of Matej anywhere all night, it is hard to credit that he would be so lackadaisical as to fail to come along to feel and deliver the sponsor love that the prestige of behind-the-scenes access often subsequently haloes with further or bigger sponsorship dollars. Making everyone come to Krsko – where even Matej allegedly views them as "country bumpkins" – for an SGP he fails to attend is either his revenge on us all or else a brief flicker of his latent but wicked sense of prankster humour.

With just over half an hour to go before tapes up, amazingly – given it was flooded yesterday – they have to water the track. It just goes to show how well gravel drains. As a possible reminder of the regional conflicts that roil this part of the world, the main grandstand walkaway has some half-hearted graffiti reminders of a visit by the self-styled "Bosnian Ultras". Helpfully but hastily written in English with black pen, the handwriting is poorly formed and artistically falls well short of the celebratory, colourful and vivacious tagging ghetto street culture that originally also gave us the elaborate handshakes Greg Hancock and Monster Joe repeatedly culturally appropriate. Beyond the smattering of Slovenian flags that adorn the grandstand and an incredibly lusty rendition of the national anthem later, this is as far as the powerfully felt regional politics visibly intrude. Though the make-up of any SGP crowd is a polyglot mix of only ever white fans drawn from the main and lesser speedway nations, understandably enough, playing the local national anthem provokes varying degrees of patriotism and national pride in the residents of the country staging any meeting. For less well-schooled visitors, it provides the requisite gravitas to go along with the exoticism and actual sound of foreignness. This even happens at Cardiff where they play the Welsh national anthem. Proudly displayed visual patriotism is a standard trope of SGP broadcasts and something BSI take no chance with as they regularly provide the crowd areas in camera shot with cheap plastic flags or suitably coloured cards to hold and wave for the cameras. Although the Slovenian flag is a simple geometric design and only three colours, its complexity, rarity or obscurity has apparently defeated and led the SGP rights holders BSI (or local promoters) not to even bother with the courtesy of such minimal niceties in Krsko. Even with such a small crowd, I am still going to guess it is a cost-cutting economy measure rather than diplomatic sensitivity towards local politics. However, whenever any national anthem is sung with this majesty and brilliance, you really don't need flags to wave to really feel the deep pride and patriotic fervour. Though at SGP events many anthems have been sung with passion, this lone female singer magnificently represents her country and easily stands out as far and away the best national anthem rendition of the whole series. It is fabulous and stirringly sung. They should book her every year. [2]

Though the prime viewing positions of the main grandstand fill out, generally this event remains noticeably sparsely attended. Even without official release of the attendance figures, despite the crowded secondary temporary grandstand or the knots of fans who occupy the stadium's grassy banks, to the naked eye it still looks easily the smallest crowd of the series to date. Casual conversation is less than easy given the power and incredible volume of stadium speakers they have apparently set up to broadcast the rider introductions, announcer banter and race results to listeners well beyond the summits of the distant surrounding hills. There is only one big screen rather than the more usual two. It is a notably small big screen too. Something the incredible stadium speaker volume fails to overcome, let alone compensate for. While we wait for something to watch beyond last-minute raking of the track or the ministrations of the officious BSI woman on the centregreen with the clipboard and what

[2] But don't in 2019.

looks like a head mike, the usual roster of SGP sponsors enjoy routine namechecks on the small screen as their logo stills play on endless rotation. Rather wonderfully this banal homage to the usual SGP sponsor and valued partner suspects is brilliantly supplemented by a wild, truly notable intrusion of a slide that reads: "Petrol Energy for Life"! What is the thinking behind this decision to pay for and then actually run such a generic advert at an international speedway meeting? Especially one where the bike fuel is actually methanol rather than petrol? Perhaps, it is a masterly spoof? Or another innovative new cost-conscious idea to "save" British speedway that for once Burbo is soft-launching in Krsko rather than via his usual route of the news pages of the *Speedway Star*? No matter what quality of racing is served up here tonight, everyone can at least go home knowing that they have been blessed with sight of arguably one of the least green and most environmentally unfriendly adverts they will ever get to see in public almost anywhere in Europe this century!

With so few fans on hand, prior to and in sharp contrast to the totally enthralling and magnificently sung national anthem, the announcer tries to amp up the atmosphere. Well, vaguely create the vestige of one by trying to conduct an aural identity parade. "Where are you fans from Sweden? [muted response] Okay. It's okay, OK? Where are you fans from UK? [air horns parp] Ha ha! Okay! Craig Cook. Where are you fans from Australia? [almost no reaction except for banshee reaction of a distressed lone stuck pig apparently sat behind me in the back row of the stand. It is such a strange almost other-worldly noise, it is initially hard to gender on the timbre of its sound alone] Okay, it's OK. Where are you fans from America? [almost nothing] Ah, okay, it is a long way." The announcer briefly goes silent to leave us to our own pre-meeting thoughts but, five minutes later, is back. "I'm sorry, I must apologise. Where are you fans from Poland? [loud greeting] I knew it! Sorry! Okay." Despite the lack of a deep and robust speedway tradition within Slovenia, the meeting does have three possible Slovenian participants – wild card Matic Ivacic along with reserves Nick Skorja and Denis Stojs who will also ride (in turn) if anyone drops out of any race during the meeting. These aren't sufficiently big name or box office, even in Krsko, to really move the stuck ticket sales dial. Poor sales are no surprise given that for most of the 2018 season Slovenian SGP tickets have been promised but remained stubbornly unavailable via the primary sales channel of the official Speedway Grand Prix website. Indeed, tickets for the next Cardiff event in September 2019 not only went on sale 15 months early but were even available on there for next year before those for this year in Krsko had even troubled the scorer. It is almost as if the rights holders BSI can't be sufficiently arsed to promote ticket sales for meetings they have licensed to third parties for a fee as they don't then, thereafter, directly benefit from the additional revenues of any incremental sales that such promotion creates.

Once the SGP schedule for any season is agreed, venue changes usually only then happen due to the ineptitude (aka "discretion") of rights holders BSI and/or their selected staging partners. These sudden changes aren't supposed to happen but sometimes do. In the past, meetings have gone from Germany to Poland or suddenly moved serious kilometres overnight to another track elsewhere within the country, as happened a few years back in Latvia. Though inconvenient for the riders, officials and broadcasters, these venue relocations have been a complete financial disaster and experiential nightmare for most paying SGP fans. Sticking to the Latvia example, fans with tickets were entitled to see the re-staging but only if they could somehow manage to arrange to travel a significant distance from where they were staying and – reasonably enough – expected to see the speedway and then travel back home much later the next day from somewhere else. Worse still, not only had they to make their way from somewhere comparatively remote to a similarly obscure place by early the next morning but they had somehow arrange to do with no notice overnight.

Public transport from that part of Latvia is sketchy to say the least at the best of times but especially on a Sunday morning and, with the sudden demand, alternative private transport options immediately disappear to those with deeper pockets, better contacts or – in the case of BSI staffers – contracts. It is, of course, a further reason to consider going to SGPs with a specialist travel tour agency as they then have the headache and responsibility to get you from A to B while still also ensuring that you are able to get transport and flights back home too. Experienced, friendly and very helpful though Travel Plus Tours and their staff are, professionally run sports events should not need fans to require such a safety net. It goes without saying that given so many SGPs – nearly 20 years after their promise of future stagings in big stadiums in major cities throughout Europe (and also globally) helped land BSI the SGP (and World Cup) rights contract from the FIM – are still primarily staged in what really are fields in the middle of nowhere. Inevitably, these faraway location decisions mean that transport difficulties and lack of effective public transport options – along with limited hotel availability and eye-watering prices for said same – still plagues the series. All of these factors combine to make going on an organised tour the eminently sensible decision for a fun and hassle-free experience that doesn't bust the bank. Obviously if there were appropriate autonomy and governance between the supervisory and regulatory authority of the FIM and rights holders BSI or between the media and BSI, then understandable anger and furore over these structural staging issues would have been addressed and possibly sorted a long time ago rather than either never mentioned or just shrugged off as the way of the world. Anyways, even with the best efforts of the UK's Travel Plus Tours and also similar specialist speedway tour travel companies from Sweden and Poland, Krsko is arguably the worst attended of the SGP of the season. Quite an achievement when you consider the obscure locations and limited stadium capacities of some of the other rival venues staging meetings during the 2018 SGP series.

My prime position grandstand seat overlooks the fourth bend exit and any race towards to start/finish line. Every fan tends to have a favoured position at their home track. Usually this is the result of who took you to speedway in the first place and where THEY preferred to stand rather than it consciously being your own choice. When you travel elsewhere stadium layouts (viewing positions; even pits location), availability (only really an issue for league meetings in Poland or occasional SGPs) and price all suddenly become factors that randomly influence where you decide to end up watching from. Rather like there is no guidebook or manual for series newbie Craig Cook to consult regarding his bike setups for SGP tracks, so it is too for first-time fans watching at these same SGP tracks. Seat comfort, stand pitch and even relationship to the setting sun all massively impact viewing comfort and pleasure. At smaller venues for fans travelling under their own steam, it is also the case that many prime seats are never available since they have been block booked. [3] Either by organised tour parties or primarily, worse still, as freebies for rights holders BSI who – understandably, in some instances – distribute them to riders, sponsors, exalted staff or hangers-on. BSI contractually have a substantial tranche of the best seats as comp tickets to distribute at each and every SGP meeting staged by third parties. This means, even at the first moment of sale, many prime seats or viewing locations are NEVER available to any ordinary fan without the connections or finance to pay the tour price premium. Of course, this is the way of sports events the world over. That said, the standard sports structural hypocrisy

---

[3] And the situation is much worse when it comes to commodious hotels – especially in obscure and remote locations – since BSI contracts stipulate that a certain number of best/better rooms in two upscale hotels in the area are reserved and paid for them by the organisers. For SGP fans, these block bookings increase prices, limit availability and add transport difficulty and cost. Weirdly when BSI CEO's Postlethwaite and Bellamy took onions from their respective pockets to opine about the allegedly usurious cost of Cardiff hotel bedrooms, they apparently overlooked their own role in both restricting availability and driving prices upwards.

of lauding the loyalty, brilliance and excitement of die-hard attending fans is thrown into sharper relief at the Speedway Grand Prix by the limited number of these best/better seats. More unforgivably, at the remoter locations where the complexity and cost of travel logistics militate against going, reduced hangers-on and notables demand – even for these FREE comp seats – means BSI don't then use up all the premium seats they have pre-reserved and acquired. Unlike, for example, aviation where yield management dictates that any empty seat effectively cost the airline the equivalent of the highest price in that class of travel, BSI can blithely ignore the collateral damage of these unfilled best seats with impunity as both the real and marginal cost to them remains nil. BSI only suffer the minor inconvenience of the non-financial cost of reputational damage – given that this is hardly in high standing, this is also negligible – if they don't have sufficient tickets on hand to satisfy any last-minute requestees. And then only if these disappointed people are deemed VIPs. Overall, the BSI SGP revenue model dictates it is fans who bear the cost of their own travel and attendance who are short-changed. Interestingly, this doesn't prevent BSI (or third-party contractors) from often levying criminally high prices for the remaining better – or VIP and hospitality box – seats at every SGP. Of course, first-time visiting fans don't necessarily choose well from these remaining available tickets even when they buy what appears at first glance by price and location to be ideal seats. Inevitably we lack the local knowledge required to make discriminating choices since each and every stadium has its less ideal seats in every price category since track shape, stand layouts along with fixed or temporary fixtures and fittings that can seriously mitigate our viewing pleasure.

My row has many late arrivals. Three seats away, one of these appears to be Adam Skornicki. Though it is hard to be sure. It could some sort of weird tribute lookalike. The context is right – after all, it is a speedway meeting. If so, "Adam" is surprisingly smartly dressed as if re-imagined as an off-duty insurance salesman. His cosplay is set off by well-shined black shoes and neatly cut hair. The only other possible clue it is him is that he has sufficient SGP connections to get to wear a deluxe green wristband. Said adornment is either some style statement against his insurance salesman uniform or the speedway equivalent of a freemason's handshake that, thereby, entitles the wearer to automatic entry at the humble event itself, premium seating as well as along to the after-show party upstairs VIP area. Where the music is fashionable, the party never stops and, like the sex and exotic drinks, is free. Either I stare along much too long or else my mental confusion easily shows as "Adam" smiles and nods encouragingly. Perhaps, this is how any imposter posing as an executive (ponytail free) version Adam Skornicki double would react to being rumbled? With the riders up at the tapes, I take the chance to look elsewhere towards where the start line should be, if only a bloke selling giant boxes of popcorn wasn't stood there completely blocking the view. You'd expect even the most dim-witted Slovenian entrepreneur would aim to have a basic understanding of the likely key moments of the event they hawk their stuff round at? Though the popcorn here is fresh and – as they say – "as cheap as chips" (cheaper, actually), latent anxiety about diabetes combines with my severe pissed-offness at the blocked view to immediately strike off this culinary option from my menu. Luckily, matey moves in time for me to see the only "action" (Freddie Lindgren blocks a brief second bend challenge from Nicki Pedersen) in a fast-looking but eminently forgettable processional first race. Welcome back to the mundanity of World Championship racing in true BSI style: lots of promise, heightened showmanship but poor delivery. Maybe this is, after all, Zen the BSI way? Who needs an exotic retreat when the premium boredom guaranteed to empty and still the mind is so freely available after an SGP race or two in the back end of beyond? Those questing their first step on the foothills of access to the nirvana of oneness with the universe via the out-of-body SGP experiences BSI put on are going to be a much more attractive prospect to global brands than the current white male and stale crowd with disposable income they currently deliver. Maybe even mandatory sips of Monster from whatever new garishly coloured can they have this week could be re-packaged as part of the abasement required to spiritually "grow"? If BSI can harness these SGP lost soul attendees this could, finally, be oft-fabled market leading innovation that finally takes speedway to the next global Gwyneth Paltrow-esque level of celebrity?

Serendipitously sat next to me is Kerry Cook with her boyfriend Dan alongside her. After a week on holiday in the region, she has come to watch her brother race overseas in this SGP. Though a digital programmer in London, whenever she can Kerry likes to see Craig race. Preferably live, if work and location allow. "I'll warn you now, I might go mad when Craig rides!" Along with Ian Corcoran (who also has a computer background), Kerry runs Craig's social media, widely praised for its fan engagement as well as its canny use as a channel to raise sponsorship and halo those activities. Heat 2 sees Maciej Janowski lead throughout until he unluckily loses a chain on the last corner. It is a heat only really notable for the enthusiastic often unbridled encouragement given throughout by the Jason Doyle uber-fan located somewhere in the back row of the grandstand. The sheer intensity of her support suggests barely hidden issues. She is so loud you half suspect the riders can hear it out on the track, despite the stadium speaker volume, the sound of four bikes and the muffling effect of the crash helmets. Craig's arrival out onto the track sees Kerry agitate in her seat but then nearly not see the race due to the sudden re-appearance of popcorn man. Again just as the riders line up at the tapes. His timing is unerring but poor. Kerry firmly requests he move before she wills Craig onwards and faster with shouts of advice, "C'mon Craig! C'mon Craig!" Kerry isn't nearly as loud as the Jason Doyle fan but is similarly passionate. Encouraged by his sister, Craig finishes third. First races haven't been his forte at the Grand Prix or elsewhere this season, so a point is a positive sign and slightly improves his series cumulative total. Zmarzlik looks incredibly fast winning a processional heat 4. After an early doors slightly stagey shoulder bump with Chris Holder, no one gets close. So far, Krsko looks like a fast one-line track where we will see very few overtakes.

The end of the fourth heat is all the encouragement Phil Morris needs to bound back out onto the track and resume issuing complex but pointless instructions to the track staff and tractor drivers accomplished via his usual hard-to-interpret gestures and perpetually impatient verbal requests. The urgency and flurry are in sharp contrast to the negligible impact, if judged by the quantity of the passing or quality of the racing at almost any of the tracks used for SGPs this season. With small pebbles easily visible in the gravel mix that is the not-so-secret sauce that underpins the performance of the Krsko track, only a pathological optimist would expect to see the sweat and toil of this virtue-signalling track-curation work dramatically improve its condition or the calibre of the racing it delivers. The primary function of Phil's song and dance is to be seen to perform his supervision and, thereby, signal a modicum of track care and dressing to watching fans, riders, officials, viewers and rights holders BSI. Experienced track staff the world over don't ever really need any second instructions about their work on their home track, especially not during the racing. Preparing a wonderful race track is a dark art that requires luck with the weather as well as skilled track-curation technique and activity during the days before any meeting. Like an iceberg, albeit of the shale variety, what you see on the night is only a fraction of what makes up the whole. During any meeting, as a track curator or staff member you do need to adapt to changing conditions brought on by the climate/weather, racing impacts and, sometimes though rarely, rider requests. During any interval break, many minor track adjustments can be accommodated. Ignoring the constituent qualities of its shale/gravel for a moment, the Krsko SGP track – like most of those elsewhere this series (except Malilla!) – is tonight essentially impervious to any significant or dramatic change. It is built to provide a hopefully crash-free smooth surface and, thereby, preserve the riders' bodies (minor consideration for BSI) and tight timings of the television broadcast schedule (major consideration for BSI). Nevertheless, Phil still power-trips on principle. Possibly just to tick the many boxes of his job-description as FIM race director at the SGP rather than for the attention and ego reasons easily imputed to his behaviour. The race director job requirements are both specific (written) but also political (unwritten). It must frustrate to be judged and held to account for factors that, ultimately, fall outside your control and that can't properly be influenced by Morris during his short attendance time. While Morris does give the temporary tracks of Warsaw, Cardiff and Horsens longer time and attention, these extra days of attention are not similarly invested elsewhere by the FIM or rights holders BSI. Mostly Morris flies in a day or two beforehand to "supervise". Doubtless, there is the cost control element behind this differential approach. A week spent at every track would require paying more. Phil's day rate times seven as well as the additional further costs of keeping him housed, fed, entertained and watered for a week rather than just the standard two or three nights. If he was allowed to do so, though some could argue that the racing and SGP product quality would improve, BSI don't want any track to have the zest exciting racing or overtakes need. Though Phil continues to issue complex instructions with the freneticism of a drowning man, his current seagull management – swoops in, squawks loudly and shits all over the place – approach (if judged by what we get to see) only really regularly delivers processional racing. To be fair, the SGP meetings are efficiently – albeit showboatily – run by Morris. If it were otherwise, fans and broadcasters would quickly complain. Of course, tracks without shale suit the highly tuned bikes of the modern era to further ensure things run very efficiently to time in processional fashion. Continuing his peculiar but apparently unpaid role as explainer, cheerleader and positive spinner for anything and everything at the SGP on the British Speedway Forum, Philip Rising sometimes tries to run with the explanation that the tracks aren't poor but that riders nowadays are too good for them! Whatever extra investments are made to improve SGP track preparation in the future – and I am going to make a wild guess that with BSI at the helm that there will be a big fat none – there really does appear to be an urgent need for someone to develop a universal track curation highway code handbook to explain Phil Morris to neutral observers. Such a manual could agree, codify and then translate into words and pictures the rich variety and range of virtuoso gestures Morris requires to create, dress, present and then maintain picture-perfect Speedway Grand Prix race tracks. In his mind if not in the actual lived reality. SGP track curation needs its bible to formalise what really is the shale gardening equivalent of combining Esperanto and sign language. The innovation of all his histrionic signing could – finally – be the way Phil Morris leaves a positive lasting legacy in the sport.

On the subject of mimes at speedway, earlier the announcer suggested we greet the "FIM officials and track staff for tonight's meeting" with whatever level of enthusiasm took our collective fancies. Given that no meeting could go ahead or then function without them and that many speedway crowds rapturously applaud eminently predictable on track accomplishments, you would think courtesy should see our greetings pitched somewhere between applause or, at least, warm acknowledgement. Instead, we acclaim them with nothing beyond studied indifference. Conversations, searches for the correct seat, honey and popcorn sales all continue unabated. They say that you don't ever notice the best referees. They say the same thing of Start Marshals as their lowly status is such as it is ensures they are regularly completely taken for granted. Except when you watch your team away in (British) speedway when they suddenly become very noticeably pernickety with almost every visiting rider. Away fans often suspect that this fastidiousness is a form of gamesmanship and bias designed to irk and, thereby, distract their riders with increased blood pressure at the very time they need calm to really concentrate up at the tapes. In a sport where fractions of a fraction of a second make all the difference between triumph and moot consolation, slight irritation isn't the emotion you want coursing through your veins towards your throttle hand. With notionally no dog in the fight as the SGP is an international meeting without home riders, FIM assessments aside, this is the last place you would expect to find serial fussiness about how exactly the riders line up at the tapes. The memo has definitely not reached the Krsko meeting mystery Start Marshal. Though he is predictably unnamed in the official programme edited by Nigel Pearson, he quickly seizes this moment of fame upon the "global" stage to really strut his pernickety stuff. With an evening of processional racing in prospect, the display and intensity of his pre-race gestures and waves adds to the visual gaiety and, arguably, gives Morris a rival for our attention. Not only does this start marshal aggressively cajole-wave riders into their infinitesimally exact correct lane position with an elaborate repertoire of hand and arm gestures but, like GPS made flesh, he then also then fine tunes each competitor's location. In relation to the tapes and, sometimes, to each other. Just when you think they are finally under orders and the race about to start, he changes his own lane position – doublechecking the riders continue to remain still and obey his placements – before he finally signals upwards to the referee that they are satisfactorily under his orders to allow the official to initiate the start lights sequence. It is quite a palaver. And definitely looks precisely the kind of wild-gesturing peacockery attention seeking busy work that the FIM race director usually makes his own. So pronounced is the start marshal's fastidious pre-race drill that the rivalry will either spur Phil Morris to even greater interval displays of his trademark frenetic but complex gestures-cum-instructions with the bemused track staff. Or, hopefully, finally allow him to realise the ridiculousness of such pointless attention-seeking and, thereby, hopefully be the antidote that is its ultimate cure.

The Austrian bloke sat next to me, Norbert Kienesberger, lets me know that he is "really good friends with Greg Hancock". It is a deep friendship possibly coincidentally related to his expensive purchase of one of Greg's bikes as a surprise 40th birthday present for his brother. More usefully, Norbert also explains that what I highlighted to him as a case of start marshal fussiness are actually speedway cultural differences in action. Apparently in Polish speedway, in the same way Jesus was God's temporary representative on earth, the start marshal is that for the referee, albeit there is less distance between the start line and the referees box than heaven and earth. Plus there is no need for the start marshal to feed the crowd as it is significantly shy of the five thousand people usually required for such miracles. Far from being ego-driven or working in mysterious ways, the start marshal has permission from Polish FIM Referee Artur Kusmierz for as much fastidiousness as he deems necessary in his pre-race marshalling routine. What to British speedway eyes looks like pedantry is, in fact, professionalism as ref and start marshal working seamlessly together in hand-in-glove fashion. Further proof that Norbert moves in higher circles than many fans, after this meeting he retires to the Jury Room where he enjoys some wine and arm-wrestling with Phil Morris until 3.30am.

Though hard to hear them properly given the announcer's English accent, it sounds like he gives airspeed times rather than race times. Maybe, he gives both. It is hard to make anything out as the stadium system as apparent surges in power has the volume randomly veer between massively over-amplified to its almost whispered opposite. Trialling air speed times at SGPs are just the sort of nonsense BSI's print media boosters Paul Burbidge and, sometimes, Peter Oakes like to "report" on as if it is yet another sign of the relentless pursuit of speedway perfection via iconoclastic innovations that is apparently both the legacy and hallmark of the SGP rights holders. Widely recognised to sometimes struggle in the real world with the basics (dry shale indoors, functioning tapes etc.), BSI make an unlikely stepping stone to our speedway futures. Opinionated fans who use online forums are quick to critique both real and imaginary problems as well as supply ludicrous and/or impractical solutions. There are groundswells for all sort of mad stuff but, without sticking my neck out or extensive research, there has been absolutely no call for airspeed times. If there were, there would already be a many paged possibly increasingly name-cally slightly xenophobic dispute – that references the brilliance of British clocks and stopwatches (made overseas) – about why we were hearing about it in kilometres (like we do in Krsko) rather than miles. Astonishingly, rather than it being an incredibly late and unfunny April Fool, it turns out that not only is this frighteningly innovative actually "technology" being trialled – *gratis*, natch – at SGPs but lack of actual "proper" news sees both Burbo and Peter Oakes express incredulity and unalloyed amazement as they hail its sheer wonder on different pages of the same issue of the *Speedway Star*. Is the first time since he became "woke" that Paul Burbidge has raised Trans issues in the magazine? Away from the track, the revolutionary technology speedway designated as a transponder is also known in the real world as a tracker. Basically the SGP media chorus get to hail the low-tech speedway bike version of the electronic tags convicted criminals wear while out on remand as something akin to military grade GPS. As ever, tame FIM officials and the riders – apparently – totally love and "embrace" the idea but, as is traditional, the extra cost is immediately an issue. More specifically, who pays? The who is invariably some – sponsor or Official Partner – mug but not SGP rights holders BSI.

In the excited rush to congratulation, it seems no one bothers to question the point of the exercise or, more importantly, if it will either attract more fans through the turnstiles or retain the diminishing band currently exploited at SGPs. Spoiler alert: it won't. Just because applications of existing technology exist, could be used or emulate similar gizmos used elsewhere – albeit used in a very poor man's variety in speedway – are "successes" in other motorsports doesn't mean that the SGP or speedway needs to use them. If we are going to start using GPS trackers at SGPs why not attach one to Phil Morris, Burbo or whoever is currently Nicki Pedersen's girlfriend so we can get intricate but illuminating heat maps of their movements? Better still, why not track Monster Joe's dresser, Tai's tattooist or whoever suggested to Freddie he put his hair up in a stumpy ponytail so we can call them to account at the inaugural session of the newly instituted SGP style crimes tribunal and – only if found guilty – deduct points from them (or their sponsored riders) championship totals? Silly ideas that only add cost, provide no benefit or extra fan interest have a rich tradition in the SGP, British speedway, on the BSF or written in green biro to the letters pages of the *Speedway Star*. These letters often get the additional attention of a withering dismissal in spidery writing a week or so later from long-time legendary promoter Len Silver. Much as he did come up with good ideas during his brief reign as co-promoter at King's Lynn speedway, Jonathan Chapman's interest in technology saw him be one of the first to advocate the use of transponders on speedway bikes to supposedly create additional fan interest and excitement via extra data produced. Unlike this pitiful SGP re-hash a decade or so later, at least Jonathan's proposed use of transponders vaguely – if looked at through an incredibly powerful telescope on a good day with the sun shining and the wind blowing in the right direction through our collective hair – added something to fan experience with lap split times. The thrill of knowing the lap times does nothing for me or the vast majority but, at least, an element of thought had gone into their value, use and roll out. The best Burbs and Poakesy can muster to justify their breathless excitement is the specious claim that though transponders will leave fans totally unmoved (actually true!) the ferocious inner competitor inside all SGP riders will somehow magically ensure lots of extra effort on track during practice the day before the SGP. Even if we ignore that very few fans voluntarily inflict attending SGP practice upon themselves – sensible given it is the shale equivalent of watching paint dry – just because something totally meaningless can be done doesn't mean it should be done to attract these stayaways along. I can understand why some more hi-tech professional dog walkers fit trackers to their charges and, afterwards, send time coded distance and speed tracker maps to proud but time-poor owners, but still struggle to see how this adds any value to riders' understandings or jeopardy to their efforts, let alone additional enjoyment to the SGP fan viewing experience at any actual meeting? That said, although race results and race times – even if sometimes forgotten and often not announced properly at SGPs – are the *lingua franca* of filling in a speedway programme the world over, this degree of extra granular detail and complexity is going to add precisely nothing to the spectacle. Knowing the winning time to three rather than two decimal places is not a revolutionary leap forward unless you are easily thrilled at the news a rider won a race in, say, 61.226 seconds rather 61.23 seconds. To further add to the empty hyperbole of Burbo and Oakes's evangelism, it is worth noting that both the SGP website and the subsequent Burbo-authored *Speedway Star* reports and results [4] often fail to provide ANY SGP race times! Just in case you are, nevertheless, still interested in this pointless appliance of science to speedway, it turns out Martin Vaculik won (surely, "output"?) his second race with an airspeed of 81.92 kilometres an hour! [5]

The second set of four races confirms that, though visually quick on the eye, we are in for another dull SGP evening of processional racing with little action and even rarer passing manoeuvres on a track set up by Phil Morris to ensure this happens as soporifically as planned. The only consolation is that we are not at home listening to Nigel and Kelvin's histrionics as they talk up minor first bend jostles for position as something astonishing on a par with the first moon landing. Heat 5 does see the actual surprise of what counts as an actual overtake – from Greg Hancock of all people – on the back straight of the first lap. The next race sees Slovenian wild card Matic Ivacic treat us to his eye-catching display of wild riding manoeuvres. We can probably already mark him down as coming last in his next three races, if he is going to ride so flamboyantly out-of-control each time he comes onto the track. At least his likely failure to score is going to entertain with its unpredictability. Wild card riders invariably share the nationality of the staging country as they get chosen for

---

[4] Though available to a revolutionary THREE decimal places, at the time of writing 2019 winning heat/race times do not appear in the nowadays revamped – with added extra "content" from Nigel Pearson, Phil Lanning and their roster of freelancers and Nigel Pearson Media staff – *Speedway Star* nor in the SGP website heat-by-heat results section. According to the British Speedway Forum, the live television graphics also apparently (I was watching live so don't see) struggled to show winning times either omitting them or through obsessing over the bright new shiny thing of individual lap times. Not that the SGP or its heavy breather reporting needs more ironies but, given BT Sports now dedicate an hour programme to practice and SGP social media perpetually hovers close meltdown over this so-called innovation, it is quite something to fail to give out heat winning race times at meetings (e.g. Prague) or fail to provide them in subsequent reports for the first meetings of 2019 (Warsaw, Krsko, Prague) on the "official SGP" website or, indeed, in the SGP report pages of the *Speedway Star*. Whoops! Of course, it goes without saying that the scorecard template Curtis Sport use in the official programmes edited by Nigel Pearson has also NOT been tweaked or updated to reflect this new reality so doesn't provide sufficient space to fill out winning times to three decimal places (if/when provided) for anyone with normal handwriting.

[5] Given certain athletics records get ruled out because of prevailing wind conditions, surely any use of transponders requires that FIM regulations specify when exactly before practice and the meeting itself wind speeds are measured? And also specify what is the maximum permitted velocity? Obviously, BSI will have to invest in – or get their individual SGP meeting sub-contractors to provide – an anemometer. Hopefully checking the legality of these measurements can easily added to the FIM Machine Examiner inspection duties? Of course, one huge benefit of introducing anemometers is that it gives the FIM Race Director greater excuse to grandstand for the cameras and SGP paying public. Luckily, Phil Morris has been extensively soft-trialling an extensive repertoire of gestures with curatorial staffs and tractors drivers throughout this season that could soon be adapted or reconfigured for wind direction and strength purposes.

their notional domestic appeal in order to notionally try to boost local media coverage and in-country ticket sales. Of course, there is cheery talk of emerging talent and nascent ability meriting its chance to strut its stuff on the international stage. But paper talk is all it is. As it is really a cynical exercise undertaken to amp up sporadic local media coverage and always in lieu of actual in-country marketing spend on event promotion by BSI and/or the staging promoters. It is also naively optimistic since countries where speedway enjoys no real profile – even as a niche sport – are not going to suddenly attract a huge surge of curiosity and interest just because someone local joins the international travelling circus for one night only when it is in town. From a rider perspective, if you can safely navigate the injury danger posed by the on-track wildness and technical roughness of wild card riders (luckily they are usually on much slower bikes), these weekend competitors should provide easier pickings in any heat you race against them. Since race points accumulation rather than race wins is the strategic way to successfully exploit the structural methodology of the current SGP format, it is good practice to maximise your points gain whenever you face these wild card riders (or, equally, newbie permanent riders) to try to ensure that you finish the season ranked eight or higher to, thereby, qualify for the next series the next year.

Heat 7 sees both Craig Cook and Jason Doyle ride so our section of the grandstand is, effectively, a head-to-head shouting match between Kerry Cook and the mystery but voluble woman with the large Australian flag. As luck would have it, Cook flies from the gate pursued by Doyle and Zmarzlik with Pedersen soon some way back. Kerry contents herself with some initial, "C'mon Craig! C'mon Craig!" before increasing her frequency and volume. Aussie woman roars her encouragement like a particularly loud but frightened koala sensing pending violent attack. It is an impressive mix of words, wild orgasm and elemental noise that includes some roars and virtuoso squeals. As expected, Aussie woman wins easily on the volume and sheer number of incredulous people turning around to look to check your sanity metrics. Though Doyle is under great pressure from Zmarzlik passing remains at a premium. Out ahead where it matters, Craig extends his lead ahead of the Doyle-Zmarzlik battle and looks increasingly comfortable right up until the last bend of lap two where he suffers an immediate engine failure. Kerry is incredulous, "What happened there? What the fark was that? He won't be happy with that!" With her hero gifted the win, in her row Aussie woman goes into loud squawk encouragement overdrive before a limbs-flailing dance-cum-fit happy finish set off with some exuberantly triumphant flag waves. She is definitely a 69 fan who knows how to wear her partiality with deafening pride. Craig cuts a disconsolate figure on the centregreen before his bike is taken off him and back to the pits. Both need some tender loving care. Kerry studiously absorbs herself in her phone.

Our digital era nowadays sees even something as old school as speedway more likely to be consumed online rather than in person. Even when there watching it live! Though screen-led digital engagement may or may not remain high, this clearly has significant implications for club revenues. With the army of lapsed or stayaway fans growing daily, consumption of contemporary speedway racing is increasingly passive. It mainly involves reading static pages on websites (forums, update boards, club, fan and the BSPA websites) and social media (Twitter, Facebook, Instagram and Snapchat) rather than watching moving pictures. These are less available. More for long-time contractual rights than demand reasons as speedway fans, like people most places, relish getting stuff free. Though Swedish and Polish meetings get televised every Sunday and Tuesday they are staged, coverage of British speedway league racing is not comprehensively shown on BT Sports. Since selling rights – including broadcast ones – is the main purpose of the sports marketing company (BSI) who currently hold all rights to the World Championships, obviously enough every SGP in the series is televised. While the rise of the attending speedway fan with internet access on their mobile phone rises inexorably amongst all age groups (like it does everywhere else beyond the speedway stadium fence), aside from the Updates website few have the time – let alone the inclination – during the meeting to live text/comment while attending the actual meeting. While the racing is on, there genuinely just isn't any time for almost anything (including fully savouring the meeting!), no matter how convenient. Though some heats occasionally do get randomly posted about in real time from the track, few attendees bother to risk the interruption never mind the wrath of the authorities and the various broadcast rights holders to film SGP (or British speedway) races live. My old-school phone is dumb but Kerry's is hi-tech and internet access enabled. This is both a function of her age demographic but also her work. Consequently, though the next race is upon us and neither the announcer nor the small-sized big screen replays provide no further insight into the whys and wherefores of Craig's sudden stoppage, the online consensus is a "lost chain". Though I wouldn't have the knowhow or fluency required even if I had the requisite phone, sat next to Kerry Cook in Krsko I get an education in the multimedia consumption of a SGP meeting. Information availability and access to the ongoing live broadcast definitely enhances the experience from a knowledge, insight and feedback point of view. Especially given the pitifully scant nature of factual announcements (in English) at any SGP meeting. Obviously, seriously bonding with the screen of your mobile phone requires that you don't any longer fully look at or concentrate upon watching what you have paid to see live in front of you inside the stadium. My waiter in a Zagreb fish restaurant the night before confidently told me "I am from the future" (before overcharging me later) and, maybe, this interactivity supplementing and mediating the live experience is really how the future will be experienced? Given the low priority given to information provision for attending SGP fans – plus how especially rushed each set of races is or how watching the severely abridged stadium big screen replays automatically means missing rider to and fro between races – online access does add a further valuable dimension. Like it does at home or work, preoccupation with the screen at hand inevitably thereby distances you from your immediate company and surroundings. Though there have always been *longueurs* between races at any speedway meeting, the sights, smells and sounds of the (hopefully) thrilling minute of each race along with the anticipation, post-race programming filling, discussion and crowd noise invariably makes going along to any speedway meeting already a truly immersive experience. Well, for me – as a fan – it does anyways! Going to any speedway meeting really truly engages all the senses (except touch). Staged as witnessed, speedway has traditionally been seen and experienced as complete in itself. The action is fast and fleeting. The brief intensity of concentration it requires absorbs and contains watchers in the joy and plenitude of the moment. In our increasingly always-on 24/7 rush-rush world, though gaining silence or achieving true stillness remains an oft-pursued but elusive goal, you can experience it briefly when fully lost in the moment of speedway contemplation during many races. Few are hippy enough to talk about it in these terms but that doesn't make it any less true. Sadly, of course, many SGP races are often so dull, mundane and processional they slowly kill our spirit and soul rather than nourish and rejuvenate them.

Sat next to an expert user of digital technology definitely supplements the lack of coherent announcements and, of course, should debate arise, the exact colour and pattern of the latest "flamboyant" shirt worn by Scott Nicholls back in the BT Sports studio. By all accounts on the British Speedway Forum (BSF), the SGP racing has been so dire this season that almost any distraction or half-reason to tune into the live broadcast is welcomed. When notable shirt design motifs outshine even the racing as the key online and social media talking point, it is a serious worry for the robust future of the sport but also raises questions about BSI's abilities as a so-called sports marketing company. It is yet another sign that things have massively jumped the SGP shark. With UK live speedway television audiences through the floor for the SGP (and British league) meetings, occasional dead cat bounces are slim consolation. With power surges regularly taking the stadium speaker volume from ear-splitting to gently susurrating, the subsequent brief power failure in the Krsko pits briefly deprives the worldwide viewers of live commentary. The sudden surge in the UK audience size this news temporarily creates, sadly, plays no part in the much hyped "official" claim of a 41 per cent increase in the UK audience for the 2018 British speedway season viewing figures. Of course, as there is absolutely no independent verification of said oft-repeated claim, we'll just have to take on trust the BSPA press release highlighting this improvement since BT Sports no longer submit viewing figures to BARB. Simple maths tells us if you start with a very low base (let's say an average of 28,250 viewers per meeting) then such high double-digit increases still only takes your audience just above pitiful and ensures speedway remains on the national profile critical list as far as big brand sponsors see things. Even if you treble F all it still remains F all. If broken out or properly verified, the actual UK SGP viewing figures would be similarly execrable. The best-ever SGP series rider line up – Nigel and Kelvin claimed; repeatedly – for the last full year of SGP viewing figures available (2017) showed an average 34,000 UK audience at BARB. As a comparison, it isn't so long ago that Philip Rising added to the gaiety of the nation by claiming on the BSF that the SGP had two million viewers in India. Culprits, of course, for these truly shocking UK SGP viewing figures abound. The poor quality of the racing. The staleness of the format. Boredom at seeing the same old riders ride (rather than race) against each other again and again and again. The lack of excitement. The heavy breathing over-excitable commentary style. The social media hyperbole. The anodyne analysis. The over-exposure of Monster Joe and Mr Morris. The dull studio discussions. There are few complaints about the actual editorial presentation. In fact, the number of cameras and angles was often praised under Sky but has, subsequently, been criticised since BT Sports took on the contract and – allegedly – cut back on camera numbers, staff and angles. Whatever the specifics or imagined defects, the overall SGP television package clearly is not fit for purpose if judged by the loss of viewers or the strict disinterest of big-name big brands. The ongoing serial lack of nationally or globally recognised sponsors for the SGP series clearly indicates that the both audience composition, size and/or trend of the speedway demographic is seen as very unappealing. Without cache or disposable income – even if segmented by country – the SGP audience (with the exception of Poland) is completely unmonetizable in terms of what it offers to boost brand recognition, drive sales and differentiation or halo product placement. Despite the claims of its boosters, the series badly lacks any credibility as a real sporting contest and worse still – since fans claim to doubters and naysayers it comes fitted as standard at every speedway meeting anywhere – excitement. That all said, the lack of inverse returns applies online as there are fleeting flurries of interest and debate, albeit only for the duration of the meeting. With Kerry sat next to me, I am tangentially able to tap into that Petri dish of contention. Well, really it is more of a slow simmer of occasional mild but often *ad hominem* disagreement.

Throughout the 2018 series, social media and the main online UK speedway forum (BSF) has made uncomfortable reading for fans, friends and family members of Craig Cook. "Expert" posters have mostly been critical and unforgiving about his performances, while they conveniently forget he starts almost without any of the insider knowledge needed to effectively compete in the SGP. Many also wilfully ignore his rightful qualification for the series and don't extend to him the same allowances made – for example – to Tai Woffinden's performances during his first SGP series (when his participation was gifted rather than gained via qualification). Then the nature of the social media is to stir disagreement and entrench positions. Without regular or explanatory announcements (in English, Polish or Slovenian) beyond the basics of race line-ups, results and times – albeit with the odd air-speed time and occasional demand we cheer thrown in for good measure – fans in the stadium are disadvantaged in terms of overall experience compared to – apparently often authoritative – non-attending armchair viewers. Those at home – or whatever institutional setting they get forced to watch the racing from – get to see the replays and some off-track pits action. Unless they watch with the sound down (or in Polish), they also have to suffer both the lack of insight on-the-hoof rider interviews inevitably provide and relentless hyperbolic commentary from Tai Woffinden's always partial press agent Nigel and his friendly sidekick Kelvin. To be fair to Kelvin, he has massively improved over the years and because his commentary work rarely requires actually appearing on screen, he has to a greater extent has conquered his default presentational nervousness whenever on screen. That said, the pressure of live commentary work means that while Kelvin's malapropisms continue they at least puncture the pomposity and matey information-lite jollity. Though much play is made of the fact that as an ex-rider Kelvin brings expertise to his analysis, it is 26 years since he rode in his last Speedway World Championship finals in Wroclaw. Dudek was born just months before this final appearance while Zmarzlik had yet to be conceived. Kerry's phone is on mute but, wherever she looks to get further information, this news adds to my experience and enjoyment of the Krsko SGP. As does being sat next to her and Dan generally. Even if the stadium small big screen was bigger or the local promoters (or BSI) had also gone to the expense of providing an accompanying screen for those at the opposite side of the stadium, it couldn't compete with the power of the internet to add valuable further insights. Any fans with online access worried by the possibility of sudden distracting information overload can, of course, retreat to the comfort of the predictable banality of the relentlessly heroic and heraldic coverage provided by the official Speedway Grand Prix Twitter account masterminded by Paul Burbidge.

The processional racing soon resumes its staccato rhythm. Only riders in red or white helmet colours won the first eight races and this trend more-or-less continues until heat 11. Before then Craig Cook bucks his usual tactic of fast starts that soon fade during the first corner by making a super almost ultra-slow departure from the tapes. So much so that though Kerry does shout words of encouragement, these are sporadic more than a continuous soundtrack. Bartosz Zmarzlik catches the eye almost every time he rides this season in the SGP. This evening is no exception. He wins easily at speed. Though nous and race savvy are all part of the appeal of watching speedway, most tracks in Poland favour brute speed so sheer pace is currently the racing vernacular there. Inevitably this places significant emphasis upon engine tuning, body weight and fast reactions. These have always been key factors but their importance trumps almost all other aspects in contemporary speedway. Consequently, riders at the top level believe they need high-performance ultra-tuned top-of-the-range engines and bikes in order to best maximise power-weight ratios and, thereby, compete effectively. There is an arms race of equipment and its bespoke preparation that along with diet and personal training sees the rich get richer as a function of the depth and calibre of their investments as much as from their knowledge, daring and skill. This is particularly so in the SGP. Top eight automatic re-qualification structurally ensures that newer entrants have a higher failure rate. Rather than easily get embedded, the SGP body rejects these newly transplanted organs. Unless knowledge is shared (a rarity) or expensive counter-measures to prevent this rejection are taken. The reality is that only riders on lucrative Polish Ekstraliga speedway contracts and sponsorships – rather than those reliant upon the truly pitiful sums of SGP prize money or payments/earnings from elsewhere – enjoy the depth of financial resource required to make the long-term equipment and staffing investments required to succeed in the World Championships. Even then, these investments are a gamble but remain sensible if leveraging the cross-subsidy racing in Poland provides. As so often, rights holders BSI are primarily free riders who rely on piggybacking upon the capital investments of others – whether riders or speedway nations – to make their business model work profitably.

It is hard to complain that the modern premium on speed has seen other things possibly permanently lost from the essential fabric of the sport – regular overtaking and random or surprise results among them – when the sport activity name (SPEEDway) foregrounds velocity as its primary attribute. To be honest, along with the lack of brakes, this speed aspect has always been a bit over-sold to outsiders. Wild talk of reaching 80 mph is just that: wild talk. While maximum speeds at the fastest point on the straight may well occasionally reach 50 or so mph, average winning speeds are much lower, despite the skilful fluency of the racing and broadsides riders execute. Actual winning speeds of 35or 40 mph sounds altogether less sexy and, visually, is what the southern European born Deliveroo lads travel at on their mopeds the wrong way down one-way streets in towns across Britain. Even a bigger sized track like Krsko struggles to get average winning speeds much above 50 mph. Indeed, professional cyclists reach much higher suicidal speeds racing down mountains on narrower gauge tyres to boot. Admittedly while they have brakes to fettle and speedway riders only have throttles to ease, their sport in its marketing and media messaging doesn't make the song and dance speedway does about either their velocity or danger of disability as a result of sudden accident or failure. Indeed, the death rate amongst professional cyclists is truly shocking and, in comparison, speedway riders are cocooned by a gamut of safety measures and devices. Smaller tracks, like those often found England (and in Scotland), further reduce average speeds compared, say, to those regularly achieved on tracks – say – in Poland. Anyways, Zmarzlik is fast, looks fast to the naked eye and, consequently, is exciting to watch! Especially if flamboyance or sheer speed is your thing. Tonight is again no exception. Outside the mandatory patriotism that infects some sections of British/English fandom, amongst speedway fans in general (whoever and wherever they are) Zmarzlik races with pizzazz, élan and passion so – for many neutrals – would be a popular choice of World Champion.

Nicki Pedersen enjoys a different kind of widespread unpopularity to Tai Woffinden. Nicki is the cartoon villain. An equal opportunities upsetter of apple carts and all-round hard rider. While some call him dangerous, others relish his competitive outlook. So-called "dangerous" and too hard riders tend to be those fans/riders don't like or are already wary of. Every successful rider is uncompromising and tough when the need or opportunity presents. Even the allegedly saintly and benign Greg Hancock has spent the entire SGP series so far hard riding the smaller fry riders whenever the chance presents. This is eminently sensible and strategic. Final ranking position determines whether you automatically get to play again next season so points accumulation is the only real game for most riders in this SGP town. There can only be one World Champion and, they say, no one really remembers who came second or third unless reminded or related. Consequently, though nowhere in status or memory stakes, eighth is as good as fourth when it comes to riding the sponsorship gravy train. Greg has (no pun intended) monstered any and every wild card or reserve in his heats almost without exception. His net points gain versus these types of riders is consistently high. You would expect that to be the case given the difference in abilities, experience, knowledge and equipment. Occasional poor starts, initial inferior track position, his age or prevailing conditions require Greg to put his throttle hand on the scales with some uncompromising close thrusts of his back wheel. It is a very simple but effective tactic to continue competing in the SGP that most lesser or inexperienced riders don't or can't take seriously enough. Inevitably this happens without (tame) media comment or even passing observation on a very regular basis this series to date. If Nicki were to do similarly, doubtless he would be vilified. Sadder to both note and notice, in the SGPs nowadays Nicki often is not as sufficiently well placed as Greg or on bikes of consistently similar speed so doesn't really get the chance to farm these easy points with basic acts of minimal vanilla aggression. Greg wins heat 10 easily from the gate. Nicki is second but offers no real challenge nor is subject to one either. The riders are strung out like the proverbial line of washing. Just the sight of Nicki not struggling really incenses the bloke next to me, Norbert Kienesberger. This is possibly partly subconscious antipathy too given his purchase of Greg's old bike for his brother as a present. "Pedersen is so bad! That's why he changes club all the time." Admittedly Nicki has again mostly struggled in the SGPs this season. This is understandable given Pedersen is coming back from serious injury but his comparatively declining powers are also a factor plus – it appears – there is a change in his psychology that sees him notice and blame imaginary equipment issues. In the toughest most competitive league in world speedway – Poland – where the big bucks are massively contested and seriously earned, Nicki is third in the Ekstraliga averages. Zmarzlik is the top rider, while Nicki is fractionally bested by fellow Dane Leon Madsen. You could genuinely argue that Nicki is actually the ONLY rider to experience the many rounds of the modern World Championships as its old one-off version. Other riders definitely all give Nicki absolutely zero favours or mulligans. They set aside their usual going-through-the-motions-when-I don't-make-the-start approach for some rediscovered real zing, zeal and zest if racing Pedersen. Beating Nicki seems to never cease to motivate as an ambition or race goal for rival SGP riders. If all riders rode with this intensity every race the SGP would – overnight – suddenly start to resemble the cut-throat winner-takes-all contest it likes to claim it is in the promotional literature and ecstatic heavy breather media reports. No other rider experiences this serial determination bordering on hostility. Nicki dishes it out but takes it back too without complaint unlike, for example, Tai. His failure to moan about any notionally tough treatment is – to my mind – hugely admirable. Many riders also dish it out but often don't see it as a two-way street.

Of course, in some quarters the perception exists that certain riders occasionally help each other out on the track in the SGPs. This is more often put down to fertile imagination or else the pragmatism of shared nationality and team sponsor rather than friendship. Such claims remain unproven. Greg's exclusion in Australia after a peculiar heat that advantaged Monster Energy team mate Chris Holder sadly further fuelled these conspiracy theory smouldering fires. If there is ever such help, it certainly doesn't go Nicki's way. Though the 2018 mostly diminished powers SGP version of Nicki is a shadow of his former hard charging imperious self, he still remains the most consistently sought and, sadly, frequently found scalp. Throughout his whole Grand Prix career, except when in his true pomp, Pedersen's points have been hard won in almost every race. There has been no "after you, Claude". Though there have been no favours, there has definitely been fear. Rightly so. But again here, whether Nicki in his prime or his decline is going to compete to the fullest. If that requires riding hard, rough or tough – and it usually does if the chance presents – so be it. Perhaps, the saddest part of watching this gradual ebb and loss of his powers is the intermittent nature of this diminution. There are races where Nicki flails his wheel but only finds the despair of empty air as opposed to the percussive clatter of bike on man or machine. There is an air of sadness to these desperate increasingly frequent misses. Or, worse still, not only do his fellow riders know and predict such tough manoeuvres but they invite his aggression only to more easily evade him. Without wishing to succumb to the ludicrous advertorial hyperbole that infects most speedway "journalism" – Nicki's win in Malilla was a thriller! And glorious to see and savour too. But, more poignantly, it was also probably his last hurrah. His final jump of the shark or, maybe, his SGP career dead cat bounce.

The last race before another extended interval of Phil Morris semaphore and circling tractors treats watching fans to a really lusty no-quarter-given four lap battle between Tai Woffinden and Jason Doyle for second place. It is all the more notable for its rarity and contrast to the standard fare of a half-hearted competitive tussle for brief supremacy. It meets with big approval from Jason's slightly deranged extra-loud uber-fan too. Last year's champion versus this year's champion (in waiting). On the telly, they would ignore that it happens at least once at every SGP and, instead, bill this race as some kind of pre-Rapture mano-a-mano battle in pursuit of some unspecified but exulted universal significance. Woffinden and Doyle race rough, ready and aggressive for their own ego superiority reasons rather than any notional bragging rights or actual points. They are two riders who grew up in Australia but gained their spurs and learnt their craft via their racing apprenticeships in England. If only all SGP races had this edge and hint of genuine passion, they could possibly then start to vaguely justify the hype and, maybe, even attract new converts. Jason Doyle's true believer in the grandstand backrow goes mental as she whoops and hollers encouragement. Kerry Cook isn't Jason's biggest admirer. "Doyle rides rough but he's hurting himself with all the broken bones. He's so thin. And too wild." By speedway standards, Doyle (like Zagar) is comparatively tall. No amount of dieting and careful nutrition can shrink your skeletal frame. But it can make the bones less padded and, possibly, more brittle when bashed. To casual observation, mindful of said fragility, Matej is the more sensible competitor since he flames out with a crash much less often than Jason.

After twelve heats, six races have been won by red from the inside gate position and five by white from gate 3 with one outlier victory from Greg Hancock in the blue helmet colour from gate 2. Unlike so many of the SGP venues, the peculiar nature of the shale and its preparation makes Krsko a track whose unpredictability defies previous experience and so resists gifting anyone too much home advantage. World Championship meetings held here have had many different winners. Arguably racing at Krsko is one of Tai Woffinden's various Achilles heels. It looks that way with only four points to his name after three rides. When the racing resumes, the manic Aussie Doyle fan is soon back into manic vocal stride. She yells, implores and shrieks her increasingly bizarre mating calls towards the object of her affections as he gains a narrow victory from the inside gate over a suddenly up-for-it Dudek. Craig Cook is second to the first bend in heat 14 but last out of the second bend. It typifies in miniature his SGP season to date. Lightning reflexes and fast starts subside with similar speed. With the bubble of first corner promise burst, the traditional script usually then sees Craig's confidence, bike speed and track position dictate further laps of fruitless pursuit from the back. Instead, this time out Craig speedily threads his bike through the eye of the proverbial needle to re-pass fellow 2018 serial struggler Piotr Pawlicki but also pass Artem Laguta and, thereby, reclaim a second place he refuses to relinquish. With dander suddenly engaged, Cook attacks the track and the bends with all the gusto and confidence he frequently exhibits away from the SGP against "lesser" riders. He looks lithe and flamboyant; the master of his bike and destiny rather than its ungainly servant. It is good to see Cook transformed back into the intuitive rider and racer whose career progression rightly brought him to this international stage rather than the recent imposter hiding in plain sight in his own shadow. Kerry is delighted. Whenever she shouts or chants words of encouragement during her brother's races, the smoother unconsciously politer London metropolitan version of Kerry's regional accent immediately reverts to the natural rawer melody of its original Cumbrian.

After yet another processional heat (15) with no overtaking and the riders strung out like a line of washing, perhaps BSI need to make a virtue of this serious shortcoming in their weekly space adverts in the *Star*? "We supply the laundry when you camp out in the wilds at SGPs". Though the joy of the countryside dictates that campsites are often located in the middle of nowhere and feel like they are at the arse-end of the universe, quite why a caravan or tent is so central to the current SGP series fan experience remains something of a mystery. After promising state-of-the-art stadia in exotic city locations when they gained the SGP rights decades back, quite how a good tent, army rations, torches, a compass and a camping stove joined airhorns, flags and programme boards as the essential accoutrements to really enjoy World Championship speedway beggars belief. The original public school ethos of the BSI executive team that saw them flirt with the Venture Scouts in their late teens – while other humans discovered sex – is, perhaps, the formative influence that continues to strongly echo in the present if their pomposity, misguidedly over-confident leadership and suggested fan accommodations are any indicator.

The greatest dramas during any SGP series are often off the track. Whether it's the spartan camping facilities, Darcy Ward's failed breathalyser, Monster Joe's airport politics, the mystery of the missing barge covers *en route* to Gelsenkirchen or Craig Boyce taking umbrage at Tomasz Gollob – off-track SGP flashpoints frequently trump on-track memories. With so many processional races and duff staging tracks, SGP races soon really badly blur into a forgettable gloop. It shouldn't be that way of course. But when revenues need maximising and no one holds BSI to account, why would it be otherwise? This season has been no exception. Apart from two brief barneys involving Nicki off the track, on whatever scant quantity of shale there is left by FIM Race Director Morris, it has all been eminently forgettable stuff. With on-track drama almost wholly structurally and methodologically absent, occasional storms in a teacup instead have to suffice as our entertainment. Prior to heat 16, with the start marshal yet again fastidiously fussing and faffing the riders into lane position, mainly by using trademark Morris-esque imploring gestures to coax them towards the tapes, Tai Woffinden is suddenly excluded by referee Artur Kusmierz while sat astride his idling bike only feet from the start line. Speedway meetings the world over regularly see riders prevaricate so they are last up to the tapes. Riders clean their goggles, adjust and tighten both real and imaginary wires, nuts and washers. They flex clutches and rev throttles. They touch and fiddle. They temporarily move away. Re-adjust the adjustments. Do some digging and scraping. They signal up to the referee's box to see the start lights lit. There is even a weird current fashion for one arm calisthenics for some riders. Anything to dawdle further. Chris Louis had such a nervously intense pre-race start line routine that he almost had to get there early in order to get his extensive repertoire of pre-start checks done in time to actually race. If you had a pound for every time you had ever seen a rider dawdle at the line, delay proceedings, fail to dig a shallow rut or briefly sit and rest as they lean their bike onto the footrest to air off their spinning back wheel – retirement would have come early to us all a long time ago. Start line gamesmanship custom and practice of whatever stripe generally gets a blind eye from referees. But not today in this speedway backwater! This comparatively inconsequential rules infraction is enough to get Tai Woffinden excluded. With only four points to his name in Krsko – now from four rides – things don't look quite so clever or bright for his championship ambitions. Given Tai is far ahead of Zmarzlik, in the cold light of day this is really only a minor bump on his road to predictable coronation. Experienced in real time in the heat of moment, incomprehension mixes with shock and *Schadenfreude* inside the stadium. We have the limited spurious evidence of our eyes but this decision is such a complete surprise that few fans know what, if anything, they have just seen? Rumours abound. Spurred wildly on by the complete lack of announcements. But also by the opinions of the chastened on social media, forums and updates boards who base their claims on the words and pictures they get from Kelvin and Tai's publicist on the telly. When the stadium speakers finally flare back into life, only the bare fact of the exclusion is confirmed but doesn't really add anything further to the sum of human knowledge or understanding. Further possible insight can only be gleaned via those connected to the internet. Luckily I am sat next to the world web enabled and digitally savvy Kerry Cook. Suddenly, I am living the future of speedway. It is a heady mix. I get to see the action live, strain to comprehend the inconclusive but boring fuzzily defined montage-cum-edit of motion pictures from the "international feed" shown on the stadium small big screen or else gawp past Kerry's hand at the even smaller screen of her phone. This multiplicity of screen access, the concatenation of fast edit footage and actual attendance is, apparently, the way evangelists claim speedway will attract back (then harvest!) the disposable income of the golden fatted calves of the elusive 18-35 age demographic that elsewhere spurs so many advertisers' wet dreams. Quite how these exalted millennials will – in the first instance – get to hear about speedway or the SGP is not explained. Nor, indeed, is why said breaking news would so thrill them that they'd be then lured to visit a small hard-to-reach provincial basic edition sports stadium built in the shadow of a cement works on the outskirts of a minor town in the middle of nowhere in a small relatively obscure Eastern European country. If this were crime fiction, we have the murder location sorted but are currently lacking sufficient victims as well as the means, motive and opportunity to then despatch them.

For once, it is a crying shame to be at the actual SGP meeting so be unable to enjoy listening to the expert *bon mots* explosively uttered by Tai Woffinden's press officer during his live television commentary. By all accounts, it was a joy to hear Nigel Pearson's incredulity and astonishment run totally, unprofessionally and wildly amok. Apparently unaware that not everyone holds his client in such godlike esteem, like a detective dog in search of a pungent deeply hidden bone or jilted lover seeing his squeeze on the arm of another in their local pub, Nigel just couldn't quite let it go for the rest of night. Though apparently Pearson fell slightly short of publicly agreeing with wilder conspiracy theorists – easily found posting illiterately on the BSF – for whom capital punishment is the only serious option. For some on the BSF or in the commentary booth, Tai's exclusion was evidence of a deliberate deep-state plot led by the Polish referee to favour rival Polish riders to deny (definitely) British Tai his crown. Apparently an unjustifiable and political decision – although really, rather inconveniently, just actually adhering to the rules – of such monumental capriciousness, it is spoken of as nearly right up there with the imprisonment of Nelson Mandela on Robben Island or all three assassinations of Malcolm X, JFK and Martin Luther King. Nigel's flabber is so completely and utterly gasted that Kelvin finds himself inadvertently thrown into the unusual position of sounding comparatively sensible and trying to dial it down a few notches rather than provide his usual Waldorf to Statler accompaniment. Given how Tai's mechanics react to some vague element of on-track speedway racing cut and thrust from Nicki with spanners drawn and biceps menacingly bulging from too-tight-fitted dark team uniforms, it would surprise few onlookers if they stormed the referee's gantry position to meet out some of the quick justice that Brexit is soon to allow more widely. Whatever happens, doubtless FIM race director Morris invariably sees spanners drawn as just larks and high jinks but comes down hard retrospectively with big fines if bad language is used (towards him) or, indeed, if any rider's dad (or mum) gets involved. [6]

Before the meeting got underway, Woffinden's lead over Zmarzlik had declined to a still incredibly comfortable 16 points and 24 points over third-placed Janowski. In this context, Woffinden's exclusion presents an immediate opportunity to gain points back over their main championship rival that both squander when the red helmeted Greg Hancock gates to beat them in the re-run. The rider with the inside gate has now won nine of the sixteen races (and white on gate 3 six of the other seven heats). To the delight of many neutrals, even a win in his last ride won't see Woffinden through to the semis. The SGP format settled on by the rights holders BSI has only once in a decade seen the whereabouts of the World Championship decided by the "drama" and race results of the last Grand Prix of the season. That season a bad "all four back" re-run decision by referee Ackroyd helped rob Nicki Pedersen of the title that instead went to Chris Holder. Occasionally, there is a fractional element of uncertainty about the likely winner that heavy breathers in the embedded speedway media require us all to relish with the mandatory suspension of belief and rational thought to and, instead, embrace the Father Christmas actually exists possibility of a run of statistically freakish results robbing the champion-in-waiting of their crown. Last season was another case in point, when Jason Doyle won at "home" in Australia. The drama of this (alleged) homecoming triumph and pathological obscurity of the winner Doyle was so underwhelming for the general Australian sports public that the subcontracting promoters there subsequently tore up the remainder of their contract to stage any further Australian SGP events on financial grounds. All that is usually left to decide by the last SGP of the season is the "race for the top eight" aka who occupies the places that guarantee automatic qualification for next season. Doing so is sensible as it avoids riders throwing themselves on the mercy of the scrupulously independent wild card jury. This is currently particularly sensible for any rider whose face doesn't fit or isn't sponsored by Monster. Though they say no one remembers who finishes second, in the SGP there are such thin pickings when it comes to either actual entertainment or notional excitement that whoever comes eighth continues to annually gain much more than a modicum of speedway fan mindshare.

Tai's cumulative points lead after Cardiff – with five grands prix still to race – was such that if there was serious national publicity to be had making such an announcement then Paddy Power would make a big show of paying out on the meagre odds they originally offered to the winning punters. Not only is there is no national interest nor any decent sized volume of wagers but the toothless speedway media must – apparently contractually – continue to pretend that there is some degree of uncertainty. A blind man on a galloping horse can see that there must be a structural organisational problem if the champion is already more-or-less decided half way through the series or, indeed, if the calibre of the field is so weak that there is no effective competition, let alone that a rider close to 50 can still be a serious contender. Given that this methodological problem with the series structure and duration has been obvious to everyone but rights-holders BSI for over a decade, its continuation clearly indicates that either indifference or revenue-maximising financial factors trump sports and entertainment ones. Obviously enough, Burbs, Pearso and Tats relentlessly ramp up the florid advertorial to pretend every meeting of the series is a thriller while strenuously maintaining that the destination of the (truly ugly looking) championship trophy is not already over bar

[6] Afterwards, Tai's "Grand Prix manager" Peter Adams will disparage the "disgraceful" decision to apply the competition rules to his rider as well as obliquely critiquing the everydayness of the majority of its races, "the referee's decision robbed the paying public of potentially the most important race of the day". Mr Adams also hailed his protégé's lack of reaction to the surprise but correct application of the rules as further sign of his burgeoning maturity. "I have often said it's like training a puppy, but he has matured fantastically well. He's a proper adult now and I thought his behaviour given what had happened to him was absolutely impeccable. I applaud him." To be honest, I had always assumed that the rigorously enforced but unimaginative "Woffy" (or is it "Wuffy"?) nickname came from Tai's surname rather than his years of dog obedience training. I now stand corrected. Like so many at the track, at the time Adams found information and analysis in short supply. "I don't watch races from inside the stadium – I have never done that. I just sit in the pit bay and watch everything on the TV. I was watching what everybody else was watching and it was just a complete mystery as to what was going on." If nothing else, this double-underlines yet again to the paying public that while watching SGPs on the telly is a low information spoken advertorial experience, these SGP meetings/races are nonetheless still best consumed via broadcast pictures than actually watched live.

Quotes from *Speedway Star* 15.09.18

the shouting. The idea that there is an element of uncertainty about the eventual winner can only really be true if serious injury suddenly intervenes. This danger is always a possibility in speedway generally and is regularly alluded to whenever Tai needs to affect human frailty in interviews set up by his press people. That said, another option to add back an element of uncertainty about the destination of the trophy could be if Tai voluntarily decided to completely miss a Grand Prix or two. Not only does his Monster Energy sponsorship contract probably prohibit such frivolity but, sadly, it would hamper the ongoing speedway celebrity rise of Joe Parsons as he'd have fewer race wins to over-celebrate and fewer "winners" to pose about with in the pits for the benefit of the cameras. Peculiarly enough, the SGP calendar is so badly organised – the majority of the events come in a cluster towards the end of the season – and the meetings so frequent that this lack of pressure or need to really compete saw Woffinden go off the boil at Malilla and continue on simmer tonight in Krsko. If Zmarzlik, Janowski and Lindgren are truly to challenge for top place on the podium – rather than provide camera-friendly fodder while remaining also-rans – then the referee and Woffinden just gifted them an ideal last opportunity to do so.

Even though the starts continue to be administered by a hyperactive start marshal, the last set of races begin with a theatrically dramatic dying swan fall for Ivacic. He stays down like a stranded upside beetle long enough to get the referee to make the all-four-back decision his theatrical performance merits. Heat 18 is serenaded by "Go, Jason!" screams and squeals from the back of the grandstand that halo his easy victory. Since Doyle led comfortably throughout, the desperation and power of this loud encouragements strikes an incongruous note. Kerry worries about Doyle's uber-fan, "I think she's got something wrong with her." As Doyle's best SGP performance of the season it merits some recognition though it comes much too late to count as any sort of defence of his World Championship crown. Afterwards, showing himself to have a possible post-speedway career as a dull motivational speaker or warm up act for the Tatum-Pearson speaking tours, Doyle chunters on in autopilot to the media about his "high standards" and learning from "mistakes". He also takes the chance to laud the renewed rejuvenating energy spewing forth from his small team but speaks darkly about the disappearance of the retinue of assorted fair-weather friends, hangers-on and "people who only like winners". These were apparently drawn towards his close inner circle by the power wattage and reflected glory of his all-too-brief glimpse of lasting fame. Heat 19 sees Pedersen continue to struggle for power and points even when drawn to race in the red helmet colour from the almost all-conquering inside gate. After a second-lap failed attempt to scythe past the third-placed Laguta only catches fresh air, and finding himself relegated further and further back at the rear of the race, Nicki ramps up his traditional pantomime engine inspection. After sufficient anxious but obsessive downward glances, he predictably retires early. With only two points to show this evening of on-track engine inspections, Nicki's faint hopes of automatic Top 8 qualification recede still further. His win at Malilla plus the fact that he is effectively the only real box-office rider currently competing in the SGP – someone who anyone and everyone always talks about (fans, riders, sponsors and tame media alike) – would, surely, in a well-run series see him automatically selected for yet another wild card? If he were a Monster Energy sponsored rider, you just know that he would definitely race in the 2019 series without cavil or question.

After appropriate fussing from the start marshal, Zmarzlik wins heat 20 to ensure he gets to the semi-finals. Before the meeting you would have expected a four lap no-holds-barred challenge from Woffinden. Instead Tai battles with Craig Cook for supremacy and second. Though Woffinden rides the faster-looking bike, Craig has the spatial awareness and track savvy to repel all the moves and feints his British compatriot employs to try to pass. Kerry mostly shouts, "C'mon Craigy!" interspersed with bend-by-bend tactical advice. "Block the inside." "You know what he's like!" "He's gonna farking take you!" Craig does indeed know the script. When Woffinden launches his expected last-gasp bend three and four outside burst, Cook angles his bike to block-cum-trap his rival near to the fence in their race to the line. Interestingly, Tai and his mechanics keep their toys in their prams over this manoeuvre. It is a fast but confident performance that Craig celebrates enthusiastically out on the track while his equally chuffed sister Kerry greets it in the stands. Her enthusiasm is as nothing compared to the cries of ecstasy that serenade Doyle's win of the first semi-final. These come from some place hidden so deep and so primal that – if only she can transfer this sincerely felt affection to Tai – you half-suspect it is an application for Nigel Pearson's SGP live commentary and Woffinden press officer jobs. Safe inside his helmet and cocooned by engine noise, Doyle is one of the few people in the Krsko area not hear these elemental screams. With an easy chance to close the points gap on Woffinden beckoning, Zmarzlik blusters but – once again when the big pressure race beckons – flounders, bottles it and is found wanting. Though on principle he challenges Hancock for second, Bartosz is eliminated. His consolation third-place point is no real use. Unless something extraordinary happens over the last two meetings of the series, Zmarzlik's challenge to become World Champion roars and flicker but won't fully flare. Bartosz's current inability to ace the challenge of the one-off must-win big race confirms him as well suited to the more neutered modern SGP era "there's always another day" ethos of points accumulation rather than the match race exceptionalism historically true of previous World Champions. With his rivals often either inconsistent, under-powered or too nervy, in contemporary Grand Prix speedway Woffinden's intermittent ability to sufficiently rouse himself to triumph in the rare but occasional must-win races that (despite the SGP format) still very occasionally arise is more than enough to make him current best-of-breed champion. But not tonight, of course. Dudek comfortably wins a processional final ahead of Doyle who is feverishly implored and worshipfully shouted home to no effect.

As the impressive fireworks light the sky, for those lucky enough to be staying in Krsko it is "And so to bed" time, as Zebedee might say. Or, given this is World Championship speedway, the freelance staffers of the BSI broadcast unit dash to their executive minibus to hit the upscale bars and theme pubs in Ljubljana for some well-deserved team-building refreshments. Helpers and staff at the club will, like the SGP roadcrew, work until nearly sunrise to remove the detritus left by the riders and fans who came along this evening. In the race aftermath, while riders are collectively briefly kept behind after class in case of the need for any post-meeting bike inspections by FIM officials in *parc ferme* (but not urine samples for drug tests as these are taken before the meeting), their mechanics strip, break down and load their bikes back into their fleet of parked-up vans as if taking part in a carefully planned heist. Burbo scuttles about nervously lurking around the various pits bays, changing room common area or "media centre" with mobile in hand in search of distracted riders he importunes into being briefly minded to answer his insightful questions ("What bike noise were you looking for tonight?", "Do you have a favourite helmet colour?" etc.). Some grudgingly share a few words that Burbs reserves the right to copy type, correct or misquote later. Experience dictates that he initially avoid Greg, otherwise there will be insufficient memory left on his phone for the few remaining riders who haven't already left. The SGP circus equipment and paraphernalia used to stage any series event gets efficiently packed away in its container ready to be shipped somewhere else ridiculously random. The airfences will – like anyone coming along expecting excitement and amazement at the calibre of the SGP racing served up in Krsko – get completely deflated. From the centregreen the stage, scaffolding-effect proscenium arch and all the various mandatory FIM official warning flags (including the black one) get packed and stored back in the trailer of the SGP lorry destined to journey like an eternally damned lost speedway soul from obscure regional European location to obscurer location. Monster Energy staff dismantle the free bar, empty the freezers and re-box the remaining brightly coloured undrunk cans of exotic fluid. The start girls signs and seats leave to get perved over another day. The madness of the unused car rally sponsors centregreen seats should, of course, on purpose get accidentally left behind but, instead, travel onwards as yet another visual reminder of Monster Joe Parsons' relentless innovative thinking and marketing brilliance. It is an appropriate legacy. All the Monster stadium luminously bright signage gets folded, stacked and packed away. All these SGP staging paraphernalia goodies just about fill out a single trailer before they wend their way from the comparative bright lights of the outskirts of Krsko to a forest car park adjacent to the remote tree-lined bowl that is Teterow to forlornly await re-use. The broadcast equipment is a purchased service and requires careful handling. Many valuable items have their own specially designed protective cases. Between now and the next SGP, these cameras, mikes and miles of cable will see service elsewhere. As will the broadcast edit suite truck that provides the race night onsite nerve centre of SGP broadcast operations. In addition to all the gear required to make their programme, the Polish speedway broadcasting team must break down and remove their distinctive look-at-us mobile outdoor studio and assorted other essential equipment. Including the presenter's optional trouser press, deluxe suit bag (small size) along with his trunk-sized screen make-up bag. While the event stage set collapses around them, even a couple of hours after the last race, all the lights inside SGP media centre blaze on. With adrenalin wildly coursing through their bloodstreams, official photographers – like Chris Horne – download, organise, curate and crop the thousands of hi-res images that very few people including those who took them will ever see again. These are the witching hours for SGP thought-leaders Burbidge and Gudgeon to mingle, glad hand, opine and/or dash off self-congratulatory tweets before Josh uploads another access-all-areas selfie to Instagram.

The morning after the night before Burbs arrives early at Franjo Tudman Airport on the outskirts of Zagreb. It's a two-storey building in the modern airport vernacular of big glass windows and showy metal to symbolise Croatia's modern era go-getting independence. Though it gleams in the early morning heat, it nonetheless still feels stuck in the middle of a far-flung field despite the cluster of warehouses and newer low-slung service office buildings that have grown up around it. Burbo is hours early for his flight so immediately heads through security to the sanctuary of the frequent-flier lounge to work his magic and/or continue his transcription work. With two media hats to heroically wear for the same event for BSI and Pinegen Ltd respectively, any SGP requires a bout of intense work climbing the trite but heraldic sounding see-no-evil-hear-no-evil advertising-cum-reportage word mountains required. Luckily prolix puffery is Paul's speciality, default setting and single gear. Florida-based Pinegen majority shareholder and *Speedway Star* Managing Editor Philip Rising is often quick to defend and praise his protégé for his ability to meet tight deadlines with content ejaculated to the appropriate word length. With its Monday print deadline and the excessive number of pages the *Speedway Star* still devote to the series run by its biggest advertiser means Burbo must breathlessly spew forth copious copy and accompanying quotes on the SGP, no matter how predictable, mundane or banal the actual event. And, of course, like so many other meetings this series, the Krsko SGP racing lacked drama while putting the capital P into Pedestrian and Processional. With so many columns to spunk up, inevitably Burbo sticks to the tried and tested formula of fraught florid heat descriptions massively padded out with trite rider reaction interviews to provide notional colour. Taped off the cuff in the immediate aftermath and heavy-fingeredly transcribed after, insights are few and far between from the riders despite their post-race adrenalin haze. If by fluke there has been a controversial minor incident, Burbs usually fails to get comment from the key rider involved in case he offends them by asking for information or reaction. Some riders avoid Burbidge interviews full stop to ensure they avoid quote-transcription errors, elisions or exaggerations. Tai Woffinden has allegedly swerved the joys of a solus Burbidge SGP interview for a few years in favour of announcements on his own website or via his chosen tame speedway scribes Lanning and Pearson. This ensures much more manicured but still anodyne statements (unless deliberately attention-seeking with some "edgy" quotes) get released into the wild to then get mostly ignored while being picked up as "exclusives" to leaven the smut on the *Daily Star* website.

Much later arrivals to the security and passport queues for the return BA flight to Heathrow are Greg Hancock's amanuensis Josh Gudgeon and his fellow SGP freelancer with the Scots accent. Josh is keen to discover more about the extent of the expenses claimed back from parties unknown (Krsko Municipality? BSI? FIM? Monster? Uncle Tom Cobley?) by his more experienced stubble chinned late thirties Scotland based travel companion ("when we go to Teterow, I get Bronze back"). Depending on the travel location and flight times, Josh's mate gleefully relates that he sometimes presents expense claims to the payees for Sunday nights away in hotels as well as Thursday nights. Apparently, they used to be hotter on questioning the level, value and validity of submitted travel expense claims back in the day. Though newer to the all-expenses-paid SGP travel game, even Josh has noticed the low supervision and interrogation levels. "I don't think she cares any more. I stayed at the Thistle and put my car in long term parking. That was £80!" This collation rather than interrogation approach towards expenses is most probably a function of a supervisory environment where efficiently documented claims are passed onto and paid by third parties. Especially when it seems these costs don't get thoroughly examined to establish if they are value-for-money, completely justifiable or could be eliminated. Given the BSI SGP accounts submitted annually to Companies House make great play of their ongoing rigorous attention to cost-cutting and their zeal for cost-control in allegedly "difficult" trading conditions – partly of their own creation, to my mind – it is possible to assume that the long tail of freelancer free-riding expenses would get better examination if BSI paid them all? With so many freelancers enjoying some aspect of their travel, accommodation and meals paid for by someone else or lost somewhere – if looked at from the macro level – in the welter of the various World Championship costs spreadsheets, no wonder SGP ticket prices paid by ordinary fans are so incredibly high. Insider access to riders, decision-makers, FIM officials and media stars like Pearson, Morris and Tatum comes with the territory but also comes with a price too. Even ignoring the event locations, speedway freelance life isn't exactly always easy street or access-all-areas glamour. Indeed, the servile nature of Josh's SGP hand-holding freelance work necessitates that even larger egos get to trump smaller ones. "Greg texted me at 2am about the Teterow hotel booking panicking! It says Rostock but I checked Google Maps and it's only a 17-minute drive."

On the plane back, even SGP big cheese Torben Olsen is among us. Keen to lead the BSI team and associated SGP freelancers by example, he too flies in economy. Differing British Airways Executive Club statuses and ticket types inevitably means SGP event staff get randomly scattered throughout the Airbus 320 before they briefly re-group Heathrow airside to wait for the terminal shuttle train. Closer to the front of the plane than them, while his other colleagues read, rest up, brown-nose or sleep, after take-off Burbo immediately gets out his robust but pleasingly unstylish ageing laptop and dons his earpiece to resume transcribing more of the many off-the-cuff interviews stored on his mobile. Favouring double-spaced and a font size so incredibly large you wonder if he is providing written flight updates on our journey for the whole of the plane sat behind him. Or, maybe, conducting *ad hoc* sight tests for the back rows of the plane? Burbo types manically throughout the duration of this two-hour flight. With touch as leaden as his prose by no stretch of the imagination is Burbo a touch-typer. The manic almost angry thud of his fingers on the keys vibrates his tray table with a turbulence and ferocity that must be really great (or soothing) for whose ever seat it is attached to. This manic staccato rhythm is easily heard above the sound of the engines and passenger chatter though located a row behind me. Monty Python famously joked that an infinite number of monkeys sat in front of an infinite number of typewriters would inevitably write the complete works of Shakespeare. Sadly the insightful questions that create Burbo's deathless prose would elude monkeys and even the exponential improvements shown by Google's latest developments in AI and machine learning. Sadly, if rumours of cost-cutting at the *Speedway Star* see the pending demise of Paul's employment over this winter are true[7], we will not see his kind again. Like the star and top speedway riders Burbo word-fellates, English language reading speedway fans are truly honoured and blessed to have had a decade or so of such an accomplished sports journalist nervily walk among us.

> **Winner:** Patryk Dudek (16 points)
>
> **Second:** Jason Doyle (17 points)
>
> **Third:** Greg Hancock (15 points)
>
> **Fourth:** Fredrik Lindgren (13 points)

[7] Luckily, this upsetting rumour proved to be completely unfounded. 2019 has seen the speedway World Championship reporting in both the *Star* and news section of the SGP website continue to be must-read copy.

CHAPTER 9

Teterow SGP 9 – 22.09.18

"Only in the sea of silence can we find the fish of peace."

Sylvie Krin

WANDERING the nearby streets of the Hamburg Hauptbahnhof on a sultry September night just before dusk in search of your hotel – allegedly only one kilometre away – delivers the kind of urban and post-industrial glamour travel experience I quite like. And attending SGPs regularly provides. Getting really lost soon takes the shine off this joy, especially if dragging a wheelie case through temporary road construction works on uneven pavements adjacent to what appears a one-way four-lane city ring road where cars observe no speed limits. The warehouses, soundproofed new-build apartments and office blocks that loom on either side of this urban freeway along with the late evening heat effects of the exhaust fumes serve to reinforce the alien unsuitability of this particular area for pedestrians (whether lost or not). Without an internet-enabled phone to give step-by-step map access when confused, my screen shots of various sections of google maps suddenly become much harder to read and interpret in the gloom. Despite assumptions to the contrary, it is an Iron Law of Foreign Lostness that the few passers-by there are don't or won't speak English. Or, sadly, understand my vaguely recalled few words of truly awful schoolboy German. Apart from basic greetings and, if I say so myself, some quite impressive counting to 30, my most confident German phrase ("the frying pan is dirty") or knowing the German for clothes-horse have little traction hereabouts. Even if useless in finding the Holiday Inn Express, *schmutzig* is a delightful and comforting word to roll around your mouth to keep any free-floating rising anxiety at bay. Making your enquiries louder or speaking faster won't help either, especially in petrol stations where, apparently, speaking to strangers isn't encouraged.

After finding English speaking locals in a distant shopping mall surprisingly still open at 9pm – albeit with big slow-moving queues and very few open checkouts – I'm sent back to the parallel lane of the freeway to quickly find the wrong nondescript three storey office block address I thought I was looking for. Either Holiday Inn Express have undergone a drastic but peculiar re-brand or else they also rather entrepreneurially codeshare their premises with a lap-dancing club and brothel-cum-hotel called "Quickie in the City". Despite its upfront in your face name, their plum-coloured back-lit hotel signage is comparatively tasteful in contrast to the large advertising hoarding that proclaims in a massive typeface, "Tastes like Somebody Cared"! This key proposition reads like the strapline from a much longer mission statement. It's not snappy but can, at least, be safely displayed in public and immediately evokes what you can roughly expect inside without going into specifics. That everything is advertised in English – rather than German – suggests, though I stand to be corrected, that its core activities are aimed at a clientele of frisky comparatively wealthy visiting foreigners rather than sex-sated locals or ageing speedway fans. Given that German people are allegedly culturally well known – in Britain – for their love of naturism (*Freikörperkultur*: aka free body culture), beer, fast cars, predictable porn storylines with men in moustaches, skilful but lucky football teams, blue- and white-collar industrial muscle, awful music tastes as well as graphic expressions of complex instructions about their sexual desires in real life, this hotel immediately ticks many of these xenophobic boxes. My first-ever business trip to the Frankfurt bookfair saw me spend three nights in a busy but cheap city-centre hotel near the main station adorned with a giant – and I mean giant – sized two-storey poster of a topless Samantha Fox. I was the only guest staying not renting their room by the hour. The reception staff were helpful, charming and sympathetic so I'd expect similar here decades later. Just before I pluck up the courage to enter, a very muscular but smartly dressed man in a tailored suit exits the building. He kindly directs me down the street to my actual hotel. The offer of wonderful entertainment options later if I return – after checking in – remains studiously unsaid.

Contrary to cultural expectations, German railways are not the ruthless model of punctuality, speed and efficiency we imagine them to be compared to those in Britain. The nature of all railways is that initial small delays can generate severe knock-on effects. More so within a much bigger network. Before I even got anywhere near to the station, Deutsche Bahn flood my inbox with service delay updates. These advisories start small a few hours before scheduled departure then cunningly build to a much lengthier delay as I walk to the station. If British trains gave out such minor delay updates, they would immediately break the internet. Sat upstairs on my late-running double-decker intercity train service awaiting departure, three heavily laden English speakers arrive in search of luggage space. They are off to a speedway event in the middle of nowhere so chose this as the best available public transport route too, albeit staying in Gustrow rather than the countryside outskirts of Teterow I chose. We have barely started on the speedway conversational pleasantries before a clipped announcement we don't understand sees everyone else leave this crowded service. In refreshing customer-friendly fashion, Deutsche Bahn tickets allow passengers to use all other available routes and services to their destinations after a cancellation or a delay of over 20 minutes. Knowing this and putting it into action in a crowd where – like SGP events – you don't speak the language and announcements non-existent is two different things. On the platform, we are all in the same boat, so it is mobile phones galore as people race to plot the best available revised travel plans. Without the required German to ask for advice from other passengers or the guards locking up our train, things are no clearer on the web beyond the sad news that a fatality has thrown the timetables into complete disarray. Fellow SGP traveller Les Howard has a new mobile device with internet access but only got it this week so is unable to navigate its screens or menus to find the DB site.

In the end, joining many others deciding similarly, we switch from bovine to decisive and elect to get the only train likely to move in the next hour or so that takes a longer completely different route and requires we change at Lubeck. Arguably Lubeck's history and rapid decline as a dominant city – by serving the interests of the privileged few and refusing to change in the face of trade disruption in contrast to its local rival Hamburg – is symbolic of the fortunes of British speedway vis-à-vis speedway in Poland changing with the times while attracting the sponsorship, TV, riders and greater interest to properly reinvent itself. Once a thriving city and definitely one of the key European trading locations, new competition, superior trading arrangements, thinking and technologies saw Lubeck's trade routes, importance and wealth evaporate. British speedway slept similarly at the wheel on more than one occasion. Lubeck's railway station has no metaphorical connection I can see with the BSPA but retains a size and grandeur at odds with its current popularity and connections. After some hanging about, we get to live out our own re-enactment of The Spice Girls classic "2 become 1" or, in our case, "7 become 2" when most passengers from our seven double-decker carriages service then somehow collectively try to board and fit themselves onto a two-carriage single-deck swishly modern tram style but ultra-sedate regional stopping train. Sensible strategic platform position pre-planning sees all four of us SGP travellers determinedly jostle like regular commuters we aren't through the impatient scrum to secure seats despite the impressive rugby maul style crush.

Determination doesn't dim with age or time. Neither do speedway memories. Hilary, daughter Kim and son-in-law Les all assume impending glory and Tai Woffinden fandom ("Are you here for Tai?") makes me want to visit far-flung Teterow. If results fall nicely, Woffinden has a very outside chance ("Tai can't gate but he can cut back") of being crowned 2018 World Champion and, though they'd all like to see that, they'll settle for his eventual series triumph in the last SGP at Torun. They have met Tai and found him charming. As they met him in a takeaway, Kim is sceptical that riders have completely got rid of their bad nutritional habits, "Even the Poole team go to McDonald's! We've seen them there." Though now Hastings based, Kim cut her speedway spurs watching the Wembley Lions. In their day, they were reputed to have a fan club of 60,000 members. Whatever the exact number, speedway is a bug that's lasted a lifetime passed on into the family by her Dad. "I think I went from 1946 to 1958 roughly. I think that's when it shut. I can remember them all. There was Waterman, Freddie and Eric Williams, Tommy Price, Brian Crutcher – my favourite because he was the younger, they were all old otherwise – Bill Kitchen was captain and Jimmy Gooch. He was at Kingsbury swimming baths once. North West nine, nearer to Colindale, it is Brent now." Les got his first speedway introduction on holiday. "I was taken to Poole as a child in the early 70s when we were staying at the Rockley Sands caravan park. Dad had a Wembley Lions plastic peel back thing in his garage so I had always been curious." Like Les – though Burgess Hill based – Kim is a Poole fan. Her 22-year-old daughter ("she's like her dad, nearly six foot") supports the Pirates too but her commitment has waned. "She doesn't have the enthusiasm since Darcy got injured." Kim likes some of the Monster Energy team sponsored riders more than others. "I'm a Tai fan but think very highly of Greg too. He's a gentleman! Dudek and Zmarzlik are both dangerous taking their leg off, they're not in control. I don't like Doyle. We watch all the GPs, mostly at home."

Hilary watches too, "The commentary is good. Who's the little short fella with the beady eyes? Um, Kelvin Tatum. And what's the other guy's name?"

[Kim] "Nigel, I like him but he's never ridden a bike."

[Hilary] "He's quite a big lad."

[Kim] "One thing I would say is that the camera work is shocking."

[Les] "They just follow the rider in the lead and ignore what's happening behind which is often what you want to see."

[Hilary] "Nicki puts it on when he falls. He takes his physio with him everywhere, she rubs him all over."

[Jeff] "That's his girlfriend not his physio."

[Hilary] "Oh. He had his wife and kids with him when he won in Malilla because he went to see them in the crowd."

Ever keen to provide fans with limited options but unique public transport travel experiences getting to their grands prix locations, rights holders BSI have excelled themselves with the obscurity of their staging choice for their latest German event. Though it is a pleasure to glide through the countryside and enjoy good conversation, once again this venue has clearly been chosen for the financial benefit of the rights holders rather than building the good name of speedway or its ease of access, let alone the quality of its facilities and track. It is the third year the small former East German town of Teterow – population less than 9,000 – in the Rostock district in the centre Mecklenburg-Western Pomerania has put on the SGP meeting. This rural town is old but beyond its existence since the 14th century is only really famous for its Teterow See (the big lake outside town). Though a couple of taxi companies are based in town, according my hotel, there is no rank at the station. This sounds strange beforehand but is immediately believable upon arrival at the neat, utilitarian but small provincial ultra-proud civic-feel compact station building. Its walkways are new-build and constructed to a high standard way in excess of likely use or demand. With a good-sized parking area under reconstruction, friends with cars wait by temporary fences where they wave to greet a smattering of the seven newly arrived disembarking Friday rush-hour passengers. It is raining heavily. Based on first impressions, the town doesn't look the best prospect ever for staging international speedway nor somewhere used to televising meetings. The Teterow club is some distance away inside a wooded clearing surrounded by many trees and good-sized fields on the edge of an industrial estate. It is really two tracks. One for speedway and the other more popular much bigger Bergring Arena grass track. With all the rain, conditions under foot in these woods get boggier by the minute.

Unusually for yet another World Championship meeting staged in a regional forest, unlike Hallstavik and Malilla, nights camping under canvas isn't a well-advertised option on the SGP website. The travel information provided for any series event on the SGP website is frankly sketchy and perfunctory at best. Any advice is also private transport biased and mostly assumes few fans stay in the local area. The sheer obscurity of many SGP series locations prevents civilising features like good standard hotels being available. And, if they are, they have already been reserved for BSI and associated imported SGP freelance workers. The few overnight accommodation recommendations that ever appear on the SGP website invariably require some form of tent or caravanning. The prime European speedway demographic is such that it is almost assumed as a fact of nature that many fans will also own camper vans, caravans or, it seems, tents to really test their lumbago. Then again, such is the make-do-and-mend attitude of speedway fans, riders and mechanics that sleeping in your caravan, camper van, van, bivouac tent or a car is always an option anywhere without need of instruction or permission. BSI Speedway Managing Director Torben Olsen needs no second invitation to sing the praises of the joys of camping at any SGP event. It is such a regular option that you half-suspect BSI and Torben run some kind of unofficial shadow Duke of Edinburgh award scheme where even attending any SGP wins badges as getting there and staying locally invariably requires great ingenuity and resilience on the part of the average speedway punter. Difficulties attending any SGP abound. Whether it is buying the tickets; organising your own travel, transport and sleeping arrangements; overcoming poor information provision and – given the wilful obscurity of many locations – just finding the track all require high level language, navigation, map reading, computer and compass skills as well as great self-reliance, energy and adaptability. Military service the world over instils the ability to look after yourself; dress neatly; follow orders; kill, prepare and eat basic nutrition on the hoof as well as adapt to changing circumstances. Though the dress tidily aspect has been quickly dropped from the speedway curriculum for fans and riders but not junior staff, BSI Speedway IMG are happy to regularly challenge the ingenuity and resilience of attendees as well as simultaneously assault their taste buds and stomachs, given the catering options offered at some SGP tracks. Though it was ever thus at speedway club catering outlets in Britain, the ability to find your own sustaining rations in a rural environment is clearly yet another carefully considered cunning challenge aspect of this SGP branded outward bound-esque forest-located fan education programme. What better way to teach self-reliance than to starve fans of decent quality racing, lodgings and comestibles while compounding the difficulty with sub-optimal hygiene considerations? Obviously, any attending ex-service people who have experienced conditions at Stoke Speedway – so already adept at coping without basic facilities like mains electricity, edible grub or even soap in the toilets – enjoy a huge natural advantage and excel on this module of the course.

If nights under canvas in wooded glades or faraway fields without facilities are synonymous with the grands prix speedway copycat Duke of Edinburgh scheme of the BSI era, privation is definitely not the option Torben Olsen chooses for himself. The International Olympic Committee (IOC) are notorious for the 700,000 page contract-cum-instruction-manual they issue to each staging city. Though slightly shorter, the BSI contract for staging franchisees is also the stuff of legend when it comes to issuing sweaty bottomed instructions. Obviously enough, BSI make lengthy extremely particular corporate identity demands and generally state the bleeding obvious but, much more excitingly, the specificity and length of their requirements when it comes to transport, deluxe accommodations and catering is quite something to behold. Especially the confidential contractual requirements of the executive staff, occasional selected FIM officials or sponsors as well as those deemed sufficiently august to be included amongst the chosen few. The best of the best is demanded, contracted and supplied. Forget the ludic abandon of rock star riders. Or even Guns N' Roses' demand for the removal of brown M&Ms – or is it blue, nowadays, in case it gets confused with their Viagra? – from their dressing-room sweet bowl as a quick stress test of the attention to detail taken by any event organiser. As befits their speedway royalty status, SGP rights holders BSI too have their oligarch level expectations for their Motley Cru of senior executives and chosen hangers-on. Just like the mystery and legend that surrounds rumours about the recipe of the elixir of eternal life and happiness (or that behind Coca-Cola), hard detail on current needs is in short supply beyond the requirement that the best rooms in the two best hotels in the area are reserved. We do, of course, on Mrs Google have the translation of BSI's requirements for the 2010 Speedway World Cup at Gorzow. [1] Given how much ticket

---

[1] After Gorzow in Poland obtained the rights to stage the 2010 Speedway World Cup event, the local newspaper *Gazeta Lubuska* revealed various details of the deal Gorzow's Mayor struck with BSI. According to a post on the British Speedway Forum by Trees on November 5, 2009 the newspaper stated: In order to obtain the rights to stage SWC, Gorzow's Town Hall (City Council) had to comply with 41 conditions put in front of them by the BSI. Among others, the Town Hall has to provide and pay for several rooms and one apartment in "the best hotel in town" for the BSI delegation at the time of the event duration, as well as for air tickets, three cars and translators. BSI will also be given, free of charge, 250 tickets for the best seats on the Main Stand, and 50 further (and more, if required) tickets at half price. The Town Hall has to "ensure availability (at no cost to BSI) of four girls to be present at the starting gate", and those girls "must be accepted in advance (of the event) by BSI. Apart from that the Town has to act according to all reasonable requests from the BSI...The most important condition is that Gorzow, for the rights of staging the event has to pay BSI 300 thousand British Pounds. But that's not the whole cost Gorzow have to bear. There are advertising boards to be bought, security forces to be hired and all other costs involved in staging such an event. The list of BSI responsibilities is much shorter and consists only of two points. The BSI is to supply their own air fence, decoration box and advertising board used as a background during TV interviews, and clothes for the track staff – if deemed necessary. They will also supply six blank advertising banners, which Gorzow can sell to interesting companies, on condition that BSI will approve them. Other conditions are no less interesting. Gorzow is not to undertake any activity, or voice opinions which might be seen as harmful to BSI reputation, renown and image. In other words, Gorzow has to keep its mouth shut. Also when it comes to disclosing any details from their agreement, which the local newspaper has just revealed. All in all the whole document consists of 15 pages. When Gorzow's mayor together with Gorzow speedway team chairman recently boasted about the news of signing the agreement with BSI, they did not reveal any details. The city councillors were not very happy when they heard that everything had already been agreed and signed behind their backs. After all, any public money which is to be spent has to be agreed by the whole Council. And councillors learned the details not at the City Council meeting, but from the local newspaper. The last nail in the coffin – so to speak – happened to be the news that the first £50,000 ought to be paid four days after signing this agreement. The newspaper revelation quickly reached the BSI who sent an email to the Gorzow Mayor with questions about how the details of their agreement leaked to the press. They were very unhappy about it and complained bitterly that the agreement was confidential.

http://www.speedway-forum.co.uk/forums/index.php?/topic/51366-details-of-bsi-deal-for-swc-at-gorzow/

prices have increased in the next nine years along with the cost-cutting and difficult trading conditions they foreground in their annual reports, it seems unlikely that BSI's contractual requirements for sub-contractor promoters support will have reduced in scope or expense. More recently, the week before the 2016 World Cup staging at Belle Vue, Manchester City Council famously baulked at the alleged six-figure financial cost of their expected support. Even if this confidential figure is wildly inflated, that gets a lot of M&Ms, fine dining and deluxe executive rooms in local top-notch hotels.

Purely in the interest of research when trying to find accommodation in the Teterow area three months before the event, the only place to stay by then available – if trying to use late Saturday night public transport – was eye-wateringly expensive even on a room-only basis. When I called them to suggest a discount, they refused but a number of factors they related secured my booking. Firstly they were friendly and seemed genuinely keen to give great customer service by phone and email as well as care for and impress possible guests. They even researched the event special service bus times – at that point not mentioned, available or listed on the SGP or club websites – and also emailed an area map with marked routes if I wished to walk there and back. It was a service level beyond any expectations. Secondly, there was no longer any other available accommodation within a 20 kilometre radius 90 or so days beforehand. However, what clinched my booking was news that the "event organisers usually stay here" but had cancelled their 2018 pre-booking to leave the hotel with said room availability. Despite the steep price, the chance to experience the Speedway World Championship weekend off-site where the GP big cheeses, tame media, *bon viveurs* or the great and good usually stay is impossible to resist. Even if only at one remove, the joy of experiencing where Torben trod, Nigel and Kelvin drank (not a small list) or Burbo slept and composed his late-night lava flow of hyperbole and *bon mots* is just too thrilling a prospect to turn down. Even better, I can eat where they ate. Judged by the hammy post-meal videos Kelvin posts on Twitter to whet fans appetites the night before any SGP restaurants he just dined deeply in as a backdrop, Kelvin has yet to eat anywhere that he doesn't consider fabulous or brilliant. It is as if anything that passes his lips takes on almost sacred status and must be excessively praised or heartily recommended. With only the table detritus and restaurant or bar background to go upon – from a detective point of view, these places are rarely those serving authentic local dishes but Eastern European curry houses or chain establishments squarely aimed at unadventurous tourists or ex-pat diners who want to only drink brand lagers they know (or Guinness). The wonder Kelvin finds in these English food dishes served in the tourist areas of foreign locations partially explains the *de facto* Pearson and Tatum in-house commentary style too. If/whenever it passes their eyes, it is thereby deemed as immediately worthy of excessive praise but little or no analysis. Once anointed and recognised as symbolic or truly significant, said race (or meal) must be described as such and honoured with the immediate excited expression of whatever happens to pass through their minds as an insight or vague thought in exaggerated language. It is an approach that lacks quality control and discrimination but sounds heroic or pertinent and, as intended, passes the time.

A quick drive up the gradual incline of tree-lined driveway to the Schlosshotel Burg Schlitz means that no one really needs George Orwell to remind themselves that all pigs aren't created equal. Set in its own 140 acres of hilly forest land, the white walled imposing Lord of the Manor meets Mary Poppins-esque main building of this Palladian property wreaks of wealth, grandeur, exclusivity and opulent luxury. Perched on its own hill, even the entrance hall is accessed by a grand staircase. Inside reception it is all high ceilings, decorative features, big windows, large substantial doors, immaculate expensive rugs precision-flung over chocolate-brown wooden floors set off with polished furniture and large realist back-lit paintings. Decorated to within an inch of its life in the English country house vernacular – albeit with incongruous touches of China in the selection of sculpture and *objets d'art* – its hushed atmosphere of well-observed splendour immediately envelopes the guest in its warm womb of opulent luxury. The public areas are all high ceilings, big doors to yet more high-ceiling rooms, lounges and drawing rooms plus private dining rooms, rug-lined walkways and signature staircases. It has three floors and a basement. The estate is so impressive that it has its own roads, fountains, woods, forest paths, stunning views as well as an imposing church/chapel next door bigger than many hotels.

The whole place has statement magnificence. Little touches abound. There are various exotic but specific purpose brushes in the wardrobe for uses unknown. The main area of the bedroom has four tables, a three-seat high-backed deep sofa and enough cushions in the room to conduct a lengthy graceful cushion auction. The ultra-soft-feel carpets delight bare feet. Various sized his and her shared mirrors including make-up ones that make your facial pores look like the cratered surface of the moon. There is even an ante-room to dress in next to the large tiled bathroom with its bath and separate power-shower closet-cum-room. Though brands I have never come across before, even the calligraphy on the bespoke "free" toiletries shouts quality and status. Disappointingly, although the writing paper is watermarked and of firm quality, there is no fountain pen or can of Monster Energy on the fold-down Georgian-style writing table. There is complementary sherry in a decanter that sits next to a small cake under its own glass dome on a small antique table by a large picture window with views of the verdant forest framed by its heavy drapes. Tasteful jazz and classical music plays from a sound and entertainment system that – when finally located – could in an emergency possibly double as an edit suite for the SGP outside broadcast unit. There are tasteful often full-colour big format books, primarily in English with emphasis upon history, geography and art. The in-room safe is well hidden inside the highly varnished chest-of-drawers-effect cupboard that also contains velvet-effect dressing gowns and retro slippers. My safe could comfortably fit a decent sized crown or tiara and is lined with snooker baize, if played on a magenta cloth. Most impressively it is locked with a substantial double-edged ornate cast key of the type that traditionally opens the fairy-tale castle gate that locks the Princess in the tower. The whole hotel has a majesty that is fit for BSI or minor royalty. This level of luxury is all the more special to me since the confirmation it has had speedway executive royalty grace its portals with their magnificent presence. To be fair, and although the British Royal Family have some notable German ancestry, it is actually way too *nouveau riche* as well as too dust-, Tupperware-, gamekeeper-, cat-, dog- and horse-free for our royals. Plus there are no dogs playing pool paintings I found. The Chinese doings about the place would also be way too *arriviste* for the comparatively simple country pursuits tastes of the majority of their highnesses. In a royal world where Pippa Middleton's mum is immediately nicknamed as "doors to manual" because of her previous earlier life as an air stewardess, this Schloss would fail to be even close to the right kind of long-held majesty. Though surely its Germanic roots would count in its favour, the Burg Schlitz would definitely immediately fail the first impression phase of its status smell test despite its many years as an old people's home or its service as a regional command centre housing senior officers during world war two. That said, this recent chequered wartime past would obviously – as it is isn't, usually – be no barrier to possible royal assent or accession. If, ultimately, your place in the hierarchy of the fixed order of beings is signalled by whether you buy or inherit your furniture, then all the tastefully chosen antiques, retro and reclaimed gear here shouts bought at auction, clearance or by appointment. Though remote, secluded and notably private, the fact the latest owners who have thoughtfully restored it to an opulence way beyond its former glory sadly excludes the Schloss from royal but not SGP itineraries. [2]

Though the owners definitely wouldn't be seen dead at any speedway or grass-track meeting staged at the Bergring Arena – and are not as open-minded and curious as the royal who once asked me, "Should I go to speedway?" – they are more than happy to take organisers Stadtwerke Teterow GmbH's money. They would have done so again this year if the organisers booking hadn't been cancelled. The endless cost-cutting that is the signature strategy of all aspects of staging any SGP event has – sadly – quickly seen off this particular line item expense from the budget spreadsheets and so deprived me of chance close encounters with the great and good of its executives and key staff at repose and, possibly, when refreshed at play. This is a very big let down. Sadly, it means I won't get to see Torben's table manners or latest choice of roll neck sweater beneath another of his casual but smartly understated jackets, nor whether the frightening officious woman with the walkie-talkie ever takes off this potent symbol of her power over the SGP weekend. Assuming she is even sufficiently part of the BSI exec in-crowd to get to stay here. The second-hand thrill of Kelvin's struggle to decipher the language and ingredients of the signature three- or four-course *menu du jour* and the six-course degustation menu as well as whether it sufficiently meets his approval to get filmed as background to his latest breathless Twitter account SGP predictions. Without Guinness on tap or a fake Blarney-stoned international Irish theme bar to settle his night-before-commentary nerves, will the spume feckle of Nigel's excitable word eruptions still be able to achieve the same heights of bombastic content-lite forced enthusiasm magic tomorrow evening? With atmospheric nooks and reading room highly polished tables galore to choose from, can the heavy-fingered clatter of Burbo's double-spaced giant type interview dictation typing avoid damaging the antique furniture or find less grandiloquence if produced in opulent surroundings? Will its creation soothe nearby boozing colleagues with its restless but syncophantic melody? All these moments and experiences remain unlived but vividly imagined. Since I am the only guest in a full hotel otherwise occupied at the wedding here scheduled for tomorrow, the hotel is so upscale that they insist I dine alone in my own deluxe private room. What manners and courtesy. Equally it spares the other guests sight of my shorts, Jason Doyle face-paint tribute and airhorn. The table seats two and – with its candles, antique lamps, Chinese lion themed pottery and signature modernist chandelier – is lit and styled for romance, affairs or marriage proposals. Should such be the order of the evening, attentive but unobtrusive service stays on the cards until discretion suddenly sees it fade away to leave only the new bottle of champagne in its ice bucket and slowly melting desserts made by the Michelin-starred female chef to feed each other by hand. When the door closes and the key half-turns must be the starters orders signal for an impromptu passionate fumble then shag on the chaise longue. That's roughly how any hotel meal alone on the night before any wedding held here plays out in most imaginations. My room mini-bar further confirms my isolation and this year's absence of the SGP crowd from the Schloss as there are no brightly coloured cans of Monster or tanning products cooling inside next to the vintage wines, slightly salty slightly sparkling water and aged cognac.

---

[2] The hotel room specification is as follows:

Double bed – From 44 to 53sqm /474 to 570sqf/Sitting area – View of landscaped park/Best sleeping comfort in TRECA de Paris beds (200 cm wide)/Spacious walk-in wardrobes – Finest handmade manufacture furniture and fine lacquered wood plank floors and hardwood floors/En-suite bathroom with bath or shower – Luxurious Penhaligon's bathroom toiletries – Bathrobe and terry slippers – SPA bag/Flat Screen TV – Telephone – Music system – Marshall Bluetooth speaker – Tablet PC with hotel information and regional excursion tips/Minibar – Shoe trees – Umbrellas/Small culinary welcome treat upon arrival in the room/Extra bed possible – Charges apply – Maximum 3 persons

Breakfast is so exotic, they serve each guest with it on a three-tier cake stand. It is ruthlessly continental. Steak tartare jostles with pates that give you an instant beard. Various raw fish fillets guarantee at least a 12-hour after-taste that the homemade breads and butters barely mute. There is definitely NO full English breakfast or anything that even heads in that direction. The hotel is so posh, it favours tea over coffee. Special kettles refuse to boil the filtered water but heat it to a maximum temperature of 85 degrees. They even have a tea sommelier to guide you through a choice of over 20 specially selected and sourced loose-leaf teas. Disappointingly, I don't get to show off my own import Chinese Green Tea as the sommelier is away ill. Some wedding guests are already dressed in their finery for the later ceremony. They are mainly a middle-aged crowd – too young to be speedway fans – with accompanying children already well into their secondary school education. The bride is absent but later her obvious age difference with the groom brings to mind Mrs Merton asking Debbie McGee, "What first attracted you to millionaire magician Paul Daniels?" It could well be the groom's third or fourth marriage. He projects confidence, wealth and health, despite being a vaper and the sort of bloke who irons his designer jeans and wears expensive box-fresh trainers to breakfast. Last-minute preparations include stunning displays of primarily white flowers. These are legion throughout the hotel and a severe departure from the strewn rose petals that traditionally greets the arrival of BSI Chief Executives John Postlethwaite, Paul Bellamy and Torben Olsen. Even the impressive number of Porsches and Lamborghinis parked outside get some tender loving care in the form of large bouquets intricately tied to their bonnets. Quite how this happens without setting off the alarms or having the car keys to hand is another marvel. Such decorations are either a German wedding transport tradition – strange given both the hotel car park is easily walkable to the next door church and ignoring that sports car bucket seats aren't bridal gown train friendly – or else its some further *ad hoc* wealth worship (and surreptitious) bill padding by the hotel management masquerading as further romantic attention to detail.

Getting to the far-flung Bergring Arena in Teterow for the SGP is comparatively easy in daylight. Getting back after dark is, by all accounts, altogether a much more testing SAS-style proposition. At one point, the Schloss suggested that, given how hard it would be to get a cab back from town afterwards, that I cycle there and back. Setting aside I don't know the area, its country roads or the return route, Australian sports photographer Chris Horne questioned the sanity of such a decision when we discussed it in Krsko. Mostly on account of the innate difficulty posed by the combination of dark conditions, narrow roads and the high proportion of speedway adrenalin-fuelled possibly drunk – or, at least, alcohol-influenced – drivers keen to get away home swiftly. Unaware I don't have media centre access, Chris kindly suggested I meet him there after the meeting and get a lift back once all his event photos have uploaded around midnight as the jams are gone and the car parks finally emptied. The Teterow German SGP is so awkward to get to that even Travel Plus Tours no longer offer a trip there. Rather diplomatically, TPT owner David Goodchild told me they don't have sufficient demand to run a trip (though they took over 150 fans to the first SGP event held here) before kindly warning of the treacherous mud-bath nature – especially so if damp under foot – of its compulsory "stubble fields" surroundings. Through bitter experience, negotiating these at night in the pitch dark after the meeting in search of your waiting coach (or the bus stop of the shuttle bus back) parked up warm and ready in a distant car park is a difficult kettle of fish that easily defeats even the able-bodied and optimistic. So much so, that according to the TPT office telephonist, it upset some attending clients at the first-ever Teterow SGP to such an extent some despaired, cried and felt frightened. Many complained. Word got about too and demand for further adventures disappeared. Though BSI have conspicuously and spectacularly failed to live up to their "global" ambitions, this location arguably wins the very strongly contested accolade for the least wheelchair- or disability-friendly speedway location. Who could have predicted that – in an intensely competitive field – it is in the area of limiting disabled access that BSI finally live up their ambition to deliver recognisable excellence on a global speedway stage?

Given all the feedback and the warnings about conditions and travel complexity, I had anxiety dreams in the weeks prior to this meeting. That's my psyche but, equally, what on earth are BSI playing at even selecting Teterow as an SGP venue? Especially if, as it seems, their prior due diligence didn't quantify risks, let alone make contingency plans. It is certainly not professional. Though graves probably aren't officially allowed in the nearby woodland or surrounding stubble fields, IMG founder Mark McCormick would surely metaphorically turn in his final resting place? Even allowing for the mandatory jolly-campers venture-scouting ethos that apparently dictates the remote venue choices of the Torben Olsen SGP era, this is well over par (a treble if not a quadruple bogey) even by BSI's low standards. Though bonkers to have to do so just to attend an allegedly professionally organised World Championship mainstream (okay, that's putting it much too strongly: ex-mainstream) sports event – forewarned and forearmed so I travel heavy with my biggest wheelie case loaded up with safety gear. Only too happy to risk its check-in gate banishment to the hold, I pack a fluorescent top, waterproof trousers with reflective strips as well as the fluorescent cycling equivalent of a hard-to-put-on baby harness. Doing so later at the meeting, amuses the watching safety stewards. Either for the origami complexity and difficulty or for my over-cautionary Peter Storm style crime. I have two torches (with spare batteries) and, from my car boot, a double-ended large torch bought in a sale by my lovely safety-conscious late mum in case of breakdown. So big, safe and substantial is this torch that it sports a shoulder strap plus various constant and intermittent light and colour (white and orange) settings including disco-style strobes and flashes. I also have a fluorescent cycling rucksack cover and sturdy boots rather than my usual trainers. Only the X-ray screening of airport security safety checks deterred me from borrowing crampons. Also packed are ropes, compass, primus stove (but no gas canister) plus assorted essential camping crockery (but no knife) and camouflage make-up. Though I want a distress flare in case I get marooned overnight, the shops in downtown Teterow aren't entrepreneurial enough to stock this essential German FIM Speedway Grand Prix safety item. I also don't bring string or shovel so potentially will have to sleep rough rather than properly bivouac down. I did bring along fleece, long-johns, gloves, beany hat, matches, insect repellent, battery-operated hand warmer, local OS map equivalent, spare mobile phone battery, fruit, water, nutritious packets of dried fruit, nuts and insects along with some fibre-rich energy bars. Bought off Amazon, I have two silver coloured vacuum-packed emergency rations that require no heat marked "breakfast" and "elevenses". These are probably British Army in origin. Best of all, since I will definitely be without the advanced filtration systems preppers usually like on-hand, I also have a wide necked empty plastic bottle for when, like Bear Grylls, I am forced to drink my own urine. And possibly – if things get desperate – use it to bathe my face or, more weirdly, my feet too in true Madonna and Audrey Hepburn fashion. It is madness that BSI's 21st century speedway grands prix requires fans to prepare and attend their events as if survivalists. Making a wild guess, though they all like to drink their own bathwater, I don't expect Torben, Phil, Nigel, Kelvin or Joe anticipate transport difficulties requiring them to drink their own urine. Should it suddenly become vital they do, obviously, Joe's work long ago pre-prepared his taste buds.

SGP meetings in Germany have a chequered history. Though it was hard to imagine BSI could ever better the self-inflicted disaster of wet shale that rather spectacularly saw their second indoor meeting in Gelsenkirchen get suddenly postponed, the initial Teterow event also attracted strong fan criticism for its disorganisation, difficulty of access and, more importantly, the dangerous possibility of getting crushed to death that some spectators believed they experienced. Strangely enough, the rights holders have previous here. When I went to watch elsewhere in Germany at their Gelsenkirchen SGP (the one they managed to stage with dry shale), so many fans were held outside the entry gate prior to entry – well after the scheduled opening time – that the crowd surge onto the perimeter fence as we tried to navigate through the narrow entrance spaces briefly threatened to crush, injure or possibly kill us too. This was entirely a function of the limited ingress points, lack of stewarding outside the rigid perimeter fences and the self-inflicted delay of the late opening that caused so many fans to muster, cluster and then impatiently surge. As my life nearly flashed before my eyes in a crushing sea of garish anoraks, Poland flag face paints and wacky headgear, in a moment of sudden clarity I recalled that minutes earlier I had seen Chris van Straaten and one of his sons walk towards these turnstiles. So immediately knew that subsequent disaster reports – as even they would struggle to pretend nothing too exceptionally negative had happened – in the *Speedway Star* would give other lesser fan deaths much lower billing than the van Straatens', if any at all. Whenever you narrowly miss such a death nearly foretold with CVS, you subsequently experience every day you are given thereafter as both a gift and blessing. Though BSI give nothing away for free unless accidentally, they have subsequently tried to give similar gifts to other fans, albeit without the correct corporate identity manual SGP brand presentation or Chris van Straaten in attendance. Colin Beveridge and his wife Sandra got first-hand experience of BSI's generous gift of lifelong spiritual re-awakening and appreciation of our shared mortality when they went to the 200th-ever SGP which was at Teterow for the first time in 2016. And got it again when they returned in 2017. [3] This must be something of what the Mayor of Teterow Andreas Lange is alluding to in his column in the programme as "the joy of speedway". Then, if judged by his paean to the SGP in Teterow, Mayor Andreas is big on fan emotion and looking on the bright side. It is all about the shared experience. Whether it is the fan feels of nearly dying in a crush beforehand or breaking bones in the struggle to leave after, Andreas informs us speedway – apparently – "evokes

---

[3] 2016

Say what you like about BSI but they really know how to throw memorable anniversary and milestone celebrations for their SGP fans. Here Colin explains the lengths BSI went to make this two-hundredth SGP the trip of a lifetime for him and his wife:

"Started badly when the train connection between Gustrow and Teterow was cancelled due to line maintenance work.

Ended up getting a taxi direct to the Stadium. Or more appropriately track with temporary stands, in a forest in the middle of nowhere. Drop off was at the North entrance where the Bus Connection from Teterow Town Centre was also dropping off. You then walk through the trees and arrive at the turnstiles above the first and second Bends.

First impression was a complete lack of Stewards and direction signage – for example to the Stadium, Fanzone etc.

We had Pit Passes to pick up but after much searching we discovered there was no SGP Office on site. We later learned that this was situated somewhere off site in the Forest 1.5 km away. Completely of no use unless you had a car.

Without exaggerating we were then involved in the most frightening crowd crush we have ever experienced at any sporting occasion. This was at the Main Entrance at the top of the hill between Bends 1 and 2. When gates opened there were only 2 Stewards at a narrow gap attempting to scan the bar code of each individual ticket. This was taking about 30 seconds per ticket. As such, crowd was building with little forward movement and come about 5pm there was at least 2000+ people pushing forward trying to get in. At this stage we were against the metal barrier funnelling posts close to the entrance. Crowd pressure was unbelievable and the posts were actually beginning to buckle.

Again without exaggerating, at that point we were literally minutes away from a major crowd disaster with numerous injuries and god forbid fatalities. Suddenly the Gates were thrown open and everyone streamed in without having their tickets scanned.

Speaking with Phil Morris later he said this was his decision as he could see the crowd numbers and pressure at the entrance building to dangerous levels.

Once inside facilities were basic but adequate. As the crowd grew though long queues formed at the catering outlets which it turned out were too few in number. Lack of Stewards was again also very obvious. As the meeting drew to close the Polish fans began climbing over the air fence and encroaching on the track. With little or no stewards to stop them this developed into a free for all. So much so that the victory parade was cancelled.

emotions and desires in many of us" and can "raise the personal mood" as well as "strengthen the feeling of togetherness".

After all my preparation for a yomp through dense woodland and over barren fields in order to establish base camp somewhere in the vicinity of the event car park, the taxi driver drops me by a roundabout close to a Ford dealership and parallel entry route through an industrial estate saying it provides a less challenging route ("mostly road") of a mile or so to the stadium. Said local Ford dealership garage specialises in vehicle servicing rather than new car sales but, though it looks closed, this afternoon has been pushed into service as the heavily disguised SGP "race office". The taxi driver is all rather Zen about previous staging mistakes, especially those at the initial event and 200th SGP meeting. "First year they had problems but they learned from their mistakes. That is what you do. There will be no repeat again." Inevitably with jet black storm clouds approaching from the distant horizon conversation quickly turns to possibly pending further weather issues. "Yesterday they had three hours of rain and the track was water so there was no practice. Today more rain is coming here but then the wind will take the clouds away."

There is little to see from the industrial estate road. Distant trees, storm clouds and a few large buildings including a modern factory-cum-warehouse building that catches the eye with its extensive but redundant Pompidou Centre effect tribute scaffolding and exposed staircases. After an easy stroll up a gradual incline the tarmac road soon narrows to a single track from where the raised banking that overlooks the last bend of the track is visible in the distance. It is a place the modestly job-titled Managing Director of Stadtwerke Teterow GmbH and 1st Chairman of MC Bergring Teterow e.V. Klaus Reinders describes in the Curtis Sport official programme edited by Nigel Pearson as, "a modern arena embedded in a wonderful landscape". Like those on foot, arriving drivers might see it differently after negotiating a series of sandy gravel tracks to the various parking options available. These are hierarchically categorised by the importance of your status as an attendee. Your position in the scale of things is identified by various matt-laminated A2 notices stuck on a series of well-spaced lampposts. Rights holders BSI like nothing better than to display their authority with

We then exited the Stadium into the pitch black. Not a light was on outside to guide you back to the Car Park/Bus Pick Up. People were stumbling and falling. You had to use the torch facility on your phone to gingerly plot a course away from the stadium. Back at the Drop Off point organized chaos was ensuing as no Buses were running to take people back into town. Unbelievably these had been chartered to get people to the meeting but not to take them back afterwards. You had hundreds of people stranded and looking for assistance. Not one SGP/FIM Official/Steward in sight. At this point I was desperately tweeting about the situation and seeking help. No response.

We ended up Googling a local taxi company and fought our way into it when it arrived about 11.30. As we left there were still about 200 people in the Car Park seeking rescue. Upon getting back to the Hotel and reconnected to Wi-Fi went into full Twitter meltdown about the situation copying Nigel Pearson/Kelvin Tatum and SGP. Not a single response.

To give Phil Morris full credit he private messaged me at lunchtime on the Sunday and asked for my mobile number. He then personally called me to discuss this issues and it was at this point he explained that it was his decision to open the main entrance due to the crowd pressure. Pit Passes were additionally organized for the next GP in Stockholm as a recompense for the issues. I cannot praise Phil Morris enough. He was the only one who stepped in.

It still amazes me how nothing else was said from any official channel about the complete fiasco that the organization of this event was and the near fatalities which resulted. I mentioned it many times since to absolutely zero response."

2017

"Against our better judgement we returned a year later. This time round we hired a car in the belief this would eliminate the location and completely inadequate public transport issues. It did to an extent but you then encounter the Parking and access problems at Teterow. Public Car Park and access is on the South side between bends 3 and 4. Car Park is a field. Because of the rain this was a quagmire. Walking up to the Stadium was like a Battle Of The Somme recreation. We booked Premium Seating at the Start/Finish line. Another disaster. Seating is positioned so that you cannot see the fourth Bend. TV Gantry and Referees Box block the view. We complained to the SGP post meeting about the issue and were given Pit Passes again as recompense. Track was a disgrace and despite the weather forecast had not been covered. Post meeting we slip slided our way back to the car and then spent 90 minutes trying to exit the car park. (One way in for all, one way out for all). We didn't return in 2018. Teterow you can keep as a GP venue."

laminated colour photocopy notices that bear their logo. Like cats territorially piss in your garden to mark it out as their own, so too it is for BSI staffers with these blu-tacked, cable-tied or taped-up signs that look made as a last-minute afterthought on the office photocopier back in the UK. The SGP untouchables – or paying fans as they are otherwise known – get to park in grassy fields furthest away from the track followed – rather ambitiously given the general lack of proper media coverage the SGP inspires throughout Europe, let alone globally – by a very generously sized "VIP Presse Helfer" in a closer grassy field. Predictably, there are very few cars currently parked up in the media section as these peeps are elsewhere deep-diving some practice hyperbole or psyching themselves up to leave every investigative and analytical stone untouched. Even if you allow for the ubiquity of Mercs, BMWs and top of the range Audis found almost anywhere in Germany, the "VIP" and "VIP Presse" cars already parked up here are upscale and expensive. Afterwards, things are so far out of hand on the show-off SGP car park mid-life-crisis executive muscle-car front that – looking out enviously from the driver's seat of his pimped-up mark two Lada with the alloy wheels, twin exhausts and go-faster racing stripe decals – even Burbs was sufficiently moved to comment slightly querulously upon the end-of-days decadence and excess of the situation. "Danish tuning wizard Flemming Graversen roared into the Teterow paddock last Saturday, proudly showing off a Mercedes AMG E63 – complete with V8 engine and personalised number plate – a car which can sell for in excess of £100,000. As the sound of the engine penetrated the forests around the Bergring Arena, there were mixed reactions in the paddock...it seems there is still money in speedway. But maybe Graversen would have better off not flaunting it quite so openly." In contrast, though BSI Speedway IMG don't flaunt their annual egregious edging eight figure (£) annual turnover nor – for example in the comparatively poor year of 2016 – that their dividend paid was still £3,953,928 on reduced turnover of £8,608,299. But, equally, their staff and other tame SGP hirelings don't ever question, mention or critically report it either. With BSI dividends per meeting on average of well over a quarter of a million per every SGP or World Cup meeting they stage, for sure there very clearly is still loads of money slopping about in the Speedway Grand Prix trough! Almost enough "dividend" to buy 40 Mercedes AMG E63s with all the trimmings per season or, perhaps – given the derisory prize money they pay competitors – award every SGP rider a Mercedes AMG E63? Doing so would still have left £2,400,000 odd in dividends to play with and transfer to BSI parent company IMG.

If this were horse racing, conditions underfoot would be classified as "soft". Ordinary fans who pay for their entry have a yomp through the forest or a faraway car park to contend with on their journeys to the turnstiles. Should it again rain heavily, VIPs and media will have only a couple of hundred yards of grassland to navigate before either slithering away afterwards or bogging down their vehicles. There are also signs that say "FIM BSI". Quite where these Holies of the Holy park up I fail to discover. The terrain between the various VIP car parks and the pits end of the track have a guard of honour formed by an impressive line of 13 blue temporary toilets. When occupants burst back out through the toilet door, they face grassland and what may later become an even more pitiful version of the type of massively scaled down fanzone area they serve up in the more remote SGP staging locations. Often revered as something akin to Woodstock by the embedded speedway media, this iteration of the fabled fanzone looks like an afterthought only begrudgingly available in Teterow for contractual reasons. There is a Monster stall of the kind of size you might put up in your back garden if wanting a slightly posher more formal welcome for a few friends coming around for casual drinks. This stall also boasts three steps up to a bijou raised platform. Only the obligatory black Monster-liveried open-backed SUV parked adjacent confirms this must be the charmed circle where fans ascend to speedway heaven via the medium of hastily scrawled rider autographs and grudging rider selfies with the punters. A small group of older fans – almost all wearing dark clothing and speedway-themed baseball caps – cluster by the only open concession stall outside the stadium perimeter fencing that serves alcohol. Close by various vehicles are parked up behind temporary wire fences that would only delay even a half-hearted jail break for approximately five seconds. These belong to the media broadcasters if judged by the single roof-mounted satellite dish. Their location is conveniently close to the back gate that gives access to the pits in one direction and a panoramic view of the man-made bowl of the stadium and its surrounding woodland in the other.

Back up by the line of temporary toilets is the four-wheel transport trailer that takes the SGP event paraphernalia from middle of nowhere place to the next out of the way location. Owning such a trailer must be a source of extreme corporate pride and joy to BSI given the blizzard of logos and accompanying repeat announcements in large size capital letters "FIM SPEEDWAY GRAND PRIX SERIES" and "SPEEDWAYGP.COM". Close by is another full body lorry with the name of a transport company or obscure DJ ("Werner Van Rennen") on its awning. Its side converts – Thunderbirds fashion – to fold out into what looks to be a temporary discotheque with the world's smallest dancefloor. Though good for an intimate smoochy dance it remains resolutely shut and also completely blocked off by an impressive number of red and white plastic moulded crash barriers. Afterwards, I am told that this vehicle folds out into the rider autograph-signing podium. Arguably for later when fans get crushed at the entrance turnstiles or the Monster rig riot really gets out of hand, there are three transit van style ambulances. With over three hours to kill before the start, bored medical staff drink coffee and wait for news of those injured with their hip bones crushed like over-dry digestive biscuits, the dying, out-of-sorts fans or riders to aid. These medical operatives wear smart motorway maintenance style orange hi-vis body suits way newer and more impressive than their vehicles.

Like any sub-cultural group, speedway fans have their tribes, codifying behaviours and dress codes. This is particularly true domestically in the UK. Many aspects of said speedway code easily translate so are also seen at tracks across Europe. Whether its Poland, Sweden, Denmark or Germany or, even, the SGPs – almost irrespective of the weather – certain garments get replicated and recognisably continue across the whole speedway firmament. Arguably, the anorak is iconic and remains king. Ideally these feature garish designs and bright colours that can be seen from space and are manufactured from synthetic materials with a strength and toxicity capable of surviving decades of landfill burial or a nuclear holocaust. The peaked cap has made great inroads into the speedway culture and fan wardrobe over recent decades. Though the glamour of international travel broadens horizons and gives possible access to new fashions, styles and cultures, the banal ubiquity of the SGP and Monster Energy logos blands out this exposure to pastures new to enforce a religiously strong degree of uniformity. Boastful tour T-shirts that list the current roster of European SGP locations (Cardiff, Great Britain anybody?) find favour among those fans keen to get a memento, boost European regional tourism or virtue signal themselves as an integral part of the SGP cognoscenti when worn back at their home tracks. With rain forecast for Teterow plus slippy conditions underfoot most speedway fashion footwear bets are on comparative hold. Seriously substantial footwear is ubiquitous. Trail boots, walking boots, DMs, hiking boots and protective footwear (even wellingtons) sensibly abound. The steel cap toe quotient is high. There are no flipflops to be seen, despite some more laid-back speedway souls – usually riders or their surfer boi beach culture aspirant sponsors, media freelancers, friends and hangers-on – keen to wear them in absolutely all weathers. It is an iron law of speedway flipflops that the further away from the sea or sunshine the pits are, the more they will be worn with pride. Whatever particular contracted or voluntary sub-cultural logo obsession people have, apart from the riders, if there is a Teterow uniform across all attendees – whether working or playing – robust waterproof boots wins the day.

Getting to the pits means running the gauntlet of three different sets of indifferent security people cosplaying as paramilitaries. They're hired from ABS according to the logos on their hi-vis tops. The first more talkative official waves away free-floating weather worries heightened by the fast approaching storm front of low but thick clouds slowly turning jet black overhead. He assumes they are about the racing rather than getting away afterwards, "It will rain like it did yesterday but they will have it on. I know of nothing for tomorrow. It is a Sunday. They will do it for sure. I think." Once past security, it is clear that arguably the best road in the surrounds and vicinity of either the Bergring Arena's speedway or grass-tracks is actually inside the stadium and constructed from concrete. This is something that would pass without comment at speedway the world over but here stands out as a towering achievement on par with Roman roads. Said concrete provides access from the pits as it slopes quite steeply down to the track. Well, to be exact, the track perimeter fence which is supplemented this evening by the further safety feature of an already inflated air fence smartly dressed out in the standard orange-and-black SGP livery. With riders passing to and fro, this section will regularly be in camera shot throughout the meeting so can expect stringent policing from Phil Morris. Lined either side by waist-high hedges, one side of this track-access route has a substantial temporary stand that overlooks bend three and a similar sized fenced-off area with rows of VIP seats. VIP seating options are a mix of basic wooden benches or plastic moulded seats put in some time ago when the stadium was built and average girths were much less. These permanent seats are so tightly packed they subsequently inspired budget airline seating configurations. The track is set in a grass bowl that in turn is surrounded by dense rings of fir trees outside the stadium perimeter and inside by a scattering of evenly spaced concession outlets housed in tents, caravans or bespoke towable metal stalls. Apart from temporary seated stands on bends one and three, fans will watch the action from large grassy banks divided off by old-school racecourse style stanchion barriers painted white. Conditions are so spartan that the only permanent building close to trackside is a narrow two-storey race-control box of the kind regularly seen in grainy colour in 1970s family holiday films made at four-wheel motor sports events. Stood alone and painted white, it really catches the eye and, in Teterow Bergring Arena terms, is the equivalent of the Taj Mahal.

The initial overall impression of the Arena is that whoever has been in charge of SGP preparations has an intense love for temporary security fencing organised into random patterns, preferably featuring different-sized squares. Possibly for a giant game of battleships later? Fences predominate. And abound. I once ate in a New York Mexican restaurant famed for its "World's Biggest Collection of Barbed Wire". They had over two hundred types looking gnarled and vicious but mainly incredibly similar to the naive untutored eye. In contrast, even to the inexpert eye, these security fences have been lovingly chosen and curated for their variety of height, colour, construction and mesh type. They hem, box off and channel the grass banks with a zeal and almost fractal complexity that obscures the original purpose for doing so. It definitely sends the message that casual access is *verboten* throughout the stadium. The spirit of authority the fences project certainly infects the staff by the track airfence who scream at me in German and then shout in English "Do not enter!" all because I have the temerity to stand and just look at the track. Its surface looks brown, damp and gritty. The first leaf fall of the autumn lies thick on the grass either side of the comparatively deluxe road running up towards the patterned paved-effect concrete flooring of the old-school pits.

The pits bays there are effectively two easy front access sheds that run parallel to each other with just about enough space for seven riders on either side plus a super small tag section for a few more riders to cram in down the end. It is very cosy. And already crowded with mechanics, hangers-on, guests and fans who got passes from BSI to recompense for bad experiences they had at SGPs elsewhere. Worn with pride on lanyards, the various rainbow hues of these passes add colour but also again demonstrate the intricate access hierarchies. Recently issued tyres ensures the pits enjoys a mannerly buzz. Even with only two bikes on hand along with all the tools and equipment required to run and service them during the meeting, it already looks a cosy squeeze for the mechanics even before the riders and their managers, press officers, nutritionists, girlfriends, personal trainers, financial advisors, psychologists, publicists, ballet tutors and visualisation coaches arrive on the scene. The central shared space of the pits is filled with late arrival vans and people unloading from them. With rain due, the pits public commons roils like a frenetic rush-hour speedway ants' nest with endless deliveries or comings and goings. It is also apparently green wheelie bin heaven. Every bay has at least one on hand. Whatever the calibre of entertainment tonight delivers, we can rest safe in the knowledge there will be much recycling.

The buildings scattered around and about the two race tracks and in the nearby woods – those that appear to be still in use – have the almost derelict look of abandoned wartime service facilities subsequently used for years by tramps and drinkers. The only obviously new building on the whole site is a large dark lime-green walled chalet with pristine tile roof close to the pits. It is big enough for a couple of large multi-generational families to take one last special but fractious holiday together. If it didn't look so new, you could half-suspect it was built for the isolation, forest views and deeply shaded unspoilt walks before the stadium, speedway and grass-tracks subsequently got constructed around it. For one day only, BSI re-designate this chalet to serve many important SGP purposes. As usual, the specifics of said activities get advised in traditional all-expenses-spared fashion of laminated A4 photocopies – gussied up in the SGP's corporate identity colours of orange and black – they blu-tac to doors, walls and windows or tape to trees. It is another sad reminder of the facts of modern business life: namely that sweaty-bottomed middle-managers and accountants have taken over almost everything everywhere nowadays. Widely spread, uninvited and unwanted, like Japanese knotweed destroys ornamental gardens and railway sidings, (mainly) style-less blokes with calculators, complex spreadsheets, limited people skills and air of quiet pathological complacency rule the business roost the world over. Whether it's the church, hospital or school, they dictate terms or try to. Their tentacles have even spread to the Bergring Arena, if we go by the white chalet door with closest proximity and access to the pits that is marked "Finanzen" in big black permanent letters. This chalet door also sports an "Environmental management map". Which, in true post-modern looking in a mirror at a mirror fashion, is a mock-architectural-plan-meets-overhead-council-maze-map that only really shows where the chalet it is pinned too is in relation to the pits, selected bits of the car park and the small section of the track that occupies the south east quadrant of the Bergring Arena. There is also another sign on the same door that says "Monster Girl". Singular. It would be something of a tragedy if cost-cutting by the accountants who normally reside inside had really let go of 80 percent of the hard-working Monster start line. More finance-driven parsimoniousness or customer service stupidity would surprise no one at any SGP. Almost anyone can make an easy case from their own GP experiences that the spreadsheet- and balance-sheet-led stringent financial demands of BSI and IMG have helped destroy the status, drama and spectacle of World Championship speedway.

There are many more deserving candidates for the chop amongst the regular roster of SGP event freelancers. As if on cue, Paul "Burbo" Burbidge scuttles nervously past and disappears into the building via another door around the corner whose sign I can't read as it's a staff-only area with a stern woman in hi-vis rigorously enforcing its borders. I am going to guess it's the chalet room temporarily designated as the "Media Centre". For some time, it was claimed that the official Speedway Grand Prix Twitter account was an experiment run by hyper-intelligent deep-mind AI bots to establish how long it took to totally alienate speedway fans with its matey deliberate relentless banality. Programmed to only use the house style (minus the orgasmic screeching) previously perfected elsewhere by the television live commentary team, the AI bots' standard vocabulary is a potent mix of empty action words, grandiloquence and heroic hyperbole at severe odds with the evidence of your own eyes. All magnificently expressed in a unique specially commissioned SGP machine code argot that mixes the cheery language of war comics and cusping pre-pubescent teenage boys to provide Trades Descriptions Act defying misleading descriptions of mundane predictable races accompanied with breathless but somehow prolix accounts of general goings on. So a bit like this book, really. "A smiling Tai salutes ecstatic fans with the magnificent specially commissioned winner's trophy that shimmers in the dying dusk sunlight as he waves it aloft in to acknowledge the roars of delight that lift off the roof". Eventually, it became clear that – despite the exponential speed of advance within Artificial Intelligence programming and machine learning – these tweets defied normal language use so could only have been created by the opposable thumbs of a human hand. Well, typed with one stabby mock-heroic finger. Given how Microsoft usually have to disconnect their self-teaching self-learning machine-learning Twitter bot experiments within the hour for tweets spewing forth premium strength racism, sexism and antisemitism, it was the lack of such content on the SGP account that gave its woke human author away. Strangely, it was the occasional Tourette tweet about the right to free speech or to bear arms guaranteed by the American constitution as much as the apparently Islamophobic critique of hijab wearers duty-free shopping habits in German airports that, if nothing else, suggested that Monster Energy's Joe Parsons emotional side and subconscious rather than a machine ran his Twitter account.

On the subject of premium strength opinion and exalted managers, FIM race director Phil Morris and Managing Director, BSI Speedway Torben Olsen stand deep in private conversation halfway down the access road to the track. It is a meeting of minds in search of a fitting metaphor. Noticeably, in the presence of true speedway greatness (albeit at one remove from Ole) and with the superior authority and influence that can directly impact his career, Phil doesn't wave his arms much or make scything gestures with his hands like he does with his direct reports or Europewide to junior track staff. Phil's body language and demeanour is attentive and earnest. Much more the keen-to-impress disciple rather than the usual track curatorial messiah. Morris definitely gives good brown nose with a fluent repertoire of head nods, laughs that fail to transfer to the eyes and knitted eyebrows as he waits the right moment to impress with carefully chosen predictable opinions or self-serving summary of his work to date. In contrast, resplendent in his small-medium sized SGP logoed jacket (deluxe padded version), Torben holds forth and is, arguably, the only man at this speedway mud fest that is the SGP in Teterow without sturdy footwear. Obviously enough, since this is the fashion top drawer of televised World Championship speedway, Torben is safe in the knowledge that he is not the only middle-aged man to sport age-inappropriate fashion statement items of clothing and footwear. Completely unlike the fervent and proudly old age pension nature of British league speedway, the SGP attracts an epidemic of age denial especially from its hangers-on, media freelancers, sponsors, mechanics, senior BSI execs and – of course, most famously – its older riders. Both Greg and Nicki are badly subject to the late stage "loud and proud" afflictions of its vice-like grip, while Freddie Lindgren is only – comparatively – still exploring the foothills by dabbling in a small but ridiculous ponytail and, fair play to him, does make it the centrepiece of his pits bay photo-hoarding. Inevitably, Monster Joe has gone all in – lifestyle, clothes, deep brown tan and opinion – so sets the standard few can meet when it comes to pride in his sub-cultural infantilism vis-à-vis his actual two score and ten age. If any of them read, Jordan Peterson would be their hero. But, instead, it seems the task of role model falls to Emile Ratelband, the 69-year old Dutch self-styled motivational speaker and television personality who wants to change his legal age on his birth certificate to 49. Apparently Ratelband wishes to do so to combat ageism; better reflect his physical appearance – as doctors told him he had the "body of a younger man" – as well as to give him a boost in life and on dating apps. Though the pursuit of youthfulness usually comes with the odour and anxiety of involuntary celibacy, speedway riders are – of course – legendarily at the opposite end of the scale when it comes the frequency and availability of shags.

Torben wears his low-cut fashion trainers with white soles with the confidence of a senior executive who has others chauffeur him from place to place on expenses. Though even Torben can't be unaware that prevailing conditions underfoot at this SGP-themed tough mudder in Teterow can err on the testy side, he also knows the distance from the pits exit to his upscale idling motor in the VIP car park is going to be nothing like the involuntary Battle of the Somme mud bath the fans have to negotiate then conquer around here on a compulsory basis. Overall, Torben's outfit – black everything – conveys the kind of meticulously observed humourless smart-casual dress-down Friday authority that avoids standard exec *faux pas* such as ironing creases into your jeans. Though his on-message SGP design deluxe anorak is zipped up, there is a high percentage likelihood of the real and present danger of a roll neck black jumper underneath. Any audition for the Milk Tray man after the meeting won't need a change of clothes. Stood close to Morris, Torben exhibits the feigned enthusiasm and forced engagement of a senior executive tasked with meeting long-serving lower middle-management staff with enhanced European employment protection on a mandatory visit to the distant under-performing regional operations of an acquired business that you know you will soon have to close down. Torben's face betrays the emotional labour required to pretend to everyone you meet in such backwater locations that you give a toss about them, their opinions, families or their futures. Though not being let go anytime soon, Morris is currently Olsen's very useful underling, albeit at one FIM remove. But even at BSI and the FIM, times, personnel and political connections change so neither will fit any and every future permutation of the SGP strategic plan (if it ever or still exists) for this business moving forwards. For as long as IMG retain the SGP rights, both strut their self-important hours upon this mediocre "global" speedway stage and give their status full-welly knowing that round here in Teterow there are no nightlife distractions to have to save themselves for afterwards.

When the forecast rain arrives a few hours before tapes up, it's torrential. There are very few places to find shelter. Those with privileges can retreat to the comfort of the chalet, while those without such access shelter outside under its eaves. During this downpour, the pits interview gazebo is protected from the worst of the elements by impressive sized clear plastic sheeting. Junior staff mooch beneath. The Monster concession stand looks forlorn as no one is keen enough to want a gratis can if it requires getting soaked first to do so. The talent in the form of mechanics and the few riders already here shelter in their respective pits bays. It is cosy with a capital C. The atmosphere is collegiate. And the collective outlook resigned patience. While everyone waits for the deluge to abate and rain clouds pass through, little work gets done. The compression and cluster of bikes, bodies and equipment means that there is little room to manoeuvre even if the inclination to continue in this confined space exists. The heavy rain sounds more torrential on the pits tin roof. The ambient temperature drops, while the proximity of the forest trees and the primarily wood construction of the pits bays adds to the sudden dank feeling. Sadly, the petrichor is an unpleasant aroma too – much more notes of decomposing body in mulch than fragrant forest glade. Will Cook shelters by Craig's bike that sits closest to the shared pits lane. As preparations for racing this evening are well in hand, he is in expansive mood so chats amiably while he half-watches the comings and goings elsewhere. "Craig was 70 kilos earlier in the week but he's 72 now. When he worked out with that Suggs he kept telling him to lose weight. Being lighter is advantage some places but not others. Sixty-seven is his ideal weight. They tested Craig at the university. They found he had incredible upper body strength for his weight and his reactions were brilliant too! It's because he rode motocross almost every day from when he was little. We were in Norfolk last week and he went clay pigeon shooting for the first time. Guess how he did? He got 14 out of 15. The bloke couldn't believe it was his first time. His hand–eye co-ordination and reactions are so good. It was the same when he went go-karting, he was a natural."

Will continues, "People say Craig won't make it at this level but I honestly think that if he got into the top eight, he'd stay there for years and years. Like Greg. He'd have the confidence. This year he's been figuring out the set ups and now knows what he can and can't push with the other riders. How they'll react. Those he can bully – I'm not saying he does – those he can push and those he can't. Look at the last GP when he blocked Tai: fair play to him. Tai would have done the same. Craig has beaten him at Belle Vue and Wolverhampton but not so much in the GPs. When we were in the Premier League, Craig rode against Doyle 30 times and I only think he beat us four times. Any rider who chases the back wheel or who takes risks is going to come off at some point. If you ride as a professional, you don't take unnecessary risks. Tai did but doesn't now. Dan [Bewley] did. He's 58 kilos and can ride the outside at Belle Vue cos he's got a three or four miles per hour advantage there. But, at the more technical tracks, he's not the same. Craig does well on those. Look at heat 13 this week, he put his arm across Doyle and fair play to him. Finally the [Belle Vue] track had an outside racing line because the weather made it rather than the track curator overwatering it." Some suggest that Craig tends to underperform in his first race of the night but Will isn't convinced. "Craig gets gate four first heat – cos Fricke needs gate two – so he has farther to go and gets covered and then it's all catch up from there. If you watch, most of this season you'll see it's mainly been racing on the inside line only there. Whereas at Glasgow – probably the number two track in the country right now – there are just so many racing lines. It's not just one line like it used to be. Craig is riding the outside and different lines too. And riders are copying him. When we went to Somerset, they prepare the inside line cos Doyle likes that but Craig just went by him on the outside so they've changed that. Look at King's Lynn. It was brilliant for the World Cup but a week later the track was so bad that Holder and that got sacked. When they're losing, Buster changes the track. The refs should stop that. Grade it – okay – but don't change it when you're losing. Scunthorpe have the Aramco wall. Someone is going to hit that one day. We all know that air fences lift so at least have something else there to protect the riders."

The Friday draw for gate positions hasn't been overly kind to Craig. "We have two gate fours here tonight. [to Craig] What's gate four like?" Craig shrugs, "dunno?" Will isn't convinced by the track preparations at Teterow. "The mechanics say they've left it rough so the rain will soak in, whereas they should have packed it down. They say it isn't up to much even when it's dry here." But what of prospects ahead over the remaining two grands prix? "I don't think that Craig will be top eight this year but he's improved every year he's rode and been learning more. Those that say he's not good enough don't know. Sometimes he hasn't been as confident as he should and can be but he has been learning. It is tough. He watches the other riders and sees what they do. Many of them having been doing it at this [SGPs] for some time. It is bound to help. Craig will be back and will do well!"

The rain has, at least, kept the guest pass visitors down. Nonetheless, it is still very crowded with limited pits space available for rubbernecking. The long hot SGP summer is definitively over. It is anoraks galore with peaked caps rampant, mostly worn backwards. The stadium is beginning to fill up but there is little to do except eat, drink or wait. There is no shelter. The route down the back straight from the pits area to the only public entrance is through the trees via a leaf covered muddy woodland path of the kind that feels like it should lead to stunning vistas or cliffside views of the sea. The going is soft to boggy underfoot. It begins to rain heavily again. Those that can seek shelter. I stop under the narrow lee of the programme shed-cum-stall roof and am soon joined by a German "Belle Vue fan" who "saw Peter Collins as a teenager". He is here with his nine-year-old son who is going to his first ever Speedway Grand Prix. With dank formative memories such as these, retaining his enthusiasm for his father's passion may prove a challenge. It's cold, damp and wet where we are stood almost equidistant between the perimeter fences of two adjacent motorcycle racing tracks in a German regional forest. Though there's a hubbub of activity, lights, sounds and food smells beyond the nearby by turnstiles, immediate entertainment prospects really don't inspire. Hopefully this youngster's imagination is vivid as well as fired by the mere proximity of pending daredevil action. Clutching for positives, his dad points out an impressive rainbow. Possible star of the future but man of few words Robert Lambert rides for their local club. That said, this season they are both more excited by Martin Smolinski's prospects in the world longtrack championships as he is currently second and they think he may even win.

When climatic conditions improve I reconnoitre the stadium environs and the route I will later need to navigate in darkness after the meeting to the shuttle bus stop back to Teterow. Though eminently sensible, what sort of madness is it that the penultimate event of the allegedly premier "global" speedway competition requires any fan to have to do so? I am well-prepared with my rucksack of torches and hi-vis clothing. Walking against the flow of fans, I have the determination of a salmon jumping fast-flowing rapids to spawn upstream. Albeit, my path is muddy and hilly not solely aquatic. It feels more golf cart track rather than public footpath. Judged by the section of the grass-track circuit I can see and its rudimentary equipment – basic bird watcher scaffolding nest for officials by the start line and five higgledy-piggledy rows of ageing wooden plank benches in need of repair on a gentle slope serves spectators as the overflow "grandstand" – the speedway stadium suddenly looks comparatively massively over-engineered, chichi and wonderfully deluxe. The grass-track centregreen must be the completely power-free camp site promised on the SGP website. It also looks totally facility-free too except for a couple of blue portaloos. Though Torben Olsen loves to sing the praises of the experience of camping out at SGPs in faraway remote locations, understandably almost sleeping rough struggles badly to gain real popularity. Vans, some old-school caravans and minibuses plus a gazebo enjoy so many acres with space to spare on the grass-track centregreen, they look truly forlorn. Further on around the corner, to show – understandably since it was founded in 1920 – that the grass-track club wears the trousers round here, there is a permanent main grandstand way better, bigger and much more impressive than that at the adjacent speedway track. Immediately contradicting this impression, close by are various careworn drab single-storey buildings with shuttered windows and locked doors whose purposes remain unknown but are clearly still in use so must be part of the regular operations of the grass-track club. The temporary bus stop area adjacent to the access road that leads to the bright lights of downtown Teterow is reached by negotiating two almost full mud-meets-waste ground sodden potholed car parks littered with big puddles and badly worn sections of crumbling tarmac. Against the flow of human traffic, it takes nearly 10 minutes in the fading light of an overcast dusk to walk.

The cheapest and most available tickets at Teterow provide access to the grass banks that primarily surround the track. With damp conditions and steep slopes, crampons and ropes are needed. These grassy banks are divided and fenced into so many different sized square-ish pens you half expect they are either breeding chickens or staging sheepdog trials not a speedway meeting here. Even with the intermittent vertical (rather than more useful lateral) steel dividing stanchions they have in place, UK health and safety would limit attendance levels to under ten thousand people. Though such UK fan-safety niceties don't apply, luckily the crowd won't get anything like that size. Shelter options if it rains again are practically non-existent. Since nothing is allocated in the various grass bank sections for the different prices paid, sensibly many fans short-cut the likely free-for-all by arriving early to bagsy their favoured viewing positions on bends one and two. By far the most popular food or drink stall inside the stadium walls is the circular Bratwurst concession with its impressive giant-sized circular pan hung over hot coals. With its smoke and subdued flame, it looks like the key artefact in a religious ceremony and is treated by its busy staff with similar diligent reverence. To untutored British eyes, they appear to serve the lengthy sausages almost raw. With time to watch closely from the slow-moving queue, it is hard to believe the time spent warming them to vaguely browned is sufficient cooking time. Pasta is fine al dente but, call me old-fashioned, processed meat is best cooked. The delicious sausages served in Landshut persuade me not to let prissy culinary niceties prompt me to abandon prior to purchase though a second bite is more than enough to make me do so after. With recycling bins aplenty in the pits, it turns out that there is a shortage of ordinary waste bins within the stadium. Another peculiar cultural tradition in full effect is the 50-cent charge for each and any use of the toilets. Even the overflow section of portaloos – without hand-washing option – adjacent to the very compact Gents toilet building enjoys zealous policing of this toll by an energetic woman who refuses to take no for an answer. It does feel a price gouge step (or stool?) too far even by the avaricious standards previously set by the SGP when it comes to their ticket prices and variable extortionate programme costs.

For my first time at Teterow, as a treat I bought a premium grandstand seat that overlooks the start gate and first bend. The ticket cost is an amazing 93 euros! I would expect to be sat next to the ref for this kind of price. Instead such tickets holders get use of a semi-permanent metal grandstand – to be fair, they are the most deluxe in the stadium – or similarly comfortable pre-fabricated cold (wet) seat, possibly bought as a job lot from the East side of pre-unification era Germany if its less than generous width is any guide. Apparently manufactured for snake hipped men and women, it easily accommodates anyone with one and half buttocks or less but otherwise offers all other derrieres a supremely snug fit. Despite the prices charged, in this unloved section, we don't even get a cheap German flag on a plastic stick to wave as these are only provided for fans in near continuous camera shot sat on the less permanent temporary stand that overlooks the third bend that sits next to the roadway down from the pits to the track used by riders, mechanics, officials, sponsors, FIM track directors and hangers-on. Inevitably the lure of the lens also attracts showboaters without flags keen to parade their access-all-areas star status on the telly and to fans sat in this particular area of the stadium.

My section is the ideal position from which to watch six members of the track staff try in vain to hand-curate the track. Their thankless task is to identify then pick stones and other rogue objects from a surface that is a slop grit mix. This is usually the kind of work given to those repaying their debt to society in blistering sunshine. The track surface looks more like the gloppy floor of a pig sty, albeit with sections of added gravel but without pigs, straw or their corrugated iron shelters. Many tracks served up by the SGP series do – to be fair – look the part but, when it comes to the actual racing, then completely fail to deliver. Unless, of course, mundane processional racing on a mostly shale-free track has been the unofficial goal in which case the organisers and rights holders have delivered another exceptional vintage. Though it has been a long hot summer, even when tracks suffer torrential rain – whether at practice or on the actual day of the meeting – generally the curators gussy up the surface into something approaching visually acceptable for the cameras, if not the riders. In Teterow even keeping up appearances while delivering sub-optimal racing conditions looks completely beyond the sub-contractors, FIM and BSI. Even theatrical sight (and occasional sound) of Phil Morris begatting the track – via his chosen medium of mime, complex hand signals and zealous authoritative verbal instruction of the curation staff – is in shockingly short supply. If Phil can't "lead by example", bark out complex orders or play charades to lead this Teterow track towards half-baked glory, who can?

Luckily, while we wait for something to watch beyond a hand search for shallow buried treasure, we have a bloke on the mike to really pep things up and along. Though bilingual, the section of the audience he chooses to fire up into something vaguely approaching sentience are the locals. Consequently, much fact or nuance is lost for non-German speakers. There is, of course, fun to be had anywhere hearing foreign language speakers say something recognisable in an otherwise incomprehensible flow. It is always a pleasure to suddenly catch "Jethro Tull", "trans exclusionary radical feminist", "delivering excellence" or "we will rock you" briefly surface from the babble. Thinking about it, if you can't suddenly notice these random incongruous words in everyday conversation at a speedway meeting in Germany, where can you properly listen to them? Despite the primary linguistic default setting of German, the presentation bursts into the kind of conversational English and enunciation that you would usually use with moody teenagers who you'd like to tell off but instead decide to try to encourage. Everything either verges on the giddy or the fascinating. "Welcome to Teterow, it's very, very interesting!" Lots is "very, very interesting". Intonation is upward so statements feel like questions and vice versa. In terms of sustained entertainment, little can match the delight the words "here's Tobi Kroner!" excite. It is a mantra so powerful that all other Grand Prix staging venues might as well adopt it or else give up competing for fan mindshare straightaway. British speedway fans the world over can immediately visualise Tobi riding towards the front of the race resplendent in his Ipswich tabard. Though a likeable and personable man known as a "perfectionist", whatever latent speedway talent Tobi promised upon arrival, his UK career mostly failed to ignite beyond itinerant jobbing rider status. After failing to make the 2010 Ipswich team, he briefly joined Belle Vue before quitting the British scene at 24 to pursue his dream of a career in banking (or, at least, embark on the training). Apparently, Tobi did this to avoid ending up looking back at 35 on "nondescript speedway career" and finding "that I'd achieved little". On the German speedway scene, in marked contrast to outside Suffolk, Tobi is looked on as something akin to a less reliable Gareth Bale. Despite that exalted status and his commentary work with Eurosport, it is strange to discover people would pay to invite Tobi along here as to provide expert analysis and colour commentary this evening. But, weirdly, they have. Well, most likely Eurosport have since BSI are notorious free riders. Whoever stumped up, we enjoy the treat of over ten minutes of Tobi's *bon mots*, insights and general thoughts. Every SGP meeting sees BSI try out local riders as a wild card in the full knowledge they are also-rans but in the vain hope of attracting further punters plus friends and family on the night to come along and see them fail dismally in the World Championship. The embedded media like to present these wild card choices as some kind of ongoing talented young rider development programme. To be fair, Kroner is an ex-German Champion (2012) and has ridden "at the highest level" – aka the inaugural Teterow German SGP in 2016 – so knows of what he speaks. I make a mental note to find out afterwards about his full World Championship record or, even, if he is now retired. His Facebook page says he is "semi-professional" which I take to mean Tobi still continues to ride at weekends. The interview is bilingual and Tobi's English is fluent. Predictably enough, the faraway audio effect of the stadium sound system works against the easy listening of any speaker in any language. Living in Ipswich, during his initial weeks in England Tobi once famously phoned the club office in a panic to exclaim, "the animals have invaded my house!" Unable or unwilling to explain further before he rang off, mystified but anxious club officials rushed round fully expecting to find a herd of galloping horses, scare off wildebeest or chase confident muntjacs but, instead, found Tobi's place had ants.

To further confirm the remoteness of Teterow (even by SGP standards) series rights holders BSI don't bother to unpack the centrepiece of their 2018 podium process: their proscenium arch. Apparently made from silver scaffolding during a tech college work experience project that won't count towards your final mark, despite the lorry load of essential equipment transported deep into the Teterow woods for the meeting, it's sheer majesty remains unseen. Unless there are some historical sensitivities that has seen an IMG corporate edict against unnecessary triumphalism in Germany, the Teterow SGP clearly must be viewed as something of a poor relation for them in the 2018 series. Given that BSI like to notionally justify the fees they charge staging promoters/clubs/councils/municipalities/governments and rentier revenues they extract from holding the SGP rights by obsessive policing of and zealous adherence to the complex detailed instructions contained in both their contract and event identity manual, it is likely to be their decision to have no arch. The arch is symbolic of much that is wrong with BSI's management of the SGP series. It adds nothing of value to the enjoyment or execution of the event for officials, print media, fans, viewers or riders. It requires many staff to erect while it potentially presents unnecessary safety issues to manage. An officious supervising manager is required but, luckily at BSI, always on hand. It is supremely pointless and seems to get used solely because it is notionally telegenic during the often dull pre- and post-meeting podium processes. This ridiculously overblown piece of kit looks more expensive than it is but seems chosen for how it adds notional flamboyance and lustre to the pretensions and self-image to these events rather than for its function. Though, heroically redundant, said arch requires detailed instructions to use and transport but is only ever temporarily installed – for riders' introductions beforehand and victory celebrations afterwards – but otherwise taken down during the meeting. Beyond this paragraph and getting hailed in the *Star* as an architectural achievement on par with building an Aztec Temple on the moon, the arch prompts no recognition, engagement or conversation with the wider general or speedway publics. If it provokes anything, like this book, it is contempt, indifference or derision. It has no real or imagined part in the tradition and history of the Speedway World Championships or, indeed, speedway full stop. It is a toy designed, bought for and played with for no discernible practical reason beyond its notional classical style. Worst of all, it completely fails to attract new fans or retain existing ones.

Even without the arch, the rider introductions proceed in the full glory of their usual predictable mundanity. Like a half-full Noah's Ark, riders are introduced one-by-one. In the journey from pit lane to the centregreen podium, not all the riders do the traditional full waving-to-the-fans-who-bothered-to-pay-top-dollar-to-see-you-here circuit of the track. Grandstanding by some of the more media-savvy (or media-needy) talent means that the introductions and riders quickly get out of synch. Such a format possibly has a tiny modicum of spectacle or drama if/when viewed on a screen. Unlike the usual line of riders and bikes introductions seen at speedway meetings the world over, watched live this approach is hard to follow and harder to clearly see. Partly because the riders haven't ridden past but mainly because how they cluster in a scrum (well, more like a loose ruck) for camera access and visuals on their podium spot marks is just plain confusing if viewed from the grandstands. As a ceremony it mostly looks like the preamble to some kind of poorly organised amateur beauty-contest-meets-charity-auction where the uglier contestants have to be hidden from prematurely prying eyes in order to maximise the winning bid that secures the main prize of a nutritionally balanced airport or service-station meal with the SGP rider of their choice.

If the organisers and rights holders can't be bothered to provide the arch, they also haven't bothered to prepare a decent track nor invest in (or provide) the full range of equipment required to provide one. Though, obviously, the track is deemed completely safe since it is fully approved by BSI's valued strategic partner – the FIM – and also meets all the existing exacting legal and regulatory obligations currently required under the rules. In some sports, track covers can be a wonder when it comes to wet and damp. Indeed, I pulled them for six tournaments as a (temporary) groundsman at the tennis at Wimbledon so have some experience to reference with vague insight. Something you only ever hear at the cricket is, "It is raining/forecast to rain but I'll go along anyway with complete confidence as they have covers". Speedway and water – in the form of rain – really aren't good friends except nowadays as a refreshing retro but natural isotonic drink after a hard personal training session. Interestingly, one of the sticks with which Paul "Burbo" Burbidge likes to troll and endlessly beat British speedway promoters with is their serial failure to invest – in a whole variety of areas – including stadiums but also track covers. To state the obvious for slower learners, covers tend to get used where there is no roof. They cost money to buy and need space to store. Speedway tracks tend to be quite big things so need a lot of covers to properly cover them. Teterow is 314 metres in length and of unknown – to me – width. Big covers need staff to put them out and again to fold as well as put them away. Covers work best when they are laid out before it rains and when the track is dry. They need skilled staff to ensure that they are applied correctly as water is a devil for finding gaps to leak through, especially if slopes, inclines, cambers or worn materials are involved. Obviously enough, though it appears to bear repeating, covers cease to work once they are removed. This is a problem if it then rains (or showers) since it renders any earlier protection irrelevant. It is worth saying again, as this key variable seems to have bypassed fevered plans to save British speedway from itself, that covers don't STOP rain. Any keenness to celebrate the Joy of Covers while trolling the notional underinvestment of the very British speedway promoters it is Burbo's notional *Speedway Star* news job to report upon, the question remains why aren't his other employer (BSI) facing similar investment demands and criticism from him for their global SGP events too? Especially when there are only ten of them now that Australia has flamed out and off the series schedule. Indeed, BSI could even make a one-off capital investment in cover or, most cost-effectively for themselves, make covers provision part of the standard SGP equipment checklist they contractually require sub-contracting promoters to adhere too? Of course, it is true covers do cost money. And depreciate so generate additional cost rather than profits. Plus the risk and cost-benefit analyses show that historically very few SGP meetings get rained off especially if the track surfaces used are comparatively shale-free.

If Teterow (or any other SGP) had covers it, arguably, wouldn't have made much difference to the track quality while news of their existence would also fail to add any additional paying spectators to the crowd. Particularly as most SGPs require advance ticket purchase to get the best seats and viewing positions. Fans keen enough to pay these eye-watering prices tend to pay for them early. Once you have a ticket for an event – often in sufficiently foreign climes that travel arrangements have to be made – you are fully invested in terms of logistics and cost so are going to go almost whatever the weather forecast. It is a truly rare beast who thinks, "Oh, I know, I won't go to the speedway but will instead have a wild night out camping in a field near Teterow, Hallstavik or Malilla instead". Given too that no SGP event is popular enough to truly sell out (Torun nearly does and, rather impressively, attracts optimistic touts on the day), walk-up impulse purchases are always possible but also expensive and something of a rarity. Something further borne out by how actual attendances and also television audiences have declined from their initial levels of enthusiasm over the past decade or so. Particularly once the reality of the racing and actual entertainment value of the fare on offer became more widely known. Who knows how many would-be impulse purchasers were lost after they thought, "I would go but it is a huge distance away, regular rain is forecast and they don't have track covers plus Tobi Kroner isn't riding so I won't"? Apologies for this fantasy world and whataboutery but, whenever taking Burbo's thoughts briefly seriously, delusional thinking is suddenly quite catching. In this parallel relentless advocacy universe, what is good enough for the BSPA servant isn't good enough for the SGP king. Nor, of course, would it work. And all this is before the lessons of history and the memorable spectre of the wet BSI shale in Gelsenkirchen saw them postpone then cancel their own indoor meeting. With the serial failure to make good on their strategic aims/promises, serial inability to find new audiences or even manage to break into new (global) markets, many doubt the leadership of BSI could organise a sherry party at a vicarage without extra help. And while we are on the subject of mandatory equipment provision, whatever happened to the BSI "promise" – following the Warsaw fiasco – to provide two complete starting gate mechanisms/sets for each and every meeting? This has been quietly forgotten plus – obviously enough – goes unreported and unquestioned by the tame embedded or "on staff" freelance speedway media.

Obligated to fulfil their bookings once they have formally signed on at any SGP, the riders slither to the start gate for the first race on what, if it were a cartoon cake, looks like a chocolate-coloured mud pie sprinkled with a dusting of icing sugar. Such a treat would soon get pressed into the face of our briefly hapless cartoon hero by someone villainous (or vice versa albeit without the haplessness). Sadly, since this is the Teterow SGP, this shale-sprinkled slop is less cinematic and an altogether less unappealing prospect to the riders. As highly experienced professionals, this troupe of skilled speedway workers can ride almost any track condition. They can't RACE it but they can ride it. They can put on the vestige of a show. Go through the motions. Appear to race. Fulfil the obligation. Allow the gate receipts to be banked rather than refunded. They will ride with care and well within themselves. It will be speedway. But, sadly, not as we really understand it. Or are sold it. In truth, this cut-down going-through-the-motions spectacle won't be that far off the ersatz version the SGP have served up to fans on sunny evenings for the last decade or so. In terms of spectacle, most SGPs have the glamour and thrill of an unexpected travel delay. BSI and their media collaborators have prepared and managed our expectations very well as many fans expect no more than this current hollowed-out simulacrum version of World Championship competition. Speedway racing with all the real excitement, devilry and goodness removed, except as it appears in the brief highlights edit of each race or the circa two-minute post-meeting showreel online. Of course, experienced live all the sights and sounds are present but without the real edge and urgency that races recognised by the riders as properly meaningful would have. When your livelihood comes from speedway, sensible professionals are going to race and ride in a manner that guards their revenue streams, longevity and health. Tomorrow is always another day. Making coin dictates not getting injured or going *hors de combat*. There have always been some fans who watch speedway for the crashes. And others who, while not specifically relishing them, fully accept them as part and parcel of the spectacle. With little to actually thrill, as a brief respite from their endless verbal exalting of the predictable and mundane, Kelvin Tatum and Nigel Pearson also relish discussing comings together, falls and crashes as these automatically add further flavour and grist into bland meal they serve up as informed analysis and discussion. The SGP feed obeys the self-imposed televisual nicety of not repeatedly showing crash slo-mo replays until the fraction of a second after the rider is confirmed up, alive and not disabled. Once this fig-leaf is quickly brushed aside and convenient fiction of sincere concern for the well-being of the fallen rider(s) fulfilled, the detailed examinations along with the sound and fury of their allocations of responsibility and opinion then get delivered up to the watching public. Said analysis is often solely in lieu of exciting race action as observed by the viewers' eyes rather than the gaslit version we are repeatedly told we are seeing via their ears. This all said, rubbernecking fans and broadcasters alike tend to prefer their crashes on decent tracks from racing incidents rather than brought on by errors resulting from sub-optimal track conditions. Though it isn't raining and hasn't for a while, it is quickly clear that this Teterow track fails the basic minimum criteria of raceable and, arguably, barely fits the latest iteration in-the-eye-of-the-beholder interpretation of "decent". It is, of course, nevertheless FIM approved and authorised by their on-site race director Morris as both legal under the existing applicable regulations and, thereby, fit for purpose.

Heat 1 is a processional almost sedate affair with riders strung out playing follow-my-leader on the inside line of the track. They mostly look fluent but also vigilant and wary. Artem Laguta rides disconsolately at the rear and retires on the last lap. Jason Doyle wins from the gate so arrives at the chequered flag in pristine condition. Even more so than usual in the SGPs, final race position is decided by speed of reaction at the start line and, thereby, the race order into the first corner. Every rider bar Doyle has much cleaning of their bikes and kevlars to do before their next race. Making sure sponsors' names appear next time out is an important task with financial imperative for all participating SGP riders. The lottery of difficult track conditions is a great equaliser as neither reputation nor high-end tuning count for aught. Przemyslaw Pawlicki's second place finishes this series won't require a second hand to count but, based on his first heat form, he should be a world championship crown contender rather than one place off bottom in the rankings. Further indication that the form book is out of the window in this mud bath, wild card Kai Huckenbeck rather easily sees off the erstwhile challenge of the highly regarded Laguta. At this stage it is a mercy that the most expensive seats in the stadium come without easy sight of the one big screen. Rather excitingly, it appears we are to be given race times to the third decimal place. The time of 59.722 is nearly two seconds outside the track record. Such ludicrously exact times raises doubts whether they are hand recorded in the traditional manner or via the oft-fabled transponder revolution. Until this pending innovative future, heat times rely continue to rely on the fallible reactions of an official timekeeper even if they bring German precision to bear.

Zagar wins heat 2 from the gate. It is the second race won easily by the rider drawn to wear the yellow helmet colour starting from gate four. Fredrik Lindgren gamely on principle attempts a first lap overtake that Woffinden repels by riding hard before the race quickly settles back into a procession. Before the third "race" even the bikes are reluctant. Holder changes his, Iversen's won't get going and Nicki nearly beats his personal best record for pointedly looking down at his engine before the third bend. The speed of the severe onset of these imaginary mechanical gremlins is impressive even by Pedersen's signature it's-not-me-it's-the-bike standards. There are no prizes for guessing Nicki is already badly fourth at the time of his realisation. For once, Nicki doesn't prematurely retire but – something of a collector's item for any rider at any speedway meeting, let alone one of his stature – Nicki is actually lapped by Zmarzlik. Suspicions remain that Nicki allowed the lapping to happen to double-underline to his fans, mechanics and engine tuners that he is yet again the innocent but talented victim of mechanical circumstance. Albeit brought on by his own bikes and tuner selection decisions. Either way, Zmarzlik is the third rider in yellow to win. Though there is an autumnal damp chill in the air, you just know that Nicki is going to need extra time with his trademark black industrial-strength handheld air-conditioner back in the pits.

Before it apparently became unworthy of comment, it often used to be said that consultants treating private patients in NHS hospitals were moonlighting on company property using skills the company paid to train them in with company equipment in company time for personal financial benefit. If not specifically in company time, then definitely denying them that overtime plus not resting so that they were at the top of their game. Though the qualifications, study and apprenticeship required to become a doctor let alone a surgeon rather than a speedway rider are vastly different, both require application and practice as well as the dedication to learn for a protracted duration. Until the ubiquitous financial dominance of Poland made the default rider ambition all-out speed on comparatively uniform large sized tracks to, thereby, become the standard experience and competitive norm: there used to be some career benefits in serving a British speedway apprenticeship. Riders racing here rode regularly while gaining experience and vital expertise upon variously sized tracks (some of them small) and a wide variety of differently prepared racing surfaces. In the early years of BSI holding the SGP rights and expanding the number of events in the series, pretty well most of SGP riders also rode in Britain. Despite being an ever-present since the inaugural event, Billy Hamill was the first to retire from the SGP series citing cost reasons as a barrier to his continued SGP participation just after the turn of the century. Though Hamill continued to ride in British speedway, Tony Rickardsson was the first to quit the UK speedway scene in 2004 to concentrate his efforts elsewhere. Others would follow. Like oil and water, the SGP and British speedway never mixed well. They were and are structurally opposed. Until Rickardsson and many riders after him bowed to the inevitable need to pare down or eliminate British riding engagements in order to fulfil their obligations in the expanded SGP series, it was common practice for "top" riders to race on our fair isle but also in Poland, Sweden and Denmark. Though fleshed out by foreign imports, our speedway rider product pipeline was in good nick compared to the present day. Though formal youth development was also better in serious European speedway countries than that provided in Britain, there was no shortage of talented – freelance – British riders keen enough to try their throttle hand and race domestically with the eventual aim of gaining sufficient abilities to try to enter the World Championships. In speedway media circles it still remains impolite to interrupt the ongoing excessive praise and hyperbole of all things SGP to note that rights holders BSI Speedway were and continue to be a completely parasitic organisation that feasts off the work and investments of other countries and organisations. Not only did they make absolutely no investments in the sport (beyond one bungled year in Reading trying to create an extension British league racing product) nor have ongoing rider salary and benefits obligations beyond the paltry SGP prize monies but they exploited existing assets – the riders as well as the ready-made speedway fan audience and sponsor pool – without need for any rental payments beyond the royalties paid to the FIM.

One of the important lessons of childhood is respect for your own property but also respect for that of others. It is as much about maintaining community values as ownership. If you break others' toys in the playground, children will often break yours back. Sadly for speedway globally, BSI's business model means that they can borrow then break any of the toys –

whether it's speedway in Britain as a whole or individual riders – with complete and total impunity. There is, of course, the fig-leaf of FIM supervision and regulation but since the FIM receive substantial annual royalty payments from BSI for the use of the rights, effectively no checks and balances or real possibility of sanction exists. If judged historically by FIM interventions to reign BSI since contract signature two decades ago. Passivity appears the extent of the FIMs supervision and pursuit of corporate good governance. In a world where BSI effectively marks its own homework, there is no penalty and, apparently, the few obligations there are aren't onerous. Worse still, even if we set aside the comparatively minor impact of the tiring travel component – since the SGP is structurally really a series of one-off events staged at increasingly remote locations – there is an overwhelming priority placed by the FIM upon the BSI's key business need that the "show must go on" from a calendar, broadcasting contracts, revenues and staging costs perspective. In such a world, though fully compliant with actual but nebulous (and hard to enforce) legal obligations as codified in the FIM regulations, questions of track quality, entertainment and rider safety appear very much secondary considerations. When the travelling circus is transient and only in town for one night only, they behave very differently towards the paying spectators and performers than if they had to permanently put on shows at the location throughout the season for the various community stakeholders (fans, club, local media, wider community, local taxpayers etc.) there. Though many of the tracks do also stage other speedway events, the extreme particularity of the SGP contract dictates compliance with its own spray-on version of event management organisation and the best practice BSI dictate. In a cynical nutshell, this means lots of freeloading, advertising signs and power tripping but little actual or metaphorical shale on the track. Contractually organisers must ensure that various chosen/selected SGP staff and freelance personnel get fed and watered in the two of the best available hotels in the local area to the standard they expect and contract. Rather than, for example, more long-term investments by rights holders BSI and/or organisers in – if we just concentrate on infrastructure alone – a stadium roof, the best available safety air fences or track covers. In effect, Torben, Burbo's, Nigel's and possibly even Kiri's transport, dinner, bed and breakfast needs take priority over additional rider safety measures, fan comfort, entertainment or additional investments – for example – in track covers or quality. Sadly, this means that the housekeeping turn-down service experienced at the hotel by the hired help is likely way better than received at the hospital by the racing talent. That it is an unfortunate fact of life doesn't make it any more acceptable. Of course, it must be noted that these freelance and ambitious riders happily compete on these terms in the same fashion we all automatically accept the Amazon or Apple terms of service. Aka if we don't agree to the version of terms presented/offered, we don't get to play. Whenever there is push back over a specific aspect of these terms and conditions, they get finessed in various ways ranging from BSI turning a tin ear, their media helpers framing or rubbishing the objections, Philip Rising posting the alleged "expert" or "insider" perspective on the BSF or BSI hiding behind FIM regulation and accreditation. For example, SGP prize money is completely derisory. Whenever this is questioned, BSI express faux concern before barely hiding behind the fig-leaf that they'd love to pay more but they are tied by the rates set by the FIM. This excuse conveniently ignores the one hand washes another nature of the claustrophobic FIM and BSI relationship, easiest seen on their balance sheet at Companies House as "royalty payments". It also forgets John Postlethwaite's original negotiating position – stated to riders' representative Hans Nielsen – that no prize monies should be paid at all by BSI because of the big-name premium-brand sponsorships that would inevitably flow from the lucrative celebrity the riders enjoyed as the SGP grew by mimicking the global success of Formula One in its revenues, worldwide expansion and live broadcasts.

One-off track quality has improved over the last two decades. There are definitely fewer falls brought on by track conditions. Early years saw these particularly prevalent on temporary tracks but also as a function of the much more competitive racing brought on by the sudden elimination intro meeting knock-out qualification process in use back then. Rider safety equipment is better – whether worn or crashed into. Injuries are less frequent generally and also at the SGP. They can still happen anywhere and at any time. It is in the nature of the beast. High-powered increasingly temperamental highly tuned performance bikes with no brakes combined with adrenalin and ambitious often competitive riders is a potent combustible mix. Luck, obviously, plays a big part in crashes and injuries too. Nevertheless, the logic of these one-off SGP stagings is that the riders – as freelance professionals – willingly sign on and knowingly compete at their own risk. It is "buyer beware" for each and every rider but not for the SGP rights holders BSI. Riders are completely expendable. It is hugely rare that the SGP show won't go after any crash or individual rider departure on a trip to the hospital. Beyond fine words and the event prize money, the SGP rights holders have zero enforceable ongoing financial and legal obligations to riders injured at their events. Neither real nor implied ethical and moral obligations form part of the BSI (or parent company IMG) calculus. Even Monster Energy saw fit to initially help their team rider Darcy Ward after his disabling injury. Trading in a world where everyone is eminently replaceable requires observing some verbal and legal niceties but also, inevitably, colours business practice. It is up to the injured rider – as professionals who make their living by racing for different employers on short-term contracts – to already have in hand their own health and/or "loss-of-earnings" insurance for whenever they find themselves on the sidelines. Given the nature of their work, injuries are inevitable. The SGP rights holders BSI are exempt from any and all the knock-on effects from any injury incurred at their events. These are borne by the rider, their loved ones and families as well as their clubs in the various national leagues they race. Sometimes the injuries prevent their teams from gaining glory while other injuries are permanently life-changing. One minute you are an able-bodied man competing in a dangerous adrenalin- and methanol-fuelled sport, the next you have to adjust to a way of living where everything you knew and took for granted has to be re-learnt and will never be the same again.

Though the UK charity Speedway Riders Benevolence Fund (SRBF) has some funds to help smooth the deepest financial troughs for both deserving and needy injured riders via loans, gifts and grants, they have limited financial resources. Like in all things, choices and decisions have to be made according to human empathy and sympathy but also the terms, conditions and exclusions of both their code of conduct and also their charitable status. Unbelievably, as more-or-less the only collective safety net available, some riders don't make themselves available to ride in the SRBF annual fundraising meeting. Other riders are always available and keen. It is human nature to shy away from considerations of mortality and fragility (except in injured rider or Tai Woffinden interviews). Perhaps, rider confidence to ignore the risks or view them with equanimity requires mental distance from the less fortunate or the possibility of misfortune. It is a given that the SGP rights holders aren't obligated to do so by the FIM so doesn't make the commercial decision to provide "tide-you-over" or compensation payments to any rider injured at one of their events. Yet more revealingly, BSI are so grasping, uncaring and un-collegiate towards British Speedway that they DON'T allow the SRBF to have collection buckets inside or outside the Cardiff Principality (Millennium as was) Stadium. It is the biggest speedway crowd every season in British speedway, yet its seven-figure revenues and profits are so completely privatised and meticulously ground out that even charitable generosity by others is absolutely verboten in case it diverts pounds that might otherwise end up in BSI coffers. Best of all the complete lack of charitable and political donations appears proudly listed as such in BSI's company accounts. Of all the real (or imaginary) shortcomings of the BSI speedway Grand Prix era this self-serving lack of generosity verging on dickishness over SRBF collections is, perhaps, the most revealing of the philosophy of grasping contempt that animates BSI's approach to speedway. Despite being a parasitic entity themselves, they treat worthier others with the contempt their own actions, attitudes and rentier philosophy deserves. And, of course, complicit silence over SRBF collections at the annual Cardiff SGP signals the complete and utter endorsement of this parlous and inequable situation by the SGP's various media fake news heavy breathers and cheerleaders. Doubtless, there is some self-serving form of carefully chosen weasel words of tosh – probably imaginary health and safety or security objections – that the rights holders can flourish about the severe danger posed by these SRBF collection buckets to "justify" their serial ongoing meanness and lack of compassionate humanity. In fact, they won't have to defend or justify their trademark avariciousness because the embedded media chumocracy won't ever ask difficult questions of any stripe, whether ethical, strategic, methodological or financial. Though the SGP wants speedway fans to be seen and heard (preferably, in bigger numbers) that is the limit of our collective sentience. As live colourful moving human scenery, our uses enjoy carefully demarcated limits. Any relationship that also involves common humanity, consultation, rights, charitable giving or independent cognition remains totally off limits.

Like dangerous, acceptable or safe beauty, what is or isn't a "good" track can to some extent be quantified and qualified but remains in the eye or under the tread of the beholder. There are many circumlocutions. Rideable. Raceable. Professional riders. Knew the risks. Same for everyone. Only one line. Conditions improved. Conditions deteriorated. Blue line appeared. What is definitely the case is that long-time participants in the series have important and advantageous prior knowledge of the regularly used SGP tracks. They know but, understandably, don't share this advantageous commercial knowledge with newbies. These various knowledges need to be individually discovered by new entrants on a trial-and-error basis over time. This applies whether it is racing lines, likely track conditions – the SGP often prepares their surfaces differently to that found during regular league meetings – and, most importantly, race set ups. Just like the "house" always enjoys an in-built structural edge at roulette in any casino (2.7% with the European single zero, and 5.26% with the American double zero slots), so too do regular top eight SGP riders when it comes to experience-led short-cuts. When prevailing conditions are neutral (aka one-off tracks) or change from the expected norm (aka weather intervenes), the advantages of experience and prior knowledge reduces closer to zero to minimise the automatic "grandfather rights" house edge enjoyed by SGP regulars. Arguably, in fact, it then switches to favour the adaptable, those without preconceptions or, indeed, the reckless. Given the points and qualification structure militates against the endlessly wild in favour of the steady accountancy of the hoarding squirrel, this evenings Teterow track probably favours "natural" motorcyclists without fear or dislike of the wet. Obviously, every rider racing here is talented and gifted on a speedway bike. They have grace, élan and sublime control. They are professionals. Being so and riding as a job dictates that some play the long game and, therefore, deliberately dial back the bravado in order to ride within themselves. That is the sensible percentage move. It isn't that they can't do otherwise, but just that they choose not to do so. It is easy to forget this aspect of their professionalism. Before they had too much money to need to do so, competitive veteran footballer indoor five-a-sides tournaments were once quite a thing. It was shocking how that likeable solid but lumbering journeyman defender you had seen so often ballooning the ball (or opposition attacker) into row Z suddenly seemed to have gained a big beer gut but also the verve, vision and skills of Lionel Messi. How on earth had you never noticed? Because they had deliberately chosen not to show that expressive side of their game. They had professionally supressed the talents that took them to centre stage and, instead, played the percentage balls for the good of the team.

Arguably, one of the riders that fits this particular temporarily reconfigured slippery unpredictable Teterow SGP bill is Craig Cook. Particularly so, given his motocross background. Perhaps, there are others with that background too. It is only my ignorance on SGP rider backgrounds and its absence from the publicity copy in the *Speedway Star*, on the SGP website or via the Pearson/Tatum TV commentary that prevents me also knowing who they possibly are. Craig has the background but also the imperative, given his current isolation at the bottom of the overall points ranking table. Stand-out stellar performances over the last two GPs could – if other results go his way – see him narrowly miss out on automatic qualification. And, thereby, this "closeness" would stake a more incontrovertible performance-based case for his possible selection as one of the four available 2019 wild cards. It is a tough task but, arguably, Craig's only route to enter the charmed circle of a season-long SGP booking. Of course, the special dispensation of a wild card is often only made to the favoured and/or face-fits few.

Predictably enough, as he has throughout the series, Cook makes a slow start in his first ride in heat 4 but Greg Hancock's struggles with track conditions allow him through to begin to chase Maciej Janowski. Cook looks fast and assured on his bike. He charges hard and quickly resumes close contact with the Pole. Cook rides his bike and prevailing conditions with confidence. It looks a question of when rather than if he'll pass. Sadly, as they exit the second bend of the third lap together, Craig accelerates at the very moment that ahead of him Maciej slows and gets more tentative. They are so close, collision automatically ensues. Craig clips Maciej's back wheel. Basic physics intervene. The sudden split-second halt dictates men and machines concatenate and then violently separate. Primal forces ensure bikes and bodies fly. Janowski is quick to his feet, while Cook gets treatment behind the screen the fleet-footed medical staff temporarily erect to protect his modesty from prying eyes. Whatever diagnosis or treatment is or isn't happening is literally shrouded in mystery, though the length of time treatment takes hints at both fastidious professionalism and possible serious injury.

Ironically, Craig Cook's wrist subsequently gets X-rayed and plastered in a lot less time than it takes the organisers to eventually stage heat 5. If this were the UK, NHS shortages, scepticism about self-inflicted rider injury by the local call handlers and deliberate under-preparation (aka not having two ambulances on hand) by promoters as a cost-control measure means that many riders similarly injured at a British meeting would experience lengthy delays just getting to the hospital. Let alone receiving treatment. The UK fans would have to patiently wait too for the legal requirement of "medical cover" to be restored at their track. Fair play, this isn't how they roll in Teterow. The fact that speedway riders the world over – in order to help "aid swift" recovery and advance alternative diagnosis by their favoured medical experts – often then hack the plaster back off again once it has dried is neither here nor there. Without access to the internet, we are deprived of the sage opinion of all the bone injury specialists watching at home who take to the British Speedway Forum Teterow SGP thread to post their immediate visual diagnoses and expert remedies. Even without this guidance, my schoolboy translation of overheard German speakers around me on the grandstand indicates that they still delight in using a lot of long complex composite descriptive words – especially those with umlauts and weird double ss's in – and body bone names in the interests of off-the-cuff medical accuracy. As I translate it, considered opinion is that Craig will struggle to walk the family dog or self-love for a while and that, somehow, a pedal bin has got broken. You never have Google Translate to hand when it is most needed.

Back in the pits a responsible rights holding organisation – I appreciate this is a wild stretch of the imagination – would rush over, open the event manual to the correct page and immediately initiate their carefully worked out accident counselling and recovery protocols for distressed mechanics, sponsors' family members or, if this were Jason Doyle, vainly attempt to reassure the various "hangers-on" that so often surround him masquerading as friends. Sadly, all those years of investment in and training for BSI's post-traumatic stress syndrome amelioration team comes to naught, not least because I have just made up their existence. Unfortunately, it transpires that far from caring for walking-wounded riders or those connected with them, the state of the track has – rather later in the day – suddenly prompted a severe outbreak of sweaty bottomed panic about over-running satellite schedules for BSI Managing Director, Torben Olsen, his correctly wristbanded and lanyarded onsite junior colleagues as well as his FIM amanuensis and tame race director Phil Morris. This is bad news for all BSI staff in attendance and, by extension, since managerial panic and shithousery inevitably quickly flows downwards to those underlings on hand in Teterow. Though apparently able to endlessly shrug off or deny any number of knickers round his ankles embarrassments, whenever race or staging issues actually impinge negatively upon live television broadcast timings or costs Torben's SGP meeting consciousness changes from its default room temperature setting of morose towards vaguely engaged man of action. Tracks Europewide can be as poor or cut up as much as they like to hamper the racing right up until the moment they start to threaten additional (satellite rental) costs. Then suddenly leadership at its very finest kicks in and, of course, flows down the chain of command from Torben. Though he needs no second invitation, this gives Phil Morris full licence to indulge in some further loud instruction giving to local track staff that his birthright of Welsh lungpower makes all the easier.

With all the diplomacy you would expect, a BSI staff member – possibly one of the "Deputy Event Delight Executives" – with a clipboard, inflated sense of power and resplendent in this season's brand compliant multi-logoed black cagoule (with orange trim) rushes round to the Cook pit bay to demand back the envelope of Torun SGP pit passes they issued earlier to save on their own postage costs. Though Craig's body is still in the early stages of its wrack with the physical and soul pain his crash inflicted – albeit in absentia with the medics – thinking ahead for once, BSI have already concluded (without waiting for any medical diagnosis) that his series is over so have come to seize back their property. Though there will be huge demand for pits access passes in Torun, running straight round to seize them back – perhaps – ill becomes the rights holders. But is, of course, very revealing of their business ethos. Only local promoter push back and squeamishness along with the petty bureaucracy of human rights legislation prevents the rights holders contractually insisting that all SGP pits have electrified fences, water cannon turrets and tear gas to repel the hordes of the insufficiently credentialed keen to illegally gain access to the riders or learn the secrets that entry into this hallowed inner SGP sanctum automatically confers. News of BSI's surmise that Cook will probably play no further part in the 2018 series travels like electronic wildfire from the Teterow woods to deep within the faraway bowels of the BSI/IMG organisation to off-duty members of its most important department. Finance. And, it's evil twin, Credit Control. Cook's accounts receivable is quickly checked for all outstanding invoices to ensure his summary of account listing can be re-tabulated and quickly despatched to the mobile he can only clutch one-handed at the hospital to demand immediate full payment of all outstanding monies owed. It is amazing to think that riders can owe BSI money, when the event offers prize monies to competitors. I am going to surmise that these prize monies are paid slowly by BSI in arrears. Of course, immediate demands to settle their accounts in full won't be what happens when SGP series regulars such a Greg or Nicki (often nowadays) require medical attention. It probably did happen with Peter Kildemand until repetitive strain injury in the accounts department brought on by the sheer volume of his crashes saw the demand for payment function disabled from his account. Better still, afterwards, Cook rather than BSI will be quickly sent a substantial three-figure (euro) bill from the ambulance company for his transport to the hospital and his treatment there. That the riders initially pay these bills directly rather than the rights holders or event organisers would be amazing if it were a surprise to learn that BSI frame and word their contracts to ensure that they can wash their hands of what the ill-informed wrongly imagine are some of the basic responsibilities and obligations they would automatically bear as rights holder licensed to stage the SGP series.

As soon as the modesty screens come down and Craig Cook is finally carted away, track conditions are so desperate that the grader immediately comes out to try to put the metaphorical poo back into the donkey. In the normal run of things during SGPs, track grades happen in the intervals after/between each set of four races. This notionally ensures that all riders experience a roughly similar (often sub-optimal) surface to race upon between track grades. That said, if the track is also watered riders who feature in heats 1, 5, 9, 13 and 17 tend to get the stickier end of the level playing field stick. Either in protest at being sent out early or possibly as a bet trying to trace a single arch of the McDonald's logo into the shale, the tractor driver circuits the track in a noticeably peculiar arc. While this curatorial Spirograph masterclass happens, the stadium tannoy crackles into life for an *ad hoc* pits interview with an unidentified rider. The sound is so bad and their accent so indistinct, it is just as likely to be with Slovenian Zagar or American Hancock as Australian Holder. Based on the honesty, I would guess Zagar. Whoever it is confirms the evidence of our eyes, "obviously, if you don't make the start you can't pass," then apparently reads our collective mind, "for the spectators, it is terrible speedway! If you try accidents can happen." You don't say.

It is, of course, worth noting yet again – while we wait like lemons in a remote regional German forest on a cold damp evening for something approaching a serviceable track to finally get properly prepared – that venue selection decision is made by rights holders BSI and appears to be made solely upon a revenue-maximising basis. They sub-contract to tracks/promoters entrepreneurial enough to risk meeting the extensive but stringent contractual obligations. And – invariably with the additional financial "support" of pliant but deluded local councils, regional governments or tourist offices with deep pockets, big egos but limited due diligence mechanisms – also able to pay the eye-watering fees and associated costs required. BSI appear to shy away from choosing venues they said they would actively seek and find, namely those in *new* speedway markets and countries or those that develop existing speedway audiences. Back in the mists of time, such selections would place additional emphasis too upon convenient major city centre locations as well as the high calibre of the racing and stadium facilities on offer. Sadly this was all mostly hooey and only the sweet nothings required for BSI to get their hands inside the FIM's knickers and, thereby, seal its shotgun marriage with the extended family of defenceless world speedway community looking on helpless. It is all very well for broadcasters and stadium announcers to prissily state that "rider safety is paramount" when they try to explain or justify the delays. That is right and proper. There is complete agreement. No fans object at all to this being paramount. However, if that really is the most important and key criteria, why is it that these conditions were considered and authorised as good enough in Teterow by the FIM Race Director in the first instance for this SGP? If there were questions about prevailing track conditions and rider safety then a few practice laps would have clarified things better. Clearly the decision taken to go ahead by Mr Morris is a function of the regulations, commercial need and pragmatism. Though Phil's riding career provides the perfect storm of zero World Championship finals experience and no track preparation apprenticeship, these don't prevent him issuing complex detailed instructions on track preparation to experienced curators around Europe. Though prevention is better than cure, the reality – as I might have previously mentioned – is that the pre-programmed timings of the SGP broadcast schedule are dictated by the television rights BSI sell/sold so the need to control associated satellite costs places a premium upon a prompt start and adherence to the race timings schedule. This commercial reality underpins, shades or trumps many factors including racing quality and rider safety so dictates preparations and decision-making. In essence, the riders and track have to be ready to race at 19.04 in order to meet those broadcast timings. Some leeway is, of course, baked into the maximum satellite booking duration of three hours. Declaring the track "fit" is one of the supervisory obligations that falls within the remit and job description of the FIM Race Director. Whether on schedule (or subsequently delayed), all SGP tracks invariably meet the existing applicable safety criteria and legislation that governs their use at the outset or, subsequently are AGAIN re-assessed as doing so after remedial work. The bottom line is that what we see at the SGP is either the performance expected or the culture tolerated. Too often at SGPs standards fall short. Many standards. Among the heavy breathers of the speedway media, if it is even acknowledged of course, any shortfalls are always blamed upon *force majeure* of external circumstance or freak happenstance. The reasons given are the legion effects – whether weather, luck, rider safety, technical glitches, promoter over ambition or error – but not its structural causes. It is NEVER presented as the responsibility and inevitable consequence of lack of investment, commercially interested decision-making or cost-controlling revenue maximising business plan of rights holders BSI.

To describe Cook's crash at Teterow as an unfortunate but impossible-to-predict "accident" is a sophist's use of language. Such a description is both accurate and a legalistic circumlocution. Accurate because this is speedway and, while crashes inevitably happen, injuries don't necessarily result. Though the law of averages dictates they do eventually. Every professional SGP rider competes knowing the risks (and benefits). All riders try to mitigate these free-floating risks by a variety of means including the standard safety equipment of crash helmet, gloves, kevlars, neck and back braces, engine cut off and, of course, the optional precautionary measure of riding possibly thoughtfully "within yourself" and known skill range, given prevailing conditions. These self-preservation ambitions can be hard to consistently apply when adrenalin spikes in the heat of the racing moment. There are also the additional off-track safety nets of health and income-protection insurances provided by specialist broking companies. These are negotiated and paid individually by each rider and, since they are freelance guns for hire, are a legitimate business expense. No compensation payments to SGP riders for loss of earnings as a result of "accidents" while on series duty are mandated, let alone made on an *ex-gratia* basis by the rights holders to any competitor. All SGP tracks are certified as safe by the FIM and then supervised by various FIM officials too. The equipment used is homologated and the air safety fences – though, arguably, not the absolute best currently available – are both authorised and a vast improvement on the concrete, brick, metal, wood, wall and wire crash fencing of yesteryear. Though never agreeable to experience, impacts with air fences tend towards the benign in comparison to any current or historic alternative. (Even the legendary cushioning effects of the collapsible blackberry growers garden style fencing Len Silver used to wax lyrical about at Rye House.)

Despite all the safety precautions currently available to all speedway riders, season- or career-ending injuries are a real and present danger. It can just be a matter of serendipity and unfortunate circumstances. Getting the Teterow meeting underway at the scheduled start time of 19.04 was, with the benefit of hindsight, sub-optimal given prevailing track condition. Though passed as "safe" and, thereby, rideable by the attending FIM supervisor authorities, to untutored eyes in the stands it still looked sloppy after the earlier heavy rain. Despite their best intentions beforehand to treat the track with caution, the ongoing need for points with only one more meeting in the series after tonight means it was inevitable that some if not all riders would attempt to race rather than just merely ride round. Subsequent lengthy repeated extensive track grades – prompted by rider difficulties and crashes – is explicit acknowledgement that the Teterow track was not in a sufficiently fit state at the outset. Obviously, so-called "accidents" and crashes had been priced into the racing equation by the organisers, promoters and rights holders. The first heat went ahead in the full knowledge that things might be tricky but that the onus to compete (or not) lay with the third parties – aka riders – they contract to perform. Clearly venue choice, equipment provision and variable weather ensures that SGPs aren't staged on a *ceteris paribus* basis. At best, tracks are adequate to good but the 2018 lived experience is that they are regularly far from ideal but suited to the efficiency that the broadcast needs require. Whatever their state or shale depth, the show invariably goes on. Craig Cook's fall sees him taken to the local hospital for examination and treatment. Said fall ends his season so results in significant loss of earnings. Such is the capricious speedway beast. However, there is a bad sting in the SGP tail. Cook's few kilometres trip from the track to the local hospital sees him sent an invoice €380 for his involuntarily use of the medically equipped transport provided at the Teterow SGP. Common sense would see almost anyone assume that this bill had been sent in error and that any/all bills resulting from the treatment of riders injured at the Teterow SGP would see the organisers (or, if not, the rights holders) liable for these medical costs. Amazingly, like polluters and avaricious rent seekers everywhere who deliberately externalise costs of their business onto third parties, FIM rules dictate that both BSI Speedway and any SGP organiser has zero responsibility to pay the medical costs of transport or treatment for any rider injured at any of their events. Let us let that sink in for a moment. What incentive do the rights holders, organisers, the FIM and its onsite supervising Track Director ultimately have to ensure rider safety is maximised rather than legally compliant if they know that they don't have any financial obligations for any and all sub-optimal rider outcomes?

Logically following through the implications of the wilful abdication of a robust duty of care further, should a spectator be injured by a flying bike at an SGP event – what faith can be placed in any of the associated notionally responsible supervisory parties (BSI Speedway; event organisers; FIM) having adequate reserve funds or insurance cover when the policy small print kicks in? Or doing the right thing by any injured, maimed or, heaven forefend, killed fans or their close families? If the riders agree – or, in the case of Cardiff, the photographers by signing into the event – to waive any rights and be treated with such contempt, then maybe unknowingly fans have too? Given we know that we can't rely on the tame speedway media to question or interrogate the situation, what assurances about the extent and terms of said insurance coverage exist? Taking this washing of hands and externalisation of risk with the competitors philosophy seriously, and since I can't see any such responsibilities printed on my ticket (or information on where to find them alluded to either), it is a sensible precaution to believe that the statement that any purchaser attends this dangerous motorsport at their own risk appears to be one of the few true, honest and accurate statements ever made by BSI or about the SGP. Going back to the €380 transport bill, final responsibility for its payment lies with the national (FIM) affiliated institution of the rider concerned. In this case, the ACU. So, both the FIM and BSI Speedway promote and operate SGPs on the basis that they have no legal liability for costs associated with rider injuries that their own governance and supervision fans might imagine would automatically give them responsibility to cover. In a nutshell, British speedway via the ACU pays for costs they neither incur or manage. On the principle that the polluter pays, this seems to run counter to natural justice and shows further complete contempt for British speedway and our club communities. It is safe to assume that the newly created limited company that nowadays runs British speedway does not have the depth of financial reserves to withstand any significant claims or liabilities, whether made by riders, fans or others. Indeed, this new-found limited company appears to have been created precisely to mitigate or possibly avoid liabilities, whether present and currently undiscovered but lurking under the rugs or in the long grass of the past.

Eventually the heat is re-run. It features something of a collector's item too, in the form of an actual overtake by Greg Hancock on a wet track. Well, a more damp than wet slurry style track. All it can really mean is that Janowski fancies things even less than Greg. It is all moot anyways as this version of heat 4 stops at the third bend when Vaculik tumbles at speed. It looks a heavy fall. And, possibly, also bad news too since he has only just fought back to fitness and up the SGP ranking table after recovering from the broken ankle he sustained in April during his first and only meeting this season for the Leicester Lions in their abandoned fixture at Swindon. It is soon rumoured in the crowd – rather than announced to us – that Vaculik, like Cook before him, has left the area for medical attention elsewhere. He too will take no further part in the meeting and, afterwards, also get a commemorative invoice for medical transport and attention services rendered. Whatever else can be said about the tracks the rights holders serve up via their third-party franchisees, no one can deny they have managed to add something to the speedway lexicon albeit with the injury equivalent of BOGOF – injure one, get one free. Whenever the race next resumes, whatever the injury situation, it will be a match race as the rules ensure that these two track condition induced falls require referee Craig Ackroyd to first exclude Cook and then Vaculik as the cause of the race stoppages. Sadly, Ackroyd has no power granted by the FIM rule book to exclude inanimate objects (the track) or the animated object that is Phil Morris.

The tractors come back out yet again to grade the shale slop slurry. Rather than the traditional agricultural blade to manicure the surface, the tractor trails behind it what appears to be a supermarket goods-in delivery cage without wheels but with retractable sides, possibly inspired by the design features of the car flown in the film *Chitty Chitty Bang Bang*. It is a shame we can't all fly away too. With nothing to feast the eyes on beyond the signature SGP sight of tractors circuiting, the stadium tannoy system comes into its own with a series of serious sounding but muffled announcements in German. To keep us vaguely alert, from the pits another on-the-spot but muffled rider interview bursts out over the tannoy. It hardly lightens the mood but is the closest we get to an update and is refreshingly candid. "I didn't make the start and after that it was survival mode." Perhaps this could become the new SGP slogan to splash as a strapline banner across their website, space adverts, Twitter header image and advertising emails? It is hard to encapsulate the regularly processional nature of most SGP heats but this does in a few words get close to their true essence. Again either indistinct sound or a lack of introductions means that the identity of the rider being interviewed is something of a mystery beyond the fact that they sound like a native English speaker. Rider accents continue to be unidentifiable. Doubtless BSI staff with clipboards rush to the pits to admonish guilty parties, cross them off the wild card candidates list (if applicable) and also ban – with immediate effect – any further pits interviews. Meantime the stadium guy switches from German to English to issue a plea for understanding. "Ladies and Gentlemen, please be patient to give us a short time for track preparation to stop the crashes."

Ninety minutes after the meeting started, there have been only three races. This is the kind of managed crisis that requires the intervention of the big boys. These big boys were, obviously, asleep at the responsibility wheel but this fiasco wakes them into vague action stations. Phil Morris carefully checks out the track by the start line as if keen to figure out where the murder weapon is hidden. He stares intensely up towards the referee's box as though wanting inspirational signals from meeting official Craig Ackroyd. Or higher powers. Since doubts exist God isn't a speedway fan, things are so serious, smart casual SGP numero uno Torben Olsen comes out to join Morris to blamestorm and somehow bodge a solution. It is a conflab of the truly important SGP people. Arguably, the best brains behind the current series in live on-the-spot action. Well, more like inaction. Beyond some innovative trademark Morris expansive waves as if using a banana to attack a sheaf of newly harvested corn to translate circumstances to an Olsen – so frozen that you half-suspect his whole body has had Botox – in simple language he can immediately grasp. "We call this a speedway track. It is quite big. But wet. We need it more dry." The situation is so desperate that Morris busts out more totally new hand signals to add to his already extensive SGP repertoire. Possibly inspired by a mix of the opening credits of *M.A.S.H.* and almost any action or war film but most likely *The Guns of Navarone*, Morris repeatedly pushes down with both hands as if trying to lever himself up from a sinking boat (or precarious cliff ledge) under enemy fire onto a rope ladder temporarily flung from the side doors of an escaping helicopter. The strong element of wish fulfilment makes it all the more wonderfully expressive. And quite something to see. Perhaps not quite enough as a substitute for speedway but visual Shakespeare in comparison to Olsen's shop dummy-like mime portrayal of "Senior Manager Receives News of Proposed Change in Accounting Report Format". Spurred on to further gesticulating excess by the immobile Torben beside him, Morris busts out a series of sweeping gestures as if he's Uri Geller levitating recalcitrant shale to the outside perimeter of the track. Though spoons bend, despite multiple sweeps, the sodden Teterow shale slurry stubbornly refuses to budge for our very own similarly credible Welsh global speedway Geller. Revised curation marching orders now discussed, agreed and delivered – in true Vulcan fashion with a tiny almost imperceptible vein movement at his temple – the SGP's less charismatic Captain Mainwaring Torben marches back off up the slope to the pits to text his driver to advise of a delayed departure while leaving Private Pike to sort the latest fine mess they've gotten into.

Even completely allowing for the ongoing lack of alternative visual stimulation, the skill of the tractor drivers verges on mesmerising. In tandem, they show sublime precision control of their vehicles – both the tractor and its strange big beast dance partner grader – and their various attachments to trace the elaborate complex patterns expert Spirograph practitioners would struggle to find enough pins and shapes to begin to emulate. Complex patterns of helixes, figure eights, circles, ovals, waves fall with geometric rigour flow effortlessly from their blades. It is more tapestry than pattern. We are witnessing master craftsmen at work. Driven this way, their tractors hypnotise as they skim and score; more oscillate than circle. Like a supportive but superfluous real-life partner offering advice from the sidelines to their well-rehearsed other half during the finale of celebrity *Strictly Come Dancing*, Morris delivers a frenzy of waves and exaggeratedly big facial movements to communicate precise but confusing instructions that boil down to "strip away all the shale slush except for the last two millimetres" or millimetric but irrelevant specificity, "particularly here rather than there". With impressive precision, the tractor drivers rigorously circuits to plough and grade the track until – finally – sparks fly as the metal blade contacts and scours its base. The announcer makes yet more of his pro-forma "Ladies and Gentlemen, please be patient" requests. Earlier wild talk of the delay also being "a short time" has vanished from the English language announcements and, most likely, the German version too. The locals get treated to a really long chat about the lengthy delays and rider jeopardy brought on by sliding their bikes in shale slurry. Though these were primarily brought about by poor track preparation, they are unsurprisingly chalked up to the UK Brexit vote, experience, inconsiderate mobile phone users not looking where they are walking and/or the weather. The English language business canard, "if you fail to prepare then prepare to fail" would be a more accurate and polite summary of the situation this evening but would, thereby, acknowledge some degree of responsibility rather than this verbal shoulder shrug of denial. These circumstances didn't just happen, it was a risk deliberately designed into this Teterow Bergring staging of the SGP cost-cutting mousetrap.

Despite our mutual reluctance, the delay is so long I attempt conversation with the German bloke next to me. "Can you can come back tomorrow?" Whether it is the sheer surprise of conversation starting after nearly two hours sat next to each other or his sincerely held religious belief about the next pending Day of Worship, he bridles at the effrontery of my suggestion. "What? Sunday? It is Sunday! No!" One of his friends further down the row adds, "It is too long, too long." As if reading the hive mind of the increasingly restive stadium crowd, the tannoy crackles back into life. "Ladies and Gentlemen, please be patient. Please be patient. The track is not in a condition for the ride, not the condition necessary for the ride!" Almost before these words have echoed through the surrounding trees, it spits on to rain. The previously remarkably patient crowd wolf-whistle. And grumble. Loudly. Despite evidence to the contrary, a man in the next row barks a gnomic, "rain not forecast". It is hard to know if he is reassuring me it's a brief shower or annoyed at the inaccuracy of these reports. The temperature falls further and the crowd are restive. Out on the track, the bowser (not spraying water!), tractor and grader deliver yet more impressive formation Busby Berkeley circles to pack down the random surf lines and mounds of shale the earlier choreographed blading scattered and piled randomly across its surface area. Rather whimsically, "Midnight Runner" blasts out over the stadium sound system.

Perhaps this is the first ever meeting where they get to award prizes for "Shale Pattern of the Night" to the most thrilling tractor driver rather than the harum-scarum daredevil rider who wins "Race of the Night"? Come to think of it, not only would this be a stunning but rare act of awareness about the actual calibre of the entertainment regularly on offer but – for once – a real *bona fide* speedway innovation from BSI! Rather than a so-called iconoclasm their media helpers spuriously claim credit on their behalf afterwards for. One of the first and universal Laws of Marketing (or Sales) is never have your customers stop and think. Invariably this is bad news and, mostly, leads to a lost sale. Even where cognition is presumed mostly *in absentia*, whenever punters have sufficient time, space and sentience to momentarily ponder their product confusion and pending act of purchase, they either walk away or select based on price. Impulse purchases do what they say on the tin and are so-called as they lack analysis or reason. The brain has been bypassed. There is no discretion. You just do it. I bought all my SGP tickets on this basis. My monkey brain – for reasons best known to itself – wished for a summer struggling to travel on public transport to obscure parts of Europe to watch gifted riders on brakeless bikes go through the motions to race processionally on mostly sub-standard tracks. Possibly that wasn't the only appeal of the SGP series to my monkey brain? Maybe it came along to drink in the razzamatazz of the caravanning-goth-bingo-meets-modern-circus rider introductions? Anyhoo. Speedway, like many sports, is followed tribally. I don't watch Sunderland to see Brazil levels of entertainment and skill (luckily) but because they are my team and loyal support of them is my default setting come what may. SGP fans usually either blindly follow speedway or their chosen rider. Some choose their favoured rider on patriotic grounds. Others on intuitive measures such as looks and actual or imputed personality. Others bandwagon jump. Of course, some like travel to laughably obscure regional European field and forest locations. In this context, it would be a slippery slope to introduce a "Race of the Night" award as not only would it invite SGP fans to stop, think and analyse but is something akin to the thankless task of vainly searching for the Beast of Bodmin or the Loch Ness monster. Even actually existing wild animals are easier to track down than a genuinely exciting SGP race. Just as the closest nowadays anyone around Dartmoor gets to Lynx is smelling it in Exeter city centre pubs, in similarly desolate natural surrounding (albeit forested ones), this evening bears are more likely to be found in the surrounding Teterow woods as a thrilling race somehow gets seen on the track. Despite authorised media claims to the contrary about "star riders" delivering mind-blowingly fabulous races, SGPs are most often consumed on a "never mind the quality feel the width" basis. If fans were encouraged to compare and contrast the notionally "best" races, even cursory analysis would quickly reveal making such selections are an almost impossible task from the 230 or so served up in any season. Go on, what are the top five SGP races of all time or this season that spring to your mind? I thought so. If you do manage to remember, is it for sheer thrill of the lusty shoulder-to-shoulder in no-quarter-given racing fashion? When we struggle to recall truly exciting races at every SGP, it is a clear sign that the gruel we get served is often thin and watery. Obviously, heavy breather commentators hail too many tracks as mind-blowingly fabulous or else impute magnificence as function of any "top" rider flinging their leg over a speedway bike to ride any SGP heat. In this world, everything is wonderful and bathes in the greater BSI SGP glory. Even if we generously extend the 2018 qualifying criteria to also include "memorable moments" that wouldn't be much help either as most would only remember Nicki's various contretemps, Greg's perma-smiles or hip-hop handshakes, the biceps and shaven hairstyles of thuggy mechanics, Phil Morris mimes, Josh's pits lane adolescence or Tai's tantrums. Just recalling the merest hint of impatient temper loss or toys leaving the Wuffy pram would also badly undo the linguistic heavy lifting and strenuous verbal gymnastics his press agent Nigel Pearson puts in during his impartial live broadcast commentary work to curate both Tai's star quality appeal while simultaneously pretending thrills levels are off the scale. If prize money came with the award then, perhaps, National Lottery style there could be rollovers until a true winner was found? Equally, given occasional first bend passes as the initial bunching dissipates are so often hailed by Kelvin and Nigel as the entertainment equivalent of a World Cup final hat-trick from Pele playing with one leg tied up maybe these first bend jostles to help further pep things up from catatonic might also merit their own award? The cash prize for "Standard Racing Pass, Jostle or Manoeuvre of the Night" would arguably roll over less often as it would be a slightly more keenly contested category.

Things don't require any pepping up in Teterow as the sheer thrill of the racing resuming is akin to the sudden discovery of a trove of nostril pin diamonds glinting on the surface of what is left of its shale. It is a fast-looking match race too. Hancock offers a brief hint of first bend pressure before he soon drops in behind Janowski to successfully harvest the race points on offer. They both know what is required so bust out some magnificently sweeping broadsides in lieu of an actual competitive race. Two and a quarter hours after the scheduled start time – around about the elapsed time it usually takes to stage a whole GP - heat 4 finally finishes. To celebrate, one German fan argues loudly with a steward before storming away and out of the stadium in a strop. Perhaps it is too close to his bedtime to continue to bear? Given the special service buses don't start to run until after 10pm, hopefully, he has his own transport or torches otherwise it's a long dark walk – albeit handily drunk-driver free at this stage of the evening – back to the town centre and what serves as civilization round these parts. I have heard of leaving before the rush – and, of course, the legendary Teterow crush is always worth missing by those who value oxygen-filled lungs – but this is still ridiculously early to leave. But, actually, thinking about it, a highly rational decision. It is cold and damp. Facilities are basic. And though speedway always looks more gladiatorial under floodlights, slurry instead of shale tends to make the racing dull and processional. That said, if instead this is an angry one-man piss-in-the-woods protest against the rigorously enforced 50 cent charge to use the portaloos or gents urinals then I can sympathise. Given those long-ago BSI Speedway promises of meetings staged in magnificent stadiums with executive boxes, food and drink nirvana concourses and state-of-the-art toilets, around 50 pence a pee is taking the proverbial, even allowing for cultural differences. In its own way, perhaps this egregious additional charge for something totally basic that pretends it is special and deluxe is the ultimate symbol of all the false promises made by BSI about their SGP? And I write this as someone broad minded and woke enough to accept women working in men's toilets long before it became fashionable to do so. I think we just know that Phil, Kelv, Burbo, Nige and Torbs aren't paying for a slash. And, if they do, then it's expensable so ultimately funded by fans – motto: "We take the pee so you can pay for it" – via the cost of their SGP tickets. Maybe fans need to collectively organise and all stage a brief walk-out protest over the poorly prepared track but also throw in a banner or two alongside about the toilet charges with the logo of whatever club is closest to our hearts? Perhaps Tai could show solidarity with the fans with a specially designed protest tattoo?

After huge delay, the Monster women return to the centregreen with blankets. Sadly, these are logo-free and not brand compliant as blue in colour rather than black/green. Many in the crowd look at these enviously. By the later intervals, it is expected that the Monster women will bring out their sleeping bags and those silver foil things they give out to marathon runners after their race to avoid hypothermia. If conditions really deteriorate, hopefully camps beds are on standby too. To pass yet more time, there is lots of intense reading of the programme. With only just over a mere third of the 52 pages given over to adverts, like the calibre of the racing usually served up at SGPs, this too delivers extremely thin-pickings and fails to live up to either value for money or expectations. Personally, I savour the German-only interview with Phil Morris that translates him as claiming, "Es ist pure Sportdrama"! And, just in case Torben Olsen reads it too, "das Format [ist] so gut". Spookily, having just read this tosh, the first race after the resumption features an actual overtake. More than one, even. In the same race. Let the full majesty of that roll around your mouth and mind for a moment. Total amazeballs. Doubtless, afterwards, thinking that BSI had successfully stamped out any hint of drama or overtaking from the SGP, Torben will demand a full enquiry into this catastrophic error. Maybe unconsciously the riders are channelling the anger, angst and pent-up frustration of the crowd into something that briefly approaches entertaining racing? Sadly, normal service immediately resumes with a mundane heat 6 only really notable for how much the riders struggle to navigate some bends. Though we have still had no updates or announcements, Martin Vaculik fails to appear for the seventh heat and is replaced by meeting first reserve Martin Smolinski. Ever dramatic in his entrances, Smolly's arrival trackside and ostentatious trip round to the tapes briefly rouses the crowd from torpor to tremulous via way of simmer before he is last by some distance and, thereby, quickly dials crowd engagement back to tepid again. Second reserve Kevin Wolbert gets an arguably bigger cheer when he replaces Craig Cook in a dull race won by Doyle after evading Zmarzlik's aggressive bisecting manoeuvre on the first bend. When running normally, there is little time between SGP races. After the delays, it is clear that things are even more on the hurry up to ensure that no drinking time is lost for the media and no additional expensive satellite time needs booking. For the attending fans, one of the many worries is that the special coaches back to town will definitely leave exactly as per the timetable schedule in 90 minutes' time, whether they have passengers or not. Incredible speed is highly prized in a getaway driver but speedway meetings run with the restless intensity of a roiled up ants nest is decidedly fan unfriendly. Though few believe it even possible, these Teterow SGP races become even more of a blur than usual. Nothing much sticks in the mind. So, though we lack contemplation time, we also lack dramatic races to replay in our minds or, for the few lucky enough to be able to see it, highlights on the big screen.

The announcer runs through the scorecard (in English) to date with the barely disguised boredom until he gets ludicrously gleeful telling us, "after two races, Nicki Pedersen has no points!" Hold the front page. Be still my beating heart. Though this joyful wonder bordering open hostility is peculiar, what is stranger is that – though it is no great shakes either – Nicki already has a point. Craig Cook and Martin Vaculik also have zero points but are spoken of as if they are still active participants rather than withdrawn *hors de combat*. With so little to entertain the crowd, perhaps the announcer is saving the thrill of this news until later? Heat 9 lacks oomph but does feature one lusty lap in the all-German duel for third place between wildcard Kai Huckenbeck and first reserve Martin Smolinski. Though even patriotic attendees would struggle to bathe in this small degree of reflected national glory, there is sufficient desultory air-horning and enough third bend grandstand German flags waved to merit panning camera shots to confirm the pre-programmed unbridled enthusiasm of local fans for the SGP home viewer narrative. Because of the cold and damp, all that is missing from this picture perfection are some ostentatiously worn lederhosen or fans waving half-eaten bratwursts.

No sooner does one heat conclude, than the riders are almost up at the tapes for the next race. With Zmarzlik Tai's only but distant rival, heat 10 is billed by the media as a high stakes head-to-head contest akin to the Ali versus Foreman Rumble in the Jungle to determine the whereabouts of the World Championship. This is more wish fulfilment than reality as – barring things not usually covered by insurance policies but mentioned in the Bible (acts of God, plagues of pestilence or the outbreak of war) – it is already pretty much definitely destined for the trophy cabinet housed inside Woffinden's 23 acre farmland estate in Staffordshire. Though Zaire is more exotic than Germany, the sub-standard nature of the Teterow track dials back the lived experience of this faux drama still further. Obviously, Zmarzlik's signature distinctive but endless and ongoing lifts of his leg off his footrest is to the fore. Depending on your point of view, his race choreography is either a pointlessly self-destructive style feature or sign of Zmarzlik's brilliant mastery of the sheer power of contemporary highly-tuned and highly strung speedway bikes. Whatever it is, with these prevailing track conditions it gives Zmarzlik noticeable last bend hiccups – as if he's suddenly been struck down by the speedway equivalent of golf's yips – on laps three and four. So much so it lets Woffinden through to take second in a processional race won by Hancock. With passing at a premium, in the next race Nicki gates then grinds out the win – in the slowest time of the night, so far – ahead of a Zagar either unable or disinclined to attempt an overtake. Niels Kristian Iversen easily wins heat 12 with the only drama a track-induced second lap wild wheelie for Doyle that nearly sees him hit the fence.

As if auditioning for a forthcoming role at BT as the speaking clock, the announcer decides to showcase his command of English diction when running through the cumulative rider scores. It's a real number festival. Not only do we get the points they have scored but we also get treated to the ridiculous personalised but unmemorable – except for Jason Doyle's 69 – individual numbers the riders have chosen for themselves too. I am guessing that these self-designated numerical "brands" have had zero impact on sponsorship revenues, rider recognition and attendances but do look nice on telly and definitely saves your mum sewing your name into your kevlars. Anyways, though Iversen's kevlars, bike covers and pits bay are plastered with the number 88 – a sign of pending vegetarianism in Chinese numerology, I believe – the announcer insists on calling him "number 19". Despite the visual evidence otherwise, the English of the man next suddenly miraculously improves when he argues that this is the completely correct nomenclature. It is true Iversen (#88) is only riding here because he has replaced the injured Patryk Dudek (#692). But it is a verbal walk round the houses to say that since wild card Wolbert is #16, first reserve Smolinski (#84 on his kevlars, bike and pits signage) is #17 and second reserve Wolbert #18 that, thereby, Iversen is #19. To further prove this moot point, he waves and flourishes his programme but is slightly let down by the fact that Iversen gets no mention in the scorecard. Apparently, that is yet further evidence of the existence of the Illuminati or governance by lizards disguised as humans. There is so little to entertain, we have been reduced to making our own fun. Before we can go full conspiracy about the moon landings, the assassination of JFK and whether Russia and/or billionaires influenced the recent Brexit referendum or the election of Trump, the racing resumes.

Sadly a track of this calibre is not going to make for epic racing even when romantically bathed by the wan light of a majestic three-quarter moon. It is just the right atmosphere for the opening scene of a horror movie. Itself set in a forest, this meeting is the latest horror show booked and inflicted on long-suffering World Championship speedway fans by the SGP rights holders BSI. Though beforehand it was hard to imagine the 20 qualifying SGP heats could get even more perfunctory than usual, the collective attitude is "make it end now!". Just get it over and done with screams rider body-language. Just tick the box and fulfil the contracted obligations. It is already 9pm. The broadcast timings are hopelessly off schedule and paying for more satellite requires extra money in the meter. Despite the rush, there is a modicum of drama in heat 13. Very much in touch with his violent street-fighter side nowadays, a slow looking Fredrik Lindgren serves up a hardscrabble battle for the glory of second place with Bartosz Zmarzlik. It is uncompromising. No quarter is given. Now as the prolix series finally wends to its banal conclusion, they are two bald men placed second and third in the overall standings battling for the consolation comb of silver. Gold is already bound for the often luxuriantly helmet-haired Woffinden. Referee Ackroyd lets the tapes go so promptly in the next it initially maroons Zagar plumb last. On the gate-and-go tracks beloved of the SGP, if you snooze you lose. Tonight this surprise works to our benefit as it rouses Zagar from his signature lackadaisical indifference. Briefly spurred into the rider his talent blesses, Zagar uses his experience, guile and track smarts to first claw his way past Pawlicki and then snatch second from nowhere on the line from an inattentive Holder. It is far and away the race of the night. So far. Next up Tai Woffinden treats us to an exhibition of wild over-riding, possibly brought on by track conditions. It is almost as if he had decided to pre-celebrate his inevitable victory on the second lap with a particularly precarious long duration wheelie. In Woffinden's man-versus-machine duel, the laws of physics and damp shale battle comes much less easily than the half the length of the straight by which he defeats Iversen, Laguta and Smolinski.

Heat 16 sees Doyle start slowly and find himself behind traffic. Not where to be as Teterow is "who gates wins" on steroids. Nor, indeed, that ideal when you still want points to finish in one of the top eight automatic qualification spots for next season. The only solution is to play the percentages and seek a professional foul. Consequently, Jason leans onto the nearest convenient rider also at the back of the bunch on bend one – Nicki Pedersen – and, though their brief touch is more of a caress than a clatter, he falls theatrically like a dying swan. Suddenly prone but also trapped like an overturned beetle under his bike, Doyle channels his inner Phil Morris with some urgent expressive signals to the nearest member of the Teterow FIM accredited track staff. He shouldn't really need telling to hurry over and help lift the bike off. By the time this impressively portly man waddles over puffing, Doyle has risen like Jesus but eschews offering any blessings in favour of his gospel of profanity. Though Doyle merits at least an eight possibly a nine for artistic merit and interpretation from the judges, under the rules referee Ackroyd must exclude him unless he deems Pedersen at fault. Instead, he – typically – bottles the decision and wrongly decides on a re-run with all four back. It's a decision that completely vindicates Doyle's gamesmanship. In combination with advances in safety (primarily air fences) and body protection allied to jockey-like control, precision and skill on and around their bikes, we nowadays see many more of these tactical falls-cum-dives from riders. Like Doyle just did and got away with, some riders definitely look for and seize the split-second opportunity for such theatrical but professionally won advantage. Many times it works, sometimes it doesn't is the calculus that more than justifies its practice. Though possibly a further sign of speedway going to hell in a handcart, at least they don't writhe like footballers after lacklustre challenges, even if speedway riders also gain from such professionalism/cheating. While he rode in the SGP series, you only had to look at Peter Kildemand for him to fall. Apparently permanently on the lookout for riders to jostle into before falling, Kildemand's offs were often at higher speed. Whether physics or theatricality, many of his featured one too many tumbles as if each race was an audition for a parallel career in film as "shot on roof baddie number three". Many hold that the velocity factor will inevitably bias the referee's decision towards the fallen rider since the visually implied danger element adds unconscious weight and veracity to whitewash such incidents from a dive to a crash. Nicki wins the re-run, while second place for Doyle further vindicates his decision to swallow dive.

Now finally up and running, the meeting continues at warp speed and flashes by so quickly, we may need to be strapped into our narrow seats. After four races in around ten minutes, while we cool and settle like freshly baked bread, the bloke next to me resumes frothing to angrily insisting that it was correct for the announcer to earlier insist Nicki hadn't scored after two rides as "he DID finish last in heat 5". Pretty well every filled-in programme around us contradicts this assertion but he refuses to check or join the rest of us from his time-lapsed worm hole eight heats later. Shortly after, the announcers *mea culpa* in German about his earlier points error elicits no matching apology but really catches my ear. Partly because of the way names and random incongruous English words – like The Steve Gibbons band, speakerphone, transgender or doxing – always stand out whenever you listen to foreign languages spoken, but mostly because the phrase, "shit happens" suddenly booms out over the stadium speakers. If any rider uttered this common language of men expression (or worse) during a live pits interview, Nigel would hitch his metaphorical skirt up to his knickers and tuck in deeply on behalf of imaginary morally disconcerted "family" viewers, apparently unaware that at this time the kids are definitely already in bed and that most find the relentless hyperbole of his heavy breather commentary much more offensive. Though I am pretty sure that public address system swearing also defies the SGP contract and corporate identity manual BSI issue and then endlessly flourish to franchisees, no such inappropriate language use apologies are forthcoming for any sensitivities or hurt feelings felt inside the stadium. Perhaps, the excitement of stadium speaker system swearing is another of those elusive and incredibly hard to pin down oft-proclaimed actual "innovations" or benefits BSI's rights ownership of the World Championship rights brings to "global" speedway?

They say you don't know what you have until it's gone. In our case, we definitely know we don't have a decent track or racing. That said, this isn't really so unusual at any SGP.

Fruitlessly scanning the centregreen for interval inspiration, the earlier absence of the proscenium arch suddenly hits home as its magnificence helps double underline the verve and splendour of each event in the series. And, of course, the thrill of rider introductions. This evening's surprise brutal absence of our iconic arch – the SGP silver scaffolding pole equivalent of the Sydney Bridge, Eiffel Tower or Pyramids – just fated things from the get-go. Also badly tempering the SGP fan experience is the absence of the Monster Energy sponsor seats from the Teterow centregreen. Once seen, this Joe Parsons inspired innovation – primarily for glad-handing sponsors and distributors – is truly unforgettable. Memorably so. Apparently designed by competitors and made at minimal expense by welding six surplus rally drivers' bucket seats together before adding a splash of colour via a smattering of logos and brand colour compliant safety harnesses. It bellows and shrieks vanity project though got breathlessly hailed – I forget by which cheerleader (probably Burbo, possibly Oakes) – in the *Speedway Star* as another revolutionary investment in the glorious future of World Championship speedway by Monster Energy. With track conditions damp under tread, there is greater chance of seeing wildly careening out-of-control bikes zip across the centregreen towards the spiritual destiny of smashing into the strapped-in but surprised big revenue valued customers brought along the Monster Energy corporation. It is another SGP Sliding Doors moment of paths not taken and destinies remaining scrupulously un-re-written thoughtlessly lost through the absence of said arch or rogue runaway bikes. There is a scandalous lack of entertainment, either of the macabrely accidental or high-speed racing on bikes without brakes variety in Teterow. Even sight of Phil Morris performatively rushing hither and thither in search of yet more incidental live screen time fails to delight like it usually does.

No sooner is it the interval than it is over again. Everyone is on the hurry up. Phil Morris briefly lurks trackside but keeps complex instructions and his accompanying arm gestures to a minimum. His damage is done. The races come thick and fast. The riders and everyone else – except, apparently, the Monster start operatives – just want to get this done. Perhaps, with the end in sight after a long term, holiday fever has kicked in. A more likely explanation is that minimising prolonged time in these dark damp dank woods appeals to everyone. Whatever the reason, even more than usual at the SGP, meaningless races blur into each other. Like blown childhood bubbles stand out for a brief instant before disappearing or burst as we fruitlessly try to catch them, these SGP heats bubble up, pass, then disappear from our collective memories, forever. With only the results in the programme to show for it. These numbers on the page are, arguably, the sole point and purpose of the exercise. It is a written historical record that – when looked back on with hindsight from the future – will get tinged and imbued with a majesty the actual experience lacked in its moment of expression. The riders will especially struggle to recall them. Except upon retirement, when their oft-retold memories will inevitably burnish and elevate the currently forgotten details of even the most humdrum and banal of these races into something truly significant and special. Each telling will bring greater imaginary clarity to the events. Heroes will separate from villains. Causes from effects. Actions from consequences. The oft-told story will race elegantly to its complex conclusion. If only Ian Perkin had been in Paris that night for Diana, the world would have complete retrospective clarity.

For now, we all just endure the races and wish them over with alacrity. Though, if the police require statements afterwards for use at Nigel or Burbo's trial for crimes against speedway or journalism, I do have contemporaneous handwritten notes I can share with the prosecution. Heat 17 sees Zagar bully NKI (as I rather over-familiarly like to know him) out of the lead, in a race otherwise notable for Martin Smolinski's only point of the night from four rides. Though svelte and remarkably toned nowadays, heat 18 sees Nicki Pedersen make another of his endlessly slow SGP starts as if somehow existentially weighed down by the guilt of past track aggressions. He gets a do over when the ref stops the race. The re-run then doesn't start when the tapes refuse to lift. Start gate failures are so yesterday. As with so much else at Teterow, things are all a bit bodged, last minute, overlooked or forgotten. This includes the complete absence of the obligatory second/reserve set of start tapes that BSI specifically promised as mandatory forever and ever amen to ensure – following the inaugural Warsaw SGP fiasco – that tapes-led delays and disasters don't recur. Quick repairs means that these aren't needed after all tonight but, fortunately, should lightning strike twice and another tapes crisis hit, we are all safe in the knowledge that we have Phil Morris in *situ* so hand signal starts are an immediately available and incredibly entertaining substitute option too. Though the tapes are quickly fixed, the Monster girls are again incredibly reluctant to take to the track with their number boards. Perhaps, they are on a work-to-rule? They do eventually rush out and perform much briefer than normal walks towards the relevant gate positions at military medium pace rather than their usual hip-swaying amble. Even their number board slow-motion twirls are perfunctory. Kevin Wolbert gates and, thereby, wins the re-re-run of heat 18. For the first time tonight, there is actually audible crowd noise to go along with the enthusiastic waves of organiser-provided cheap plastic German flags on the third bend grandstand. These three points make Wolbert the best performing German rider at this particular German SGP and for the whole 2018 series. Doubtless, Tobi Kroner is barely able to contain his excitement in the Eurosport commentary booth at the German speedway renaissance this surprise race win must surely herald. Heat 19 has an intense first bend before Emil wins it in what looks like superfast style but is really over a second slower than the winning times to three decimal places served up on the problem version of the track in opening few heats. With all points at a premium, through willpower and determination as much as track craft, Zmarzlik fights his way through to finish second. From the gate Jason Doyle wins the last heat before the knock-out races but nearly doesn't after a signature surprise sneak attack-cum-rush to the line by an until then apparently malingering Tai Woffinden.

Tonight even the draw for gate position – which is usually heralded on the telly as something visually akin to or on par with the opening ceremony at the Olympics – must have been hugely rushed since the riders are almost back out on track moments after they had just left. Fans scramble to fill out their programmes as the riders search for wisps of shale to dig and scuffle about at the start gate. Only the Monster start team are unhurried. They are so slow from their seats that, if only they kept glancing back down towards them, you could half-suspect it is some kind of inspired tribute to late era Nicki Pedersen. The first semi-final sees what actually appears to be something approaching a proper race, albeit ONLY down the back straight of the first lap when Greg Hancock and Niels Kristian Iversen briefly ride side by side at speed. There is nothing more magnificent than older riders racing flat out. Really competing handlebar-to-handlebar with passion and verve. Sadly, such sights are implied but almost completely absent from each and every SGP race. Not only does the SGP format not require such effort or risk, it also disincentivises such all-out action. By the time they hit the third bend, Greg bullies then easily brushes NKI aside. Given Greg has much more harshness than his Nice Guy give-some-racing-room public persona suggests, he prefers to gate and win or else flat track bully the lesser lights. Even allowing for notional SGP rustiness – this is a stretch – Greg quickly identifies his easy marks and how to best them. Like so many other SGP riders, Greg knows the real threat level NKI poses since he has already his number in triplicate for quite some time. As a speedway fan, it is *déjà vu* all over again when it comes to NKI. He looks the part and also appears fast on good equipment but, as sure as eggs are eggs, and though he has won five GPs (two of them in

2013), ultimately whenever the going gets tough against the better riders NKI mostly flatters to deceive before he psychologically crumbles then folds. This applies as much at the SGPs as elsewhere. Iversen has rightly qualified on merit for the 2019 series but – though looking slim, speedy and sometimes stylish (breakdown traffic repairman orange kevlar sleeve aside) – won't regularly threaten the podium unless, of course, he is consistently much tougher in the first corner or when subject to intense pressure. Of course, dogged professionalism and thoughtful, sincere application means – based on his current reinvigorated form – Iversen may well automatically re-qualify next season by the same SGP Challenge route rather than finishing in the top eight. For sensible insurance reasons, it is certain that Iversen will also compete in the SGP Challenge as well as the SGP next season.

The second semi-final is only really notable for the third lap battle for the non-qualifying third place between Zagar and Lindgren. Anticipating the predictable wildly aggressive response that his desire to pass will inevitably provoke from Freddie, Zagar feints to the outside then fractionally pauses to let Lindgren blast across him much too wide to provide the space he can use to then cut back and exit the corner ahead. It is a wonderful example of using your opponent's power to defeat them without need of contact. Speedway tai chi in action. Before the final, there is just enough time to invest yet further monies (50 cents) into the joy of micturition as well as fully engage my Teterow SGP walk-home safety procedures. I don my various items of fluorescent clothing as well as get my various torches to hand before resuming my seat apparently dressed for a trip down the pit. Collective nerves and anxiety off the track about the walk away from the stadium are much greater than those of the riders under starters orders at the tapes for the final. Out there Greg Hancock fails to gate and then suddenly remembers the track is damp so trails in at the back. Woffinden wins the final to move ten points up with only the Torun SGP still to go this season. Though berating myself for not investing in a head torch, the walk to the waiting special bus service area is muddy, puddle strewn and partly but sufficiently lit. Contrary to expectations, in my direction of travel, I see no able-bodied fallers nor older less able bodied people get flung to the ground when their wheelchairs or walking sticks suddenly stick in the mud of the notorious Teterow paths or stubble fields. Indeed, there are many buses and they run efficiently. Back in Teterow town centre, the two taxi companies completely fail to cope with demand. Volumes of wannabe punters are such that they can hang up on non-German speakers as well as complex or long-distance requests with insouciance. To add to the fun, the last train to Gustrow gets cancelled without warning for reasons unknown to all but DBahn.

The next morning, the station looks similarly train-free though they are now apparently back running again. The only other passenger is a young woman who sofa-surfed last night with local friends. She went last year and thought it so exciting she took her sister this year. They decided to go at the last minute and, though there were plenty of tickets still available, she felt they were hugely expensive. She still likes the "exciting" Polish riders best and, though a fan of the SGP and firmly part of its ideal future demographic, isn't sure that she will definitely go again. "Why not make the track best before? It was too long and cold to do it then in the meeting! There were many races where they did it from the start rather than overtaking. I like to see the tactics of the overtaking more often. The crowd were quiet except for some Polish people following a rider. Or when the reserve won. The buses were organised well this time."

> **First:** Tai Woffinden (16 points)
>
> **Second:** Jason Doyle (16 points)
>
> **Third:** Bartosz Zmarzlik (15 points)
>
> **Fourth:** Greg Hancock (12 points)

CHAPTER 10

Torun SGP 10 – 06.10.18

"Mr Pearson, one of the best commentators in the world!"

Torben Olsen

RENOWNED as the birthplace of Renaissance mathematician and astronomer Nicolaus Copernicus, Torun is one of the oldest cities in Poland set in the centre of a valley bisected by the impressively wide Vistula river. On a sunny early autumn Saturday afternoon, though the old quarter is a UNESCO Heritage site (so boasts visitor attractions such as the Cathedral and the world-famous Gingerbread Museum), since it is too far to sensibly walk, tourists and locals alike crowd routes to the city outskirts for the speedway. Whether in cars, old-school Eastern European trams, minibuses or taxis, people flock towards the Mariana Rose MotoArena. Though hard to exactly place, you can even feel a buzz of anticipation in the traffic queues. Windows are down, music blares and everyone speeds between the red stop lights. I even see a sign for SGP Turkish tyre sponsor Anlas out in the wild – probably not such a coincidence – rather than labelling a forlorn pile of unwrapped tyres dumped aside in a corner of some SGP pits.

Though it is over three hours to tapes up, a substantial number of fans already drink, hang out and enjoy the vibe of the merchandise and refreshments area directly adjacent to the stadium. There is quite a buzz, plus an incredible array of fencing and crash barriers as well as a substantial police platoon, mainly in riot gear. Even the less paramilitary looking police dress for trouble with a capital T. They wear stab vests and carry an impressive array of crowd-control equipment on their belts including handcuffs, truncheon and a spray unlikely to be antiperspirant. The fan dress code is casual. Black, red and white dominate the colour palate. Polish national flags are rampant. They come in a wide variety types and sizes to get waved, worn, adorned or draped. Face painters struggle with demand. Serious coin is being made from food, drink and merchandise sales even before the turnstiles open. Many advertisers have stalls too. Most are notionally or tangentially relevant to speedway, motorsports and our so-called fan lifestyles. Other stallholders show ambition by being here but remain either irrelevant or completely obscure. There is, of course, inevitably a gingerbread stall with speedway-themed metal presentation boxes to vaguely help justify steep prices – noticeably higher than even those found in the tourist old quarter – or, possibly, pay for the full-page advert they have in the programme. The variety and range of adverts in the programme is a joy to behold. Everything from the exclusive Arena Prestige Club ("high standards and the highest quality services for the most demanding customers") to heartrending charity appeals in words and pictures ("with a very rare genetic disease which deformed her body") as well as all the usual forklift trucks and industrial washers. Over 50 percent of the good value – aka priced at 15zl – 72-page official programme is taken up with advertising. More shockingly, there is original and, arguably, unique information inside. This is precisely the kind of thing BSI and editor Nigel Pearson's commissioning decisions (such as they are) usually stamps out. Without his claustrophobic but gossamer-touch supervision, this local produced programme has gone rogue and revealed that Nicki Pedersen claims to have the nickname

"Power". Perhaps, something has been lost in translation? Or else Nicki is having one of his rare "jokes"? This truly hard to believe something this ridiculously high-blown, verbose and incongruently grandiose could be allowed to exist in speedway outside my books or Burbo tweets and SGP news reports. I reckon Nicki is obliquely letting us all know that he admires Nigel Pearson's commentary style so much that he is contemplating a second sports career in darts. If so (and also if the approach to speedway his rivals ascribe to him translates to the oche), then expect to see darts occasionally spearing opponents' hands or other extremities plus the odd barney when feelings run high. Other SGP rider nicknames imaginatively include Doyley, Tajski, Bartus and Rosyjska torpedo. Only Zagar has the common sense and, strangely, ego modesty to admit to no nickname. If ever there was a clear signal that interviewing him might be a slow bordering on unrewarding experience, my other favourite nickname is Artem "Artem" Laguta.

To further double-underline the sense of occasion and celebration, ticket touts are out and about in full effect. Ticket touts at an SGP meeting! Amazeballs! At many SGP events this season it would almost be quicker to introduce the crowd to the riders rather than vice versa. The touts aggressively mingle and promote their wares but don't appear to work in concert. These entrepreneurial sole traders are – even more amazingly – keener to buy (for 120zl) than sell. At every other SGP in Europe, you can walk up and have your choice of last-minute tickets, even at the more popular earlier season Polish meetings held in Warsaw and Gorzow. Though later there are more empty upper tier seats in Torun than you would expect to see at a sold-out meeting, the touts show ludicrous zeal to try to buy any spares. Given you could put a pig on a bike and attract close to a sell-out crowd here (I'd definitely go and watch), people tell me that this demand is a function of the sheer popularity of speedway in Poland rather than for the SGP series *per se*. Even more astonishingly, vendors actively give away free 28-page full-colour speedway magazines specially produced for this Grand Prix! Though written for its target audience in Polish, for the non-native speaker it nevertheless still looks entertaining, professionally produced and informative. Even the rider profiles have insights and definitely are a notch above the usual cut-and-paste repetitious profiles beloved by the official programmes. The fact that this gratis speedway magazine is dated suggests that it might even be a weekly magazine specialising in the Speedway Grand Prix? If so, even in speedway mad Poland, surely this would be overkill? Giveaways to boost further or future subscriber demand is sensible in country famed for its love of its speedway. Though the magazine carries some adverts, these aren't excessive in the manner of the official 2018 SGP programmes primarily edited on auto-pilot by Nigel Pearson and produced by his current UK "favourite" speedway programme printers Curtis Sport. In every official SGP various columns and many adverts repeat with alteration to really bulk out the page extent. Fewer adverts litter the occasional one-off commemorative "specials" produced by Curtis Sports under Pearson's editorship. A casual look through the (Polish language) contents of this gratis SGP magazine shows it contains more original bespoke content than that often found in the over copious *Speedway Star* SGP news reporting.

Purpose built for speedway, the stadium is reputed to house one of the best race tracks in the world. Indeed, the Motorarena is spoken of in such hushed and reverential tones in the media but also crucially amongst the rider and fans, that you half-suspect Jesus may choose to hold his next resurrection here if Catholics rather than Mormons or the Born Again win preferment. It is a definitely real/proper speedway destination well known for both its racing and atmosphere. Even if we take the passion of local fans and Poles generally for speedway as a given (but not for granted), then this stadium is one of the canonical places of speedway worship. Though reputed to exhibit the atmospheric equivalent of the Nou Camp on derby day for almost any speedway league meeting held, the last SGP of the 2018 season channels and leverages this pre-existing passion rather than invents or pacifies it. Though from the outside it presents as a lower slung more modest stadium building than positive noises might indicate to those who haven't previously visited, its modern design signature glass roof immediately catches the eye and impresses with its visual grandeur. This architectural feature alone confirms its cradle and cathedral of speedway status and reputation.

In comparison, the pits lane that runs parallel to the back straight and sits in the lee of the rear aspect of some of the stadium offices has the look of an open-to-the-elements service-access route. And feels altogether something of an afterthought. It is as if after they made the roof, they then almost ran out of money for other construction. Upon further investigation, it turns out that though the club boasts state-of-the-art permanent rider workshops and deluxe pit bays for all their riders, these facilities get shuttered whenever the World Championships are back in town. As a result, the SGP riders do literally have to make do with temporary comparatively sub-standard pit facilities based in the club service tunnel! Worse still, the highly acclaimed food served by the club cafeteria is apparently also out of bounds too. Whatever the SGP pits lack in space, convenience and visual majesty, they make up for with the throng of people on the afternoon of race day. Though it is a place for older men it is not suited to claustrophobics. There are so many well-wishers, rubberneckers, sponsors, mechanics, media, guests, photographers, stadium and security staff that pit lane verges on gridlocked. Progress is extremely slow especially if you wish to embrace your inner Phil Morris to rush hither and thither promenading with barely suppressed masterful gait or try to see and be seen.

It seems everyone is here but the riders. According to Surrey-based Craig Cook Crew members Adriana and Ben – two ordinary speedway fans who sponsor the Cumbrian so get to see their names listed on his kevlars, special issue T-shirts and van as part of his crew – yesterday's practice or this morning in their hotel (Filmar) is where to go for unfettered access to riders. These are some of the few remaining ways to overcome and compensate for the increasingly rare sightings of this increasingly elusive species in the wild. "Freddie's staying there. Freddie didn't seem that optimistic at breakfast at our hotel. He told us, 'It will be what it is.' We know him from Wolverhampton so he came over to chat when he saw us. There's someone else's van in our car park but we can't figure out whose. We saw Zagar this morning too. They were all out here yesterday for practice. We spotted Bartosz's dad a mile off as he looks exactly like him. He speaks exactly like him too! And Max Fricke. Going to practice is the only way to really see them properly as I don't think any of the riders are going to come out in this. It's too small a space for the number of people. It's crowded but has no atmosphere."

It is unusual for a speedway rider to own a van and then not plaster it with various sponsor logos and decals plus – for the forgetful – their own name. And, of course, if still comparatively new to the speedway game the key words: "International Speedway Rider". Perhaps, all SGP riders are well past this newbie boasting phase of their career, not forgetting that many top riders often get others to drive their equipment to their meetings in undecorated vans. Equally, it probably pays not to advertise your van contents. Poland is definitely one of the few places where the value of speedway bikes and equipment is commonly recognised. Demand for keepsakes and memorabilia runs so high hereabouts that reports of ex-riders getting burgled or robbed of their trophy collections and equipment is more common than in the UK. This could either be a function of the any-excuse-to-issue-trophies-for-meaningless-meetings that besets speedway generally or, maybe, the higher calibre of their workmanship and innate resale value for a widely popular sport in a much bigger memorabilia market.

Though enjoying their third Grand Prix of this season with guest pits access, Adriana and Ben are disappointed that injury means Cook swaps a bay in the Torun pits for the bright lights of the BT Sports studio for his stint of expert analysis alongside Natalie Quirk and Scott Nicholls. "We've got the GP on record. He's absolutely gutted not to be here. I would like to think that Craig will get a wild card but, really, it depends on who just misses out. Has Pedersen finally run out of chances, I wonder? Pedersen has had them before but, this time, has actually finished the season rather than got one through injury. It's just unlucky for Craig that the wrist injury has knocked him out completely. He puts much too much pressure on himself and never enjoys anything because of that. We've been seeing him every week or every other week. The Belle Vue aways, some home meetings, some Glasgow and the [Speedway of] Nations where it was £60 or £70 a ticket! GP prices! I'm a carer for adults with learning difficulties and take Katie, Katie Robertson – she's got Downs, who loves the GPs – to speedway. We've been to Poole versus Somerset and Rye House away. She really loves to meet Craig. She absolutely loves him! He's brilliant. She likes to help in the pits and help pack his stuff up after. We sponsored him at the Test Match and are part of his crew for the year. He's really given us a lot more than we've given him. When it comes to favourite bits and memories and notable things, I'd say that was Cookie nearly winning a race and then his chain going in Slovenia or all of his races in Cardiff. Having pits access thanks to Craig has been great! Now I just need Magic to complete my set of rider selfies. Might as well while we're here. Our favourite Pole is Dudek. He's very shy!"

If there is a World Championship mentor-motivator-cum-horse-whisperer figure then – over recent decades – that accolade falls to Peter Adams. A taciturn modest man more comfortable in his own company, Peter slips almost unnoticed through the Torun pits throng to rest up in the Woffinden pits bay. If there is a secret weapon to his track record of World Championship success – managing Olsen, Nielsen and Woffinden to glory – it might well be bringing along home comforts such as the packet of chocolate digestives he clutches. It is hard to see whether Tai and Pete prefer the milk or dark chocolate variety but, whatever flavour, it seems contrary to the fashion for calorie counting that currently runs rampant throughout the current younger generation of speedway riders. Even with calorie control and lots of gym visits, the lifestyle demands of late nights, early starts and extensive travel impacts upon body clocks and physiology so almost inevitably results in some weight gain for riders during any season. Adams was in Tai's corner – possibly with chocolate digestives – for his 2013 and 2015 title wins before they split by "mutual agreement" at the end of 2016 so Woffinden could search for – but fail to find – a new advisor with different ideas and biscuits to inspire him to further SGP glory. If Woffinden triumphs tonight, over the last six years he will have won three times or else finished in the rostrum places except for the year when he lost a run-off for third with Nicki in Poland after they tied on cumulative points in the final standings.

Until the lower-tier access guest pass holders are summarily dismissed by a choreographed but fierce line of security staff in hi-vis, the deep shade of narrow pits lane is thronged. Suddenly available Polish SGP riders adds greater force to the waves of admirers. Trapped by the adulation, these riders press the flesh, sign programmes or patiently pose for selfies with warm but dutiful smiles. While all this goes on, mechanics virtue signal some last-minute minor adjustments or just look plain bored. The more exalted riders chosen to staff the Monster rig finally show up in pit lane to muster only to then immediately depart with their important bubble of personal assistants and helpers in tow. Blokes employed by the club vigilantly scan the crowd for infractions unknown, clutching walkie-talkies. Ignored in the hubbub but rammed onto the ledge of one of the anonymous office windows, there is an informal collection of an impressive number of random trophies and shields not august enough to make it out elsewhere onto public display. Friendly Eastbourne Eagles fan, Anita Dennington is here with her partner Ian. She still works at some SGPs and is also newly installed as Events co-ordinator for the Great Britain Speedway Team. She is access all areas, a good hire and enthusiastic about the future prospects of the newly privatised national team ("the riders are really getting behind it"). Her son Sam works at the SGPs too. "He's six foot one now, you wouldn't recognise him. He's had a full-time job with BSI since January. It's all early starts and late finishes with lots of travel and heat this summer."

The pits gate is a couple of rows deep with fans but that is nothing compared to the crowds that now crush out the refreshment and merchandise stalls fanzone area. Only a short while ago, the vast number of cordons and crash barriers looked like overkill but seem a sensible crowd management precaution. For the first and only time this season, a large Monster Energy riders rig is truly rammed. Security men vainly try to hold back the line of frenzied admirers beneath the raised dais-cum-stage from where Monster start line women and their rider accomplices navigate the mosh pit of grasping raised hands. It appears like a sold-out concert. And sounds like it too. Upbeat atonal electronic music with a hint of metal blasts out from powerful speakers. The vibe is ludic. The adulation is severe. Fervour levels are off the scale. Monster women run quick sorties to the edge of the stage to fire tee-shirts into the crowd as they evade – with practised skill – the sea of imploring hands. Despite their gung-ho adrenalin-fuelled derring-do on the track, the riders hang back or warily hand over pre-signed postcards in the manner of nervous children warily feeding grass to hungry horses they expect to get bitten by. On the edge of the crowd, cannier semi-professional memorabilia collectors clutch, sift and sort their piles of early arrival booty. Many have multiples of the pre-signed rider postcards they immediately sell on rather than trade with fans at the periphery unable or unwilling to risk the crush. As informal price and popularity market research, I stand and watch their trades. Woffinden cards are especially prized. Prices per card vary from 5zl to 10zl depending on the seller or rider card. It is fan-level speedway capitalism in action. In sharp contrast a few yards round the corner at front of the stadium, apart from queues at programme sales windows, it is surprisingly empty. The crowd self-selects. Those with no interest in buying souvenir gingerbread or hoovering up any of the free stress relievers, pens, key rings and brochures that advertise obscure non-descript companies tangentially related to speedway but keen to bask in its notional greater glory, walk around in comfort and leisure. Friends meet and chat. Ex-riders arrive, sign the odd autograph then scuttle away to the safety of the stadium reception area. Garry Stead parks up in a disabled bay and people help unload the wheelchair that is the barely hidden price of his speedway racing career. Garry is warmly greeted rather than ignored. Polish fans know, respect and celebrate their shale idols, fallen or otherwise. There is an *ad hoc* bucket collection for totemic Polish speedway racer Tomasz Gollob, arguably one of the most gifted, skilled and exciting riders ever.

The stadium authorities ban a variety of items including (hurrah!) "larger flag sticks". On a non-returnable basis, persons trying to sneak in "klaxon horns", big flags or drinks "will be asked to deposit them in a refuse skip provided for this purpose". I don't manage to spot the skips but do notice that there are close inspections at multiple stadium entrances. The queues are notably long. After bag checks, onwards access to the functional concourse is smooth and efficient with only a further short walk to the back edge of the seats to reveal the stadium and track below. On first sight on a warm evening, it all looks rather magnificent. Though new build and with a comparatively compact two-tiered all-seater stadium capacity of 15,500, the combined effect of the man-made bowl of the stadium – overlooking an impressive but pristine dark-hued shale track – and the design flair of the signature glass roof projects a speedway amphitheatre air. Simultaneously gladiatorial and deluxe, to the casual admiring glance everything appears thoroughly considered and well-prepared. Given the track is the stage upon which speedway riders strut their stuff – and as much as dirt ever can – it looks manicured and almost pristine. As the shale gradually dries out from damp, the compact contours of the track look conducive to finally delivering the exciting racing the SGP series has so far lacked almost everywhere this season. The track typology is all elegant curves and straights as if lovingly mapped out by experts determined to maximise the speed of its racing lines and, thereby, tip its scales toward numerous passing opportunities. The start line area is flat before it slopes gently upwards towards a narrowish entry into a slightly elevated but generously wide flared corner. Exiting the savannah of the bend apex down the flat back straight, riders enjoy a slight lateral rise towards the safety fence. Flat and fast, it then gently rises towards similarly shaped companion bends three and four. The track salutes its creators and curators with its elegant design and not quite perfectly oval shaped grassed centregreen.

Everything is primped, primed and ready for action. The ambient temperature is warm and the concourse crowd atmosphere bubbly. The green of the centregreen grass makes a striking colour contrast set against the dark shale but also against the blue and yellow Torun club colour stadium seats. Aural and visual verve strikes the senses. Placed on each seat is an A3 sized card in red or white for fans to "spontaneously" wave later for the benefit of the TV cameras to perform our die-hard Polish patriotism. The rays of the setting sun glint and refract through the glass roof. Phil Morris is deep conversation with Kelvin Tatum arms thrashing like parallel metronomes as though repeatedly demonstrating to a slow learner how to do crawl swimming legs properly. Kelvin carries a large rucksack that bulges as if concerns about his hotel room security means he feels safer bringing all his possessions along with him to the stadium. Sat in the front row of the lower grandstand seats at the exit of bend two, an Ellis Perks lookalike showily rests up his leg in plaster cast on the stanchion with the pride of someone who knows this studied insouciance about injury definitely marks him out as a rider to passing strangers. Equally, occupying the seat someone else has paid for also soon gets attention. Ellis or this Ellis wannabe has the facial hair styling – angular cut moustache with narrow cut sideburns – of an extra playing bar-fight baddie number four in a straight-to-video forgettable western. Ellis barely looks up from his phone apart from a lengthy chat with a younger Jan Staechmann look-a-like. Screen focus means he ignores the swarm of riders who suddenly all decide to take a sedate track inspection walk at roughly the same time but not speak to each other. Almost every rider has an entourage, albeit numbers and fellow walker prestige vary. Though, apparently, size isn't always everything, Tai Woffinden has the biggest. Three smartly dressed mechanics – if imaginary speedway celebrity ever reaches the fever pitch of mechanics going on a close season after-dinner speaking tour to deliver turgid insights (like commentators do nowadays), these are the likeliest candidates – are accompanied by a surprisingly voluble and almost animated Peter Adams (without his digestives) along with Tai himself apparently casually dressed for a beachside bar. Born in Britain but made in Australia, yet again Tai foregrounds his pride in and affinity with his fair dinkum but adopted surfer dude roots. Though notionally on a track walk, Tai barely glances at the shale surface, let alone checks it, as he is deep in conversation on his mobile. Occasional enthusiastic air-horn parped greetings merit a distracted but regal wave towards the rough stand vicinity of the noise. From the centregreen, Woffinden's Press Officer Nigel Pearson catches Tai's eye. Though primarily wearing his SGP commentary duties freelance hat tonight, Nigel is important enough for Tai to leave the track and his entourage to walk over to greet. The perma-smile has barely made it onto Nigel's face but not his eyes before it freezes into a rictus grin as Tai takes another call that requires a wave and immediate departure towards the (faraway) bend three grandstand. On the stanchions to my right, some twatty but patriotic Brits sitting elsewhere come down to tie up a generously sized Union Flag that escaped the bag check skips replete with their home town (I am guessing Staines but can't be bothered to look) and favourite rider name (I am guessing Tai as it is short enough to remember and write) details. Their passion virtue signalled, they quickly retreat having blocked the view of the track for the duration of the meeting for anyone who wants to look in that direction sat in the first two rows of that section of low-lying seats. If the flag is important enough to customise and bring along, then farking block your own view with it at the football. These are precisely the kind of xenophobic selfish carnts that give some British speedway fans a bad name in certain quarters.

The Monster Energy start operatives go out onto the centregreen weirdly early. Over 30 minutes before the rider introductions and massively before the official scheduled tapes up time of 19.04 (local time). Possibly, since unlike the actual competition SGP itself, there can be quite a lot of churn in their squad during the close season, this might be their last chance to watch everybody's favourite erection: that of BSI's pretentious silver scaffold pole proscenium arch. Apparently thought to add majesty to the podium procedures – rider intros and post-meeting award ceremony – as well as breath-taking lustre to the televisual experience of said same, inside the sweeping sight lines of this purpose-built speedway stadium the arch looks pitiful and even sillier than usual. It's silver-coated scaffold pole faux classicism jars against the brutalist lines of the stadium proper and the comparative elegance of the signature roof. Perhaps, the Monster team are out there to see off the brief parade of two similarly objectified women from an unknown (to me anyways) rival sponsor who happily proclaim, "We Deliver". Quite what they deliver other than another blast of off-the-shelf everyday sexism remains unexplained. These women have on less practical footwear than the more SGP experienced Monster staff who – in full foreknowledge of the highly likely varying track and centregreen conditions – wear sturdier black boots, albeit with the fashionable addition of stack soles to deliver the desired "sexy" high-heel height effect. If stack soles are the crack cocaine of the speedway fashion footwear world for the Monster women, they are at least worn openly in contrast to diminutive men – speedway riders included – the world over who prefer secret inner foot-lifts to give them those additional inches of extra confidence. If nothing else, the "We Deliver" women teach us once more that actual high heels struggle with grass and shale, irrespective of the moisture content. Beyond the disposable ersatz camaraderie of the Monster-sponsored rider squad, you wouldn't expect to find team spirit in a World Championship notionally premised upon individual winner-takes-all competition. The exception to this all-against-all rule are the Monster women who throughout the SGP series work hard, stick together, act professionally, appear to look out for each other as well as take time and patience to fulfil their public duties with thoroughness and some grace. Well, as much as you can in such tight work clothes. They work long hours but appear to enjoy it, while having a laugh too. They easily slough off and elegantly evade the low-level overly touchy-feely admiration-cum-objectification that their dress code apparently both permits and invites. To be fair, the mechanics also have their bantz but equally also have friendships and cliques that run counter to their employ and notional rider loyalties. Otherwise though the SGPs are matey meet and greets central – plus the obligatory travel discussions, hip-hop handshakes and expert insider insights – collegiality is conspicuous by its absence among the various upper orders of the skilled freelancers that staff behind the scenes. Such as it is, their collegiality comes across as the speedway equivalent of air-kissing. Working long hours and always on show as well as probably shockingly low paid (doubtless explained as the paid-in-kind career benefit of prolonged international media exposure), the Monster women belie my prior expectations. Apart from the standing army unpaid volunteers required at every track without whom no event would take place, the Monster start women seem to me the SGP people who mostly closely represent the better more traditional speedway values of community, humour, respect for others and humility that are often frequently absent in and around this World Championship competition. In contrast, the dominant off-track ethos and values generally feel much more centred around surface show and appearances, assertion of power, revenue maximisation, entitlement, vanity and elitism. In a line of work primarily judged by surface appearances, my observation of the whole series from behind the scenes suggests that these Monster women have and exhibit the values of modesty, depth and humanity that is usually projected by fans and media alike onto the riders.

Ten minutes before the rider parade, Burbo does his media walk of shame across the centregreen. Many media types promenade billy big bollocks fashion as if we are here to see them. In contrast, Burbo scuttles nervously hunch-shouldered across at some pace as if anxious the reporting gods may strike him down for his ongoing transgressions. He soon escapes to a prime viewing position that overlooks the vicinity of the start line. With cost-cutting editorial changes already in train at the *Speedway Star*, I am surprised to feel sympathy at the rumours that – despite his pliability – Paul might also be let go from his Chief News Writer position there. Some suggest the declining circulation is an inevitable consequence of many factors including his bombastic reporting masquerade that all things SGP = wonderful, while British speedway generally (but especially without "top riders") = bad. Additionally, there are his slew of mad ideas to "save" the sport. These are invariably costly to implement or ill-conceived proposals that he has half-understood when overheard or else, weirdly, often dovetail with either the SGP's and Poole's organisational needs or commercial interests. Whether Burbs stays or goes, the calibre and integrity of the reporting probably won't get better there as plans are to eliminate the page extents taken by the club/match reports provided by experienced long-serving freelance club reporters. These loyal long servers were mostly let go by an end-of-season email as a cost-cutting measure. The often locally based team news reporting provided by these experienced freelance writers is to be replaced by the much more anodyne cut and paste job lot individual club reporting already provided elsewhere by the shifting staff of Nigel Pearson Media, Nigel Pearson and Phil Lanning. The window-dressing to justify this to the readers is to be a design revamp plus yet more bland rider-led interviews and double-page feature coverage. Specially produced dog food is to be replaced by extra burps of an own label version already consumed without satisfaction in programmes, the odd local regional newspaper and club websites elsewhere. A long time ago, Eastbourne Eagles Head of Speedway Jon Cook advised I avoid speaking to the riders for my books as they all more-or-less said the same bland things. Endlessly. Obviously, it isn't that they lack insights (who better to ask?) but that they are primarily focussed on either the short term or their own self-interest rather than taking wider or more strategic perspectives. Soon the spoil heaps created by the Pearson and Lanning speedway word-mining production line – which spans programmes, websites, broadcast, print and social media – will be visible from outer space. If Burbo's features and reports leave the *Star* I will miss them. They are compulsory reading. They brighten the universe. Partly for all they completely miss out reporting but mostly for their mix of grandiloquence and confident banality as much as their lawyerly tangential focus, peculiar factual assertions and relentless but mis-placed hyperbole. And, of course, for Burbo's delightful refusal to reflect or analyse while thinking that he actually is. But most of all because whatever Paul suggests as essential or worthwhile invariably means that the diametric opposite is true or should happen for the good of the sport. Burbo will, hopefully, retain his SGP website and social media propaganda responsibilities – at least until some other more professional and ambitious sports marketing company or One Sport get awarded the SGP rights by the FIM – so the joy of his work for future generations won't initially be completely lost to speedway.

Six pick-up trucks form the cortège to ferry the riders on an ultra-slow lap of honour to pretty good levels of adoration. The departure of the procession of gleaming vehicles from the pits is lovingly shown on the stadium big screen. Initially the pictures are slightly grainy as if a visual recognition that this journey is almost as significant as the first moon landing. You could do make up from your reflection in the highly polished bodywork of the trucks. These trucks glisten like hearses under the lights even more than the box-fresh ultra-pristine rider kevlars. Greg Hancock is the only rider with a selfie-stick, apparently live streaming the thrill of the rider parade – as if it is the second wedding of minor royalty to a much younger bride – to audiences unknown via some form of social media. Greg is truly relentless in his outreach. Usually in the hunt for innovation and more fan engagement so that he can then big these factors up when trying to monetise them into further lucrative sponsorships. Naturally the pictures will strongly feature Greg and (most importantly) his sponsors' logos but does also provide some idea of the presentation experience from a rider perspective. If nothing else, this defies both the footage and visual editorial convention of its portrayal on the telly. For all we know, there may be sound too though the strong rumble of the crowd noise would interfere with easy listening. Said film is not for his podcast since this medium requires no pictures. There we get weekly fluent doses of unexpurgated Greg. Along with lengthy but pathologically matey conversations with occasional guests. These are mostly friends or sponsors from Greg's lengthy speedway career. His notional co-presenter Stefan is there mainly in his role as the totally-in-awe straight man. He asks easy segue questions, endlessly expresses amazement, always wants updates on rides from last week and generally makes Greg sound vaguely compelling. We all knew beforehand, that of all contemporary speedway riders Greg does enjoy the gift of loquacity. Once you apply yourself to get over the cloying bonhomie and everything being "rad", the podcasts do have a low-fi charm. Some insights do also lurk beneath the circuitous exposition, pathologically tame observations and effortless rambling.

If only more riders did these podcasts, we could start to re-feel greater affinity, learn more and not have to suffer the formula translation effects of official comment or occasional insights gleaned via the Boys Own rhetoric of the print and broadcast speedway media. And again fair play to him, Greg records a new podcast every week. He has done so for over a year, mostly throughout 2018. Some are enjoyable but, mostly, they are less rad to be honest. Overall, Greg is likeable, engaging and, comparatively, open. Listeners definitely get to know Greg the man. And whatever is passing through his mind at that moment. For the attentive listener, there are always little new facts. For example, there was a lengthy but sometimes fascinating conversation with Monster Joe Parsons. Though a patriotic American and US passport holder, Parsons revealed that he was born in Pakistan. We also learnt the primary and – it sounded – most exciting aspect of his work for Monster is actually his annual extensive involvement with and in the Dakar rally for the Monster Energy Honda Team rather than that he undertakes (whatever it is) at the SGP. Though less so than his roots in skateboarding, surfing and Californian lifestyle generally, speedway is clearly also something close to Joe's personal and corporate hearts. Sadly, Greg's podcast can also go briefly but badly off-piste. Most recently, when he expressed brief but sincere sympathy for Roseanne Barr while apparently claiming the dark forces of political correctness had misrepresented her racist tweet and taken her opinion out of context in order to get her fired from her US TV show.

On the stadium big screen we get treated to the best SGP world feed live montages available. Mainly footage of the trucks, plus rider close ups and so many further long shots that reveal the true majesty of the six-truck cortège that you could half-suspect it is a commercial not a parade. From my position trackside, varying levels of actual rider enthusiasm about said journey are easier to spot. Matej Zagar, Nicki Pedersen and Chris Holder all share the back of the same truck, possibly a not-so-subtle pre-meeting message from BSI about the likely unavailability of wild cards next year for these riders? If this were the football World Cup, it could be dubbed "the truck of death". If Zagar is actually worried that his final cumulative points total may yet fall short of automatic qualification, his body language gives nothing away. Neither does his facial expression which is, as ever, set to his default haughty. As if playing his own internal mental game of "when the music stops", Matej holds his hand in a spookily frozen position of half-acknowledgement for the whole lap of honour. The arduousness of regular waving at public events means that Royal Family members often suffer work-related aches, arthritis and wrist injuries unless they develop a repertoire of low impact movements more akin to a visible twitch than a wave to protect their various carpal bones. They are reluctant handshakers and obsessive hand sanitisers too. For similar repetitive strain industrial injury reasons, Zagar is obviously cut from regal cloth and, if he obviously channels the approach any British royal personage towards the public, it is – drinking aside – the refreshingly abrupt Princess Margaret. On this basis, assuming the tradition that actual nationality is no bar to membership of the British Royal Family, Greg is Charles, Tai is Prince Harry, Niels Kristian Iversen is Prince Edward and Nicki is James Hewitt. From the stage truck help, Phil Morris is Prince Andrew, while Nigel Pearson is Nicholas Whitchell. Oblivious to the crowd or his lack of blue blood, Nicki stretches and flexes his shoulders throughout this brief truck road trip rather than bothering to wave. He does these truck bed calisthenics with such energy that you suspect that he is a black belt at reformer Pilates and keen to rival SGP tv pits interviewer Kiri Bloore. Otherwise Nicki noisily cracks his shoulder blades – like boxers do their arthritic knuckles – to try to psyche out his fellow riders. Throughout the slow circuit as he waits his call to finally mount the podium, Greg continues to live stream for posterity the almost complete lack of compelling action along with the hammy intro ceremony via a mobile he holds aloft on a selfie stick in the manner of a Black Power Olympic protest. Thousands of miles away in a variety different time zones, captive audiences unable to control what they watch – whether service station urinal users, or worried coma patients family members sat helplessly alongside the endless road to recovery – are forced to watch auteur Greg's random filmmaking. Imagine how tough it is for those with locked-in syndrome to blink their urgent request to change the channel or, at least for God's sake, mute the sound? At least, prisoners can riot.

While he waits for his introduction, Tai Woffinden – for the first time I can recall him hinting at either athleticism or a warm up (except for that amusing exercise bands and ball catching post-privatisation video from the Glasgow pits for Team GB earlier this season) – goes through stretching exercises apparently modelled upon John Cleese in the Ministry of Silly Walks. If it wasn't October, the shapes Tai throws totally look like an April Fool or, possibly, a dare. After each theatrical lunge of his (leading) leg, Tai twists from the waist in Daniel Craig fashion to shoot imaginary enemy agents queueing for beers on the stadium catering concourse with his invisible gun before he segues into some kind of football-esque inner thigh stretch (for same leg) that requires a ballet barre. Woffinden then alternates legs. The overall effect is to suggest attempting a particularly limber ante-natal class exercise for supportive dads negotiating a squat toilet on a moving train. Equally, perhaps, Tai just has severe wind? For sure, it is NOT going to instil fear in his rivals, whatever obscure muscle groups are supposedly getting stretched or warmed for action here. That said, given the rebelliousness and notorious plain-speaking so often cited by tame journos or his publicist, perhaps Tai's "exercises" are an oblique protest against his wider boredom with speedway life and this rider intro ceremony in particular?

Either as a result of the BSI's SGP planning unit off-site strategy workshop awayday or as an IMG local school geography flag project to inspire the elusive audiences of tomorrow, the last meeting at Torun has been chosen to "soft" trial a totally new presentation style. Though the specifics of this new dynamic idea are hard to exactly intuit, it basically appears to involve having whatever random national flag is on hand dominate the camera shot. Quickly followed by an upwards directional crotch shot that requires riders to attempt but fail to properly photo-bomb the foreground by contorting their head and one shoulder dramatically downwards while pretending to gut an imaginary fish with their teeth. The closing shot of the sequence then sees the flag dominate the foreground while the rider gurns or lurks indistinctly in the background. Looked at holistically, this clearly some sort of subliminal but weird visual flag recognition test for cunningly deep purposes – as yet unknown but loftily highlighted in the latest stunning innovations plan – dreamt up by BSI to add further lustre and appeal to the SGP for infants and the unborn. Equally it could be an induction test for the newly minted BSI Speedway IMG manager primarily tasked to book bespoke travel itineraries for its executives next season? Whatever the deeper meaning or plans, seeing a couple of the less handsome riders this way may be sensible but for all 16 – especially for the lookers or vain – it is nonsensical. Luckily, inside the stadium one of the few benefits of attending in person is that it isn't mandatory to watch or listen to the world feed transmission on the big screen. From the stands, we can survey the scene that unfolds before us at our leisure and as we chose without being told what to think or marvel at. Viewers elsewhere aren't so lucky except for those who watch Polish transmissions or choose to make a cuppa or do something useful before the actual racing starts. Those tuned into wherever Greg is live streaming continue to be treated to whatever random footage he captures via his selfie-stick atmosphere "rad" cam instead. Given BSI's relentless pursuit of pointless or destructive SGP innovations, surely it can't be long until their quest for cinematic presentational gold sees tail cams attached to a troupe of hyperactive Monster-sponsored skittish puppies to appeal to those slighted bored by the current Phil Morris version of The Truman Show.

In the investment arms race that is speedway nowadays, the latest must-have accessory is your own personal trainer along at the meeting with you. If there wasn't so little to cook, doubtless riders would soon also all get their own personal chefs too. Apparently, the less ambitious or poorer SGP rider makes do with only specially developed personal exercise programmes tailored to their exact needs and specifications in lieu of no one on hand to motivate and mentor. And, since we are in the conspicuous consumption area, all these programmes and routines are always billed as coming with a proven mainstream sports pedigree from elsewhere you had never noticed previously and, thereby, vital in the hyperactive quest for marginal gains. Personal trainers and nutritionists we haven't even heard of when they allegedly worked for a decade making the Scottish badminton, Welsh lacrosse or England U18 frisbee teams so special invariably manage to parlay these tremendously weak almost spoof curricula vitae into world-beating expertise as soon as they arrive through the speedway pits gate. In the food chain of world class athletes, it appears speedway riders often get the dregs, chancers, never were's and never will be's. It goes without saying, and irrespective of who writes your programme, regular exercise gives numerous health benefits and an endorphin high so can often breed a touch of obsessiveness. The roving pits cam apparently attached to the bridle of an excitable pony earlier gave us glorious pictures on the stadium big screens of Bartosz skipping intensely while wearing giant headphones. Whether these were specially designed head weights worn as part of his pre-meeting warm-up regime or a fashion statement, either way he looked supremely silly. The frenzy of his skipping was almost tantamount to a concession of defeat to Woffinden. What kind of universe do we live in where riders believe that skipping, diets and more slices of brown bread can land them the World Championship? Worse still, this nonsense runs rampant throughout the sport in Britain at all levels. Before too long and know it, track rakers, stadium music operatives and referees are going to start doing specially designed warm-up calisthenics to isolate and maximise the twitch performances of vital specific body parts they deem supremely important to delivering excellence in their performances too!

Without wishing to state the bleedin' obvious, modern speedway bikes weigh something around 77 kilos give or take the odd kilo. Until they invent even lighter (and doubtless much more expensive) bike parts, one of the few variables that remain within a rider's control is their body weight. Physics tells us that generally the lighter the rider, the better the power weight ratio. Albeit this isn't an immutable law since the track also needs to be dry and slick to almost shale-free too. Anyways, with a powerful beast of a bike to wrangle, riders also need notable upper body and core strength allied to ultra-quick ("fast twitch") reactions. Given heats are only ever raced in the same direction, only one side of the riders body needs to be trained to take account of these velocity load factors. Beyond this, all the usual stuff you can read in almost any newspaper or magazine feature about sensible food choices, the healing power of sauerkraut or enough vegetables, quinoa and fruit in your diet plus enough sleep and hydration applies. Speedway rider frequent-flier lifestyles – late nights, early starts, unprotected sex with strangers, sponsors with distinctive ambient particulates and lots of flights – don't help peak performance. Like race horse jockeys the world over, the ideal rider is short, light, lean and powerful with the grace of a ballet dancer on their steed. Beyond these key attributes, it is often the case that luck, psychology and rider quality apply in spades. No matter which era of speedway you consider, even with iron will and dedication, current or recent national team managers like Neil Middleditch, Alun Rossiter or Mark Lemon couldn't diet or exercise themselves into World Champions. Special ingredient X or Y can't be magically imported as a winning template from obscure sports elsewhere to ensure speedway excellence. Let alone taught by an over-confident personal trainer (or nutritionist) with a snappy haircut and nice choice in athletewear based in Umea, Basingstoke or Krakow with big ideas, framed certificates, national team sports pedigree, reassuring matside manner and wildly exaggerated credentials. Though easy to measure, the requirements needed to hone the speedway body to perfection are ludicrously hard to specify and are only a small part of a complex equation primarily founded upon equipment excellence, fast reactions, good fortune and racing intelligence. The best trainers, psychologists and nutritionists can shade the sports performance percentages but won't turn base metal into speedway gold. Star speedway riders are born not made. On shale, nature mostly trumps nurture. The current fad for trainers, psychologists and nutritionists is – for most British riders – the speedway equivalent of mis-sold PPI or the sheds full of revolutionary engines bought by the BSPA so come without the chance of recompense down the line for the unnecessary time and expense. Emphasis upon the importance of this area also functions to distract from or in lieu of investment in (for example) actual speedway training facilities, health insurance or full-time proper contracts with bona fide employment obligations for the sport governing bodies and existing league clubs.

Eventually this innovative but weirdly random rider introduction ceremony ends. Nicki wins by a close head the unofficial race back to the pits from the podium by setting off on a sprint as soon as the last bars of the Polish national anthem start to fade away. He is closely pursued by Bartosz who – infected by a burning desire to win everything tonight – competes strongly. Given the 18-year age difference between them, this performance doesn't bode well for Zmarzlik's evening ahead. While we wait for the racing to finally get underway, security in stab vests loiter at the top of the stairways to ensure last-minute arrivals take their seats with due obedience. The big screen flares back into life with an all-action commercial montage of "danger" sports from Monster before it settles back into a soporific rolling montage of "event" and "partner" sponsor logo stills played on a loop. All the usual anonymous SGP sponsor suspects flicker forgettably by albeit with pointless addition of adverts for the city of Torun and SGP merchandise. Given we are already visiting Torun (or live here) or that the merch is only available beforehand outside the stadium and, if on unlikely sale after, is located somewhere well away from sensible (aka the stadium exits and all routes back to the city). Still, this is way above par when it comes to the definitely not subliminal power of product placement that the SGP offers advertisers. After the endless montage of dull logos finally ceases and desists, a dull but pre-recorded pre-packaged interview with Fredrik Lindgren booms over the stadium speakers. Judged by his reflections, Freddie has spent his recent recuperation avidly watching mindfulness videos on You Tube. "The injury I sustained is very hard to overcome. It's been very difficult. Looking back, I do appreciate the last two seasons' achievements."

The first race of the night is hugely important to Bartosz Zmarzlik. If he is to capitalise on the outside possibility of becoming World Champion, he needs to pretty well win all his races but also hope that Tai Woffinden has a nightmare night or withdraws injured. Despite the need to win, his prospects don't look good but would be deserving as he has been the consistently most exciting rider to watch in the SGP this season. Victory would be a real surprise statistically but also because, so far this season, whenever Zmarzlik faces a must-win race, he fails to gate or goes missing. Maciek Janowski is taking things so seriously he brings two bikes out for the race. "Magic" flies from the tapes on the machine he eventually chose at the last possible moment but it comes to nought when, watching the replays, we can all see that the referee has incorrectly stopped the race. The crowd is of sufficient size and knowledge that their boos about the decision during the replay are audible. The big-screen race footage continues to enjoy a retro but snowy resolution kind of picture you get if your portable telly doesn't have an outside aerial. Arguably, this decision also robs Janowski of his chance of third place overall in the final standing. Tied on points with Lindgren coming into the meeting, gaining an immediate points and psychological advantage in the first race would have been handy and merited by such a fast start. It is definitely a reprieve for Zmarzlik who, predictably enough, made a poor fist of it. In the re-run, Bartosz doubles down to make an even worse start that relegates him to the back of the bunch. Counter-intuitively, this is excellent news for neutral speedway fans, especially those tired of Woffinden's room temperature mostly excitement-free march to glory. Though it has taken until the last meeting of the 2018 SGP season, we finally get to see a race heat with an element of jeopardy and edge as a result of circumstances that force and require determined skilful overtaking rather than positional acceptance and points accumulation. Bartosz really doesn't disappoint. He serves up a thrilling spectacle and totally brilliant minute of high-speed virtuoso outside manoeuvres and overtakes going from more-or-less last to winning by winding it on to overtake all and sundry including Lindgren on their dash to the chequered flag. The crowd erupts. It is – arguably – the best race of the SGP season. Throughout Zmarzlik gave us the speedy probing manoeuvres in the search for real or imagined gaps through which to execute his dare devil outside overtakes. It is the type of brilliantly thrilling speedway race action that catches the breath anywhere. Just the kind of harum-scarum body-on-the-line exciting racing that boosters and advocates suggest comes fitted as standard at SGPs but is really only notable by its almost complete absence.

It isn't just that our stressed lifestyles mean that we are increasingly getting less attentive or more forgetful, but this (2018) season there really just aren't any really memorable SGP races. It is all gate and go. The format ensures BSI maximise their income from TV rights sales, promoters fees and sponsorship payments, but ensures the actual racing in every SGP meeting is all about playing the percentages and settling for position. Lukewarm leftovers with the odd extra fresh ingredient rather than the gourmet feast promised. Obviously, the "fake news" providers from the embedded speedway media – whether written, broadcast or on social media – garnish the gruel of this stale rather pitiful SGP cake with the marzipan of lustrous visual tropes made in the edit (rather than on the track) topped off with their traditional garnish of word slurry decorative icing. But, despite the presentational élan, the hyperbole can't alter the lived visual experience that has seen both television audiences and crowds steadily decline. Putting lipstick on the SGP pig, still leaves it a pig despite ferocious protestations it is a roaring lion. But, hold on, if the SGP meetings are as dire as I claim, how come there was such a breath-taking race? To my mind, the brilliance and sheer entertainment of this particular heat is despite the SGP rather than because of its platform. Enthralling speedway usually requires committed competitive racing, exciting but well-matched riders/ equipment, a sense of jeopardy and something vaguely worth winning along with a good well-prepared track that permits close racing and overtakes plus – but not necessarily – some shale and a buoyant atmosphere. That said, while Polish speedway definitely has the sponsorships, high-worth contracts and financial incentives to regularly deliver ferocious races and memorable competition, it isn't a fail-safe or fool-proof magic formula for them either. They also have (many) dull first from the gate processional races too. The banal reality is that these mundane heats often look better as they get haloed by the big crowd atmosphere of passionate fans still able to support clubs and club riders they really believe in. In essence, this particular SGP race thrills because it has a rider who knows he needs to win plus it is staged inside the already highly successful fully functioning upscale speedway mousetrap used week in and week out by Torun for the Ekstraliga. The combination of track, stadium, riders, club loyalty and crowd passion sees the speedway gods align here. The difference to almost every other SGP heat 1 to heat 20 is that Bartosz had to immediately win his first race tonight rather just ride in it. He had to – as the self-aggrandising often say – go hard or go home. This evening he had fight back through the field or, at least, try to – otherwise, his quest for SGP glory was over. This assumes, of course, that his World Championship ambitions are sincere. This is not a given in an SGP grace-and-favour world where a stale unchanging field of riders forms the main body of this competition. If this has been earlier in this much too lengthy series, Zmarzlik would have just settled for second (or third) and lived to fight another day. It isn't just a function of speedway racing in Poland either. Even in front of the big passionate crowds in Warsaw (meeting 1) and Gorzow (meeting 7), we didn't get a race like this since neither rider engagement nor series format didn't enable or require it from the riders. With our collective heartbeats aflutter, this one swallow has to make our SGP summer.

Sadly, though it continues to look fast and side-by-side competitive, we also really don't get any other similarly thrilling SGP race of this quality – let alone fourth to first overtaking panache – here this evening in Torun either! For a sold-out event that had touts outside, there are a surprising number of empty seats dotted about the stadium. Those not here definitely miss out on the vibe, if nothing else. They also miss out on quite a bit of dust. This is pretty amazing to see or breathe in given its pre-meeting look as well as media happy talk about the manicured brilliance of the Mariana Rose Motorarena track. We also get a long delay when Vaclic Milik punctures the air fence after he clips the labouring back wheel of the slow-starting Nicki Pedersen. The air fence panel in question advertises "Visit Wales" dot com. It is the kind of prime-time negative association mindshare that advertisers would usually pay to avoid. Lucky, the power of SGP space adverts, air fence banners and sponsorships are notoriously ineffective and, worse still, nebulously unquantifiable not anything like increased revenues or even the fool's gold of greater mindshare, if using industry standard advertising metrics. The exception to this iron rule is, of course, Monster Energy who are, apparently, happy to use the SGP as an "extreme" action sport backdrop they leverage using their own marketing smarts and proven channels be loathed and detested – on the grounds of taste, arrogance and ubiquity – by pretty well all who follow speedway and still possess taste buds. If it had been Greg Hancock (rather than Milik) who punctured this air fence panel, suspicions of some kind of attempt at infinitesimally impactful brand awareness raising sponsorship with the Welsh tourist office would arise. Greg has long set the standard for organic but crowbarred product placement, whenever or wherever live television cameras abound. Every surface is a billboard for Greg and, of course, has its quoted price. Sponsors know that Greg will relentlessly showcase their brand and, thereby, deliver both real and imagined value as well generally give good sponsor gladhand too. It is one of the many ways Greg Hancock stands apart from the competition but also skilfully monetises his sponsorship proposition. When BSI Speedway made a brief but embarrassingly expensive one season complete dog's dinner of running a top-flight British speedway club – and also rechristened the Reading Racers the Reading Bulldogs – at televised meetings Greg often accidentally suddenly made pre-race lingering bike adjustments-cum-checks right by the same air fence panel before many races. While Greg delivers exceptional and extensive visual love-bombing for sponsors, Milik is inexperienced in the brutal ways of the speedway rider sponsorship world so rather than just linger by them, he dramatically punctures airfences for free. If previously sponsored by Visit Wales, this greater drama could even be contracted and merit bonus payments. As it is, Milik gets the wear and tear plus an exclusion for his troubles. If this is – as rumours suggest – Nicki Pedersen's last ever SGP, he fails to take any advantage of his reprieve in the re-run. Tonight, we appear to have been re-gifted the out-of-sorts with the world and his equipment version of Nicki that has dogged and plagued his latter-day injury afflicted SGP years.

While the media and many fans take an unduly reverential and uncritical view of the heroic nature of riders that often borders on a polite form of non-denominational worship, it is the race programme that guides our engagement and enjoyment of the service. During any speedway meeting, for speedway fans the programme race card effectively functions as a cross between the TV listings and the Book of Common Prayer. Plus, even better, we are encouraged and allowed to write in ours. Often. Even at SGPs, the race card is our compass, reference and guide to proceedings, though the stringent TV time schedules and poor information provision leaves little or no time for its completion. I flatter myself that I am not as obsessive as many other speedway fans for a variety of reasons including just using the programme as a tool to record and follow the meeting as it goes along rather than the creation of a holy object for use and reverence forever after. More fastidious fans fill their programmes in using pencil during the meeting before using the official results to complete it properly after. These official figures are getting much harder to source nowadays – as they no longer appear with race times on the official BSPA and SGP websites nor in the *Speedway Star* – so this habit is likely to gradually die out. Other fastidious fans buy two programmes at each meeting – one for use there and another for best in their collection. Even more serious hobbyist collector types buy three in order to preserve the third in all its original pristine glory inside individual transparent plastic presentation envelopes. At a rough guess, there are so many obsessively compiled speedway programme collections in Britain that – if all were thrown away at once – this flood of speedway memorabilia would quickly overwhelm existing UK recycling and waste disposal sites. If football joined in too, these programmes would be the straw that broke the already under strain landfill camel's back. Thoughts of souvenir programmes and collections immediately brings to mind the late speedway track impresario Dave Rattenberry. He was a canny businessman-trader with an extensive speedway trackshop and memorabilia empire to match. So much so, he even managed to return unsold books to me from beyond the grave six months after his death and eight years since he had bought them! He was also a football ground hopper and once explained to me that the definition of "going to a match" – something that you would imagine is obvious and self-evident – was the subject of serious debate and dispute due to different recognition philosophies. Some hoppers count it as going if they went through the turnstiles then left after five minutes. For others, it only ever counts as a ground visit if they stayed to the end and saw the game finish. Abandonments at remote locations were a particular bugbear for these particular more completist types as the match then didn't count as a visited ground. Yet other hoppers, had to also BUY a programme for the visit to count. If an obscure club or its crowds were too meagre to justify or require producing said programme, then Dave had an ingenious friend who got round this by producing his own bespoke programmes (ten, usually) that he then brought along to give to the club to sell at the match in order that he could then buy one back – as they were, thereby, both official and "on sale" – to further round out his programme collection as well as properly evidence his ground visit to his philosophical satisfaction.

Anyways, though not as extreme as some, it always puts a slight dent in my enjoyment of any speedway meeting when I make unforced errors in my own programme. I take little responsibility for my mistakes elsewhere in life except, of course, for my speedway programme crossings out. Even then, I struggle to take ownership. For maddening reasons beyond the comprehension of mere human minds, rights holders BSI Speedway Limited apparently labour under the ego-led delusion that there is a burgeoning SGP forgery market for their meeting race cards. This imaginary market has existed for well over a decade now; roughly the time period that programmes for each SGP have been sold without the most important news of which rider actually rides in which heat! While speedway fans accept, nay relish, filling out race details and also happily make changes to the race line ups from what is already printed there – providing nothing is beyond unacceptable. That said, this is no surprise as we already know that fans are very low down on the SGP agenda beyond their film back-drop status and imputed rider adoration capabilities. To make matters harder, if you attend these meetings without internet access then you have to rely on fleeting sight – often so quick you could suspect it is a subliminal message – of the line up as it flashes up on the big screen before each of the first four heats in order to figure out who rides where. Already time-poor, hurried and compressed when watched in the flesh due to live broadcast and satellite access requirements, this distracts from the lived experience of enjoying watching the riders come round and dig about the start gates prior to lining up at the tapes for these races. The false justification given way back when in the dim mists of time – obviously the embedded media swerve any hint of customer unfriendliness, wherever and despite how often it appears – was that the draw for race position during the Friday practice provided surety that the process was honest, fair and above board. It also ruled out the possibility that lengthy foreknowledge of the gate positions for the opening four heats could lead rogue ground staff in the pay of the deep state to doctor the gate position(s) to the advantage of their favoured rider(s). This happens as often as asteroids hit BSI headquarters in London, the SGP UK television audience increases or the BSI exec team find or develop new markets. To be fair, statistically the asteroid is a more likely outcome. BSI spokespeople sold the Friday practice race position draw as a further thrilling addition to the series and yet another fan-friendly reason to attend without ever quite explaining how a draw you can't see in a place you can't access that results in an incomplete programme excites crowds or adds to the entertainment?

The real reason for the lack of a printed race card turned out to be much more prosaic. But revealing. Namely BSI could print the whole thing much more cheaply weeks beforehand rather than have the time, logistics and expense of bespoke printing the just drawn race line up and inserting said race card into the programme during the night before the event. They also apparently worried about lost programme revenues if/when fans brought along their own pre-printed race card sheet – having gained the information on the internet – and, therefore, didn't buy a programme. Obviously, though people can still access the world wide web between Friday practice and the Saturday evening of the meeting – BSI would ban this too, if they could (except for their own website and Twitter account) – if you are on the road, it is a faff to do so or, for that matter, find a print shop open. Inertia wins. In pretty well every SGP series location, programmes are ludicrously expensive compared to the notional value of their content. I enjoy meaningless self-deluding guff from the big FIM and BSI big cheeses along with cut-and-paste columns and rider profiles produced on auto-pilot, so am a very happy purchaser. Without the utility of the race information, it is a sorrier purchase. Except, of course, for programme collectors and speedway memorabilia-ists. There are massive unexplained and un-investigated (by the embedded speedway media) price differentials. What is more or less the same programme – different local advertisers aside – costs £3 in Poland yet is sold for £10 in Cardiff. Some element of pricing to market is understandable and common practice the world over. Price-gouging by BSI – whether stupidly expensive ticket prices or these programme costs – is par for their course for their long-time business model. Though attendance decline is denied, premium pricing of tickets, programmes and memorabilia is a compounding factor along with the predictability and lack of entertainment the series offers.

After a season following the SGP, I am now wise to the pre-prepared trap of the inconsistency of the race card format. It is annoyingly won bitter experience. Given riders get listed from number 1 to number 16 and the first heat sees riders one to four race in helmet colour order of red, blue, white and yellow, you would expect this to repeat down the race card for all four of the first heats for the riders numbered five to sixteen. Whereas, in fact, possibly for imaginary forgery fraud protection reasons, it goes down the race card – for heats two to four – as RWBY, WRBY and YBRW. Effectively, for the remainder of the race card only rider numbers five, eight, twelve and fourteen follow the race position-helmet colour logic expected. So, if as a fan, you use your eyes to visually assign rider race position numbers by sight as the riders take to the track – sensible common practice at speedway meetings but harder to do correctly at SGPs because of the frenetic rush of batches of four heats – and write them into your programme, you'll create an error-strewn document before the second race has even started. Perhaps, this programme defacing/damage is deliberately intended by the FIM and BSI to make attending memorable? There is definitely no warning or guidance about this quirk in this standard key advice section of the programme. Though there is guidance on how points are scored and how "gate position" is chosen by "participating riders" for the final three heats. There is a small measure of smug satisfaction in a swiftly and correctly completed programme that avoids the pending predictable errors of other less experienced fans. To get better calligraphy and to try to avoid errors, the "Be Prepared" ex-cub scout in me tends to copy out the rider draw information onto my race card from better informed nearby fans during the wait before the meeting starts rather than rush as the riders take the track or the details flash upon the stadium big screens. In this instance, the closest fan with a pre-completed programme race card is a blonde woman sat a row in front to my right here with her friend and a biggish Swedish flag to support Fredrik Lindgren. Sadly, this choice means my race card quickly descends into a spider's web of amends and crossings out, almost nearly as intensely decorated as Tai Woffinden's body is tattooed. It is a complete mess. I glare quizzical evils over at the back of the blonde head of my information supplier though, really, my own blind faith in the knowledge and expertise of other fans has inflicted this programme crazy patterning. Trust is a laudable value but, when it comes to the good faith of BSI towards speedway generally or their SGP programmes, misplaced.

I try to visibly intuit if she has yet also realised that exactly half of her 16 programme entries are totally wrong. Quite how you recognise such dawning realisation from a stranger's body language while they watch the racing or wave their flag at Freddie is a conundrum. After the first race thriller, the heats settle down into the sludge of their usual more workaday rhythm. Visually the colour and speed of the riders on the track along with the variety of the racing lines they explore as well as the haloing effect of the crowded stadium under dark night-time skies provides some degree of entertainment. Sadly, race thrills aren't really on offer. It is still mainly mundane, workaday processional stuff. And very dusty too. Blizzards of flung shale initially pocks fans sat in the lower rows of seats before these give way to a dust particle after-wave. Everywhere speedway is staged, the sheer velocity of rapidly spinning back wheels quickly buffs tracks of loose shale and flings it to all quarters, the air fence and stands. Though comparatively shale free before a throttle has even been twisted in anger, Torun is no exception so the race surface is soon buffed smooth. Sure, the meeting packaging is better, the atmosphere enthusiastic and the media claims grandiloquent but the SGP racing fare even at Torun is – looked at coldly – still very stale. The speedway entertainment prize heifer has lipstick but still covers us in excrement if wrestled. Looking to the bright side, for nearly a decade the World Champion has already been known well before the final meeting and often before the penultimate one too. At least tonight we have the vague outside statistical possibility of drama, albeit that the SGP format inevitably presents this as a war of points-accumulation attrition rather than head-to-head decisive combat. Though Woffinden and Zmarzlik get to race each other in heat 11, it is a duel at one remove. Bartosz is the football fan hoping that the results go his way and his team doesn't get relegated due to freak results delivered by others. Except – in that analogy – he is the team, there are no promotions and, perhaps, whisper it softly, all other riders won't necessarily race to the maximum or, indeed, don't necessarily share his objectives. It would only be human nature if his fellow Polish SGP competitors – Janowski or Pawlicki – saw no benefit in his triumph for their own careers.

Worse still, the possibly illusory, oft-denied but barely disguised stench of the possible undue influence Monster Energy "team" sponsorship of individual SGP riders again rears its ugly head. Apparently Hancock, Holder, Dudek (not riding tonight) and Woffinden only ever race and compete with solely their own World Championship ambitions at heart rather than ever consider their wider career interests. And definitely without pressure or instruction to do otherwise by Monster Energy or their representative on Eastern European earth Joe Parsons. They may, of course, appear to race in a way that benefits another rider in the Monster SGP team voluntarily or accidentally, albeit unconsciously like a surprise teenage nocturnal emission. Though the oldest rider in the SGP even back then, it is not so long ago that – when already guaranteed to be World Champion that season Greg – suddenly had his own version of a wet dream in Melbourne. Holder passing as Hancock theatrically slowed (for safety reasons) so concerned the referee and FIM, they penalised him in a manner that implied on balance they saw his actions as cheating. In turn, the violent unfairness of this perspective of the FIM officialdom so disgusted Greg that he refused to ride further and, instead, strumped off out of the meeting – and should, thereby, if one reading of the rules was correctly applied, have cost him his World Championship – claiming that he never cheated and didn't even fancy Chris Holder anyway. In fact, caught up in the white heat of the race moment, Greg temporarily wasn't really aware that Holder was human let alone riding in the World Championships as his Monster Energy teammate – despite their many promotional appearances together – or, indeed, that Holder urgently required these race points to ensure he made the top eight to qualify for next season. Not only had all this completely passed Greg by but – when he put the safety of others first by temporarily slowing, repeatedly looking back and then moving aside to let to Holder pass for further mystery safety reasons – bitter ignoramuses imputed foul motives to his careful respectful sensible precautions. Of course, these allegedly actions (and petulant walkout) went against and badly impugned Greg's relentlessly wholesome character. Anyways, though another Monster Energy team rider directly benefitted that is and was just a fluke one-off never-to-be-repeated coincidence. We also know that honesty and integrity if rather edgy or extreme are the values that drive the Monster Energy vibe. Even before you consider Joe Parsons ferocious advocacy of and his team riders unconditional adherence to all the Queensbury rules of speedway. So, take it all back, there is definitely no whiff of Bartosz finding tougher riding Monster Energy opponents than Tai discovers. As if to prove the point, setting aside what Paul Burbidge describes as the "personal issues" that regularly harsh his on-track mojo, Holder races Woffinden really hard for about half a lap – his standard unit of competitiveness in the SGPs over recent years – in heat 4 before letting him go to then trail back off to third.

The first interval gives the stadium to chance to collectively struggle badly to get any network signal as we stretch their legs or grab a beer and a bite. Stewards in hi-vis stab vests assert their authority on the stairs but find no use for the handcuffs or truncheons hung from their over-sized belts. Also keen to be a touch authoritarian for the benefit of the cameras is FIM Track Director Phil Morris, who is out quickly to supervise and photogenically wave his arms. From this distance, his gestures look like the driver hand signals you require if your car indicators stop working just as you have to pass a horse. It is a life lesson especially handy for any rural dwellers about to sit classroom-based international driving theory tests. Sadly, Phil's audience is mostly the hundreds watching the world feed live broadcast, the bowser operative and a few bored track men who studiously continue to reserve judgement on his ability to either lead them or work curatorial miracles. Given the sheer amount of dust experienced by the crowd, the Torun bowser is remarkably small. So bijou, that it only contains enough liquid to damp down the inside line. Oblivious to the lack of water, Phil throws himself into a frenzy of complex traffic directions more suitable to managing the 12 exits of the Arc de Triomphe roundabout in rush hour. Inevitably it is a lengthy display. Often furious but ultimately futile. Morris's serial inability to effect positive change is demonstrated by every SGP track but emphasized in Torun given the size of its surface area and limited water available. This ongoing lack of positive results for his track work doesn't dim his self-belief or kink the ardour of Phil's zeal. He is a speedway Sisyphus endlessly shifting shale to no end except regular camera time and further rehearsals of his supreme race directorship power. Each and every SGP meeting provides an astonishing minimum of 45 minutes tractor/bowser formation displays, racing and track grading out of a total event run time of around 130-150 minutes to get through the whole shebang. Previous incumbents of the FIM Track Director position – Ole Olsen and Tony (no relation) Olsson – were very rarely seen giving such ludicrously performative look-at-me displays. In contrast, whenever the blinking red light of a live camera beckons, Morris struts his stuff. Given the track grades takes up a minimum of 30 percent of any SGP, this effectively ensures Morris appears on screen/track for longer than individual rider at every meeting. Though Morris never qualified for a World Championship final – despite being Welsh National Champion – in only a few years as FIM

Race Director he has almost had more track and camera time than any rider in Speedway World Championship history. Even during the actual racing, Morris regularly appears on screen whenever he inserts himself into the meeting to and fro. The only surprise is that he doesn't hover by the podium to supervise the post-meeting trophy presentations. Returning to the reality that BSI's SGP series are really tractor display events cunningly disguised as a World Championship speedway meeting: if we compare actual minutes raced by riders versus the lapsed time taken up by grading then the percentage comparison is madness. Effectively each ticket pays for nearly twice as much tractors as bikes! This really isn't mentioned in the terms and conditions small print. Given roughly only three to five races a season of the 230 raced really truly excite and entertain, it could be argued that the tractors manoeuvres and Phil's signals are sufficiently varied to make this component of the SGP show is similarly or possibly just as enthralling as most of the races served up. Given this excessive camera dwell time upon him, no wonder Morris so fancies his seriousness and importance. Despite never having ridden at them officially, the reality Morris is twice as important to every SGP than the riders based on time spent on the track and, possibly, camera. There are 16 racers and only ONE Morris. It is no surprise that his apparent fear of anonymity means that he would happily dance in front of a mirror in a phone box with cameras running. [1]

For a better view of these signals and racing afterwards, I move back from the front row into one of the many empty seats in the row behind. Fredrik Lindgren's cousin Petronella Gudmundsson courteously comes over to apologise about the programme mess we share. She is in Torun with her friend Hanna Paloraara. They hope to see Freddie ride well enough this evening to end his season on the podium afterwards (holding whatever grotesquely designed trophy they award for finishing third in the World Championship). Petronella complains she copied the duff information we both used to obliterate our programme score cards "directly from the SGP website on Friday AFTER the draw." It is hard to credit that the rights holders BSI might have inaccurate info on their official website. To be fair, this more often takes the form of omissions, deliberate exaggerations and portentous claims rather than easily avoidable basic errors. TripAdvisor don't need to quake in their boots just yet, as travel information – for both directions and accommodation – on the SGP site are so pitiful and sketchy that some suspect that BSI have mistaken them for state secrets that if ever released threaten to imperil national security. Clearly some dim bulb at BSI – or whomever they have sub-contracted the work to on a cost-cutting rather than quality or expertise basis – doesn't understand speedway (surprise!) or even their own unnecessarily complex race draw rules. Still, we can rest easy in our beds clutching our scribbled-out documents secure in the knowledge that programme sales continue to get maximised for the greater good of the BSI bottom line and also to help ensure those seven-figure dividends continue to get paid.

After all the excitable pre-meeting talk of multiple racing lines and endless opportunities for thrilling overtakes, the races still mostly stick rigidly to one racing line to keep things boringly processional. Spectacle is minimal. Greg gates and goes to beat Nicki in their (last ever, it turns out) battle of the SGP Elders. Hancock and Pedersen are so long in the tooth that their ages are higher and, arguably, more distinctive than the race numbers chosen by their younger rivals to decorate their bikes, kevlars and race suits in their forlorn attempts to further brand their identities into our collective unconscious. Even businesses with serious

---

[1] If we assume an average SGP meeting duration of 150 minutes, the actual racing only takes up around 20 per cent of that time! Though the disequilibrium of this comparison is a fact of speedway life generally, it is compounded at SGPs by the races getting rushed through without pre- or post-meeting ceremony as television needs are being prioritised over the live fan experience. Phil Morris executes this running an efficient meeting for the television schedules aspect of his duties with relish, even though it bastardises the overall SGP fan journey and customer experience.

budgets know that – in reality – branding is only for cattle. Quite how designating your World Championship number as 444 then plastering all over every available surface is going to add cache, sponsors or grab mindshare has still to be adequately explained, let alone monetised. The memorability of Jason Doyle's 69 comes pre-installed so is, of course, the exception that proves this rule and continues to roll off many tongues. During the race Petronella leaps, implores and semaphores encouragement to her uncle Freddie but, sadly, to no avail. Tai wins the next processional race easily to elicit almost no reaction from the crowd. Even the most fervent Woffinden fan – unless they have a vested interest or microphone to hand in the commentary booth – surely struggles to summon up too much excitement for his dull workmanlike progress towards the final goal of his third championship title? If, as banker and poet T. S. Eliot suggested, the world ends with a whimper not a bang, then SGP-style speedway lives that dream. Given how the World Championship format rights holders finally settled upon (after many false starts and tweaks) by BSI maximises their television and sponsorship revenues to the detriment of excitement and entertainment, perhaps there is a case to say that Tai's new money wins are really only worth half of Ivan Mauger's old money wins? I have yet to hear a compelling case why there shouldn't be a discounted tariff applied beyond the tin justification and airy talk of you can only win under the rules that apply in each different era racing against the riders who are your contemporaries. Though dislikeable to many fans both then and now as a person (if judged by his public and social media persona), Darcy Ward's injury and enforced premature retirement surely deprived him of the many World Championships that his talent on a bike merited. And that, otherwise, have mostly gone to Tai. All other things being equal, doubtless, while there are significant monies to be easily made Tai will continue to grind away, flog off his recently worn gear on eBay and eventually beat the record of six World Championship wins held jointly by Mauger and Tony Rickardsson. If he does, and it currently looks likely, this achievement will receive widespread indifference from the general public and the real – aka uncompromised, independent and national – media. If Woffinden continues to mirror the trajectory of his previous triumphs to date, these will be just as notable for the lack of thrills, daring and emotional engagement as the significance and scale of the achievement.

Heat 7 sees Zmarzlik again gate poorly. Luckily for him Zagar goes out of his way to clip the back wheel of Holder which allows Bartosz to escape to victory. The stadium celebrates while Zmarzlik frenetically rabbit punches the air. Even allowing for the fact that his other hand holds the bike, his vigorous but wild technique suggests he isn't a natural boxer. The track looks poor and the crowd continue to get showered in shale dust. Heat 8 sees Emil give Doyle a masterclass in how to exploit the lauded multiple Torun racing lines. It is a decent race. By SGP standards, actual entertainment in five percent of the races is exceptional. Of course, it wouldn't be "speedway at the highest level" unless SGP fans suffered the consequences of easily predictable Keystone Kops style blunders. By BSI standards, and though these snafus are usually blamed on a third party, the ongoing struggles of the mobile network with the volume of stadium traffic is small beer and won't force an abandonment or compromise the racing. Being freed from always-on demands of wi-fi and mobiles is a lifestyle choice of the wealthy but somewhat less helpful when forced upon Torun attendees. Ironically, the SGP live interview booth backdrop relentlessly tells watching fans to "join the conversation" on the SGP Twitter account. Other than endless phone screen refreshes, the interval passes in a blizzard of big-screen adverts for also-ran companies with ego and budget enough to also want to remain (un)known while reaching the exalted heights of being second- and third-tier SGP sponsors. Ultimately, SGP sponsorship is corporate ambition at its self-deluding best for almost every company but Monster. We also get treated to another eight minutes of extensive formation tractor activity out on the track. Sensible fans don't ever hold their breath in the expectation of any dramatic improvement in the track surface. More on principle than impact, Phil Morris energetically signals and signs his way through what looks like the speedway version of a pre-flight passenger safety briefing with especial emphasis upon the dynamics of evacuation procedure etiquette.

With experience and a good understanding of the Torun track topology, Hancock fails to gate but cuts back sharply inside to force the race leaders towards the fence so he can pass them. This is the sum total of the race "thrills" we get to witness. Impartial observers with or without spectacles – rather than those who purport to be sports journalists but instead prefer product advocacy and advertorial in lieu of analytical reporting – know that there is a severe problem with the speedway spectacle served up by the SGP series. Fortunately, what Heat 10 lacks in thrills or drama is made up in my section of the Torun grandstands by Petronella and Hanne as this heat features Freddie. Together they channel their inner Phil Morris to amp up the excitement and atmosphere via the medium of exaggerated gesture. Lindgren's cousin Petronella is so engaged before, during and after each race featuring cousin Lindgren that she has even brought a change of shoes. Black ninja style flat ones so she can leap and clamber more safely onto the nearby stadium stanchion bars to deliver her brand of vigorous encouragement (and delight in victories) from a greater height along with wild swishes of her generous sized Swedish flag. Before any athletic jump up onto the stadium furniture, prior to each Freddie heat Petronella has a set routine that requires she intensely concentrate upon the start line as if able to project mind control powers. To ensure the absolute focus of her gaze upon Lindgren and the soon-to-rise tapes, Petronella holds her hands to her eyes like binocular-cum-blinders most often seen in old war films before she flings her hand as if firing her playground cartoon gun at the instant they rise. Despite the heat map created by her frenetic foot-to-foot hops, leaps and shouts, it remains a processional race throughout won by Laguta.

The next race has been baked in by the media as well as the SGP on their website and Twitter account as a clash-of-the-titans encounter of Zmarzlik and Woffinden somewhat akin to a motorsports version of the Rumble-in-the-Jungle of Ali versus Frazier. Come to think of it, Manila is a much easier place to access than Malilla (or Teterow, Hallstavik and Krsko). Apparently forgetting his big race voodoo, Zmarzlik leads after he shrugs off brief pressure from Doyle. Keen to really compete in this race, behind them Woffinden actually appears to race flat out along the back straight – arguably edging over into wild over-riding – before hitting a bend three track bump that flings him from the bike like a rag doll. It looks the kind of crash that snaps collarbones as well as dents spinal cords along with composure. Completely confounding the impression given by his nightclub bouncer aura and muscle bulk, Tai's mechanic Konrad Darwinski sprints brilliantly across the centregreen from a standing start from by the pits gate. It is a genuinely impressive all-out full-gas power sprint that easily sees off the chasing group of other keen to impress but altogether less speedy runners. If they ever decide to hold foot races amongst Woffinden's staff, only short odds will be available on Konrad. The care and humanity the sight of this all-out determination to reach his stricken master implies is cut short when Konrad completely ignores Woffinden to rush past him to retrieve the bike. Konrad then bullets back at notable speed with little more than a perfunctory backward glance towards the fallen Tai. Woffinden's tall rake-thin Groot-lookalike chief mechanic Jacek Trojanowski ambles over much more sedately then lingers the two or so minutes it takes for his employer to rise Lazarus-like from the shale. Tai makes an ultra-slow slightly hammy walk back to the pits interspersed by broad smiles or hand bumps on his heart to acknowledge the crescendo of get-well-soon air-horn greetings. His stately progress back to the pits gives ample additional time for bike assessments, any repairs and welcome brief extra moments of injury recovery. Whether or not Tai is in severe pain, without wishing to come over all cod-psychologist like Pearson and Tatum love to do during their live commentary-cum-rider-mind-reading sessions, the doublethink of marginal gains, toxic masculinity and also gamesmanship requires Woffinden continue to project absolute confidence and indifference to his fall – irrespective of his real feelings – just for his closely watching rivals to observe. Whatever conclusions are drawn, the re-run sees Zmarzlik win easily after he overcomes a poor gate with a full speed outside pass of Martin Vaculik. It also means that, after over 50 laps of four bikes back tyres polishing the track surface, the last few remnants of loose shale finally get sprayed into the lower-tier grandstand seats. Closely followed by a shale dust shock wave to lightly dust the fans too. Heat 12 is a fast full gas win for Niels Kristian Iversen. With his two SGP wins a long distant memory, "fast full gas" isn't a phrase that automatically springs to mind about Niels at any SGP nowadays.

Apart from watching the tractors or network access icon circle aimlessly, there nothing to do during the interval beyond joining one of the lengthy queues for the various rows of temporary water-free unisex toilets. Quite how you design a purpose-built 15,500 seater speedway stadium but forget to provide adequate bog facilities is a decidedly contrary omission, especially when the programme boasts of "42 sets of toilet facilities". Though hardly a surprise, it seems that even here BSI's strategic big promise of a superior stadia fan experience – in terms of comfortable seating, catering and toilets – is still not anything like a reality even when they sub-contract to notable Polish speedway clubs. Now that the track Brazilian has finished, the lure of a ten-minute queue means tearing yourself away from the wonder of watching Phil Morris cajole nearby track staff on how to use a rake. The Joy of Raking is a new practical addition to his usual repertoire of complex but redundant hand gestures. Better still, Morris gives the fans and track staff our very own virtuoso masterclass in the dark of arts of curation raking. It is compulsive viewing, almost on par with a demonstration on how to pick your nose. It's hard to resist enjoying the full majesty of every last second his masterclass. Out on the dingy concourse, catchy albeit melodramatic backing music makes me glance back towards the big screens to see what exactly is being shown. Dang, if it isn't the standard Monster Energy advert they show at every SGP. The one without any real speedway footage in its fast-edit Beginner's Guide to Extreme Sports action montage. Speedway Grands Prix races are so unappealing – even to the "partner" sponsor's in-house video staff – that speedway conspicuously fails to pass muster as a visual trope in the edit suite. I do worry that the endless contractual repetition of this Monster commercial at every SGP has unconsciously trained me into brand loyalty, despite never having touched a drop of this "renowned" dark fluid. I am Pavlov's Dog. Well, Parsons' Dog. Easily distracted by the implied visual messaging, psychologically happy to wag my metaphorical tail at the merest hint of this elixir of the gods, albeit without the reward of a biscuit or eternal life. I then worry that, maybe, I have somehow been (further) mentally damaged without even a sip of the noxious liquid passing my lips. If Coca-Cola want to teach the world to sing, then the Monster mission is to get us to grimace. The only real way to resist their indoctrination and try to wipe it from the deep recesses of our collective brains is to wipe – Men in Black fashion – our collective memories by gazing upon the sun-kissed tyre knobbles of the Anlas advert, when and wherever it appears.

Just as the riders take to the track, the tractor completing its last circuit accidentally dumps a sizeable foot or so mound of shale at the exit of bend two. Such a pile would fail to register if this were MotoX but represents almost a season's worth of shale at the SGP. Like Sirens on the rocks calling unwary sailors, it is deposited in one particularly dangerous but magnetic lump. Excess grip is an anathema for modern high powered bikes. Any rider hugging the inside race line – and there are lots of these the world over, even at SGPs – would immediately come a cropper just as they really accelerate towards maximum velocity. If this were golf, you would get a free drop without penalty. In speedway, your drop would be literal, painful, possibly career-costly as well as result in an automatic exclusion. To properly clear said mound properly should require a delay but, since satellite broadcast timings invariably trump minor rider health and safety concerns, time – no matter how briefly – waits for no man/FIM race director so doesn't here either. Instead Morris sets about the pile with the gusto of a political prisoner facing immediate summary execution. In leadership terms, Phil appears to be the exception to the rule that all good managers use their experience and smarts to motivate and lead by example. Unless, of course, the real purpose of this example is show how to nearly spear the feet or ankles of anyone silly enough to stand too close. Quizzical but statuesque members of the curation team foolish enough to linger nearly gain career-ending injuries. Like a rabbit manically digging a new hole or a frenzied hound in pursuit of a fox down one, Morris rakes and dangerously flings the fallen shale off the track with the feverish ferocity of a cartoon character. His manic energy disinvites help but severely tests both his deodorant and mood. As the saying goes in the white-collar executive suite, if you want something blue-collar poorly done then make sure you three-quarters bodge it yourself. The race starts moments later without any hazard warning given to the competitors, though the remedial track work has not yet been fully completed by the FIM race director. Even slight slippy patches in shopping malls get those warning yellow hazard signs, yet the supposed crème de la crème competing in the biggest/best global speedway event (Phil's modest post-season description of the SGP series on his Twitter account) don't even get a quiet word of warning about the mogul run ahead. This is particularly peculiar given Morris gets regular camera time informing riders what they can easily see with a glance at the exclusion lights. Yet, when it comes to a sudden safety matter that the referee can't highlight unless informed about it, Mr Morris uses his judgement to decide not to alert the riders nor the referee. Instead he decides to stay silent on this possible safety matter and, thereby, avoids any jeopardy to the tight programming of the television schedules and commercial breaks. Out on the track, it is – as ever – always rider beware when it comes to seeing and overcoming hazards. Making things look alright but leaving essential snagging work unchecked, forgotten or undone has long been claimed by critics to be the lingua franca of SGP rights holders BSI. Of course, by its very nature the unforeseen happens. Sometimes often. And not in a good way. Though not on the scale of the Gelsenkirchen postponement or the start gates and crowd control failures at the respective inaugural Warsaw and Teterow stagings, the lumpy turd of shale left behind as a memento after remedial work by the FIM race director is symbolic of a lack of detailed disaster recovery planning in a world where – no matter what – those expensive tightly scheduled satellite timings dictate the SGP show must almost immediately always go on.

Since the riders in heat 13 manage to avoid the shale dump lump, it is yet another processional race. Tai tries his trademark first bend cut back but fails to gain any benefit. He's marooned in fourth until he passes – since normal Iversen SGP service has resumed – an out-of-sorts Niels Kristian. Heat 14 features a lusty battle for third between Doyle and Zagar but otherwise it is mundane follow-my-leader stuff, albeit enlivened off the track by the enthusiastic voluble support of Petronella for her uncle. The interval dance cam has got so little traction in Torun, there is a strong case for in future only filming the reactions of riders' relatives and family members in the crowd. Petronella's section of the grandstand, let alone her seat, can barely contain her. She mimics and mirrors her uncle. Stock still concentration – her uncle at the tapes, she in her seat – transitions into all-out action as they rise. Freddie releases his clutch to fire towards the first bend while Petronella leaps impressively with the urgency of a salmon called to die as it spawns upstream. Beneath his helmet, Lindgren is less expressive than his cousin who gurns, implores and dances him to the chequered flag. To celebrate she flies, flutters and jiggles her Swedish flag with the intensity shipwrecked mariners signal passing planes to their desert island. On the second bend of the second lap of the next race (heat 15), apparently under the strong impression he is still the defending champion, Pedersen brutally cuts off Zmarzlik to relegate him to last place and, thereby, almost guarantee Tai definitely wins the world title. At least that looks the case right until Bartosz fires down the length of the straight to power under and clatter Pawlicki. Looked at in real time directly across from this coming together, Zmarzlik is definitely the transgressor and should be excluded. Watched in the snowy vision of the big screen, the replay could be viewed to suggest that an experimental film-maker has commandeered the stadium cameras to snatch some silent action footage for a re-make of one of the industrial scenes of Vertov's 1929 classic "The Man with the Movie Camera". The snatch of action we see suggests that Piotr Pawlicki is marginally at fault and this is the safer decision referee Jesper Steentoft chooses. Continuing to ride under the delusion it is his crown to cede, Nicki again races ultra-hard, fast and aggressive in the re-run. It is the kind of lusty competitive battle for position and points that riders in the SGP should serve up almost every time they take to the track. And is just the type of gung-ho, all-out action that the promotional literature and media boosters claim gets served up every time, yet doesn't. Many other similarly frequent meaningless races have similar ingredients: good track, talented professional riders with competitive mindsets at the near height of their speedway career astride highly tuned engines mounted inside superbly well-maintained bikes but then don't deliver a modicum of this taste of passion and drama. Actually, to be fair, most SGP races lack a good quality race track with multiple racing lines. Plus, of course, the series format deliberately neuters the testosterone urge – let alone the need or imperative to ride with all-out fervour – as BSI prefer the predictability of regular –servings of another humdrum day at the office. It is almost as if maximising sponsorship, staging and television SGP fees required BSI to emasculate World Championship speedway of its propulsive drama and jeopardy. For ill or ill, this nothing-added-everything-taken-away mundanely processional iteration is de facto currently the dominant contemporary global representation of speedway that conspicuously fails to attract or excite the audiences the sport needs to survive (let alone thrive).

With only the final set of races plus the semi-finals and finals of the 2018 SGP series left, it takes quite a leap to claim that there is either uncertainty or tension when it comes to the whereabouts of either the world championship crown or thinner gruel of the final ranking outcomes. Tedium tends to be the default setting. Barring a meteor strike, Tai will become World Champion, despite the best efforts of Bartosz. Compared to previous SGP series where the World Champion is known two, three or four events beforehand, this year there is – if you listen carefully enough – a vague whisper of mathematical mystery. Leading up to Torun, Tai's press team made a virtue of the fact that Woffinden would eschew all media interviews in order to concentrate on the task at hand. Ha ha. All fair and good, of course. Such a decision and its public statement shows some vanity and pretention since there is, as usual, approximately zero demand from any proper national/independent media – of any stripe (broadcast, print or online – even podcasts) – for any exposure to Tai's thoughts, anxieties, bon mots or reticent off-hand insouciance about the tasks at hand.

Inevitably, talking up this decision to seek monastic "concentration" massively occupied the tame trade press, SGP website and Twitter account plus Nigel Pearson's seasonal weekly column in the Wolverhampton Express & Star as well as the excitable posters on the British Speedway Forum. Such interest is predictable and the equivalent in news or excitement terms of a single tree falling down (of its own accord) in the Amazonian rain forest. Woffinden's pitiful media profile is often blamed by the *Speedway Star*, Peter Oakes and low-information BSF posters on an alleged media conspiracy against speedway, whereas really the blame mostly lies with the decline of speedway's ability to set or be part of the national consciousness as much as the culpability of his publicist and media team. Clearly both speedway and Tai have no meaningful existing profile to leverage for traction. This is hardly a surprise since their national media outreach to new contacts is pitiful to non-existent while their media messaging is both predictably banal and infrequent. Though they do get the odd post-triumph high profile national media slot, Tai's tendency to the monosyllabic and his reluctance to engage ensures little passing audience interest and even fewer repeat bookings.

As a further predictable but bracingly xenophobic string to Woffinden's media messaging bow, his press team talked up the cauldron of antipathy and hate Tai would have to overcome from the Torun crowd in order to land the title he already effectively had anyways. Beyond the fact that it is obviously a nonsense to suggest that passionate partisan noise from Polish fans would gain any influence beneath Woffinden's helmet above the roar of the bikes, Zmarzlik's home town crowd was found elsewhere earlier in the series at Gorzow. Obviously, this doesn't stop Burbo uncritically lapping it up or repeating it as gospel across his SGP promotional channels (*Speedway Star* "reports", Twitter and the "news" section of the SGP website). [2] To be fair to Zmarzlik, unlike Woffinden, he is born and bred in his country of origin (Poland) so is always likelier to attract more floating patriotic support in his home country on an *ad hoc* basis rather than if he was born there but badged as Polish when really brought up elsewhere as, culturally, Australian. Such "cauldron of hate" talk and comment also ignores the unfailing general politeness of speedway fans, almost everywhere. Afterwards, Tai, his media team and his trade media advocates would express surprise at the complete absence of hostility and vituperation they warned about. Indeed, they would – surprise, surprise – praise how Polish fans generously celebrated his triumph. Of course, quite how you can tell the nationality of one cheer from another is a mystery for another day. It is a tried and tested fake news technique, of course. The *Sunday Sport* famously had a front-page headline one weekend that stated (and I paraphrase) "World War 2 Bomber Found on Moon" with accompanying blurry pictures followed in the next weekend's edition by "World War 2 Bomber Found on Moon Vanishes" complete with crystal clear moon surface stock photo. At least, this deception had a modicum of wit, if no less commercial basis. Even if the media currency the Woffinden press team wish to trade in is counterfeit, generating fake news stories poorly serves the long term interests of their media profile building on behalf of their client. Looking to the bright side, this fake news is much more wholesome and less icky than Tai banging on in media interviews about how he knows the danger of competing in speedway could lead him to permanently land in a wheelchair. Though serious sporting injuries are always possible in speedway, the superstitious might suggest that such statements invite bad luck while others feel it is in plain bad taste given other riders have, do and will find themselves in the reality of that unfortunate position. Given we all cope with grief and the loss of our parents differently, the go to Woffinden backstory-cum-meme about the ongoing impact of his teen years loss of his Dad to cancer is actual sad lived experience rather than emotional but imaginary fiction.

---

[2] It is regularly overlooked in speedway circles (whether promoters, BSPA, riders or media) that repeating something as fact doesn't make it so no matter how breathlessly or often it is stated with a straight face. Or, indeed, how much vested interests along with the speedway media sincerely believe such truths. In the real world of fact-checking, independent sources and corroboration are required. For example, just to pick one such thing at random, claims on the BSPA website that BT Sports saw a 41 per cent increase in their audience during 2018 couldn't be independently verified by the *Guardian* for a news item when they tried to establish the veracity of this statement.

News stories that reveal Tai still discusses his thoughts, feelings and events in his life with his Dad arguably tell us something, whereas reading of Tai's magnanimous acceptance that his choice of career could mean life in a wheelchair is much less so.

Back at the drama face of the notional mystery whereabouts and composition of the final rankings, at least this SGP season there is an outside element of statistical uncertainty about the final destination of the awful-looking – specially commissioned by Monster to be a design abomination – World Championship trophy until during this final meeting. Given the series format rarely boosts entertainment or excitement, the thin pickings of this last meeting hint of uncertainty is – by SGP standards – a sumptuous banquet. Usually, all that is left by the end of a long series is for the identity of the rider occupying the final automatic qualification ranking place of eighth position to be discovered. If generally no one in sports remembers who came second, how can landing up eighth be seen as an achievement, let alone a thrilling spectacle to follow for fans inside the stadium or elsewhere? Of course, such pitiful "excitements" expose the reality and transactional banality of this accountancy led BSI World Championship. It applies across the board. Since the riders ride to maximise their points, second and third place points cumulatively suffice – this is the Greg Hancock model – rather than the need to perpetually race to win. Concomitantly, rights holders BSI finagle and leverage the duration and multiple locations that their expanded SGP series format offers to intensively farm the various revenue streams. The only vaguely world standard on display at the SGP under BSI is the financial engineering rather than speedway action. Even the rider who finishes sixth or tenth struggles to remember that fact in their van just afterwards. Of course, they have to remember to do so as all riders need to be able to parrot news of this "achievement" in conversation and writing as somehow thrilling as it is fundamental to their own product pitch to existing or would-be sponsors. The basic SGP rider come-and-get-me sponsor proposition takes the form of declaring that they ride in the "Speedway World Championship" while talking up the number of events broadcast live rather than the pitiful audiences these attract. Fleeting glimpses of your logo trailed off at the back of a processional race in a forest on the outskirts of an obscure European regional town surprisingly continues to be a powerful sponsor aphrodisiac. Such spin also conveniently forgets that not only do BSI enjoy five "wild card" picks (four permanent and one random) but as the top eight riders automatically qualify for re-enrolment, there is no white heat of competition as the so-called Speedway World Championship is effectively an invitation-only event. Indeed, the series format and qualification criteria is deliberately one that does NOT showcase the most in-form riders but a formula to provide the predictability and stability that suits the existing rights holder, sponsors, embedded media and chosen riders alike.

After a long interval the racing resumes just before 9pm. It is possibly Chris Holder's last ever proper World Championship appearance as a regular member of the circus. The MotoArena was the scene of his only world crown triumph and also the controversial referee decision that helped give him it in 2012. The intervening track years have not been kind with bad crashes and leg breaks hampering his form and earnings as well as leading to a court case with Coventry speedway he lost. Plus his close friend on and off the track Darcy Ward sustained career-ending injuries. In this context, understandably recent years have seen him struggle to retain his enthusiasm or place in the series. Two years ago, the dead cat bounce of a late season run saw Holder finish fourth in the rankings as well as finish the last Grand Prix meeting of the season in Melbourne with a win. Holder's 2017 was another annus horribilis with off-track worries plaguing his on-track form to the extent that against expectations or current future potential, he was coincidentally awarded a wild card his riding did not merit during a period that also featured contract renewal negotiations between Monster Energy and SGP rights holders BSI. In his pomp and prime, Holder was compulsive viewing. Early in his UK career, I used to take every chance I could to watch him ride. For example, when setting out on their long career road ahead, both he and Jason Doyle were worth the proverbial admission money every time they took to the Smallbrook track on the Isle of Wight. That carefree daredevil and fearless Holder disappeared a long time ago, ground down by the long-distance travel but also banished by the realities of life as a professional speedway rider. Proud parenthood and family responsibilities saw the off-track high jinks dialled back too. Heat 17 sees Holder briefly roll back the years and – most recently mentioned in a Fathers for Justice style interview article with Phil Lanning – off-track hurt. Holder races like a champion he once was. Fast, hard and confident. For two laps he battles Doyle before besting him. It is a rare glimpse of the gifts of his innate racing talent and a welcome change from the fare of his recent SGP seasons as well as the mostly mundane processional races served up in Torun tonight.

To add further notional excitement this year, the whereabouts of the consolation third – bronze (plated) – position is also still up for grabs. This is particularly good news for those of us sat close to Fredrik Lindgren's cousin Petronella (and, to some extent, her friend Hanna) who lives each and every race with visible passion and notable intensity. The podium place will go to Freddie if he scores more points than Janowski. After being robbed by the ref in the initial running of heat 1, Maciej has – by his high standards – struggled for points. Lindgren leads him by three points with one race to go. In the first running of heat 18, Niels Kristian Iversen has his helmet visor and white helmet colour ripped off by the rising tapes and is – eventually, after some contemplation by the referee – excluded for his trouble. Despite the big-screen replays showing his bike didn't move, getting binned by the ref for your intention to move – as signalled by moving your head – at the start line is an altogether new level of harsh. The strenuously polite Niels clearly thinks so too as the decision prompts him to protest to FIM race director Phil Morris before he is banished back to the pits. For once Morris is lost for a mystifying but putatively authoritative arm gesture in response and instead shrugs. Other than to milk the attention of the additional camera time, Morris' need to histrionically re-communicate each refereeing decision to the riders like a sympathetic marriage guidance counsellor reluctantly confirming divorce proceedings are definitely going ahead adds nothing. Especially so as – with helmets still on – any message is at best muffled and totally ignores that speedway tracks have long had exclusion lights to very effectively visually communicate these refereeing decisions. Arguably, Morris relentlessly seeking the spotlight of his "accidental" SGP notoriety and celebrity is one of the rare iconoclasms of the BSI SGP era. It is pure grandstanding but, perhaps, symbolic of the actual value BSI bought to speedway and delivered via their version of the World Championship. On first glance it appears professional but, upon examination, is just adventitious officious busy work to justify position and income that adds little or nothing to the drama, spectacle, status, popularity and integrity of the event.

It is definitely refreshing to see that Iversen is old school and parsimonious enough to still use helmet colours. Nowadays it is apparently a rite of passage and sign of profligacy (or sponsor generosity) for every SGP rider to have four different helmets on hand in their pit bay coloured red, blue, white and yellow. They probably have reserve helmets in these standard colours too. I wouldn't be surprised. The re-run sees the wonderfully named Torun first reserve Igor Kopec-Sobczynski take to the track on the noisiest bike of the 2018 SGP series. It serenades us with the very very throaty roar of its engine. So much so it sounds simultaneously oversized and under-tuned. You half suspect, Igor made it the night before with his dad as a course requirement of his speedway apprenticeship. Igor's loud rumble echoes pleasingly around inside the stadium bowl. His extremely comprehensive last place suggests there won't be a queue of new customers at the door of his engine tuner for a while just yet. Freddie's much quieter second place prompts Petronella to make noise. She yells, shakes her fists, yelps then climbs onto the dangerously high bar of the nearby stanchion with the grace and confidence of a gymnast to wave her Swedish flag in wild semaphore salute as Lindgren passes by obliviously lost in his own moment of celebration. Her earlier change into flat martial arts type shoes makes these precariously balanced virtuoso routines on the stadium furniture much safer to perform. Her displays of unbridled enthusiasm definitely gifts her honorary Polish speedway fan status. She certainly defies the cliché image of staid Swedes with the joy of her celebrations. Statistically, Petronella's delight is – perhaps – premature as a win for Janowski in his last race (heat 20) could still see him qualify for the semi-finals and possible further catch up points.

Offering further proof that must-win big races currently aren't ever nailed on whenever Zmarzlik races them, Bartosz trails in behind Laguta in a processional heat 19. With fourteen points and a seven point lead, Zmarzlik's ideal heat 20 would see Woffinden fail to score and, thereby, miss the additional points opportunity of the semi-finals. Any other outcome, more-or-less glues the crown onto Tai's head. It remains unclear what – if any – after effects Tai suffers as a result of his earlier crash. His form tonight, so far, has been win-win-crash/exclusion-third. The mystery – such as it is – is soon solved when the practised ease of Woffinden's winning ways return. Janowski finishes in third to, thereby, guarantee Lindgren's podium place bronze medal in the final standings. Petronella flutters her Swedish flag in brief acknowledgement of either Tai's win, Janowski's third or Freddie's absent triumph. Lindgren taking to the track ahead of the first semi-final has Petronella revert to full jack-in-the-box mode. Unable to settle or sit still. Though Laguta gates and goes, by the time Freddie leads Emil out of the second bend she switches into full on exultant triumph. Petronella's premature carnival-meets-full-independence celebrations immediately get cut short when Emil returns the favour to re-secure the qualifying second place. Emil is untroubled thereafter. Petronella stands agog. Frozen. Amazed, but not in a good way. Even when Freddie passes on his lap of honour waving vigorously, she refuses to jiggle her flag or even return the gesture.

Tai Woffinden wins the second semi-final like a World Champion. His crew – and, of course, Joe Parsons – mob the track in ecstasy. Though his publicist Nigel Pearson remains stuck elsewhere in the live commentary booth by virtue of the Venn diagram of his aggressively intersecting other speedway media commitments, I don't doubt his full spectrum triumphalism. Tai's crew administer the bumps then ostentatiously put on their specially designed pre-prepared "Tai Woffinden 2018 World Champion" T-shirts they brought along to wear tonight. In true Aussie Pat Cash Wimbledon tennis or – recalling a more apposite historic example – Irish Alex Higgins bring me my baby daughter Sheffield Crucible snooker style, Tai storms into the crowd to embrace his friends and loved ones. Wife Faye, baby daughter Rylee and mum Sue. Seeing the vulnerable Tai immediately seek out the embrace of his family makes me feel almost tearful. Like many of the Polish fans around me, I kill any lingering emotion by joining the lengthy unisex toilet queues ahead of the final. When I return, my section has been annexed by fanatical French speedway fans here from Toulouse via Stansted, where they slept the night. France and speedway fans aren't words that usually go together in the same sentence easily. They are a tad defensive when I express my unfeigned surprise, "We are so excellent at rugby and football, we need new challenges". As if to prove their implied point about my ignorance, I immediately badly fail their "name the famous French speedway riders you know" test. I write Dimitri Berge and David Bellagio on the back of my postage stamp but, stupidly, forget the three Tresarrieu brothers!

Tai wins the final race to further emphasise his world champion credentials. It is the third World Championship win of his career. This year he has actually won the most grands prix (three) of any of his seasons so far but, since he competes in an era where points accumulation trumps outright victories, such feats are no longer essential. Woffinden now has ten SGP wins, three World Championships and two wild card nominations to his World Championship name. With a top-performing off-track crew and bikes/engines plus mentor Peter Adams back in his fold, without serious or effective challenge from his contemporary speedway rivals (since the career-ending injuries to Darcy Ward), it really seems that the only contemporary rider who can regularly defeat Tai – if fit to ride – is Tai himself. Whenever he puts family or property restoration ahead of speedway, gets injured or lacks a mentor, other riders emerge triumphant. Jason Doyle last season and Greg Hancock the year before. Someone else next. The majority of the crowd herald Woffinden's triumph enthusiastically as the speedway fans they are rather than the partisan Zmarzlik biased Polish patriots Tai's media boosters lazily claimed they were. Other fans rush out into the temperate night ahead of the presentations and post-meeting crush to head home or into the city centre for another long night on the town.

Winner: Tai Woffinden

Second: Artem Laguta

Third: Emil Sayfutdinov

Fourth: Niels Kristian Iversen

World Champion: Tai Woffinden

Runner up: Bartosz Zmarzlik

Third: Fredrik Lindgren

Afterword

SPEEDWAY loves stats and the SGP is no different. I thought a brief snapshot of random numbers might illuminate (or shade) the 2018 season just gone. Tai Woffinden won the World Championship for the third time. Interestingly Tai has never formally qualified for the SGP as he has either automatically re-qualified as function of his place in the final standings or else – twice – been the recipient of a wild card from BSI and the FIM.

Prize money at the SGP continues to be a scandal – and illogical to explain to outsiders too – but, obviously, though there is a welter of information on the official SGP website it isn't mentioned there and, predictably, is not covered by the embedded speedway media.

For winning the 2018 series Tai won $84,900 in prize money. Second-placed Bartosz Zmarzlik won $55,450 in prize money, and third-placed Fredrik Lindgren got $62,200. None of these prizes come anywhere close to covering costs of participation in the SGP for any of these riders. As a comparison, it is said that top/star riders racing in the Ekstraliga in Poland usually race in five heats per meeting and earn £1,000 a point (aka £3,000 for a race win or paid-win). Before the start of the 2018 season, it was reported on the sport.pl website that Tai Woffinden had a contract with Wroclaw for 1,900,000zl.

Digging fractionally deeper into the SGP prize money, Nicki Pedersen won $ in prize money for the 2018 series to take his all-time SGP career prize money to $820,950. This places him second on the all-time list behind almost ever-present Greg Hancock on $906,300 (who won $50,100 in prize money in 2018). Looking at Nicki's SGP career for a moment: he is a three-times World Champion (2003, 2007 and 2008), three-times bronze medallist and one-time runner up. Nicki has had 17 SGP wins – his latest in Malilla - and reached the final 64 times. He has won over a third (336 wins) of his 1,015 SGP heats for a total points tally of 1,972. If we remember that prize money is weighted to incentivise and "reward" those riders that qualify for the knockout stages of the semi-final and final, though Nicki has excelled at this metric it still means in effect that BSI has only "paid" Nicki $809 a race or $416 a point. Hardly a king's ransom, let alone adequate reward for efforts. In comparison, if we look at Craig Cook we find that his prize money total for the 2018 season totalled $27,550. This works out at $656 per race and $917 per point.

Completely ignoring ALL my travel expenses – not an insignificant sum (!) – I spent £457.66 on SGP admissions. This was the cost of admission when I often bought the cheapest tickets available at the time of pre-purchase, I could easily have paid significantly more to see these meetings. For this total expenditure (using the figures quoted in the Speedway Star), I could have gained one adult admission to every single British speedway club – all thirty three of them - racing in the Championship, Premiership and National Leagues in 2018 and still had over £20 left. Indeed, for the price of the most expensive adult ticket to see the SGP in Cardiff (and a programme), if I invested a further £6 I could go along to watch a meeting at every British National League club. In heat terms, this admission money buys 495 heats of British Speedway or 230 heats of the Speedway Grand Prix. Very few of these 230 SGP heats in 2018 were vaguely memorable in my opinion and experience. Given British Speedway naysayers regularly acknowledge the thrills served up by the racing in all three of its current leagues, even if there was only one thrilling heat – and, surely, this is an underestimate? - per meeting attended this would deliver at least three times the thrills of going to watch the SGPs. Anyways, though these things are ultimately always in the eyes of the beholder, with many British Speedway clubs struggling financially and some even closing, not only it has never been more true that it is a case of 'use it or lose it' but also any monies paid remain within the sport. This is the zero sum game of contemporary speedway finance, every £ spent with BSI/IMG is effectively another £ nail in the coffin of British Speedway and a stake through the heart of the echo of the happy speedway memories that took you along to be short-changed at the SGP. That so many people with vested commercial interests – especially, I may have mentioned, the embedded media and retinue of helpers and fellow travellers – insist otherwise does not make this less so. If you must SGP, maybe please also think of going to however many British Speedway club meetings it is for you that represents a similar total spend (aka all travel and accommodation costs plus entry, programme, food and drink).

When it comes to 2018 SGP programme prices, these vary massively by location though most are printed by Curtis Sport. I spent a total of £69.10. Though paper stock varies, on the whole – and to be fair – the SGP programmes are well-designed and professionally produced. Personally, I take this as basic/minimum requirement rather than something to make a song and dance about. What makes the SGP programmes poor value generally is not only the number of pages taken up with adverts but the dearth of new content. If something can be cut and pasted with minor tweaks, it is. Where the SGP programmes truly flop as memorabilia is this ongoing absence of new or compelling content. This seems to be a function of the lack of editorial vision as running on auto-pilot is preferred to creativity and originality. Again in fairness, I suspect demand might be inelastic so extra thought, time and effort achieves little additional financial reward, so why bother? If we set aside my gripe about the blank race cards in every SGP programme – though still asking a question I know the answer to: why can't BSI print a colour insert overnight to supply to every purchaser? – then space adverts took up an incredible 42 per cent (!!) of total number of available programme pages for the 2018 series. If ever time permits, I plan to briefly review the contents along with the highlights and lowlights of the 2018 and 2019 SGP programmes on my blog.

Acknowledgements

THOUGH all mistakes are my own, this book wouldn't have come out as it did without the help, guidance, encouragement and advice of many people including: Robert Bamford, Mr. S Bear, Per-Arne Bernhardsson, Colin & Sandra Beveridge, Toby Bowen, Tom Buckle, Brian Burford, Jess Cassidy, Ian Corcoran, Craig Cook, Kerry Cook, Will Cook, Alan Crooks, Richard Cotton, Jade Delmage, Claire Dunn, Chris Durno, Emma & Dennis Edvardsson, Wendy Fowler, Ove Fundin, David Goodchild, Ursula Gruener, Petronella Gudmundsson, Ian & Nikki Gyte, James Hawkes, Melanie Hecke, Vicky Holtham, Chris Horne, Les & Kim Howard and Hilary, Billy Jenkins, Igor & Nataly Kalashnik, Norbert Kienesberger, Adriana Merritt, Michael Payne, Sophie Pell, Andy Riddle, Graham Russel, Julie Sweet, Reverend Michael Whawell, Eric & friends in Landshut as well as an off-duty DSB bloke on the train to Horsens. I have been blessed to have enjoyed numerous random acts of kindness from strangers during my SGP travels. Obviously, many apologies for the error of my oversight if I have missed anyone out here.